"Father Copleston gives us an objective, yet critical, exposition of a very important philosophical period in this seventh volume of his well-known history of western thought."

Best Sellers

"No English philosopher writing today can match the industry of Fr. Copleston . . . To the discussion of these difficult thinkers, he brings not only his well-known gifts for exposition but also the authority of a specialist. Many of us who are already deeply indebted to Fr. Copleston for the earlier volumes of his history will owe him for this volume an even greater debt in proportion to our unfamiliarity with the period which it treats . . . there is always something to inform and fascinate."

The [London] Tablet

"Fr. Copleston continues to write with the assured air of a teacher in complete mastery of his material."

The Catholic Messenger

"Father Copleston's virtues as a historian are well known from his previous volumes. His erudition, objectivity, lucidity and powers of exposition have been praised by all. These admirable qualities are to be seen here also."

The Irish Ecclesiastical Record

"The addition of this work to the previous volumes of Dr. Copleston's history is perhaps a more significant event than the publication of the previous volumes. Not only is the treatment as impartial, as judicious in emphasis and in scale, as accurate and as well illustrated as in the previous volumes, but it also brings into the ken of those who need general piloting an orientation in philosophy of a sphere of thinkers who are as great as they are strange, and as worth knowing as they are hard to know. The whole of nineteenth-century German philosophy . . ."

Heythrop's

Volumes of A HISTORY OF PHILOSOPHY now available in
Image Books:

A History of Philosophy

VOLUME VII

Modern Philosophy

PART I

Fichte to Hegel

by Frederick Copleston, S. J.

IMAGE BOOKS
A Division of Doubleday & Company, Inc.
Garden City, New York

Image Books Edition
by special arrangement with The Newman Press
Image Books Edition published September 1965

CONTENTS

PREFACE

As Volume 6 of this *History of Philosophy* ended with Kant, the natural procedure was to open the present volume with a discussion of post-Kantian German idealism. I might then have turned to the philosophy of the first part of the nineteenth century in France and Great Britain. But on reflection it seemed to me that nineteenth-century German philosophy could reasonably be treated on its own, and that this would confer on the volume a greater unity than would otherwise be possible. And in point of fact the only non-German-speaking philosopher considered in the book is Kierkegaard, who wrote in Danish.

The volume has been entitled *Fichte to Nietzsche*, as Nietzsche is the last world-famous philosopher who is considered at any length. It might indeed have been called *Fichte to Heidegger*. For not only have a good many philosophers been mentioned who were chronologically posterior to Nietzsche, but also in the last chapter a glance has been taken at German philosophy in the first half of the twentieth century. But I decided that to call the volume *Fichte to Heidegger* would tend to mislead prospective readers. For it would suggest that twentieth-century philosophers such as Husserl, N. Hartmann, Jaspers and Heidegger are treated, so to speak, for their own sake, in the same way as Fichte, Schelling and Hegel, whereas in fact they are discussed briefly as illustrating different ideas of the nature and scope of philosophy.

In the present work there are one or two variations from the pattern generally followed in preceding volumes. The introductory chapter deals only with the idealist movement, and it has therefore been placed within Part I, not before it. And though in the final chapter there are some retrospective reflections, there is also, as already indicated, a preview of thought in the first half of the twentieth century. Hence I have called this chapter 'Retrospect and Prospect' rather than 'Concluding Review'. Apart from the reasons given in the text for referring to twentieth-century thought there is the reason that I do not propose to include within this *History* any full-scale treatment of the philosophy of the present century. At the same time I did not wish to end the volume abruptly without any reference at all to later developments. The result is, of course, that one lays oneself open to the comment that it would be better to say nothing about these developments than to make some sketchy and inadequate remarks. However, I decided to risk this criticism.

To economize on space I have confined the Bibliography at the end of the book to general works and to works by and on the major figures. As for minor philosophers, many of their writings are mentioned at the appropriate places in the text. In view of the number both of nineteenth-century philosophers and of their publications, and in view of the vast literature on some of the major figures, anything like a full bibliography is out of the question. In the case of the twentieth-century thinkers mentioned in the final chapter, some books are referred to in the text or in footnotes, but no explicit bibliography has been given. Apart from the problem of space I felt that it would be inappropriate to supply, for example, a bibliography on Heidegger when he is only briefly mentioned.

The present writer hopes to devote a further volume, the eighth in this *History*, to some aspects of French and British thought in the nineteenth century. But he does not propose to spread his net any farther. Instead he plans, circumstances permitting, to turn in a supplementary volume to what may be called the philosophy of the history of philosophy, that is, to reflection on the development of philosophical thought rather than to telling the story of this development.

A final remark. A friendly critic observed that this work would be more appropriately called A *History of Western Philosophy* or A *History of European Philosophy* than A *History of Philosophy* without addition. For there is no mention, for instance, of Indian philosophy. The critic was, of course, quite right. But I should like to remark that the omission of Oriental philosophy is neither an oversight nor due to any prejudice on the author's part. The composition of a history of Oriental philosophy is a work for a specialist and requires a knowledge of the relevant languages which the present writer does not possess. Bréhier included a volume on Oriental philosophy in his *Histoire de la philosophie*, but it was not written by Bréhier.

Finally I have pleasure in expressing my gratitude to the Oxford University Press for their kind permission to quote from Kierkegaard's *The Point of View* and *Fear and Trembling* according to the English translations published by them, and to the Princeton University Press for similar permission to quote from Kierkegaard's *Sickness unto Death, Concluding Unscientific Postscript* and *The Concept of Dread*. In the case of quotations from philosophers other than Kierkegaard I have translated the passages myself. But I have frequently given page-references to existing English translations for the benefit of readers who wish to consult a translation rather than the original. In the case of minor figures, however, I have generally omitted references to translations.

Part I

POST-KANTIAN IDEALIST SYSTEMS

Chapter One

INTRODUCTION

Preliminary remarks – Kant's philosophy and idealist meta-physics – The meaning of idealism, its insistence on system and its confidence in the power and scope of philosophy – The idealists and theology – The romantic movement and German idealism – The difficulty in fulfilling the idealist pro-gramme – The anthropomorphic element in German idealism – Idealist philosophies of man.

1. In the German philosophical world during the early part of the nineteenth century we find one of the most remark-able flowerings of metaphysical speculation which have oc-curred in the long history of western philosophy. We are presented with a succession of systems, of original interpre-tations of reality and of human life and history, which pos-sess a grandeur that can hardly be called in question and which are still capable of exercising on some minds at least a peculiar power of fascination. For each of the leading phi-losophers of the period professes to solve the riddle of the world, to reveal the secret of the universe and the meaning of human existence.

True, before the death of Schelling in 1854 Auguste Comte in France had already published his *Course of Positive Phi-losophy* in which metaphysics was represented as a passing stage in the history of human thought. And Germany was to have its own positivist and materialist movements which, while not killing metaphysics, would force metaphysicians to reflect on and define more closely the relation between phi-losophy and the particular sciences. But in the early decades of the nineteenth century the shadow of positivism had not yet fallen across the scene and speculative philosophy enjoyed a period of uninhibited and luxuriant growth. With the great German idealists we find a superb confidence in the power of the human reason and in the scope of philosophy. Looking on reality as the self-manifestation of infinite reason, they thought that the life of self-expression of this reason could be retraced in philosophical reflection. They were not nervous men looking over their shoulders to see if critics were whispering that they were producing poetic effusions under the thin disguise of theoretical philosophy, or that their profundity and obscure language were a mask for lack of clarity of thought. On the contrary, they were convinced that the human spirit had at last come into its own and that the nature of reality was at last clearly revealed to human consciousness. And each set out his vision of the Universe with a splendid confidence in its objective truth.

It can, of course, hardly be denied that German idealism makes on most people today the impression of belonging to another world, to another climate of thought. And we can say that the death of Hegel in 1831 marked the end of an epoch. For it was followed by the collapse of absolute idealism[1] and the emergence of other lines of thought. Even metaphysics took a different turn. And the superb confidence in the power and range of speculative philosophy which was characteristic of Hegel in particular has never been regained. But though German idealism sped through the sky like a rocket and after a comparatively short space of time disintegrated and fell to earth, its flight was extremely impressive. Whatever its shortcomings, it represented one of the most sustained attempts which the history of thought has known to achieve a unified conceptual mastery of reality and experience as a whole. And even if the presuppositions of idealism are rejected, the idealist systems can still retain the power of stimulating the natural impulse of the reflective mind to strive after a unified conceptual synthesis.

Some are indeed convinced that the elaboration of an overall view of reality is not the proper task of scientific philosophy. And even those who do not share this conviction may well think that the achievement of a final systematic synthesis lies beyond the capacity of any one man and is more of an ideal goal than a practical possibility. But we should be prepared to recognize intellectual stature when we meet it. Hegel in particular towers up in impressive grandeur above the vast majority of those who have tried to belittle him. And we can always learn from an outstanding philosopher, even if it is only by reflecting on our reasons for disagreeing with him. The historical collapse of metaphysical idealism does not necessarily entail the conclusion that the great idealists have nothing of value to offer. German idealism has its fantastic aspects, but the writings of the leading idealists are very far from being all fantasy.

2. The point which we have to consider here is not, however, the collapse of German idealism but its rise. And this indeed stands in need of some explanation. On the one hand the immediate philosophical background of the idealist movement was provided by the critical philosophy of Immanuel Kant, who had attacked the claims of metaphysicians to provide theoretical knowledge of reality. On the other hand the German idealists looked on themselves as the true spiritual successors of Kant and not as simply reacting against his ideas. What we have to explain, therefore, is how metaphysical idealism could develop out of the system of a thinker whose name is for ever associated with scepticism about metaphysics' claim to provide us with theoretical knowledge about reality as a whole or indeed about any reality other than the *a priori* structure of human knowledge and experience.[2]

The most convenient starting-point for an explanation of the development of metaphysical idealism out of the critical philosophy is the Kantian notion of the thing-in-itself.[3] In Fichte's view Kant had placed himself in an impossible position by steadfastly refusing to abandon this notion. On the one hand, if Kant had asserted the existence of the thing-in-itself as cause of the given or material element in sensation, he would have been guilty of an obvious inconsistency. For according to his own philosophy the concept of cause cannot be used to extend our knowledge beyond the phenomenal sphere. On the other hand, if Kant retained the idea of the thing-in-itself simply as a problematical and limiting notion, this was tantamount to retaining a ghostly relic of the very dogmatism which it was the mission of the critical philosophy to overcome. Kant's Copernican revolution was a great step forward, and for Fichte there could be no question of moving backwards to a pre-Kantian position. If one had any understanding of the development of philosophy and of the demands of modern thought, one could only go forward and complete Kant's work. And this meant eliminating the thing-in-itself. For, given Kant's premisses, there was no room for an unknowable occult entity supposed to be independent of mind. In other words, the critical philosophy had to be transformed into a consistent idealism; and this meant that things had to be regarded in their entirety as products of thought.

Now, it is immediately obvious that what we think of as the extramental world cannot be interpreted as the product of conscious creative activity by the human mind. As far as ordinary consciousness is concerned, I find myself in a world of objects which affect me in various ways and which I spontaneously think of as existing independently of my thought and will. Hence the idealist philosopher must go behind consciousness, as it were, and retrace the process of the unconscious activity which grounds it.

But we must go further than this and recognize that the production of the world cannot be attributed to the individual self at all, even to its unconscious activity. For if it were attributed to the individual finite self as such, it would be very difficult, if not impossible, to avoid solipsism, a position which can hardly be seriously maintained. Idealism is thus compelled to go behind the finite subject to a supra-individual intelligence, an absolute subject.

The word 'subject', however, is not really appropriate, except as indicating that the ultimate productive principle lies, so to speak, on the side of thought and not on the side of the sensible thing. For the words 'subject' and 'object' are correlative. And the ultimate principle is, considered in itself, without object. It grounds the subject-object relationship and, in itself, transcends the relationship. It is subject and object in identity, the infinite activity from which both proceed.

Post-Kantian idealism was thus necessarily a metaphysics. Fichte, starting from the position of Kant and developing it into idealism, not unnaturally began by calling his first principle the ego, turning Kant's transcendental ego into a metaphysical or ontological principle. But he explained that he meant by this the absolute ego, not the individual finite ego. But with the other idealists (and with Fichte himself in his later philosophy) the word 'ego' is not used in this context. With Hegel the ultimate principle is infinite reason, infinite spirit. And we can say that for metaphysical idealism in general reality is the process of the self-expression or self-manifestation of infinite thought or reason.

This does not mean, of course, that the world is reduced to a process of thinking in the ordinary sense. Absolute thought or reason is regarded as an activity, as productive reason which posits or expresses itself in the world. And the world retains all the reality which we see it to possess. Metaphysical idealism does not involve the thesis that empirical reality consists of subjective ideas; but it involves the vision of the world and human history as the objective expression of creative reason. This vision was fundamental in the outlook of the German idealist: he could not avoid it. For he accepted the necessity of transforming the critical philosophy into idealism. And this transformation meant that the world in its entirety had to be regarded as the product of creative thought or reason. If, therefore, we look on the need for transforming the philosophy of Kant into idealism as a premiss, we can say that this premiss determined the basic vision of the post-Kantian idealists. But when it comes to explaining what is meant by saying that reality is a process of creative thought, there is room for different interpretations, for the several particular visions of the different idealist philosophers.

The direct influence of Kant's thought was naturally felt more strongly by Fichte than by Schelling or Hegel. For Schelling's philosophizing presupposed the earlier stages of Fichte's thought, and Hegel's absolute idealism presupposed the earlier phases of the philosophies of both Fichte and Schelling. But this does not alter the fact that the movement of German idealism as a whole presupposed the critical philosophy. And in his account of the history of modern philosophy Hegel depicted the Kantian system as representing an advance on preceding stages of thought and as demanding to be itself developed and surpassed in succeeding stages.

In this section reference has been made so far only to the process of eliminating the thing-in-itself and transferring Kant's philosophy into metaphysical idealism. But it was certainly not my intention to suggest that the post-Kantian idealists were influenced only by the idea that the thing-in-itself had to be eliminated. They were also influenced by other aspects of the critical philosophy. For example, Kant's doctrine of the primacy of the practical reason had a powerful appeal for Fichte's strongly-marked ethical outlook. And we find him interpreting the absolute ego as an infinite practical reason or moral will which posits Nature as a field and instrument for moral activity. In his philosophy the concepts of action, of duty and of moral vocation are extremely prominent. And we are perhaps entitled to say that Fichte turned Kant's second *Critique* into a metaphysics, employing his development of the first *Critique* as a means of doing so. With Schelling, however, the prominence given to the philosophy of art, to the role of genius and to the metaphysical significance of aesthetic intuition and artistic creation links him with the third *Critique* rather than with the first or second.

But instead of dwelling at length on the particular ways in which different parts or aspects of Kant's philosophy influenced this or that idealist, it will be more appropriate in our introductory chapter if we take a broader and more general view of the relation between the critical philosophy and metaphysical idealism.

The desire to form a coherent and unified interpretation of reality is natural to the reflective mind. But the actual task to be performed presents itself in different ways at different times. For example, the development of physical science in the post-mediaeval world meant that the philosopher who wished to construct an overall interpretation had to grapple with the problem of reconciling the scientific view of the world as a mechanical system with the demands of the moral and religious consciousness. Descartes was faced with this problem. And so was Kant.[4] But though Kant rejected the ways of dealing with this problem which were characteristic of his philosophical predecessors and offered his own original solution, it is arguable that in the long run he left us with 'a bifurcated reality'.[5] On the one hand we have the phenomenal world, the world of Newtonian science, governed by necessary causal laws.[6] On the other hand there is the supersensuous world of the free moral agent and of God. There is no valid reason for asserting that the phenomenal world is the only reality.[7] But at the same time there is no theoretical proof of the existence of a supersensuous reality. It is a matter of practical faith, resting on the moral consciousness. It is true that in the third *Critique* Kant endeavoured to bridge the gulf between the two worlds to the extent in which he considered this to be possible for the human mind.[8] But it is understandable if other philosophers were not satisfied with his performance. And the German idealists were able to proceed beyond Kant by means of their development and transformation of his philosophy. For if reality is the unified process by which absolute thought or reason manifests itself, it is intelligible. And it is intelligible by the human mind, provided that this mind can be regarded as the vehicle, as it were, of absolute thought reflecting on itself.

This condition possesses an obvious importance if there is to be any continuity between Kant's idea of the only possible scientific metaphysics of the future and the idealists' conception of metaphysics. For Kant the metaphysics of the future is a transcendental critique of human experience and knowledge. We can say in fact that it is the human mind's reflective awareness of its own spontaneous formative activity. In metaphysical idealism, however, the activity in question is productive in the fullest sense (the thing-in-itself having been eliminated); and this activity is attributed, not to the finite human mind as such, but to absolute thought or reason. Hence philosophy, which is reflection by the human mind, cannot be regarded as absolute thought's reflective awareness of itself unless the human mind is capable of rising to the absolute point of view and becoming the vehicle, as it were, of absolute thought or reason's reflective awareness of its own activity. If this condition is fulfilled, there is a certain continuity between Kant's idea of the only possible scientific type of metaphysics and the idealist conception of metaphysics. There is also, of course, an obvious inflation, so to speak. That is to say, the Kantian theory of knowledge is inflated into a metaphysics of reality. But the process of inflation retains a certain measure of continuity. While going far beyond anything that Kant himself envisaged, it is not a simple reversion to a pre-Kantian conception of metaphysics.

The transformation of the Kantian theory of knowledge into a metaphysics of reality carries with it, of course, certain important changes. For example, if with the elimination of the thing-in-itself the world becomes the self-manifestation of thought or reason, the Kantian distinction between the *a priori* and the *a posteriori* loses its absolute character. And the categories, instead of being subjective forms or conceptual moulds of the human understanding, become categories of reality; they regain an objective status. Again, the teleological judgment is no longer subjective, as with Kant. For in metaphysical idealism the idea of purposiveness in Nature cannot be simply a heuristic or regulative principle of the human mind, a principle which performs a useful function but the objectivity of which cannot be theoretically proved. If Nature is the expression and manifestation of thought or reason in its movement towards a goal, the process of Nature must be teleological in character.

It cannot indeed be denied that there is a very great difference between Kant's modest idea of the scope and power of metaphysics and the idealists' notion of what metaphysical philosophy is capable of achieving. Kant himself repudiated Fichte's demand for the transformation of the critical philosophy into pure idealism by the elimination of the thing-in-itself. And it is easy to understand the attitude of the neo-Kantians who, later in the century, announced that they had had enough of the airy metaphysical speculations of the idealists and that it was time to return to the spirit of Kant himself. At the same time the development of Kant's system into metaphysical idealism is not unintelligible, and the remarks in this section may have helped to explain how the idealists were able to look on themselves as Kant's legitimate spiritual successors.

3. It will be clear from what has been said about the development of metaphysical idealism that the post-Kantian idealists were not subjective idealists in the sense of holding that the human mind knows only its own ideas as distinct from extramentally existing things. Nor were they subjective idealists in the sense of holding that all objects of knowledge are the products of the finite human subject. True, Fichte's use of the word 'ego' in his earlier writings tended to give the impression that this was precisely what he did hold. But the impression was mistaken. For Fichte insisted that the productive subject was not the finite ego as such but the absolute ego, a transcendental and supra-individual principle. And as for Schelling and Hegel, any reduction of things to products of the individual finite mind was entirely foreign to their thought.

But though it is easily understood that post-Kantian idealism did not involve subjective idealism in either of the senses alluded to in the last paragraph, it is not so easy to give a general description of the movement which will apply to all the leading idealist systems. For they differ in important respects. Moreover, the thought of Schelling in particular moved through successive phases. At the same time there is, of course, a family likeness between the different systems. And this fact justifies one in venturing on some generalizations.

Inasmuch as reality is looked on as the self-expression or self-unfolding of absolute thought or reason, there is a marked tendency in German idealism to assimilate the causal relation to the logical relation of implication. For example, the empirical world is conceived by Fichte and by Schelling (in at any rate the earlier phases of the latter's thought) as standing to the ultimate productive principle in the relation of consequent to antecedent. And this means, of course, that the world follows necessarily from the first productive principle, the priority of which is logical and not temporal. Obviously, there is not and cannot be any question of external compulsion. But the Absolute spontaneously and inevitably manifests itself in the world. And there is really no place for the idea of creation in time, in the sense of there being an ideally assignable first moment of time.[9]

This notion of reality as the self-unfolding of absolute reason helps to explain the idealists' insistence on system. For if philosophy is the reflective reconstruction of the structure of a dynamic rational process, it should be systematic, in the sense that it should begin with the first principle and exhibit the essential rational structure of reality as flowing from it. True, the idea of a purely theoretical deduction does not in practice occupy such an important place in metaphysical idealism as the foreground dialectical process of Fichte and above all Hegel tends to suggest. For idealist philosophy is the conceptual reconstruction of a dynamic activity, a self-unfolding infinite life, rather than a strict analysis of the meaning and implications of one or more initial basic propositions. But the general world-view is embryonically contained in the initial idea of the world as the process of absolute reason's self-manifestation. And it is the business of philosophy to give systematic articulation to this idea, reliving the process, as it were, on the plane of reflective awareness. Hence, though it would be possible to start from the empirical manifestations of absolute reason and work backwards, metaphysical idealism naturally follows a deductive form of exposition, in the sense that it systematically retraces a teleological movement.

Now, if we assume that reality is a rational process and that its essential dynamic structure is penetrable by the philosopher, this assumption is naturally accompanied by a confidence in the power and scope of metaphysics which contrasts sharply with Kant's modest estimate of what it can achieve. And this contrast is obvious enough if one compares the critical philosophy with Hegel's system of absolute idealism. Indeed, it is probably true to say that Hegel's confidence in the power and reach of philosophy was unequalled by any previous philosopher of note. At the same time we have seen in the last section that there was a certain continuity between Kant's philosophy and metaphysical idealism. And we can even say, though it is a paradoxical statement, that the closer idealism kept to Kant's idea of the only possible form of scientific metaphysics, the greater was its confidence in the power and scope of philosophy. For if we assume that philosophy is thought's reflective awareness of its own spontaneous activity, and if we substitute a context of idealist metaphysics for the context of Kant's theory of human knowledge and experience, we then have the idea of the rational process, which is reality, becoming aware of itself in and through man's philosophical reflection. In this case the history of philosophy is the history of absolute reason's self-reflection. In other words, the Universe knows itself in and through the mind of man. And philosophy can be interpreted as the self-knowledge of the Absolute.

True, this conception of philosophy is characteristic more of Hegel than of the other leading idealists. Fichte ended by insisting on a divine Absolute which in itself transcends the reach of human thought, and in his later philosophy of religion Schelling emphasized the idea of a personal God who reveals himself to man. It is with Hegel that the idea of the philosopher's conceptual mastery of all reality and the interpretation of this mastery as the self-reflection of the Absolute become most prominent. But to say this is simply to say that it is in Hegelianism, the greatest achievement of metaphysical idealism, that the faith in the power and scope of speculative philosophy which inspired the idealist movement finds its purest and most grandiose expression.

4. Mention has just been made of Fichte's later doctrine of the Absolute and of Schelling's philosophy of religion. And it is appropriate to say something here of the relations be-

tween German idealism and theology. For it is important to
understand that the idealist movement was not simply the
result of a transformation of the critical philosophy into
metaphysics. All three of the leading idealists started as students of theology, Fichte at Jena, Schelling and Hegel at
Tübingen. And though it is true that they turned very
quickly to philosophy, theological themes played a conspicuous role in the development of German idealism. Nietzsche's
statement that the philosophers in question were concealed
theologians was misleading in some respects, but it was not
altogether without foundation.

The importance of the role played by theological themes
in German idealism can be illustrated by the following contrast. Though not a professional scientist Kant was always interested in science. His first writings were mainly concerned
with scientific topics,[10] and one of his primary questions was
about the conditions which render scientific knowledge possible. Hegel, however, came to philosophy from theology. His
first writings were largely theological in character, and he was
later to declare that the subject-matter of philosophy is God
and nothing but God. Whether the term 'God', as here used,
is to be understood in anything approaching a theistic sense
is not a question which need detain us at present. The point
to be made is that Hegel's point of departure was the theme
of the relation between the infinite and the finite, between
God and creatures. His mind could not remain satisfied with
a sharp distinction between the infinite Being on the one
hand and finite beings on the other, and he tried to bring
them together, seeing the infinite in the finite and the finite
in the infinite. In the theological phase of his development
he was inclined to think that the elevation of the finite to
the infinite could take place only in the life of love, and he
then drew the conclusion that philosophy must in the long
run yield to religion. As a philosopher, he tried to exhibit the
relation between the infinite and the finite conceptually, in
thought, and tended to depict philosophical reflection as a
higher form of understanding than the way of thinking which
is characteristic of the religious consciousness. But the gen-

eral theme of the relation between the infinite and the finite which runs through his philosophical system was taken over, as it were, from his early theological reflections.

It is not, however, simply a question of Hegel. In Fichte's earlier philosophy the theme of the relation between the infinite and the finite is not indeed conspicuous, for he was primarily concerned with the completion, as he saw it, of Kant's deduction of consciousness. But in his later thought the idea of one infinite divine Life comes to the fore, and the religious aspects of his philosophy were developed. As for Schelling, he did not hesitate to say that the relation between the divine infinite and the finite is the chief problem of philosophy. And his later thought was profoundly religious in character, the ideas of man's alienation from and return to God playing a prominent role.

Being philosophers, the idealists tried, of course, to understand the relation between the infinite and the finite. And they tended to view it according to the analogy of logical implication. Further, if we make the necessary exception for Schelling's later religious philosophy, we can say that the idea of a personal God who is both infinite and fully transcendent seemed to the idealists to be both illogical and unduly anthropomorphic. Hence we find a tendency to transform the idea of God into the idea of the Absolute, in the sense of the all-comprehensive totality. At the same time the idealists had no intention of denying the reality of the finite. Hence the problem which faced them was that of including, as it were, the finite within the life of the infinite without depriving the former of its reality. And the difficulty of solving this problem is responsible for a good deal of the ambiguity in metaphysical idealism when it is a question of defining its relation to theism on the one hand and pantheism on the other. But in any case it is clear that a central theological theme, namely the relation between God and the world, looms large in the speculations of the German idealists.

It has been said above that Nietzsche's description of the German idealists as concealed theologians is misleading in some respects. For it suggests that the idealists were concerned with reintroducing orthodox Christianity by the backdoor, whereas in point of fact we find a marked tendency to substitute metaphysics for faith and to rationalize the revealed mysteries of Christianity, bringing them within the scope of the speculative reason. To use a modern term, we find a tendency to demythologize Christian dogmas, turning them in the process into a speculative philosophy. Hence we may be inclined to smile at J. H. Stirling's picture of Hegel as the great philosophical champion of Christianity. We may be more inclined to accept McTaggart's view, and also Kierkegaard's, that the Hegelian philosophy undermined Christianity from within as it were, by professing to lay bare the rational content of the Christian doctrines in their traditional form. And we may feel that the connection which Fichte sought to establish between his later philosophy of the Absolute and the first chapter of St. John's Gospel was somewhat tenuous.

At the same time there is no cogent reason for supposing, for instance, that Hegel had his tongue in his cheek when he referred to St. Anselm and to the process of faith seeking understanding. His early essays showed marked hostility to positive Christianity; but he came to change his attitude and to take the Christian faith under his wing, so to speak. It would be absurd to claim that Hegel was in fact an orthodox Christian. But he was doubtless sincere when he represented the relation of Christianity to Hegelianism as being that of the absolute religion to the absolute philosophy, two different ways of apprehending and expressing the same truth-content. From an orthodox theological standpoint Hegel must be judged to have substituted reason for faith, philosophy for revelation, and to have defended Christianity by rationalizing it and turning it, to borrow a phrase from McTaggart, into exoteric Hegelianism. But this does not alter the fact that Hegel thought of himself as having demonstrated the truth of the Christian religion. Nietzsche's statement, therefore, was not altogether wide of the mark, especially if one takes into account the development in the religious aspects of

Fichte's thought and the later phases of Schelling's philosophy. And in any case the German idealists certainly attributed significance and value to the religious consciousness and found a place for it in their systems. They may have turned from theology to philosophy, but they were very far from being irreligious men or rationalists in a modern sense.

5. But there is another aspect of metaphysical idealism which must also be mentioned, namely its relation to the romantic movement in Germany. The description of German idealism as the philosophy of romanticism is indeed open to serious objection. In the first place it suggests the idea of a one-way influence. That is to say, it suggests that the great idealist systems were simply the ideological expression of the romantic spirit, whereas in point of fact the philosophies of Fichte and Schelling exercised a considerable influence on some of the romantics. In the second place, the leading idealist philosophers stood in somewhat different relations to the romantics. We can say indeed that Schelling gave notable expression to the spirit of the romantic movement. But Fichte indulged in some sharp criticism of the romantics, even if the latter had derived inspiration from certain of his ideas. And Hegel had scant sympathy with some aspects of romanticism. In the third place it is arguable that the term 'philosophy of romanticism' would be better applied to the speculative ideas developed by romantics such as Friedrich Schlegel (1772–1829) and Novalis (1772–1801) than to the great idealist systems. At the same time there was undoubtedly some spiritual affinity between the idealist and romantic movements. The romantic spirit as such was indeed an attitude towards life and the universe rather than a systematic philosophy. One may perhaps borrow Rudolf Carnap's terms and speak of it as a *Lebensgefühl* or *Lebenseinstellung*.[11] And it is perfectly understandable that Hegel saw a considerable difference between systematic philosophical reflection and the utterances of the romantics. But when we look back on the German scene in the first part of the nineteenth century, we are naturally struck by affinities as well as by differences. After all, metaphysical idealism and romanticism were more or less

contemporary German cultural phenomena, and an underlying spiritual affinity is only what one might expect to find.

The romantic spirit is notoriously difficult to define. Nor
indeed should one expect to be able to define it. But one
can, of course, mention some of its characteristic traits. For
example, as against the Enlightenment's concentration on
the critical, analytic and scientific understanding the romantics exalted the power of the creative imagination and the
role of feeling and intuition.[12] The artistic genius took the
place of *le philosophe*. But the emphasis which was laid on
the creative imagination and on artistic genius formed part
of a general emphasis on the free and full development of
the human personality, on man's creative powers and on en-
joyment of the wealth of possible human experience. In
other words, stress was laid on the originality of each human
person rather than on what is common to all men. And this
insistence on the creative personality was sometimes associated with a tendency to ethical subjectivism. That is to say,
there was a tendency to depreciate fixed universal moral laws
or rules in favour of the free development of the self in
accordance with values rooted in and corresponding to the
individual personality. I do not mean to imply by this that
the romantics had no concern for morality and moral values.
But there was a tendency, with F. Schlegel for example, to
emphasize the free pursuit by the individual of his own moral
ideal (the fulfilment of his own 'Idea') rather than obedience
to universal laws dictated by the impersonal practical reason.

In developing their ideas of the creative personality some
of the romantics derived inspiration and stimulus from
Fichte's early thought. This is true of both F. Schlegel and
Novalis. But it does not follow, of course, that the use which
they made of Fichte's ideas always corresponded with the
philosopher's intentions. An example will make this clear.
As we have seen, in his transformation of the Kantian philosophy into pure idealism Fichte took as his ultimate creative principle the transcendental ego, considered as unlimited
activity. And in his systematic deduction or reconstruction of
consciousness he made copious use of the idea of the pro-

ductive imagination. Novalis seized on these ideas and represented Fichte as opening up to view the wonders of the
creative self. But he made an important change. Fichte was
concerned with explaining on idealist principles the situation
in which the finite subject finds itself in a world of objects
which are given to it and which affect it in various ways, as in
sensation. He therefore represented the activity of the so-
called productive imagination, when it posits the object as
affecting the finite self, as taking place below the level of
consciousness. By transcendental reflection the philosopher
can be aware *that* this activity takes place, but neither he
nor anyone else is aware of it *as* taking place. For the positing
of the object is logically prior to all awareness or consciousness. And this activity of the productive imagination is certainly not modifiable at the will of the finite self. Novalis,
however, depicted the activity of the productive imagination
as modifiable by the will. Just as the artist creates works of
art, so is man a creative power not only in the moral sphere
but also, in principle at least, in the natural sphere. Fichte's
transcendental idealism was thus turned into Novalis's 'magi-
cal idealism'. In other words, Novalis seized on some of
Fichte's philosophical theories and used them in the service
of a poetic and romantic extravaganza, to exalt the creative
self.

Further, the romantics' emphasis on the creative genius
links them with Schelling much more than with Fichte. As
will be seen in due course, it was the former and not the
latter who laid stress on the metaphysical significance of art
and on the role of artistic genius. When Friedrich Schlegel
asserted that there is no greater world than the world of art
and that the artist exhibits the Idea in finite form, and when
Novalis asserted that the poet is the true 'magician', the
embodiment of the creative power of the human self, they
were speaking in ways which were more in tune with the
thought of Schelling than with the strongly ethical outlook
of Fichte.

Emphasis on the creative self was, however, only one aspect of romanticism. Another important aspect was the ro-

mantics' conception of Nature. Instead of conceiving Nature simply as a mechanical system, so that they would be forced to make a sharp contrast (as in Cartesianism) between man and Nature, the romantics tended to look on Nature as a living organic whole which is in some way akin to spirit and which is clothed in beauty and mystery. And some of them showed a marked sympathy with Spinoza, that is, a romanticized Spinoza.

This view of Nature as an organic totality akin to spirit again links the romantics with Schelling. The philosopher's idea of Nature below man as slumbering spirit and the human spirit as the organ of Nature's consciousness of herself was thoroughly romantic in tone. It is significant that the poet Hölderlin (1770–1843) was a friend of Schelling when they were fellow-students at Tübingen. And the poet's view of Nature as a living comprehensive whole seems to have exercised some influence on the philosopher. In turn Schelling's philosophy of Nature exercised a powerful stimulative influence on some of the romantics. As for the romantic's sympathy with Spinoza, this was shared by the theologian and philosopher Schleiermacher. But it was certainly not shared by Fichte who had a profound dislike for anything approaching a divinization of Nature, which he looked on simply as a field and instrument for free moral activity. In this respect he was anti-romantic in his outlook.

The romantics' attachment to the idea of Nature as an organic living totality does not mean, however, that they emphasized Nature to the detriment, so to speak, of man. We have seen that they also stressed the free creative personality. In the human spirit Nature reaches, as it were, its culmination. Hence the romantic idea of Nature could be and was allied with a marked appreciation of the continuity of historical and cultural development and of the significance of past cultural periods for the unfolding of the potentialities of the human spirit. Hölderlin, for example, had a romantic enthusiasm for the genius of ancient Greece,[13] an enthusiasm which was shared by Hegel in his student days. But special attention can be drawn here to the reawakened interest in the Middle Ages. The man of the Enlightenment had tended to see in the mediaeval period a dark night which preceded the dawn of the Renaissance and the subsequent emergence of *les philosophes*. But for Novalis the Middle Ages represented, even if imperfectly, an ideal of the organic unity of faith and culture, an ideal which should be recovered. Further, the romantics showed a strong attachment to the idea of the spirit of a people (*Volksgeist*) and an interest in the cultural manifestation of this spirit, such as language. In this respect they continued the thought of Herder[14] and other predecessors.

The idealist philosophers not unnaturally shared this appreciation of historical continuity and development. For history was for them the working-out in time of a spiritual Idea, a *telos* or end. Each of the great idealists had his philosophy of history, that of Hegel being particularly notable. As Fichte looked on Nature primarily as an instrument for moral activity, he naturally laid more emphasis on the sphere of the human spirit and on history as a movement towards the realization of an ideal moral world-order. In Schelling's philosophy of religion history appears as the story of the return to God of fallen humanity, of man alienated from the true centre of his being. With Hegel the idea of the dialectic of national spirits plays a prominent role, though this is accompanied by an insistence on the part played by so-called world-historical individuals. And the movement of history as a whole is depicted as a movement towards the realization of spiritual freedom. In general, we can say, the great idealists regarded their epoch as a time in which the human spirit had become conscious of the significance of its activity in history and of the meaning or direction of the whole historical process.

Above all perhaps romanticism was characterized by a feeling for and longing for the infinite. And the ideas of Nature and of human history were brought together in the conception of them as manifestations of one infinite Life, as aspects of a kind of divine poem. Thus the notion of infinite Life served as a unifying factor in the romantic world-outlook. At first sight perhaps the romantics' attachment to the idea of the *Volksgeist* may appear to be at variance with their emphasis on the free development of the individual personality. But there was really no radical incompatibility. For the infinite totality was conceived, generally speaking, as infinite Life which manifested itself in and through finite beings but not as annihilating them or as reducing them to mere mechanical instruments. And the spirits of peoples were conceived as manifestations of the same infinite Life, as relative totalities which required for their full development the free expression of the individual personalities which were the bearers, so to speak, of these spirits. And the same can be said of the State, considered as the political embodiment of the spirit of a people.

The typical romantic was inclined to conceive the infinite totality aesthetically, as an organic whole with which man felt himself to be one, the means of apprehending this unity being intuition and feeling rather than conceptual thought. For conceptual thought tends to fix and perpetuate defined limits and boundaries, whereas romanticism tends to dissolve limits and boundaries in the infinite flow of Life. In other words, romantic feeling for the infinite was not infrequently a feeling for the indefinite. And this trait can be seen as well in the tendency to obscure the boundary between the infinite and the finite as in the tendency to confuse philosophy with poetry or, within the artistic sphere itself, to intermingle the arts.

Partly, of course, it was a question of seeing affinities and of synthesizing different types of human experience. Thus F. Schlegel regarded philosophy as akin to religion on the ground that both are concerned with the infinite and that every relation of man to the infinite can be said to belong to religion. Indeed art too is religious in character, for the creative artist sees the infinite in the finite, in the form of beauty. At the same time the romantics' repugnance to definite limits and clear-cut form was one of the reasons which led Goethe to make his famous statement that the classical is the healthy and the romantic the diseased. For the matter of that, some of the romantics themselves came to feel the need for giving definite shape to their intuitive and rather hazy visions of life and reality and for combining the nostalgia for the infinite and for the free expression of the individual personality with a recognition of definite limits. And certain representatives of the movement, such as F. Schlegel, found in Catholicism a fulfilment of this need.

The feeling for the infinite obviously constitutes common ground for romanticism and idealism. The idea of the infinite Absolute, conceived as infinite Life, comes to the fore in Fichte's later philosophy, and the Absolute is a central theme in the philosophies of Schelling, Schleiermacher and Hegel. Further, we can say that the German idealists tend to conceive the infinite not as something set over against the finite but as infinite life or activity which expresses itself in and through the finite. With Hegel especially there is a deliberate attempt to mediate between the finite and the infinite, to bring them together without either identifying the infinite with the finite or dismissing the latter as unreal or illusory. The totality lives in and through its particular manifestations, whether it is a question of the infinite totality, the Absolute, or of a relative totality such as the State.

The spiritual affinity between the romantic and idealist movements is thus unquestionable. And it can be illustrated by many examples. For instance, when Hegel depicts art, religion and philosophy as concerned with the Absolute, though in different ways, we can see an affinity between his view and the ideas of F. Schlegel to which reference was made in the last paragraph. At the same time it is necessary to emphasize an important contrast between the great idealist philosophers and the romantics, a contrast which can be illustrated in the following manner.

Friedrich Schlegel assimilated philosophy to poetry and dreamed of their becoming one. In his view philosophizing was primarily a matter of intuitive insights, not of deductive reasoning or of proof. For every proof is a proof of something, and the intuitive grasp of the truth to be proved precedes all argument, which is a purely secondary affair.[15] As Schlegel put it, Leibniz asserted and Wolff proved. Evidently, this remark was not intended as a compliment to Wolff. Further, philosophy is concerned with the Universe, the totality. And we cannot prove the totality: it is apprehended only in intuition. Nor can we describe it in the same way in which we can describe a particular thing and its relations to other particular things. The totality can in a sense be displayed or shown, as in poetry, but to say precisely what it is transcends our power. The philosopher, therefore, is concerned with attempting to say what cannot be said. And for this reason philosophy and the philosopher himself are for the true philosopher a matter for ironic wit.

When, however, we turn from Friedrich Schlegel, the romantic, to Hegel, the absolute idealist, we find a resolute insistence on systematic conceptual thought and a determined rejection of appeals to mystical intention and feeling. Hegel is indeed concerned with the totality, the Absolute, but he is concerned with *thinking* it, with expressing the life of the infinite and its relation to the finite in conceptual thought. It is true that he interprets art, including poetry, as having the same subject-matter as philosophy, namely absolute Spirit. But he also insists on a difference of form which it is essential to preserve. Poetry and philosophy are distinct, and they should not be confused.

It may be objected that the contrast between the romantics' idea of philosophy and that of the great idealists is not nearly so great as a comparison between the views of F. Schlegel and Hegel tends to suggest. Fichte postulated a basic intellectual intuition of the pure or absolute ego an idea which was exploited by some of the romantics. Schelling insisted, at least in one stage of his philosophizing, that the Absolute can be apprehended in itself only in mystical intuition. And he also emphasized an aesthetic intuition through which the nature of the Absolute is apprehended not in itself but in symbolic form. For the matter of that, romantic traits can be discerned even within the Hegelian dialectical logic, which is a logic of movement, designed to exhibit the inner life of the Spirit and to overcome the conceptual antitheses which ordinary logic tends to render fixed and permanent. Indeed, the way in which Hegel depicts the human spirit as passing successively through a variety of attitudes and as restlessly moving from position to position can reasonably be regarded as an expression of the romantic outlook. Hegel's logical apparatus itself is alien to the romantic spirit, but this apparatus belongs to the foreground of his system. Underneath we can see a profound spiritual affinity with the romantic movement.

It is not, however, a question of denying the existence of a spiritual affinity between metaphysical idealism and romanticism. We have already argued that there is such an affinity. It is a question of pointing out that, in general, the idealist philosophers were concerned with systematic thought whereas the romantics were inclined to emphasize the role of intuition and feeling and to assimilate philosophy to poetry. Schelling and Schleiermacher stood indeed closer to the romantic spirit than did Fichte or Hegel. It is true that Fichte postulated a basic intellectual intuition of the pure or absolute ego; but he did not think of this as some sort of privileged mystical insight. For him it was an intuitive grasp of an activity which manifests itself to the reflective consciousness. What is required is not some mystical or poetic capacity but transcendental reflection, which is open in principle to all. And in his attack on the romantics Fichte insisted that his philosophy, though demanding this basic intellectual intuition of the ego as activity, was a matter of logical thought which yielded science, in the sense of certain knowledge. Philosophy is the knowledge of knowledge, the basic science; it is not an attempt to say what cannot be said. As for Hegel, it is doubtless true that we, looking back, can discern romantic traits even within his dialectic. But this does not alter the fact that he insisted that philosophy is not a matter of apocalyptic utterances or poetic rhapsodies or mystical intuitions but of systematic logical thought which thinks its subject-matter conceptually and makes it plain to view. The philosopher's business is to understand reality and to make others understand it, not to edify or to suggest meaning by the use of poetic images.

6. As we have seen, the initial transformation of Kant's philosophy into pure idealism meant that reality had to be looked on as a process of productive thought or reason. In other words, being had to be identified with thought. And the natural programme of idealism was to exhibit the truth of this identification by means of a deductive reconstruction of the essential dynamic structure of the life of absolute thought or reason. Further, if the Kantian conception of philosophy as thought's reflective awareness of its own spontaneous activity was to be retained, philosophical reflection had to be represented as the self-awareness or self-consciousness of absolute reason in and through the human mind. Hence it pertained also to the natural programme of idealism to exhibit the truth of this interpretation of philosophical reflection.

When, however, we turn to the actual history of the idealist movement, we see the difficulty encountered by the idealists in completely fulfilling this programme. Or, to put the matter in another way, we see marked divergences from the pattern suggested by the initial transformation of the critical philosophy into transcendental idealism. For example, Fichte starts with the determination not to go beyond consciousness, in the sense of postulating as his first principle a being which transcends consciousness. He thus takes as his first principle the pure ego as manifested in consciousness, not as a thing but as an activity. But the demands of his transcendental idealism force him to push back, as it were, the ultimate reality behind consciousness. And in the later form of his philosophy we find him postulating absolute infinite Being which transcends thought.

With Schelling the process is in a sense reversed. That is to say, while at one stage of his philosophical pilgrimage he asserts the existence of an Absolute which transcends human thought and conceptualization, in his subsequent religious philosophy he attempts to reconstruct reflectively the essence and inner life of the personal Deity. At the same time, however, he abandons the idea of deducing in a *a priori* manner the existence and structure of empirical reality and emphasizes the idea of God's free self-revelation. He does not entirely abandon the idealist tendency to look on the finite as though it were a logical consequence of the infinite; but once he has introduced the idea of a free personal God his thought necessarily departs to a large extent from the original pattern of metaphysical idealism.

Needless to say, the fact that both Fichte and Schelling, especially the latter, developed and changed their initial positions does not by itself constitute any proof that the developments and changes were unjustified. My point is rather that these illustrate the difficulty in carrying through to completion what I have called the idealist programme. One can say that neither with Fichte nor with Schelling is being in the long run reduced to thought.

It is with Hegel that we find by far the most sustained attempt to fulfil the idealist programme. He has no doubt that the rational is the real and the real the rational. And in his view it is quite wrong to speak of the human mind as merely finite and on this ground to question its power to understand the self-unfolding life of the infinite Absolute. The mind has indeed its finite aspects, but it is also infinite, in the sense that it is capable of rising to the level of absolute thought, at which level the Absolute's knowledge of itself and man's knowledge of the Absolute are one. And Hegel makes what is undoubtedly a most impressive attempt to show in a systematic and detailed way how reality is the life of absolute reason in its movement towards the goal of self-knowledge, thus becoming in actual existence what it always is in essence, namely self-thinking thought.

Clearly, the more Hegel identifies the Absolute's knowledge of itself with man's knowledge of the Absolute, the more completely does he fulfil the demand of the idealist programme that philosophy should be represented as the self-reflection of absolute thought or reason. If the Absolute were a personal God, eternally enjoying perfect self-awareness quite independently of the human spirit, man's knowledge of God would be an outside view, so to speak. If, however, the Absolute is all reality, the Universe, interpreted as the self-unfolding of absolute thought which attains self-reflection in and through the human spirit, man's knowledge of the Absolute is the Absolute's knowledge of itself. And philosophy is productive thought thinking itself.

But what is then meant by productive thought? It is arguable at any rate that it can hardly mean anything else but the Universe considered teleologically, that is, as a process moving towards self-knowledge, this self-knowledge being in effect nothing but man's developing knowledge of Nature, of himself and of his history. And in this case there is nothing behind the Universe, as it were, no thought or reason which expresses itself in Nature and human history in the way that an efficient cause expresses itself in its effect. Thought is teleologically prior, in the sense that man's knowledge of the world-process is represented as the goal of the process and as giving it its significance. But that which is actually or historically prior is Being in the form of objective Nature. And in this case the whole pattern of idealism, as suggested by the initial transformation of Kant's philosophy, is changed. For this transformation inevitably suggests the picture of an activity of infinite thought which produces or creates the objective world, whereas the picture described above is simply the picture of the actual world of experience interpreted as a teleological process. The *telos* or goal of the process is indeed depicted as the world's self-reflection in and through the human mind. But this goal or end is an ideal which is never complete at any given moment of time. Hence the identification of being and thought is never actually achieved.

7. Another aspect of the divergences from the natural pattern of post-Kantian idealism can be expressed in this way. F. H. Bradley, the English absolute idealist, maintained that the concept of God inevitably passes into the concept of the Absolute. That is to say, if the mind tries to think the infinite in a consistent manner, it must in the end acknowledge that the infinite cannot be anything else but the universe of being, reality as a whole, the totality. And with this transformation

of God into the Absolute religion disappears. 'Short of the Absolute God cannot rest, and, having reached that goal, he is lost and religion with him.'[16] A similar view was expressed by R. G. Collingwood. 'God and the absolute are not identical but irretrievably distinct. And yet they are identical in this sense: God is the imaginative or intuitive form in which the absolute reveals itself to the religious consciousness.'[17] If we preserve speculative metaphysics, we must admit in the long run that theism is a half-way house between the frank anthropomorphism of polytheism on the one hand and the idea of the all-inclusive Absolute on the other.

It is indeed obvious that in the absence of any clear idea of the analogy of being the notion of a finite being which is ontologically distinct from the infinite cannot stand. But let us pass over this point, important as it is, and note instead that post-Kantian idealism in what one might call its natural form is thoroughly anthropomorphic. For the pattern of human consciousness is transferred to reality as a whole. Let us suppose that the human ego comes to self-consciousness only indirectly. That is to say, attention is first directed to the not-self. The not-self has to be posited by the ego or subject, not in the sense that the not-self must be ontologically created by the self but in the sense that it must be recognized as an object if consciousness is to arise at all. The ego can then turn back upon itself and become reflectively aware of itself in its activity. In post-Kantian idealism this process of human consciousness is used as a key-idea for the interpretation of reality as a whole. The absolute ego or absolute reason or whatever it may be called is regarded as positing (in an ontological sense) the objective world of Nature as a necessary condition for returning to itself in and through the human spirit.

This general scheme follows naturally enough from the transformation of the Kantian philosophy into metaphysical idealism. But inasmuch as Kant was concerned with human knowledge and consciousness, the inflation of his theory of knowledge into cosmic metaphysics inevitably involves interpreting the process of reality as a whole according to the pattern of human consciousness. And in this sense post-Kantian idealism contains a marked element of anthropomorphism, a fact which it is just as well to notice in view of the not uncommon notion that absolute idealism is much less anthropomorphic than theism. Of course, we cannot conceive God other than analogically; and we cannot conceive the divine consciousness except according to an analogy with human consciousness. But we can endeavour to eliminate in thought the aspects of consciousness which are bound up with finitude. And it is arguable, to put it mildly, that to attribute to the infinite a process of becoming self-conscious is an evident expression of anthropomorphic thinking.

Now, if there is a spiritual reality which is at any rate logically prior to Nature and which becomes self-conscious in and through man, how are we to conceive it? If we conceive it as an unlimited activity which is not itself conscious but grounds consciousness, we have more or less Fichte's theory of the so-called absolute ego.

But the concept of an ultimate reality which is at the same time spiritual and unconscious is not easily understood. Nor, of course, does it bear much resemblance to the Christian concept of God. If, however, we maintain with Schelling in his later religious philosophy that the spiritual reality which lies behind Nature is a personal Being, the pattern of the idealist scheme is inevitably changed. For it cannot then be maintained that the ultimate spiritual reality becomes self-conscious in and through the cosmic process. And inasmuch as Schelling outlived Hegel by more than twenty years we can say that the idealist movement which immediately followed the critical philosophy of Kant ended, chronologically speaking, in a reapproximation to philosophical theism. As we have seen, Bradley maintained that the concept of God is required by the religious consciousness but that, from the philosophical point of view, it must be transformed into the concept of the Absolute. Schelling would have accepted the first contention but rejected the second, at least as understood by Bradley. For in his later years Schelling's philosophy was pretty well a philosophy of the religious consciousness. And he believed that the religious consciousness demanded the transformation of his own former idea of the Absolute into the idea of a personal God. In his theosophical speculations he undoubtedly introduced obvious anthropomorphic elements, as will be seen later. But at the same time the movement of his mind towards theism represented a departure from the peculiar brand of anthropomorphism which was characteristic of post-Kantian idealism.

There is, however, a third possibility. We can eliminate the idea of a spiritual reality, whether unconscious or conscious, which produces Nature, and we can at the same time retain the idea of the Absolute becoming self-conscious. The Absolute then means the world, in the sense of the universe. And we have the picture of man's knowledge of the world and of his own history as the self-knowledge of the Absolute. In this picture, which represents the general line of one of the main interpretations of Hegel's absolute idealism,[18] nothing is added, as it were, to the empirical world except a teleological account of the world-process. That is to say, no existent transcendent Being is postulated; but the universe is interpreted as a process moving towards an ideal goal, namely complete self-reflection in and through the human spirit.

This interpretation can hardly be taken as merely equivalent to the empirical statements that in the course of the world's history man has as a matter of fact appeared and that as a matter of fact he is capable of knowing and of increasing his knowledge of himself, his history and his environment. For presumably none of us, whether materialists or idealists, whether theists, pantheists or atheists, would hesitate to accept these statements. At the very least the interpretation is meant to suggest a teleological pattern, a movement towards human knowledge of the universe, considered as the universe's knowledge of itself. But unless we are prepared to admit that this is only one possible way of regarding the world-process and thus to lay ourselves open to the objection that our choice of this particular pattern is determined by an intellectualist prejudice in favour of knowledge for the sake of knowledge (that is, by a particular valuational judgment), we must claim, it appears, that the world moves by some inner necessity towards the goal of self-knowledge in and through man. But what ground have we for making this claim unless we believe either that Nature itself is unconscious mind (or, as Schelling put it, slumbering Spirit) which strives towards consciousness or that behind Nature there is unconscious mind or reason which spontaneously posits Nature as a necessary precondition for attaining consciousness in and through the human spirit? And if we accept either of these positions, we transfer to the universe as a whole the pattern of the development of human consciousness. This procedure may indeed be demanded by the transformation of the critical philosophy into metaphysical idealism; but it is certainly not less anthropomorphic in character than philosophical theism.

8. In this chapter we have been mainly concerned with German idealism as a theory, or rather set of theories, about reality as a whole, the self-manifesting Absolute. But a philosophy of man is also a prominent feature of the idealist movement. And this is indeed only what one would expect if one considers the metaphysical premisses of the several philosophers. According to Fichte, the absolute ego is an unlimited activity which can be represented as striving towards consciousness of its own freedom. But consciousness exists only in the form of individual consciousness. Hence the absolute ego necessarily expresses itself in a community of finite subjects or selves, each of which strives towards the attainment of true freedom. And the theme of moral activity inevitably comes to the fore. Fichte's philosophy is essentially a dynamic ethical idealism. Again, for Hegel the Absolute is definable as Spirit or as self-thinking Thought. Hence it is more adequately revealed in the human spirit and its life than in Nature. And more emphasis must be placed on the reflective understanding of man's spiritual life (the life of man as a rational being) than on the philosophy of Nature. As for Schelling, when he comes to assert the existence of a personal and free God, he occupies himself concurrently with the

problem of freedom in man and with man's fall from and return to God.

In the idealist philosophies of man and society insistence on freedom is a conspicuous feature. But it does not follow, of course, that the word 'freedom' is used throughout in the same sense. With Fichte the emphasis is on individual freedom as manifested in action. And we can doubtless see in this emphasis a reflection of the philosopher's own dynamic and energetic temperament. For Fichte man is from one point of view a system of natural drives, instincts and impulses; and if he is looked at simply from this point of view, it is idle to talk about freedom. But as spirit man is not tied, so to speak, to the automatic satisfaction of one desire after another: he can direct his activity to an ideal goal and act in accordance with the idea of duty. As with Kant, freedom tends to mean rising above the life of sensual impulse and acting as a rational, moral being. And Fichte is inclined to speak as though activity were its own end, emphasizing free action for the sake of free action.

But though Fichte's primary emphasis is on the individual's activity and on his rising above the slavery of natural drive and impulse to a life of action in accordance with duty, he sees, of course, that some content has to be given to the idea of free moral action. And he does this by stressing the concept of moral vocation. A man's vocation, the series of actions which he ought to perform in the world, is largely determined by his social situation, by his position, for example, as the father of a family. And in the end we have the vision of a multiplicity of moral vocations converging towards a common ideal end, the establishment of a moral world-order.

As a young man Fichte was an enthusiastic supporter of the French Revolution which he regarded as liberating men from forms of social and political life which hindered their free moral development. But then the question arose, what form of social, economic and political organization is best fitted to favour man's moral development? And Fichte found himself compelled to lay increasing emphasis on the positive role of political society as a morally educative power. But though in his later years reflection on contemporary political events, namely the Napoleonic domination and the war of liberation, was partly responsible for the growth in his mind of a nationalistic outlook and for a strong emphasis on the cultural mission of a unified German State in which alone the Germans could find true freedom, his more characteristic idea was that the State is a necessary instrument to preserve the system of rights as long as man has not attained his full moral development. If man as a moral being were fully developed, the State would wither away.

When we turn to Hegel, however, we find a different attitude. Hegel too was influenced in his youth by the ferment of the French Revolution and the drive to freedom. And the term 'freedom' plays a conspicuous role in his philosophy. As will be seen in due course, he represents human history as a movement towards the fuller realization of freedom. But he distinguishes sharply between negative freedom, as mere absence of restraint, and positive freedom. As Kant saw, moral freedom involves obeying only that law which one gives oneself as a rational being. But the rational is the universal. And positive freedom involves identifying oneself with ends that transcend one's desires as a particular individual. It is attained, above all, by identifying one's particular will with Rousseau's General Will which finds expression in the State. Morality is essentially social morality. The formal moral law receives its content and field of application in social life, especially in the State.

Both Fichte and Hegel, therefore, attempt to overcome the formalism of the Kantian ethic by placing morality in a social setting. But there is a difference of emphasis. Fichte places the emphasis on individual freedom and action in accordance with duty mediated by the personal conscience. We have to add as a corrective that the individual's moral vocation is seen as a member of a system of moral vocations, and so in a social setting. But in Fichte's ethics the emphasis is placed on the individual's struggle to overcome himself, to bring his lower self, as it were, into tune with the free will which aims at complete freedom. Hegel, however, places the emphasis on man as a member of political society and on the social aspects of ethics. Positive freedom is something to be attained through membership in a greater organic whole. As a corrective or counterweight to this emphasis we must add that for Hegel no State can be fully rational unless it recognizes the value of and finds room for subjective or individual freedom. When at Berlin Hegel lectured on political theory and described the State in highfaluting terms, he was concerned with making his hearers socially and politically conscious and with overcoming what he regarded as an unfortunate one-sided emphasis on the inwardness of morality rather than with turning them into totalitarians. Further, political institutions constitute, according to Hegel, the necessary basis for man's higher spiritual activities, art, religion and philosophy, in which the freedom of the spirit reaches its supreme expression.

What one misses, however, in both Fichte and Hegel is perhaps a clear theory of absolute moral values. If we talk with Fichte about action for action's sake, freedom for the sake of freedom, we may show an awareness of the unique character of each human being's moral vocation. But at the same time we run the risk of emphasizing the creative personality and the uniqueness of its moral vocation at the expense of the universality of the moral law. If, however, we socialize morality with Hegel, we give it concrete content and avoid the formalism of the Kantian ethic, but at the same time we run the risk of implying that moral values and standards are simply relative to different societies and cultural periods. Obviously, some would maintain that this is in fact the case. But if we do not agree, we require a clearer and more adequate theory of absolute values than Hegel actually provides.

Schelling's outlook was rather different from that either of Fichte or of Hegel. At one period of his philosophical development he utilized a good many of the former's ideas and represented the moral activity of man as tending to create a second Nature, a moral world-order, a moral world within the physical world. But the difference between his attitude and

Fichte's showed itself in the fact that he proceeded to add a philosophy of art and of aesthetic intuition to which he attributed a great metaphysical significance. With Fichte the emphasis was placed on the moral struggle and on free moral action, with Schelling it was placed on aesthetic intuition as a key to the ultimate nature of reality, and he exalted the artistic genius rather than the moral hero. When, however, theological problems came to absorb his interest, his philosophy of man naturally took on a marked religious colouring. Freedom, he thought, is the power to choose between good and bad. And personality is something to be won by the birth of light out of darkness, that is, by a sublimation of man's lower nature and its subordination to the rational will. But these themes are treated in a metaphysical setting. For example, the views on freedom and personality to which allusion has just been made lead Schelling into theosophical speculation about the nature of God. In turn, his theories about the divine nature react on his view of man.

To return to Hegel, the greatest of the German idealists. His analysis of human society and his philosophy of history are certainly very impressive. Many of those who listened to his lectures on history must have felt that the significance of the past and the meaning of the movement of history were being revealed to them. Moreover, Hegel was not exclusively concerned with understanding the past. As has already been remarked, he wished to make his students socially, politically and ethically conscious. And he doubtless thought that his analysis of the rational State could furnish standards and aims in political life, especially in German political life. But the emphasis is placed on understanding. Hegel is the author of the famous saying that the owl of Minerva spreads her wings only with the falling of the dusk, and that when philosophy spreads her grey on grey, then has a shape of life grown cold. He had a vivid realization of the fact that political philosophy is apt to canonize, as it were, the social and political forms of a society or culture which is about to pass away. When a culture or society has become mature and ripe, or even over-ripe, it becomes conscious of itself in and through philosophical reflection, just at the moment when the movement of life is demanding and bringing forth new societies or new social and political forms.

With Karl Marx we find a different attitude. The business of the philosopher is to understand the movement of history in order to change existing institutions and forms of social organization in accordance with the demands of the teleological movement of history. Marx does not, of course, deny the necessity and value of understanding, but he emphasizes the revolutionary function of understanding. In a sense Hegel looks backward, Marx forward. Whether Marx's idea of the philosopher's function is tenable or not is a question which we need not discuss here. It is sufficient to note the difference between the attitudes of the great idealist and the social revolutionary. If we wish to find among the idealist philosophers something comparable to Marx's missionary zeal, we have to turn to Fichte rather than to Hegel. As will be seen in the relevant chapters, Fichte had a passionate belief in the saving mission of his own philosophy for human society. But Hegel felt, as it were, the weight and burden of all history on his shoulders. And looking back on the history of the world, his primary aim was to understand it. Further, though he certainly did not imagine that history had stopped with the coming of the nineteenth century, he was too historically minded to have much faith in the finality of any philosophical Utopia.

Chapter Two

FICHTE (1)

Life and writings – On looking for the fundamental principle of philosophy; the choice between idealism and dogmatism – The pure ego and intellectual intuition – Comments on the theory of the pure ego; phenomenology of consciousness and idealist metaphysics – The three fundamental principles of philosophy – Explanatory comments on Fichte's dialectical method – The theory of science and formal logic – The general idea of the two deductions of consciousness – The theoretical deduction – The practical deduction – Comments on Fichte's deduction of consciousness.

1. Johann Gottlieb Fichte was born in 1762 at Rammenau in Saxony. He came of a poor family, and in the ordinary course of events he could hardly have enjoyed facilities for pursuing advanced studies. But as a small boy he aroused the interest of a local nobleman, the Baron von Miltitz, who undertook to provide for his education. At the appropriate age Fichte was sent to the famous school at Pforta where Nietzsche was later to study. And in 1780 he enrolled as a student of theology in the University of Jena, moving later to Wittenberg and subsequently to Leipzig.

During his studies Fichte came to accept the theory of determinism. To remedy this sad state of affairs a good clergyman recommended to him an edition of Spinoza's *Ethics* which was furnished with a refutation by Wolff. But as the refutation seemed to Fichte to be extremely weak, the effect of the work was the very opposite of that intended by the pastor. Determinism, however, was not really in tune with Fichte's active and energetic character or with his strong ethical interests, and it was soon replaced by an insistence on moral freedom. He was later to show himself a vigorous opponent of Spinozism, but it always represented for him one of the great alternatives in philosophy.

For financial reasons Fichte found himself compelled to take a post as tutor in a family at Zürich where he read Rousseau and Montesquieu and welcomed the news of the French Revolution with its message of liberty. His interest in Kant was aroused when a student's request for the explanation of the critical philosophy led him to study it for the first time. And in 1791, when returning to Germany from Warsaw, where he had a brief and rather humiliating experience as tutor in a nobleman's family, he visited Kant at Königsberg. But he was not received with any enthusiasm. And he therefore attempted to win the great man's favour by writing an essay to develop Kant's justification of faith in the name of the practical reason. The resulting *Essay towards a Critique of all Revelation (Versuch einer Kritik aller Offenbarung)* pleased Kant, and after some difficulties with the theological censorship it was published in 1792. As the name of the author was not given, some reviewers concluded that the essay had been written by Kant. And when Kant proceeded to correct this error and to praise the real author, Fichte's name became at once widely known.

In 1793 Fichte published his *Contributions Designed to Correct the Judgment of the Public on the French Revolution*. This work won for him the reputation of being a democrat and Jacobin, a politically dangerous figure. In spite of this, however, he was appointed professor of philosophy at Jena in 1794, partly owing to a warm recommendation by Goethe. In addition to his more professional courses of lectures Fichte gave a series of conferences on the dignity of man and the vocation of the scholar, which were published in the year of his appointment to the chair. He was always something of a missionary or preacher. But the chief publication of 1794 was the *Basis of the Entire Theory of Science (Grundlage der gesammten Wissenschaftslehre)* in which he presented his idealist development of the critical philosophy of Kant. His predecessor in the chair of philosophy at Jena, K. L.

Reinhold (1758–1823), who had accepted an invitation to Kiel, had already demanded that the Kantian criticism should be turned into a system, that is to say, that it should be derived systematically from one fundamental principle. And in his theory of science Fichte undertook to fulfil this task more successfully than Reinhold had done.[1] The theory of science was conceived as exhibiting the systematic development from one ultimate principle of the fundamental propositions which lie at the basis of and make possible all particular sciences or ways of knowing. But to exhibit this development is at the same time to portray the development of creative thought. Hence the theory of science is not only epistemology but also metaphysics.

But Fichte was very far from concentrating exclusively on the theoretical deduction of consciousness. He laid great stress on the moral end of the development of consciousness or, in more concrete terms, on the moral purpose of human existence. And we find him publishing in 1796 the *Basis of Natural Right (Grundlage des Naturrechts)* and in 1798 *The System of Ethics (Das System der Sittenlehre)*. Both subjects are said to be treated 'according to the principles of the theory of science'. And so no doubt they are. But the works are much more than mere appendages to the *Wissenschaftslehre*. For they display the true character of Fichte's philosophy, that is, as a system of ethical idealism.

Complaints have often been made, and not without reason, of the obscurity of the metaphysical idealists. But a prominent feature of Fichte's literary activity was his unremitting efforts to clarify the ideas and principles of the theory of science.[2] For instance, in 1797 he published two introductions to the *Wissenschaftslehre* and in 1801 his *Sonnenklarer Bericht, A Report, Clear as the Sun, for the General Public on the Real Essence of the Latest Philosophy: An Attempt to Compel the Reader to Understand*. The title may have been over-optimistic, but at any rate it bore witness to the author's efforts to make his meaning clear. Moreover, in the period 1801–13 Fichte composed, for his lecture courses, several revised versions of the *Wissenschaftslehre*. In

1810 he published *The Theory of Science in Its General Lines* (*Die Wissenschaftslehre in ihrem allgemeinen Umrisse*) and the *Facts of Consciousness* (*Tatsachen des Bewusstseins*, second edition, 1813).

In 1799 Fichte's career at Jena came to an abrupt end. He had already aroused some antagonism in the university by his plans to reform the students' societies and by his Sunday discourses which seemed to the clergy to constitute an act of trespass on their preserves. But his crowning offence was the publication in 1798 of an essay *On the Ground of Our Belief in a Divine World-Order* (*Ueber den Grund unseres Glaubens an eine göttliche Weltregierung*). The appearance of this essay led to a charge of atheism, on the ground that Fichte identified God with a moral world-order to be created and sustained by the human will. The philosopher tried to defend himself, but without success. And in 1799 he had to leave Jena and went to Berlin.

In 1800 Fichte published *The Vocation of Man* (*Die Bestimmung des Menschen*). The work belongs to his so-called popular writings, addressed to the general educated public rather than to professional philosophers; and it is a manifesto in favour of the author's idealist system as contrasted with the romantics' attitude to Nature and to religion. Fichte's exalted language may indeed easily suggest a romantic pantheism, but the significance of the work was understood well enough by the romantics themselves. Schleiermacher, for example, saw that Fichte was concerned with repudiating any attempt to achieve a fusion of Spinozism and idealism, and in a sharply critical review he maintained that Fichte's hostile reaction to the idea of the universal necessity of Nature was really caused by his predominating interest in man as a finite, independent being who had at all costs to be exalted above Nature. In Schleiermacher's opinion Fichte should have sought for a higher synthesis which would include the truth in Spinozism while not denying moral freedom, instead of simply opposing man to Nature.

In the same year, 1800, Fichte published his work on *The Closed Commercial State* (*Der geschlossene Handelsstaat*) in

which he proposed a kind of State socialism. It has already
been remarked that Fichte was something of a missionary.
He regarded his system not only as the philosophical truth
in an abstract, academic sense, but also as the saving truth,
in the sense that the proper application of its principles would
lead to the reform of society. In this respect at least he resembles Plato. Fichte had once hoped that Freemasonry
might prove an apt instrument for promoting moral and social
reform by taking up and applying the principles of the *Wissenschaftslehre*. But he was disappointed in this hope and
turned instead to the Prussian government. And his work was
really a programme offered to the government for implemen-
tation.

In 1804 Fichte accepted the offer of a chair at Erlangen.
But he was not actually nominated professor until April 1805,
and he employed the interval by lecturing at Berlin on the
Characteristics of the Present Age (*Grundzüge des gegen-
wärtigen Zeitalters*). In these lectures he attacked the view
of romantics such as Novalis, Tieck and the two Schlegels.
Tieck introduced Novalis to Boehme's writings, and some of
the romantics were enthusiastic admirers of the mystical
shoemaker of Görlitz. But their enthusiasm was not shared by
Fichte. Nor had he any sympathy with Novalis's dream of the
restoration of a theocratic Catholic culture. His lectures were
also directed against the philosophy of Nature which had been
developed by Schelling, his former disciple. But these polem-
ics are in a sense incidental to the general philosophy of history which is sketched in the lectures. Fichte's 'present age'
represents one of the epochs in the development of man towards the goal of history described as the ordering of all human relations with freedom according to reason. The lectures
were published in 1806.

At Erlangen Fichte lectured in 1805 *On the Nature of the
Scholar* (*Ueber das Wesen des Gelehrten*). And in the winter
of 1805–6 he gave a course of lectures at Berlin on *The Way
to the Blessed Life or The Doctrine of Religion* (*Die An-
weisung zum seligen Leben, oder auch die Religionslehre*).
At first sight at least this work on religion seems to show a rad-

ical change from the philosophy expounded in Fichte's early
writings. We hear less about the ego and much more about
the Absolute and life in God. Indeed, Schelling accused
Fichte of plagiarism, that is, of borrowing ideas from Schelling's theory of the Absolute and trying to graft them on to
the *Wissenschaftslehre*, oblivious of the incompatibility between the two elements. Fichte, however, refused to admit
that his religious ideas, as set forth in *The Doctrine of Religion*, were in any way inconsistent with his original philosophy.

When Napoleon invaded Prussia in 1806, Fichte offered to
accompany the Prussian troops as a lay preacher or orator.
But he was informed that the King considered it a time for
speaking by acts rather than by words, and that oratory would
be better suited for celebrating victory. When events took a
menacing turn Fichte left Berlin; but he returned in 1807,
and in the winter of 1807–8 he delivered his *Addresses to the
German Nation* (*Reden an die deutsche Nation*). These discourses, in which the philosopher speaks in exalted and glow-
ing terms of the cultural mission of the German people,[3]
have lent themselves to subsequent exploitation in an extreme nationalist sense. But in justice to him we should remember the circumstances in which they were delivered,
namely the period of Napoleonic domination.

The year 1810 saw the foundation of the University of
Berlin, and Fichte was appointed dean of the philosophical
faculty. From 1811 to 1812 he was rector of the university.
At the beginning of 1814 he caught typhus from his wife who
had contracted the disease while nursing the sick, and on
January 29th of that year he died.

2. Fichte's initial conception of philosophy has little in
common with the romantic idea of the kinship between it
and poetry. Philosophy is, or at least ought to be, a science.
In the first place, that is to say, it should be a body of propositions which form a systematic whole of such a kind that
each proposition occupies its proper place in a logical order.
And in the second there must be a fundamental or logically
prior proposition. 'Every science must have a fundamental

proposition [*Grundsatz*]. . . . And it cannot have more than one fundamental proposition. For otherwise it would be not one but several sciences.'[4] We might indeed wish to question the statement that every science must have one, and only one basic proposition; but this is at any rate part of what Fichte means by a science.

This idea of science is obviously inspired by a mathematical model. Indeed, Fichte takes geometry as an example of a science. But it is, of course, a particular science, whereas philosophy is for Fichte the science of science, that is, the knowledge of knowledge or doctrine of knowledge (*Wissenschaftslehre*). In other words, philosophy is the basic science. Hence the fundamental proposition of philosophy must be indemonstrable and self-evidently true. 'All other propositions will possess only a mediate certainty, derived from it, whereas it must be immediately certain.'[5] For if its fundamental proposition were demonstrable in another science, philosophy would not be the basic science.

As will be seen in the course of the exposition of his thought, Fichte does not actually adhere to the programme suggested by this concept of philosophy. That is to say, his philosophy is not in practice a strict logical deduction such as could in principle be performed by a machine. But this point must be left aside for the moment. The immediate question is, what is the basic proposition of philosophy?

But before we can answer this question we must decide in what direction we are going to look for the proposition which we are seeking. And here, according to Fichte, one is faced with an initial option, one's choice depending on what kind of a man one is. A man of one type will be inclined to look in one direction and a man of another type in another direction. But this idea of an initial option stands in need of some explanation. And the explanation throws light on Fichte's conception of the task of philosophy and of the issue with which contemporary thought is faced.

In his *First Introduction to the Theory of Science* Fichte tells us that philosophy is called upon to make clear the ground of all experience (*Erfahrung*). But the word experience is here used in a somewhat restricted sense. If we consider the contents of consciousness, we see that they are of two kinds. 'We can say in brief: some of our presentations [*Vorstellungen*] are accompanied by the feeling of freedom, while others are accompanied by the feeling of necessity.'[6] If I construct in imagination a griffin or a golden mountain, or if I make up my mind to go to Paris rather than to Brussels, such presentations seem to depend on myself. And, as depending on the subject's choice, they are said to be accompanied by the feeling of freedom. If we ask why they are what they are, the answer is that the subject makes them what they are. But if I take a walk along a London street, it does not depend simply on myself what I see or hear. And such presentations are said to be accompanied by the feeling of necessity. That is to say, they appear to be imposed upon me. The whole system of these presentations is called by Fichte 'experience' even if he does not always use the term in this limited sense. And we can ask, what is the ground of experience? How are we to explain the obvious fact that a very large class of presentations seem to be imposed on the subject? 'To answer this question is the task of philosophy.'[7]

Now, two possibilities lie open to us. Actual experience is always experience of something by an experiencer: consciousness is always consciousness of an object by a subject or, as Fichte sometimes puts it, intelligence. But by a process which Fichte calls abstraction the philosopher can isolate conceptually the two factors which in actual consciousness are always conjoined. He can thus form the concepts of intelligence-in-itself and thing-in-itself. And two paths lie before him. Either he can try to explain experience (in the sense described in the last paragraph) as the product of intelligence-in-itself, that is, of creative thought. Or he can try to explain experience as the effect of the thing-in-itself. The first path is obviously that of idealism. The second is that of 'dogmatism'. And in the long run dogmatism spells materialism and determinism. If the thing, the object, is taken as the fundamental principle of explanation, intelligence will ultimately be reduced to a mere epiphenomenon.

This uncompromising Either-Or attitude is characteristic of Fichte. There is for him a clear-cut option between two opposed and mutually exclusive positions. True, some philosophers, notably Kant, have endeavoured to effect a compromise, to find, that is to say, a middle path between pure idealism and a dogmatism which ends in deterministic materialism. But Fichte has no use for such compromises. If a philosopher wishes to avoid dogmatism with all its consequences, and if he is prepared to be consistent, he must eliminate the thing-in-itself as a factor in the explanation of experience. The presentations which are accompanied by a feeling of necessity, by the feeling of being imposed upon or affected by an object existing independently of mind or thought, must be accounted for without any recourse to the Kantian idea of the thing-in-itself.

But on what principle is the philosopher to make his choice between the two possibilities which lie open to him? He cannot appeal to any basic theoretical principle. For we are assuming that he has not yet found such a principle but has to decide in what direction he is going to look for it. The issue must, therefore, be decided 'by inclination and interest'.[8] That is to say, the choice which the philosopher makes depends on what kind of a man he is. Needless to say, Fichte is convinced that the superiority of idealism to dogmatism as an explanation of experience becomes evident in the process of working out the two systems. But they have not yet been worked out. And in looking for the first principle of philosophy we cannot appeal to the theoretical superiority of a system which has not yet been constructed.

What Fichte means is that the philosopher who is maturely conscious of his freedom as revealed in moral experience will be inclined to idealism, while the philosopher who lacks this mature moral consciousness will be inclined to dogmatism. The 'interest' in question is thus interest in and for the self, which Fichte regards as the highest interest. The dogmatist, lacking this interest, emphasizes the thing, the not-self. But the thinker who has a genuine interest in and for the free moral subject will turn for his basic philosophical principle to intelligence, the self or ego, rather than to the not-self.

Fichte's preoccupation with the free and morally active self is thus made clear from the start. Underlying and inspiring his theoretical inquiry into the ground of experience there is a profound conviction of the primary significance of man's free moral activity. He continues Kant's insistence on the primacy of the practical reason, the moral will. But he is convinced that to maintain this primacy one has to take the path to pure idealism. For behind Kant's apparently innocent retention of the thing-in-itself Fichte sees the lurking spectre of Spinozism, the exaltation of Nature and the disappearance of freedom. If we are to exorcize this spectre, compromise must be rejected.

We can, of course, detach Fichte's idea of the influence exercised by 'inclination and interest' from his historically-conditioned picture of the initial option with which philosophers are faced. And the idea can then be seen as opening up fascinating vistas in the field of what Karl Jaspers calls 'the psychology of world-views'. But in a book of this kind one must resist the temptation to embark on a discussion of this attractive topic.

3. Assuming that we have chosen the path of idealism, we must turn for the first principle of philosophy to intelligence-in-itself. But it is better to drop this cumbersome term and to speak, as Fichte proceeds to do, of the *I* or ego. We are committed, therefore, to explaining the genesis of experience from the side, so to speak, of the self. In reality Fichte is concerned with deriving consciousness in general from the ego. But in speaking of experience, in the restricted sense explained above, he lays his finger on the crucial difficulty which pure idealism has to face, namely the evident fact that the self finds itself in a world of objects which affect it in various ways. If idealism is incapable of accounting adequately for this fact, it is evidently untenable.

But what is the ego which is the foundation of philosophy? To answer this question we obviously have to go behind the objectifiable self, the ego as object of introspection or of empirical psychology, to the pure ego. Fichte once said to his students: 'Gentlemen, think the wall.' He then proceeded: 'Gentlemen, think him who thought the wall.' Clearly, we could proceed indefinitely in this fashion. 'Gentlemen, think him who thought him who thought the wall', and so on. In other words, however hard we may try to objectify the self, that is, to turn it into an object of consciousness, there always remains an *I* or ego which transcends objectification and is itself the condition of all objectifiability and the condition of the unity of consciousness. And it is this pure or transcendental ego which is the first principle of philosophy.

It is clearly idle to object against Fichte that we cannot find a pure or transcendental ego by peering about. For it is precisely Fichte's contention that the pure ego cannot be found in this way, though it is the necessary condition of our being able to do any peering about. But for this very reason it may appear that Fichte has gone beyond the range of experience (in a wide sense) or consciousness and has failed to observe his own self-imposed limitations. That is to say, having re-affirmed the Kantian view that our theoretical knowledge cannot extend beyond experience, he now seems to have transgressed this limit.

But this, Fichte insists, is not the case. For we can enjoy an intellectual intuition of the pure ego. This is not, however, a mystical experience reserved for the privileged few. Nor is it an intuition of the pure ego as an entity existing behind or beyond consciousness. Rather is it an awareness of the pure ego or *I* principle as an activity within consciousness. And this awareness is a component element in all self-consciousness. 'I cannot take a pace, I cannot move hand or foot, without the intellectual intuition of my self-consciousness in these actions. It is only through intuition that I know that I perform the action. . . . Everyone who ascribes activity to himself appeals to this intuition. In it is the foundation of life, and without it is death.'[9] In other words, anyone who is conscious of an action as his own is aware of himself acting. In this sense he has an intuition of the self as activity. But it does not follow that he is reflectively aware of this intuition as a component element in consciousness. It is only the philosopher who is reflectively aware of it, for the simple reason that transcendental reflection, by which the attention is reflected onto the pure ego, is a philosophical act. But this reflection is directed, so to speak, to ordinary consciousness, not to a privileged mystical experience. Hence, if the philosopher wishes to convince anyone of the reality of this intuition, he can only draw the man's attention to the data of consciousness and invite him to reflect for himself. He cannot show the man the intuition existing in a pure state, unmixed with any component elements; for it does not exist in this state. Nor can he convince the other man by means of some abstract proof. He can only invite the man to reflect on his own self-consciousness and to see that it includes an intuition of the pure ego, not as a thing, but as an activity. 'That there is such a power of intellectual intuition cannot be demonstrated through concepts, nor can its nature be developed by means of concepts. Everyone must find it immediately in himself or he will never be able to know it.'[10]

Fichte's thesis can be clarified in this way. The pure ego cannot be turned into an object of consciousness in the same way that a desire, for example, can be objectified. It would be absurd to say that through introspection I see a desire, an image and a pure ego. For every act of objectification presupposes the pure ego. And for this reason it can be called the transcendental ego. But it does not follow that the pure ego is an inferred occult entity. For it manifests itself in the activity of objectification. When I say, 'I am walking', I objectify the action, in the sense that I make it object-for-a-subject. And the pure *I* reveals itself to reflection in this activity of objectification. An activity is intuited, but no entity behind consciousness is inferred. Hence Fichte concludes that the pure ego is not something which acts but simply an activity or doing. 'For idealism the intelligence is a doing [*Thun*] and absolutely nothing else; one should not even call it an active thing [*ein Tätiges*].'[11]

At first sight at least Fichte appears to contradict Kant's denial that the human mind possesses any faculty of intellectual intuition. In particular, he seems to be turning into an object of intuition the transcendental ego which for Kant was simply a logical condition of the unity of consciousness and could be neither intuited nor proved to exist as a spiritual substance. But Fichte insists that his contradiction of Kant is really only verbal. For when Kant denied that the human mind possesses any faculty of intellectual intuition, he meant that we do not enjoy any intellectual intuition of supersensible entities transcending experience. And the *Wissenschaftslehre* does not really affirm what Kant denied. For it is not claimed that we intuit the pure ego as a spiritual substance or entity transcending consciousness but simply as an activity within consciousness, which reveals itself to reflection. Further, apart from the fact that Kant's doctrine of pure apperception[12] gives us at any rate a hint of intellectual intuition, we can easily indicate the place, Fichte claims, at which Kant ought to have spoken of and admitted this intuition. For he asserted that we are conscious of a categorical imperative; and if he had considered the matter thoroughly, he should have seen that this consciousness involves the intellectual intuition of the pure ego as activity. Indeed, Fichte goes on to suggest a specifically moral approach to the topic. 'In the consciousness of this law . . . is grounded the intuition of self-activity and freedom. . . . It is only through the medium of the moral law that I apprehend *myself*. And if I apprehend myself in this way, I necessarily apprehend myself as self-active. . . .'[13] Once again, therefore, the strongly ethical bent of Fichte's mind finds clear expression.

4. If we look at the matter from the point of view of phenomenology of consciousness, Fichte is, in the opinion of the present writer, perfectly justified in affirming the I-subject or transcendental ego. Hume, looking into his mind, so to speak, and finding only psychical phenomena, tried to reduce the self to the succession of these phenomena.[14] And it is understandable that he acted in this way. For part of his programme was to apply to man the empirical method, as he conceived it, which had proved so successful in 'experimental philosophy' or natural science. But the direction of his atten-

tion to the objects or data of introspection led him to slur
over the fact, all-important for the philosopher, that psychical
phenomena become phenomena (appearing to a subject)
only through the objectifying activity of a subject which transcends objectification in the same sense. Obviously, there is
no question of reducing the human being to a transcendental
or metaphysical ego. And the problem of the relation between
the self as pure subject and other aspects of the self is one
that cannot be evaded. But this does not alter the fact that a
recognition of the transcendental ego is essential to an adequate phenomenology of consciousness. And in regard to this
point Fichte shows a degree of insight which Hume lacked.

But Fichte is not, of course, simply concerned with the
phenomenology of consciousness, that is, with a descriptive
analysis of consciousness. He is concerned also with developing a system of idealist metaphysics. And this point has an
important bearing on his theory of the transcendental ego.
From a purely phenomenological point of view talk about
'the transcendental ego' no more commits us to saying that
there is one and only one such ego than a medical writer's
generalizations about 'the stomach' commit him to holding
that there is one and only one stomach. But if we propose to
derive the whole sphere of the objective, including Nature
and all selves in so far as they are objects for a subject, from
the transcendental ego, we must either embrace solipsism or
interpret the transcendental ego as a supra-individual productive activity which manifests itself in all finite consciousnesses. As, therefore, Fichte has no intention of defending
solipsism, he is bound to interpret the pure ego as a supra-
individual absolute ego.

To be sure, Fichte's use of the term *I* or ego not unnaturally suggested to many of his readers that he was talking
about the individual self or ego. And this interpretation was
facilitated by the fact that the more metaphysical aspects of
his thought were comparatively inconspicuous in his earlier
writings. But the interpretation, Fichte insisted, was erroneous. Lecturing in the winter of 1810–11 and looking back at
the criticism that had been levelled against the *Wissen-*

schaftslehre he protested that he had never intended to say that the creative ego is the individual finite self. 'People have generally understood the theory of science as attributing to the individual effects which could certainly not be ascribed to it, such as the production of the whole material world. . . . They have been completely mistaken: it is not the individual but the one immediate spiritual Life which is the creator of all phenomena, including phenomenal individuals.'[15]

It will be noticed that in this passage the word 'Life' is used instead of 'ego'. Starting, as he did, from the position of Kant and being concerned with transforming it into pure idealism, he not unnaturally began by talking about the pure or absolute ego. But in the course of time he saw that it was inappropriate to describe the infinite activity which grounds consciousness, including the finite self, as itself an ego or subject. However, we need not dwell at present on this point. It is sufficient to note Fichte's protest against what he considered to be a fundamental misinterpretation of his theory. The absolute ego is not the individual finite self but an infinite (better, unlimited) activity.

Fichte's *Wissenschaftslehre* is thus both a phenomenology of consciousness and an idealist metaphysics. And to a certain extent at any rate the two aspects can be separated. Hence it is possible to attach some value to a good deal of what Fichte has to say without committing oneself to his metaphysical idealism. We have already indicated this in regard to the theory of the transcendental ego. But the distinction has a wider field of application.

5. In the second section of this chapter it was remarked that philosophy, according to Fichte, must have a fundamental and indemonstrable proposition. And the thought may have occurred to the reader that whatever else the ego may be, it is not a proposition. This is, of course, true. We have still to ascertain what is the basic proposition of philosophy. But we know at any rate that it must be the expression of the original activity of the pure ego.

Now, we can distinguish between the spontaneous activity of the pure ego on the one hand and the philosopher's philosophical reconstruction or thinking of this activity on the other. The spontaneous activity of the pure ego in grounding consciousness is not, of course, itself conscious. As spontaneous activity the pure ego does not exist 'for itself'. It comes to exist for itself, as an ego, only in the intellectual intuition by which the philosopher in transcendental reflection apprehends the ego's spontaneous activity. It is through the act of the philosopher, 'through an activity directed towards an activity . . . that the ego first comes to be *originally* [*ursprünglich*] for itself'.[16] In intellectual intuition, therefore, the pure ego is said to posit itself (*sich setzen*). And the fundamental proposition of philosophy is that 'the ego simply posits in an original way its own being'.[17] In transcendental reflection the philosopher goes back, as it were, to the ultimate ground of consciousness. And in his intellectual intuition the pure ego affirms itself. It is not demonstrated as a conclusion from premises: it is seen as affirming itself and so as existing. 'To *posit itself* and to *be* are, as said of the ego, completely the same.'[18]

But though by means of what Fichte calls an activity directed towards an activity[19] the pure ego is, so to speak, made to affirm itself, the ego's original spontaneous activity is not in itself conscious. Rather is it the ultimate ground of consciousness, that is, of ordinary consciousness, one's natural awareness of oneself in a world. But this consciousness cannot arise unless the non-ego is opposed to the ego. Hence the second basic proposition of philosophy is that 'a non-ego is simply opposed to the ego'.[20] This oppositing must, of course, be done by the ego itself. Otherwise pure idealism would have to be abandoned.

Now, the non-ego of which the second proposition speaks is unlimited, in the sense that it is objectivity in general rather than a definite object or set of finite objects. And this unlimited non-ego is opposed to the ego within the ego. For we are engaged in the systematic reconstruction of consciousness; and consciousness is a unity, comprising both ego and non-ego. Hence the unlimited activity which constitutes the pure or absolute ego must posit the non-ego within itself.

But if both are unlimited, each will tend, as it were, to fill all reality to the exclusion of the other. They will tend to cancel one another out, to annihilate one another. And consciousness will be rendered impossible. Hence, if consciousness is to arise, there must be reciprocal limitation of ego and non-ego. Each must cancel the other out, but only in part. In this sense both ego and non-ego must be 'divisible' (theilbar). And in his Basis of the Entire Theory of Science Fichte offers the following formulation of the third basic proposition of philosophy. 'I posit in the ego a divisible non-ego as opposed to a divisible ego.'[21] That is to say, the absolute ego posits within itself a finite ego and a finite non-ego as reciprocally limiting and determining one another. Fichte obviously does not mean that there can be only one of each. Indeed, as will be seen later, he maintains that for self-consciousness the existence of the Other (and so of a plurality of finite selves) is required. His point is that there can be no consciousness unless the absolute ego, considered as unlimited activity, produces within itself the finite ego and the finite non-ego.

6. If we mean by consciousness, as Fichte means by it, human consciousness, the assertion that the non-ego is a necessary condition of consciousness is not difficult to understand. To be sure, the finite ego can reflect on itself, but this reflection is for Fichte a bending back of the attention from the not-self. Hence the non-ego is a necessary condition even of self-consciousness.[22] But we can very well ask why there should be consciousness at all. Or, to put the question in another way, how can the second basic proposition of philosophy be deduced from the first?

Fichte answers that no purely theoretical deduction is possible. We must have recourse to a practical deduction. That is to say, we must see the pure or absolute ego as an unlimited activity striving towards consciousness of its own freedom through moral self-realization. And we must see the positing of the non-ego as a necessary means to the attainment of this end. True, the absolute ego in its spontaneous activity does not act consciously for any end at all. But the philosopher consciously rethinking this activity sees the total movement as directed towards a certain goal. And he sees that self-consciousness demands the non-ego, from which the otherwise unlimited activity of the ego, comparable to a straight line stretching out indefinitely, can recoil, as it were, onto itself. He sees too that moral activity requires an objective field, a world, in which actions can be performed.

Now, the second basic proposition of philosophy stands to the first as antithesis to thesis. And we have seen that the ego and non-ego tend to cancel one another out, if both are unlimited. It is this fact that drives the philosopher to enunciate the third basic proposition, which stands to the first and second propositions as synthesis to thesis and antithesis. But Fichte does not mean to imply that the non-ego ever exists in such a way that it annihilates the pure ego or threatens to do so. It is because this annihilation would take place if an unlimited non-ego were posited within the ego that we are compelled to proceed to the third proposition. In other words, the synthesis shows what the antithesis must mean if the contradiction between an unlimited ego and an unlimited non-ego is not to arise. If we assume that consciousness is to arise at all, the activity which grounds consciousness must produce the situation in which an ego and a non-ego limit one another.

Looked at under one aspect, therefore, Fichte's dialectic of thesis, antithesis and synthesis[23] takes the form of a progressive determination of the meanings of the initial propositions. And the contradictions which arise are resolved in the sense that they are shown to be only apparent. 'All contradictions are reconciled by determining more closely the contradictory propositions.'[24] Speaking, for example, of the statements that the ego posits itself as infinite and that it posits itself as finite, Fichte remarks that 'were it posited as both infinite and finite in one and the same sense, the contradictions could not be resolved. . . .'[25] The apparent contradiction is resolved by so defining the meanings of the two statements that their mutual compatibility becomes evident.

In the case in question we have to see the one infinite activity expressing itself in and through finite selves.

Yet it would not be accurate to say that in actual fact Fichte's dialectic consists simply in the progressive determination or clarification of meanings. For he introduces by the way ideas which cannot be obtained through strict analysis of the initial proposition or propositions. For instance, in order to proceed from the second basic proposition to the third Fichte postulates a limiting activity on the part of the ego, though the idea of limitation cannot be obtained simply through logical analysis of either the first or the second proposition.

This procedure was criticized by Hegel as being insufficiently speculative, that is, philosophical. In Hegel's opinion it was unworthy of a philosopher to offer a deduction which was admittedly no strict theoretical deduction[26] and to introduce, like a *deus ex machina*, undeduced activities of the ego to make possible the transition from one proposition to another.

It can hardly be denied, I think, that Fichte's actual procedure does not square very well with his initial account of the nature of philosophy as a deductive science. At the same time we must remember that for him the philosopher is engaged in consciously reconstructing, as it were, an active process, namely the grounding of consciousness, which in itself takes place unconsciously. In doing so the philosopher has his point of departure, the self-positing of the absolute ego, and his point of arrival, human consciousness as we know it. And if it is impossible to proceed from one step to another in the reconstruction of the productive activity of the ego without attributing to the ego a certain function or mode of activity, then this must be done. Thus even if the concept of limitation is not obtained through strict logical analysis of the first two basic propositions, it is none the less required, from Fichte's point of view, to clarify their meaning.

7. When outlining Fichte's theory of the three basic propositions of philosophy I omitted the logical apparatus which is employed in the *Basis of the Entire Theory of Science* and

which figures prominently in some accounts of his philosophy. For this apparatus is not really necessary, as is shown by the fact that Fichte himself omits it in some of the expositions of his system. At the same time something ought to be said about it because it serves to clarify Fichte's idea of the relations between philosophy and formal logic.

In the *Basis of the Entire Theory of Science* Fichte approaches the first fundamental proposition of philosophy by reflecting on an indemonstrable logical proposition, the truth of which would be admitted by all. This is the principle of identity, stated in the form A *is* A or $A = A$. Nothing is said about the content of A; nor is it asserted that A exists. What is asserted is a necessary relation between A and itself. If there is an A, it is necessarily self-identical. And this necessary relation between A as subject and A as predicate is referred to by Fichte as X.

This judgment is asserted or posited only in and through the I or ego. Thus the existence of the ego is affirmed in its activity of judging, even if no value has been assigned to A. 'If the proposition $A = A$ is certain, so also must the proposition I *am* be certain.'[27] In affirming the principle of identity the ego affirms or posits itself as self-identical.

While, therefore, the formal principle of identity is used by Fichte as a means or device for arriving at the first basic proposition of philosophy, the principle of identity is not itself this proposition. Indeed, it is sufficiently obvious that one would not get very far with a deduction or reconstruction of consciousness if one proposed to use the formal principle of identity as a starting-point or foundation.

At the same time the relation between the formal principle of identity and the first basic proposition of philosophy is closer, according to Fichte, than the description of the former as a means or device for arriving at the latter tends to suggest. For the principle of identity is, so to speak, the first basic proposition of philosophy with variables substituted for definite values or content. That is to say, if we took the first basic proposition of philosophy and rendered it purely formal, we would obtain the principle of identity. And in this sense the latter is grounded in the former and derivable from it.

Similarly, what Fichte calls the formal axiom of opposition, $Not-A$ $not = A$, is used to arrive at the second basic proposition. For the positing of $Not -A$ presupposes the positing of A and is thus an oppositing to A. And this oppositing takes place only in and through the ego. At the same time the formal axiom of opposition is said to be grounded in the second proposition of philosophy which affirms the ego's oppositing to itself of the non-ego in general. Again, the logical proposition which Fichte calls the axiom of the ground or of sufficient reason, A in $part = -A$, and conversely, is said to be grounded in the third basic proposition of philosophy, in the sense that the former is derived by abstracting definite content from the latter and substituting variables instead.

In brief, therefore, Fichte's view is that formal logic is dependent on and derived from the *Wissenschaftslehre*, and not the other way round. This view of the relation between formal logic and basic philosophy is indeed somewhat obscured by the fact that in the *Basis of the Entire Theory of Science* Fichte starts by reflecting on the principle of identity. But in his subsequent discussion he proceeds to make his view of the derivative character of formal logic quite clear. And this view is in any case entailed by his insistence that the *Wissenschaftslehre* is the fundamental science.

We may add that in his deduction of the fundamental propositions of philosophy Fichte begins to deduce the categories. In his opinion Kant's deduction was insufficiently systematic. If, however, we start with the self-positing of the ego, we can deduce them successively in the course of the reconstruction of consciousness. Thus the first basic proposition gives us the category of reality. For 'that which is posited through the mere positing of a thing . . . is its reality, its essence [*Wesen*]'.[28] The second proposition obviously gives us the category of negation and the third that of limitation or determination.

8. The idea of reciprocal limitation provides the basis for

the twofold deduction of consciousness which Fichte considers necessary. Take the statement that the absolute ego posits within itself a finite ego and a finite non-ego as reciprocally limiting or determining one another. This implies two propositions. One is that the absolute ego posits itself as limited by the non-ego. The other is that the absolute ego posits (within itself) the non-ego as limited or determined by the (finite) ego. And these two propositions are respectively the basic propositions of the theoretical and practical deductions of consciousness. If we consider the ego as affected by the non-ego, we can proceed to the theoretical deduction of consciousness which considers what Fichte calls the 'real' series of acts, that is, the acts of the ego as determined by the non-ego. Sensation, for example, belongs to this class of acts. If, however, we consider the ego as affecting the non-ego, we can proceed to the practical deduction of consciousness which considers the 'ideal' series of acts, including, for instance, desire and free action.

The two deductions are, of course, complementary, forming together the total philosophical deduction or reconstruction of consciousness. At the same time the theoretical deduction is subordinated to the practical. For the absolute ego is an infinite striving towards self-realization through free moral activity, and the non-ego, the world of Nature, is a means or instrument for the attainment of this end. The practical deduction gives us the reason why the absolute ego posits the non-ego as limiting and affecting the finite ego; and it leads us to the confines of ethics. Indeed, Fichte's theories of rights and of morals are a continuation of the practical deduction as contained in the *Wissenschaftslehre* proper. As already mentioned, Fichte's philosophy is essentially a dynamic ethical idealism.

It is not possible to discuss here all the stages of Fichte's deduction of consciousness. And even if it were possible, it would scarcely be desirable. But in the next two sections some features of the theoretical and practical deductions will be mentioned, to give the reader some idea of Fichte's line of thought.

9. In Fichte's idealist system all activity must be referred ultimately to the ego itself, that is, to the absolute ego, and the non-ego must exist only for consciousness. For to admit the idea of a non-ego which exists quite independently of all consciousness and which affects the ego would be to readmit the idea of the thing-in-itself and to abandon idealism. At the same time it is obvious that from the point of view of ordinary consciousness there is a distinction between presentation (*Vorstellung*) and thing. We have the spontaneous belief that we are acted upon by things which exist independently of the ego. And to all appearances this belief is fully justified. Hence it is incumbent on Fichte to show, in a manner consistent with the idealist position, how the point of view of ordinary consciousness arises, and how from this point of view our spontaneous belief in an objective Nature is in a sense justified. For the aim of idealist philosophy is to explain the facts of consciousness on idealist principles, not to deny them.

Obviously, Fichte must attribute to the ego the power of producing the idea of an independently existing non-ego when in point of fact it is dependent on the ego, so that the non-ego's activity is ultimately the activity of the ego itself. Equally obviously, this power must be attributed to the absolute ego rather than to the individual self, and it must work spontaneously, inevitably and without consciousness. To put the matter crudely, when consciousness comes on the scene the work must be already done. It must take place below the level of consciousness. Otherwise it would be impossible to explain our spontaneous belief in a Nature existing independently of the ego. In other words, for empirical consciousness Nature must be something given. It is only the philosopher who in transcendental reflection retraces with consciousness the productive activity of the absolute ego, which in itself takes place without consciousness. For the non-philosopher, and for the empirical consciousness of the philosopher himself, the natural world is something given, a situation in which the finite ego finds itself.

This power is called by Fichte the power of imagination

or, more appropriately, the productive power of imagination or power of productive imagination. The power of imagination was prominent in the philosophy of Kant, where it served as an indispensable link between sensibility and understanding.[29] But with Fichte it assumes an all-important role in grounding ordinary or empirical consciousness. It is not, of course, a kind of third force in addition to the ego and non-ego: it is the activity of the ego itself, that is, the absolute ego. In his earlier writings Fichte may sometimes give the impression that he is talking about the activity of the individual self, but when he reviews the development of his thought he protests that he never meant this.

In what he calls a pragmatic history of consciousness[30] Fichte pictures the ego as spontaneously limiting its own activity and thus positing itself as passive, as affected. Its state is then that of sensation (*Empfindung*). But the ego's activity reasserts itself, as it were, and objectifies sensation. That is to say, in the outwardly-directed activity of intuition the ego spontaneously refers sensation to a non-ego. And this act grounds the distinction between representation or image (*Bild*) and thing. In empirical consciousness, the finite self regards the distinction between image and thing as a distinction between a subjective modification and an object which exists independently of its own activity. For it is ignorant of the fact that the projection of the non-ego was the work of the productive imagination functioning on an infra-conscious level.

Now, consciousness requires not simply an indeterminate non-ego but definite and distinct objects. And if there are to be distinguishable objects, there must be a common sphere in which and in relation to which objects mutually exclude one another. Hence the power of imagination produces space, extended, continuous and indefinitely divisible, as a form of intuition.

Similarly, there must be an irreversible time series of such a kind that successive acts of intuition are possible and that if a particular act of intuition occurs at any moment, every other possibility is excluded as far as this moment is concerned. Hence the productive imagination conveniently posits time as a second form of intuition. Needless to say, the forms of space and time are produced spontaneously by the activity of the pure or absolute ego: they are not consciously and deliberately posited.

The development of consciousness, however, requires that the product of the creative imagination should be rendered more determinate. And this is effected by means of the powers of understanding and judgment. At the level of understanding the ego 'fixes' (*fixiert*) presentations as concepts, while the power of judgment is said to turn these concepts into *thought* objects, in the sense that they come to exist not only *in* but also *for* the understanding. Both understanding and judgment, therefore, are required for understanding in the full sense. 'Nothing in the understanding, no power of judgment: no power of judgment, nothing in the understanding *for the understanding*. . . .'[31] Sensible intuition is riveted, as it were, to particular objects; but at the level of understanding and judgment we find abstraction from particular objects and the making of universal judgments. Thus in the pragmatic history of consciousness we have seen the ego rising above the unconscious activity of the productive imagination and acquiring, so to speak, a certain freedom of movement.

Self-consciousness, however, requires more than the power to abstract from particular objects in favour of the universal. It presupposes the power to abstract from the object in general, in order to achieve reflection on the subject. And this power of absolute abstraction, as Fichte calls it, is reason (*Vernunft*). When reason abstracts from the sphere of the non-ego, the ego remains, and we have self-consciousness. But one cannot totally eliminate the ego-object and identify oneself in consciousness with the ego-subject. That is to say, pure self-consciousness, in which the I-subject would be completely transparent to itself, is an ideal which can never be actually achieved, but to which one can only approximate. 'The more a determinate individual can think himself (as object) away, the closer does his empirical self-consciousness approximate to pure self-consciousness.'[32]

It is, of course, the power of reason which enables the philosopher to apprehend the pure ego and to retrace, in transcendental reflection, its productive activity in the movement towards self-consciousness. But we have seen that the intellectual intuition of the absolute ego is never unmixed with other elements. Not even the philosopher can achieve the ideal of what Fichte calls pure self-consciousness.

10. The practical deduction of consciousness goes behind, as it were, the work of the productive imagination and reveals its ground in the nature of the absolute ego as an infinite striving (*ein unendliches Streben*). True, if we speak of striving, we naturally tend to think of striving after something. That is to say, we presuppose the existence of the non-ego. But if we start with the absolute ego as infinite striving, we obviously cannot presuppose the existence of the non-ego. For to do this would be to reintroduce the Kantian thing-in-itself. At the same time striving, Fichte insists, demands a counter-movement, a counter-striving, a check or obstacle. For if it met with no resistance, no obstacle or check, it would be satisfied and would cease to be a striving. But the absolute ego cannot cease to be a striving. Hence the very nature of the absolute ego necessitates the positing of the non-ego by the productive imagination, that is, by the absolute ego in its 'real' activity.

The matter can be expressed in this way. The absolute ego is to be conceived as activity. And this activity is fundamentally an infinite striving. But striving, according to Fichte, implies overcoming, and overcoming requires an obstacle to overcome. Hence the ego must posit the non-ego, Nature, as an obstacle to be overcome, as a check to be transcended. In other words, Nature is a necessary means or instrument to the moral self-realization of the ego. It is a field for action.

Fichte does not, however, proceed directly from the idea of the ego as striving to the positing of the non-ego. He argues first that striving takes the determinate form of infra-conscious impulse or drive (*Trieb*) and that this impulse exists 'for the ego' in the form of feeling (*Gefühl*). Now, impulse or drive aims, as Fichte puts it, at being causality, at effecting something outside itself. Yet it cannot, considered simply as impulse, effect anything. Hence the feeling of impulse or drive is a feeling of constraint, of not-being-able, of being hindered. And the feeling ego is compelled to posit the non-ego as a felt I-know-not-what, a felt obstacle or check. And impulse can then become 'impulse *towards the object*'.[33]

It is worth noting that for Fichte feeling is the basis of all belief in reality. The ego feels impulse or drive as power or force (*Kraft*) which is hindered. The feeling of force and the feeling of hindrance go together. And the total feeling is the foundation of belief in reality. 'Here lies the ground of all reality. Only through the relation of feeling to the ego . . . is reality possible for the ego, whether of the ego or of the non-ego.'[34] Belief in reality is based ultimately on feeling, not on any theoretical argument.

Now, the feeling of impulse as force represents a rudimentary grade of reflection. For the ego is itself the impulse which is felt. Hence the feeling is self-feeling. And in successive sections of the practical deduction of consciousness Fichte traces the development of this reflection. We see, for instance, impulse or drive as such becoming more determinate in the form of distinct impulses and desires, and we see the development in the ego of distinct feelings of satisfaction. But inasmuch as the ego is infinite striving, it is unable to rest in any particular satisfaction or group of satisfactions. And we see it as reaching out towards an ideal goal through its free activity. Yet this goal always recedes. Indeed, it must do so, if the ego is infinite or endless striving. In the end, therefore, we have action for the sake of action, though in his ethical theory Fichte shows how the infinite striving of the absolute ego after complete freedom and self-possession is fulfilled, so far as it can be, through the series of determinate moral actions in the world which it has posited, through, that is to say, the convergence of the determinate moral vocations of finite subjects towards an ideal goal.

In its detailed development Fichte's practical deduction of

consciousness is notoriously difficult to follow. But it is clear enough that for him the ego is from the start the morally active ego. That is to say, it is potentially this. And it is the actualization of the ego's potential nature which demands the positing of the non-ego and the whole work of the productive imagination. Behind, as it were, the theoretical activity of the ego lies its nature as striving, as impulse or drive. For example, the production of the presentation (*Vorstellung*) is the work of the theoretical power, not of the practical power or impulse as such. But the production presupposes the drive to presentation (*der Vorstellungstrieb*). Conversely, the positing of the sensible world is necessary in order that the fundamental striving or drive can take the determinate form of free moral activity directed towards an ideal goal. Thus the two deductions are complementary, though the theoretical deduction finds its ultimate explanation in the practical. In this sense Fichte endeavours to satisfy in his own way the demands of Kant's doctrine of the primacy of the practical reason.

We can also say that in his practical deduction of consciousness Fichte tries to overcome the dichotomy, present in the Kantian philosophy, between the higher and lower nature of man, between man as a moral agent and man as a complex of instincts and impulses. For it is the self-same fundamental drive which is represented as assuming different forms up to that of free moral activity. In other words, Fichte sees the moral life as a development out of the life of instinct and impulse rather than as a counterblast to it. And he even finds a prefiguring of the categorical imperative on the level of physical longing (*Sehnen*) and desire. In his ethics he has, of course, to allow for the fact that there may be, and often is, a conflict between the voice of duty and the claims of sensual desire. But he tries to resolve the problem within the framework of a unified view of the ego's activity in general.

11. From one point of view Fichte's deduction of consciousness can be regarded as a systematic exhibition of the conditions of consciousness as we know it. And if it is regarded simply in this way, questions about the temporal or

historical relations between the different conditions are ir-relevant. For example, Fichte takes it that the subject-object relationship is essential to consciousness. And in this case there must be both subject and object, ego and non-ego, if there is to be consciousness. The historical order in which these conditions appear is irrelevant to the validity of this statement.

But, as we have seen, the deduction of consciousness is also idealist metaphysics, and the pure ego has to be inter-preted as a supra-individual and transfinite activity, the so-called absolute ego. Hence it is understandable if the stu-dent of Fichte asks whether the philosopher regards the absolute ego as positing the sensible world before the finite ego or simultaneously with it or through it.

At first sight at least this may seem to be a silly question. The temporal, historical point of view, it may be said, pre-supposes for Fichte the constitution of empirical conscious-ness. Hence the transcendental deduction of empirical con-sciousness necessarily transcends the temporal and historical order and possesses the timelessness of a logical deduction. After all, the time-series is itself deduced. Fichte has no in-tention of denying the point of view of empirical conscious-ness, for which Nature precedes finite selves. He is concerned with grounding it, not with denying it.

But the matter is not quite so simple. In the Kantian phi-losophy it is the human mind which exercises a constitutive activity in giving its *a priori* form to phenomenal reality. True, in this activity the mind acts spontaneously and un-consciously, and it acts as mind as such, as the subject as such, rather than as the mind of Tom or John. But it is none the less the human mind, not the divine mind, which is said to exercise this activity. And if we eliminate the thing-in-it-self and hypostatize Kant's transcendental ego as the meta-physical absolute ego, it is quite natural to ask whether the absolute ego posits Nature immediately or through the infra-conscious levels, as it were, of the human being. After all, Fichte's deduction of consciousness not infrequently sug-gests the second of these alternatives. And if this is what the philosopher really means, he is faced with an obvious difficulty.

Happily, Fichte answers the question in explicit terms. At the beginning of the practical deduction of consciousness he draws attention to an apparent contradiction. On the one hand the ego as intelligence is dependent on the non-ego. On the other hand the ego is said to determine the non-ego and must thus be independent of it. The contradiction is resolved (that is, shown to be only apparent) when we understand that the absolute ego determines immediately the non-ego which enters into representation (*das vorzustellende Nicht-Ich*), whereas it determines the ego as intelligence (the ego as representing, *das vorstellende Ich*) *mediately*, that is, by means of the non-ego. In other words, the absolute ego does not posit the world through the finite ego, but immediately. And the same thing is clearly stated in a passage of the lectures on *The Facts of Consciousness*, to which allusion has already been made. 'The material world has been deduced earlier on as an absolute limitation of the productive power of imagination. But we have not yet stated clearly and explicitly whether the productive power in this function is the self-manifestation of the one Life as such or whether it is the manifestation of individual life; whether, that is to say, a material world is posited through one self-identical Life or through the individual as such. . . . It is not the individual as such but the one Life which intuits the objects of the material world.'[35]

The development of this point of view obviously requires that Fichte should move away from his Kantian point of departure, and that the pure ego, a concept arrived at through reflection on human consciousness, should become absolute Being which manifests itself in the world. And this is indeed the path which Fichte takes in the later philosophy, to which the lectures on *The Facts of Consciousness* belong. But, as will be seen later, he never really succeeds in kicking away the ladder by which he has climbed up to metaphysical idealism. And though he clearly thinks of Nature as being posited by the Absolute as a field for moral activity, he maintains to the end that the world exists only in and for consciousness. Apart, therefore, from the explicit denial that material things are posited 'through the individual as such', his position remains ambiguous. For though consciousness is said to be the Absolute's consciousness, the Absolute is also said to be conscious through man, and not in itself considered apart from man.

Chapter Three

FICHTE (2)

Introductory remarks – The common moral consciousness and the science of ethics – Man's moral nature – The supreme principle of morality and the formal condition of the morality of actions – Conscience as an unerring guide – The philosophical application of the formal moral law – The idea of moral vocation and Fichte's general vision of reality – A community of selves in a world as a condition of self-consciousness – The principle or rule of right – The deduction and nature of the State – The closed commercial State – Fichte and nationalism.

1. In the section on Fichte's life and writings we saw that he published the *Basis of Natural Right* in 1796, two years before the publication of *The System of Ethics*. In his opinion the theory of rights and of political society could be, and ought to be, deduced independently of the deduction of the principles of morality. This does not mean that Fichte thought of the two branches of philosophy as having no connection at all with each other. For one thing the two deductions possess a common root in the concept of the self as striving and as free activity. For another thing the system of rights and political society provides a field of application for the moral law. But it was Fichte's opinion that his field is external to morality, in the sense that it is not a deduction from the fundamental ethical principle but a framework within which, and in regard to which, the moral law can be applied. For example, man can have moral duties towards the State and the State should bring about those conditions in which the moral life can develop. But the State itself is deduced as a hypothetically necessary contrivance or means to

guard and protect the system of rights. If man's moral nature were fully developed, the State would wither away. Again, though the right of private property receives from ethics what Fichte calls a further sanction, its initial deduction is supposed to be independent of ethics.

One main reason why Fichte makes this distinction between the theory of rights and political theory on the one hand and ethics on the other is that he looks on ethics as concerned with interior morality, with conscience and the formal principle of morality, whereas the theory of rights and of political society is concerned with the external relations between human beings. Further, if the comment is made that the doctrine of rights can be regarded as applied ethics, in the sense that it is deducible as an application of the moral law, Fichte refuses to admit the truth of this contention. The fact that I have a right does not necessarily mean that I am under an obligation to exercise it. And the common good may demand on occasion a curtailment of or limitation on the exercise of rights. But the moral law is categorical: it simply says, 'Do this' or 'Do not do that'. Hence the system of rights is not deducible from the moral law, though we are, of course, morally obliged to respect the system of rights as established in a community. In this sense the moral law adds a further sanction to rights, but it is not their initial source.

In Hegel's opinion Fichte did not really succeed in overcoming the formalism of the Kantian ethics, even if he provided some of the material for doing so. And it was indeed Hegel rather than Fichte who synthesized the concepts of right, interior morality and society in the general concept of man's ethical life. But the chief reason why I have dwelt in the first section of this chapter on Fichte's distinction between the doctrine of rights and ethical theory is that I propose to treat of the philosopher's moral theory before outlining his theory of rights and of the State. And this procedure might otherwise give the erroneous impression that Fichte regarded the theory of rights as a deduction from the moral law.

2. A man can have knowledge, Fichte says, of his moral

nature, of his subjection to a moral imperative, in two ways.
In the first place he can possess this knowledge on the level
of common moral consciousness. That is to say, he can be
aware through his conscience of a moral imperative telling
him to do this or not to do that. And this immediate awareness is quite sufficient for a knowledge of one's duties and
for moral behaviour. In the second place a man can assume
the ordinary moral consciousness as something given and inquire into its grounds. And a systematic deduction of the
moral consciousness from its roots in the ego is the science of
ethics and provides 'learned knowledge'.[1] In one sense, of
course, this learned knowledge leaves everything as it was before. It does not create obligation, nor does it substitute a
new set of duties for those of which one is already aware
through conscience. It will not give a man a moral nature.
But it can enable him to understand his moral nature.

3. What is meant by man's moral nature? Fichte tells us
that there is in man an impulsion to perform certain actions
simply for the sake of performing them, without regard to
external purposes or ends, and to leave undone other actions
simply for the sake of leaving them undone, again without
regard to external purposes or ends. And the nature of man
in so far as this impulsion necessarily manifests itself within
him is his 'moral or ethical nature'.[2] To understand the
grounds of this moral nature is the task of ethics.

The ego is activity, striving. And as we saw when considering the practical deduction of consciousness, the basic form
taken by the striving which constitutes the ego is infra-conscious impulse or drive. Hence from one point of view man
is a system of impulses, the impulse which can be ascribed to
the system as a whole being that of self-preservation. Considered in this light, man can be described as an organized
product of Nature. And as conscious of myself as a system of
impulses I can say, 'I find myself as an organized product of
Nature'.[3] That is to say, I posit or affirm myself as being this
when I consider myself as object.

But man is also intelligence, a subject of consciousness.
And as subject of consciousness the ego necessarily tends or is

impelled to determine itself through itself alone; that is, it is a striving after complete freedom and independence. Inasmuch, therefore, as the natural impulses and desires which belong to man as a product of Nature aim at satisfaction through some relation to a determinate natural object and consequently appear to depend on the object, we understandably contrast these impulses with the spiritual impulse of the ego as intelligence, the impulse, that is to say, to complete self-determination. We speak of lower and higher desires, of the sphere of necessity and the sphere of freedom, and introduce a dichotomy into human nature.

Fichte does not deny, of course, that such distinctions have, so to speak, a cash value. For one can look at man from two points of view, as object and as subject. As we have seen, I can be conscious of myself as an object in Nature, as an organized product of Nature, and I can be aware of myself as a subject for whose consciousness Nature, including myself as object, exists. To this extent Kant's distinction between the phenomenal and noumenal aspects of man is justified.

At the same time Fichte insists that this distinction is not ultimate. For instance, the natural impulse which aims at satisfaction and the spiritual impulse which aims at complete freedom and independence are from the transcendental or phenomenal point of view one impulse. It is a great mistake to suppose that man as an organized product of Nature is the sphere of mere mechanism. As Fichte puts it, 'I do not hunger because food exists for me, but a certain object becomes food for me because I am hungry.'[4] The organism asserts itself: it tends to activity. And it is fundamentally the same impulse to self-activity which reappears in the form of the spiritual impulse to the realization of complete freedom. For this basic impulse cannot be stilled and brought to quiescence by temporary sense satisfaction, but reaches out, as it were, to infinity. It is true, of course, that the basic impulse or striving could not take the form of the higher spiritual impulse without consciousness. Consciousness is indeed a dividing-line between man as an organized product of Nature and man as a rational ego, as spirit. But from the philosophical point of view there is ultimately only one impulse, and man is subject and object in one. 'My impulse as a being of Nature and my tendency as pure spirit: are they two different impulses? No, from the transcendental point of view both are one and the same original impulse which constitutes my being: it is only regarded from two different sides. That is to say, I am subject-object, and in the identity and inseparability of both consists my true being. If I regard myself as an *object*, completely determined through the laws of sense intuition and discursive thinking, then that which is actually my one impulse becomes for me a natural impulse, because from this point of view I myself am Nature. If I regard myself as subject, the impulse becomes for me a purely spiritual impulse or the law of self-determination. All the phenomena of the ego rest simply on the reciprocity of these two impulses, and this is really the reciprocal relation *of one and the same impulse to itself*.'[5]

This theory of the unity of man in terms of one impulse has an important bearing on ethics. Fichte makes a distinction between formal and material freedom. Formal freedom requires only the presence of consciousness. Even if a man always followed his natural impulses as directed to pleasure, he would do so freely, provided that he did so consciously and deliberately.[6] Material freedom, however, is expressed in a series of acts tending to the realization of the ego's complete independence. And these are moral acts. Now, if we pressed this distinction, we should be faced with the difficulty of giving any content to the moral act. For we should have on the one hand actions performed in accordance with natural impulse, which are rendered determinate by their reference to particular objects, and on the other actions which exclude all determination by particular objects and are performed solely in accordance with the idea of freedom for freedom's sake. And this second class of actions would appear to be completely indeterminate. But Fichte answers that we have to effect a synthesis which is demanded by the fact that the impulse or tendency which constitutes man's nature is ultimately one impulse. The lower impulse or lower form of the one impulse must sacrifice its end, namely pleasure, while the higher impulse or form of the one impulse must sacrifice its purity, that is, its lack of determination by any object.

Expressed in this abstract way Fichte's idea of a synthesis may seem extremely obscure. But the fundamental notion is clear enough. For example, it is clearly not demanded of the moral agent that he should cease to perform all those actions to which natural impulse prompts him, such as eating and drinking. It is not demanded of him that he should try to live as a disembodied spirit. What is demanded is that his actions should not be performed simply for the sake of immediate satisfaction, but that they should be members of a series converging towards the ideal end which man sets before himself as a spiritual subject. In so far as he fulfils this demand man realizes his moral nature.

This suggests, of course, that the moral life involves substituting one end for another, a spiritual ideal for natural satisfaction and pleasure. And this idea may seem to be at variance with Fichte's picture of morality as demanding the performance of certain actions simply for the sake of performing them and the non-performance of other actions simply for the sake of not performing them. But the spiritual ideal in question is for Fichte self-activity, action determined through the ego alone. And his point is that such action must take the form of a series of determinate actions in the world, though at the same time they must be determined by the ego itself and express its freedom rather than subjection to the natural world. This means in effect that the actions should be performed for the sake of performing them.

One can say, therefore, that Fichte makes a resolute attempt to exhibit the unity of human nature and to show that there is continuity between the life of man as a natural organism and the life of man as spiritual subject of consciousness. At the same time the influence of the Kantian formalism is strongly marked. And it shows itself clearly in Fichte's account of the supreme principle of morality.

4. Speaking of the ego when it is thought only as *object*

Fichte asserts that 'the essential character of the ego, by
which it is distinguished from everything external to itself,
consists in a tendency to self-activity [*Selbstthätigkeit*] for
the sake of self-activity; and it is this tendency which is
thought when the ego is thought in and for itself without
relation to anything outside it'.[7] But it is the ego as subject,
as intelligence, which thinks itself as object. And when it
thinks itself as a tendency to self-activity for the sake of self-
activity, it necessarily thinks itself as free, as able to realize absolute self-activity, as a power of self-determination.
Further, the ego cannot conceive itself in this way without
conceiving itself as subject to law, the law of determining itself in accordance with the concept of self-determination.
That is to say, if I conceive my objective essence as a power
of self-determination, the power of realizing absolute self-
activity, I must also conceive myself as obliged to actualize
this essence.

We have, therefore, the two ideas of freedom and law. But
just as the ego as subject and the ego as object, though distinguished in consciousness, are inseparable and ultimately
one, so are the ideas of freedom and law inseparable and
ultimately one. 'When you think yourself as free, you are
compelled to think your freedom as falling under a law; and
when you think this law, you are compelled to think yourself
as free. Freedom does not follow from the law any more than
the law follows from freedom. They are not two ideas, of
which the one can be thought as dependent on the other, but
they are one and the same idea; it is a complete synthesis.'[8]

By this somewhat tortuous route Fichte deduces the fundamental principle of morality, 'the necessary idea of the intelligence that it ought to determine its freedom purely and
without exception in accordance with the concept of independence [*Selbständigkeit*]'.[9] The free being ought to bring
its freedom under a law, namely the law of complete self-
determination or absolute independence (absence of determination through any external object). And this law should
admit of no exception because it expresses the very nature of
the free being.

Now, a finite rational being cannot ascribe freedom to itself without conceiving the possibility of a series of determinate free actions, caused by a will which is capable of exercising real causal activity. But the realization of this possibility demands an objective world in which the rational being can tend towards its goal through a series of particular actions. The natural world, the sphere of the non-ego, can thus be regarded as the material or instrument for the fulfilment of our duty, sensible things appearing as so many occasions for specifying the pure ought. We have already seen that according to Fichte the absolute ego posits the world as an obstacle or check which renders possible the recoil of the ego onto itself in self-consciousness. And we now see the positing of the world in a more specifically ethical context. It is the necessary condition for the rational being's fulfilment of its moral vocation. Without the world it could not give content, as it were, to the pure ought.

To be a moral action, each of these particular actions must fulfil a certain formal condition. '*Act always according to your best conviction of your duty* or Act according to your conscience. This is the formal condition of the morality of our actions. . . .'[10] The will which so acts is the good will. Fichte is obviously writing under the influence of Kant.

5. 'Act according to your conscience.' Fichte defines conscience as 'the immediate consciousness of our determinate duty'.[11] That is to say, conscience is the immediate awareness of a particular obligation. And from this definition it obviously follows that conscience never errs and cannot err. For if conscience is defined as an immediate awareness of one's duty, it would be contradictory to say that it can be a non-awareness of one's duty.

It is clear that Fichte wishes to find an absolute criterion of right and wrong. It is also clear that he wishes, like Kant, to avoid heteronomy. No external authority can be the required criterion. Further, the criterion must be at the disposal of all, unlearned as well as learned. Fichte fixes, therefore, upon conscience and describes it as an immediate feeling (*Gefühl*). For inasmuch as the practical power has priority over the theoretical power, it is the former which must be the source of conscience. And as the practical power does not judge, conscience must be a feeling.

Fichte's description of conscience as an immediate feeling does indeed fit in with the way in which the ordinary man is accustomed to speak about his moral convictions. A man might say, for example, 'I feel that this is the right thing to do. I feel that any other course of action would be wrong.' And he may very well feel certain about it. At the same time one might wish to comment that feeling is scarcely an un-erring criterion of duty. Fichte, however, argues that the im-mediate feeling in question expresses the agreement or har-mony between 'our empirical ego and the pure ego. And the pure ego is our only true being; it is all possible being and all possible truth.'[12] Hence the feeling which constitutes con-science can never be erroneous or deceptive.

To understand Fichte's theory we must understand that he is not excluding from man's moral life all activity by the theoretical power. The ego's fundamental tendency to com-plete freedom and independence stimulates this power to look for the determinate content of duty. After all, we can and do reflect about what we ought to do in this or that set of cir-cumstances. But any theoretical judgment which we make may be mistaken. The function of argument is to draw at-tention to the different aspects of the situation under dis-cussion and so to facilitate the attunement, so to speak, of the empirical ego with the pure ego. This attunement ex-presses itself in a feeling, the immediate consciousness of one's duty. And this immediate awareness puts a stop to theoretical inquiry and argument which might otherwise be prolonged indefinitely.

Fichte will not admit that anyone who has an immediate consciousness of his duty can resolve not to do his duty pre-cisely because it is his duty. 'Such a maxim would be diaboli-cal; but the concept of the devil is self-contradictory.'[13] At the same time 'no man, indeed no finite being so far as we know, is confirmed in good'.[14] Conscience as such cannot err, but it can be obscured or even vanish. Thus the concept of duty may remain, though the consciousness of its connection with some particular action may be obscured. To put the matter crudely, I may not give my empirical ego the chance to click with the pure ego.[15] Further, the consciousness of duty may practically vanish, in which case 'we then act either according to the maxim of self-advantage or according to the blind impulse to assert everywhere our lawless will'.[16] Thus even if the possibility of diabolical evil is excluded, the doctrine of infallibility of conscience does not exclude the possibility of acting wrongly. For I may be accountable for allowing my conscience to become obscured or even to vanish altogether.

According to Fichte, therefore, the ordinary man has at his disposal, if he chooses to make use of it, an infallible criterion for assessing his particular duties, which does not depend on any knowledge of the science of ethics. But the philosopher can inquire into the grounds of this criterion. And we have seen that Fichte offers a metaphysical explanation.

6. Conscience is thus the supreme judge in the practical moral life. But its dictates are not arbitrary and capricious. For the 'feeling' of which Fichte speaks is really the expression of our implicit awareness that a particular action falls inside or outside the series of actions which fulfil the fundamental impulse of the pure ego. Hence even if conscience is a sufficient guide for moral conduct, there is no reason why the philosopher should be unable to show theoretically that actions of a certain type belong or do not belong to the class of actions which lead to the ego's moral goal. He cannot deduce the particular obligations of particular individuals. This is a matter for conscience. But a philosophical application of the fundamental principle of morality is possible, within the limits of general principles or rules.

To take an example. I am under an obligation to act, for only through action can I fulfil the moral law. And the body is a necessary instrument for action. On the one hand, therefore, I ought not to treat my body as if it were itself my final end. On the other hand I ought to preserve and foster the body as a necessary instrument for action. Hence self-mutilation, for example, would be wrong unless it were required for the preservation of the body as a whole. Whether in this or that particular instance self-mutilation is justified is, however, a matter for conscience rather than for the philosopher. I can only consider the situation under its different aspects and then act according to my immediate consciousness of my duty, confident, according to Fichte, that this immediate 'feeling' cannot err.

Similarly, one can formulate general rules in regard to the use of the cognitive powers. Fichte's profound respect for the vocation of the scholar is expressed in his insistence on the need for combining complete freedom of thought and research with the conviction that 'knowledge of my duty must be the final end of all my knowledge, all my thought and research'.[17] The synthesizing rule is that the scholar should pursue his researches in a spirit of devotion to duty and not out of mere curiosity or to have something to do.

7. The philosopher, therefore, can lay down certain general rules of conduct as applications of the fundamental principle of morality. But an individual's moral vocation is made up of countless particular obligations, in regard to which conscience is the unerring guide. Thus each single individual has his own real moral vocation, his own personal contribution to make to converging series of actions which tend to realize a moral world-order, the perfect rule of reason in the world. The attainment of this ideal goal requires, as it were, a division of moral labour. And we can reformulate the fundamental principle of morality in this way: 'Always fulfil your moral vocation.'[18]

The general outlines of Fichte's vision of reality should now be clear. The ultimate reality, which can be described, according to our point of view, as the absolute ego or as infinite Will, strives spontaneously towards perfect consciousness of itself as free, towards perfect self-possession. But self-consciousness, in Fichte's view, must take the form of finite self-consciousness, and the infinite Will's self-realization can take place only through the self-realization of finite wills. Hence the infinite activity spontaneously expresses itself in a multiplicity of finite selves or rational and free beings. But self-consciousness is not possible without a non-ego, from which the finite ego can recoil onto itself. And the realization of the finite free will through action requires a world in and through which action is possible. Hence the absolute ego or infinite Will must posit the world, Nature, if it is to become conscious of its own freedom through finite selves. And the moral vocations of finite selves in a common goal can be seen as the way in which the absolute ego or infinite Will moves towards its goal. Nature is simply the condition, though a necessary condition, for the expression of the moral will. The really significant feature in empirical reality is the moral activity of human beings, which is itself the expression of the infinite Will, the form which the infinite Will, an activity or doing rather than a being which acts, spontaneously and necessarily assumes.

8. We can turn now to the theory of right and the deduction of the State, to a consideration, that is to say, of the framework within which man's moral life is developed. But the theory of right and political theory, treating, as they do, of relations between human beings, presupposes a plurality of selves. Hence it is appropriate to begin by saying a little more about Fichte's deduction of this plurality.

As we have seen, the absolute ego must limit itself in the form of the finite ego if self-consciousness is to arise. But 'no free being becomes conscious of itself without at the same time becoming conscious of other similar beings'.[19] It is only by distinguishing myself from other beings which I recognize as rational and free that I can become conscious of myself as a determinate free individual. Intersubjectivity is a condition of self-consciousness. A community of selves is thus required if self-consciousness is to arise. Intelligence, as existing, is a manifold. In fact it is 'a closed manifold, that is, a *system* of rational beings'.[20] For they are all limitations of the one absolute ego, the one infinite activity.

This recognition of oneself as a member of a community or system of rational beings requires in turn, as a precondition, the sensible world. For I perceive my freedom as manifested in actions which interlock, so to speak, with the actions of others. And for such a system of actions to be possible there must be a common sensible world in which distinct rational beings can express themselves.

9. Now, if I cannot become conscious of myself as free without regarding myself as a member of a community of free rational beings, it follows that I cannot ascribe to myself alone the totality of infinite freedom. 'I limit myself in my appropriation of freedom by the fact that I also recognize the freedom of others.'[21] At the same time I must also conceive each member of the community as limiting the external expression of his freedom in such a way that all other members can express their freedom.

This idea of each member of the community of rational beings limiting the expression of his freedom in such a way that all other members can also express their freedom is the concept of right. And the principle or rule of right (*Rechtsregel*) is stated by Fichte in this way: 'Limit your freedom through the concept of the freedom of all other persons with whom you come into relation.'[22] The concept of right for Fichte is essentially a social concept. It arises together with the idea of other rational beings who are capable of interfering with one's own activity, and with whose activities one is oneself capable of interfering. If I think away all other rational beings save myself, I have *powers*, and I may have a moral duty to exercise them or some of them. But it is inappropriate in this context to speak of my having a *right* to exercise them. For instance, I have the power of free speech. But if I think away all other rational beings, it is absurd, according to Fichte, to speak of my having a right to free speech. For the concept makes no sense unless I conceive the existence of other beings capable of interfering with my exercise of the power to speak my mind freely. Similarly, it makes no sense to speak of a right to private property except in a social context. True, if I were the only rational being I should have a duty to act and to use material things, expressing my freedom in and through them. I should have possessions. But the concept of the right of private property in the strict sense arises only when I conceive other human beings to whom I have to ascribe similar rights. What can private property mean outside a social context?

Now, though the existence of a community of free selves demands that each member should take the rule of right as the operative principle of his conduct, no individual will is necessarily governed by the rule. Fichte argues, however, that the union of many wills into one can produce a will constantly directed by the rule. 'If a million men are together, it may well be that each one wills for himself as much freedom as possible. But if we unite the will of all in one concept as one will, this will divides the sum of possible freedom into equal parts. It aims at all being free in such a way that the freedom of each individual is limited by the freedom of all the rest.'[23] This union expresses itself in mutual recognition of rights. And it is this mutual recognition which gives rise to the right of private property, considered as the right to exclusive possession of certain things.[24] 'The right of exclusive possession is brought into being *through mutual recognition:* and it does not exist without this condition. All property is grounded on the union of many wills into one will.'[25]

10. If the stability of rights rests on sustained common recognition, reciprocal loyalty and trust are required in the persons concerned. But these are moral conditions on which one cannot count with certainty. Hence there must be some power which can enforce respect for rights. Further, this power must be the expression of the freedom of the human person: it must be established freely. We thus require a compact or contract whereby the contracting parties agree that anyone who infringes the rights of another should be treated in accordance with coercive law. But such a contract can be effective only when it takes the form of the social contract whereby the State is established,[26] furnished with the requisite power to secure the attainment of the end desired by the general will, namely the stability of the system of rights and the protection of the freedom of all. The union of all wills into one thus takes the form of the General Will as embodied in the State.

The influence of Rousseau[27] is obvious, both in Fichte's theory of the General Will and in his idea of the social contract. But the ideas are not introduced simply out of reverence for the name of the French philosopher. For Fichte's deduction of the State consists in a progressive argument showing that the State is a necessary condition for maintaining relations of right without which a community of free persons cannot be conceived. And this community is itself depicted as a necessary condition for the self-realization of the absolute ego as infinite freedom. The State must thus be interpreted as the expression of freedom. And Rousseau's theories of the Social Contract and General Will lend themselves for this purpose.

Fichte does indeed speak of the State as a totality, and he compares it with an organized product of Nature. We cannot say, therefore, that the organic theory of the State is absent from Fichte's political thought. At the same time he emphasizes the fact that the State not only expresses freedom but also exists to create a state of affairs in which each citizen can exercise his personal freedom so far as this is consistent with the freedom of others. Further, the State, considered as a coercive power, is only hypothetically necessary. That is to say, it is necessary on the hypothesis that man's moral development has not reached a point at which each member of society respects the rights and liberties of others from moral motives alone. If this condition were fulfilled, the State, as a coercive power, would no longer be necessary. Indeed, as one of the functions of the State is to facilitate man's moral development, we can say that for Fichte the State should endeavour to bring about the conditions for its own demise. To use Marxist language, Fichte looks forward to the withering away of the State, at least as an ideal possibility. He cannot, therefore, regard it as an end in itself.

Given these premises, Fichte naturally rejects despotism. What may seem surprising in a sympathizer with the French Revolution is that he also rejects democracy. 'No State may be ruled either *despotically* or *democratically*.'[28] But by democracy he understands direct rule by the whole people. And his objection to it is that in a literal democracy there would be no authority to compel the multitude to observe its own laws. Even if many citizens were individually well disposed, there would be no power capable of preventing the degeneration of the community into an irresponsible and capricious mob. Provided, however, that the two extremes of unqualified despotism and democracy are avoided, we cannot say what form of constitution is the best. It is a matter of politics, not of philosophy.

At the same time reflection on the possibility of abuse of power by the civil authority led Fichte to lay great stress on the desirability of establishing a kind of supreme court or tribunal, the 'Ephorate'. This would possess no legislative, executive or judicial power in the ordinary sense. Its function would be to watch over the observance of the laws and constitution, and in the event of a serious abuse of power by the civil authority the Ephors would be entitled to suspend it from the exercise of its functions by means of a State interdict. Recourse would then be had to a referendum to ascertain the people's will concerning a change in the constitution, the law or the government, as the case might be.

That Fichte shows no inclination to deify the State is clear enough. But his political theory, as so far outlined, may suggest that he is committed to minimizing the functions of the State by defending a purely *laissez-faire* policy. But this conclusion does not represent his mind. He does indeed maintain that the purpose of the State is to maintain public security and the system of rights. And from this it follows that interference with the freedom of the individual should be limited to what is required for the fulfilment of this purpose. But the establishment and maintenance of a system of rights and its adjustment to the common good may require a very considerable amount of State activity. It is idle, for example, to insist that everyone has a right to live by his labour if conditions are such that many people cannot do so. Further, though the State is not the fount of the moral law, it is its business to promote the conditions which facilitate the moral development without which there is no true freedom. In particular it should attend to the matter of education.

11. Hence it is not really so astonishing if in his *Closed Commercial State* we find Fichte envisaging a planned economy. He presupposes that all human beings have a right not simply to live but to live a decent human life. And the question then arises how this right can be most effectively realized. In the first place, as Plato recognized centuries ago, there must be division of labour, giving rise to the main economic classes.[29] And in the second place a state of harmony or balance must be maintained. If one economic class grows disproportionately large, the whole economy may be upset. In *The System of Ethics* Fichte emphasized the individual's duty to choose his profession in accordance with his talents and circumstances. In *The Closed Commercial State* he is concerned rather with the common good, and he stresses the State's need to watch over and regulate the division of labour for the good of the community. True, changing circumstances will demand changes in the State's regulations. But supervision and planning are in any case indispensable.

In Fichte's opinion a balanced economy, once established, cannot be maintained unless the State has the power to prevent its being upset by any individual or set of individuals. And he draws the conclusion that all commercial relations with foreign countries should be in the hands of the State or subject to strict State control. 'In the rational State immediate trade with a foreign subject cannot be permitted to the individual citizen.'[30] Fichte's ideal is that of a closed economy in the sense of a self-sufficient economic community.[31] But if there has to be trade with foreign countries, it should not be left to the private initiative and judgment of individuals.

What Fichte envisages, therefore, is a form of national socialism. And he thinks of a planned economy as calculated to provide the material conditions required for the higher intellectual and moral development of the people. In fact, by 'the rational State' (*der Vernunftstaat*) he really means a State directed according to the principles of his own philosophy. We may not feel particularly optimistic about the results of State patronage of a particular philosophical system. But in Fichte's opinion rulers who were really conversant with the principles of transcendental idealism would never abuse their power by restricting private freedom more than was required for the attainment of an end which is itself the expression of freedom.

12. Regarded from the economic point of view, Fichte can be spoken of as one of Germany's first socialist writers. Politically speaking, however, he moved from an earlier cosmopolitan attitude towards German nationalism. In the *Basis of Natural Right* he interpreted the idea of the General Will as leading to the idea of the union of all human wills in a universal community, and he looked forward to a confederation of nations. The system of rights, he thought, could be rendered really stable only through the establishment of a worldwide community. And to a certain extent he always retained this wide outlook. For his ideal was always that of the advance of all men to spiritual freedom. But he came to think that the ideals of the French Revolution, which had aroused his youthful enthusiasm, had been betrayed by Napoleon and that the Germans were better qualified than the French for leading mankind towards its goal. After all, were not the Germans best suited for understanding the principles of the *Wissenschaftslehre* and so for enlightening mankind and teaching it by example what the saving truth could effect? In other words, he thought of Germany as having a cultural mission. And he was convinced that this mission could not be effectively fulfilled without the political unity of the German people. Cultural and linguistic unity go together, and no culture can be unified and lasting without the backbone of political unity. Hence Fichte looked forward to the formation of one German *Reich* which would put an end to the existing division of the Germans into a multiplicity of States. And he hoped for the emergence of a leader who would achieve this political unification of the Germans into one 'rational State'.

If we look back on Fichte's hopes and dreams in the light

of Germany's history in the first half of the twentieth century, they obviously tend to appear as sinister and ominous. But, as has already been remarked, we should bear in mind the historical circumstances of his own time. In any case further reflections on this matter can be left to the reader.

Fichte's early ideas on religion – God in the first version of the theory of science – The charge of atheism and Fichte's reply – The infinite Will in The Vocation of Man *– The development of the philosophy of Being, 1801–5 – The Doctrine of Religion – Later writings – Explanatory and critical comments on Fichte's philosophy of Being.*

1. In 1790 Fichte wrote some notes or *Aphorisms on Religion and Deism (Aphorismen über Religion und Deismus)* which express clearly enough a sense of tension between simple Christian piety and speculative philosophy or, to use a rather hackneyed phrase, between the God of religion and the God of the philosophers. 'The Christian religion seems to be designed more for the heart than for the understanding.'[1] The heart seeks a God who can respond to prayer, who can feel compassion and love; and Christianity fulfils this need. But the understanding, as represented by what Fichte calls deism, presents us with the concept of a changeless necessary Being who is the ultimate cause of all that happens in the world. Christianity offers us the picture of an anthropomorphic Deity, and this picture is well adapted to religious feeling and its exigencies. Speculative philosophy offers us the idea of a changeless first cause and of a system of finite beings which is governed by determinism. And this idea of the understanding does not meet the needs of the heart. True, the two are compatible, in the sense that speculative philosophy leaves untouched the subjective validity of religion. And for the pious Christian who knows little or nothing of philosophy there is no problem. But what of the man whose heart desires a God conceived in human terms but who is at the same time

so constituted that the inclination to philosophical reflection is part of his nature? It is all very well to say that he should set limits to philosophical reflection. 'But can he do so, even if he wishes?'[2]

Fichte's own reflection, however, led him in the direction of the Kantian conception of God and of religion rather than in that of deism, which belonged to the pre-Kantian era. And in his *Essay towards a Critique of All Revelation* (*Versuch einer Kritik aller Offenbarung*, 1792) he attempted to develop Kant's point of view. In particular he made a distinction between 'theology' and religion. The idea of the possibility of a moral law demands belief in God not only as the Power which dominates Nature and is able to synthesize virtue and happiness but also as the complete embodiment of the moral ideal, as the all-holy Being and supreme Good. But assent to propositions about God (such as 'God is holy and just') is not the same thing as religion which 'according to the meaning of the word [*religio*] should be something which *binds* us, and indeed binds us *more strongly* than we would otherwise be bound'.[3] And this binding is derived from the acceptance of the rational moral law as God's law, as the expression of the divine will.

Needless to say, Fichte does not mean that the content of the moral law is arbitrarily determined by the divine will, so that it cannot be known without revelation. Nor does he propose to substitute the concept of heteronomy, of an authoritarian ethics, for the Kantian concept of the autonomy of the practical reason. To justify his position, therefore, he has recourse to the idea of a radical evil in man, that is, to the idea of the ingrained possibility of evil, owing to the strength of natural impulse and passion, and to the idea of the consequent obscuring of man's knowledge of the moral law. The concept of God as the moral legislator and of obedience to the all-holy will of God helps man to fulfil the moral law and grounds the additional element of binding which is peculiar to religion. Further, as the knowledge of God and his law can be obscured, God's revelation of himself as moral legislator is desirable if it is possible.

This may sound as though Fichte is going well beyond Kant. But the difference is much less than may appear at first. Fichte does not decide where revelation is to be found. But he gives general criteria for deciding whether an alleged revelation is really what it claims to be. For example, no alleged revelation can possibly be what it is claimed to be if it contradicts the moral law. And any alleged revelation which goes beyond the idea of the moral law as the expression of the divine will is not revelation. Hence Fichte does not really transcend the limits of Kant's conception of religion. And the sympathy which he was later to show for Christian dogmas is absent at this stage of his thought.

Obviously, it can be objected against Fichte's position that to decide whether revelation really is revelation or not we have first to know the moral law. Hence revelation adds nothing except the idea of fulfilling the moral law as the expression of the all-holy will of God. True, this additional element constitutes what is peculiar to religion. But it seems to follow, on Fichte's premises, that religion is, as it were, a concession to human weakness. For it is precisely human weakness which needs strengthening through the concept of obedience to the divine legislator. Hence if Fichte is not prepared to abandon the Kantian idea of the autonomy of the practical reason and if at the same time he wishes to retain and support the idea of religion, he must revise his concept of God. And as will be seen presently, his own system of transcendental idealism, in its first form at least, left him no option but to do this.

2. In Fichte's first exposition and explanations of the *Wissenschaftslehre* there is very little mention of God. Nor indeed is there much occasion for mentioning God. For Fichte is concerned with the deduction or reconstruction of consciousness from a first principle which is immanent in consciousness. As we have seen, the pure ego is not a being which lies behind consciousness but an activity which is immanent in consciousness and grounds it. And the intellectual intuition by which the pure ego is apprehended is not a mystical apprehension of the Deity but an intuitive grasping of

the pure I-principle revealing itself as an activity or doing (*Thun*). Hence if we emphasize the phenomenological aspect of Fichte's theory of science or knowledge, there is no more reason for describing his pure ego as God than there is for so describing Kant's transcendental ego.

The phenomenological aspect is not indeed the only aspect. In virtue of his elimination of the thing-in-itself and his transformation of the critical philosophy into idealism Fichte is bound to attribute to the pure ego an ontological status and function which was not attributed by Kant to the transcendental ego as logical condition of the unity of consciousness. If the thing-in-itself is to be eliminated, sensible being must be derived, in all the reality which it possesses, from the ultimate principle on the side of the subject; that is, from the absolute ego. But the word 'absolute' must be understood as referring in the first place to that which is fundamental in the transcendental deduction of consciousness from a principle which is immanent in consciousness, not as referring to a Being beyond all consciousness. To postulate such a Being in a system of transcendental idealism would be to abandon the attempt to reduce being to thought.

It is true, of course, that the more the metaphysical implications of the theory of the absolute ego are developed, the more does it take on, as it were, the character of the divine. For it then appears as the infinite activity which produces within itself the world of Nature and of finite selves. But while Fichte is primarily engaged in transforming the system of Kant into idealism and in deducing experience from the transcendental ego, it would hardly occur to him to describe this ego as God. For, as the very use of the word 'ego' shows, the notion of the pure, transcendental or absolute ego is so entangled, as it were, with human consciousness that such a description necessarily appears as extremely inappropriate.

Further, the term 'God' signifies for Fichte a personal self-conscious Being. But the absolute ego is not a self-conscious being. The activity which grounds consciousness and is a striving towards self-consciousness cannot itself be conscious. The absolute ego, therefore, cannot be identified with God. What is more, we cannot even think the idea of God. The concept of consciousness involves a distinction between subject and object, ego and non-ego. And self-consciousness presupposes the positing of the non-ego and itself involves a distinction between the I-subject and the me-object. But the idea of God is the idea of a Being in which there is no such distinction and which is perfectly self-luminous quite independently of the existence of a world. And we are unable to think such an idea. We can *talk* about it, of course; but we cannot be said to *conceive* it. For once we try to *think* what is said, we necessarily introduce the distinctions which are verbally denied. The idea of a subject to which nothing is opposed is thus 'the unthinkable idea of the Godhead'.[4]

It should be noted that Fichte does not say that God is impossible. When Jean-Paul Sartre says that self-consciousness necessarily involves a distinction and that the idea of an infinite self-consciousness in which there is perfect coincidence of subject and object without any distinction is a contradictory idea, he intends this as a proof of atheism, if, that is to say, theism is understood as implying the idea which is alleged to be contradictory. But Fichte carefully avoids saying that it is impossible that there should be a God. He appears to leave open the possibility of a Being which transcends the range of human thought and conception. In any case Fichte does not assert atheism.

At the same time it is easily understandable that Fichte was accused of atheism. And we can turn to a brief consideration of the famous atheism controversy which resulted in the philosopher having to abandon his chair at Jena.

3. In his paper *On the Basis of Our Belief in a Divine Providence* (1798) Fichte gave an explicit account of his idea of God. Let us assume first of all that we are looking at the world from the point of view of ordinary consciousness, which is also that of empirical science. From this point of view, that is, for empirical consciousness, we find ourselves as being in the world, the universe, and we cannot transcend it by means of any metaphysical proof of the existence of a

supernatural Being. 'The world is, simply because it is; and it is what it is, simply because it is what it is. From this point of view we start with an absolute being, and this absolute being is the world: the two concepts are identical.'⁵ To explain the world as the creation of a divine intelligence is, from the scientific point of view, 'simply nonsense' (*totaler Unsinn*). The world is a self-organizing whole which contains in itself the ground of all the phenomena which occur in it.

Now let us look at the world from the point of view of transcendental idealism. The world is then seen as existing only for consciousness and as posited by the pure ego. But in this case the question of finding a cause of the world apart from the ego does not arise. Therefore neither from the scientific nor from the transcendental point of view can we prove the existence of a transcendent divine Creator.

There is, however, a third point of view, the moral. And when looked at from this point of view the world is seen to be 'the sensible material for (the performance of) our duty'.⁶ And the ego is seen to belong to a supersensible moral order. It is this moral order which is God. The 'living and operative moral order is itself God. We need no other God, and we cannot conceive any other.'⁷ 'This is the true faith; this moral order is the *divine*. . . . It is constructed by right action.'⁸ To speak of God as substance or as personal or as exercising with foresight a benevolent providence is so much nonsense. Belief in divine providence is the belief that moral action always has good results and that evil actions can never have good results.

That such statements led to a charge of atheism is not altogether surprising. For to most of Fichte's readers God seemed to have been reduced to a moral ideal. And this is not what is generally meant by theism. After all, there are atheists with moral ideals. Fichte, however, was indignant at the accusation and answered it at considerable length. His replies did not achieve the desired result of clearing his name in the eyes of his opponents; but this is irrelevant for our purposes. We are concerned only with what he said.

In the first place Fichte explained that he could not describe God as personal or as substance because personality was for him something essentially finite and substance meant something extended in space and time, a material thing. In fact, none of the attributes of things or beings could be predicated of God. 'Speaking in a purely philosophical manner one would have to say of God: He is . . . not a being but a *pure activity*, the life and principle of a supersensible world-order.'[9]

In the second place Fichte maintained that his critics had misunderstood what he meant by a moral world-order. They had interpreted him as saying that God is a moral order in a sense analogous to the order created by a housewife when she arranges the furniture and other objects in a room. But what he had really meant was that God is an active ordering, an *ordo ordinans*, a living and active moral order, not an *ordo ordinatus*, something merely constructed by human effort. God is *ein tätiges Ordnen*, an active ordering, rather than an *Ordnung*, an order constructed by man.[10] And the finite ego, considered as acting in accordance with duty, is 'a member of that supersensible world-order'.[11]

In Fichte's idea of God as the moral world-order we can perhaps see the fusion of two lines of thought. First there is the concept of the dynamic unity of all rational beings. In the *Basis of the Entire Theory of Science* Fichte had not much occasion for dwelling on the plurality of selves. For he was primarily concerned with an abstract deduction of 'experience' in the sense already explained. But in the *Basis of Natural Right* he insisted, as we have seen, on the necessity of a plurality of rational beings. 'Man becomes man only amongst men; and as he can be nothing else but man and would not exist at all if he were not man, *there must be a plurality of men if there is to be man at all*.'[12] Hence Fichte was naturally impelled to reflect on the bond of union between men. In *The Science of Ethics* he was primarily concerned with the moral law as such and with personal morality; but he expressed his conviction that all rational beings have a common moral end, and he spoke of the moral law as using the individual as a tool or instrument for its self-realization in the sensible world. And from this notion there is an easy transition to the idea of a moral world-order which fulfils itself in and through rational beings and unites them in itself.

The second line of thought is Fichte's strongly moralistic conception of religion. At the time when he wrote the essay which occasioned the atheism-controversy he tended, like Kant before him, to equate religion with morality. Not prayer but the performance of one's duty is true religion. True, Fichte allowed that the moral life has a distinguishable religious aspect, namely the belief that whatever appearances may suggest performance of one's duty always produces a good result because it forms part, as it were, of a self-realizing moral order. But, given Fichte's moralistic interpretation of religion, faith in this moral world-order would naturally count for him as faith in God, especially as on his premises he could not think of God as a personal transcendent Being.

This moralistic conception of religion finds clear expression in an essay to which the title *From a Private Paper* (1800) has been given. The place or locus of religion, Fichte asserts, is found in obedience to the moral law. And religious faith is faith in a moral order. In action considered from a purely natural and non-moral point of view man reckons on the natural order, that is, on the stability and uniformity of Nature. In moral action he reckons on a supersensible moral order in which his action has a part to play and which ensures its moral fruitfulness. 'Every belief in a divine being *which contains more* than this concept of the moral order is to that extent imagination and superstition.'[13]

Obviously, those who described Fichte as an atheist were from one point of view quite justified. For he refused to assert what theism was generally taken to mean. At the same time his indignant repudiation of the charge of atheism is understandable. For he did not assert that nothing exists except finite selves and the sensible world. There is, at least as an object of practical faith, a supersensible moral world-order which fulfils itself in and through man.

4. But if the moral world-order is really an *ordo ordinans*, a truly active ordering, it must obviously possess an ontologi-

cal status. And in *The Vocation of Man* (1800) it appears
as the eternal and infinite Will. 'This Will binds me in union
with itself: it also binds me in union with all finite beings
like myself and is the common mediator between us all.'[14]
It is infinite Reason. But dynamic creative Reason is Will.
Fichte also describes it as creative Life.

If we took some of Fichte's expressions literally, we should
probably be inclined to interpret his doctrine of the infinite
Will in a theistic sense. He even addresses the 'sublime and
living Will, named by no name and compassed by no concept'.[15] But he still maintains that personality is something
limited and finite and cannot be applied to God. The infinite
differs from the finite in nature and not merely in degree.
Further, the philosopher repeats that true religion consists in
the fulfilment of one's moral vocation. At the same time this
idea of doing one's duty and so fulfilling one's moral vocation is undoubtedly infused with a spirit of devout abandonment to and trust in the divine Will.

To appreciate the role of *The Vocation of Man* in the development of Fichte's later philosophy it is important to understand that the doctrine of the infinite Will is described as
a matter of faith. This somewhat strange and turgid work,
which is introduced by the remarks that it is not intended for
professional philosophers and that the *I* of the dialogue por-
tions should not be taken without more ado to represent the
author himself, is divided into three parts, entitled respectively *Doubt, Knowledge* and *Faith*. In the second part idealism is interpreted as meaning that not only external objects
but also one's own self, so far as one can have any idea of it,
exist only for consciousness. And the conclusion is drawn that
everything is reduced to images or pictures (*Bilder*) without
there being any reality which is pictured. 'All reality is transformed into a wonderful dream, without a life which is
dreamed of and without a mind which dreams it, into a dream
which consists of a dream of itself. *Intuition* is the dream;
thought—the source of all the being and all the reality which
I imagine to myself, of *my* being, my power, my purpose—
is the dream of that dream.'[16] In other words, subjective

idealism reduces everything to presentations without there being anything which does the presenting or to which the presentations are made. For when I try to grasp the self for whose consciousness the presentations exist, this self necessarily becomes one of the presentations. Knowledge, therefore, that is, idealist philosophy, can find nothing abiding, no being. But the mind cannot rest in such a position. And practical or moral faith, based on consciousness of myself as a moral will subject to the moral imperative, asserts the infinite Will which underlies the finite self and creates the world in the only way in which it can do so, 'in the finite reason'.[17]

Fichte thus retains idealism but at the same time goes beyond the ego-philosophy to postulate the infinite underlying and all-comprehensive Will. And with this postulate the atmosphere, so to speak, of his original philosophy changes dramatically. I do not mean to imply that there is no connection. For the theory of the Will can be regarded as implicit in the practical deduction of consciousness in the original *Wissenschaftslehre*. At the same time the ego retreats from the foreground and an infinite reality, which is no longer described as the absolute ego, takes its place. 'Only Reason exists; the infinite in itself, the finite in it and through it. Only in our minds does He create a world, at least that *from which* and that *by which* we unfold it: the voice of duty, and harmonious feelings, intuition and laws of thought.'[18]

As already mentioned, this dynamic panentheistic idealism is for Fichte a matter of practical faith, not of knowledge. To fulfil properly our moral vocations, we require faith in a living and active moral order which can only be interpreted as infinite dynamic Reason, that is, as infinite Will. This is the one true Being behind the sphere of presentation, creating and sustaining it through finite selves which themselves exist only as manifestations of the infinite Will. The development of Fichte's later philosophy is largely conditioned by the need to *think* this concept of absolute Being, to give it philosophical form. In *The Vocation of Man* it remains within the sphere of moral faith.

5. In the *Exposition of the Theory of Science*[19] which he composed in 1801 Fichte clearly states that 'all knowledge presupposes . . . its own being'.[20] For knowledge is 'a being *for itself* and *in itself*':[21] it is being's 'self-penetration'[22] and is thus the expression of Freedom. Absolute knowledge, therefore, presupposes absolute Being: the former is the latter's self-penetration.

Here we have a clear reversal of the position adopted by Fichte in the earlier form of his doctrine of knowledge. At first he maintained that all being is being for consciousness. Hence it was not possible for him to admit the idea of an absolute divine Being behind or beyond consciousness. For the very fact of conceiving such a Being made it conditioned and dependent. In other words, the idea of absolute Being was for him contradictory. Now, however, he asserts the primacy of Being. Absolute Being comes to exist 'for itself' in absolute knowledge. Hence the latter must presuppose the former. And this absolute Being is the divine.

It does not follow, of course, that absolute Being is for Fichte a personal God. Being 'penetrates itself', comes to knowledge or consciousness of itself, in and through human knowledge of reality. In other words, absolute Being expresses itself in and bears within itself all finite rational beings, and their knowledge of Being is Being's knowledge of itself. At the same time Fichte insists that absolute Being can never be wholly understood or comprehended by the finite mind. In this sense God transcends the human mind.

Evidently, there is some difficulty here. On the one hand absolute Being is said to penetrate itself in absolute knowledge. On the other hand absolute knowledge seems to be ruled out. If, therefore, we exclude Christian theism, according to which God enjoys perfect self-knowledge independently of the human spirit, it appears that Fichte should logically adopt the Hegelian conception of philosophical knowledge as penetrating the inner essence of the Absolute and as being the Absolute's absolute knowledge of itself. But in point of fact Fichte does not do this. To the very end he maintains that absolute Being in itself transcends the reach of the hu-

man mind. We know images, pictures, rather than the reality
in itself.

In the lectures on the *Wissenschaftslehre* which he delivered in 1804 Fichte emphasizes the idea of absolute Being as Light,[23] an idea which goes back to Plato and the
Platonic tradition in metaphysics. This living Light in its radiation is said to divide itself into Being and Thought (*Den-
ken*). But conceptual thought, Fichte insists, can never grasp
absolute Being in itself, which is incomprehensible. And this
incomprehensibility is 'the negation of the concept'.[24] One
might expect Fichte to draw the conclusion that the human
mind can approach the Absolute only by way of negation.
But in point of fact he makes a good many positive statements, telling us, for example, that Being and Life and *esse*
are one, and that the Absolute *in itself* can never be subject
to division.[25] It is only in its appearance, in the radiation of
Light, that division is introduced.

In *The Nature of the Scholar* (1806), the published version of lectures delivered at Erlangen in 1805, we are again
told that the one divine Being is Life and that this Life is
itself changeless and eternal. But it externalizes itself in the
life of the human race throughout time, 'an endlessly self-
developing life which always advances towards a higher self-
realization in a never-ending stream of time'.[26] In other
words, this external life of God advances towards the realization of an ideal which can be described, in anthropomorphic
language, as 'the Idea and fundamental notion of God in the
production of the world, God's purpose and plan for the
world'.[27] In this sense the divine Idea is 'the ultimate and
absolute foundation of all appearances'.[28]

6. These speculations were worked out more at length in
The Way to the Blessed Life or the Doctrine of Religion
(1806), which comprises a series of lectures delivered at Berlin. God is absolute Being. And to say this is to say that God
is infinite Life. For 'Being and Life are one and the same'.[29]
In itself this Life is one, indivisible and unchanging. But it
expresses or manifests itself externally. And the only way in
which it can do this is through consciousness which is the

ex-istence (*Dasein*) of God. 'Being ex-ists [*ist da*] and the ex-istence of Being is necessarily consciousness or reflection.'[30] In this external manifestation distinction or division appears. For consciousness involves the subject-object relation.

The subject in question is obviously the limited or finite subject, namely the human spirit. But what is the object? It is indeed Being. For consciousness, the divine *Dasein*, is consciousness of Being. But Being in itself, the immediate infinite Life, transcends the comprehension of the human mind. Hence the object of consciousness must be the image or picture or *schema* of the Absolute. And this is the world. 'What does this consciousness contain? I think that each of you will answer: the world and nothing but the world. . . . In consciousness the divine Life is inevitably transformed into an abiding world.'[31] In other words, Being is objectified for consciousness in the form of the world.

Although Fichte insists that the Absolute transcends the grasp of the human mind, he says a good deal about it. And even if the finite spirit cannot know the infinite Life as it is in itself, it can at least know that the world of consciousness is the image or *schema* of the Absolute. Hence there are two main forms of life which lie open to man. It is possible for him to immerse himself in apparent life (*das Scheinleben*), life in the finite and changeable, life directed towards the gratification of natural impulse. But because of its unity with the infinite divine Life the human spirit can never be satisfied with love of the finite and sensible. Indeed, the endless seeking for successive finite sources of satisfaction shows that even apparent life is informed or carried along, as it were, by the longing for the infinite and eternal which is 'the innermost root of all finite existence'.[32] Hence man is capable of rising to true life (*das wahrhaftige Leben*) which is characterized by love of God. For love, as Fichte puts it, is the heart of life.

If it is asked in what this true life precisely consists, Fichte's reply is still given primarily in terms of morality. That is to say, true life consists primarily in a man's fulfilling his moral vocation, by which he is liberated from the servitude of the sensible world and in which he strives after the attainment of ideal ends. At the same time the markedly moralistic atmosphere of Fichte's earlier accounts of religion tends to disappear or at any rate to diminish. The religious point of view is not simply identical with the moral point of view. For it involves the fundamental conviction that God alone is, that God is the one true reality. True, God as he is in himself is hidden from the finite mind. But the religious man knows that the infinite divine Life is immanent in himself, and his moral vocation is for him a divine vocation. In the creative realization of ideals or values through action[33] he sees the image or *schema* of the divine Life.

But though *The Doctrine of Religion* is permeated with a religious atmosphere, there is a marked tendency to subordinate the religious point of view to the philosophical. Thus, according to Fichte, while the religious point of view involves belief in the Absolute as the foundation of all plurality and finite existence, philosophy turns this belief into knowledge. And it is in accordance with this attitude that Fichte attempts to show the identity between Christian dogmas and his own system. To be sure, this attempt can be regarded as the expression of a growth in sympathy with Christian theology; but it can also be regarded as an essay in 'demythologization'. For instance, in the sixth lecture Fichte refers to the prologue to St. John's Gospel and argues that the doctrine of the divine Word, when translated into the language of philosophy, is identical with his own theory of the divine ex-istence or *Dasein*. And the statement of St. John that all things were made in and through the Word means, from the speculative point of view, that the world and all that is in it exist only in the sphere of consciousness as the ex-istence of the Absolute.

However, with the development of the philosophy of Being there goes a development in Fichte's understanding of religion. From the religious point of view moral activity is love of God and fulfilment of his will, and it is sustained by faith and trust in God. We exist only in and through God, infinite Life, and the feeling of this union is essential to the religious or blessed life (*das selige Leben*).

7. *The Way to the Blessed Life* is a series of popular lectures, in the sense that it is not a work for professional philosophers. And Fichte is obviously concerned with edifying and uplifting his hearers, as well as with reassuring them that his philosophy is not at variance with the Christian religion. But the fundamental theories are common to Fichte's later writings: they are certainly not put forward simply for the sake of edification. Thus in *The Facts of Consciousness* (1810) we are told that 'knowledge is certainly not merely knowledge of itself . . . it is knowledge of a *Being*, namely of the one Being which truly is, God'.[34] But this object of knowledge is not grasped in itself; it is splintered, as it were, into forms of knowledge. And 'the demonstration of the necessity of these forms is precisely philosophy or the *Wissenschaftslehre*'.[35] Similarly, in *The Theory of Science in its General Outline* (1810) we read that 'only one Being exists purely through itself, God. . . . And neither within him nor outside him can a new being arise.'[36] The only thing which can be external to God is the *schema* or picture of Being itself, which is 'God's Being outside his Being',[37] the divine self-externalization in consciousness. Thus the whole of the productive activity which is reconstructed or deduced in the theory of science is the schematizing or picturing of God, the spontaneous self-externalization of the divine life.

In the *System of Ethics* of 1812 we find Fichte saying that while from the scientific point of view the world is primary and the concept a secondary reflection or picture, from the ethical point of view the Concept is primary. In fact 'the Concept is ground of the world or of Being'.[38] And this assertion, if taken out of its context, appears to contradict the doctrine which we have been considering, namely that Being is primary. But Fichte explains that 'the proposition in question, namely that the Concept is ground of Being, can be expressed in this way: Reason or the Concept is practical'.[39] He further explains that though the Concept or Reason is in fact itself the picture of a higher Being, the picture of God, 'ethics can and should know nothing of this. . . . Ethics must know nothing of God, but take the Concept itself as the Absolute.'[40] In other words, the doctrine of absolute Being, as expounded in the *Wissenschaftslehre*, transcends the sphere of ethics which deals with the causality of the Concept, the self-realizing Idea or Ideal.

8. Fichte's later philosophy has sometimes been represented as being to all intents and purposes a new system which involved a break with the earlier philosophy of the ego. Fichte himself, however, maintained that it was nothing of the kind. In his view the philosophy of Being constituted a development of his earlier thought rather than a break with it. If he had originally meant, as most of his critics took him to mean, that the world is the creation of the finite self as such, his later theory of absolute Being would indeed have involved a radical change of view. But he had never meant this. The finite subject and its object, the two poles of consciousness, had always been for him the expression of an unlimited or infinite principle. And his later doctrine of the sphere of consciousness as the ex-istence of infinite Life or Being was a development, not a contradiction, of his earlier thought. In other words, the philosophy of Being supplemented the *Wissenschaftslehre* rather than took its place.

It is indeed arguable that unless Fichte was prepared to defend a subjective idealism which it would have been difficult to dissociate from a solipsistic implication, he was bound in the long run to transgress his initial self-imposed limits, to go behind consciousness and to find its ground in absolute Being. Further, he explicitly admitted that the absolute ego, as transcending the subject-object relationship which it grounds, must be the identity of subjectivity and objectivity. Hence it is not unnatural that in proportion as he developed the metaphysical aspect of his philosophy he should tend to discard the word 'ego' as an appropriate descriptive term for his ultimate principle. For this word is too closely associated with the idea of the subject as distinct from the object. In this sense his later philosophy was a development of his earlier thought.

At the same time it is also arguable that the philosophy of Being is superimposed on the *Wissenschaftslehre* in such a way that the two do not really fit together. According to the *Wissenschaftslehre* the world exists only for consciousness. And this thesis really depends on the premiss that being must be reduced to thought or consciousness. Fichte's philosophy of absolute Being, however, clearly implies the logical priority of being to thought. True, in his later philosophy Fichte does not deny his former thesis that the world has reality only within the sphere of consciousness. On the contrary, he re-affirms it. What he does is to depict the whole sphere of consciousness as the externalization of absolute Being in itself. But it is very difficult to understand this idea of externalization. If we take seriously the statement that absolute Being is and eternally remains one and immutable, we can hardly interpret Fichte as meaning that Being *becomes* conscious. And if the sphere of consciousness is an eternal reflection of God, if it is the divine self-consciousness eternally proceeding from God as the Plotinian *Nous* emanates eternally from the One, it seems to follow that there must always have been a human spirit.

Fichte could, of course, depict absolute Being as an infinite activity moving towards self-consciousness in and through the human spirit. But then it would be natural to conceive the infinite Life as expressing itself immediately in objective Nature as a necessary condition for the life of the human spirit. In other words, it would be natural to proceed in the direction of Hegel's absolute idealism. But this would involve a greater change in the *Wissenschaftslehre* than Fichte was prepared to make. He does indeed say that it is the one Life, and not the individual as such, which 'intuits' the material world. But he maintains to the end that the world, as the image or *schema* of God, has reality only within the sphere of consciousness. And as absolute Being in itself is not conscious, this can only mean human consciousness. Until this element of subjective idealism is abandoned, the transition to the absolute idealism of Hegel is not possible.

There is indeed another possibility, namely that of conceiving absolute Being as eternally self-conscious. But Fichte can hardly take the path of traditional theism. For his idea of what self-consciousness essentially involves prevents him from attributing it to the One. Hence consciousness must be derivative. And this is human consciousness. But there can be no being apart from God. Hence human consciousness must be in some sense the Absolute's consciousness of itself. But in what sense? It does not seem to me that any clear answer is forthcoming. And the reason is that Fichte's later philosophy of Being could not be simply superimposed on the *Wissenschaftslehre*. A much greater measure of revision was required.

It may be objected that to interpret Fichte's philosophy as demanding revision either in the direction of Hegel's absolute idealism or in that of theism is to fail to do justice to its intrinsic character. And this is true in a sense. For Fichte has his own ethical vision of reality, to which attention has been drawn in these chapters. We have seen the infinite Will expressing itself in finite selves for which Nature forms the scene and material for the fulfilment of their several moral vocations. And we have seen these vocations converging towards the realization of a universal moral order, the goal, as it were, of the infinite Will itself. And the grandeur of this vision of reality, of Fichte's dynamic ethical idealism in its main lines, is not in question. But Fichte did not offer his philosophy simply as an impressionistic vision or as poetry, but as the truth about reality. Hence criticism of his theories is quite in place. After all, it is not the vision of the realization of a universal ideal, a moral world-order, which has been subjected to adverse criticism. This vision may well possess an abiding value. And it can serve as a corrective to an interpretation of reality simply in terms of empirical science. One can certainly derive stimulus and inspiration from Fichte. But to draw profit from him one has to discard a good deal of the theoretical framework of the vision.

It has been stated above that Fichte could hardly take the path of traditional theism. But some writers have maintained that his later philosophy is in fact a form of theism. And in support of this contention they can appeal to certain statements which represent the philosopher's firm convictions and

are not simply *obiter dicta* or remarks calculated to reassure
his more orthodox readers or hearers. For example, Fichte
constantly maintains that absolute Being is unchangeable and
that it can suffer no self-diremption. It is the eternal immutable One; not a static lifeless One but the fullness of infinite
Life. True, creation is free only in the sense that it is spontaneous; but creation does not effect any change in God. To
be sure, Fichte refuses to predicate personality of God, even
if he frequently employs Christian language and speaks of
God as 'He'. But as he regards personality as necessarily finite,
he obviously cannot attribute it to infinite Being. But this
does not mean that he looks on God as infra-personal. God is
supra-personal, not less than personal. In Scholastic language,
Fichte has no analogical concept of personality, and this prevents him from using theistic terms. At the same time the
concept of absolute Being which transcends the sphere of the
distinctions which necessarily exist between finite beings is
clearly a move in the direction of theism. The ego no longer
occupies the central position in Fichte's picture of reality: its
place is taken by infinite Life which in itself suffers no change
or self-diremption.

This is all very well as far as it goes. And it is true that
Fichte's refusal to predicate personality of God is due to the
fact that personality for him involves finitude. God transcends the sphere of personality rather than falls short of it.
But it is also the absence of any clear idea of analogy which
involves Fichte's thought in a radical ambiguity. God is infinite Being. Therefore there can arise no being apart from
God. If there were such a being, God would not be infinite.
The Absolute is the sole Being. This line of thought clearly
points in the direction of pantheism. At the same time Fichte
is determined to maintain that the sphere of consciousness,
with its distinction, between the finite ego and the world, is
in some sense outside God. But in what sense? It is all very
well for Fichte to say that the distinction between the divine Being and the divine ex-istence arises only for consciousness. The question inevitably suggests itself, are finite selves

beings or are they not? If they are not, monism results. And it is then impossible to explain how consciousness, with the distinctions which it introduces, arises. If, however, finite selves are beings, how are we to reconcile this with the statement that God is the only Being unless we have recourse to a theory of analogy? Fichte wishes to have things both ways. That is, he wishes to say at the same time that the sphere of consciousness, with its distinction between the finite self and its object, is external to God and that God is the only Being. Hence his position in regard to the issue between theism and pantheism inevitably remains ambiguous. This is not to deny, of course, that the development of Fichte's philosophy of Being conferred on his thought a much greater resemblance to theism than would be suggested by his earlier writings. But it seems to me that if a writer who admires Fichte for his use of the transcendental method of reflection or for his ethical idealism proceeds to interpret his later philosophy as a clear statement of theism, he is going beyond the historical evidence.

If, finally, it is asked whether in his philosophy of Being Fichte abandons idealism, the answer should be clear from what has been already said. Fichte does not repudiate the *Wissenschaftslehre*, and in this sense he retains idealism. When he says that it is the one Life, and not the individual subject, which 'intuits' (and so produces) the material world, he is obviously accounting for the fact that the material world appears to the finite subject as something given, as an already constituted object. But he had proclaimed from the beginning that this is the crucial fact which idealism has to explain, and not to deny. At the same time the assertion of the primacy of Being and of the derivative character of consciousness and knowledge is a move away from idealism. Hence we can say that in so far as this assertion proceeded from the exigencies of his own thought, idealism with Fichte tended to overcome itself. But this is not to say that the philosopher ever made a clear and explicit break with idealism. In any case we may well feel that though in recent times there has been a tendency to emphasize Fichte's later thought, his impressive vision of reality is his system of ethical idealism rather than his obscure utterances about absolute Being and the divine *Dasein*.

Chapter Five

SCHELLING (1)

Life and writings – The successive phases in Schelling's thought – Early writings and the influence of Fichte.

1. Friedrich Wilhelm Joseph von Schelling, son of a learned Lutheran pastor, was born in 1775 at Leonberg in Württemberg. A precocious boy, he was admitted at the age of fifteen to the Protestant theological foundation at the University of Tübingen where he became a friend of Hegel and Hölderlin, both of whom were five years older than himself. At the age of seventeen he wrote a dissertation on the third chapter of Genesis, and in 1793 he published an essay *On Myths* (*Ueber Mythen*). This was followed in 1794 by a paper *On the Possibility of a Form of Philosophy in General* (*Ueber die Möglichkeit einer Form der Philosophie überhaupt*).

At this time Schelling was more or less a disciple of Fichte, a fact which is apparent in the title of a work published in 1795, *On the Ego as Principle of Philosophy* (*Vom Ich als Prinzip der Philosophie*). In the same year there appeared his *Philosophical Letters on Dogmatism and Criticism* (*Philosophische Briefe über Dogmatismus und Kritizismus*), dogmatism being represented by Spinoza and criticism by Fichte.

But though Fichte's thought formed a point of departure for his reflections, Schelling very soon showed the independence of his mind. In particular, he was dissatisfied with Fichte's view of Nature as being simply an instrument for moral action. And his own view of Nature as an immediate manifestation of the Absolute, as a self-organizing dynamic and teleological system which moves upwards, as it were, to the emergence of consciousness and to Nature's knowledge of herself in and through man, found expression in a series of works on the philosophy of Nature. Thus in 1797 he published *Ideas towards a Philosophy of Nature* (*Ideen zu einer Philosophie der Natur*), in 1798 *On the World-Soul* (*Von der Weltseele*), and in 1799 a *First Sketch of a System of the Philosophy of Nature* (*Erster Ertwurf eines Systems der Naturphilosophie*) and an *Introduction to the Sketch of a System of the Philosophy of Nature, or On the Concept of Speculative Physics* (*Einleitung zu dem Entwurf eines Systems der Naturphilosophie oder über den Begriff der spekulativen Physik*).

It will be noted that the title of the last work refers to speculative physics. And a similar term occurs in the full title of the work *On the World-Soul*, the world-soul being said to be an hypothesis of 'the higher physics'. One can hardly imagine Fichte giving much attention to speculative physics. Yet the series of publications on the philosophy of Nature does not indicate a complete break with Fichte's thought. For in 1800 Schelling published his *System of Transcendental Idealism* (*System des transzendentalen Idealismus*) in which the influence of Fichte's *Wissenschaftslehre* is obvious. Whereas in his writings on the philosophy of Nature Schelling moved from the objective to the subjective, from the lowest grades of Nature up to the organic sphere as a preparation for consciousness, in the *System of Transcendental Idealism* he began with the ego and proceeded to trace the process of its self-objectification. He regarded the two points of view as complementary, as is shown by the fact that in 1800 he also published a *General Deduction of the Dynamic Process* (*Allgemeine Deduktion des dynamischen Prozesses*), which was followed in 1801 by a short piece *On the True Concept of the Philosophy of Nature* (*Ueber den wahren Begriff der Naturphilosophie*). In the same year he also published *An Exposition of My System of Philosophy* (*Darstellung meines Systems der Philosophie*).

In 1798 Schelling was appointed to a chair in the University of Jena. He was only twenty-three, but his writings had won him the commendation not only of Goethe but also of Fichte. From 1802 to 1803 he collaborated with Hegel in editing the *Critical Journal of Philosophy*. And during the period of his professorship at Jena he was in friendly relations with the circle of the romantics, such as the two Schlegels and Novalis. In 1802 Schelling published, *Bruno, or On the Divine and Natural Principle of Things* (*Bruno, oder über das göttliche und natürliche Prinzip der Dinge*) and also a series of *Lectures on the Method of Academic Study* (*Vorlesungen über die Methode des akademischen Studiums*) in which he discussed the unity of the sciences and the place of philosophy in academic life.

It has been mentioned that in his *System of Transcendental Idealism* Schelling started with the ego and utilized ideas taken from Fichte's *Wissenschaftslehre* in his reconstruction of the ego's self-objectification, for example in morals. But this work culminated in a philosophy of art, to which Schelling attached great importance. And in the winter of 1802–3 he lectured at Jena on the philosophy of art. At this time he looked on art as the key to the nature of reality. And this fact alone is sufficient to show the marked difference between Schelling's outlook and that of Fichte.

In 1803 Schelling married Caroline Schlegel after the legal dissolution of her marriage with A. W. Schlegel, and the pair went to Würzburg, where Schelling lectured for a period in the University. About this time he began to devote his attention to problems of religion and to the theosophical utterances of the mystical shoemaker of Görlitz, Jakob Boehme.[1] And in 1804 he published *Philosophy and Religion* (*Philosophie und Religion*).

Schelling left Würzburg for Munich in 1806. His reflections on freedom and on the relation between human freedom and the Absolute found expression in *Philosophical Inquiries into the Nature of Human Freedom* (*Philosophische Untersuchungen über das Wesen der menschlichen Freiheit*), a work which was published in 1809. But by this time his star had begun to grow dim. We have seen that he collaborated with Hegel for a short period in editing a philosophical journal. But in 1807 Hegel, who had previously been little known, published his first great work, *The Phenomenology of Spirit*.

And this work not only formed the first stage in its author's rise to fame as Germany's leading philosopher but also represented his intellectual break with Schelling. In particular, Hegel gave a somewhat caustic expression to his opinion of Schelling's doctrine of the Absolute. And Schelling, who was the very opposite of thick-skinned, took this betrayal, as he saw it, very much to heart. In the years that followed, as he witnessed the growing reputation of his rival, he became obsessed by the thought that his former friend had foisted on a gullible public an inferior system of philosophy. Indeed, his bitter disappointment at Hegel's rise to a pre-eminent position in the philosophical world of Germany probably helps to explain why, after a remarkable burst of literary activity, he published comparatively little.

Schelling continued, however, to lecture. Thus a course of lectures which he gave at Stuttgart in 1810 is printed in his collected Works. In 1811 he wrote The Ages of the World (Die Zeitalter), but the work remained unfinished and was not published during his lifetime.

During the period 1821–6 Schelling lectured at Erlangen. In 1827 he returned to Munich to occupy the chair of philosophy and zestfully set about the congenial task of undermining the influence of Hegel. He had become convinced that a distinction must be made between negative philosophy, which is a purely abstract conceptual construction, and positive philosophy, which treats of concrete existence. The Hegelian system, needless to say, was declared to be an example of the first type.

The death of Schelling's great rival[2] in 1831 should have facilitated his task. And ten years later, in 1841, he was appointed professor of philosophy at Berlin with the mission of combating the influence of Hegelianism by expounding his own religious system. In the Prussian capital Schelling began lecturing as a prophet, as one announcing the advent of a new era. And he had among his audience professors, statesmen and a number of hearers whose names were to become famous, such as Sören Kierkegaard, Jakob Burckhardt, Friedrich Engels and Bakunin. But the lectures were not as successful as Schelling hoped that they would be, and the audience started to diminish. In 1846 he abandoned lecturing, except for occasional discourses at the Berlin Academy. Later he retired to Munich and busied himself with preparing manuscripts for publication. He died in 1854 at Ragaz in Switzerland. His *Philosophy of Revelation* (*Philosophie der Offenbarung*) and *Philosophy of Mythology* (*Philosophie der Mythologie*) were published posthumously.

2. There is no one closely-knit system which we can call Schelling's system of philosophy. For his thought passed through a succession of phases from the early period when he stood very much under the influence of Fichte up to the final period which is represented by the posthumously published lectures on the philosophy of revelation and mythology. There has been no general agreement among historians about the precise number of phases which should be distinguished. One or two have contented themselves with Schelling's own distinction between negative and positive philosophy; but this distinction fails to take account of the variety of phases in his thought before he set about expounding his final philosophy of religion. Hence it has been customary to make further divisions. But though there certainly are distinct phases in Schelling's thought, it would be a mistake to regard these phases as so many independent systems. For there is a visible continuity. That is to say, reflection on a position already adopted led Schelling to raise further problems, the solution of which required fresh moves on his part. True, in his later years he emphasized the distinction between negative and positive philosophy. But though he regarded a good deal of his own previous thought as negative philosophy, he stressed the distinction in the course of his polemic against Hegel; and what he desired was not so much a complete rejection of so-called negative philosophy as its incorporation into and subordination to positive philosophy. Further, he claimed that some inkling at least of positive philosophy could be found in his early *Philosophical Letters on Dogmatism and Criticism*, and that even in his first philo-

sophical essays his inclination towards the concrete and historical had manifested itself.

In 1796, when Schelling was twenty-one, he drew up for
himself a programme for a system of philosophy. The projected system would proceed from the idea of the ego or self
as an absolutely free being by way of the positing of the non-
ego to the sphere of speculative physics. It would then proceed
to the sphere of the human spirit. The principles of historical
development would have to be laid down, and the ideas of a
moral world, of God and of the freedom of all spiritual beings
would have to be developed. Further, the central importance
of the idea of beauty would have to be shown, and the
aesthetic character of the highest act of reason. Finally, there
would have to be a new mythology, uniting philosophy and
religion.

This programme is illuminating. On the one hand it illustrates the element of discontinuity in Schelling's thought.
For the fact that he proposes to start from the ego reveals
the influence of Fichte, an influence which grew progressively less as time went on. On the other hand the programme
illustrates the element of continuity in Schelling's philosophizing. For it envisages the development of a philosophy of
Nature, a philosophy of history, a philosophy of art, a philosophy of freedom and a philosophy of religion and mythology, themes which were to occupy his attention in turn. In
other words, though Schelling at first gave the impression of
being a disciple of Fichte, his interests and bent of mind
were already apparent at the beginning of his career.

The upshot of all this is that time spent on discussing
exactly how many phases or 'systems' there are in Schelling's
philosophizing is time wasted. There certainly are distinct
phases, but a genetic account of his thought can do justice
to these distinctions without its being implied that Schelling
jumped from one self-enclosed system to another. In fine, the
philosophy of Schelling is a philosophizing rather than a finished system or succession of finished systems. In a sense the
beginning and the end of his pilgrimage coincide. We have
seen that in 1793 he published an essay *On Myths*. In his

old age he returned to this subject and lectured on it at length. But in between we find a restless process of reflection moving from the ego-philosophy of Fichte through the philosophy of Nature and of art to the philosophy of the religious consciousness and a form of speculative theism, the whole being linked together by the theme of the relation between the finite and the infinite.

3. In his essay *On the Possibility of a Form of Philosophy in General* (1794) Schelling follows Fichte in asserting that philosophy, being a science, must be a logically unified system of propositions, developed from one fundamental proposition which gives expression to the unconditioned. This unconditioned is the self-positing ego. Hence 'the fundamental proposition can only be this: I is I'.[3] In the work *On the Ego as Principle of Philosophy* (1795) this proposition is formulated in the less peculiar form, 'I am I or I am'.[4] And from this proposition Schelling proceeds to the positing of the non-ego and argues that ego and non-ego mutually condition one another. There is no subject without an object and no object without a subject. Hence there must be a mediating factor, a common product which links them together; and this is representation (*Vorstellung*). We thus have the form of the fundamental triad of all science or knowledge, namely subject, object and representation.

The influence of Fichte is obvious enough. But it is worth noting that from the very start Schelling emphasizes the difference between the absolute and the empirical ego. 'The completed system of science starts with the absolute ego.'[5] This is not a thing but infinite freedom. It is indeed one, but the unity which is predicated of it transcends the unity which is predicated of the individual member of a class. The absolute ego is not and cannot be a member of any class: it transcends the concept of class. Further, it transcends the grasp of conceptual thought and can be apprehended only in intellectual intuition.

None of this contradicts Ficte; but the point is that Schelling's metaphysical interests are revealed from the beginning of his career. Whereas Fichte, starting from the phi-

losophy of Kant, gave so little prominence at first to the
metaphysical implications of his idealism that he was widely
thought to be taking the individual ego as his point of departure, Schelling emphasizes at once the idea of the Absolute, even if, under Fichte's influence, he describes it as
the absolute ego.

It will be noted that in the essay *On the Possibility of a
Form of Philosophy in General* Schelling follows Fichte in
deducing the presentation or representation. But his real interest is ontological. In the early *Wissenschaftslehre* Fichte
declared that the task of philosophy is to explain experience
in the sense of the system of presentations which are accompanied by a feeling of necessity. And he did so by showing
how the ego gives rise to these presentations through the
activity of the productive imagination which works unconsciously, so that for empirical consciousness the world inevitably possesses an appearance of independence. But in his
Philosophical Letters on Dogmatism and Criticism (1795)
Schelling roundly declares that the 'chief business of all philosophy consists in solving the problem of the existence of
the world'.[6] In one sense, of course, the two statements
come to the same thing. But there is a considerable difference
in emphasis between saying that the business of philosophy
is to explain the system of presentations which are accompanied by a feeling of necessity and saying that the business
of philosophy is to explain the existence of the world. And
with the help of a little hindsight at any rate we can discern
beneath all the Fichtean trappings of Schelling's early thought
the same metaphysical bent of mind which led him to say at
a later stage that the task of philosophy is to answer the
question, why there is something rather than nothing. True,
Fichte himself came to develop the metaphysical implications of his philosophy. But when he did so, Schelling accused
him of plagiarism.

Schelling's *Philosophical Letters* is an illuminating work.
It is in a sense a defence of Fichte. For Schelling contrasts
criticism, represented by Fichte, with dogmatism, represented
chiefly by Spinoza. And he comes down on the side of Fichte.

At the same time the work reveals the author's profound sympathy with Spinoza and an at any rate latent dissatisfaction with Fichte.

Dogmatism, says Schelling, involves in the long run the absolutization of the non-ego. Man is reduced to a mere modification of the infinite Object, Spinoza's substance, and freedom is excluded. It is true that Spinozism, which aims at the attainment of peace and tranquillity of soul through 'quiet self-surrender to the absolute Object',[7] possesses an aesthetic appeal and can exercise a powerful attraction on some minds. But ultimately it means the annihilation of the human being as a free moral agent. Dogmatism has no room for freedom.

But it does not follow that dogmatism can be theoretically refuted. The philosophy of Kant 'has only weak weapons against dogmatism',[8] and can achieve nothing more than a negative refutation. For example, Kant shows that it is impossible to disprove freedom in the noumenal sphere, but he admits himself that he can give no positive theoretical proof of freedom. Yet 'even the completed system of criticism cannot refute dogmatism *theoretically*',[9] even if it can deliver some shrewd blows. And this is not at all surprising. For as long as we remain on the theoretical plane dogmatism and criticism lead, Schelling maintains, to much the same conclusion.

In the first place both systems try to make the transition from the infinite to the finite. But 'philosophy cannot proceed from the infinite to the finite'.[10] We can, of course, invent reasons why the infinite must manifest itself in the finite, but they are simply ways of covering up an inability to bridge the gulf. It appears, therefore, that we must proceed the other way round. But how is this to be done when the traditional *a posteriori* demonstrations have been discredited? Obviously what is required is the suppression of the problem. That is to say, if the finite can be seen in the infinite and the infinite in the finite, the problem of bridging the gulf between them by means of a theoretical argument or demonstration no longer arises.

This need is fulfilled by intellectual intuition, which is an intuition of the identity of the intuiting with the intuited self. But it is interpreted in different ways by dogmatism and criticism. Dogmatism interprets it as an intuition of the self as identical with the Absolute conceived as absolute Object. Criticism interprets it as revealing the identity of the self with the Absolute as absolute Subject, conceived as pure free activity.

Though, however, dogmatism and criticism interpret intellectual intuition in different ways, the two interpretations lead to much the same theoretical conclusion. In dogmatism the subject is ultimately reduced to the object, and with this reduction one of the necessary conditions of consciousness is cancelled out. In criticism the object is ultimately reduced to the subject, and with this reduction the other necessary condition of consciousness is cancelled out. In other words, both dogmatism and criticism point to the theoretical annihilation of the finite self or subject. Spinoza reduces the finite self to the absolute Object: Fichte reduces it to the absolute Subject or, more precisely (since the absolute ego is not properly a subject), to infinite activity or striving. In both cases the self is swamped, so to speak, in the Absolute.

But though from the purely theoretical point of view the two systems lead by different routes to much the same conclusion, their practical or moral demands are different. They express different ideas of man's moral vocation. Dogmatism demands of the finite self that it should surrender itself to the absolute causality of the divine substance and renounce its own freedom that the divine may be all in all. Thus in the philosophy of Spinoza the self is called on to recognize an already existing ontological situation, namely its position as a modification of infinite substance, and to surrender itself. Criticism, however, demands that man shall realize the Absolute in himself through constant free activity. For Fichte, that is to say, the identity of the finite self with the Absolute is not simply an existing ontological situation which has only to be recognized. It is a goal to be achieved through moral effort. Moreover, it is an always receding goal. Hence even if the philosophy of Fichte points to the identification of the self with the Absolute as a theoretical ideal, on the practical plane it demands unceasing free moral activity, unceasing fidelity to one's personal moral vocation.

In a sense, therefore, the choice between dogmatism and criticism is for the finite self a choice between non-being and being. That is to say, it is a choice between the ideal of self-surrender, of absorption in the impersonal Absolute, of renunciation of personal freedom as illusion, and the ideal of constant free activity in accordance with one's vocation, of becoming more and more the moral agent who rises free and triumphant over the mere object. 'Be! is the highest demand of criticism.'[11] With Spinoza the absolute Object carries all before it: with Fichte Nature is reduced to a mere instrument for the free moral agent.

Obviously, if a man accepts the demand of criticism, he is thereby committed to rejecting dogmatism. But it is also true that dogmatism cannot be refuted, even on the moral or practical plane, in the eyes of the man 'who can tolerate the idea of working at his own annihilation, of annulling in himself all free causality, and of being the modification of an object in the infinity of which he sooner or later finds his moral destruction'.[12]

This account of the issue between dogmatism and criticism obviously echoes Fichte's view that the sort of philosophy which a man chooses depends on the sort of man that one is. Further, we can, if we wish, link up Schelling's contention that neither dogmatism nor criticism is theoretically refutable and that the choice between them must be made on the practical plane with the view which has sometimes been advanced in much more recent times that we cannot decide between metaphysical systems on the purely theoretical plane but that moral criteria can be used to judge between them when they serve as backgrounds for and tend to promote different patterns of conduct. But for our present purpose it is more relevant to note that though the *Philosophical Letters* was written in support of Fichte and though Schelling comes down ostensibly on his side, the work implies the unspoken,

but none the less clear, criticism that both the philosophy of
Spinoza and the transcendental idealism of Fichte are one-
sided exaggerations. For Spinoza is depicted as absolutizing
the object and Fichte as absolutizing the subject. And the
implication is that the Absolute must transcend the distinction between subjectivity and objectivity and be subject and
object in identity.[13]

In other words, the implication is that some sort of synthesis must be effected which will reconcile the conflicting
attitudes of Spinoza and Fichte. Indeed, we can see in the
Philosophical Letters evidence of a degree of sympathy with
Spinoza which was alien to Fichte's mind. And it is in no way
surprising if we find Schelling very soon devoting himself to
the publication of works on the philosophy of Nature. For
the Spinozistic element in the foreshadowed synthesis will be
the attribution to Nature as an organic totality of an ontological status which was denied it by Fichte. Nature will be
shown as the immediate objective manifestation of the Absolute. At the same time the synthesis, if it is to be a synthesis at all, must depict Nature as the expression and manifestation of Spirit. A synthesis must be idealism, if it is not
to represent a return to pre-Kantian thought. But it must not
be a subjective idealism in which Nature is depicted as no
more than an obstacle posited by the ego in order that it
may have something to overcome.

These remarks may perhaps seem to go beyond what the
early writings of Schelling entitle one to say. But we have
already seen that in the programme which Schelling drew up
for himself in 1796, very shortly after the writing of *Philosophical Letters*, he explicitly envisaged the development of
a speculative physics or philosophy of Nature. And it is quite
evident that dissatisfaction with Fichte's one-sided attitude
to Nature was already felt by Schelling within the period of
his so-called Fichtean phase.

Chapter Six

SCHELLING (2)

The possibility and metaphysical grounds of a philosophy of Nature – The general outlines of Schelling's philosophy of Nature – The system of transcendental idealism – The philosophy of art – The Absolute as identity.

1. It is the growth of reflection, Schelling maintains, that has introduced a rift between the subjective and the objective, the ideal and the real. If we think away the work of reflection, we must conceive man as one with Nature. That is to say, we must conceive him as experiencing this unity with Nature on the level of the immediacy of feeling. But through reflection he has distinguished between the external object and its subjective representation, and he has become an object for himself. In general, reflection has grounded and perpetuated the distinction between the objective external world of Nature and the subjective inner life of representation and self-consciousness, the distinction between Nature and Spirit. Nature thus becomes externality, the opposite of Spirit, and man, as a self-conscious reflective being, is alienated from Nature.

If reflection is made an end in itself, it becomes 'a spiritual malady'.[1] For man is born for action, and the more he is turned in on himself in self-reflection, the less active he is. At the same time it is the capacity for reflection which distinguishes man from the animal. And the rift which has been introduced between the objective and the subjective, the real and the ideal, Nature and Spirit, cannot be overcome by a return to the immediacy of feeling, to the childhood, as it were, of the human race. If the divided factors are to be reunited and the original unity restored, this must be achieved on a higher plane than feeling. That is to say, it must be achieved by reflection itself in the form of philosophy. After all, it is reflection which raises the problem. At the level of ordinary commonsense there is no problem of the relation between the real and the ideal order, between the thing and its mental representation. It is reflection which raises the problem, and it is reflection which must solve it.

One's first impulse is to solve the problem in terms of causal activity. Things exist independently of the mind and cause representations of themselves: the subjective is causally dependent on the objective. But by saying this one simply gives rise to a further problem. For if I assert that external things exist independently and cause representations of themselves in me, I necessarily set myself above thing and representation. And I thus implicitly affirm myself as spirit. And the question at once arises, how can external things exercise a determining causal activity on spirit?

We can indeed attempt to tackle the problem from the other side. Instead of saying that things cause representations of themselves we can say with Kant that the subject imposes its cognitive forms on some given matter of experience and so creates phenomenal reality. But we are then left with the thing-in-itself. And this is inconceivable. For what can a thing possibly be apart from the forms which the subject is said to impose?

There have been, however, two notable attempts to solve the problem of the correspondence between the subjective and the objective, the ideal and the real, without having recourse to the idea of causal activity. Spinoza explained the correspondence by means of the theory of parallel modifications of different attributes of one infinite substance, while Leibniz had recourse to the theory of a pre-established harmony. But neither theory was a genuine explanation. For Spinoza left the modifications of Substance unexplained, while Leibniz, in Schelling's opinion, simply postulated a pre-established harmony.

At the same time both Spinoza and Leibniz had an inkling of the truth that the ideal and the real are ultimately one. And it is this truth which the philosopher is called upon to exhibit. He must show that Nature is 'visible Spirit' and Spirit 'invisible Nature'.[2] That is to say, the philosopher must show how objective Nature is ideal through and through in the sense that it is a unified dynamic and teleological system which develops upwards, so to speak, to the point at which it returns upon itself in and through the human spirit. For, given this picture of Nature, we can see that the life of representation is not something which is simply set over against and alien to the objective world, so that there arises the problem of correspondence between the subjective and the objective, the ideal and the real. The life of representation is Nature's knowledge of itself; it is the actualization of Nature's potentiality, whereby slumbering Spirit awakens to consciousness.

But can we show that Nature is in fact a teleological system, exhibiting finality? We cannot indeed accept as adequate the purely mechanistic interpretation of the world. For when we consider the organism, we are driven to introduce the idea of finality. Nor can the mind remain content with a dichotomy between two sharply divided spheres, namely those of mechanism and teleology. It is driven on to regard Nature as a self-organizing totality in which we can distinguish various levels. But the question arises whether we are not then simply reading teleology into Nature, first into the organism and then into Nature as a whole. After all, Kant admitted that we cannot help thinking of Nature as if it were a teleological system. For we have a regulative Idea of purpose in Nature, an Idea which gives rise to certain heuristic maxims of judgment. But Kant would not allow that this subjective Idea proves anything about Nature in itself.

Schelling is convinced that all scientific inquiry presupposes the intelligibility of Nature. Every experiment, he insists, involves putting a question to Nature which Nature is forced to answer. And this procedure presupposes the belief that Nature conforms to the demands of reason, that it is intelligible and in this sense ideal. This belief is justified if we once assume the general view of the world which has been outlined above. For the idea of Nature as an intelligible teleological system then appears as Nature's self-reflection, as Nature knowing itself in and through man.

But we can obviously ask for a justification of this general view of Nature. And the ultimate justification is for Schelling a metaphysical theory about the Absolute. 'The first step towards philosophy and the indispensable condition for even arriving at it is to understand that the Absolute in the ideal order is also the Absolute in the real order.'[3] The Absolute is the 'pure identity'[4] of subjectivity and objectivity. And this identity is reflected in the mutual interpenetration of Nature and Nature's knowledge of itself in and through man.

In itself the Absolute is one eternal act of knowledge in which there is no temporal succession. At the same time we can distinguish three moments or phases in this one act, provided that we do not look on them as succeeding one another temporally. In the first moment the Absolute objectifies itself in ideal Nature, in the universal pattern, as it were, of Nature, for which Schelling uses Spinoza's term *Natura naturans*. In the second moment the Absolute as objectivity is transformed into the Absolute as subjectivity. And the third moment is the synthesis 'in which these two absolutenesses (absolute objectivity and absolute subjectivity) are again one absoluteness'.[5] The Absolute is thus an eternal act of self-knowledge.

The first moment in the inner life of the Absolute is expressed or manifested in *Natura naturata*, Nature as a system of particular things. This is the symbol or appearance of *Natura naturans*, and as such it is said to be 'outside the Absolute'.[6] The second moment in the inner life of the Absolute, the transformation of objectivity into subjectivity, is expressed externally in the world of representation, the ideal world of human knowledge whereby *Natura naturata* is represented in and through the human mind and the particular is taken up, as it were, into the universal, that is, on the conceptual level. We have, therefore, two unities, as Schelling calls them, objective Nature and the ideal world of representation. The third unity, correlated with the third moment in the inner life of the Absolute, is the apprehended interpenetration of the real and the ideal.

It can hardly be claimed, I think, that Schelling makes the relation between the infinite and the finite, between the Absolute in itself and its self-manifestation, crystal clear. We have seen indeed that *Natura naturata*, considered as the symbol or appearance of *Natura naturans*, is said to be outside the Absolute. But Schelling also speaks of the Absolute as expanding itself into the particular. Clearly, Schelling wishes to make a distinction between the unchanging Absolute in itself and the world of finite particular things. But at the same time he wishes to maintain that the Absolute is the all-comprehensive reality. But we shall have to return later to this topic. For the moment we can content ourselves with the general picture of the Absolute as eternal essence or Idea objectifying itself in Nature, returning to itself as subjectivity in the world of representation and then knowing itself, in and through philosophical reflection, as the identity of the real and the ideal, of Nature and Spirit.[7]

Schelling's justification of the possibility of a philosophy of Nature or of the so-called higher physics is thus admittedly metaphysical in character. Nature (that is, *Natura naturata*) must be ideal through and through. For it is the symbol or appearance of *Natura naturans*, ideal Nature: it is the 'external' objectification of the Absolute. And as the Absolute is always one, the identity of objectivity and subjectivity, *Natura naturata*, must also be subjectivity. This truth is manifested in the process by which Nature passes, as it were, into the world of representation. And the culmination of this process is the insight by which it is seen that human knowledge of Nature is Nature's knowledge of itself. There is really no rift between the objective and the subjective. From the transcendental point of view they are one. Slumbering Spirit becomes awakened Spirit. The distinguishable moments in the supra-temporal life of the Absolute as pure essence are manifested in the temporal order, which stands to the Absolute in itself as consequent to antecedent.

2. To develop a philosophy of Nature is to develop a sys-

tematic ideal construction of Nature. In the *Timaeus* Plato
sketched a theoretical construction of bodies out of fundamental qualities. And Schelling is concerned with the same
sort of thing. A purely experimental physics would not deserve
the name of science. It would be 'nothing but a collection of
facts, of reports on what has been observed, of what has
happened either under natural or under artificially-produced
conditions'.[8] Schelling admits indeed that physics as we
know it is not purely experimental or empirical in this sense.
'In what is now called physics empiricism [*Empirie*] and science are mixed up.'[9] But there is room, in Schelling's opinion, for a purely theoretical construction or deduction of matter and of the fundamental types of bodies, the inorganic
and the organic. Moreover, this speculative physics will not
simply assume natural forces, such as gravitation, as something given. It will construct them from first principles.

According to Schelling's intentions at least this construction does not involve producing a fanciful and arbitrary deduction of the fundamental levels of Nature. Rather does
it mean letting Nature construct itself before the watchful
attention of the mind. Speculative or higher physics cannot
indeed explain the basic productive activity which gives rise
to Nature. This is a matter for metaphysics rather than for
the philosophy of Nature proper. But if the development of
the natural system is the necessary progressive self-expression
of ideal Nature, *Natura naturans*, it must be possible to retrace systematically the stages of the process by which ideal
Nature expresses itself in *Natura naturata*. And to do this is
the task of speculative physics. Schelling is obviously well
aware that it is through experience that we become acquainted with the existence of natural forces and of inorganic and organic things. And it is not the philosopher's task
to tell us the empirical facts for the first time, so to speak, or
to work out *a priori* a natural history which can be developed
only on the basis of empirical investigation. He is concerned
with exhibiting the fundamental and necessary teleological
pattern in Nature, in Nature, that is to say, as known in the
first instance by experience and empirical inquiry. One might

say that he is concerned with explaining to us the why and
wherefore of the facts.

To exhibit Nature as a teleological system, as the necessary
self-unfolding of the eternal Idea, involves showing that the
explanation of the lower is always to be found in the higher.
For instance, even if from the temporal point of view the
inorganic is prior to the organic, from the philosophical point
of view the latter is logically prior to the former. That is to
say, the lower level exists as a foundation for the higher
level. And this is true throughout Nature. The materialist
tends to reduce the higher to the lower. For example, he tries
to explain organic life in terms of mechanical causality, without introducing the concept of finality. But he has the wrong
point of view. It is not, as he is inclined to imagine, a question of denying the laws of mechanics or of regarding them
as suspended in the organic sphere, if one introduces the
concept of finality. Rather is it a question of seeing the sphere
of mechanics as the necessary setting for the realization of
the ends of Nature in the production of the organism. There
is continuity. For the lower is the necessary foundation for
the higher, and the latter subsumes the former in itself. But
there is also the emergence of something new, and this new
level explains the level which it presupposes.

When we understand this, we see that 'the opposition between mechanism and the organic sphere disappears'.[10] For
we see the production of the organism as that at which Nature unconsciously aims through the development of the inorganic sphere, with the laws of mechanics. And it is thus
truer to say that the inorganic is the organic *minus* than that
the organic is the inorganic *plus*. Yet even this way of speaking can be misleading. For the opposition between mechanism and the organic sphere is overcome not so much by the
theory that the former exists for the latter as by the theory
that Nature as a whole is an organic unity.

Now, the activity which lies at the basis of Nature and
which 'expands' itself in the phenomenal world is infinite or
unlimited. For Nature is, as we have seen, the self-objectification of the infinite Absolute which, as an eternal *act*, is

activity or willing. But if there is to be any objective system of Nature at all, this unlimited activity must be checked. That is to say, there must be a checking or limiting force. And it is the interaction between the unlimited activity and the checking force which gives rise to the lowest level of Nature, the general structure of the world and the series of bodies,[11] which Schelling calls the first potency (*Potenz*) of Nature. Thus if we think of the force of attraction as corresponding to the checking force and the force of repulsion as corresponding to the unlimited activity, the synthesis of the two is matter in so far as this is simply mass.

But the drive of the unlimited activity reasserts itself, only to be checked at another point. And the second unity or potency in the construction of Nature is universal mechanism, under which heading Schelling deduces light and the dynamic process or the dynamic laws of bodies. 'The dynamic process is nothing else but the second construction of matter.'[12] That is to say, the original construction of matter is repeated, as it were, at a higher level. On the lower level we have the elementary operation of the forces of attraction and repulsion and their synthesis in matter as mass. At the higher level we find the same forces showing themselves in the phenomena of magnetism, electricity and chemical process or the chemical properties of bodies.

The third unity or potency of Nature is the organism. And on this level we find the same forces further actualizing their potentialities in the phenomena of sensibility, irritability and reproduction. This unity or level of Nature is represented as the synthesis of the two others. Hence it cannot be said that at any level Nature is simply lifeless. It is a living organic unity which actualizes its potentialities at ascending levels until it expresses itself in the organism. We must add, however, that there are obviously distinguishable levels within the organic sphere itself. On the lower levels reproductivity is particularly conspicuous whereas sensibility is comparatively undeveloped. The individual organisms are lost, as it were, in the species. On the higher levels the life of the senses is more developed, and the individual organism is, so to speak, more of an individual and less a mere particular member of an indefinite class. The culminating point is reached in the human organism, which most clearly manifests the ideality of Nature and forms the point of transition to the world of representation or subjectivity, Nature's reflection on itself.

Throughout his construction of Nature Schelling employs the idea of the polarity of forces. But 'these two conflicting forces . . . lead to the idea of an *organizing principle* which makes the world a system'.[13] And to this principle we can conveniently give the time-hallowed name of world-soul. It cannot indeed be discovered by empirical investigation. Nor can it be described in terms of the qualities of phenomena. It is a postulate, 'an hypothesis of the higher physics for explaining the universal organism'.[14] This so-called world-soul is not in itself a conscious intelligence. It is the organizing principle which manifests itself in Nature and which attains consciousness in and through the human ego. And unless we postulated it, we could not look on Nature as a unified, self-developing super-organism.

It may have occurred to the reader to wonder how Schelling's theory of Nature stands to the theory of evolution in the sense of the transformation of forms or the emergence of higher from lower forms. And it is clearly arguable not only that a theory of emergent evolution would fit in very well with Schelling's interpretation but that it is demanded by his view of the world as a self-developing organic unity. Indeed, he explicitly refers to the possibility of evolution. He observes, for instance, that even if man's experience does not reveal any case of the transformation of one species into another, lack of empirical evidence does not prove that such a transformation is impossible. For it may well be that such changes can take place only in a much longer period of time than that covered by man's experience. At the same time Schelling goes on to remark, 'however, let us pass over these possibilities'.[15] In other words, while he allows for the possibility of emergent evolution, he is primarily concerned not with a genetic history of Nature but with an ideal or theoretical construction.

This construction is indeed rich in ideas. It echoes much past speculation about the world. For instance, the pervasive idea of the polarity of forces recalls Greek speculation about Nature, while the theory of Nature as slumbering Spirit recalls certain aspects of Leibniz's philosophy. Schelling's interpretation of Nature also looks forward to later speculation. For example, there is some family resemblance between Schelling's philosophy of Nature and Bergson's picture of inorganic things as representing, as it were, the extinguished sparks thrown off by the *élan vital* in its upward flight.

At the same time Schelling's construction of Nature inevitably appears so fanciful and arbitrary to the scientific mentality that there does not seem to be any justification for devoting space here to further detailed treatment of it.[16] It is not that the philosopher fails to incorporate into his philosophy of Nature theories and hypotheses taken from science as he knows it. On the contrary, he borrows and utilizes ideas taken from contemporary physics, electrodynamics, chemistry and biology. But these ideas are fitted into a dialectical scheme, and they are often held together by the application of analogies which, however ingenious and perhaps sometimes suggestive, tend to appear fanciful and farfetched. Hence discussion of the details is more a matter for a specialized treatment of Schelling and of his relations to scientists such as Newton and to contemporary writers such as Goethe than for a general history of philosophy.

To say this is not, however, to deny the importance of Schelling's philosophy of Nature in its general outlines. For it shows clearly that German idealism does not involve subjectivism in the ordinary sense. Nature is the immediate and objective manifestation of the Absolute. It is indeed ideal through and through. But this does not mean that Nature is in any sense the creation of the human ego. It is ideal because it expresses the eternal Idea and because it is orientated towards self-reflection in and through the human mind. Schelling's view of the Absolute as the identity of objectivity and subjectivity demands, of course, that the Absolute's self-objectification, namely Nature, should reveal this identity.

But the identity is revealed through the teleological pattern of Nature, not through its reduction to human ideas. Nature's representation in and through the human mind presupposes the objectivity of the world, though at the same time it presupposes the intelligibility of the world and its intrinsic orientation to self-reflection.

Further, if we prescind from Schelling's rather fanciful speculations about magnetism, electricity and so on, that is, from the details of his theoretical construction of Nature, the general view of Nature as an objective manifestation of the Absolute and as a teleological system possesses an abiding value. It is obviously a metaphysical interpretation, and as such it can hardly commend itself to those who reject all metaphysics. But the general picture of Nature is not unreasonable. And if we once accept with Schelling, and afterwards with Hegel, the idea of a spiritual Absolute, we should expect to find in Nature a teleological pattern, though it does not necessarily follow that we can deduce the forces and phenomena of Nature in the way that Schelling thought that speculative physics is capable of doing.

3. In view of the fact that Schelling's philosophy of Nature represents his divergence from Fichte and his own original contribution to the development of German idealism it is at first sight surprising to find him publishing in 1800 a *System of Transcendental Idealism* in which he starts from the ego and proceeds to elaborate 'the continuous history of self-consciousness'.[17] For it looks as though he is adding to the philosophy of Nature an incompatible system inspired by the influence of Fichte. In Schelling's opinion, however, transcendental idealism forms a necessary complement to the philosophy of Nature. In knowledge itself subject and object are united: they are one. But if we wish to explain this identity, we have first to think it away. And then we are faced with two possibilities. Either we can start with the objective and proceed towards the subjective, asking how unconscious Nature comes to be represented. Or we can start with the subjective and proceed towards the objective, asking how an object comes to exist for the subject. In the first case we

develop the philosophy of Nature, showing how Nature develops the conditions for its own self-reflection on the subjective level. In the second case we develop the system of transcendental idealism, showing how the ultimate immanent principle of consciousness produces the objective world as the condition of its attainment of self-consciousness. And the two lines of reflection are and must be complementary. For if the Absolute is the identity of subjectivity and objectivity, it must be possible to start from either pole and to develop a philosophy in harmony with the philosophy developed by starting from the other pole. In other words, it is Schelling's conviction that the mutually complementary characters of the philosophy of Nature and the system of transcendental idealism manifest the nature of the Absolute as identity of subject and object, of the ideal and the real.

As transcendental idealism is described as the science of knowledge, it prescinds from the question whether there is an ontological reality behind the whole sphere of knowledge. Hence its first principle must be immanent within this sphere. And if we are to proceed from the subjective to the objective by transcendental deduction, we must start with the original identity of subject and object. This identity within the sphere of knowledge is self-consciousness, wherein subject and object are the same. And self-consciousness is described by Schelling as the ego. But the term 'ego' does not signify the individual self. It signifies 'the act of *self-consciousness in general*'.[18] 'The self-consciousness which is our point of departure is *one absolute act*.'[19] And this absolute act is a production of itself as object. 'The ego is nothing else but a producing which becomes its own object.'[20] It is in fact 'an intellectual intuition'.[21] For the ego exists through knowing itself, and this self-knowledge is the act of intellectual intuition, which is 'the organ of all transcendental thought'[22] and freely produces as its object what is otherwise no object. Intellectual intuition and the production of the object of transcendental thought are one and the same. Hence a system of transcendental idealism must take the form of a production or construction of self-consciousness.

Schelling makes a wider use than Fichte had made of the idea of intellectual intuition. But the general pattern of his transcendental idealism is obviously based on Fichte's thought. The ego is in itself an unlimited act or activity. But to become its own object it must limit this activity by setting something over against itself, namely the non-ego. And it must do so unconsciously. For it is impossible to explain the givenness of the non-ego within the framework of idealism unless we assume that the production of the non-ego is an unconscious and necessary production. The non-ego is a necessary condition of self-consciousness. And in this sense the limitation of the infinite or unlimited activity which constitutes the ego must always remain. But in another sense the limitation must be transcended. That is to say, the ego must be able to abstract from the non-ego and recoil, as it were, on to itself. Self-consciousness, in other words, will take the form of human self-consciousness which presupposes Nature, the non-ego.

In the first part of the system of transcendental idealism, which corresponds to Fichte's theoretical deduction of consciousness in the *Wissenschaftslehre*, Schelling traces the history of consciousness in three main epochs or stages. Many of Fichte's themes reappear, but Schelling is naturally at pains to correlate his history of consciousness with the philosophy of Nature. The first epoch ranges from primitive sensation up to productive intuition. And it is correlated with the construction of matter in the philosophy of Nature. In other words, we see the production of the material world as the unconscious activity of Spirit. The second epoch ranges from productive intuition up to reflection. The ego is here conscious on the level of sense. That is to say, the sensible object appears as distinct from the act of productive intuition. And Schelling deduces the categories of space, time and causality. A universe begins to exist for the ego. Schelling also occupies himself with the deduction of the organism as a necessary condition for the ego's return on itself. This takes place in the third epoch which culminates in the act of absolute abstraction by which the ego reflectively differentiates itself from the object or non-ego as such and recognizes itself as intelligence. It has become object to itself.

The act of absolute abstraction is explicable only as an act of the self-determining will. And we thus pass to the idea of the ego or intelligence as an active and free power, and so to the second or practical part of the system of transcendental idealism. After treating of the part played by the consciousness of other selves, other free wills, in the development of self-consciousness Schelling goes on to discuss the distinction between natural impulse and the will considered as an idealizing activity (*eine idealisierende Tätigkeit*), that is, as seeking to modify or change the objective in accordance with an ideal. The ideal belongs to the side of the subjective: it is in fact the ego itself. Hence in seeking to actualize the ideal in the objective world the ego also realizes itself.

This idea sets the stage for a discussion of morality. How, asks Schelling, can the will, namely the ego as self-determining or self-realizing activity, become objectified for the ego as intelligence? That is to say, how can the ego become conscious of itself as will? The answer is, through a demand, the demand that the ego should will nothing else but self-determination. 'This demand is nothing else but the categorical imperative or the moral law which Kant expresses in this way: you ought to will only that which other intelligences can will. But that which all intelligences can will is only pure self-determination, pure conformity to law. Through the law of morality, therefore, pure self-determination . . . becomes an object for the ego.'[23]

But self-determination or self-realization can be achieved only through concrete action in the world. And Schelling proceeds to deduce the system of rights and the State as conditions for moral action. The State is, of course, an edifice built by human hands, by the activity of the Spirit. But it is a necessary condition for the harmonious realization of freedom by a plurality of individuals. And though it is an edifice built by human hands, it should become a second Nature. In all our actions we count on the uniformity of Nature, on the reign of natural laws. And in our moral activity we ought to be able to count on the rule of rational law in society. That is to say, we ought to be able to count on the rational State, the characteristic of which is the rule of law.

Yet even the best-ordered State is exposed to the capricious and egoistic wills of other States. And the question arises, how can political society be rescued, as far as this is possible, from this condition of instability and insecurity? The answer can be found only in 'an organization which transcends the individual State, namely a federation of all States',[24] which will do away with conflicts between nations. Only in this way can political society become a second Nature, something on which we can count.

For this end to be attained, however, two conditions are required. First, the fundamental principles of a truly rational constitution must be generally acknowledged, so that all individual States will have a common interest in guaranteeing and protecting one another's law and rights. Secondly, individual States must submit themselves to a common fundamental law in the same way that individual citizens submit themselves to the law of their own State. And this means in effect that the federation will have to be a 'State of States',[25] in ideal at least a world-organization with sovereign power. If this ideal could be realized, political society would become a secure setting for the full actualization of a universal moral order.

Now, if this ideal is to be realized at all, it must obviously be realized within history. And the question arises whether we can discern in human history any necessary tendency towards the attainment of this goal. In Schelling's opinion 'there lies in the concept of history the concept of endless *progress*'.[26] Obviously, if this statement meant that the word 'history', as ordinarily used, necessarily includes as part of its meaning the concept of endless progress towards a predetermined goal, its truth would be open to question. But Schelling is looking on history in the light of his theory of the Absolute. 'History as a whole is a continual revelation of the Absolute, a revelation which gradually discloses itself.'[27] As the Absolute is the pure identity of the ideal and the real, history must be a movement towards the creation of a second Nature, a perfect moral world-order in the framework of a rationally-organized political society. And as the Absolute is infinite, this movement of progress must be endless. If the Absolute were perfectly revealed in its true nature, the point of view of human consciousness, which presupposes a distinction between subject and object, would no longer exist. Hence the revelation of the Absolute in human history must be in principle endless.

But are we not then faced with a dilemma? If on the one hand we assert that the human will is free, must we not admit that man can thwart the ends of history and that there is no necessary progress towards an ideal goal? If on the other hand we assert that history necessarily moves in a certain direction, must we not deny human freedom and explain away the psychological feeling of freedom?

In dealing with this problem Schelling has recourse to the idea of an absolute synthesis, as he puts it, of free actions. Individuals act freely. And any given individual may act for some purely private and selfish end. But there is at the same time a hidden necessity which achieves a synthesis of the apparently unconnected and often conflicting actions of human beings. Even if a man acts from purely selfish motives, he will none the less unconsciously contribute, even though against his will, to the fulfilment of the common end of human history.[28]

Up to this point we have been considering briefly the parts of the system of transcendental idealism which cover more or less the ground covered by Fichte in his theoretical and practical deductions of consciousness and in his works on the theory of rights and on ethics, though Schelling makes, of course, some changes and introduces and develops ideas of his own. But Schelling adds a third part which is his own peculiar contribution to transcendental idealism and which serves to underline the difference between his general outlook and that of Fichte. The philosophy of Nature deals with slumbering or unconscious Spirit. In the system of transcendental idealism as hitherto outlined we see conscious Spirit objectifying itself in moral action and in the creation of a moral world-order, a second Nature. But we have yet to find an intuition in which the identity of the unconscious and of the conscious, of the real and of the ideal, is presented in a concrete manner to the ego itself. And in the third part of the system of transcendental idealism Schelling locates what he is seeking in aesthetic intuition. Thus transcendental idealism culminates in a philosophy of art, to which Schelling attaches great importance. And provided that the statement is not taken as implying that the philosopher sets out to minimize the significance of moral activity, we can say that with Schelling, as contrasted with Fichte, the emphasis shifts from ethics to aesthetics, from the moral life to artistic creation, from action for the sake of action to aesthetic contemplation.

From one point of view it would be desirable to treat first of Schelling's philosophy of art as given in the third part of the *System of Transcendental Idealism* and later of his aesthetic ideas as expressed in his lectures on *The Philosophy of Art*. For in the meantime he had developed his theory of the Absolute, and this fact is reflected in the lectures. But it is more convenient to outline his ideas on art in one section, though I shall draw attention to their historical development.

4. In the *System of Transcendental Idealism* we read that 'the objective world is only the original, still unconscious poetry of the Spirit: the universal organon of philosophy—and the keystone of the whole arch—is *the philosophy of art*'.[29] But the view that the philosophy of art is 'the true organon of philosophy'[30] stands in need of some explanation.

In the first place art is grounded on the power of productive intuition which is the indispensable organ or instrument of transcendental idealism. As we have seen, transcendental idealism comprises a history of consciousness. But the stages of this history are not present from the start to the ego's vision as so many already constituted objects at which it only needs to look. The ego or intelligence has to produce them, in the sense that it has to re-create or, to use a Platonic term, re-collect them in a systematic manner. And this task of re-creation or re-collection is performed by the power of productive intuition. Aesthetic intuition is an activity of the same power, though there it is directed outwards, as it were, rather than inwards.

In the second place aesthetic intuition manifests the basic truth of the unity of the unconscious and the conscious, of the real and the ideal. If we consider aesthetic intuition from the side of the creative artist, the genius, we can see that in a real sense he knows what he is doing: he acts consciously and deliberately. When Michelangelo made the statue of Moses, he knew what he was about. At the same time, however, we can equally well say that the genius acts unconsciously. Genius is not reducible to a technical proficiency which can be imparted by instruction: the creative artist is, as it were, the vehicle of a power which acts through him. And for Schelling this is the same power which operates in Nature. In other words, the same power which acts without consciousness in producing Nature, the unconscious poetry of the Spirit, acts with consciousness in producing the work of art. That is to say, it acts through the consciousness of the artist. And this illustrates the ultimate unity of the unconscious and the conscious, of the real and the ideal.

The matter can be considered from another point of view. We can ask why it is that contemplation of a work of art is accompanied by 'the feeling of infinite satisfaction',[31] why it is that 'every impulse to produce is stilled with the completion of the product, that all contradictions are reconciled and all riddles solved'.[32] In other words, why is it that in contemplating a work of art the mind, whether of the artist himself or of someone else, enjoys a feeling of finality, the feeling that nothing should be added or subtracted, the feeling that a problem is solved, even if the problem cannot be stated? In Schelling's opinion the answer is that the completed work of art is the intelligence's supreme objectification of itself to itself, that is, as the identity of the unconscious and the conscious, the real and the ideal, the objective and the subjective. But as the intelligence or ego does not know this reflectively, it simply feels a boundless satisfaction, as though some unstated mystery had been revealed, and ascribes the production of the work of art to some power which acts through it.

The philosophy of art is thus the culmination of the *System of Transcendental Idealism*. It will be remembered that transcendental idealism starts with the idea of the so-called ego or intelligence considered as an absolute act of self-consciousness in which subject and object are one. But this absolute act is a producing: it has to produce its object. And the supreme objectification is the work of art. True, the organism, as considered in the philosophy of Nature, is a partial manifestation of the identity of the real and the ideal. But it is ascribed to an unconscious productive power which does not work with freedom, whereas the work of art is the expression of freedom: it is the free ego's manifestation of itself to itself.

Transcendental idealism, as was remarked in the last section, starts with the first immanent principle within the sphere of knowledge, namely with the absolute act which becomes an object for itself, and prescinds from the question whether there is a reality behind, as it were, this absolute act or ego.[33] But by the time (1802–3) that Schelling came to deliver the lectures which were eventually published as the *Philosophy of Art* he had developed his theory of the Absolute, and we find him emphasizing the metaphysical significance of the work of art as the finite manifestation of the infinite Absolute. The Absolute is the 'indifference' (that is to say, the ultimate identity) of the ideal and the real, and 'the indifference of the ideal and the real, as indifference, is expressed in the ideal world through art'.[34] Schelling is not contradicting what he has previously said about art. But in the lectures he transcends the self-imposed Fichtean limitations of the *System of Transcendental Idealism* and adopts the frankly metaphysical point of view which is really characteristic of his thought.

In *Bruno* (1802) Schelling introduced the notion of divine ideas and asserted that things are beautiful in virtue of their participation in these ideas. And this theory reappears in the lectures on art. Thus we are told that 'beauty exists where the particular (the real) is so in accord with its idea that this idea itself, as infinite, enters into the finite and is intuited *in concreto*'.[35] Aesthetic intuition is thus the intuition of the infinite in a finite product of intelligence. Further, the conformity of a thing with its eternal idea is its truth. Hence beauty and truth[36] are ultimately one.

Now, if the creative genius exhibits in the work of art an eternal idea, he must be akin to the philosopher. But it does not follow that he is a philosopher. For he does not apprehend the eternal ideas in an abstract form but only through a symbolic medium. Artistic creation requires the presence of a symbolic world, a world of 'poetic existence'[37] which mediates between the universal and the particular. The symbol represents neither the universal as such nor the particular as such, but both in unity. We must distinguish, therefore, between the symbol and the image. For the image is always concrete and particular.

This symbolic world of poetic existence is provided by mythology which is 'the necessary condition and primary matter [*Stoff*] of all art'.[38] Schelling dwells at length on Greek mythology, but he does not confine the symbolic world which in his view forms the material for artistic creation to the mythology of the Greeks. He includes, for instance, what he calls Jewish and Christian mythology. The Christian mind has constructed its own symbolic world which has proved a fruitful source of material for the artist.

This emphasis on mythology in Schelling's account of the symbolic world of poetic existence may well appear too narrow. But it illustrates Schelling's constant interest in myths as being at the same time imaginative constructions and intimations or expressions of the divine. In his later years he makes a distinction between myth and revelation. But his interest in the significance of mythology is a lasting element in his thought. And we shall have to return to the subject in connection with his later philosophy of religion.

In this outline of Schelling's aesthetic philosophy the terms 'art' and 'artist' have been used in a wider sense than is customary in ordinary English. But it would not, I think, be very profitable to devote space here to Schelling's discussion of the particular fine arts which he divides into those belonging to the real series, such as painting and sculpture, and those belonging to the ideal series, such as poetry.[39] For general purposes it is sufficient to understand how Schelling makes aesthetic theory an integral part of his philosophy. In the third *Critique* Kant had indeed discussed the aesthetic judgment, and he can be said to have made aesthetics an integral part of the critical philosophy. But the nature of Kant's system made it impossible for him to develop a metaphysics of art in the way that Schelling does. Kant allowed, it is true, that from the subjective point of view we can see a hint of noumenal reality, of the so-called supersensible substrate. But with Schelling the product of artistic genius becomes a clear revelation of the nature of the Absolute. And in his exaltation of the genius, in his partial assimilation of the artistic genius to the philosopher and his insistence on the metaphysical significance of aesthetic intuition we can see clear evidence of his romantic affiliations.

5. In the foregoing sections reference has frequently been made to Schelling's theory of the Absolute as the pure identity of subjectivity and objectivity, of the ideal and the real. In a sense these references were premature. For in the preface to his *Exposition of My System of Philosophy* (1801) Schelling speaks of expounding 'the system of absolute identity'.[40] And this way of speaking shows that he does not regard himself as simply repeating what he has already said. At the same time the so-called system of identity can be looked on as an inquiry into and exposition of the metaphysical implications of the conviction that the philosophy of Nature and the system of transcendental idealism are mutually complementary.

'The standpoint of philosophy,' says Schelling, 'is the standpoint of Reason.'[41] That is to say, philosophical knowledge of things is knowledge of them as they are in Reason. 'I give the name of Reason [*Vernunft*] to the absolute Reason or to

Reason in so far as it is conceived as the total indifference of the subjective and objective.'[42] In other words, philosophy is knowledge of the relation between things and the Absolute or, as the Absolute is infinite, between the finite and the infinite. And the Absolute is to be conceived as the pure identity or indifference (lack of all difference) of subjectivity and objectivity.

In attempting to describe the relation between the finite and the infinite Schelling is in a very difficult position. On the one hand there can be nothing outside the Absolute. For it is infinite reality and must contain all reality within itself. Hence it cannot be the external cause of the universe. 'The absolute identity is not the cause of the universe but the universe itself. For everything which exists is the absolute identity itself. And the universe is everything which is.'[43] On the other hand, if the Absolute is pure identity, all distinctions must be outside it. 'Quantitative difference is possible only outside the absolute totality.'[44] Hence finite things must be external to the Absolute.

Schelling cannot say that the Absolute somehow proceeds outside itself. For he maintains that 'the fundamental error of all philosophy is the proposition that the absolute identity has really gone out of itself. . . .'[45] Hence he is forced to say that it is only from the point of view of empirical consciousness that there is a distinction between subject and object and that there are subsistent finite things. But this really will not do. For the emergence of the point of view of empirical consciousness and its ontological status remain unexplained. It is all very well for Schelling to say that quantitative difference is posited 'only in appearance'[46] and that the Absolute is 'in no way affected by the opposition between subjectivity and objectivity'.[47] If appearance is anything at all, it must, on Schelling's premises, be within the Absolute. And if it is not within the Absolute, the Absolute must be transcendent and unidentifiable with the universe.

In *Bruno* (1802) Schelling makes play with the theory of divine Ideas, taken over from the Platonic and Neo-Platonic traditions. Considered from one point of view at least, the Absolute is the Idea of ideas, and finite things have eternal existence in the divine Ideas. But even if we are prepared to admit that this theory of divine Ideas is compatible with the view of the Absolute as pure identity, a view which is re-affirmed in *Bruno*, there is still the temporal status of finite things and their quantitative differentiation to be explained. In the dialogue Bruno tells Lucian that individual finite things are separate 'only for you'[48] and that for a stone noth-ing proceeds out of the darkness of absolute identity. But we can very well ask how empirical consciousness, with the distinctions which it involves, can arise either within the Ab-solute, if it is pure identity, or outside it, if it is the totality.

Schelling's general point of view is that absolute Reason, as the identity of subjectivity and objectivity, is self-conscious-ness, the absolute act in which subject and object are one. But Reason is not itself actually self-conscious: it is simply the 'indifference' or lack of difference between subject and object, the ideal and the real. It attains actual self-conscious-ness only in and through human consciousness, the immedi-ate object of which is the world. In other words, the Absolute manifests itself or appears in two series of 'potencies', the real series, which is considered in the philosophy of Nature, and the ideal series, which is considered in transcendental idealism. And from the standpoint of empirical consciousness the two series are distinct. We have subjectivity on the one hand and objectivity on the other. And the two together con-stitute 'the universe', which, as everything that is, is the Ab-solute. If, however, we try to transcend the standpoint of empirical consciousness, for which distinctions exist, and to grasp the Absolute as it is in itself rather than in its appear-ance, we can conceive it only as the indifference or vanishing-point of all difference and distinctions. True, the concept has then no positive content. But this simply shows that by con-ceptual thought we can apprehend only the appearance of the Absolute, the absolute identity as it appears in its 'ex-ternal' being, and not as it is in itself.

In Schelling's opinion the theory of identity enables him

to transcend all disputes between realism and idealism. For such controversy assumes that the distinction made by empirical consciousness between the real and the ideal can be overcome only by subordinating or even reducing the one to the other. But once we understand that the real and the ideal are one in the Absolute, the controversy loses its point. And the system of identity can thus be called real-idealism (*Realidealismus*).

But though Schelling himself was pleased with the system of identity, there were others who were not so appreciative. And the philosopher set himself to explain his position in such a way as to meet what he regarded as the misunderstandings of his critics. Further, his own reflections on his position drove him to develop fresh lines of thought. Maintaining, as he did, that the relation between the finite and the infinite or the problem of the existence of the world of things is the fundamental problem of metaphysics, he could hardly rest content with the system of identity. For it seemed to imply that the universe is the actualization of the Absolute, while it also asserted that the distinction between potentiality and act falls outside the Absolute in itself. Some more satisfactory account of the relation between the finite and the infinite was obviously required. But a sketch of Schelling's further philosophical journeying is best reserved for the next chapter.

Chapter Seven

SCHELLING (3)

The idea of the cosmic Fall – Personality and freedom in man and God; good and evil – The distinction between negative and positive philosophy – Mythology and revelation – General remarks on Schelling – Notes on Schelling's influence and on some kindred thinkers.

1. In his work on *Philosophy and Religion* (1804) Schelling explains that the description of the Absolute as pure identity does not mean either that it is a formless stuff, composed of all phenomena fused together, or that it is a vacuous nonentity. The Absolute is pure identity in the sense that it is an absolutely simple infinity. We can approach it in conceptual thought only by thinking away and denying of it the attributes of finite things; but it does not follow that it is in itself empty of all reality. What follows is that it can be apprehended only by intuition. 'The nature of the Absolute *itself*, which as ideal is also immediately real, cannot be known by explanations, but only through intuition. For it is only the composite which can be known by description. The simple must be intuited.'[1] This intuition cannot be imparted by instruction. But the negative approach to the Absolute facilitates the act of intuition of which the soul is capable through its fundamental unity with the divine reality.

The Absolute as ideal manifests or expresses itself immediately in the eternal ideas. Strictly speaking, indeed, there is only one Idea, the immediate eternal reflection of the Absolute which proceeds from it as the light flows from the sun. 'All ideas are one Idea.'[2] But we can speak of a plurality of ideas inasmuch as Nature with all its grades is eternally present in the one Idea. This eternal Idea can be described as the divine self-knowledge. 'But this self-knowledge must not be conceived as a mere accident or attribute of the Absolute-ideal but as itself a subsistent Absolute. For the Absolute cannot be the ideal ground of anything which is not like itself, absolute.'[3]

In developing this theory of the divine Idea, which, as we have seen, was first expounded in *Bruno*, Schelling draws attention to its origins in Greek philosophy. No doubt he has also at the back of his mind the Christian doctrine of the divine Word; but the description of the eternal Idea as a second Absolute is more akin to the Plotinian theory of *Nous* than to the Christian doctrine of the second Person of the Trinity. Further, the ideas of the negative approach to the Absolute and of intuitive apprehension of the supreme Godhead also go back to Neo-Platonism, though the first idea at any rate reappears in Scholasticism, as well, of course, as the theory of divine ideas.

However, in spite of its venerable history Schelling's theory of the eternal Idea cannot by itself explain the existence of finite things. For Nature as present in the eternal Idea is *Natura naturans* rather than *Natura naturata*. And from ideas, Schelling sensibly maintains, we can derive by deduction only other ideas. He therefore has recourse to the speculations of Jakob Boehme and introduces the notion of a cosmic Fall. The origin of the world is to be found in a falling-away or breaking-away (*Abbrechen*) from God, which can also be described as a leap (*Sprung*). 'From the Absolute to the real there is no continuous transition; the origin of the sensible world is thinkable only as a complete breaking-away from Absoluteness by means of a leap.'[4]

Schelling does not mean that a part of the Absolute breaks away or splits off. The Fall consists in the emergence of a dim image of an image, resembling the shadow which accompanies the body. All things have their eternal ideal existence in the Idea or divine ideas. Hence the centre and true reality of any finite thing is in the divine Idea, and the essence of the finite thing may thus be said to be infinite rather than finite. Considered, however, precisely as a finite thing, it is the image of an image (that is, an image of the ideal essence which is itself a reflection of the Absolute). And its existence as a distinct finite thing is an alienation from its true centre, a negation of infinity. True, finite things are not simply nothing. They are, as Plato said, a mixture of being and not-being. But particularity and finitude represent the negative element. Hence the emergence of *Natura naturata*, the system of particular finite things, is a Fall from the Absolute.

It must not be thought, however, that the cosmic Fall, the emergence of an image of an image, is an event in time. It is 'as eternal (outside all time) as the Absolute itself and the world of Ideas'.[5] The Idea is an eternal image of God. And the sensible world is an indefinite succession of shadows, images of images, without any assignable beginning. This means that no finite thing can be referred to God as its immediate cause. The origin of any given finite thing, a man for instance, is explicable in terms of finite causes. The thing, in other words, is a member in the endless chain of causes and effects which constitutes the sensible world. And this is why it is psychologically possible for a human being to look upon the world as the one reality. For it possesses a relative independence and self-subsistence. But this point of view is precisely the point of view of a fallen creature. From the metaphysical and religious standpoints we must see in the world's relative independence a clear sign of its fallen nature, of its alienation from the Absolute.

Now, if creation is not an event in time, the natural conclusion is that it is a necessary external self-expression of the eternal Idea. And in this case it should be in principle deducible, even if the finite mind is unable actually to perform the deduction. But we have seen that Schelling refuses to allow that the world is deducible even in principle from the Absolute. 'The Fall cannot be, as they say, explained.'[6] Hence the origin of the world must be ascribed to freedom. 'The ground of the possibility of the Fall lies in freedom.'[7] But in what sense? On the one hand this freedom cannot be exercised by the world itself. Schelling may sometimes speak as though the world broke away from the Absolute. But as it is the very existence and origin of the world which are in question, we can hardly conceive it as freely leaping away, as it were, from the Absolute. For *ex hypothesi* it does not yet exist. On the other hand, if we ascribe the timeless origination of the world to a free creative act of God, in a theistic sense, there is no very obvious reason for speaking about a cosmic Fall.

In treating of this problem Schelling appears to connect the Fall with a kind of double-life led by the eternal Idea considered as 'another Absolute'.[8] Regarded precisely as the eternal reflection of the Absolute, as the eternal Idea, its true life is in the Absolute itself. But regarded as 'real', as a second Absolute, as Soul, it strives to produce, and it can produce only phenomena, images of images, 'the nothingness of sensible things'.[9] It is, however, only the *possibility* of finite things which can be 'explained', that is, deduced from the second Absolute. Their actual existence is due to freedom, to a spontaneous movement which is at the same time a lapse.

Creation is thus a Fall in the sense that it is a centrifugal movement. The absolute identity becomes differentiated or splintered on the phenomenal level, though not in itself. But there is also a centripetal movement, the return to God. This does not mean that particular finite material things as such return to the divine Idea. We have seen that no particular sensible thing has God for its immediate cause. Similarly, no particular sensible thing, considered precisely as such, returns immediately to God. Its return is mediate, by means of the transformation of the real into the ideal, of objectivity into subjectivity, in and through the human ego or reason which is capable of seeing the infinite in the finite and referring all images to the divine exemplar. As for the finite ego itself, it represents from one point of view 'the point of furthest alienation from God'.[10] For the apparent independence of the phenomenal image of the Absolute reaches its culminating-point in the ego's conscious self-possession and self-assertion. At the same time the ego is one in essence with infinite Reason, and it can rise above its egoistic point of view, returning to its true centre from which it has been alienated.

This point of view determines Schelling's general conception of history, which is well illustrated by the following oft-quoted passage. 'History is an epic composed in the mind of God. Its two main parts are: first, that which depicts the departure of humanity from its centre up to its furthest point of alienation from this centre, and, secondly, that which depicts the return. The first part is the *Iliad*, the second the *Odyssey* of history. In the first the movement was centrifugal, in the second it is centripetal.'[11]

In grappling with the problem of the One and the Many or of the relation between the infinite and the finite Schelling is obviously concerned with allowing for the possibility of evil. The idea of the Fall and of alienation allows for this possibility. For the human self is a fallen self, entangled, as it were, in particularity; and this entanglement, this alienation from the self's true centre, renders possible selfishness, sensuality and so on. But how can man be really free if the Absolute is the totality? And if there is a real possibility of evil, must it not have a ground in the Absolute itself? If so, what conclusions must we draw about the nature of the Absolute or God? In the next section we can consider Schelling's reflections on these problems.

2. In the Preface to his *Philosophical Inquiries into the Nature of Human Freedom* (1809) Schelling frankly admits that *Philosophy and Religion* was deficient in clarity. He intends, therefore, to give another exposition of his thought in the light of the idea of human freedom.[12] This is especially desirable, he says, in view of the accusation that his system is pantheistic and that there is accordingly no room in it for the concept of human freedom.

As for the charge of pantheism, this is, Schelling remarks, an ambiguous term. On the one hand it might be used to describe the theory that the visible world, *Natura naturata*, is identical with God. On the other hand it might be understood as referring to the theory that finite things do not exist at all but that there is only the simple indifferentiated unity

of the Godhead. But in neither sense is Schelling's philosophy
pantheistic. For he neither identifies the visible world with
God nor teaches acosmism, the theory of the non-existence
of the world. Nature is a consequence of the first principle,
not the first principle itself. But it is a real consequence. God
is the God of the living, not of the dead: the divine Being
manifests itself and the manifestation is real. If, however,
pantheism is interpreted as meaning that all things are immanent in God, Schelling is quite prepared to be called a
pantheist. But he proceeds to point out that St. Paul himself
declared that in God we live and move and have our being.

To clarify his position, Schelling reinterprets the principle
of identity. 'The profound logic of the ancients distinguished
subject and predicate as antecedent and consequent (*ante-
cedens et consequens*) and thereby expressed the real meaning of the principle of identity.'[13] God and the world are
identical; but to say this is to say that God is the ground or
antecedent and the world the consequent. The unity which
is asserted is a creative unity. God is self-revealing or self-
manifesting life. And though the manifestation is immanent
in God, it is yet distinguishable from him. The consequent
is dependent on the antecedent, but it is not identical with
it in the sense that there is no distinction between them.

This theory, Schelling insists, in no way involves the denial
of human freedom. For by itself it says nothing about the nature of the consequent. If God is free, the human spirit,
which is his image, is free. If God is not free, the human
spirit is not free.

Now, in Schelling's view the human spirit is certainly free.
For 'the real and living concept [of freedom] is that it is a
power of good and evil.'[14] And it is evident that man possesses this power. But if this power is present in man, the
consequent, must it not also be present in God, the antecedent? And the question then arises, whether we are forced
to draw the conclusion that God can do evil.

To answer this question, let us first look more closely at the
human being. We talk about human beings as persons, but
personality, Schelling maintains, is not something given from

the start, it is something to be won. 'All birth is birth out of darkness into light',[15] and this general proposition is true of the birth of human personality. There is in man a dark foundation, as it were, the unconscious and the life or urge and natural impulse. And it is on this foundation that personality is built. Man is capable of following sensual desire and dark impulse rather than reason: he is able to affirm himself as a particular finite being to the exclusion of the moral law. But he also has the power of subordinating selfish desire and impulse to the rational will and of developing his true human personality. He can do this, however, only by strife, conflict and sublimation. For the dark foundation of personality always remains, though it can be progressively sublimated and integrated in the movement from darkness to light.

As far as man is concerned, what Schelling has to say on this subject obviously contains a great deal of truth. But stimulated by the writings of Boehme and impelled by the exigencies of his theory of the relation between the human spirit and God, he applies this notion of personality to God himself. There is in God a ground of his personal existence,[16] which is itself impersonal. It can be called will, but it is a 'will in which there is no understanding'.[17] It can be conceived as an unconscious desire or yearning for personal existence. And the personal divine existence must be conceived as rational will. The irrational or unconscious will can be called 'the egoism in God'.[18] And if there were only this will in God, there would be no creation. But the rational will is the will of love, and as such it is 'expansive',[19] self-communicating.

The inner life of God is thus conceived by Schelling as a dynamic process of self-creation. In the ultimate dark abyss of the divine Being, the primal ground or *Urgrund*, there is no differentiation but only pure identity. But this absolutely undifferentiated identity does not exist as such. 'A division, a difference must be posited, that is, if we wish to pass from essence to existence.'[20] God first posits himself as object, as the unconscious will. But he cannot do this without at the same time positing himself as subject, as the rational will of love.

There is, therefore, a likeness between the divine and the human conquest of personality. And we can even say that 'God makes himself.'[21] But there is also a great difference. And an understanding of this difference shows that the answer to the question whether God can do evil is that he cannot.

In God the conquest of personality is not a temporal process. We can distinguish different 'potencies' in God, different moments in the divine life, but there is no temporal succession. Thus if we say that God first posits himself as unconscious will and then as rational will, there is no question of temporally successive acts. 'Both acts are one act, and both are absolutely simultaneous.'[22] For Schelling the unconscious will in God is no more temporally prior to the rational will than the Father is temporally prior to the Son in the Christian theology of the Trinity. Hence, though we can distinguish different moments in the 'becoming' of the divine personality, one moment being logically prior to another, there is no becoming at all in the temporal sense. God is eternally love, and 'in love there can never be the will to evil'.[23] Hence it is metaphysically impossible for God to do evil.

But in God's external manifestation the two principles, the lower and the higher wills, are and must be separable. 'If the identity of the two principles were as indissoluble in the human spirit as in God, there would be no distinction (that is, between God and the human spirit); that is to say, God would not manifest himself. Therefore the unity which is indissoluble in God must be dissoluble in man. And this is the possibility of good and evil.'[24] This possibility has its ground in God, but as a realized possibility it is present only in man. Perhaps one can express the matter by saying that whereas God is necessarily an integrated personality, man need not be. For the basic elements are separable in man.

It would, however, be erroneous to conclude that Schelling attributes to man a complete liberty of indifference. He is too fond of the idea of antecedent and consequent to admit the concept of freedom as 'a completely indeterminate power of willing one or other of two contradictory things without determining grounds and simply because it is willed'.[25] Schelling rejects this concept and finds the determining ground of a man's successive choices in his intelligible essence or character which stands to his particular acts as antecedent to consequent. At the same time he does not wish to say that it is God who predetermines a man's acts by conceiving him in the eternal Idea. Hence he is forced to depict a man's intelligible character as due to an original self-positing of the ego, as the result of an original choice by the ego itself. He can thus say both that a man's actions are in principle predictable and that they are free. They are necessary; but this necessity is an inner necessity, imposed by the ego's original choice, not a necessity externally imposed by God. 'This inner necessity is itself freedom, the essence of man is essentially *his own act*; necessity and freedom are mutually immanent, as one reality which appears as one or the other only when looked at from different sides. . . .'[26] Thus Judas's betrayal of Christ was necessary and inevitable, given the historical circumstances; but at the same time he betrayed Christ 'willingly and with complete freedom'.[27] Similarly it was inevitable both that Peter would deny Christ and that he would repent of this denial; yet both the denial and the repentance, being Peter's own acts, were free.

If the theory of an intelligible character is given a purely psychological interpretation, it can be made at any rate very plausible. On the one hand we not infrequently say of a given man that he could not act in this or that manner, meaning that such a way of acting would be quite contrary to his character. And if after all he does act in this way, we are inclined to say that his character was not what we supposed. On the other hand we come to know not only other people's characters but also our own through their and our acts. And we might wish to draw the conclusion that in each man there is, as it were, a hidden character which manifests itself progressively in his acts, so that his acts stand to his character in a relation analogous to that between consequent and ground or antecedent. The objection can indeed be made that this presupposes that character is something fixed and settled

from the start (by heredity, environment, very early experi-
ences and so on), and that this presupposition is false. But
as long as the theory is presented as a psychological theory,
it is a matter for empirical investigation. And it is clear that
some empirical data count in its favour, even if others tell
against it. It is a question of weighing, interpreting and co-
ordinating the available evidence.

But Schelling does not present his theory simply as an empirical hypothesis. It is a metaphysical theory. At least it depends in part on metaphysical theories. For example, the
theory of identity is influential. The Absolute is the identity
of necessity and freedom, and this identity is reflected in man.
His acts are both necessary and free. And Schelling draws the
conclusion that a man's intelligible essence, which determines
his particular acts, must itself have, as it were, an aspect of
freedom, in that it is the result of the ego's self-positing. But
this original choice of itself by the ego is neither a conscious
act nor an act in time. According to Schelling, it is outside
time and determines all consciousness, though a man's acts
are free inasmuch as they issue from his own essence or self.
But it is extremely difficult to see what this primeval act of
will can possibly be. Schelling's theory bears some resemblance
to M. Sartre's interpretation of freedom in his existentialist
philosophy; but the setting is much more metaphysical. Schelling develops Kant's distinction between the intelligible and
phenomenal spheres in the light of his theory of identity and
of his preoccupation with the idea of ground and consequent,
and the resulting theory is extremely obscure. It is indeed
clear that Schelling wishes to avoid the Calvinist doctrine of
divine predestination on the one hand and the theory of liberty of indifference on the other, while at the same time he
wishes to allow for the truths which find expression in these
positions. But it can hardly be claimed that the conclusion
of his reflections is crystal clear. True, Schelling did not claim
that everything in philosophy could be made crystal clear.
But the trouble is that it is difficult to assess the truth of
what is said unless one understands what is being said.

As for the nature of evil, Schelling experienced considerable difficulty in finding a satisfactory descriptive formula. As he did not look on himself as a pantheist in the sense of one who denies any distinction between the world and God, he felt that he could affirm the positive reality of evil without committing himself to the conclusion that there is evil in the divine Being itself. At the same time his account of the relation between the world and God as being that of consequent or ground to antecedent implies that if evil is a positive reality it must have its ground in God. And the conclusion might be thought to follow that 'in order that evil should not be, God would have not to be himself'.[28] In the Stuttgart lectures Schelling attempts to steer a middle course between asserting and denying the positive reality of evil by saying that it is 'from one point of view nothing, from another point of view an extremely real being'.[29] Perhaps we can say that he was feeling after the Scholastic formula which describes evil as a privation, though a real privation.

In any case evil is certainly present in the world, whatever its precise nature may be. Hence the return to God in human history must take the form of the progressive triumph of good over evil. 'The good must be brought out of darkness into actuality that it may live everlastingly with God; and evil must be separated from the good that it may be cast into not-being. For this is the final end of creation.'[30] In other words, the complete triumph of the rational will over the lower will or urge, which is eternally accomplished in God, is the ideal goal of human history. In God the sublimation of the lower will is eternal and necessary. In man it is a temporal process.

3. We have already had occasion to note Schelling's insistence that from ideas we can deduce only ideas. It is not surprising, therefore, if in his later years we find him emphasizing the distinction, to which allusion was made in the section on his life and writings, between negative philosophy, which is confined to the world of concepts and essences, and positive philosophy, which stresses existence.

All philosophy worthy of the name, Schelling maintains, is concerned with the first or ultimate principle of reality. Negative philosophy, however, discovers this principle only as a supreme essence, as the absolute Idea. And from a supreme essence we can deduce only other essences, from the Idea only other ideas. From a *What* we cannot deduce a *That*. In other words, negative philosophy is quite incapable of explaining the existent world. Its deduction of the world is not a deduction of existents but only of what things must be if they exist. Of being outside God the negative philosopher can only say that '*if* it exists, it can exist only in this way and only as such and such'.[31] His thought moves within the realm of the hypothetical. And this is especially clear in the case of the Hegelian system which, according to Schelling, by-passes the existential order.

Positive philosophy, however, does not start simply with God as Idea, as a *What* or essence, but rather with God 'as a pure That',[32] as pure act or being in an existential sense. And from this supreme existential act it passes to the concept or nature of God, showing that he is not an impersonal Idea or essence but a creative personal Being, the existing 'Lord of being',[33] where 'being' means the world. Schelling thus connects positive philosophy with the concept of God as a personal Being.

Schelling does not mean to imply that he is the first to discover positive philosophy. On the contrary, the whole history of philosophy manifests the 'combat between negative and positive philosophy'.[34] But the use of the word 'combat' must not be misunderstood. It is a question of emphasis and priority rather than of a fight to the death between two completely irreconcilable lines of thought. For negative philosophy cannot be simply rejected. No system can be constructed without concepts. And even if the positive philosopher places the emphasis on existence, he obviously does not and cannot disdain all consideration of what exists. Hence we have 'to assert the connection, yes the unity, between the two',[35] that is, between positive and negative philosophy.[36]

But how, Schelling asks, are we to make the transition from negative to positive philosophy? It cannot be made merely by thinking. For conceptual thought is concerned with es-

sences and logical deductions. Hence we must have recourse
to the will, 'a will which demands with inner necessity that
God should not be a mere idea'.[37] In other words, the initial
affirmation of the divine existence is based on an act of faith
demanded by the will. The ego is conscious of its fallen condition, of its state of alienation, and it is aware that this
alienation can be overcome only by God's activity. It demands, therefore, that God should be not simply a transmun-
dane ideal but an actually existing personal God through
whom man can be redeemed. Fichte's ideal moral order will
not satisfy man's religious needs. The faith which lies at the
basis of positive philosophy is faith in a personal creative and
redeeming God, not in Fichte's ideal moral order, nor in
Hegel's absolute Idea.

At first sight at least Schelling may appear to be repeating
Kant's theory of practical or moral faith. But Schelling makes
it clear that he regards the critical philosophy as an example
of negative philosophizing. Kant does indeed affirm God on
faith, but simply as a postulate, that is, as a possibility. Further, Kant affirms God as an instrument, as it were, for synthesizing virtue and happiness. In his religion within the
limits of bare reason there is no room for genuine religion.
The truly religious man is conscious of his profound need of
God, and he is brought by this consciousness and by his longing for God to a personal Deity. 'For the person seeks a person.'[38] The truly religious man does not affirm God simply
as an instrument for apportioning happiness to virtue: he
seeks God for himself. The ego 'demands God himself. *Him,
him*, will it have, the God who acts, who exercises providence,
who, as being himself real, can meet the reality of the Fall.
. . . In this God alone does the ego see the *real* supreme
good.'[39]

The distinction between positive and negative philosophy
thus turns out to be a distinction between philosophy which
is truly religious and philosophy which cannot assimilate the
religious consciousness and its demands. Schelling says this
quite explicitly with an evident reference to Kant. 'The longing for the real God and for redemption through him is, as

you see, nothing else but the expression of the need of *religion*. . . . Without an active God . . . there can be no religion, for religion presupposes an actual, real relationship of man to God. Nor can there be any history in which God is providence. . . . At the end of negative philosophy I have only possible and not actual religion, religion only "within the limits of bare reason". . . . It is with the transition to positive philosophy that we first enter the sphere of religion.'[40]

Now, if positive philosophy affirms the existence of God as a first principle, and if the transition to positive philosophy cannot be made by thinking but only by an act of the will issuing in faith, Schelling obviously cannot turn negative into positive philosophy by supplementing the former by a natural theology in the traditional sense. At the same time there can be what we may call an empirical proof of the rationality of the will's act. For the demand of the religious man is for a God who reveals himself and accomplishes man's redemption. And the proof, if one may so put it, of God's existence will take the form of showing the historical development of the religious consciousness, the history of man's demand for God and of God's answer to this demand. 'Positive philosophy is historical philosophy.'[41] And this is the reason why in his later writings Schelling devotes himself to the study of mythology and revelation. He is trying to exhibit God's progressive self-revelation to man and the progressive work of divine redemption.

This is not to say that Schelling abandons all his earlier speculations in favour of an empirical study of the history of mythology and revelation. As we have seen, his thesis is that negative and positive philosophy must be combined. And his earlier religious speculations are not jettisoned. For example, in the essay entitled *Another Deduction of the Principles of Positive Philosophy* (1841) he takes as his point of departure 'the unconditioned existent'[42] and proceeds to deduce the moments or phases of God's inner life. He does indeed lay emphasis on the primacy of being in the sense of existence, but the general scheme of his earlier philosophy of religion, with the ideas of the moments in the divine life, of the cosmic Fall and of the return to God, is retained. And though in his lectures on mythology and religion he concerns himself with the empirical confirmation, as it were, of his religious philosophy, he never really frees himself from the idealist tendency to interpret the relation between God and the world as a relation of ground or antecedent to consequent.

The reader may be inclined to share Kierkegaard's disappointment that after making his distinction between negative and positive philosophy Schelling proceeds to concentrate on the study of mythology and revelation instead of radically rethinking his philosophy in the light of this distinction. At the same time we can understand the philosopher's point of view. The philosophy of religion has come to occupy the central position in his thought. And the self-manifesting impersonal Absolute has become the self-revealing personal God. Schelling is anxious, therefore, to show that man's faith in God is historically justified and that the history of the religious consciousness is also the history of the divine self-revelation to man.

4. If, however, we speak of Schelling's philosophy of mythology and revelation as an empirical study, the word 'empirical' must be understood in a relative sense. Schelling has not abandoned deductive metaphysics for pure empiricism. Far from it. For example, the deduction of three 'potencies' in the one God is presupposed. It is also presupposed that if there is a self-manifesting God, this necessary nature of an absolute Being will be progressively revealed. Hence when Schelling turns to the study of mythology and revelation, he already possesses the scheme, as it were, of what he will find. The study is empirical in the sense that its matter is provided by the actual history of religion as known through empirical investigation. But the framework of interpretation is provided by the supposedly necessary deductions of metaphysics. In other words, Schelling sets out to find in the history of religion the self-revelation of one personal God, whose unity does not exclude three distinguishable potencies or moments. And he has, of course, no difficulty in discovering expressions of

this conception of the Deity in the development of religious beliefs from the ancient mythologies of East and West up to the Christian dogma of the Trinity. Similarly, he has no difficulty in finding expressions of the ideas of a Fall and of a return to God.

If Schelling's premises are once assumed, this procedure is, of course, justified. For, as we have seen, he never intended to jettison metaphysics, the abstract philosophy of reason, which, to use modern jargon, shows us what must be the case if anything is the case. Hence from Schelling's point of view metaphysical presuppositions are quite in order. For philosophy as a whole is a combination of negative and positive philosophy. At the same time Schelling's procedure is doubtless one reason why his philosophy of mythology and revelation exercised comparatively little influence on the development of the study of the history of religion. This is not to say that metaphysical presuppositions are illegitimate. Whether one thinks that they are legitimate or illegitimate obviously depends on one's view of the cognitive value of metaphysics. But it is easy to understand that Schelling's *philosophy* of mythology and revelation was looked at askance by those who wished to free the study of the history of religion from the presuppositions of idealist metaphysics.

A distinction is drawn by Schelling between mythology on the one hand and revelation on the other. 'Everything has its time. Mythological religion had to come first. In mythological religion we have blind (because produced by a necessary process), *unfree* and *unspiritual* religion.'[43] Myths are not simply arbitrary and capricious products of the imagination. But neither are they revelation, in the sense of a freely-imparted knowledge of God. They can, of course, be consciously elaborated, but fundamentally they are the product of an unconscious and necessary process, successive forms in which an apprehension of the divine imposes itself on the religious consciousness. In other words, mythology corresponds to the dark or lower principle in God, and it has its roots in the sphere of the unconscious. When, however, we pass from mythology to revelation, we pass 'into a completely different sphere'.[44] In mythology the mind 'had to do with a necessary process, here with something which exists only as the result of an absolutely free will'.[45] For the concept of revelation presupposes an act whereby God 'freely gives or has given himself to mankind'.[46]

Inasmuch as mythological religion and revealed religion are both religion, it must be possible, Schelling insists, to subsume them under a common idea. And in fact the whole history of the religious consciousness is a second theogony or birth of God, in the sense that the eternal and timeless becoming or birth of God in himself[47] is represented in time in the history of religion. Mythology, as rooted in the unconscious, represents a moment in the divine life. It logically precedes revelation and is a preparation for it. But it is not itself revelation. For revelation is essentially God's free manifestation of himself as infinite, personal and free creator and lord of being. And, as a free act on God's part, it is not simply a logical consequence of mythology. At the same time revelation can be described as the truth of mythology. For mythology is, as it were, the exoteric element which veils the revealed truth. And in paganism the philosopher can find mythological representations or anticipations of the truth.

In other words, Schelling wishes to represent the whole history of the religious consciousness as God's revelation of himself, while at the same time he wishes to leave room for a specifically Christian concept of revelation. On the one hand revelation, in what we might perhaps call a weak sense of the term, runs through the whole history of religion. For it is the inner truth of mythology. On the other hand revelation in a strong sense of the term is found in Christianity. For it is in the Christian religion that this inner truth first comes to the clear light of day. Christianity thus gives the truth of mythology, and it can be described as the culmination of historical religion. But it does not follow that Christianity is an automatic consequence of mythology. Mythology as such is, as we have seen, a necessary process. But in and through Christ the personal God freely reveals himself. Obviously, if Schelling wishes to represent the whole history of religion as

the temporal representation of the divine life, it is very difficult for him to avoid asserting a necessary connection between
pagan mythology and Christianity. The former would represent God as unconscious will, while the latter would represent
God as free will, the will of love. At the same time Schelling
tries to preserve an essential distinction between mythology
and revelation by insisting that the concept of revelation is
the concept of a free act on God's part. Revelation is the
truth of mythology in the sense that it is that at which mythology aims and that which underlies the exoteric clothing
of myth. But it is in and through Christ that the truth is
clearly revealed, and it is revealed freely. Its truth could not
be known simply by logical deduction from the pagan myths.

But though Schelling certainly tries to allow for a distinction between mythology and revelation, there is a further important point to make. If we mean by revelation Christianity
simply as a fact which stands over against the fact of paganism, there is room for a higher standpoint, namely that of
reason understanding both mythology and revelation. And
this higher standpoint is positive philosophy. But Schelling
is careful to explain that he is not referring to a rationalistic
interpretation of religion from outside. He is referring to the
activity of the religious consciousness whereby it understands
itself from within. The philosophy of religion is thus for
Schelling not only philosophy but also religion. It presupposes
Christianity and cannot exist without it. It arises within
Christianity, not outside it. 'Philosophical religion is therefore
historically mediated through revealed religion.'[48] But it cannot be simply identified with Christian belief and life as facts.
For it takes these facts as subject-matter for free reflective
understanding. In contrast, therefore, with the simple acceptance of the original Christian revelation on authority philosophical religion can be called 'free' religion. 'The free
religion is only *mediated* through Christianity; it is not immediately *posited* by it.'[49] But this does not mean that philosophical religion rejects revelation. Faith seeks understanding;
but understanding from within does not annul what is understood.

This process of understanding, of free reflection, has its own history, ranging through Scholastic theology and metaphysics, up to Schelling's own later religious philosophy. And in this philosophy we can discern Schelling's hankering after a higher wisdom. There was always something of the Gnostic in his mental make-up. Just as he was not content with ordinary physics but expounded a speculative or higher physics, so in later years he expounded an esoteric or higher knowledge of God's nature and of his self-revelation.

It is not surprising, therefore, to find Schelling giving an interpretation of the history of Christianity which in certain respects is reminiscent of the theories of the twelfth-century Abbot Joachim of Flores. According to Schelling there are three main periods in the development of Christianity. The first is the Petrine, characterized by the dominating ideas of law and authority and correlated with the ultimate ground of being in God, which is itself identified with the Father of Trinitarian theology. The second period, the Pauline, starts with the Protestant Reformation. It is characterized by the idea of freedom and correlated with the ideal principle in God, identified with the Son. And Schelling looks forward to a third period, the Johannine, which will be a higher synthesis of the first two periods and unite together law and freedom in the one Christian community. This third period is correlated with the Holy Spirit, the divine love, interpreted as a synthesis of the first two moments in God's inner life.

5. If we look at Schelling's philosophical pilgrimage as a whole, there is obviously a very great difference between its point of departure and its point of arrival. At the same time there is a certain continuity. For we can see how fresh problems arise for him out of positions already adopted, and how his solutions to these problems demand the adoption of new positions which involve modifications in the old or display them in a new light. Further, there are certain pervasive fundamental problems which serve to confer a certain unity on his philosophizing in spite of all changes.

There can be no reasonable objection to this process of development as such, unless we are prepared to defend as reasonable the thesis that a philosopher should expound a rigid closed system and never change it. Indeed, it is arguable that Schelling did not make sufficient changes. For he showed a tendency to retain ideas already employed even when the adoption of a new idea or set of ideas might well have suggested the advisability of discarding them. This characteristic may not be peculiar to Schelling: it is likely to be found in any philosopher whose thought passed through a variety of distinct phases. But it leads to a certain difficulty in assessing Schelling's precise position at a given moment. For instance, in his later thought he emphasizes the personal nature of God and the freedom of God's creative act. And it is natural to describe the evolution of his thought in its theological aspects as being a movement from pantheism to speculative theism. At the same time his insistence on the divine freedom is accompanied by a retention of the idea of the cosmic Fall and by a persistent inclination to look on the relation between the world and God as analogous to that between consequent and antecedent. Hence, though it seems to me more appropriate to describe his later thought in terms of the ideas which are new rather than in terms of those which are retained for the past, he provides material for those who maintain that even in the last phase of his philosophizing he was a dynamic pantheist rather than a theist. It is, of course, a question partly of emphasis and partly of terminology. But the point is that Schelling himself is largely responsible for the difficulty in finding the precise appropriate descriptive term. However, perhaps one ought not to expect anything else in the case of a philosopher who was so anxious to synthesize apparently conflicting points of view and to show that they were really complementary.

It scarcely needs saying that Schelling was not a systematizer in the sense of one who leaves to posterity a closed and rigid system of the take-it-or-leave-it type. But it does not necessarily follow that he was not a systematic thinker. True, his mind was notably open to stimulus and inspiration from a variety of thinkers whom he found in some respects congenial. For example, Plato, the Neo-Platonists, Giordano

Bruno,[50] Jakob Boehme, Spinoza and Leibniz, not to speak of Kant and Fichte, were all used as sources of inspiration. But this openness to the reception of ideas from a variety of sources was not accompanied by any very pronounced ability to weld them all together into one consistent whole. Further, we have seen that in his later years he showed a strong inclination to take flight into the cloudy realm of theosophy and gnosticism. And it is understandable that a man who drew heavily on the speculations of Jakob Boehme can exercise only a very limited appeal among philosophers. At the same time it is necessary, as Hegel remarks, to make a distinction between Schelling's philosophy and the imitations of it which consist in a farrago of words about the Absolute or in the substitution for sustained thought of vague analogies based on alleged intuitive insights. For though Schelling was not a systematizer in the sense that Hegel was, he none the less thought systematically. That is to say, he made a real and sustained effort to understand his material and to think through the problems which he raised. It was always systematic understanding at which he aimed and which he tried to communicate. Whether he succeeded or not, is another question.

Schelling's later thought has been comparatively neglected by historians. And this is understandable. For one thing, as was remarked in the introductory chapter, Schelling's philosophy of Nature, system of transcendental idealism and theory of the Absolute as pure identity are the important phases of his thought if we choose to regard him primarily as a link between Fichte and Hegel in the development of German idealism. For another thing, his philosophy of mythology and revelation, which in any case belonged to a period when the impetus of metaphysical idealism was already spent, has seemed to many not only to represent a flight beyond anything which can be regarded as rational philosophy but also to be hardly worth considering in view of the actual development of the history of religion in subsequent times.

But though this neglect is understandable, it is also perhaps regrettable. At least it is regrettable if one thinks that there is room for a philosophy of religion as well as for a purely historical and sociological study of religions or a purely psychological study of the religious consciousness. It is not so much a question of looking to Schelling for solutions to problems as of finding stimulus and inspiration in his thought, points of departure for independent reflection. And possibly this is a characteristic of Schelling's philosophizing as a whole. Its value may be primarily suggestive and stimulative. But it can, of course, exercise this function only for those who have a certain initial sympathy with his mentality and an appreciation of the problems which he raised. In the absence of this sympathy and appreciation there is a natural tendency to write him off as a poet who chose the wrong medium for the expression of his visions of the world.

6. In the introductory chapter some mention was made of Schelling's relations with the romantic movement as represented by F. Schlegel, Novalis, Hölderlin and so on. And I do not propose either to repeat or to develop what was then said. But some remarks may be appropriate in this last section of the present chapter on Schelling's influence on some other thinkers both inside and outside Germany.

Schelling's philosophy of Nature exercised some influence on Lorenz Oken (1779–1851). Oken was a professor of medicine at Jena, Munich and Zürich successively; but he was deeply interested in philosophy and published several philosophical works, such as On the Universe (Ueber das Universum), 1808. In his view the philosophy of Nature is the doctrine of the eternal transformation of God into the world. God is the totality, and the world is the eternal appearance of God. That is to say, the world cannot have had a beginning because it is the expressed divine thought. And for the same reason it can have no end. But there can be and is evolution in the world.

Schelling's judgment of Oken's philosophy was not particularly favourable, though he made use of some of Oken's ideas in his lectures. In his turn Oken refused to follow Schelling into the paths of his later religious philosophy.

The influence of Schelling's philosophy of Nature was also

felt by Johann Joseph von Görres (1776–1848), a leading Catholic philosopher of Munich.[51] But Görres is chiefly known as a religious thinker. At first somewhat inclined to the pantheism of Schelling's system of identity, he later expounded a theistic philosophy, as in the four volumes of his *Christian Mysticism* (*Christliche Mystik*, 1836–42), though, like Schelling himself, he was strongly attracted to theosophical speculation. Görres also wrote on art and on political questions. Indeed he took an active part in political life and interested himself in the problem of the relations between Church and State.

Görres's abandonment of the standpoint represented by Schelling's system of identity was not shared by Karl Gustav Carus (1789–1860), a doctor and philosopher who defended pantheism throughout his career. He is of some importance for his work on the soul (*Psyche*, 1846) in which he maintains that the key to the conscious life of the soul is to be found in the sphere of the unconscious.

Turning to Franz von Baader (1765–1841) who, like Görres, was an important member of the circle of Catholic thinkers and writers at Munich, we find a clear case of reciprocal influence. That is to say, though Baader was influenced by Schelling, he in turn influenced the latter. For it was Baader who introduced Schelling to the writings of Boehme and so helped to determine the direction taken by his thought.

It was Baader's conviction that since the time of Francis Bacon and Descartes philosophy had tended to become more and more divorced from religion, whereas true philosophy should have its foundations in faith. And in working out his own philosophy Baader drew on the speculations of thinkers such as Eckhart and Boehme. In God himself we can distinguish higher and lower principles, and though the sensible world is to be regarded as a divine self-manifestation it none the less represents a Fall. Again, just as in God there is the eternal victory of the higher principle over the lower, of light over darkness, so in man there should be a process of spiritualization whereby the world would return to God. It is evident that Baader and Schelling were kindred souls who drank from the same spiritual fountain.

Baader's social and political writings are of some interest. In them he expresses a resolute opposition to the theory of the State as a result of a social compact or contract between individuals. On the contrary, the State is a natural institution in the sense that it is grounded in and proceeds from the nature of man: it is not the product of a convention. At the same time Baader strongly attacks the notion that the State is the ultimate sovereign power. The ultimate sovereign is God alone, and reverence for God and the universal moral law, together with respect for the human person as the image of God, are the only real safeguards against tyranny. If these safeguards are neglected, tyranny and intolerance will result, no matter whether sovereignty is regarded as residing with the monarch or with the people. To the atheistic or secular power-State Baader opposes the ideal of the Christian State. The concentration of power which is characteristic of the secular or the atheistic national State and which leads to injustice at home and to war abroad can be overcome only if religion and morality penetrate the whole of human society.

One can hardly call Karl Christian Friedrich Krause (1781–1832) a disciple of Schelling. For he professed to be the true spiritual successor of Kant, and his relations with Schelling, when at Munich, were far from friendly. However, he was wont to say that the approach to his own philosophy must be by way of Schelling, and some of his ideas were akin to those of Schelling. The body, he maintained, belongs to the realm of Nature, while the spirit or ego belongs to the spiritual sphere, the realm of 'reason'. This idea echoes indeed Kant's distinction between the phenomenal and noumenal spheres. But Krause argued that as Spirit and Nature, though distinct and in one sense opposed, react on one another, we must look for the ground of both in a perfect essence, God or the Absolute. Krause also expounded a 'synthetic' order, proceeding from God or the Absolute to the derived essences, Spirit and Nature, and to finite things. He insisted on the unity of all humanity as the goal of history, and after abandoning his hope of this end being attained through Freemasonry, issued a manifesto proclaiming a League of Humanity (*Menschheitsbund*). In Germany his philosophy was overshadowed by the systems of the three great idealists, but it exercised, perhaps somewhat surprisingly, a wide influence in Spain where 'Krausism' became a fashionable system of thought.

In Russia Schelling appealed to the pan-Slavist group, whereas the westernizers were influenced more by Hegel. For instance, in the early part of the nineteenth century Schelling's philosophy of Nature was expounded at Moscow by M. G. Pavlov (1773–1840), while the later religious thought of Schelling exercised some influence on the famous Russian philosopher Vladimir Soloviev (1853–1900). It would certainly not be accurate to call Soloviev a disciple of Schelling. Apart from the fact that he was influenced by other non-Russian thinkers, he was in any case an original philosopher and not the 'disciple' of anyone. But in his tendency to theosophical speculation[52] he showed a marked affinity of spirit with Schelling, and certain aspects of his profoundly religious thought are very similar to positions adopted by the German philosopher.

In Great Britain the influence of Schelling has been negligible. Coleridge, the poet, remarks in his *Biographia Literaria* that in Schelling's philosophy of Nature and system of transcendental idealism he found 'a genial coincidence' with much that he had worked out for himself, and he praises Schelling at the expense of Fichte, whom he caricatures. But it can hardly be said that professional philosophers in this country have shown any enthusiasm for Schelling.

In recent times there has been a certain renewal of interest in Schelling's philosophy of religion. For instance, it acted as a stimulus in the development of the thought of the Protestant theologian Paul Tillich. And in spite of Kierkegaard's attitude there has been a tendency to see in Schelling's distinction between negative and positive philosophy, in his insistence on freedom and in his emphasis on existence, an anticipation of some themes of existentialism. But though this interpretation has some limited justification, the desire to find anticipations of later ideas in illustrious minds of the past should not blind us to the great differences in atmosphere between the idealist and existentialist movements. In any case Schelling is perhaps most notable for his transformation of the impersonal Absolute of metaphysical idealism into the personal God who reveals himself to the religious consciousness.

Chapter Eight

SCHLEIERMACHER

Life and writings – The basic religious experience and its interpretation – The moral and religious life of man – Final remarks.

1. Concerned as they were with the Absolute, with the relation between the infinite and the finite and with the life of the spirit, the three great German idealists naturally devoted attention to religion as an expression of the finite spirit's relation to the divine reality. And as all three were professors of philosophy and constructors of philosophical systems, it was also natural that they should interpret religion in the light of the fundamental principles of these systems. Thus in accordance with the spirit of his ethical idealism Fichte tended to reduce religion to ethics,[1] while Hegel tended to depict it as a form of knowledge. Even Schelling, whose thought, as we have seen, became more and more a philosophy of the religious consciousness and who laid emphasis on man's need of a personal God, tended to interpret the development of the religious consciousness as the development of a higher knowledge. With Schleiermacher, however, we find an approach to the philosophy of religion from the point of view of a theologian and preacher, a man who in spite of his strongly-marked philosophical interests retained the imprint of his pietistic upbringing and who was concerned with making a sharp distinction between the religious consciousness on the one hand and metaphysics and ethics on the other.

Friedrich Daniel Ernst Schleiermacher was born at Breslau on November 21st, 1768. His school education was entrusted by his parents to the Moravian Brotherhood. In spite of a loss of faith in some fundamental Christian doctrines he then proceeded to Halle for the study of theology, though during his first two years at the university he interested himself in Spinoza and Kant more than in purely theological subjects. In 1790 he passed his examinations at Berlin and then took a post as tutor in a family. From 1794 until the end of 1795 he acted as pastor at Landsberg near Frankfurt on the Oder, and from 1796 until 1802 he held an ecclesiastical position at Berlin.

During this period at Berlin Schleiermacher was in relation with the circle of the romantics, particularly with Friedrich Schlegel. He shared the general romantic concern with the totality, and he had a profound sympathy with Spinoza. At the same time he had been attracted from an early age by Plato's view of the world as the visible image of the ideal realm of true being. And Spinoza's Nature was conceived by him as the reality which reveals itself in the phenomenal world. But as an admirer of Spinoza he was faced with the task of reconciling his philosophical outlook with the religion which he was commissioned to teach. Nor was this simply a matter of satisfying his professional conscience as a Protestant clergyman. For he was a sincerely religious man who, as already remarked, retained the lasting imprint of the piety of his family and of his early teachers. He had therefore to think out the intellectual framework for the religious consciousness as he conceived it. And in 1799 he published his *Discourses on Religion* (*Reden über die Religion*), of which there were several subsequent editions.

This work was followed in 1800 by *Monologues* (*Monologen*) treating of problems connected with the relation between the individual and society, and in 1801 by Schleiermacher's first collection of sermons. Schleiermacher was not, however, what would generally be considered an orthodox Protestant theologian, and the years 1802–4 were passed in retirement. In 1803 he published *Outlines of a Critique of the Doctrine of Morals up to Present* (*Grundlinien einer Kritik der bisherigen Sittenlehre*). He also occupied himself with translating into German the dialogues of Plato, furnished with introductions and notes. The first part appeared in 1804, the second in 1809 and the third in 1828.

In 1804 Schleiermacher accepted a chair at the University of Halle. And when Napoleon closed the university, he remained in the town as a preacher. In 1807, however, he returned to Berlin where he took part in political life and collaborated in the foundation of the new university. In 1810 he was appointed professor of theology in the university and he held this post until his death in 1834. In 1821–2 he published his *Christian Faith according to the Principles of the Evangelical Church* (*Der christliche Glaube nach den Grundsätzen der evangelischen Kirche*), a second edition of which appeared in 1830–1. He also published further collections of sermons. His lecture-courses at the university, which covered not only theological but also philosophical and educational themes, were published after his death.

2. Thought and being, Schleiermacher maintains, are correlative. But there are two ways in which thought can be related to being. In the first place thought can conform itself to being, as in scientific or theoretical knowledge. And the being which corresponds to the totality of our scientific concepts and judgments is called Nature. In the second place thought can seek to conform being to itself. And this is verified in the thinking which lies at the basis of our moral activity. For through moral action we seek to realize our ethical ideals and purposes, endeavouring in this way to conform being to our ideas rather than the other way round. 'Thought which aims at knowledge relates itself to a being which it presupposes; the thought which lies at the root of our actions relates itself to a being which is to come about through us.'[2] And the totality of that which expresses itself in thought-directed action is called Spirit.

We are thus presented, at first sight at least, with a dualism. On the one hand we have Nature, on the other Spirit. But though Spirit and Nature, thought and being, subject and object, are distinct and different notions for conceptual thinking, which is unable to transcend all distinction and oppositions, the dualism is not absolute. The ultimate reality is the identity of Spirit and Nature in the Universe or God. Conceptual thought cannot apprehend this identity. But the identity can be felt. And this feeling is linked by Schleiermacher with self-consciousness. It is not indeed reflective self-awareness, which apprehends the identity of the ego in the diversity of its moments or phases. But at the basis of reflective self-awareness there lies an 'immediate self-consciousness, which equals feeling'.[3] In other words, there is a fundamental immediacy of feeling, at which level the distinctions and oppositions of conceptual thought have not yet emerged. We can speak of it as an intuition. But if we do, we must understand that it is never a clear intellectual intuition. Rather is it the feeling-basis, so to speak, in self-consciousness, and it cannot be separated from consciousness of the self. That is to say, the self does not enjoy any intellectual intuition of the divine totality as direct and sole object, but it feels itself as dependent on the totality which transcends all oppositions.

This feeling of dependence (*Abhängigkeitsgefühl*) is the 'religious side'[4] of self-consciousness: it is in fact 'the religious feeling'.[5] For the essence of religion is 'neither thought nor action but intuition and feeling. It seeks to intuit the Universe. . . .'[6] And the Universe, as Schleiermacher uses the term, is the infinite divine reality. Hence religion is for him essentially or fundamentally the feeling of dependence on the infinite.

In this case it is obviously necessary to make a sharp distinction between religion on the one hand and metaphysics and ethics on the other. True, metaphysics and ethics have 'the same subject-matter as religion, namely the Universe and man's relation to it'.[7] But their approaches are quite different. Metaphysics, says Schleiermacher with an obvious reference to Fichte's idealism, 'spins out of itself the reality of the world and its laws'.[8] Ethics 'develops out of the nature of man and his relation to the Universe a system of duties; it commands and prohibits actions. . . .'[9] But religion is not concerned with metaphysical deduction, nor is it concerned with using the Universe to derive a code of duties. It is neither knowledge nor morality: it is feeling.

We can say, therefore, that Schleiermacher turns his back on the tendency shown by Kant and Fichte to reduce religion to morals, just as he rejects any attempt to exhibit the essence of religion as a form of theoretical knowledge, and that he follows Jacobi in finding the basis of faith in feeling. But there is an important difference between Schleiermacher and Jacobi. For while Jacobi grounded all knowledge on faith, Schleiermacher wishes to differentiate between theoretical knowledge and religious faith and finds in feeling the specific basis of the latter. We can add that though for Schleiermacher the religious consciousness stands closer to the aesthetic consciousness than to theoretical knowledge, the feeling on which the religious consciousness is based, namely the feeling of dependence on the infinite, is peculiar to it. Hence Schleiermacher avoids the romantic tendency to confuse the religious with the aesthetic consciousness.

It must not be concluded from what has been said that in Schleiermacher's view there is no connection at all between religion on the one hand and metaphysics and ethics on the other. On the contrary, there is a sense in which both metaphysics and ethics stand in need of religion. Without the fundamental religious intuition of the infinite totality metaphysics would be left hanging in the air, as a purely conceptual construction. And ethics without religion would give us a very inadequate idea of man. For from the purely ethical point of view man appears as the free and autonomous master of his fate, whereas religious intuition reveals to him his dependence on the infinite Totality, on God.

Now, when Schleiermacher asserts that religious faith is grounded on the feeling of dependence on the infinite, the word 'feeling' must obviously be understood as signifying the immediacy of this consciousness of dependence rather than as excluding any intellectual act. For, as we have seen, he also talks about 'intuition'. But this intuition is not an apprehension of God as a clearly-conceived object: it is a consciousness of self as essentially dependent on infinite being in an indeterminate and unconceptualized sense. Hence the feeling of dependence stands in need of interpretation on the conceptual level. And this is the task of philosophical theology. It is arguable, of course, that Schleiermacher's account of the basic religious experience already comprises a conspicuous element of interpretation. For turning away from the moralism of Kant and the metaphysical speculation of Fichte and inspired by the thought of 'the holy, rejected Spinoza'[10] he identifies that on which the self is felt to depend with the infinite totality, the divine Universe. 'Religion is feeling and taste for the infinite';[11] and of Spinoza we can say that 'the infinite was his beginning and end; the Universe was his only and eternal love. . . .'[12] Thus the basic religious feeling of dependence is initially described in a manner inspired by a romanticized Spinoza. At the same time the influence of Spinoza should not be overestimated. For whereas Spinoza set the 'intellectual love of God' at the summit of the mind's ascent, Schleiermacher finds the feeling of dependence on the infinite at the basis of the religious view of the world. And the question arises, how are we to think or conceive this immediate consciousness of dependence?

A difficulty immediately arises. The basic religious feeling is one of dependence on an infinite in which there are no oppositions, the self-identical totality. But conceptual thought at once introduces distinctions and oppositions: the infinite unity falls apart into the ideas of God and the world. The world is thought of as the totality of all oppositions and differences, while God is conceived a simple unity, as the existing negation of all opposition and distinction.

As conceptual thought cannot do away altogether with the distinction to which it necessarily gives rise, it must conceive God and the world as correlates. That is to say, it must conceive the relation between God and the world as one of mutual implication and not as one of mere compresence, nor even as a one-way relation of dependence, that is, of the world's dependence on God. 'No God without the world, and no world without God.'[13] At the same time the two ideas, namely of God and the world, must not be identified: 'therefore neither complete identification nor complete separation of the two ideas.'[14] In other words, as conceptual thought necessarily conceives the Universe through two ideas, it should not confuse them. The unity of the Universe of being must be conceived in terms of their correlation rather than of their identification.

At first sight at least this suggests that for Schleiermacher the distinction between God and the world exists only for human reflection, and that in reality there is no distinction. In point of fact, however, Schleiermacher wishes to avoid both the reduction of the world to God and the reduction of God to the world. On the one hand an acosmistic theory which simply denied any reality to the finite would be unfaithful to the basic religious consciousness. For this would inevitably be misinterpreted by a theory which left nothing at all of which it could be said that it was dependent. On the other hand a simple identification of God with the spatio-temporal system of finite things would leave no room for an underlying undifferentiated unity. Hence the distinction between God and the world must be something more than the expression of a defect in conceptual thought. True, conceptual thought is quite unable to attain an adequate understanding of the totality, the divine Universe. But it can and should correct its tendency to separate completely the ideas of God and the world by conceiving them as correlates and seeing the world as standing to God in the relation of consequent to antecedent, as the necessary self-manifestation of an undifferentiated unity, or, to use Spinoza's terms, as *Natura naturata* in relation to *Natura naturans*. This is, as it were, the best that conceptual thought can do, avoiding, that is to say, both complete separation and complete identification. The divine reality in itself transcends the reach of our concepts.

The really interesting and significant feature in Schleiermacher's philosophy of religion is the fact that it is for him the explicitation of a fundamental religious experience. In interpreting this experience he is obviously influenced by Spinoza. And, like Spinoza, he insists that God transcends all human categories. As God is the unity without differentiation or opposition, none of the categories of human thought, such as personality, can really apply to him. For they are bound up with finitude. At the same time God is not to be conceived as static Substance but as infinite Life which reveals itself necessarily in the world. In this respect Schleiermacher stands closer to Fichte's later philosophy than to the system of Spinoza, while the theory of God or the Absolute as the undifferentiated self-identity to which the world stands as consequent to antecedent resembles the speculations of Schelling. But Schelling's later gnosticism would hardly have met with Schleiermacher's full approval. Religion for Schleiermacher really consists in the appropriation of the basic feeling of dependence on the infinite. It is an affair of the heart rather than of the understanding, of faith rather than knowledge.

3. Though he refuses to ascribe personality to God, except in a symbolic sense, Schleiermacher lays great stress on the value of the individual personality when he is considering human beings as moral agents. The totality, the universal, is indeed immanent in all finite individuals. And for this reason sheer egoism, involving the deification of one finite self, cannot possibly be the moral ideal for man. At the same time every individual is a particular manifestation of God, and he has his own special gifts, his own particularity (*Eigentümlichkeit*). It is thus his duty to develop his individual talents. And education should be directed to the formation of fully developed and harmoniously integrated individual personalities. Man combines in himself Spirit and Nature, and his moral development requires their harmonization. From the metaphysical point of view Spirit and Nature are ultimately one. Hence the human personality cannot be properly developed if we make so sharp a distinction between, say, reason and natural impulse as to imply that morality consists in disregarding or opposing all natural impulses. The moral ideal is not conflict but harmonization and integration. In other words, Schleiermacher has little sympathy with the rigoristic morality of Kant and with his tendency to assert an antithesis between reason and inclination or impulse. If God is the positive negation, so to speak, of all differences and oppositions, man's moral vocation involves expressing the di-

vine nature in finite form through the harmonization in an
integrated personality of reason, will and impulse.

But though Schleiermacher stresses the development of the
individual personality, he also insists that individual and society are not contradictory concepts. For particularity 'exists
only in relation to others'.[15] On the one hand a man's element of uniqueness, that which distinguishes him from other
men, presupposes human society. On the other hand society,
being a community of distinct individuals, presupposes individual differences. Hence individual and society imply one
another. And self-expression or self-development demands not
only the development of one's individual gifts but also respect
for other personalities. In other words, every human being
has a unique moral vocation, but this vocation can be fulfilled
only within society, that is, by man as member of a community.

If we ask what is the relation between morality as depicted
by the philosopher and specifically Christian morality, the answer is that they differ in form but not in content. The content of Christian morality cannot contradict the content of
'philosophical' morality, but it has its own form, this form
being furnished by the elements in the Christian consciousness which mark it off from the religious consciousness in
general. And the specific note of the Christian consciousness
is that 'all community with God is regarded as conditioned
by Christ's redemptive act'.[16]

As regards historical religions, Schleiermacher's attitude is
somewhat complex. On the one hand he rejects the idea of a
universal natural religion which should be substituted for historical religions. For there are only the latter; the former is
a fiction. On the other hand Schleiermacher sees in the series
of historical religions the progressive revelation of an ideal
which can never be grasped in its entirety. Dogmas are necessary in one sense, namely as concrete symbolic expressions
of the religious consciousness. But they can at the same time
become fetters preventing the free movement of the spirit.
An historical religion such as Christianity owes its origin and
impetus to a religious genius, analogous to an artistic genius;

and its life is perpetuated by its adherents steeping themselves in the spirit of the genius and in the vital movement which stems from him rather than by subscription to a certain set of dogmas. It is true that as time went on Schleiermacher came to lay more stress on the idea of the Church and on specifically Christian belief; but he was and remained what is sometimes called a liberal theologian. And as such he has exercised a very considerable influence in German Protestant circles, though this influence has been sharply challenged in recent times by the revival of Protestant orthodoxy.

4. In his attempt to interpret what he regarded as the basic religious consciousness Schleiermacher certainly attempted to develop a systematic philosophy, a coherent whole. But it can hardly be claimed that this philosophy is free from internal strains and stresses. The influence of a romanticized Spinoza, the man possessed by a passion for the infinite, impelled him in the direction of pantheism. At the same time the very nature of the fundamental feeling or intuition which he wished to interpret militated against sheer monism and demanded some distinction between God and the world. For unless we postulate some distinction, how can we sensibly speak of the finite self as conscious of its dependence on the infinite? Again, whereas the pantheistic aspects of Schleiermacher's thought were unfavourable to the admission of personal freedom, in his moral theory and in his account of the relations between human beings he needed and used the idea of freedom. In other words, the pantheistic elements in his metaphysics were offset by his emphasis on the individual in his theories of moral conduct and of society. There was no question of the theory of the divine Universe being reflected in political totalitarianism. On the contrary, quite apart from his admission of the Church as a society distinct from the State, he emphasized the concept of the 'free society', the social organization which gives free play to the expression of the unique character of each individual personality.

The strains in Schleiermacher's philosophy were not, however, peculiar to it. For any philosophy which tried to combine the idea of the divine totality with personal freedom and the idea of an ultimate identity with a full recognition of the value of the distinct finite particular was bound to find itself involved in similar difficulties. But Schleiermacher could hardly evade the problem by saying that the universal exists only in and through the particulars. For he was determined to justify the feeling of dependence on a reality which was not identifiable with the spatio-temporal world. There had to be something 'behind' the world. Yet the world could not be something outside God. Hence he was driven in the same direction taken by Schelling. Perhaps we can say that Schleiermacher had a profound quasi-mystical consciousness of the One as underlying and expressing itself in the Many, and that this was the foundation of his philosophy. The difficulties arose when he tried to give theoretical expression to this consciousness. But, to do him justice, he readily admitted that no adequate theoretical account was possible. God is the object of 'feeling' and faith rather than of knowledge. Religion is neither metaphysics nor morals. And theology is symbolical. Schleiermacher had indeed obvious affinities with the great idealists, but he was certainly not a rationalist. Religion was for him the basic element in man's spiritual life; and religion, he insisted, is grounded on the immediate intuitive feeling of dependence. This feeling of absolute dependence was for him the food, as it were, of philosophical reflection. And this is not, of course, a view which can be summarily dismissed as the amiable prejudice of a man who attributed to the pious feelings of the heart a cosmic significance which the reflective reason denies them. For it is at any rate arguable that speculative metaphysics is, in part at least, a reflective explicitation of a preliminary apprehension of the dependence of the Many on the One, an apprehension which for want of a better word can be described as intuitive.

Chapter Nine

HEGEL (1)

Life and writings – Early theological writings – Hegel's relations to Fichte and Schelling – The life of the Absolute and the nature of philosophy – The phenomenology of consciousness.

1. Georg Wilhelm Friedrich Hegel, greatest of German idealists and one of the most outstanding of western philosophers, was born at Stuttgart on August 27th, 1770.[1] His father was a civil servant. In his school years at Stuttgart the future philosopher did not distinguish himself in any particular way, but it was at this period that he first felt the attraction of the Greek genius, being especially impressed by the plays of Sophocles, above all by the *Antigone*.

In 1788 Hegel enrolled as a student in the Protestant theological foundation of the University of Tübingen where he formed relations of friendship with Schelling and Hölderlin. The friends studied Rousseau together and shared a common enthusiasm for the ideals of the French Revolution. But, as at school, Hegel gave no impression of exceptional ability. And when he left the university in 1793, his certificate mentioned his good character, his fair knowledge of theology and philology and his inadequate grasp of philosophy. Hegel's mind was not precocious like Schelling's: it needed more time to mature. There is, however, another side to the picture. He had already begun to turn his attention to the relation between philosophy and theology, but he did not show his jottings or notes to his professors, who do not appear to have been remarkable in any way and in whom he doubtless did not feel much confidence.

After leaving the university Hegel gained his livelihood as a family tutor, first at Berne in Switzerland (1793–6) and then at Frankfurt (1797–1800). Though outwardly uneventful these years constituted an important period in his philosophical development. The essays which he wrote at the time were published for the first time in 1907 by Hermann Nohl under the title *Hegel's Early Theological Writings* (*Hegels theologische Jugendschriften*), and something will be said about their content in the next section. True, if we possessed only these essays we should not have any idea of the philosophical system which he subsequently developed, and there would be no good reason for devoting space to him in a history of philosophy. In this sense the essays are of minor importance. But when we look back on Hegel's early writings in the light of our knowledge of his developed system, we can discern a certain continuity in his problematics and understand better how he arrived at his system and what was his leading idea. As we have seen, the early writings have been described as 'theological'. And though it is true that Hegel became a philosopher rather than a theologian, his philosophy was always theology in the sense that its subject-matter was, as he himself insisted, the same as the subject-matter of theology, namely the Absolute or, in religious language, God and the relation of the finite to the infinite.

In 1801 Hegel obtained a post in the University of Jena, and his first published work, on the *Difference between the Philosophical Systems of Fichte and Schelling* (*Differenz des Fichteschen und Schellingschen Systems*) appeared in the same year. This work gave the impression that he was to all intents and purposes a disciple of Schelling. And the impression was strengthened by his collaboration with Schelling in editing the *Critical Journal of Philosophy* (1802–3). But Hegel's lectures at Jena, which were not published before the present century, show that he was already working out an independent position of his own. And his divergence from Schelling was made clear to the public in his first great work, *The Phenomenology of Spirit* (*Die Phänomenologie des Geistes*), which appeared in 1807. Further reference to this remarkable book will be made in the fifth section of this chapter.

After the Battle of Jena, which brought the life of the university to a close, Hegel found himself practically destitute; and from 1807 to 1808 he edited a newspaper at Bamberg. He was appointed rector of the *Gymnasium* at Nuremberg, a post which he held until 1816. (In 1811 he married.) As rector of the *Gymnasium* Hegel promoted classical studies, though not, we are told, to the detriment of study of the students' mother tongue. He also gave instruction to his pupils in the rudiments of philosophy, though more, it appears, out of deference to the wish of his patron Niethammer than from any personal enthusiasm for the policy of introducing philosophy into the school curriculum. And one imagines that most of the pupils must have experienced great difficulty in understanding Hegel's meaning. At the same time the philosopher pursued his own studies and reflections, and it was during his sojourn at Nuremberg that he produced one of his main works, the *Science of Logic* (*Wissenschaft der Logik*, 1812–16).

In the year in which the second and final volume of this work appeared Hegel received three invitations to accept a chair of philosophy, from Erlangen, Heidelberg and Berlin. He accepted the one from Heidelberg. His influence on the general body of the students does not seem to have been very great, but his reputation as a philosopher was steadily rising. And it was enhanced by the publication in 1817 of the *Encyclopaedia of the Philosophical Sciences in Outline* (*Enzyklopädie der philosophischen Wissenschaften im Grundriss*) in which he gave a conspectus of his system according to its three main divisions, logic, philosophy of Nature and philosophy of Spirit. We may also note that it was at Heidelberg that Hegel first lectured on aesthetics.

In 1818 Hegel accepted a renewed invitation to Berlin, and he occupied the chair of philosophy in the university until his death from cholera on November 14th, 1831. During this period he attained an unrivalled position in the philosophical world not only of Berlin but also of Germany as a whole. To

some extent he was looked on as a kind of official philosopher.
But his influence as a teacher was certainly not due to his
connections with the government. Nor was it due to any outstanding gift of eloquence. As an orator he was inferior to
Schelling. His influence was due rather to his evident and
uncompromising devotion to pure thought, coupled with his
remarkable ability for comprising a vast field within the scope
and sweep of his dialectic. And his disciples felt that under
his tuition the inner nature and process of reality, including
the history of man, his political life and spiritual achieve-
ments, were being revealed to their understanding.

During his tenure of the chair of philosophy at Berlin Hegel
published comparatively little. His *Outlines of the Philosophy
of Right* (*Grundlinien der Philosophie des Rechts*) appeared
in 1821, and new editions of the *Encyclopaedia* were published in 1827 and 1830. At the time of his death Hegel was
revising *The Phenomenology of Spirit*. But he was, of course,
lecturing during the whole of this period. And the texts of
his courses, partly based on the collated notes of students,
were published posthumously. In their English translations
the lectures on the philosophy of art comprise four volumes,
those on the philosophy of religion and on the history of
philosophy three volumes each, and those on the philosophy
of history one volume.

In Hölderlin's opinion Hegel was a man of calm prosaic
understanding. In ordinary life at least he never gave the impression of exuberant genius. Painstaking, methodical, conscientious, sociable, he was from one point of view very much
the honest *bourgeois* university professor, the worthy son of a
good civil servant. At the same time he was inspired by a profound vision of the movement and significance of cosmic and
human history, to the expression of which he gave his life.
This is not to say that he was what is usually meant by a visionary. Appeals to mystical intuitions and to feelings were
abhorrent to him, so far as philosophy at any rate was concerned. He was a firm believer in the unity of form and content. The content, truth, exists for philosophy, he was
convinced, only in its systematic conceptual form. The real

is the rational and the rational the real; and reality can be apprehended only in its rational reconstruction. But though Hegel had little use for philosophies which took short-cuts, as it were, by appealing to mystical insights or for philosophies which, in his opinion, aimed at edification rather than at systematic understanding, the fact remains that he presented mankind with one of the most grandiose and impressive pictures of the Universe which are to be met with in the history of philosophy. And in this sense he was a great visionary.

2. We have seen that Hegel was attracted by the Greek genius while he was still at school. And at the university this attraction exercised a marked influence on his attitude towards the Christian religion. The theology which he heard from his professors at Tübingen was for the most part Christianity adapted to the ideas of the Enlightenment, that is to say, rationalistic theism with a certain infusion of or tincture of Biblical supernaturalism. But this religion of the understanding, as Hegel described it, seemed to him to be not only arid and barren but also divorced from the spirit and needs of his generation. And he contrasted it unfavourably with Greek religion which was rooted in the spirit of the Greek people and formed an integral part of their culture. Christianity is, he thought, a book-religion, and the book in question, namely the Bible, is the product of an alien race and out of harmony with the Germanic soul. Hegel was not, of course, proposing a literal substitute of Greek religion for Christianity. His point was that Greek religion was a *Volksreligion*, a religion intimately related to the spirit and genius of the people and forming an element of this people's culture, whereas Christianity, at least as presented to him by his professors, was something imposed from without. Moreover, Christianity was, he thought, hostile to human happiness and liberty and indifferent to beauty.

This expression of Hegel's early enthusiasm for the Greek genius and culture was soon modified by his study of Kant. While not abandoning his admiration for the Greek spirit, he came to regard it as lacking in moral profundity. In his opinion this element of moral profundity and earnestness had been supplied by Kant who had at the same time expounded an ethical religion which was free from the burdens of dogma and Bible-worship. Obviously, Hegel did not mean to imply that mankind had to wait till the time of Kant for the appearance of moral profundity. On the contrary, he attributed a Kantian-like emphasis on morality to the Founder of Christianity. And in his *Life of Jesus* (*Das Leben Jesu*, 1795), which was written while he was a family tutor at Berne, he depicted Christ as being exclusively a moral teacher and almost as an expounder of the Kantian ethics. True, Christ insisted on his personal mission; but according to Hegel he was forced to do so simply because the Jews were accustomed to think of all religions and moral insights as revealed, as coming from a divine source. Hence to persuade the Jews to listen to him at all Christ had to represent himself as the legate or messenger of God. But it was not really his intention either to make himself the unique mediator between God and man or to impose revealed dogmas.

How, then, did Christianity become transformed into an authoritarian, ecclesiastical and dogmatic system? Hegel considered this question in *The Positivity of the Christian Religion* (*Die Positivität der christlichen Religion*), the first two parts of which were composed in 1795–6 and the third somewhat later, in 1798–9. As one would expect, the transformation of Christianity is attributed in large part to the apostles and other disciples of Christ. And the result of the transformation is depicted as the alienation of man from his true self. Through the imposition of dogmas liberty of thought was lost, and through the idea of a moral law imposed from without moral liberty perished. Further, man was regarded as alienated from God. He could be reconciled only by faith and, in Catholicism at least, by the sacraments of the Church.

During his Frankfurt period, however, Hegel's attitude towards Christianity underwent a certain change, which found expression in *The Spirit of Christianity and Its Fate* (*Der Geist des Christentums und sein Schicksal*, 1800). In this essay Judaism with its legalistic morality becomes the villain

of the piece. For the Jew God was the master and man the
slave who had to carry out his master's will. For Christ God
is love, living in man; and the alienation of man from God,
as of man from man, is overcome by the union and life of
love. Kant's insistence on law and duty and the emphasis
which he lays on the overcoming of passion and impulse seem
now to Hegel to express an inadequate notion of morality
and to smack in their own way of the master-slave relationship
which was characteristic of the Jewish outlook. Christ, however, rises above both Jewish legalism and Kantian moralism.
He recognizes, of course, the moral struggle, but his ideal is
that morality should cease to be a matter of obedience to
law and should become the spontaneous expression of a life
which is itself a participation in the infinite divine life. Christ
does not abrogate morality in regard to its content, but he
strips it of its legal form, substituting the motive of love for
that of obedience to law.

It will be noted that Hegel's attention is already directed
to the themes of alienation and to the recovery of a lost unity.
At the time when he was contrasting Christianity with Greek
religion to the detriment of the former he was already dissatisfied with any view of the divine reality as a remote and
purely transcendent being. In the poem entitled *Eleusis* which
he wrote at the end of his sojourn at Berne and which he
dedicated to Hölderlin he expressed his feeling for the infinite Totality. And at Frankfurt he represented Christ as
preaching the overcoming of the gulf between man and God,
the infinite and the finite, by the life of love. The Absolute
is infinite life, and love is the consciousness of the unity of
this life, of unity with the infinite life itself and of unity
with other men through this life.

In 1800, while still at Frankfurt, Hegel wrote some notes
to which Hermann Nohl gave the title *Fragment of a System*
(*Systemfragment*). For on the strength of an allusion in a
letter from Hegel to Schelling, Nohl and Dilthey thought
that the extant notes represented the sketch of a completed
system. This conclusion seems to be based on somewhat in-
sufficient evidence, at least if the word 'system' is understood

in terms of Hegel's developed philosophy. At the same time
the notes are of considerable interest, and deserve some
mention.

Hegel is grappling with the problem of overcoming oppositions or antitheses, above all the opposition between the finite
and the infinite. If we put ourselves in the position of spec-
tators, the movement of life appears to us an infinite organized multiplicity of finite individuals, that is, as Nature. Indeed, Nature can well be described as life posited for
reflection or understanding. But the individual things, the
organization of which is Nature, are transitory and perishing.
Thought, therefore, which is itself a form of life, thinks the
unity between things as an infinite, creative life which is free
from the mortality which affects finite individuals. And this
creative life, which is conceived as bearing the manifold
within itself and not as a mere conceptual abstraction, is
called God. It must also be defined as Spirit (*Geist*). For it
is neither an external link between finite things nor the
purely abstract concept of life, an abstract universal. Infinite
life unites all finite things from within, as it were, but without
annihilating them. It is the living unity of the manifold.

Hegel thus introduces a term, namely Spirit, which is of
great importance in his developed philosophy. But the question arises whether we are able by conceptual thought so to
unify the infinite and the finite that neither term is dissolved
in the other while at the same time they are truly united.
And in the so-called *Fragment of a System* Hegel maintains
that it is not possible. That is to say, in denying the gulf
between finite and infinite conceptual thought inevitably
tends to merge them without distinction or to reduce the one
to the other, while if it affirms their unity it inevitably tends
to deny their distinction. We can see the necessity for a synthesis in which unity does not exclude distinction, but we
cannot really think it. The unification of the Many within
the One without the former's dissolution can be achieved
only by living it, that is, by man's self-elevation from finite
to infinite life. And this living process is religion.

It follows from this that philosophy stops short of religion, and that in this sense it is subordinate to religion. Philosophy shows us what is demanded if the opposition between finite and infinite is to be overcome, but it cannot itself fulfil this demand. For its fulfilment we have to turn to religion, that is, to the Christian religion. The Jews objectified God as a being set over above and outside the finite. And this is the wrong idea of the infinite, a 'bad' infinity. Christ, however, discovered the infinite life within himself as source of his thought and action. And this is the right idea of the infinite, namely as immanent in the finite and as comprising the finite within itself. But this synthesis can only be lived as Christ lived it: it is the life of love. The organ of mediation between finite and infinite is love, not reflection. True, there is a passage where Hegel foreshadows his later dialectical method, but he asserts at the same time that the complete synthesis transcends reflection.

Yet if it is presupposed that philosophy demands the overcoming of the oppositions which it posits, it is only to be expected that philosophy will itself try to fulfil this demand. And even if we say that the life of love, the religious life, fulfils the demand, philosophy will attempt to understand what religion does and how it does it. It is thus not surprising if Hegel soon tries to accomplish by reflection what he had previously declared to be impossible. And what he requires for the fulfilment of this task is a new form of logic, a logic which is able to follow the movement of life and does not leave opposed concepts in irremediable opposition. The adoption of this new logic signifies the transition from Hegel the theologian to Hegel the philosopher or, better, from the view that religion is supreme and that philosophy stops short of it to the view that speculative philosophy is the supreme truth. But the problem remains the same, namely the relation of the finite to the infinite. And so does the idea of the infinite as Spirit.

3. Some six months after his arrival at Jena Hegel published his work on the *Difference between the Philosophical Systems of Fichte and Schelling* (1801). Its immediate aim was twofold; first to show that these systems really were dif-

ferent and not, as some people supposed, the same, and secondly to show that the system of Schelling represented an advance on that of Fichte. But Hegel's discussion of these topics naturally leads him into general reflections on the nature and purpose of philosophy.

The fundamental purpose of philosophy, Hegel maintains, is that of overcoming oppositions and divisions. 'Division [*Entzweiung*] is the source of *the need of philosophy*.'[2] In the world of experience the mind finds differences, oppositions, apparent contradictions, and it seeks to construct a unified whole, to overcome the splintered harmony, as Hegel puts it. True, division and opposition present themselves to the mind in different forms in different cultural epochs. And this helps to explain the peculiar characteristics of different systems. At one time the mind is confronted, for instance, with the problem of the division and opposition between soul and body, while at another time the same sort of problem presents itself as that of the relation between subject and object, intelligence and Nature. But in whatever particular way or ways the problem may present itself, the fundamental interest of reason (*Vernunft*) is the same, namely to attain a unified synthesis.

This means in effect that 'the Absolute is to be constructed for consciousness; such is the task of philosophy'.[3] For the synthesis must in the long run involve reality as a whole. And it must overcome the basic opposition between the finite and the infinite, not by denying all reality to the finite, not by reducing the infinite to the multiplicity of finite particulars as such, but by integrating, as it were, the finite into the infinite.

But a difficulty at once arises. If the life of the Absolute is to be constructed by philosophy, the instrument will be reflection. Left to itself, however, reflection tends to function as understanding (*Verstand*) and thus to posit and perpetuate oppositions. It must therefore be united with transcendental intuition which discovers the interpenetration of the ideal and the real, idea and being, subject and object. Reflection is then raised to the level of reason (*Vernunft*), and we have a speculative knowledge which 'must be conceived as identity of reflection and intuition'.[4] Hegel is evidently writing under the influence of Schelling's ideas.

Now, in the Kantian system, as Hegel sees it, we are repeatedly confronted with unreconciled dualisms or oppositions, between phenomena and noumena, sensibility and understanding, and so on. Hegel shows therefore a lively sympathy with Fichte's attempt to remedy this state of affairs. He entirely agrees, for instance, with Fichte's elimination of the unknowable thing-in-itself, and regards his system as an important essay in genuine philosophizing. 'The absolute principle, the one real foundation and firm standpoint of philosophy is, in the philosophy of Fichte as in that of Schelling, intellectual intuition or, in the language of reflection, the identity of subject and object. In science this intuition becomes the object of reflection, and philosophical reflection is thus itself transcendental intuition which makes itself its own object and is one with it. Hence it is speculation. Fichte's philosophy, therefore, is a genuine product of speculation.'[5]

But though Fichte sees that the presupposition of speculative philosophy is an ultimate unity and starts with the principle of identity, 'the principle of identity is not the principle of the system: directly the construction of the system begins, identity disappears'.[6] In the theoretical deduction of consciousness it is only the idea of the objective world which is deduced, not the world itself. We are left simply with subjectivity. In the practical deduction we are indeed presented with a real world, but Nature is posited only as the opposite of the ego. In other words, we are left with an unresolved dualism.

With Schelling, however, the situation is very different. For 'the principle of identity is the absolute principle of the *whole* system of Schelling. Philosophy and system coincide: identity is not lost in the parts, and much less in the result.'[7] That is to say, Schelling starts with the idea of the Absolute as the identity of subjectivity and objectivity, and it persists as the guiding-idea of the parts of the system. In the philosophy of Nature Schelling shows that Nature is not simply the opposite of the ideal but that, though real, it is also ideal through and through: it is visible Spirit. In the system of transcendental idealism he shows how subjectivity objectifies itself, how the ideal is also the real. The principle of identity is thus maintained throughout the whole system.

In his works on the systems of Fichte and Schelling there are indeed signs of Hegel's divergence from Schelling. For instance, it is clear that intellectual intuition does not mean for him a mystical intuition of a dark and impenetrable abyss, the vanishing-point of all differences, but rather reason's insight into antitheses as moments in the one all-comprehensive life of the Absolute. But as the work is designed to illustrate the superiority of Schelling's system to that of Fichte, Hegel naturally does not make explicit his points of divergence from the former's thought. The independence of his own standpoint is, however, clearly revealed in the lectures of his Jena period.

In the Jena lectures Hegel argues, for example, that if finite and infinite are set over against one another as opposed concepts, there is no passage from one to the other. A synthesis is impossible. But in point of fact we cannot think the finite without thinking the infinite: the concept of the finite is not a self-contained and isolated concept. The finite is limited by what is other than itself. In Hegel's language, it is affected by negation. But the finite is not simply negation. Hence we must negate the negation. And in doing so we affirm that the finite is more than finite. That is to say, it is a moment in the life of the infinite. And from this it follows that to construct the life of the Absolute, which is the task of philosophy, is to construct it in and through the finite, showing how the Absolute necessarily expresses itself as Spirit, as self-consciousness, in and through the human mind. For the human mind, though finite, is at the same time more than finite and can attain the standpoint at which it is the vehicle, as it were, of the Absolute's knowledge of itself.

To a certain extent, of course, this is in harmony with Schelling's philosophy. But there is also a major difference. For Schelling the Absolute in itself transcends conceptual thought, and we must approach the absolute identity by the *via negativa*, thinking away the attributes and distinctions of the finite.[8] For Hegel the Absolute is not an identity about which nothing further can be said: it is the total process of its self-expression or self-manifestation in and through the finite. It is not surprising, therefore, to find in the Preface to *The Phenomenology of Spirit* a sharp rejection of Schelling's view of the Absolute. True, Schelling is not mentioned by name, but the reference is clear enough. It was clear to Schelling himself, who felt deeply wounded. Hegel speaks of a monotonous formalism and abstract universality which are said to constitute the Absolute. All the emphasis is placed on the universal in the bare form of identity. 'And we see speculative contemplation identified with the dissolution of the distinct and determinate, or rather with hurling it down, without more ado and without justification, into the abyss of vacuity.'[9] To consider a thing as in the Absolute is taken to mean considering it as dissolved in an undifferentiated self-identical unity. But 'to pit this one piece of knowledge, namely that in the Absolute all is one, against determinate and complete knowledge or knowledge which at least seeks and demands completion—to proclaim the *Absolute* as the night in which, as we say, all cows are black—this is the naïvety of empty knowledge'.[10] It is not by plunging ourselves into a mystical night that we can come to know the Absolute. We come to know it only by understanding a determinate content, the self-developing life of the Absolute in Nature and Spirit. True, in his philosophy of Nature and in his system of transcendental idealism Schelling considered determinate contents, and in regard to these contents he attempted a systematic demonstration of the identity of the ideal and the real. But he conceived the Absolute in itself as being, for conceptual thought at least, a blank identity, a vanishing-point of all differences, whereas for Hegel the Absolute is not an impenetrable reality existing, as it were, above and behind its determinate manifestations: it *is* its self-manifestation.

4. This point is of great importance for understanding

Hegel. The subject-matter of philosophy is indeed the Absolute. But the Absolute is the Totality, reality as a whole, the universe. 'Philosophy is concerned with the true and the true is the whole.'[11] Further, this totality or whole is infinite life, a process of self-development. The Absolute is 'the process of its own becoming, the circle which presupposes its end as its purpose and has its end as its beginning. It becomes concrete or actual only by its development and through its end.'[12] In other words, reality is a teleological process; and the ideal term presupposes the whole process and gives to it its significance. Indeed we can say that the Absolute is 'essentially a result'.[13] For if we look on the whole process as the self-unfolding of an essence, the actualization of an eternal Idea, we can see that it is the term or end of the process which reveals what the Absolute really is. True, the whole process is the Absolute; but in a teleological process it is the *telos* or end which shows its nature, its meaning. And philosophy must take the form of a systematic understanding of this teleological process. 'The true form in which truth exists can only be the scientific system of the same.'[14]

Now, if we say that the Absolute is the whole of reality, the Universe, it may seem that we are committed to Spinozism, to the statement that the Absolute is infinite Substance. But this is for Hegel a very inadequate description of the Absolute. 'In my view—a view which can be justified only through the exposition of the system itself—everything depends on grasping the true not merely as *Substance* but as *Subject* as well.'[15] But if the Absolute is subject, what is its object? The only possible answer is that its object is itself. In this case it is Thought which thinks itself, self-thinking Thought. And to say this is to say that the Absolute is Spirit, the infinite self-luminous or self-conscious subject. The statement that the Absolute is Spirit is for Hegel its supreme definition.

In saying that the Absolute is self-thinking Thought Hegel is obviously repeating Aristotle's definition of God, a fact of which he is, of course, well aware. But it would be a great mistake to assume that Hegel is thinking of a transcendent

Deity. The Absolute is, as we have seen, the Totality, the whole of reality; and this totality is a process. In other words, the Absolute is a process of self-reflection: reality comes to know itself. And it does so in and through the human spirit. Nature is a necessary precondition of human consciousness in general: it provides the sphere of the objective without which the sphere of the subjective cannot exist. But both are moments in the life of the Absolute. In Nature the Absolute goes over into, as it were, or expresses itself in objectivity. There is no question with Hegel of Nature being unreal or merely idea in a subjectivist sense. In the sphere of human consciousness the Absolute returns to itself, that is, as Spirit. And the philosophical reflection of humanity is the Absolute's self-knowledge. That is to say, the history of philosophy is the process by which the Absolute, reality as a whole, comes to think itself. Philosophical reason comes to see the whole history of the cosmos and the whole history of man as the self-unfolding of the Absolute. And this insight is the Absolute's knowledge of itself.

One can put the matter in this way. Hegel agrees with Aristotle that God is self-thinking Thought,[16] and that this self-thinking Thought is the *telos* or end which draws the world as its final cause. But whereas the self-thinking Thought of Aristotle is, so to speak, an already constituted self-consciousness which does not depend on the world, the self-thinking Thought of Hegel is not a transcendent reality but rather the universe's knowledge of itself. The whole process of reality is a teleological movement towards the actualization of self-thinking Thought; and in this sense the Thought which thinks itself is the *telos* or end of the universe. But it is an end which is immanent within the process. The Absolute, the universe or totality, is indeed definable as self-thinking Thought. But it is Thought which comes to think itself. And in this sense we can say, as Hegel says, that the Absolute is essentially a result.

To say, therefore, that the Absolute is self-thinking Thought is to affirm the identity of the ideal and the real, of subjectivity and objectivity. But this is an identity-in-difference, not a blank undifferentiated identity. Spirit sees itself in Nature: it sees Nature as the objective manifestation of the Absolute, a manifestation which is a necessary condition for its own existence. In other words, the Absolute knows itself as the Totality, as the whole process of its becoming; but at the same time it sees the distinctions between the phases of its own life. It knows itself as an identity-in-difference, as the unity which comprises distinguishable phases within itself.

As we have seen, the task of philosophy is to construct the life of the Absolute. That is to say, it must exhibit systematically the rational dynamic structure, the teleological process or movement of the cosmic Reason, in Nature and the sphere of the human spirit, which culminates in the Absolute's knowledge of itself. It is not, of course, a question of philosophy trying to do over again, or to do better, the work accomplished by empirical science or by history. Such knowledge is presupposed. Rather is it philosophy's task to make clear the basic teleological process which is immanent in the material known in other ways, the process which gives to this material its metaphysical significance. In other words, philosophy has to exhibit systematically the self-realization of infinite Reason in and through the finite.

Now if, as Hegel believes, the rational is the real and the real the rational, in the sense that reality is the necessary process by which infinite Reason, the self-thinking Thought, actualizes itself, we can say that Nature and the sphere of the human spirit are the field in which an eternal Idea or an eternal essence manifests itself. That is to say, we can make a distinction between the Idea or essence which is actualized and the field of its actualization. We then have the picture of the eternal Idea or *Logos* manifesting itself in Nature and in Spirit. In Nature the *Logos* goes over, as it were, into objectivity, into the material world, which is its antithesis. In Spirit (the sphere of the human spirit) the *Logos* returns to itself, in the sense that it manifests itself as what it essentially is. The life of the Absolute thus comprises three main phases: the logical Idea or Concept or Notion,[17] Nature and Spirit. And the system of philosophy will fall into three main parts:

logic, which for Hegel is metaphysics in the sense that it studies the nature of the Absolute 'in itself', the philosophy of Nature and the philosophy of Spirit. These three parts together form the philosophical construction of the life of the Absolute.

Obviously, if we talk about the eternal Idea 'manifesting itself' in Nature and Spirit, we imply that the *Logos* possesses an ontological status of its own, independently of things. And when Hegel uses, as he so frequently does, the language of religion and speaks of the logical Idea as God-in-himself, he inevitably tends to give the impression that the *Logos* is for him a transcendent reality which manifests itself externally in Nature. But such use of religious language does not necessarily justify this conclusion about his meaning. However, I do not wish to discuss this disputed problem here. For the moment we can leave undecided the question whether or not the self-thinking Thought which forms the culminating category of Hegel's logic can properly be said to exist, that is, independently of the finite. It is sufficient to have noticed the three main parts of philosophy, each of which is concerned with the Absolute. Logic studies the Absolute 'in itself'; the philosophy of Nature studies the Absolute 'for itself'; and the philosophy of Spirit studies the Absolute 'in and for itself'. Together they constitute the complete construction of the life of the Absolute.

Philosophy must, of course, exhibit this life in conceptual form. There is no other form in which it can present it. And if the life of the Absolute is a necessary process of self-actualization, this necessity must be reflected in the philosophical system. That is to say, it must be shown that concept A gives rise to concept B. And if the Absolute is the Totality, philosophy must be a self-contained system, exhibiting the fact that the Absolute is both Alpha and Omega. A truly adequate philosophy would be the total system of truth, the whole truth, the perfect conceptual reflection of the life of the Absolute. It would in fact be the Absolute's knowledge of itself in and through the human mind; it would be the self-mediation of the Totality. Hence, on Hegelian principles, there would be no question of comparing the absolute philosophy with the Absolute, as though the former were a purely external account of the latter, so that we had to compare them to see whether the philosophy fitted the reality which it described. For the absolute philosophy would *be* the Absolute's knowledge of itself.

But if we say that philosophy must exhibit the life of the Absolute in conceptual form, a difficulty at once arises. The Absolute is, as we have seen, identity-in-difference. For instance, it is the identity-in-difference of the infinite and the finite, of the One and the Many. But the concepts of infinite and finite, as of the One and the Many, seem to be mutually exclusive. If, therefore, philosophy operates with clearly-defined concepts, how can it possibly construct the life of the Absolute? And if it operates with vague, ill-defined concepts, how can it be an apt instrument for understanding anything? Would it not be better to say with Schelling that the Absolute transcends conceptual thought?

In Hegel's view this difficulty does indeed arise on the level of understanding (*Verstand*). For understanding posits and perpetuates fixed static concepts of such a kind that it cannot itself overcome the oppositions which it posits. To take the same example which has already been given, for understanding the concepts of the finite and the infinite are irrevocably opposed. If finite, then not infinite: if infinite, then not finite. But the conclusion to be drawn is that understanding is an inadequate instrument for the development of speculative philosophy, not that philosophy is impossible. Obviously, if the term 'understanding' is taken in a wide sense, philosophy is understanding. But if the term is taken in the narrow sense of *Verstand*, the mind, functioning in this way, is unable to produce the understanding (in the wide sense) which is, or ought to be, characteristic of philosophy.

Hegel has, of course, no intention of denying that understanding, in the sense of the mind operating as *Verstand*, has its uses in human life. For practical purposes it is often important to maintain clear-cut concepts and oppositions. The opposition between the real and the apparent might be a case in point. Moreover, a great deal of scientific work, such as mathematics, is based on *Verstand*. But it is a different matter when the mind is trying to grasp the life of the Absolute, the identity-in-difference. It cannot then remain content with the level of understanding, which for Hegel is a superficial level. It must penetrate deeper into the concepts which are categories of reality, and it will then see how a given concept tends to pass over into or to call forth its opposite. For example, if the mind really thinks through, so to speak, the concept of the infinite, it sees it losing its rigid self-containedness and the concept of the infinite emerging. Similarly, if the mind really thinks through the concept of reality as opposed to appearance, it will see the absurd or 'contradictory' character of a reality which in no way at all appears or manifests itself. Again, for common sense and practical life one thing is distinct from all other things; it is self-identical and negates all other things. And so long as we are not concerned with thinking what this really means, the idea has its practical uses. But once we really try to think it, we see the absurdity of the notion of a completely isolated thing, and we are forced to negate the original negation.

Thus in speculative philosophy the mind must elevate itself from the level of understanding in the narrow sense to the level of dialectical thinking which overcomes the rigidity of the concepts of the understanding and sees one concept as generating or passing into its opposite. Only so can it hope to grasp the life of the Absolute in which one moment or phase passes necessarily into another. But this is obviously not enough. If for the understanding concepts A and B are irrevocably opposed whereas for the deeper penetration of dialectical thought A passes into B and B into A, there must be a higher unity or synthesis which unites them without annulling their difference. And it is the function of reason (*Vernunft*) to grasp this moment of identity-in-difference. Hence philosophy demands the elevation of understanding through dialectical thinking to the level of reason or speculative thought which is capable of apprehending identity-in-difference.[18]

It is perhaps unnecessary to add that from Hegel's point of view it is not a question of producing a new species of logic out of the hat to enable him to establish an arbitrarily preconceived view of reality. For he sincerely believes that dialectical thought gives a deeper penetration of the nature of reality than understanding in the narrow sense can possibly do. For example, it is not for Hegel a question of insisting that the concept of the finite must pass over into or call forth the concept of the infinite simply because of a preconceived belief that the infinite exists in and through the finite. For it is his conviction that we cannot really think the finite without relating it to the infinite. It is not we who do something to the concept, juggling about with it, as it were: it is the concept itself which loses its rigidity and breaks up before the mind's attentive gaze. And this fact reveals to us the nature of the finite: it has a metaphysical significance.

In his account of dialectical thinking Hegel makes a rather disconcerting use of the word 'contradiction'. Through what he calls the power of the negative a concept of the understanding is said to give rise to a contradiction. That is to say, the contradiction implicit in the concept becomes explicit when the concept loses its rigidity and self-containedness and passes into its opposite. Further, Hegel does not hesitate to speak as though contradictions are present not only in conceptual thought or discourse about the world but in things themselves. And indeed this must be so in some sense if the dialectic mirrors the life of the Absolute. Moreover, this insistence on the role of contradiction is not simply incidental to Hegel's thought. For the emergence of contradiction is the motive force, as it were, of the dialectical movement. The conflict of opposed concepts and the resolution of the conflict in a synthesis which itself gives rise to another contradiction is the feature which drives the mind restlessly onwards towards an ideal term, an all-embracing synthesis, the complete system of truth. And, as we have noted, this does not mean that contradiction and conflict are confined to discourse about reality. When philosophy considers, for example, the history of man, it discovers a dialectical movement at work.

This use of the word 'contradiction' has led some critics of Hegel to accuse him of denying the logical principle of non-contradiction by saying that contradictory notions or propositions can stand together. And in refutation of this charge it has often been pointed out that for Hegel it is precisely the impossibility of being satisfied with a sheer contradiction which forces the mind onwards to a synthesis in which the contradiction is overcome. This answer, however, lays itself open to the retort that Hegel does not share Fichte's tendency to argue that the contradictions or antinomies which arise in the course of dialectical thinking are merely apparent. On the contrary, he insists on their reality. And in the syntheses the so-called contradictory concepts are preserved. In turn, however, it can be replied that though the concepts are preserved, they are not preserved in a relation of mutual exclusiveness. For they are shown to be essential and complementary moments in a higher unity. And in this sense the contradiction is resolved. Hence the simple assertion that Hegel denies the principle of non-contradiction gives a quite inaccurate view of the situation. What Hegel does is to give a dynamic interpretation of the principle in place of the static interpretation which is characteristic of the level of understanding. The principle operates in dialectical thinking, but it operates as a principle of movement.

This discussion might be prolonged. But it would be pointless to do so without first inquiring in what sense Hegel actually understands the term 'contradiction' when he is engaged in working out his dialectical philosophy rather than in talking abstractly about dialectical thought. And it is a notorious fact that the result of such an inquiry is to show that there is no single precise and invariable sense in which Hegel uses the term. Occasionally indeed we find a verbal contradiction. Thus the concept of Being is said to give rise to and pass into the concept of Not-being, while the concept of Not-being passes into the concept of Being. And this dialectical oscillation gives rise to the concept of Becoming which synthesizes Being and Not-being. But, as will be seen in the section on Hegel's logic in the next chapter, the meaning of this dialectical performance is easily intelligible, whether we agree or not with what Hegel has to say. In any case Hegel's so-called contradictions are much more often contraries than contradictions. And the idea is that one contrary demands the other, an idea which, whether true or false, does not amount to a denial of the principle of non-contradiction. Again, the so-called contradictory or opposed concepts may be simply complementary concepts. A one-sided abstraction evokes another one-sided abstraction. And the one-sidedness of each is overcome in the synthesis. Further, the statement that every thing is contradictory sometimes bears the meaning that a thing in a state of complete isolation, apart from its essential relations, would be impossible and 'contradictory'. Reason cannot remain in the idea of a completely isolated finite thing. Here again there is no question of denying the principle of non-contradiction.

We have used the word 'synthesis' for the moment of identity-in-difference in the dialectical advance. But in point of fact the terms 'thesis', 'antithesis' and 'synthesis' are more characteristic of Fichte than of Hegel, who seldom uses them. At the same time the most cursory inspection of the Hegelian system reveals his preoccupation with triads. Thus there are three main phases in the construction of the life of the Absolute: the logical Idea, Nature and Spirit. And each phase is divided and subdivided into triads. Moreover, the whole system is, or aims at, a necessary development. That is to say, for philosophical reflection one stage reveals itself as demanding the next by an inner necessity. Thus, in theory at least, if we start with the first category of the *Logic*, the inner necessity of dialectical development forces the mind to proceed not simply to the final category of the *Logic* but also to the ultimate phase of the philosophy of Spirit.

As for Hegel's preoccupation with triadic development, we may think that it is unnecessary and that it sometimes produces highly artificial results, but we obviously have to accept it as a fact. But though it is a fact that he develops his system according to this pattern, it obviously does not follow that the development always possesses the character of necessity which Hegel implies that it ought to have. And if it does not, this is easily understandable. For when Hegel is concerned, for example, with the life of the Spirit in art or in religion, he is faced with a multitude of historical data which he takes over, as it were, from the relevant sources and which he then interprets according to a dialectical pattern. And it is clear that there might be various possible ways of grouping and interpreting the data, no one of which was strictly necessary. The discovery of the best way will be a matter of reflection and insight rather than of strict deduction. To say this is not necessarily to condemn Hegel's practice. For in point of fact his interpretations of vast masses of data can sometimes be illuminating and are often stimulating even when we do not agree with them. At the same time the transitions between the stages of his dialectic are by no means always of the logical type suggested by his claim that philosophy is a necessary deductive system, even if the persistent observance of the same external pattern, namely the triadic arrangement, tends to obscure the underlying complexity.

Of course, when Hegel claims that philosophy is or ought to be a necessary deductive system, he does not really mean that it is the sort of deductive system which could be worked out by a machine. If it were, then it would belong to the sphere of understanding rather than to that of reason. Philosophy is concerned with the life of absolute Spirit, and to discern the unfolding of this life in, say, human history, *a priori* deduction is obviously not enough. The empirical material cannot be supplied by philosophy, though philosophy discerns the teleological pattern which works itself out in this material. At the same time the whole dialectical movement of the Hegelian system should, in theory at least, impose itself on the mind by its own inner necessity. Otherwise the system could hardly be, as Hegel claims that it is, its own justification. Yet it is clear that Hegel comes to philosophy with certain basic convictions; that the rational is the real and the real the rational, that reality is the self-manifestation

of infinite reason, and that infinite reason is self-thinking
Thought which actualizes itself in the historical process. True,
it is Hegel's contention that the truth of these convictions is
demonstrated in the system. But it is arguable that the system really depends upon them, and that this is one of the
main reasons why those who do not share, or at least are not
sympathetically disposed towards, Hegel's initial convictions
are not much impressed by what we may call his empirical
confirmation of his general metaphysical scheme. For it seems
to them that his interpretations of the material are governed
by a preconceived scheme, and that even if the system is a
remarkable intellectual *tour-de-force*, it demonstrates at best
only on what lines we must interpret the various aspects of
reality if we have already made up our minds that reality as
a whole is of a certain nature. This criticism would indeed
be invalidated if the system really showed that Hegel's interpretation of the process of reality was the only interpretation which satisfied the demands of reason. But it may well
be doubted whether this can be shown without giving to the
word 'reason' a meaning which would beg the whole question.

One might perhaps neglect or pass over Hegel's theory of
the necessity inherent in the dialectical development of the
system and view his philosophy simply as one of the possible
ways of satisfying the mind's impulse to obtain conceptual
mastery over the whole wealth of empirical data or to interpret the world as a whole and man's relation to it. And we
could then compare it with other large-scale interpretations
or visions of the universe and try to find criteria for judging
between them. But though this procedure may seem eminently reasonable to many people, it does not square with
Hegel's own estimation of his own philosophy. For even if he
did not think that his presentation of the system of philosophy was the whole truth in its final form, he certainly thought
that it represented the highest stage which the Absolute's
developing knowledge of itself had reached up to date.

This may seem to be an extremely bizarre notion. But we
have to bear in mind Hegel's view of the Absolute as identity-
in-difference. The infinite exists in and through the finite,

and infinite Reason or Spirit knows itself in and through the finite spirit or mind. But it is not every sort of thinking by the finite mind which can be said to form a moment in the developing self-knowledge of the infinite Absolute. It is man's knowledge of the Absolute which is the Absolute's knowledge of itself. Yet we cannot say of any finite mind's knowledge of the Absolute that it is identical with the Absolute's knowledge of itself. For the latter transcends any given finite mind or set of finite minds. Plato and Aristotle, for example, are dead. But according to Hegel's interpretation of the history of philosophy the essential elements in their respective apprehensions of reality were taken up into and persist in the total dialectical movement of philosophy through the centuries. And it is this developing movement which is the Absolute's developing knowledge of itself. It does not exist apart from all finite minds, but it is obviously not confined to any given mind or set of minds.[19]

5. We can speak, therefore, of the human mind rising to a participation in the self-knowledge of the Absolute. Some writers have interpreted Hegel on more or less theistic lines. That is to say, they have understood him to mean that God is perfectly luminous to himself quite independently of man, though man is capable of participating in this self-knowledge. But I have interpreted him here as meaning that man's knowledge of the Absolute and the Absolute's knowledge of itself are two aspects of the same reality. Even, however, on this interpretation we can still speak of the finite mind rising to a participation in the divine self-knowledge. For, as we have seen, it is not every sort of idea and thought in man's mind which can be regarded as a moment in the Absolute's self-knowledge. It is not every level of consciousness which is a participation in the divine self-consciousness. To achieve this participation the finite mind has to rise to the level of what Hegel calls absolute knowledge.

In this case it is possible to trace the successive stages of consciousness from the lowest to the highest levels. And this is what Hegel does in *The Phenomenology of Spirit*, which can be described as a history of consciousness. If we consider the mind and its activity in themselves, without relation to an object, we are concerned with psychology. If, however, we consider mind as essentially related to an object, external or internal, we are concerned with consciousness. And phenomenology is the science of consciousness in this sense. Hegel begins with the natural unscientific consciousness and proceeds to trace the dialectical development of this consciousness, showing how the lower levels are subsumed in the higher according to a more adequate point of view, until we reach the level of absolute knowledge.

In a certain sense *The Phenomenology* can be regarded as an introduction to philosophy. That is to say, it systematically traces the development of consciousness up to the level of what we might call the properly philosophical consciousness. But it is certainly not an introduction to philosophy in the sense of being an external preparation for philosophizing. Hegel did not believe that an introduction in this sense was possible. And in any case the work is itself an outstanding example of sustained philosophical reflection. It is, we may say, the philosophical consciousness reflecting on the phenomenology of its own genesis. Moreover, even if the work is in some sense an introduction to the point of view required by the Hegelian system, there is an overlapping. The system itself finds a place for the phenomenology of consciousness, and *The Phenomenology* contains an outline of a certain amount of material which is later treated by Hegel at greater length. The religious consciousness is a case in point. Lastly, by no stretch of the imagination can *The Phenomenology* be described as an introduction to philosophy in the sense of a work of philosophy-without-tears. On the contrary, it is a profound work and often extremely difficult to understand.

The Phenomenology falls into three main parts, corresponding with the three main phases of consciousness. The first of these phases is consciousness of the object as a sensible thing standing over against the subject. And it is to this phase that Hegel appropriates the name 'consciousness' (*Bewusstsein*). The second phase is that of self-consciousness (*Selbstbewusstsein*). And here Hegel has a lot to say about social consciousness. The third phase is that of Reason (*Vernunft*), which is represented as the synthesis or unity of the preceding phases on a higher level. In other words, Reason is the synthesis of objectivity and subjectivity. Needless to say, each of these main divisions of the work has its subdivisions. And Hegel's general procedure is first to describe the spontaneous attitude of consciousness at a given level and then to institute an analysis of it. The result of the analysis is that the mind is compelled to proceed to the next level, considered as a more adequate attitude or point of view.

Hegel begins with what he calls sense-certainty, the uncritical apprehension by the senses of particular objects, which to the naïve consciousness appears to be not only the most certain and basic form of knowledge but also the richest. Analysis, he argues, shows that it is in fact a peculiarly empty and abstract form of knowledge. The naïve consciousness feels certain that it is directly acquainted through sense-apprehension with a particular thing. But when we try to say what it is that we know, that is, to describe the particular object with which we claim to be immediately acquainted, we find that we can describe it only in universal terms which are applicable to other things as well. We can, of course, attempt to pin the object down, as it were, by using words such as 'this', 'here', and 'now', accompanying them perhaps with an ostensive gesture. But a moment later the same words apply to another object. Indeed, it is impossible, Hegel argues, to give even to words like 'this' a genuinely particular significance, however much we may wish and try to do so.

We might wish to say that Hegel is simply calling attention to a feature of language. And he is, of course, perfectly well aware that he is saying something about language. But his main concern is epistemological. He wishes to show that the claim of 'sense-certainty' to be knowledge *par excellence* is a bogus claim. And he draws the conclusion that this level of consciousness, on the path towards becoming genuine knowledge, must pass into the level of perception for which the object is a thing conceived as the centre of distinct properties and qualities. But analysis of this level of consciousness shows that it is not possible, as long as we remain simply on the level of sense, to reconcile in any satisfactory manner the elements of unity and multiplicity which are postulated by this view of the object. And the mind passes, therefore, by various stages to the level of scientific understanding which invokes metaphenomenal or unobservable entities to explain sense-phenomena.

For instance, the mind sees sense-phenomena as the manifestations of hidden forces. But, Hegel maintains, the mind cannot rest here and proceeds instead to the idea of laws. Yet natural laws are ways of ordering and describing phenomena; they are not explicative. Hence they cannot perform the function for which they have been invoked, namely to explain sense-phenomena. Hegel obviously does not mean to deny that the concept of natural laws has a useful function to perform at the appropriate level. But it does not give the sort of knowledge which, in his opinion, the mind is seeking.

In the end the mind sees that the whole realm of the metaphenomenal which has been invoked to explain sense-phenomena is the product of the understanding itself. Consciousness is thus turned back on itself as the reality behind the veil of phenomena and becomes self-consciousness.

Hegel begins with self-consciousness in the form of desire (*Begierde*). The self is still concerned with the external object, but it is characteristic of the attitude of desire that the self subordinates the object to itself, seeking to make it minister to its satisfaction, to appropriate it, even to consume it. And this attitude can be shown, of course, in regard to living and non-living things. But when the self is confronted with another self, this attitude breaks down. For the presence of the Other is for Hegel essential to self-consciousness. Developed self-consciousness can arise only when the self recognizes selfhood in itself and others. It must take the form, therefore, of a truly social or we-consciousness, the recognition at the level of self-consciousness of identity-in-difference. But in the dialectical evolution of this phase of consciousness developed self-consciousness is not attained immediately. And Hegel's study of the successive stages forms one of the most interesting and influential parts of *The Phenomenology*.

The existence of another self is, we have mentioned, a condition of self-consciousness. But the first spontaneous reaction of a self confronted with another self is to assert its own existence as a self in face of the other. The one self desires to cancel out or annihilate the other self as a means to the triumphant assertion of its own selfhood. But a literal destruction would defeat its own purpose. For consciousness of one's own selfhood demands as a condition the recognition of this selfhood by another self. There thus arises the master-slave relationship. The master is the one who succeeds in obtaining recognition from the other, in the sense that he imposes himself as the other's value. The slave is the one who sees his own true self in the other.

Paradoxically, however, the original situation changes. And it must do so because of the contradictions concealed in it. On the one hand, by not recognizing the slave as a real person the master deprives himself of that recognition of his own freedom which he originally demanded and which is required for the development of self-consciousness. He thus debases himself to an infra-human condition. On the other hand, by carrying out his master's will the slave objectifies himself through labour which transforms material things. He thus forms himself and rises to the level of true existence.[20]

It is obvious that the concept of the master-slave relationship has two aspects. It can be considered as a stage in the abstract dialectical development of consciousness. And it can also be considered in relation to history. But the two aspects are by no means incompatible. For human history itself reveals the development of Spirit, the travail of the Spirit on the way to its goal. Hence we need not be surprised if from the master-slave relationship in its primary form Hegel passes to an attitude or state of consciousness to which he gives a name with explicit historical associations, namely the Stoic consciousness.

In the Stoic consciousness the contradictions inherent in the slave relationship are not really overcome: they are overcome only to the extent that both master (typified by Marcus

Aurelius) and slave (typified by Epictetus) take flight into interiority and exalt the idea of true interior freedom, internal self-sufficiency, leaving concrete relationships unchanged. Hence, according to Hegel, this negative attitude towards the concrete and external passes easily into the Sceptical consciousness for which the self alone abides while all else is subjected to doubt and negation.

But the Sceptical consciousness contains an implicit contradiction. For it is impossible for the sceptic to eliminate the natural consciousness; and affirmation and negation coexist in the same attitude. And when this contradiction becomes explicit, as it must do, we pass to what Hegel calls 'the unhappy consciousness' (*das unglückliche Bewusstsein*), which is a divided consciousness. At this level the masterslave relationship, which has not been successfully overcome by either the Stoic or the Sceptical consciousness, returns in another form. In the master-slave relationship proper the elements of true self-consciousness, recognition of selfhood and freedom both in oneself and in the Other, were divided between two individual consciousnesses. The master recognized selfhood and freedom only in himself, not in the slave, while the slave recognized them only in the master, not in himself. In the so-called unhappy consciousness, however, the division occurs in the same self. For example, the self is conscious of a gulf between a changing, inconsistent, fickle self and a changeless, ideal self. The first appears as in some sense a false self, something to be denied, while the second appears as the true self which is not yet attained. And this ideal self can be projected into an other-worldly sphere and identified with absolute perfection, God considered as existing apart from the world and the finite self.[21] The human consciousness is then divided, self-alienated, 'unhappy'.

The contradictions or divisions implicit in self-consciousness are overcome in the third phase of *The Phenomenology* when the finite subject rises to universal self-consciousness. At this level self-consciousness no longer takes the form of the one-sided awareness of oneself as an individual subject threatened by and in conflict with other self-conscious beings.

Rather is there a full recognition of selfhood in oneself and in others; and this recognition is at least an implicit awareness of the life of the universal, the infinite Spirit, in and through finite selves, binding them together yet not annulling them. Present implicitly and imperfectly in the developed moral consciousness, for which the one rational will expresses itself in a multiplicity of concrete moral vocations in the social order, this awareness of the identity-in-difference which is characteristic of the life of the Spirit attains a higher and more explicit expression in the developed religious consciousness, for which the one divine life is immanent in all selves, bearing them in itself while yet maintaining their distinctness. In the idea of a living union with God the division within the unhappy or divided consciousness is overcome. The true self is no longer conceived as an ideal from which the actual self is hopelessly alienated, but rather as the living core, so to speak, of the actual self, which expresses itself in and through its finite manifestations.

This third phase of the phenomenological history of consciousness, to which, as we have seen, Hegel gives the general name of Reason, is represented as the synthesis of consciousness and self-consciousness, that is, of the first two phases. In consciousness in the narrow sense (*Bewusstsein*) the subject is aware of the sensible object as something external and heterogeneous to itself. In self-consciousness (*Selbstbewusstsein*) the subject's attention is turned back on itself as a finite self. At the level of Reason it sees Nature as the objective expression of infinite Spirit with which it is itself united. But this awareness can take different forms. In the developed religious consciousness the subject sees Nature as the creation and self-manifestation of God, with whom it is united in the depth of its being and through whom it is united with other selves. And this religious vision of reality is true. But at the level of the religious consciousness truth finds expression in the form of figurative or pictorial thought (*Vorstellung*), whereas at the supreme level of 'absolute knowledge' (*das absolute Wissen*) the same truth is reflectively apprehended in philosophical form. The finite subject is explicitly aware

of its inmost self as a moment in the life of the infinite and
universal Spirit, as a moment in absolute Thought. And, as
such, it sees Nature as its own objectification and as the precondition of its own life as actually existing Spirit. This does
not mean, of course, that the finite subject considered precisely as such sees Nature as its own product. Rather does it
mean that the finite subject, aware of itself as more than
finite, as a moment in the innermost life of absolute Spirit,
sees Nature as a necessary stage in the onward march of Spirit
in its process of self-actualization. In other words, absolute
knowledge is the level at which the finite subject participates
in the life of self-thinking Thought, the Absolute. Or, to put
the matter in another way, it is the level at which the Absolute, the Totality, thinks itself as identity-in-difference in
and through the finite mind of the philosopher.

As in the previous main phases of the phenomenology of
consciousness Hegel develops the third phase, that of Reason,
through a series of dialectical stages. He treats first of observing Reason which is seen as obtaining some glimpse at any
rate of its own reflection in Nature (through the idea of
finality, for example), then as turning inwards in the study
of formal logic and of empirical psychology, and finally as
manifesting itself in a series of practical ethical attitudes,
ranging from the pursuit of happiness up to that criticism of
the universal moral laws dictated by the practical reason
which follows from recognition of the fact that a universal
law stands in need of so many qualifications that it tends to
lose all definite meaning. This sets the stage for the transition
to concrete moral life in society. Here Hegel moves from the
unreflective ethical life in which human beings simply follow
the customs and traditions of their community to the form of
culture in which individuals are estranged from this unreflective background and pass judgments about it. The two
moments are synthesized in the developed moral consciousness for which the rational general will is not something over
and above individuals in society but a common life binding
them together as free persons. In the first moment, we can
say, Spirit is unreflective, as in the ancient Greek morality

before the time of the so-called Sophists. In the second moment Spirit is reflective but at the same time estranged from actual society and its traditions, on which it passes judgment. In the extreme case, as in the Jacobin Terror, it annihilates actual persons in the name of abstract freedom. In the third moment, however, Spirit is said to be ethically sure of itself. It takes the form of a community of free persons embodying the general will as a living unity.

This living unity, however, in which each member of the community is for the others a free self demands an explicit recognition of the idea of identity-in-difference, of a life which is present in all as their inner bond of unity though it does not annihilate them as individuals. It demands, that is to say, an explicit recognition of the idea of the concrete universal which differentiates itself into or manifests itself in its particulars while uniting them within itself. In other words, morality passes dialectically into religion, the moral into the religious consciousness, for which this living unity is explicitly recognized in the form of God.

In religion, therefore, we see absolute Spirit becoming explicitly conscious of itself. But religion, of course, has its history; and in this history we see earlier phases of the dialectic being repeated. Thus Hegel moves from what he calls 'natural religion', in which the divine is seen under the form of perceptual objects or of Nature, to the religion of art or of beauty, in which, as in Greek religion, the divine is seen as the self-conscious associated with the physical. The statue, for example, represents the anthropomorphic deity. Finally, in the absolute religion, Christianity, absolute Spirit is recognized for what it is, namely Spirit; Nature is seen as a divine creation, the expression of the Word; and the Holy Spirit is seen as immanent in and uniting together finite selves.

But the religious consciousness expresses itself, as we have seen, in pictorial forms. And it demands to be transmuted into the pure conceptual form of philosophy which at the same time expresses the transition from faith to knowledge or science. That is to say, the pictorial idea of the transcendent personal Deity who saves man by a unique Incarnation and the power of grace passes into the concept of absolute Spirit, the infinite self-thinking Thought which knows itself in Nature (as its objectification and as the condition for its own actualization) and recognizes in the history of human culture, with its successive forms and levels, its own Odyssey. Hegel is not saying that religion is untrue. On the contrary, the absolute religion, Christianity, is the absolute truth. But it is expressed in the imaginative or pictorial form which is correlative to the religious consciousness. In philosophy this truth becomes absolute knowledge which is 'Spirit knowing itself in the form of Spirit.'[22] The Absolute, the Totality, comes to know itself in and through the human spirit, in so far, that is to say, as the human spirit rises above its finitude and identifies itself with pure Thought. God cannot be equated with man. For God is Being, the Totality, and man is not. But the Totality comes actually to know itself in and through the spirit of man; on the level of pictorial thought in the evolution of the religious consciousness, on the level of science or pure conceptual knowledge in the history of philosophy which has as its ideal term the complete truth about reality in the form of the Absolute's knowledge of itself.

In *The Phenomenology*, therefore, Hegel starts with the lowest levels of human consciousness and works dialectically upwards to the level at which the human mind attains the absolute point of view and becomes the vehicle, as it were, of infinite self-conscious Spirit. The connections between one level and the next are often very loose, logically speaking. And some of the stages are obviously suggested not so much by the demands of a dialectical development as by Hegel's reflections on the spirits and attitudes of different cultural phases and epochs. Further, some of the topics of which Hegel treats strike the modern reader as somewhat odd. There is, for example, a critical treatment of phrenology. At the same time, as a study of the Odyssey of the human spirit, of the movement from one attitude or outlook, which proves to be one-sided and inadequate, to another, the work is both impressive and fascinating. And the correlations between stages of the dialectic of consciousness and historically-manifested attitudes (the spirit of the Enlightenment, the romantic spirit, and so on) add to its interest. One may be suspicious of Hegel's summaries and interpretations of the spirits of epochs and cultures, and his exaltation of philosophical knowledge may strike one as having a comical aspect; but in spite of all reservations and disagreements the reader who really tries to penetrate into Hegel's thought can hardly come to any other conclusion than that *The Phenomenology* is one of the great works of speculative philosophy.

Chapter Ten

HEGEL (2)

The logic of Hegel – The ontological status of the Idea or Absolute in itself and the transition to Nature – The philosophy of Nature – The Absolute as Spirit; subjective Spirit – The concept of right – Morality – The family and civil society – The State – Explanatory comments on Hegel's idea of political philosophy – The function of war – Philosophy of history – Some comments on Hegel's philosophy of history.

1. As we have seen, Hegel rejected the view, advanced by Schelling in his so-called system of identity, that the Absolute in itself is for conceptual thought the vanishing-point of all differences, an absolute self-identity which cannot properly be described except in negative terms and which can be positively apprehended only, if at all, in mystical intuition. Hegel was convinced that the speculative reason can penetrate the inner essence of the Absolute, the essence which manifests itself in Nature and in the history of the human spirit.

The part of philosophy which is concerned with laying bare the inner essence of the Absolute is for Hegel logic. To anyone who is accustomed to regard logic as a purely formal science, entirely dissociated from metaphysics, this must seem an extraordinary and even absurd point of view. But we have to bear in mind the fact that for Hegel the Absolute is pure Thought. This Thought can be considered in itself, apart from its externalization or self-manifestation. And the science of pure Thought in itself is logic. Further, inasmuch as pure Thought is the substance, as it were, of reality, logic necessarily coincides with metaphysics, that is, with metaphysics as concerned with the Absolute in itself.

The matter can be made clearer by relating Hegel's concep-

tion of logic to Kant's view of transcendental logic. In the
philosophy of Kant the categories which give shape and form
to phenomena are *a priori* categories of human thought. The
human mind does not create things-in-themselves, but it determines the basic character of the phenomenal world, the
world of appearance. On Kant's premises, therefore, we have
no warrant for assuming that the categories of the human
mind apply to reality in itself; their cognitive function is limited to the phenomenal world. But, as was explained in the
introductory chapter, with the elimination of the unknowable
thing-in-itself and the transformation of the critical philosophy into pure idealism the categories become the categories
of creative thought in the full sense. And if a subjectivist
position, threatening to lead to solipsism, is to be avoided,
creative thought must be interpreted as absolute Thought.
The categories, therefore, become the categories of absolute
Thought, the categories of reality. And logic, which studies
them, becomes metaphysics. It discloses the essence or nature
of the absolute Thought which manifests itself in Nature and
history.

Now, Hegel speaks of the Absolute in itself as God in himself. The subject-matter of logic is 'the truth as it is without
husk and for itself. One can therefore express the matter by
saying that its content is the presentation of God as he is in
his eternal essence before the creation of Nature and of a
finite spirit.'[1] And this manner of speaking tends to suggest
the very odd picture of the logician penetrating the inner
essence of a transcendent Deity and describing it in terms of
a system of categories. But Hegel's use of religious language
can be misleading. We have to remember that though his
Absolute is certainly transcendent in the sense that it cannot
be identified with any particular finite entity or set of entities, it is not transcendent in the sense in which the God
of Christianity is said to transcend the created universe.
Hegel's Absolute is the Totality, and this Totality is depicted
as coming to know itself in and through the finite spirit, in
so far as the finite spirit attains the level of 'absolute knowledge'. Logic, therefore, is the Absolute's knowledge of itself

in itself, in abstraction from its concrete self-manifestation in Nature and history. That is to say, logic is absolute Thought's knowledge of its own essence, the essence which exists concretely in the process of reality.

If we use the word 'category' in a somewhat wider sense than that in which it is used by Hegel himself, we can say, therefore, that his logic is the system of categories. But if we say this, it is essential to understand that the whole system of categories is a progressive definition of the Absolute in itself. Hegel starts with the concept of being because it is for him the most indeterminate and the logically prior concept. And he then proceeds to show how this concept passes necessarily into successive concepts until we reach the absolute Idea, the concept or category of self-knowledge or self-consciousness, self-thinking Thought. But the Absolute is not, of course, a string or chain of categories or concepts. If we ask what the Absolute is, we can answer that it is being. And if we ask what being is, we shall in the end be forced to answer that being is self-thinking Thought or Spirit. The process of showing that this is the case, as worked out by the logician, is obviously a temporal process. But the Absolute in itself does not, to put the matter crudely, start as being at seven in the morning and end as self-thinking Thought at seven in the evening. To say that the Absolute is being is to say that it is self-thinking Thought. But the logician's demonstration of the fact, his systematic dialectical elucidation of the meaning of being, is a temporal process. It is his business to show that the whole system of categories turns in on itself, so to speak. The beginning is the end, and the end is the beginning. That is to say, the first category or concept contains all the others implicitly, and the last is the final explicitation of the first: it gives its true meaning.

The point is easily understood if we employ the religious or theological language which Hegel not infrequently uses. God is being, he is also self-thinking Thought. But the word 'also' is really inappropriate. For to say that God is being is to say that he is self-thinking Thought. The systematic exhibition of this fact by the philosopher is a temporal process.

But this temporality obviously does not affect the divine essence in itself. There is, of course, a great difference between Hegel's Absolute and the God of Christian theology. But though Hegel's Absolute is said to be the process of its own becoming, we are not concerned in logic with this actual process, the actualization of the *Logos:* we are concerned with the Absolute 'in itself', with the logical Idea. And this is not a temporal process.

The dialectical movement of Hegel's logic can be illustrated by means of the first three categories. The logically prior concept of the Absolute is the concept of being. But the concept or category of pure being (*reines Sein*) is wholly indeterminate. And the concept of wholly indeterminate being passes into the concept of not-being. That is to say, if we try to think being without any determination at all, we find that we are thinking nothing. The mind passes from being to not-being and from not-being back to being: it can rest in neither, and each disappears, as it were, in its opposite. 'Their truth is thus this *movement* of the immediate disappearing of the one into the other.'[2] And this movement from being to not-being and from not-being to being is becoming. Becoming is thus the synthesis of being and not-being; it is their unity and truth. Being must therefore be conceived as becoming. In other words, the concept of the Absolute as being is the concept of the Absolute as becoming, as a process of self-development.[3]

According to our ordinary way of looking at things a contradiction brings us to a full stop. Being and not-being are mutually exclusive. But we think in this way because we conceive being as determinate being and not-being as the not-being of this determination. Pure being, however, is for Hegel indeterminate, empty or vacuous; and it is for this reason that it is said to pass into its opposite. But contradiction is for Hegel a positive force which reveals both thesis and antithesis as abstract moments in a higher unity or synthesis. And this unity of the concepts of being and not-being is the concept of becoming. But the unity gives rise in turn to a 'contradiction', so that the mind is driven onwards in its search for the mean-

ing of being, for the nature or essence of the Absolute in
itself.

Being, not-being or nothing and becoming form the first
triad of the first part of Hegel's logic, the so-called logic of
being (*die Logik des Seins*). This part is concerned with the
categories of being-in-itself, as distinct from the categories of
relation. And the three main classes of categories in this part
of logic are those of quality, which include the above-men-
tioned triad, quantity and measure. Measure is described as
the synthesis of quality and quantity. For it is the concept of
a specific quantum determined by the nature of the object,
that is, by its quality.

In the second main part of the *Logic*, the logic of essence
(*die Logik des Wesens*), Hegel deduces pairs of related categories, such as essence and existence, force and expression,
substance and accident, cause and effect, action and reaction.
These categories are called categories of reflection because
they correspond with the reflective consciousness which penetrates beneath the surface, as it were, of being in its immediacy. Essence, for example, is conceived as lying behind
appearance, and force is conceived as the reality displayed in
its expression. In other words, for the reflective consciousness
being-in-itself undergoes self-diremption, breaking up into related categories.

But the logic of essence does not leave us with the division
of being into inner essence and outward phenomenal existence. For the last main subdivision is devoted to the category
of actuality (*die Wirklichkeit*) which is described as 'the
unity of essence and existence'.[4] That is to say, the actual is
the inner essence which ex-ists, the force which has found
complete expression. If we identify being with appearance,
with its external manifestation, this is a one-sided abstraction.
But so is the identification of being with a hidden essence
underlying appearance. Being as actuality is the unity of the
inner and the outer; it is essence manifesting itself. And it
must manifest itself.

It is under the general heading of the category of actuality
that Hegel deduces the categories of substance and accident,

cause and effect, and action and reaction or reciprocal action. And as we have said that his logic is a progressive definition or determination of the nature of the Absolute in itself, the impression may be given that for him there is only one substance and one cause, namely the Absolute. In other words the impression may be given that Hegel embraces Spinozism. But this would be an incorrect interpretation of his meaning. The deduction of the categories of substance and cause is not intended to imply, for example, that there can be no such thing as a finite cause. For the Absolute as actuality is essence manifesting itself; and the manifestation is the universe as we know it. The Absolute is not simply the One. It is the One, but it is also the Many: it is identity-in-difference.

From the logic of essence Hegel passes to the logic of the Concept (*die Logik des Begriffs*) which is the third main part of his work. In the logic of being each category is at first sight independent, standing on its own feet, as it were, even if the dialectical movement of thought breaks down this apparent self-containedness. In the logic of essence we are concerned with obviously related categories, such as cause and effect or substance and accident. We are thus in the sphere of mediation. But each member of a pair of related categories is conceived as mediated 'by another', that is, by something different from itself. The cause, for example, is constituted as a cause by passing into its opposite, namely the effect, which is conceived as something different from the cause. Similarly, the effect is constituted as an effect by its relation to something different from itself, namely the cause. The synthesis of the spheres of immediacy and of mediation by another will be the sphere of self-mediation. A being is said to be self-mediating when it is conceived as passing into its opposite and yet as remaining identical with itself even in this self-opposition. And the self-mediating is what Hegel calls the Concept or the Notion.[5]

Needless to say, the logic of the Notion has three main subdivisions. In the first Hegel considers the Notion as 'subjectivity', as thought in its formal aspects. And this part corresponds more or less with logic in the ordinary sense. Hegel tries to show how the general idea of being going out from itself and then returning to itself at a higher level is verified in a formal manner in the movement of logical thought. Thus the unity of the universal concept is divided in the judgment and is re-established at a higher level in the syllogism.

Having considered the Notion as subjectivity, Hegel goes on to consider it as objectivity. And as in the first phase or part of the logic of the Notion he finds three moments, the universal concept, the judgment and syllogistic inference, so in this second phase or part he finds three moments, namely mechanism, chemism and teleology. He thus anticipates the main ideas of the philosophy of Nature. But he is concerned here with the thought or concept of the objective rather than with Nature considered as an empirically-given existing reality. The nature of the Absolute is such that it comprises the concept of self-objectification.

Given the character of the Hegelian dialectic, the third phase of the logic of the Notion will obviously be the synthesis or unity on a higher plane of subjectivity and objectivity. As such the Notion is called the Idea. In the Idea the one-sided factors of the formal and the material, the subjective and the objective, are brought together. But the Idea too has its phases or moments. And in the final subdivision of the logic of the Notion Hegel considers in turn life, knowledge and their unity in the absolute Idea which is, as it were, the union of subjectivity and objectivity enriched with rational life. In other words, the absolute Idea is the concept or category of self-consciousness, personality, self-thinking Thought which knows itself in its object and its object as itself. It is thus the category of Spirit. In religious language, it is the concept of God in and for himself, knowing himself as the totality.

After a long dialectical wandering, therefore, being has at length revealed itself as the absolute Idea, as self-thinking Thought. The Absolute is being, and the meaning of this statement has now been made explicit. 'The absolute Idea alone is *being*, eternal *life*, *self-knowing truth*, and it is *all truth*. It is the one subject-matter and content of philosophy.'[6] Hegel does not mean, of course, that the logical Idea, considered precisely as such, is the one subject-matter of philosophy. But philosophy is concerned with reality as a whole, with the Absolute. And reality, in the sense of Nature and the sphere of the human spirit, is the process by which the logical Idea or *Logos* actualizes itself. Hence philosophy is always concerned with the Idea.

2. Now, if we speak of the logical Idea or *Logos* as manifesting or expressing itself in Nature and in the sphere of the human spirit, we are obviously faced with the question, what is the ontological status of the logical Idea or the Absolute in itself? Is it a reality which exists independently of the world and which manifests itself in the world, or is it not? If it is, how can there be a subsistent Idea? If it is not, how can we speak of the Idea as manifesting or actualizing itself?

At the end of the *Logic* in the *Encyclopaedia of the Philosophical Sciences*[7] Hegel asserts that the Idea 'in its absolute freedom . . . *resolves* to let its moment of particularity . . . the immediate Idea as its reflected image, go forth freely out of itself as Nature'.[8] In this passage, therefore, Hegel seems to imply not only that Nature is ontologically derived from the Idea but also that the Idea freely posits Nature. And if this implication were taken literally, we should clearly have to interpret the Idea as a name for the personal creative Deity. For it would be preposterous to speak of an Idea in any other sense as 'resolving' to do something.

But consideration of the Hegelian system as a whole suggests that this passage represents an intrusion, as it were, of the way of speaking which is characteristic of the Christian religious consciousness, and that its implications should not be pressed. It seems to be clear enough that according to Hegel the doctrine of free creation by God belongs to the figurative or pictorial language of the religious consciousness. It expresses indeed a truth, but it does not do so in the idiom of pure philosophy. From the strictly philosophical point of view the Absolute in itself manifests itself necessarily in Nature. Obviously, it is not constrained to do so by anything external to itself. The necessity is an inner necessity of nature.

The only freedom in the *Logos'* self-manifestation is the freedom of spontaneity. And from this it follows that from the philosophical point of view there is no sense in speaking of the Absolute in itself as existing 'before' creation. If Nature is derived ontologically from the Idea, the latter is not temporally prior to the former.[9] Further, though some writers have interpreted Hegel in a theistic sense, as holding, that is to say, that the Absolute in itself is a personal Being, existing independently of Nature and of the sphere of the human spirit, it does not seem to me that this interpretation is correct. True, there are passages which can be cited in support of it. But these passages can equally well be interpreted as expressions of the religious consciousness, as pictorial or figurative statements of the truth. And the nature of the system as a whole clearly suggests that the Absolute attains actual self-consciousness only in and through the human spirit. As has already been explained, this does not mean that human consciousness can be identified without more ado with the divine self-consciousness. For the Absolute is said to know itself in and through the human mind in so far as this mind rises above mere finitude and particularity and reaches the level of absolute knowledge. But the point is that if the Absolute becomes actually existent only in and through the human spirit, the Absolute in itself, the logical Idea, cannot properly be said to 'resolve' to posit Nature, which is the objective precondition for the existence of the sphere of Spirit. If such language is used, it is a concession, as it were, to the mode of thought which is characteristic of the religious consciousness.

If, however, we exclude the theistic interpretation of the Absolute in itself,[10] how are we to conceive the transition from the logical Idea to Nature? If we conceive it as a real ontological transition, that is to say, if we conceive a subsistent Idea as manifesting itself necessarily in Nature, we are obviously attributing to Hegel a thesis which, to put it mildly, is somewhat odd. We expose him at once to the criticism made by Schelling in his polemic against 'negative philosophy', that from ideas we can deduce only other ideas, and that it is quite impossible to deduce an existing world from an Idea.

It is understandable, therefore, that some writers have endeavoured to exclude altogether the concept of an ontological derivation of Nature from the Idea. The Absolute is the totality, the universe. And this totality is a teleological process, the actualization of self-thinking Thought. The essential nature of this process can be considered in abstraction. It then takes the form of the logical Idea. But it does not exist as a subsistent reality which is logically prior to Nature and which is the efficient cause of Nature. The Idea reflects the goal or result of the process rather than a subsistent reality which stands at its beginning. Hence there is no question of an ontological derivation of Nature from the logical Idea as efficient cause. And the so-called deduction of Nature from the Idea is really an exhibition of the fact, or alleged fact, that Nature is a necessary precondition for the realization of the goal of the total process of reality, the universe's knowledge of itself in and through the human spirit.

It seems to the present writer that the foregoing line of interpretation must be accepted in so far as it denies the separate existence of the logical Idea as a reality quite distinct from the world or as an external efficient cause of the world. For Hegel the infinite exists in and through the finite; the universal lives and has its being, as it were, in and through the particulars. Hence there is no room in his system for an efficient cause which transcends the world in the sense that it exists quite independently of it. At the same time, even though the infinite exists in and through the finite, it is obvious that finite things arise and perish. They are, so to speak, transitory manifestations of an infinite Life. And Hegel certainly tends to speak of the *Logos* as though it were pulsating Life, dynamic Reason or Thought. It exists, it is true, only in and through its manifestations. But inasmuch as it is a continuous Life, Being actualizing itself as what it potentially is, namely Spirit, it is quite natural to look on the passing manifestations as ontologically dependent on the one immanent Life, as an 'outside' in relation to an 'inside'. And Hegel can thus speak of the *Logos* spontaneously expressing itself in or going over into Nature. For Being, the Absolute, the infinite Totality, is not a mere collection of finite things, but one infinite Life, self-actualizing Spirit. It is the universal of universals; and even though it exists only in and through the particulars, it itself persists whereas the particulars do not. Hence it is perfectly reasonable to speak of the *Logos* as expressing or manifesting itself in finite things. And inasmuch as it is absolute Spirit which comes to exist as such through the process of its own self-development, material Nature is naturally conceived as its opposite, the opposite which is a precondition for the attainment of the end or *telos* of the process.

This line of interpretation may seem to be an attempt to have things both ways. On the one hand it is admitted that the logical Idea does not exist as a subsistent reality which creates Nature from outside, as it were. On the other hand, it is claimed that the logical Idea, in the sense of the essential structure or meaning of Being as grasped by the metaphysician, represents a metaphysical reality which, though it exists only in and through its self-manifestation, is in a certain sense logically prior to its manifestation. But I do not think that we can exclude metaphysics from Hegelianism or eliminate altogether a certain element of transcendence. The attempt to do this seems to me to make nonsense of Hegel's doctrine of the infinite Absolute. The Absolute is indeed the totality, the universe, considered as the process of its own self-development; but in my opinion we cannot escape making a distinction between inner and outer, between, that is to say, the one infinite Life, self-actualizing Spirit, and the finite manifestations in and through which it lives and has its being. And in this case we can equally well say that the finite manifestations derive their reality from the one Life which expresses itself in them. If there is a certain element of ambiguity in Hegel's position, this is scarcely surprising. For if there were no such element, his philosophy would hardly have given rise to divergent interpretations.

3. 'Nature,' says Hegel, 'is *in itself*, in the Idea, divine.

. . . But as it exists, its being does not correspond with its concept.'[11] In the language of religion, the idea of Nature in the divine mind is divine, but the objectification of this idea in existing Nature cannot be called divine. For the fact that the idea is expressed in the material world, in that which is most unlike God, means that it is only inadequately expressed. God cannot be adequately manifested in the material world. In the language of philosophy, the Absolute is defined as Spirit. Hence it can manifest itself adequately only in the sphere of Spirit. Nature is a precondition of the existence of this sphere, but it is not in itself Spirit, though in its rational structure it bears the imprint of Spirit. One might say with Schelling that it is slumbering Spirit or visible Spirit; but it is not Spirit proper, Spirit as awoken to consciousness of itself.

Spirit is freedom: Nature is the sphere of necessity rather than of freedom. It is also the sphere of contingency (*Zufälligkeit*). For example, it does not exhibit in any uniformly clear-cut way the distinctions postulated by a purely rational pattern. There are, for instance, 'monsters' in Nature which do not conform clearly to any one specific type. And there are even natural species which seem to be due to a kind of Bacchic dance or revel on Nature's part, and not to any rational necessity. Nature appears to run riot as much in the wealth of forms which she produces as in the number of individual members of given species. They elude all logical deduction. Obviously, an empirical explanation of any natural object can be given in terms of physical causality. But to give an empirical explanation in terms of physical causality is not the same thing as to give a logical deduction.

Obviously, Nature cannot exist without particular things. Immanent teleology, for instance, cannot exist without particular organisms. The universal exists only in and through its particulars. But it does not follow that any given individual is logically deducible from the concept of its specific type or from any more general concept. It is not simply a question of its being very difficult or practically impossible for the finite mind to deduce particulars which could in principle be deduced by an infinite mind. For Hegel seems to say that par-

ticular objects in Nature are not deducible even in principle, even though they are physically explicable. To put the
matter somewhat paradoxically, contingency in Nature is necessary. For without it there could be no Nature. But contingency is none the less real, in the sense that it is a factor in
Nature which the philosopher is unable to eliminate. And
Hegel ascribes it to 'the *impotence* of Nature'[12] to remain
faithful to the determination of the Notion. He is speaking
here about the way in which Nature mixes specific types,
producing intermediate forms. But the main point is that contingency is ascribed to the impotence of Nature itself and
not to the finite mind's incapability of giving a purely rational
account of Nature. Whether on his principles Hegel ought
to have admitted contingency in Nature is disputable, but
the fact that he did so is not open to doubt. And this is why
he sometimes speaks of Nature as a Fall (*Abfall*) from the
Idea. In other words, contingency represents the externality
of Nature in relation to the Idea. And it follows that Nature
'is not to be deified'.[13] Indeed, it is a mistake, Hegel says, to
regard natural phenomena such as the heavenly bodies as
works of God in a higher sense than the creations of the human spirit, such as works of art or the State. Hegel certainly
followed Schelling in attributing to Nature a status which it
did not enjoy in the philosophy of Fichte. At the same time
he shows no inclination to share the romantic divinization of
Nature.

But though Hegel rejects any deification of existing Nature,
the fact remains that if Nature is real it must be a moment
in the life of the Absolute. For the Absolute is the totality.
Hegel is thus placed in a difficult position. On the one hand
he has no wish to deny that there is an objective Nature. Indeed, it is essential to his system to maintain that there is. For
the Absolute is the identity-in-difference of subjectivity and
objectivity. And if there is real subjectivity, there must be
real objectivity. On the other hand it is not easy for him to
explain how contingency can have any place in a system of
absolute idealism. And it is understandable if we can discern
a marked tendency to adopt a Platonic position by distinguish-

ing between the inside, as it were, of Nature, its rational structure or reflection of the Idea, and its outside, its contingent aspect, and by relegating the latter to the sphere of the irrational and unreal. There must indeed be an objective Nature. For the Idea must take the form of objectivity. And there cannot be an objective Nature without contingency. But the philosopher cannot cope with this element, beyond registering the fact that it is there and must be there. And what Professor Hegel cannot cope with he tends to dismiss as irrational and so as unreal. For the rational is the real and the real the rational. Obviously, once contingency has been admitted Hegel is driven either to admit some kind of dualism or to slide over the contingent element in Nature as though it were not 'really real'.

However this may be, Nature, in so far as it can be treated by the philosopher, 'is to be considered as a system of stages, of which one proceeds necessarily from the other'.[14] But it must be clearly understood that this system of stages or levels in Nature is a dialectical development of concepts and not an empirical history of Nature. It is indeed somewhat amusing to find Hegel dismissing the evolutionary hypothesis in a cavalier manner.[15] But a physical hypothesis of this kind is in any case irrelevant to the philosophy of Nature as expounded by Hegel. For it introduces the idea of temporal succession which has no place in the dialectical deduction of the levels of Nature. And if Hegel had lived to a time when the evolutionary hypothesis had won wide acceptance, it would have been open to him to say: 'Well, I dare say that I was wrong about evolution. But in any case it is an empirical hypothesis, and its acceptance or rejection does not affect the validity of my dialectic.'

As one would expect, the main divisions of Hegel's philosophy of Nature are three in number. In the *Encyclopaedia* they are given as mathematics, physics and organic physics, while in the lectures on the philosophy of Nature they are given as mechanics, physics and organics. In both cases, however, Hegel starts with space, with what is most removed from mind or Spirit, and works dialectically up to the animal organism which of all levels of Nature is the closest to Spirit. Space is sheer externality: in the organism we find internality. Subjectivity can be said to make its appearance in the animal organism, though not in the form of self-consciousness. Nature brings us to the threshold of Spirit, but only to the threshold.

It is hardly worth while following Hegel into the details of his philosophy of Nature. But attention should be drawn to the fact that he is not trying to do the work of the scientist all over again by some peculiar philosophical method of his own. He is concerned rather with finding in Nature as known through observation and science the exemplification of a dynamic rational pattern. This may sometimes lead to bizarre attempts to show that natural phenomena are what they are, or what Hegel believes that they are, because it is rational and, so to speak, for the best that they should be what they are. And we may well feel somewhat sceptical about the value of this kind of speculative or higher physics, as well as amused at the philosopher's tendency to look down on empirical science from a superior position. But it is as well to understand that Hegel takes empirical science for granted, even if he sometimes takes sides, and not always to the advantage of his reputation, in controversial issues. It is more a question of fitting the facts into a conceptual scheme than of pretending to deduce the facts in a purely *a priori* manner.

4. 'The Absolute is Spirit: this is the highest definition of the Absolute. To find this definition and to understand its content was, one may say, the final motive of all culture and philosophy. All religion and science have striven to reach this point.'[16] The Absolute in itself is Spirit, but it is potential rather than actual Spirit.[17] The Absolute for itself, Nature, is Spirit, but it is 'self-alienated Spirit',[18] in religious language it is, as Hegel puts it, God in his otherness. Spirit begins to exist as such only when we come to the human spirit, which is studied by Hegel in the third main part of his system, the philosophy of Spirit.

The philosophy of Spirit, needless to say, has three main parts or subdivisions. 'The two first parts of the doctrine of

Spirit treat of the finite spirit',[19] while the third part deals with absolute Spirit, the *Logos* in its concrete existence as self-thinking Thought. In this section we shall be concerned only with the first part, to which Hegel gives the title 'subjective Spirit'.

This first part of the philosophy of Spirit is subdivided, according to Hegel's pervasive dialectical scheme, into three subordinate parts. Under the heading of anthropology he treats of the soul (*Seele*) as sensing and feeling subject. The soul is, as it were, a point of transition from Nature to Spirit. On the one hand it reveals the ideality of Nature, while on the other hand it is 'only the *sleep* of the Spirit'.[20] That is to say, it enjoys self-feeling (*Selbstgefühl*) but not reflective self-consciousness. It is sunk in the particularity of its feelings. And it is actual precisely as embodied, the body being the externality of the soul. In the human organism soul and body are its inner and outer aspects.

From the concept of the soul in this restricted sense Hegel passes to the phenomenology of consciousness, resuming some of the themes already treated in *The Phenomenology of Spirit*. The soul of the section on anthropology was subjective spirit considered on its lowest level, as a yet undifferentiated unity. On the level of consciousness, however, subjective spirit is confronted by an object, first by an object regarded as external to and independent of the subject, then, in self-consciousness, by itself. Finally, the subject is depicted as rising to universal self-consciousness in which it recognizes other selves as both distinct from and one with itself. Here, therefore, consciousness (consciousness, that is, of something external to the subject) and self-consciousness are unified on a higher level.

The third section of the philosophy of subjective Spirit is entitled 'mind' or 'spirit' (*Geist*), and it considers the powers or general modes of activity of the finite spirit as such. We are no longer concerned simply with slumbering spirit, the 'soul' of the section on anthropology, nor, as in phenomenology, with the ego or subject in relation to an object. We have returned from the finite spirit as term of a relation to spirit in itself but at a higher level than that of soul. In a sense we are concerned with psychology rather than with the phenomenology of consciousness. But the psychology in question is not empirical psychology but a dialectical deduction of the concepts of the logically successive stages in the activity of the finite spirit in itself.

Hegel studies the activity of the finite spirit or mind in both its theoretical and its practical aspects. Under the theoretical aspect he treats, for instance, of intuition, memory, imagination and thought, while under the practical aspect he considers feeling, impulse and will. And his conclusion is that 'the actual free will is the unity of the theoretical and practical spirit; *free will which exists for itself as free will*'.[21] He is speaking, of course, of the will as conscious of its freedom. And this is '*will* as free *intelligence*'.[22] We can say, therefore, that the concept of Spirit in itself is the concept of the rational will (*der vernünftige Wille*).

But 'whole regions of the world, Africa and the East, have never had this idea and do not yet have it. The Greeks and the Romans, Plato and Aristotle, also the Stoics, did not have it. On the contrary, they knew only that man is actually free by birth (as a citizen of Athens or Sparta and so on) or through strength of character, education or philosophy (the wise man is free even when he is a slave and in chains). This idea entered the world through Christianity, according to which the individual *as such* possesses an *infinite* value, . . . that is, that man *in himself* is destined to the highest freedom.'[23] This idea of the realization of freedom is a key-idea in Hegel's philosophy of history.

5. We have seen that the Absolute in itself objectifies or expresses itself in Nature. So also does Spirit in itself objectify or express itself, issuing, as it were, out of its state of immediacy. Thus we come to the sphere of 'objective Spirit', the second main part of the philosophy of Spirit as a whole.

The first phase of objective Spirit is the sphere of right (*das Recht*). The person, the individual subject conscious of his freedom, must give external expression to his nature as free spirit; he must 'give himself an external sphere of free-

dom'.[24] And he does this by expressing his will in the realm
of material things. That is to say, he expresses his free will by
effectively appropriating and using material things. Personality confers the capacity for having and exercising rights such
as that of property. A material thing, precisely because it is
material and not spiritual, can have no rights: it is an instrument for the expression of rational will. By its being
taken possession of and used a thing's non-personal nature
is actually revealed and its destiny fulfilled. Indeed, it is in a
sense elevated by being thus set in relation to a rational will.

A person becomes the owner of a thing not by a merely
internal act of will but by effective appropriation, by embodying his will in it, as it were.[25] But he can also withdraw
his will from the thing, thereby alienating it. And this is
possible because the thing is external to him. A man can re-
linquish his right, for example, to a house. He can also re-
linquish his right to his labour for a limited time and for a
specified purpose. For his labour can then be looked upon as
something external. But he cannot alienate his total freedom
by handing himself over as a slave. For his total freedom is
not and cannot properly be regarded as something external to
himself. Nor can his moral conscience or his religion be regarded as an external thing.[26]

In Hegel's somewhat odd dialectical progression the concept of alienation of property leads us to the concept of contract (*Vertrag*). True, alienation of property might take the
form of withdrawing one's will, as it were, from a thing and
leaving it ownerless. I might alienate an umbrella in this way.
But we then remain within the sphere of the abstract concept of property. We advance beyond this sphere by introducing the concept of the unity of two or more individual wills
in respect of property, that is, by developing the concept of
contract. When a man gives, sells or exchanges by agreement, two wills come together. But he can also agree with
one or more persons to possess and use certain property in
common for a common end. And here the union of wills,
mediated by an external thing, is more evident.

But though contract rests on a union of wills, there is ob-

viously no guarantee that the particular wills of the contracting parties will remain in union. In this sense the union of
wills into a common will is contingent. And it comprises
within itself the possibility of its own negation. This negation is actualized in wrong. The concept of wrong, however,
passes through several phases; and Hegel considers in turn
civil wrong (which is the result of incorrect interpretation
rather than of evil intent or disrespect of other persons'
rights), fraud and crime and violence. The notion of crime
brings him to the subject of punishment, which he interprets as a cancellation of wrong, a cancellation which is said
to be demanded even by the implicit will of the criminal
himself. A criminal, according to Hegel, is not to be treated
like an animal which has to be deterred or reformed. As a
rational free being, he implicitly consents to and even demands the annulment of his crime through punishment.

Now, it is easy to see how Hegel is led from the concept of
contract to that of wrong. For contract, as a free act, involves
the possibility of its violation. But it is not so easy to see how
the concept of wrong can reasonably be regarded as the unity
on a higher plane of the concepts of property and contract.
However, it is obvious that Hegel's dialectic is often a process of rational reflection in which one idea leads more or less
naturally to another than a process of strictly necessary deduction. And even though he persists in observing his uniform
triadic scheme, there is not much point in pressing it.

6. In wrong there is an opposition between the particular
will and the universal will, the principle of rightness, which
is implicit in the common will expressed in contract. This is
true at least of wrong in the form of crime. The particular
will negates right, and in doing so it negates the conception
or notion of the will, which is universal, the rational free will
as such. As we have seen, punishment is the negation of this
negation. But punishment is external, in the sense that it is
inflicted by an external authority. The opposition or negation
can be adequately overcome only when the particular will is
in harmony with the universal will, that is, when it becomes
what it ought to be, namely in accord with the concept of the

will as raised above mere particularity and selfishness. Such a will is the moral will. We are thus led to make the transition from the concept of right to that of morality (*Moralität*).

It is important to note that the term 'morality' is used by Hegel in a much more restricted sense than it bears in ordinary usage. True, the term can be used in a variety of ways in ordinary language. But when we think of morality, we generally think of the fulfilment of positive duties, especially in a social setting, whereas Hegel abstracts from particular duties, towards the family, for example, or the State, and uses the term for what he calls 'a determination of the will [*Willensbestimmtheit*], so far as it is in the interior of the will in general'.[27] The moral will is free will which has returned on itself, that is, which is conscious of itself as free and which recognizes only itself, and no external authority, as the principle of its actions. As such the will is said to be 'infinite' or universal not only in itself but also for itself. 'The moral standpoint is the standpoint of the will in so far as it is *infinite* not simply *in itself* but *for itself*.'[28] It is the will as conscious of itself as the source of its own principle of action in an unrestricted way. Hegel does indeed introduce in passing the topic of obligation or ought (*Sollen*). For the will considered as a particular finite will may not be in accordance with the will considered as universal; and what is willed by the latter thus appears to the former as a demand or obligation. And, as will be seen presently, he discusses action from the point of view of the responsibility of the subject for its action. But in his treatment of morality he is concerned with the autonomous free will in its subjective aspect, that is, with the purely formal aspect of morality (in the wider sense of the term).

This purely formal treatment of morality is, of course, an unfortunate legacy from the Kantian philosophy. It is all the more important, therefore, to understand that morality, as Hegel uses the term, is a one-sided concept in which the mind cannot rest. It is certainly not his intention to imply that morality consists simply of 'interiority'. On the contrary, it is his intention to show that the purely formal concept of morality is inadequate. And we can say, therefore, that he treats the Kantian ethic as a one-sided moment in the dialectical development of the full moral consciousness. If, then, we use the term 'morality' to mean the whole ethical life of man, it would be quite incorrect to say that Hegel makes it entirely formal and 'interior' or subjective. For he does nothing of the kind. At the same time it is arguable that in the transition from morality in the restricted sense (*Moralität*) to the concrete ethical life (*Sittlichkeit*) some important elements in the moral consciousness are omitted or at least slurred over.

The subjective will externalizes itself in action. But the free will, as self-determined, has the right to regard as its own action, for which it can be held accountable, only those acts which stand in certain relations to it. We can say, therefore, that Hegel raises the question, for what actions can a person rightly be held accountable? Or, what are, properly speaking, the actions of a person? But it must be remembered that Hegel is thinking of the general formal characteristics of actions, and that he is not concerned at this stage with indicating where a person's concrete moral duties lie. For the matter of that, a person can be accountable for bad as well as for good actions. Hegel is, as it were, going behind the moral distinction between good and bad to the characteristics of action which make it possible for us to say that a person has acted morally or immorally.

In the first place any change or alteration in the world which the subject brings about can be called his 'deed' (*Handlung*). But he has the right to recognize as his 'action' (*That*) only that deed which was the purpose (*Vorsatz*) of his will. The external world is the sphere of contingency, and I cannot hold myself responsible for the unforeseeable consequences of my action. It does not follow, of course, that I can disavow all its consequences. For some consequences are simply the outward shape which my acting necessarily assumes, and they must be counted as comprised within my purpose. But it would be contrary to the idea of the self-determining free will to hold myself responsible for the unforeseeable conse-

quences or alterations in the world which are in some sense
my deed but which were certainly not comprised within my
purpose.

Purpose is thus the first phase of morality. The second is
intention (*Absicht*) or, more accurately, intention and welfare or well-being (*das Wohl*). It seems true to say that we
generally use the words 'purpose' and 'intention' synony-
mously. But Hegel distinguishes between them. If I apply a
lighted match to inflammable material in the grate, the natural and foreseen consequence of my action is the ensuing fire.
My purpose was to light the fire. But I should not perform
this action except in view of an intended end, such as warming myself or drying the room. And my intention is relevant
to the moral character of the action. It is not, of course, the
only relevant factor. Hegel is far from saying that any sort of
action is justified by a good intention. But intention is none
the less a moment or relevant factor in morality.

Hegel assumes that intentions are directed to welfare or
well-being. And he insists that the moral agent has a right to
seek his own welfare, the satisfaction of his needs as a human
being. He is not suggesting, of course, that egoism is the norm
or morality. But at present we are considering morality apart
from its social framework and expression. And when Hegel
insists that a man has a right to seek his own welfare, he is
saying that the satisfaction of one's needs as a human being
belongs to morality and is not opposed to it. In other words,
he is defending a point of view comprised in Greek ethics as
represented by Aristotle and rejecting the Kantian notion that
an act loses its moral value if performed from inclination. In
his opinion it is quite wrong to suppose that morality consists
in a constant warfare against inclinations and natural impulses.

But though the individual is entitled to seek his own welfare, morality certainly does not consist in the particular will
seeking its particular good. At the same time this idea has to
be preserved and not simply negated. Hence we must proceed
to the idea of the particular will identifying itself with the
rational and so universal will and aiming at universal wel-

fare. And the unity of the particular will with the concept of the will in itself (that is, with the rational will as such) is the good (*das Gute*), which can be described as 'the realization of freedom, the absolute final purpose of the world'.[29]

The rational will as such is a man's true will, his will as a rational, free being. And the need for conforming his particular will, his will as this or that particular individual, to the rational will (to his true self, one might say) presents itself as duty or obligation. Inasmuch, therefore, as morality abstracts from all concrete positive duties, we can say that duty should be done for duty's sake. A man ought to conform his particular will to the universal will, which is his true or real will; and he ought to do so simply because it is his duty. But this, of course, tells us nothing about what a man ought to will in particular. We can only say that the good will is determined by the subject's inward certainty, which is conscience (*Gewissen*). 'Conscience expresses the absolute right of subjective self-consciousness to know *in itself* and *through itself* what is right and duty, and to recognize nothing as good other than what it knows to be good, at the same time asserting that what it knows and wills as good is in truth right and duty.'[30]

Hegel thus incorporates into his account of morality what we may perhaps call the Protestant insistence on inwardness and on the absolute authority of conscience. But pure subjectivism and inwardness are really abhorrent to him. And he proceeds immediately to argue that to rely on a purely subjective conscience is to be potentially evil. If he had contented himself with saying that a person's conscience can err and that some objective norm or standard is required, he would have been expounding a familiar and easily intelligible position. But he gives the impression of trying to establish a connection between undiluted moral inwardness and wickedness, at least as a possible conjunction. Exaggeration apart, however, his main point is that we cannot give a definite content to morality on the level of pure moral inwardness. To do so, we have to turn to the idea of organized society.

The concepts of abstract right and of morality are thus

for Hegel one-sided notions which have to be unified on a higher level in the concept of ethical life (*die Sittlichkeit*). That is to say, in the dialectical development of the sphere of objective Spirit they reveal themselves as moments or phases in the development of the concept of concrete ethics, phases which have at the same time to be negated, preserved and elevated.

Concrete ethics is for Hegel social ethics. It is one's position in society which specifies one's duties. Hence social ethics is the synthesis or unity at a higher level of the one-sided concepts of right and morality.

7. Hegel's way of dealing with the concrete life is to deduce the three moments of what he calls 'the ethical substance' (*die sittliche Substanz*). These are the family, civil society and the State. One might perhaps expect him to consider man's concrete duties in this social setting. But what he actually does is to study the essential natures of the family, civil society and the State and to show how one concept leads to another. It is not necessary, he remarks, to add that a man has these or those duties towards his family or towards the State. For this will be sufficiently evident from a study of the natures or essences of these societies. In any case it cannot properly be expected of the philosopher that he should draw up a code of particular duties. He is concerned with the universal, with the dialectical development of concepts, rather than with moralizing.

The family, the first moment in 'the ethical substance' or union of moral subjectivity and objectivity, is said to be 'the immediate or natural ethical spirit'.[31] In the social sphere the human spirit, issuing, as it were, out of its inwardness, objectifies itself first of all in the family. This is not to say that in Hegel's opinion the family is a transitory institution which passes away when other types of society have reached their full development. It is to say that the family is the logically prior society inasmuch as it represents the universal in its logically first moment of immediacy. The members of the family are considered as one, united primarily by the bond of feeling, that is, by love.[32] The family is what one might call a feeling-totality. It is, as it were, one person whose will is expressed in property, the common property of the family.

But if we consider the family in this way, we must add that it contains within itself the seeds of its own dissolution. Within the family, considered as a feeling-totality and as representing the moment of universality, the children exist simply as members. They are, of course, individual persons, but they are such *in* themselves rather than *for* themselves. In the course of time, however, they pass out of the unity of family life into the condition of individual persons, each of whom possesses his own plans in life and so on. It is as though the particulars emerge out of the universality of family life and assert themselves as particulars.

The notion of the comparatively undifferentiated unity of the family breaking up through the emergence of particularity is not in itself, of course, the notion of a society. Rather is it the notion of the dissolution or negation of a society. But this negation is itself negated or overcome in what Hegel calls 'civil society' (*die bürgerliche Gesellschaft*) which represents the second moment in the development of social ethics.

To understand what Hegel means by civil society we can first picture a plurality of individuals, each of whom seeks his own ends and endeavours to satisfy his own needs. We must then conceive them as united in a form of economic organization for the better furtherance of their ends. This will involve specialization of labour and the development of economic classes and corporations. Further, an economic organization of this kind requires for its stability the institution of law and the machinery of law-enforcements, namely law-courts, a judiciary and police.

Inasmuch as Hegel considers the political constitution and government under the heading of the State and not under that of civil society, we may be inclined to comment that the latter could never exist. For how can there be laws and the administration of justice except in a State? The answer is, of course, that there cannot. But Hegel is not concerned with maintaining that civil society ever existed in the precise form in which he describes it. For the concept of civil society is for him a one-sided and inadequate concept of the State itself. It is the State 'as external State'.[33] That is to say, it is the State with the latter's essential nature omitted.

In other words, Hegel is concerned with the dialectical development of the concept of the State. And he does so by taking two one-sided concepts of society and showing that both represent ideas which are united on a higher plane in the concept of the State. The family, of course, persists in the State. So does civil society. For it represents an aspect of the State, even though it is only a partial aspect. But it does not follow that this aspect, taken in isolation and called 'civil society', ever actually existed precisely as such. The dialectical development of the concept of the State is a conceptual development. It is not equivalent to the statement that, historically speaking, the family existed first, then civil society, then the State, as though these concepts were all mutually exclusive. If we interpret Hegel in this way, we shall probably be inclined to think that he is concerned with expounding a thoroughly totalitarian theory of the State as against, for example, the sort of theory advanced by Herbert Spencer which more or less corresponds, though with certain important qualifications, to the concept of civil society. But though Hegel would doubtless have regarded Spencer's theory of society as very inadequate, he thought of the moment of particularity, represented by the concept of civil society, as being preserved, and not simply cancelled out, in the State.

8. The family represents the moment of universality in the sense of undifferentiated unity. Civil society represents the moment of particularity. The State represents the unity of the universal and the particular. Instead of undifferentiated unity we find in the State differentiated universality, that is, unity in difference. And instead of sheer particularity[34] we find the identification of the particular with the universal will. To put the matter in another way, in the State self-consciousness has risen to the level of universal self-consciousness. The individual is conscious of himself as being a member of the totality in such a way that his selfhood is not

annulled but fulfilled. The State is not an abstract universal standing over against its members: it exists in and through them. At the same time by participation in the life of the State the members are elevated above their sheer particularity. In other words, the State is an organic unity. It is a concrete universal, existing in and through particulars which are distinct and one at the same time.

The State is said to be 'the self-conscious ethical substance.'[35] It is 'ethical mind as substantial will manifest and clear to itself, which thinks and knows itself and accomplishes what it knows in so far as it knows it'.[36] The State is the actuality of the rational will when this has been raised to the plane of universal self-consciousness. It is thus the highest expression of objective Spirit. And the preceding moments of this sphere are resumed and synthesized in it. For instance, rights are established and maintained as the expression of the universal rational will. And morality obtains its content. That is to say, a man's duties are determined by his position in the social organism. This does not mean, of course, that a man has duties only to the State and none to his family. For the family is not annulled in the State: it is an essential, if subordinate, moment in the State's life. Nor does Hegel mean to imply that a man's duties are determined once and for all by an unchangeable social position. For though he insists that the welfare of the whole social organism is paramount, he also insists that the principle of individual freedom and personal decision is not annihilated in the State but preserved. The theory of 'my station and its duties', to use Bradley's famous phrase, does not imply acceptance of some sort of caste system.

It is indeed undeniable that Hegel speaks of the State in the most exalted terms. He even describes it, for instance, as 'this actual God'.[37] But there are several points to be borne in mind. In the first place the State, as objective Spirit, is necessarily 'divine' in some sense. And just as the Absolute itself is identity-in-difference, so is the State, though on a more restricted scale. In the second place it is essential to remember that Hegel is speaking throughout of the concept of the State, its ideal essence. He has no intention of suggesting that historical States are immune from criticism. Indeed, he makes this point quite clear. 'The State is no work of art; it stands in the world, and so in the sphere of caprice, contingency and error; it can be disfigured by evil conduct in many respects. But the ugliest human being, the criminal, the diseased and the cripple, each is still a living man. The positive element, life, remains in spite of the privation; and it is with this positive element that we have to do here.'[38]

In the third place we must bear in mind Hegel's insistence on the fact that the mature or well-developed State preserves the principle of private liberty in the ordinary sense. He maintains indeed that the will of the State must prevail over the particular will when there is a clash between them. And inasmuch as the will of the State, the universal or general will, is for him in some sense the 'real' will of the individual, it follows that the individual's identification of his interests with those of the State is the actualization of freedom. For the free will is potentially universal, and, as universal, it wills the general good. There is a strong dose of Rousseau's doctrines in Hegel's political theory. At the same time it is unjust to Hegel to draw from the highfaluting way in which he speaks of the majesty and divinity of the State the conclusion that his ideal is a totalitarian State in which private freedom and initiative are reduced to a minimum. On the contrary, a mature State is for Hegel one which ensures the maximum development of personal liberty which is compatible with the sovereign rights of the universal will. Thus he insists that while the stability of the State requires that its members should make the universal end their end[39] according to their several positions and capacities, it also requires that the State should be in a real sense the means to the satisfaction of their subjective aims.[40] As already remarked, the concept of civil society is not simply cancelled out in the concept of the State.

In his treatment of the State Hegel discusses first the political constitution. And he represents constitutional monarchy as being the most rational form. But he regards a corporative State as more rational than democracy after the English model. That is to say, he maintains that the citizens should participate in the affairs of the State as members of subordinate wholes, corporations or Estates, rather than as individuals. Or, more accurately, representatives should represent corporations or Estates rather than the individual citizens precisely as such. And this view seems to be required by Hegel's dialectical scheme. For the concept of civil society, which is preserved in that of the State, culminates in the idea of the corporation.

It has frequently been said that by deducing constitutional monarchy as the most rational form of political organization Hegel canonized the Prussian State of his time. But though he may, like Fichte, have come to regard Prussia as the most promising instrument for educating the Germans to political self-consciousness, his historical sense was far too strong to allow him to suppose that one particular type of constitution could be profitably adopted by any given nation without regard to its history, traditions and spirit. He may have talked a good deal about the rational State, but he was far too reasonable himself to think that a constitution could be imposed on all nations simply because it corresponded best with the demands of abstract reason. 'A constitution *develops* out of the spirit of a nation *only* in identity with this spirit's own development; and it runs through, together with this spirit, the grades of formation and the alterations required by its spirit. It is the indwelling spirit and the history of the nation (and, indeed, the history is simply the history of this spirit) by which constitutions have been and are made.'[41] Again, 'Napoleon wished to give the Spaniards, for example, a constitution *a priori*, but the attempt fared badly enough. For a constitution is no mere artificial product; it is the work of centuries, the idea and the consciousness of the rational in so far as it has been developed in a people. . . . What Napoleon gave the Spaniards was more rational than what they had before, and yet they rejected it as something alien to them.'[42]

Hegel further observes that from one point of view it is

idle to ask whether monarchy or democracy is the best form of government. The fact of the matter is that any constitution is one-sided and inadequate unless it embodies the principle of subjectivity (that is, the principle of personal freedom) and answers to the demands of 'mature reason'.[43] In other words, a more rational constitution means a more liberal constitution, at least in the sense that it must explicitly allow for the free development of individual personality and respect the rights of individuals. Hegel was by no means so reactionary as has sometimes been supposed. He did not hanker after the *ancien régime*.

9. It is worth drawing attention to Hegel's general idea of political theory. His insistence that the philosopher is concerned with the concept or ideal essence of the State may suggest that in his opinion it is the philosopher's business to show politicians and statesmen what they should aim at, by portraying more or less in detail a supposedly ideal State, subsisting in some Platonic world of essences. But if we look at the preface to *The Philosophy of Right* we find Hegel denying in explicit terms that it is the philosopher's business to do anything of the kind. The philosopher is concerned with understanding the actual rather than with offering political schemes and panaceas. And in a sense the actual is the past. For political philosophy appears in the period of a culture's maturity, and when the philosopher attempts to understand the actual, it is already passing into the past and giving place to new forms. In Hegel's famous words, 'when philosophy paints its grey on grey, then has a shape of life grown old. And by this grey on grey it can only be understood, not rejuvenated. The owl of Minerva spreads its wings only with the falling of the dusk.'[44]

Some thinkers, of course, have supposed that they were delineating an eternal pattern, a changeless ideal essence. But in Hegel's opinion they were mistaken. 'Even the Platonic *Republic*, which passes proverbially as an *empty ideal*, was in essence nothing but an interpretation of Greek ethical life.'[45] After all, 'every individual is a son of his time [and] it is just as foolish to suppose that a philosophy can transcend its contemporary world as it is to suppose that an individual can overleap his own time. . . .'[46]

The clear expression of this view obviously constitutes an answer to those who take too seriously Hegel's apparent canonization of the Prussian State. For it is difficult to suppose that a man who understood very well that Aristotle, for example, canonized the Greek *polis* or City-State at a time when its vigorous life was already on the decline really supposed that the contemporary State of his own period represented the final and culminating form of political development. And even if Hegel did think this, there is nothing in his philosophy as such to warrant his prejudice. On the contrary, one would expect the sphere of objective Spirit to undergo further developments as long as history lasts.

Given this interpretation of political philosophy, the natural conclusion to draw is that the philosopher is concerned with making explicit what we may call the operative ideal of the culture or nation to which he belongs. He is an interpreter of the spirit of his time (*die Zeitgeist*). In and through him the political ideals of a society are raised to the level of reflective consciousness. And a society becomes self-conscious in this way only when it has reached maturity and looks back, as it were, on itself, at a time, that is to say, when a form of life has already actualized itself and is ready to pass into or give way to another.

No doubt, this is partly what Hegel means. His remarks about Plato's *Republic* show that it is. But in this case, it may be asked, how can he at the same time speak of the political philosopher as being concerned with the concept or essence of the State?

The answer to this question must be given, I think, in terms of Hegel's metaphysics. The historical process is the self-actualization of Spirit or Reason. 'What is rational is real and what is real is rational.'[47] And the concept of Spirit is the concept of identity-in-difference at the level of rational life. Objective Spirit, therefore, which culminates in the State tends towards the manifestation of identity-in-difference in political life. And this means that a mature or rational

State will unite in itself the moments of universality and difference. It will embody universal self-consciousness or the self-conscious General Will. But this is embodied only in and through distinct finite spirits, each of which, as spirit, possesses 'infinite' value. Hence no State can be fully mature or rational (it cannot accord with the concept of the State) unless it reconciles the conception of the State as an organic totality with the principle of individual freedom. And the philosopher, reflecting on the past and present political organizations, can discern how far they approximate to the requirements of the State as such. But this State as such is not a subsistent essence, existing in a celestial world. It is the *telos* or end of the movement of Spirit or Reason in man's social life. The philosopher can discern this *telos* in its essential outline, because he understands the nature of reality. But it does not follow that he is in a better position, as a philosopher, than is anyone else to prophesy the future or to tell statesmen and politicians what they ought to do. 'Philosophy always comes too late on the scene to do so.'[48] Plato may indeed have told contemporary Greeks how they ought, in his opinion, to organize the City-State. But he was in any case too late. For the shape of life which he dreamed of reorganizing was growing cold and would before long be ripe for decay. Utopian schemes are defeated by the movement of history.

10. Each State is in relation to other States a sovereign individual and demands recognition as such. The mutual relations between States are indeed partly regulated by treaties and by international law, which presuppose acceptance by the States concerned. But if this acceptance is refused or withdrawn, the ultimate arbiter in any dispute is war. For there is no sovereign power above individual States.

Now, if Hegel was simply registering an obvious empirical fact in the international life of his time, there would be no reason for adverse comment. But he goes on to justify war, as though it were an essential feature of human history. True, he admits that war can bring with it much injustice, cruelty and waste. But he argues that it has an ethical aspect and that it should not be regarded as 'an absolute evil and as a mere external contingent fact'.[49] On the contrary, it is a rational necessity. 'It is *necessary* that the finite, property and life, should be *posited* as contingent. . . .'[50] And this is precisely what war does. It is 'the condition in which we have to take seriously the vanity of temporal goods and things, which otherwise is usually only an edifying phrase'.[51]

It should be noted that Hegel is not simply saying that in war a man's moral qualities can be displayed on an heroic scale, which is obviously true. Nor is he saying merely that war brings home to us the transitory character of the finite. He is asserting that war is a necessary rational phenomenon. It is in fact for him the means by which the dialectic of history gets, so to speak, a move on. It prevents stagnation and preserves, as he puts it, the ethical health of nations. It is the chief means by which a people's spirit acquires renewed vigour or a decayed political organism is swept aside and gives place to a more vigorous manifestation of the Spirit. Hegel rejects, therefore, Kant's ideal of perpetual peace.[52]

Obviously, Hegel had no experience of what we call total war. And he doubtless had the Napoleonic Wars and Prussia's struggle for independence fresh in his mind. But when one reads the passages in which he speaks of war and dismisses Kant's ideal of perpetual peace it is difficult to avoid the impression, partly comical and partly unpleasant, of a university professor romanticizing a dark feature of human history and decking it out with metaphysical trappings.[53]

11. Mention of international relations and of war as an instrument by which the historical dialectic progresses brings us to the subject of Hegel's concept of world-history.

Hegel distinguishes three main types of history or, rather, historiography. First there is 'original history', that is to say, descriptions of deeds and events and states of society which the historian had before his eyes. Thucydides' history represents this type. Secondly there is 'reflective history'. A general history, extending beyond the limits of the historian's experience, belongs to this type. So, for instance, does didactic history. Thirdly, there is 'philosophical history' or the philosophy of history. This term, says Hegel, signifies 'nothing else but the thoughtful consideration of history'.[54] But it can hardly be claimed that this description, taken by itself, is very enlightening. And, as Hegel explicitly admits, something more must be said by way of elucidation.

To say that the philosophy of history is the thoughtful consideration of history is to say that a thought is brought to this consideration. But the thought in question, Hegel insists, is not a preconceived plan or scheme into which the facts have somehow to be fitted. 'The only idea which philosophy brings with it [that is, to the contemplation of history] is the simple idea of reason, that reason dominates the world and that world-history is thus a rational process.'[55] As far as philosophy is concerned, this truth is provided in metaphysics. But in history as such it is an hypothesis. Hence the truth that world-history is the self-unfolding of Spirit must be exhibited as the result of reflection on history. In our reflection history 'must be taken as it is; we must proceed historically, empirically'.[56]

The obvious comment on this is that even if Hegel disclaims any desire to force history into a preconceived mould, the thought or idea which the philosopher brings to the study of history must obviously exercise a great influence on his interpretation of events. Even if the idea is professedly proposed as an empirically verifiable hypothesis, the philosopher who, like Hegel himself, believes that its truth has been demonstrated in metaphysics will undoubtedly be prone to emphasize those aspects of history which seem to offer support for the hypothesis. Moreover, for the Hegelian the hypothesis is really no hypothesis at all but a demonstrated truth.

Hegel remarks, however, that even the would-be 'impartial' historians bring their own categories to the study of history. Absolute impartiality is a myth. And there cannot be a better principle of interpretation than a proven philosophical truth. Evidently, Hegel's general idea is more or less this. As the philosopher knows that reality is the self-unfolding of infinite reason, he knows that reason must operate in human history. At the same time we cannot tell in advance how it operates. To discover this, we have to study the course of events as depicted by historians in the ordinary sense and try to discern the significant rational process in the mass of contingent material. In theological language, we know in advance that divine providence operates in history. But to see how it operates we must study the historical data.

Now, world-history is the process whereby Spirit comes to actual consciousness of itself as freedom. Hence 'world-history is progress in the consciousness of freedom'.[57] This consciousness is attained, of course, only in and through the mind of man. And the divine Spirit, as manifested in history through the consciousness of man, is the World-Spirit (*der Weltgeist*). History, therefore, is the process whereby the World-Spirit comes to explicit consciousness of itself as free.

But though the *Weltgeist* attains consciousness of itself as free only in and through the human mind, the historian is concerned with nations rather than with individuals. Hence the unit, so to speak, in the concrete development of the World-Spirit is the national spirit or the spirit of a people (*der Volksgeist*). And by this Hegel means in part a people's culture as manifested not only in its political constitution and traditions but also in its morality, art, religion and philosophy. But a national spirit is not, of course, resident simply in legal forms, works of art and so on. It is a living totality, the spirit of a people as living in and through that people. And the individual is a bearer of the *Weltgeist* in so far as he participates in this more limited totality, the *Volksgeist*, which is itself a phase or moment in the life of the World-Spirit.

Hegel does indeed assert that 'in world-history the individuals with whom we have to do are peoples, the totalities which are States'.[58] But he can use the terms 'State' and 'national spirit' more or less interchangeably because the first term signifies for him something much more than the juridical State. He understands by the State in this context a totality which exists in and through its members, though it is not identical with any given set of citizens existing here and now, and which gives concrete form to the spirit and culture of a people or nation.

It should be noted, however, that one important reason why Hegel insists that world-history is concerned with States is that in his view a national spirit exists for itself (that is, as conscious of itself) only in and through the State. Hence those peoples which do not constitute national States are practically excluded from consideration in world-history. For their spirits are only implicit: they do not exist 'for themselves'.

Each national spirit, therefore, embodied in a State, is a phase or moment in the life of the *Weltgeist*. Indeed, this World-Spirit is really a *result* of the interplay of national spirits. They are, so to speak, the moments in its actualization. National spirits are limited, finite 'and their fates and deeds in their relations to one another reveal the dialectic of the finitude of these spirits. Out of this dialectic there arises the *Universal Spirit*, the unlimited *World-Spirit* which pronounces its judgment—and its judgment is the highest— upon the finite national spirits. It does so within *world-history* which is the *world's court of* judgment.'[59] The judgment of the nations is for Hegel immanent in history. The actual fate of each nation constitutes its judgment.

Spirit, therefore, in its progress towards full and explicit self-consciousness takes the form of limited and one-sided manifestations of itself, the several national spirits. And Hegel assumes that in any given epoch one particular nation represents in a special way the development of the World-Spirit. 'This people is the dominant people in world-history for this epoch—*and it is only once that it can make its hour strike.*'[60] Its national spirit develops, reaches its zenith and then declines, after which the nation is relegated to the background of the historical stage. Hegel is doubtless thinking of the way in which Spain, for instance, developed into a great empire, with a peculiar stamp and culture of its own, and then declined. But he assumes without more ado that a nation cannot occupy the centre of the stage more than once. And this assumption is perhaps disputable, unless, of course, we choose to make it necessarily true by maintaining that a nation which enjoys a second period of outstanding importance is really a different nation with a different spirit. In any case Hegel's desire to find a particular world-historical nation for each epoch has a narrowing effect on his conception of history.

To say this is not, however, to deny that in his lectures on the philosophy of history Hegel covers a wide field. As he is dealing with world-history, this is obviously bound to be the case. The first part of his work is devoted to the Oriental world, including China, India, Persia, Asia Minor, Palestine and Egypt. In the second part he treats of the Greek world, and in the third of the Roman world, including the rise of Christianity to the position of an historical power (*eine geschichtliche Macht*). The fourth part is devoted to what Hegel calls the Germanic world. The period covered stretches from the Byzantine Empire up to the French Revolution and the Napoleonic Wars inclusively. Mohammedanism receives a brief treatment in this fourth part.

The Orientals, according to Hegel, did not know that man as such is free. And in the absence of this knowledge they were not free. They knew only that *one* man, the despot, was free. 'But for this very reason such freedom is only caprice, ferocity or brutal passion—or a mildness and tameness in the passions which is itself only an accident of Nature or caprice. This *one* is, therefore, only a despot, he is not a free man, a true human being.'[61]

In the Greco-Roman world there arises the consciousness of freedom. But the Greeks and Romans of classical times knew only that *some* men are free, namely the free men as opposed to the slaves. Even Plato and Aristotle exemplify this inadequate phase in the growth of the consciousness of freedom.

In Hegel's view it was the 'Germanic' peoples who under the influence of Christianity first arrived at the conscious awareness that man as such is free. But though this principle was recognized from the start in Christianity, it does not follow that it immediately found expression in laws, government and political organization and institutions. The awareness of the freedom of the spirit arose first in religion, but a long process of development was required for it to attain explicit practical recognition as the basis of the State. And this process of development is studied in history. The inner consciousness of the freedom of the spirit had to give itself explicit objectification, and here Hegel attributes a leading role to the so-called Germanic peoples.

Now, we have seen that the units to which primary consideration is given in world-history are national States. But it is a notorious fact that Hegel emphasizes the role of what he calls the world-historical individuals (*die weltgeschichtlichen Individuen*), men such as Alexander the Great, Julius Caesar and Napoleon. And this may seem to involve him in some inconsistency. But national spirits and the World-Spirit which arises out of their dialectic exist and live and operate only in and through human beings. And Hegel's point of view is that the World-Spirit has used certain individuals as its instruments in a signal way. In theological language, they were the special instruments of divine providence. They had, of course, their subjective passions and private motives. Napoleon, for example, may have been dominated to a great extent by personal ambition and megalomania. But though the private motives, conscious and unconscious, of a Caesar or a Napoleon are of interest to the biographer and the psychologist, they are not of much importance or relevance for the philosopher of history who is interested in such men for what they accomplished as instruments of the World-Spirit. Nothing great, Hegel remarks, is accomplished in this world without passion. But the passions of the great figures of history are used as instruments by the World-Spirit and exhibit 'the cunning of Reason'. Whatever motives Julius Caesar may have had for crossing the Rubicon his action had an historical importance which probably far transcended anything that he understood. Whatever his private interests may have been, the cosmic Reason or Spirit in its 'cunning' used these interests to transform the Republic into the Empire and to bring the Roman genius and spirit to the peak of its development.

If we abstract from all questionable metaphysics, Hegel is obviously saying something quite sensible. It is certainly not absurd to claim, for example, that the historian is or ought to be more interested in what Stalin actually accomplished for Russia than in the psychology of that unpleasing tyrant. But Hegel's teleological view of history implies in addition, of course, that what Stalin accomplished *had* to be accomplished, and that the Russian dictator, with all his unpleasant characteristics, was an instrument in the hands of the World-Spirit.[62]

12. In view of the already somewhat inordinate length of this chapter I have no wish either to repeat or to amplify the general remarks about the philosophy of history which I made in the preceding volume.[63] But one or two comments relating to Hegel's concept of world-history may be appropriate.

In the first place, if history is a rational process in the sense of being a teleological process, a movement towards a goal which is determined by the nature of the Absolute rather than by human choice, it may appear that all that occurs is justified by the very fact that it occurs. And if the history of the world is itself the highest court of judgment, the judgment of the nations, it may appear to follow that might is right. For example, if one nation succeeds in conquering another, it seems to follow that its action is justified by its success.

Now, the saying 'might is right' is perhaps generally understood as being an expression of that type of cynical outlook which is manifested by Callicles in Plato's *Gorgias*. For this outlook the notion of a universally obligatory and fundamentally unchanging moral law is the creation of a self-defensive instinct on the part of the weak who try by this means to enslave the strong and free. The really free and strong man sees through this notion of morality and rejects it. He sees that the only right is might. In his judgment the weak, nature's slaves, implicitly admit the truth of this judgment, though they are not consciously aware of the fact. For, individually weak, they try to exercise a collective might by imposing on the strong an ethical code which is of advantage to themselves.

But Hegel was no cynic. As we have seen, he was convinced of the value of the human person as such, not merely of the value of some human beings. And it can be reasonably claimed that with him it is not so much a question of the cynical view that might is right as of the exaggeratedly optimistic view that in history right, in the form of the rational, is the necessarily dominant factor.

Yet it is arguable, of course, that in the long run it comes more or less to the same thing, even if there is a difference of attitude between Hegel and the cynic. If right always prevails in history, then successful might is justified. It is justified because it is right rather than because it is might; but it is none the less justified. Hegel does indeed allow, for example, that moral judgments can be passed on what he calls world-historical individuals. But he also makes it clear that such judgments possess for him only a purely formal rectitude, as he puts it. From the point of view of a given system of social ethics a great revolutionary, for example, may be a bad man. But from the point of view of world-history his deeds are justified, for he accomplishes what the universal Spirit requires. And if one nation conquers another, its action is justified inasmuch as it is a moment in the dialectic of world-history, whatever moral judgments are passed on the actions of the individuals involved when they are considered, so to speak, in their private capacities. Indeed, world-history is not interested in this second aspect of the situation.

We can say, therefore, that it is Hegel's metaphysical views rather than any cynical outlook which involve him in justifying all the events in which the world-historian or philosopher of history is interested. Hegel argues indeed that he is simply taking seriously and applying to history as a whole the Christian doctrine of divine providence. But there are obvious differences. Once the transcendent God has been transformed into the Hegelian Absolute and judgment has been made purely immanent in history itself, no escape is left from the conclusion that from the world-historical point of view all the events and actions which form moments in the self-manifestation of the Absolute are justified. And moral questions which possess importance from the Christian point of view become practically irrelevant. I do not mean to imply, of course, that this shows of itself that Hegel's point of view is false. Nor do I mean to imply that a Christian historian is committed to moralizing. But Hegel's philosophy of history is much more than what historians generally understand by history. It is a metaphysical interpretation of history. And my point is that Hegel's metaphysics drives him to conclusions to which the Christian theologian is not committed. True, Hegel thought that he was giving the philosophical essence, as it were, of the Christian doctrine of providence. But in point of fact this 'demythologization' was a transformation.

Mention of Hegel's metaphysics suggests another comment. If, as Hegel maintains, world-history is the process by which the universal Spirit actualizes itself in time, it is difficult to understand why the goal of the process should not be a universal world-State or world-society in which personal freedom would be perfectly realized within an all-embracing unity. Even if Hegel wishes to insist that the universal is manifested in its particulars and that the particulars in question are national spirits, it would seem that the ideal end of the whole movement should be a world-federation, representing the concrete universal.

Hegel did not, however, adopt this point of view. World-history is for him essentially the dialectic of national spirits, of States, which are the determinate shape which Spirit assumes in history. If we consider Spirit as rising above these particular finite forms, we enter the sphere of absolute Spirit, which will be the theme of the next chapter.

Chapter Eleven

HEGEL (3)

The sphere of absolute Spirit – The philosophy of art – The philosophy of religion – The relation between religion and philosophy – Hegel's philosophy of the history of philosophy – The influence of Hegel and the division between right-wing and left-wing Hegelians.

1. As we have seen, difficulties arise directly we begin to probe beneath the surface of the outlines of Hegel's system. For example, when we start to inquire into the ontological reference of the logical Idea and the precise relation between the *Logos* and Nature, several possible lines of interpretation present themselves to the mind. But this does not alter the fact that a preliminary statement of the outline of the system can be easily made. The Absolute is Being. Being, considered first (though not in a temporal sense) as the Idea, objectifies itself in Nature, the material world. As the objectification of the Idea, Nature manifests the Idea. At the same time it cannot do so adequately. For Being, the Absolute, is defined as Spirit, as Thought which thinks itself. And it must come to exist as such. It cannot do so in Nature, though Nature is a condition for its doing so. Being comes to exist as Spirit and thus to manifest its essence adequately only in and through the human spirit. But Being as Spirit can be conceived in different ways. It can be conceived 'in itself', in the form of the finite spirit in its inwardness or subjectivity. This is the sphere of subjective Spirit. It can be conceived as issuing out of itself and objectifying itself in the institutions, above all the State, which it posits or creates. This is the sphere of objective Spirit. And it can be conceived as rising above finitude and knowing itself as Being, the totality. And this is the sphere of

absolute Spirit. Absolute Spirit exists only in and through the human spirit, but it does so at the level at which the individual human spirit is no longer a finite mind, enclosed in its own private thoughts, emotions, interests and purposes, but has become a moment in the life of the infinite as an identity-in-difference which knows itself as such. In other words, absolute Spirit is Spirit at the level of that absolute knowledge of which Hegel wrote in *The Phenomenology of Spirit*. And we can thus say that man's knowledge of the Absolute and the Absolute's knowledge of itself are two aspects of the same reality. For Being actualizes itself as concretely existing self-thinking Thought through the human spirit.

For the sake of clarity the following point must be made clear. I am conscious of myself as a finite being: I have, so to speak, my own self-consciousness which is quite different from the self-consciousness of any other human being. But though, like anything else, this subjective self-consciousness must be within the Absolute, it is not at all what Hegel means by absolute knowledge. This arises when I am aware, not simply of myself as a finite individual standing over against other finite persons and things, but rather of the Absolute as the ultimate and all-embracing reality. My knowledge, if I attain it, of Nature as the objective manifestation of the Absolute and of the Absolute as returning to itself as subjectivity in the form of Spirit, existing in and through the spiritual life of man in history, is a moment in absolute self-consciousness, that is, in the self-knowledge of Being or the Absolute.

The matter can be put in this way. We have seen that according to Hegel the World-Spirit arises out of the dialectic of national spirits. And in the comments at the end of the last chapter it was remarked that this view might reasonably be expected to involve the conclusion that the end or goal of history is a universal society, a world-State or at least a world-federation of States. But this was not Hegel's point of view. National spirits are limited and finite. And when the World-Spirit is conceived as rising above this finitude and limitation and existing as infinite Spirit, it must be conceived as knowledge, as self-thinking Thought. We thus pass out of the political sphere. The State is indeed described by Hegel as the self-conscious ethical substance, in the sense that it conceives its own ends and consciously pursues them. But it cannot be described as self-thinking Thought or as personality. Self-thinking Thought is Spirit knowing itself as Spirit and Nature as its objectification and as the condition for its own concrete existence as Spirit. It is the Absolute knowing itself as the Totality, that is, as identity-in-difference: it is infinite Being reflectively conscious of the distinct phases or moments in its own life. It is Spirit set free, as it were, from the limitations of the finitude which characterizes the national spirit.

Absolute Spirit is thus the synthesis or unity of subjective Spirit and objective Spirit on a higher plane. It is subjectivity and objectivity in one. For it is Spirit knowing itself. But whereas in the spheres of subjective Spirit and objective Spirit we are concerned with the finite Spirit, first in its inwardness, then in its self-manifestation in objective institutions, such as the family and the State, in the sphere of absolute Spirit we are concerned with infinite Spirit knowing itself as infinite. This does not mean that infinite Spirit is something set over against, opposed to and existing entirely apart from the finite spirit. The infinite exists in and through the finite. But in the sphere of absolute Spirit the infinite is reflectively conscious of itself as such. Hence absolute Spirit is not a repetition, so to speak, of subjective Spirit. It is Spirit's return to itself at a higher level, a level at which subjectivity and objectivity are united in one infinite act.

To speak, however, of one infinite act can be misleading. For it suggests the idea of an eternally changeless self-intuition on the part of the Absolute, whereas for Hegel absolute Spirit is the life of the Absolute's developing self-knowledge. It is the process whereby the Absolute actualizes itself precisely as self-thinking Thought. And it does so at three main levels, those of art, religion and philosophy.

What Hegel means by this can most easily be understood if we approach the matter from the point of view of man's knowledge of the Absolute. First, the Absolute can be apprehended under the sensuous form of beauty as manifested in Nature or, more adequately, in the work of art. Hegel thus accepts Schelling's theory of the metaphysical significance of art. Secondly, the Absolute can be apprehended in the form of pictorial or figurative thought which finds expression in the language of religion. Thirdly, the Absolute can be apprehended purely conceptually, that is, in speculative philosophy. Art, religion and philosophy are thus all concerned with the Absolute. The infinite divine Being is, as it were, the content or subject-matter of all three spiritual activities. But though the content is the same, the form is different. That is to say, the Absolute is apprehended in different ways in these activities. As having the same content or subject-matter, art, religion and philosophy all belong to the sphere of absolute Spirit. But the differences in form show that they are distinct phases in the life of absolute Spirit.

The philosophy of absolute Spirit, therefore, consists of three main parts, the philosophy of art, the philosophy of religion and what we may call the philosophy of philosophy. And as Hegel proceeds dialectically, showing how art passes into or demands the transition to religion and how religion in turn demands the transition to philosophy, it is important to understand in what sense the time element enters into this dialectic and in what sense it does not.

In his philosophy of art Hegel does not confine himself to a purely abstract account of the essence of the aesthetic consciousness. He surveys the historical development of art and tries to show a development in the aesthetic consciousness up to the point at which it demands the transition to the religious consciousness. Similarly, in his philosophy of religion he does not confine himself to delineating the essential features or moments of the religious consciousness: he surveys the history of religion from primitive religion up to the absolute religion, Christianity, and endeavours to make clear a dialectical pattern of development in the religious consciousness up to the point at which it demands a transition to the standpoint of speculative philosophy. There is, therefore, a mixture of the temporal and the non-temporal. On the one hand the actual historical developments of art, religion and philosophy are all temporal processes. This is sufficiently obvious. For instance, classical Greek art temporally preceded Christian art, and Greek religion temporally preceded the Christian religion. On the other hand Hegel is not so foolish as to suppose that art ran through all its forms before religion appeared on the scene or that there was no philosophy before the appearance of the absolute religion. He is as well aware as anyone else that Greek temples were associated with Greek religion, and that there were Greek philosophers. The dialectical transition from the concept of art to the concept of religion and from the concept of religion to that of philosophy is in itself timeless. That is to say, it is in essence a conceptual, and not a temporal or historical, progression.

The point can be expressed in this way. Hegel might have confined himself to a purely conceptual movement, in which the only priority involved would be logical, not temporal. But the life of the Spirit is an historical development in which one form of art succeeds another, one stage in the evolution of the religious consciousness succeeds another stage, and one philosophical system succeeds another philosophical system. And Hegel is anxious to show the dialectical patterns exhibited in the history of art, the history of religion and the history of philosophy. Hence the philosophy of absolute Spirit, as he expounds it, cannot abstract from all temporal succession. And it has, therefore, two aspects. It may not indeed be always a simple matter to sort them out. But in any case we only make nonsense of Hegel's doctrine if we take him to mean, for example, that religion started only when art stopped. And whatever some writers may think that Hegel ought to have said, in my opinion he looked on art, religion and philosophy as permanent activities of the human spirit. He may have thought that philosophy is the highest of these activities. But it does not follow that he imagined that man would ever become pure thought.

By way of conclusion to this section it is worth drawing attention to the following point. It is a mistake to think that according to Hegel the State is the highest of all realities and political life the highest activity of man. For, as we have seen, the sphere of objective Spirit leads on to the sphere of absolute Spirit. And while organized society in some form is for Hegel a condition for art, religion and philosophy, these three activities are the highest expression of Spirit. Hegel doubtless exalted the State, but he exalted philosophy still more.

2. Dialectically or logically speaking, the Absolute is manifested first of all in the form of immediacy, under the guise, that is to say, of objects of sense. As such, it is apprehended as beauty, which is 'the sensuous semblance [*Scheinen*] of the Idea'.[1] And this sensuous appearance of the Idea, this shining of the Absolute through the veils of sense, is called the Ideal. Looked at from one point of view the Idea as beauty is, of course, identical with the Idea as truth. For it is the same Absolute which is apprehended as beauty by the aesthetic consciousness and as truth in philosophy. But the forms or modes of apprehension are distinct. Aesthetic intuition and philosophy are not the same thing. Hence the Idea as beauty is termed the Ideal.

While not denying that there can be such a thing as beauty in Nature, Hegel insists that beauty in art is far superior. For artistic beauty is the immediate creation of Spirit; it is Spirit's manifestation of itself to itself. And Spirit and its products are superior to Nature and its phenomena. Hegel confines his attention, therefore, to beauty in art. It may indeed be regrettable that he under-estimates natural beauty as a manifestation of the divine. But, given the construction of his system, he can hardly do anything else but concentrate on artistic beauty. For he has left the philosophy of Nature behind him and is concerned with the philosophy of Spirit.

But, we may ask, if artistic beauty is said to be the sensuous semblance or appearance of the Idea, what does this proposition mean? Is it anything more than a high-sounding but vague statement? The answer is fairly simple. The Idea is the unity of subjectivity and objectivity. And in the beautiful work of art this unity is expressed or represented in the union of spiritual content with external or material embodiment. Spirit and matter, subjectivity and objectivity, are fused together in a harmonious unity or synthesis. 'Art has the task of presenting the Idea to immediate intuition in sensuous form, and not in the form of thought or pure spirituality. And the value and dignity of this presentation lie in the correspondence and unity of the two aspects of ideal content and its embodiment, so that the perfection and excellence of art and the conformity of its products with its essential concept depend on the degree of inner harmony and unity with which the ideal content and sensuous form are made to interpenetrate.'[2]

Obviously, Hegel does not mean to imply that the artist is consciously aware of the fact that his product is a manifestation of the nature of the Absolute. Nor does he mean to imply that a man is unable to appreciate the beauty of a work of art unless he has this conscious awareness. Both the artist and the beholder may feel that the product is, so to speak, just right or perfect, in the sense that to add or subtract anything would be to impair or disfigure the work of art. Both may feel that spiritual content and sensuous embodiment are perfectly fused. And they may both feel that the product is in some undefined sense a manifestation of 'truth'. But it by no means follows that either of them can state the metaphysical significance of the work of art, whether to himself or to anyone else. Nor does this indicate any defect in the aesthetic consciousness. For it is philosophy, and not the aesthetic consciousness, which explicitly or reflectively apprehends the metaphysical significance of art. In other words, this apprehension arises from philosophical reflection *about* art. And this is something very different from artistic creation. A great artist may be a very bad philosopher or no philosopher at all. And a great philosopher may well be incapable of painting a beautiful picture or composing a symphony.

In the perfect work of art, therefore, there is complete harmony between ideal content and its sensuous form or embodiment. The two elements interpenetrate and are fused into one. But this artistic ideal is not always attained. And the different possible types of relation between the two elements give us the fundamental types of art.

First we have the type of art in which the sensuous element predominates over the spiritual or ideal content, in the sense that the latter has not mastered its medium of expression and does not shine through the veils of sense. In other words, the artist suggests rather than expresses his meaning. There is ambiguity and an air of mystery. And this type of art is *symbolic* art. It can be found, for example, among the ancient Egyptians. 'It is in *Egypt* that we have to look for the perfect exemplification of the symbolic mode of expression, in regard both to its peculiar content and to its form. Egypt is the land of symbol which sets itself the spiritual task of the self-interpretation of Spirit, without really being able to fulfil it.'[3] And Hegel finds in the Sphinx 'the symbol of the symbolic itself'.[4] It is 'the objective riddle'.[5]

Hegel subdivides symbolic art into subordinate phases and discusses the difference between Hindu and Egyptian art and the religious poetry of the Hebrews. But we cannot follow him into details. It is sufficient to notice that according to him symbolic art is best suited to the early ages of humanity when the world and man itself, Nature and Spirit, are felt as mysterious and enigmatic.

Secondly we have the type of art in which spiritual or ideal content are fused into a harmonious unity. This is *classical* art. Whereas in symbolic art the Absolute is conceived as a mysterious, formless One which is suggested rather than expressed in the work of art, in classical art Spirit is conceived in concrete form as the self-conscious individual spirit, whose sensuous embodiment is the human body. This type of art, therefore, is predominantly anthropomorphic. The gods are simply glorified human beings. And the leading classical art is thus *sculpture*, which presents Spirit as the finite embodied spirit.

Just as Hegel associates symbolic art with the Hindus and Egyptians, so he associates classical art with the ancient Greeks. In the great works of Greek sculpture we find the perfect marriage, as it were, of Spirit and matter. The spiritual content shines through the veils of sense: it is expressed, not merely suggested in symbolic form. For the human body, as represented by a Praxiteles, is the clear expression of Spirit.

Yet 'classical art and its religion of beauty do not satisfy wholly the depths of the Spirit'.[6] And we have the third main type of art, namely *romantic* art, in which Spirit, felt as infinite, tends to overflow, as it were, its sensuous embodiment and to abandon the veils of sense. In classical art there is a perfect fusion of ideal content and sensuous form. But Spirit is not merely the particular finite spirit, united with a particular body: it is the divine infinite. And in romantic art, which is to all intents and purposes the art of Christendom, no sensuous embodiment is felt to be adequate to the spiritual content. It is not, as in symbolic art, a case of the spiritual content having to be suggested rather than expressed because Spirit has not yet been conceived as such and remains enigmatic, a riddle or problem. Rather is it that Spirit has been conceived as what it is, namely infinite spiritual Life as God, and therefore as overflowing any finite sensuous embodiment.

Romantic art, according to Hegel, is concerned with the life of the Spirit, which is movement, action, conflict. Spirit must, as it were, die to live. That is to say, it must go over into what is not itself that it may rise again to become itself, a truth which is expressed in Christianity, in the doctrine of self-sacrifice and resurrection, exemplified above all in the life, death and resurrection of Christ. The typical romantic arts, therefore, will be those which are best adapted to expressing movement, action and conflict. And these are painting, music and poetry. Architecture is least adapted for expressing the inner life of the Spirit and is the typical form of symbolic art. Sculpture, the typical form of classical art, is better adapted than architecture for this purpose, but it concentrates on the external, on the body, and its expression of movement and life is very limited. In poetry, however, the medium consists of words, that is, of sensuous images expressed in language; and it is best suited for expressing the life of the Spirit.

This association of particular arts with definite general types of art must not, however, be understood in an exclusive sense. Architecture, for example, is particularly associated with symbolic art because, while capable of expressing mystery, it is of all the fine arts the least fitted for expressing the life of the Spirit. But to say this is not to deny that there are forms of architecture which are characteristic of classical and romantic art. Thus the Greek temple, the perfect house for the anthropomorphic deity, is an obvious example of classical architecture, while the Gothic, an example of romantic architecture, expresses the feeling that the divine transcends the sphere of finitude and of matter. In contrast with the Greek temple we can see how 'the romantic character of Christian churches consists in the way in which they arise out of the soil and soar into the heights'.[7]

Similarly, sculpture is not confined to classical art, even if it is the characteristic classical art-form. Nor are painting, music and poetry confined to romantic art. But we cannot follow Hegel any further into his lengthy discussion of the particular fine arts.

Now, if we are considering art simply in itself, we must say that the highest type of art is that in which spiritual content and sensuous embodiment are in perfect harmonious accord. And this is classical art, the leading characteristic form of which is sculpture. But if we are considering the aesthetic consciousness as a stage in the self-manifestation of God or as a level in man's developing knowledge of God, we must say that romantic art is the highest type. For, as we have seen, in romantic art infinite Spirit tends to drop the veils of sense, a fact which becomes most evident in poetry. Of course, as long as we remain in the sphere of art at all, the veils of sense are never completely abandoned. But romantic art provides the point of transition from the aesthetic to the religious consciousness. That is to say, when the mind perceives that no material embodiment is adequate to the expression of Spirit, it passes from the sphere of art to that of religion.[8] Art cannot satisfy the Spirit as a means of apprehending its own nature.

3. If the Absolute is Spirit, Reason, self-thinking Thought, it can be adequately apprehended as such only by thought

itself. And we might perhaps expect Hegel to make a direct transition from art to philosophy, whereas in point of fact he makes the transition to philosophy by way of an intermediate mode of apprehending the Absolute, namely religion. 'The sphere of conscious life which is nearest in ascending order to the realm of art is religion.'[9] Obviously, Hegel is not simply concerned with completing a triad, so that the sphere of absolute Spirit may conform to the general pattern of the system. Nor is it simply that he sees the need for a philosophy of religion in view of the importance of religion in the history of mankind, and of the obvious fact that it is concerned with the divine. The insertion of religion between art and philosophy is due above all to Hegel's conviction that the religious consciousness exemplifies an intermediate way of apprehending the Absolute. Religion in general is or essentially involves the self-manifestation of the Absolute in the form of *Vorstellung*, a word which can be translated in this context as figurative or pictorial thought. On the one hand the religious consciousness differs from the aesthetic in that it *thinks* the Absolute. On the other hand the thought which is characteristic of religion is not pure conceptual thought as found in philosophy. It is thought clothed, as it were, in imagery: it is, one may say, the product of a marriage between imagination and thought. A *Vorstellung* is a concept, but it is not the pure concept of the philosopher. Rather is it a pictorial or imaginative concept.

For example, the truth that the logical Idea, the *Logos*, is objectified in Nature is apprehended by the religious consciousness (at least in Judaism, Christianity and Mohammedanism) in the form of the imaginative or pictorial concept of the free creation of the world by a transcendent Deity. Again, the truth that the finite spirit is in essence a moment in the life of infinite Spirit is apprehended by the Christian consciousness in the form of the doctrine of the Incarnation and of man's union with God through Christ. For Hegel the truths are the same in content, but the modes of apprehension and expression are different in religion and in philosophy. For instance, the idea of God in the Christian consciousness

and the concept of the Absolute have for Hegel exactly the
same content: they refer to or mean the same reality. But
this reality is apprehended and described in different ways.

As for the existence of God, there is an obvious sense in
which Hegel needs no proof, no proof, that is to say, in addition to his system itself. For God is Being, and the nature
of Being is demonstrated in logic or abstract metaphysics. At
the same time Hegel devotes a good deal of attention to traditional proofs of God's existence. Nowadays, he remarks,
these proofs have fallen into discredit. They are regarded not
only as completely antiquated from a philosophical point of
view but also, from a religious standpoint, as irreligious and
practically impious. For there is a strong tendency to substitute unreasoned faith and pious feelings of the heart for any
attempt to give faith a rational foundation. Indeed, so un-
fashionable has this business of proof become that 'the proofs
are here and there hardly even known as historical data; and
even by theologians, people, that is to say, who profess to
have a scientific knowledge of religious truths, they are sometimes unknown'.[10] Yet the proofs do not merit this con-
tempt. For they arose 'out of the need to satisfy thought,
reason',[11] and they represent the elevation of the human
mind to God, making explicit the immediate movement of
faith.

Speaking of the cosmological proof, Hegel remarks that its
essential defect in its traditional forms is that it posits the
finite as something existing on its own and then tries to make
a transition to the infinite as something different from the
finite. But this defect can be remedied if we once understand
that 'Being is to be defined not only as finite but also as
infinite.'[12] In other words, we have to show that 'the being
of the finite is not only its being but also the being of the
infinite'.[13] Conversely, of course, it has to be shown that infinite Being unfolds itself in and through the finite. The ob-
jections against making the transition from the finite to the
infinite or from the infinite to the finite can be met only by a
true philosophy of Being which shows that the supposed gulf

between the finite and the infinite does not exist. Kant's criticism of the proofs then falls to the ground.

This amounts to saying that the true proof of the existence of God is, as was remarked above, the Hegelian system itself. And to expound this system is obviously a philosophical task. Hence the philosophy of religion proper is concerned more with the religious consciousness and its mode or modes of apprehending God than with proving God's existence.

Considered abstractly, the religious consciousness comprises three main moments or phases. The first, as the normal scheme of the Hegelian dialectic would lead one to expect, is the moment of universality. God is conceived as the undifferentiated universal, as the infinite and only true reality. The second moment is that of particularity. In conceiving God I distinguish between myself and him, between the infinite and the finite. He becomes for me an object over against me. And my consciousness of God as 'outside' me or over against me involves the consciousness of myself as separated or alienated from him, as a sinner. Finally, the third moment is that of individuality, of the return of the particular to the universal, of the finite to the infinite. Separation and alienation are overcome. For the religious consciousness this is accomplished in worship and in the way of salvation, that is, by the variety of means by which man conceives himself as entering into union with God.

The mind thus moves from the bare abstract thought of God to the consciousness of itself and God in separation, and thence to awareness of itself as one with God. And this movement is the essential movement of the religious consciousness. Its three moments or phases, one may note, correspond with the three moments of the Idea.

But religion is not, of course, simply religion in the abstract. It takes the form of definite religions. And in his lectures on the philosophy of religion Hegel traces the development of the religious consciousness through different types of religion. He is primarily concerned with exhibiting a logical or conceptual sequence; but this sequence is developed through reflection on the historical religions of mankind, the existence and nature of which is obviously known by other means than *a priori* deduction. Hegel's concern is to exhibit the dialectical pattern exemplified in the empirical or historical data.

The first main phase of definite or determinate religion is called by Hegel the religion of Nature (*die Naturreligion*), this phrase being used to cover any religion in which God is conceived as less than Spirit. It is subdivided into three phases. First there is immediate religion or magic. Secondly there is the religion of substance, under which heading Hegel considers in turn Chinese religion, Hinduism and Buddhism. Thirdly there are the religions of Persia, Syria and Egypt in which there can be found some glimmering of the idea of spirituality. Thus while in Hinduism Brahman is the purely abstract undifferentiated One, in the Persian religion of Zoroastrianism God is conceived as the Good.

The religion of Nature can be said to correspond with the first moment of the religious consciousness as described above. In the characteristic *Naturreligion*, namely the religion of substance, God is conceived as the undifferentiated universal. This is pantheism in the sense that the finite being is regarded as swallowed up by or as purely accidental to the divine Being. At the same time, though in Hinduism Brahman is conceived in a way corresponding to the first moment of the religious consciousness, this does not mean that the other moments are altogether absent.

The second main phase of definite religion is the religion of spiritual individuality. Here God is conceived as Spirit, but in the form of an individual person or of individual persons. The inevitable triad comprises the Jewish, Greek and Roman religions, entitled respectively the religions of sublimity, beauty and utility. Thus Jupiter Capitolinus has as his function the preservation of the safety and sovereignty of Rome.[14]

These three types of religion correspond to the second moment of the religious consciousness. The divine is conceived as being over against or apart from the human. In Jewish religion, for example, God is exalted above the world and man in transcendent sublimity. At the same time the other moments of the religious consciousness are also represented. Thus in Judaism there is the idea of man's reconciliation with God through sacrifice and obedience to the divine law.

The third main phase of definite religion is absolute religion, namely Christianity. In Christianity God is conceived as what he really is, infinite Spirit which is not only transcendent but also immanent. And man is conceived as united with God by participating in the divine life through the grace received from Christ, the God-man. Hence the Christian religion corresponds above all with the third moment of the religious consciousness, which is the synthesis or unity of the first two moments. God is not looked on as an undifferentiated unity, but as the Trinity of Persons, as infinite spiritual Life. And the infinite and finite are not regarded as set over against one another, but as united without confusion. As St. Paul says, in him we live and move and have our being.

To say that Christianity is the absolute religion is to say that it is the absolute truth. And Hegel fulminates against preachers and theologians who pass lightly over the Christian dogmas or who whittle them down to suit the outlook of a supposedly enlightened age. But we must add that Christianity expresses the absolute truth under the form of *Vorstellung*. There arises, therefore, the demand for a transition to philosophy which thinks the content of religion in pure conceptual form. The attempt to do so is, according to Hegel, the continuation of the pioneer work of men such as St. Anselm who consciously set out to understand and justify by necessary reasons the content of faith.

4. As we have seen, the transition from religion to philosophy is in no way a transition from one subject-matter to another. The subject-matter is in both cases the same, 'the *eternal truth* in its objectivity, God and nothing but God and the unfolding [*die Explication*] of God'.[15] In this sense, therefore, 'religion and philosophy come to the same thing'.[16] 'Philosophy unfolds only itself when it unfolds religion; and when it unfolds itself, it unfolds religion.'[17]

The distinction between them lies in the different ways in which they conceive God, 'in the peculiar ways in which they occupy themselves with God'.[18] For example, the change from *Vorstellung* to pure thought involves the replacement of the form of contingency by that of logical sequence. Thus the theological concept of divine creation as a contingent event, in the sense that it might or might not have taken place, becomes in philosophy the doctrine that the *Logos* is necessarily objectified in Nature, not because the Absolute is subject to compulsion but because it is what it is. Speculative philosophy, in other words, strips away the imaginative or pictorial element which is characteristic of religious thought and expresses the truth, the same truth, in purely conceptual form.

It does not follow, however, that philosophy is irreligious. In Hegel's opinion the notion that philosophy and religion are incompatible or that the former is hostile or dangerous to the latter rests on a misconception of their respective natures. Both treat of God and both are religion. 'What they have in common is that both are religion; what distinguishes them lies only in the kind and manner of religion which we find in each.'[19] It is indeed this difference in their respective ways of apprehending and expressing the truth which gives rise to the idea that philosophy threatens religion. But philosophy would be a threat to religion only if it professed to substitute truth for falsity. And this is not the case. The truth is the same, though the religious consciousness demands a mode of expression which must be distinguished from that of philosophy.

One may be inclined to comment that Hegel uses the term 'religion' ambiguously. For he uses it to cover not only religious experience, faith and cult but also theology. And while a plausible case can be made out for saying that philosophy is not hostile to religious experience as such, or even to pure faith, it must necessarily be hostile to religion if religion is taken to mean or include theology and if philosophy proposes to reveal the unvarnished truth, as it were, which is contained in the doctrines which theologians believe to be the best possible expression of the truth in human language.

As regards the first point, Hegel insists that '*knowledge* is an essential part of the Christian religion itself'.[20] Christianity strives to understand its own faith. And speculative philosophy is a continuation of this attempt. The difference lies in the fact that philosophy substitutes the form of pure thought for the form of *Vorstellung*, pictorial or figurative thought. But this does not mean that speculative philosophy takes the place of Christianity in the sense that the latter is simply discarded in favour of the former. Christianity is the absolute religion and absolute idealism is the absolute philosophy. Both are true, and their truth is the same. The forms of conception and expression may differ, but it does not follow that Christianity is superseded by absolute idealism. For the human being is not simply pure thought: he is by no means only a philosopher, even if he is a philosopher at all. And for the religious consciousness Christian theology is the perfect expression of the truth. This is why preachers, who are addressing themselves to the religious consciousness, have no business to tamper with Christian dogmas. For Christianity is the revealed religion, in the sense that it is the perfect self-manifestation of God to the religious consciousness.

It is not my intention to imply that Hegel's attitude is consistent with the standpoint of Christian orthodoxy. For I am convinced that it is not. I agree with McTaggart, who was not himself a Christian believer, when he points out that as an ally of Christianity Hegelianism is 'an enemy in disguise —the least evident but the most dangerous. The doctrines which have been protected from external refutation are found to be transforming themselves till they are on the point of melting away. . . .'[21] Thus Hegel gives philosophical proofs of such doctrines as the Trinity, the Fall and the Incarnation. But when he has finished with stating them in the form of pure thought, they are obviously something very different from the doctrines which the Church believes to be the correct statement of the truth in human language. In other words, Hegel makes speculative philosophy the final arbiter of the inner meaning of Christian revelation. Absolute idealism is presented as esoteric Christianity and Christianity as exoteric Hegelianism; and the mystery insisted on by theology is subordinated to a philosophical clarification which amounts in fact to a transformation.

At the same time there is, in my opinion at least, no cogent reason for accusing Hegel of personal insincerity. I do not believe that when he posed as a champion of orthodoxy he had his tongue in his cheek. As was noted in the introductory chapter, Benedetto Croce argued that there could be no valid reason for retaining an inferior form of thought, namely religion, along with science, art and philosophy. If philosophy really gives the inner meaning of religious beliefs, then religion must give place to philosophy. That is to say, the two cannot coexist in the same mind. A man may think in the categories of religion or he may think in the categories of philosophy. But he cannot think in both. But while Croce's comments are by no means without point, it does not necessarily follow that they represent Hegel's real, though concealed, opinion. After all, Croce, though not a believing Catholic, was accustomed to the idea of ecclesiastical authority as the final arbiter of religious truth and its statement. And it is perfectly obvious that Hegel's theory of the relation of speculative philosophy to Christianity is incompatible with *this* idea. But Hegel was a Lutheran. And though the superiority of speculative philosophy to faith is very far from being a Lutheran idea, it was much easier for him than it would have been for Croce to be sincerely convinced that his view of the relation between the absolute philosophy and the absolute religion was acceptable from the Christian standpoint. He doubtless thought of himself as continuing the work of the theologians who in their accounts of the Christian dogmas endeavoured to avoid the crudely imaginative forms in which these dogmas were pictured by the theologically uneducated religious consciousness.

5. But the absolute philosophy is no more the only manifestation of the speculative reason than is the absolute religion the only manifestation of the religious consciousness. Just as art and religion have their history, so has philosophy. And this history is a dialectical process. From one point of view it is the process by which infinite Thought comes to

think itself explicitly, moving from one inadequate conception of itself to another and then uniting them in a higher
unity. From another point of view it is the process by which
the human mind moves dialectically towards an adequate conception of the ultimate reality, the Absolute. But these two
points of view represent simply different aspects of one process. For Spirit, self-thinking Thought, becomes explicit in
and through the reflection of the human mind on the level of
absolute knowledge.

This means, of course, that the different one-sided and inadequate concepts of reality which emerge at different stages
of the history of philosophy are taken up and preserved in
the succeeding higher stages. 'The last philosophy is the result of all earlier ones: nothing is lost, all principles are preserved.'[22] 'The general result of the history of philosophy is
this. First, throughout all time there has been only one philosophy, the contemporary differences of which represent the
necessary aspects of the one principle. Secondly, the succession of philosophical systems is no matter of chance but exhibits the necessary succession of stages in the development
of this science. Thirdly, the final philosophy of a period is
the result of this development and is truth in the highest
form which the self-consciousness of Spirit affords. The final
philosophy, therefore, contains the ones which went before;
it embraces in itself all their stages; it is the product and
result of all the philosophies which preceded it.'[23]

Now, if the history of philosophy is the development of
the divine self-knowledge, of absolute self-consciousness, the
successive stages in this history will tend to correspond with
the successive phases or moments in the Notion or logical
Idea. We find, therefore, that Hegel represents Parmenides
as the first genuine philosopher, the man who apprehended
the Absolute as Being, while Heraclitus affirms the Absolute
as Becoming. If this is taken as a statement of chronological
sequence, it is open to criticism. But it illustrates Hegel's
general procedure. Like Aristotle before him, he looks on his
predecessors as bringing to light aspects of truth which are
preserved, elevated and integrated with complementary as-

pects in his own system. Needless to say, the explicit and adequate recognition of the category of Spirit is reserved for German idealism. And the philosophies of Fichte and Schelling are treated as moments in the development of absolute idealism.

Hegel's history of philosophy is thus an integral part of his system. It is not simply an account of what philosophers have held, of the factors which influenced their thought and led them to think in the ways that they did, and of their influence on their successors and perhaps on society at large. It is a sustained attempt to exhibit a necessary dialectical advance, a teleological development, in the data of the history of philosophy. And this enterprise is obviously carried out in the light of a general philosophy. It is the work of a philosopher looking back on the past from the vantage-point of a system which he believes to be the highest expression of the truth up to date and seeing this system as the culmination of a process of reflection which, in spite of all contingent elements, has been in its essential outlines a necessary movement of Thought coming to think itself. Hegel's history of philosophy is thus a philosophy of the history of philosophy. If it is objected that the selection of the essential elements in a given system is governed by philosophical preconceptions or principles, Hegel can, of course, answer that any history of philosophy worthy of the name necessarily involves not only interpretation but also a separation of the essential from the unessential in the light of beliefs about what is philosophically important and what is not. But such an answer, though reasonable enough, would not be adequate in the context. For just as Hegel approaches the philosophy of history with the belief that the history of mankind is a rational teleological process, so does he approach the history of philosophy with the conviction that this history is 'the temple of self-conscious reason',[24] the dialectically continuous and progressive determination of the Idea, 'a logical progress impelled by an inherent necessity',[25] the one true philosophy developing itself in time, the dynamic process of self-thinking Thought.

Does this conception of the history of philosophy imply the conclusion that for Hegel his philosophy is the final system, the system to end all systems? He has sometimes been represented as thinking precisely this. But it seems to me that this picture is a caricature. He does indeed depict German idealism in general, and his own system in particular, as the highest stage yet reached in the historical development of philosophy. In view of his interpretation of the history of philosophy he cannot do anything else. And he makes remarks which lend themselves for use by those who wish to ascribe to him the absurd idea that with Hegelianism philosophy comes to an end. 'A new epoch has arisen in the world. It seems that the World-Spirit has now succeeded in freeing itself from all alien objective existence and in apprehending itself at last as absolute Spirit. . . . The strife between the finite self-consciousness and the absolute self-consciousness, which seemed to finite self-consciousness to lie outside it, now ceases. Finite self-consciousness has ceased to be finite, and thereby absolute self-consciousness on the other hand has attained the reality which it formerly lacked.'[26] But though this passage clearly states that absolute idealism is the culmination of all preceding philosophy, Hegel goes on to speak of 'the whole history of the World in general and of the history of philosophy in particular up to the present'.[27] And is it probable that a man who stated roundly that 'philosophy is *its own time expressed in thoughts*'[28] and that it is just as foolish to suppose that a philosophy can transcend its contemporary world as it is to suppose that an individual can overleap his own time seriously thought that philosophy had come to an end with himself? Obviously, on Hegel's principles subsequent philosophy would have to incorporate absolute idealism, even if his system revealed itself as a one-sided moment in a higher synthesis. But to say this is not the same as to deny that there could be or would be any subsequent philosophy.

There is, however, this point. If Christianity is the absolute religion, Hegelianism, as esoteric Christianity, must be the absolute philosophy. And if we take the word 'absolute' in this context as meaning truth in the highest form which it has yet attained rather than as meaning the final or terminal statement of the truth, Christianity is no more the final religion than is Hegelianism the final philosophy. On Hegel's own principles Christianity and absolute idealism stand or fall together. And if we wish to say that Christianity cannot be surpassed whereas Hegelianism can, we cannot at the same time accept Hegel's account of the relation between the two.

6. In view of the comprehensive character of Hegel's system and of the commanding position which he came to occupy in the German philosophical world it is not surprising that his influence was felt in a variety of fields. As one would expect in the case of a man whose thought centred round the Absolute and who appeared, to the not too critical or too orthodox observer, to have provided a rational justification of Christianity in terms of the most up-to-date philosophy, his sphere of influence included the theological field. For example, Karl Daub (1765–1836), professor of theology at Heidelberg, abandoned the ideas of Schelling and endeavoured to use the dialectical method of Hegel in the service of Protestant theology. Another eminent theologian who was converted or seduced, according as one chooses to regard the matter, by the attraction of Hegel was Philipp Konrad Marheineke (1780–1846) who became a professor of theology at Berlin and who helped to edit the first general edition of Hegel's works. In his posthumously published *System of Christian Dogmatics* Marheineke attempted to translate Hegelianism into the terms of Christian theology and at the same time to interpret the content of Christian dogma in the Hegelian manner. For instance, he represented the Absolute as attaining full consciousness of itself in the Church, which was for him the concrete actualization of Spirit, this Spirit being interpreted as the Third Person of the Trinity.

The history of ethical systems was studied from an Hegelian point of view by Leopold von Henning (1791–1866) who followed Hegel's courses at Berlin and became one of his most fervent admirers. In the field of law Hegel's influence was considerable. Prominent among his disciples was the cele-

brated jurist Eduard Gans (1798–1839) who obtained a chair
of law at Berlin and published a well-known work on the
right of inheritance.[29] In the field of aesthetics Heinrich
Theodor Rötscher (1803–71) may be mentioned as one of
those who derived inspiration from Hegel. In the history of
philosophy Hegel's influence was felt by such eminent historians as Johann Eduard Erdmann (1805–92), Eduard Zel-
ler (1814–1908) and Kuno Fischer (1824–1907). Whatever
one may think of absolute idealism, one cannot deny Hegel's
stimulating effect on scholars in a variety of fields.

To return to the theological field. We have noted that the
Hegelian system left room for dispute about its precise relation to Christian theism. And in point of fact controversy
arose on this topic even before Hegel's death, though this
event naturally gave it fresh impetus. Some writers, who are
generally classified as belonging to the Hegelian right wing,
maintained that absolute idealism could be legitimately interpreted in a sense compatible with Christianity. While
Hegel was still alive Karl Friedrich Göschel (1784–1861)
tried to interpret the philosopher's theory of the relation between the form of thought peculiar to the religious consciousness and pure thought or knowledge in such a way as not to
imply that religion is inferior to philosophy. And this defence
of Hegel met with a warm response from the philosopher.
After Hegel's death Göschel published writings designed to
show that Hegelianism was compatible with the doctrines of
a personal God and of personal immortality. Mention can
also be made of Karl Ludwig Michelet (1801–93), a Berlin
professor, who identified the Hegelian triad with the Persons
of the Trinity (as indeed Hegel himself had done) and tried
to show that there was no incompatibility between Hegelianism and Christian theology.

The left wing was represented, for example, by David
Friedrich Strauss (1808–74), author of the celebrated *Life of
Jesus* (1835). According to Strauss the Gospel stories were
myths, and he explicitly connected this view with Hegel's
theory of *Vorstellung* and represented his own dissolution of
historic Christianity as a genuine development of Hegel's

thought. He thus provided valuable ammunition for the Christian writers who refused to accept the contention of the right-wing Hegelians that Hegelianism and Christianity were compatible.

The centre of the Hegelian movement can be represented by the name of Johann Karl Friedrich Rosenkranz (1805–79), biographer of Hegel and a professor at Königsberg. As a pupil of both Schleiermacher and Hegel he tried to mediate between them in his development of the Hegelian system. In his *Encyclopaedia of the Theological Sciences* (1831) he distinguished between speculative, historical and practical theology. Speculative theology exhibits the absolute religion, Christianity, in an *a priori* form. Historical theology deals with the temporal objectification of this Idea or concept of the absolute religion. In his evaluation of historic Christianity Rosenkranz was more restrained than Strauss, who looked on him as belonging to the centre of the Hegelian school. Later on Rosenkranz attempted to develop Hegel's logic, though his efforts in this direction were not much appreciated by other Hegelians.

We can say, therefore, that the split between right- and left-wing Hegelians concerned first of all the interpretation, evaluation and development of Hegel's position in regard to religious and theological problems. The right wing interpreted Hegel in a sense more or less compatible with Christianity, which meant that God had to be represented as a personal, self-conscious Being in his own right, so to speak. The left wing maintained a pantheistic interpretation and denied personal immortality.

The left wing, however, soon went beyond pantheism to naturalism and atheism. And at the hands of Marx and Engels the Hegelian theories of society and history were revolutionized. The left wing is thus of much greater historical importance than the right wing. But the radical thinkers of the former group must be accorded separate treatment and not treated as disciples of Hegel, who would scarcely have recognized them as such.

Under the heading of the influence of Hegel we might

refer, of course, to the British idealism of the second half of the nineteenth century and of the first two decades of the present century, to Italian philosophers such as Benedetto Croce (1866–1952) and Giovanni Gentile (1875–1944) and to recent French works on Hegel, not to mention other examples of the philosopher's long-term influence. But these topics would take us outside the scope of the present volume. Instead we can turn to consideration of the reaction against metaphysical idealism and of the emergence of other lines of thought in the German philosophical world of the nineteenth century.

APPENDIX

A SHORT BIBLIOGRAPHY

General Works

Abbagnano, N. *Storia della filosofia:* II, *parte seconda.* Turin, 1950.

Adamson, R. *The Development of Modern Philosophy, with other Lectures and Essays.* Edinburgh, 1908 (2nd edition).

Alexander, A. B. D. *A Short History of Philosophy.* Glasgow, 1922 (3rd edition).

Bosanquet, B. *A History of Aesthetic.* London, 1892.

Bréhier, E. *Histoire de la philosophie:* II, *deuxième partie.* Paris, 1944. (Bréhier's work is one of the best histories of philosophy, and it contains brief, but useful, bibliographies.)

Histoire de la philosophie allemande. Paris, 1933 (2nd edition).

Castell, A. *An Introduction to Modern Philosophy in Six Problems.* New York, 1943.

Catlin, G. *A History of the Political Philosophers.* London, 1950.

Collins, J. *A History of Modern European Philosophy.* Milwaukee, 1954. (This work by a Thomist can be highly recommended. It contains useful bibliographies.)

God in Modern Philosophy. London, 1960. (In the relevant period this work contains treatments of Hegel, Feuerbach, Marx and Kierkegaard.)

De Ruggiero, G. *Storia della filosofia:* IV, *la filosofia moderna. L'età del romanticismo.* Bari, 1943.

Hegel. Bari, 1948.

Deussen, P. *Allgemeine Geschichte der Philosophie:* II, 3, *Neuere Philosophie von Descartes bis Schopenhauer.* Leipzig, 1922 (3rd edition).

Devaux, P. *De Thalès à Bergson. Introduction historique à la philosophie.* Liège, 1948.

Erdmann, J. E. *A History of Philosophy:* II, *Modern Philosophy,* translated by W. S. Hough. London, 1889, and subsequent editions.

Falckenberg, R. *Geschichte der neuern Philosophie.* Berlin, 1921 (8th edition).

Fischer, K. *Geschichte der neuern Philosophie.* 10 vols. Heidelberg, 1897–1904. (This work includes separate volumes on Fichte, Schelling, Hegel and Schopenhauer, as listed under these names.)

Fischl, J. *Geschichte der Philosophie,* 5 vols. III, *Aufklärung und deutscher Idealismus.* IV, *Positivismus und Materialismus.* Vienna, 1950.

Fuller, B. A. G. *A History of Philosophy.* New York, 1945 (revised edition).

Hegel, G. W. F. *Lectures on the History of Philosophy,* translated by E. S. Haldane and F. H. Simson. Vol. III. London, 1895. (Hegel's history of philosophy forms part of his system.)

Heimsoeth, H. *Metaphysik der Neuzeit.* Munich, 1929.

Hirschberger, J. *The History of Philosophy,* translated by A. Fuerst, 2 vols. Milwaukee, 1959. (The second volume treats of modern philosophy.)

Höffding, H. *A History of Philosophy* (modern), translated by B. E. Meyer, 2 vols. London, 1900 (American reprint, 1924).
    A Brief History of Modern Philosophy, translated by C. F. Sanders, London, 1912.

Jones, W. T. *A History of Western Philosophy:* II, *The Modern Mind.* New York, 1952.

Klimke, F., S.J. and Colomer, E., S.J. *Historia de la filosofía.* Barcelona, 1961 (3rd edition).

Marías, J. *Historia de la filosofía.* Madrid, 1941.

Meyer, H. *Geschichte der abendländischen Weltanschauung:* IV, *Von der Renaissance zum deutschen Idealismus:* V, *Die Weltanschauung der Gegenwart.* Würzburg, 1950.

Oesterreich, T. K. *Die deutsche Philosophie des XIX Jahr-*

hunderts. Berlin, 1923 (reproduction, 1953). (This is the fourth volume of the new revised edition of Ueberweg's *Grundriss der Geschichte der Philosophie*. It contains extensive bibliographies and is useful as a work of reference.)

Randall, H., Jr. *The Making of the Modern Mind*. Boston, 1940 (revised edition).

Rogers, A. K. *A Student's History of Philosophy*. New York, 1954 (3rd edition reprinted). (A straightforward textbook.)

Russell, Bertrand. *History of Western Philosophy and Its Connection with Political and Social Circumstances from the Earliest Times to the Present Day*. London, 1946, and reprints.

    Wisdom of the West. An Historical Survey of Western Philosophy in Its Social and Political Setting. London, 1959. (For German philosophy in the nineteenth century the last-named work is to be preferred to the first.)

Sabine, G. H. *A History of Political Theory*. London, 1941. (A valuable study of the subject.)

Schilling, K. *Geschichte der Philosophie*: II, *Die Neuzeit*. Munich, 1953. (Contains useful bibliographies.)

Souilhé, J. *La philosophie chrétienne de Descartes à nos jours*. 2 vols. Paris, 1934.

Thilly, F. *A History of Philosophy*, revised by L. Wood. New York, 1951.

Thonnard, F. J. *Précis d'histoire de la philosophie*. Paris, 1941 (revised edition).

Turner, W. *History of Philosophy*. Boston and London, 1903.

Vorländer, K. *Geschichte der Philosophie*: II, *Philosophie der Neuzeit*. Leipzig, 1919 (5th edition).

Webb, C. C. J. *A History of Philosophy*. (Home University Library.) London, 1915 and reprints.

Windelband, W. *A History of Philosophy, with especial reference to the Formation and Development of its Problems and Conceptions*, translated by J. A. Tufts. New York and London, 1952 (reprint of 1901 edition). (This

notable work treats the history of philosophy according
to the development of problems.)

Lehrbuch der Geschichte der Philosophie, edited by H.
Heimsoeth with a concluding chapter, *Die Philosophie
im 20 Jahrhundert mit einer Uebersicht über den Stand
der philosophie-geschichtlichen Forschung.* Tübingen,
1935.

Wright, W. K. *A History of Modern Philosophy.* New York,
1941.

Chapter I: General Works Relating to the German Idealist Movement

Benz, R. *Die deutsche Romantik*, Leipzig, 1937.

Cassirer, E. *Das Erkenntnisproblem in der Philosophie und
Wissenschaft der neueren Zeit:* III, *Die nachkantischen
Systeme.* Berlin, 1920.

Delbos, V. *De Kant aux Postkantiens.* Paris, 1940.

Flügel, O. *Die Religionsphilosophie des absoluten Idealismus: Fichte, Schelling, Hegel, Schopenhauer.* Langen-
salza, 1905.

Gardeil, H.-D. *Les étages de la philosophie idéaliste.* Paris,
1935.

Groos, H. *Der deutsche Idealismus und das Christentum.*
Munich, 1927.

Hartmann, N. *Die Philosophie des deutschen Idealismus.*
Berlin, 1960. 2nd edition (originally 2 vols., 1923–9).

Haym, R. *Die romantische Schule.* Berlin, 1928 (5th edition).

Hirsch, E. *Die idealistische Philosophie und das Christentum.*
Gütersloh, 1926.

Kircher, E. *Philosophie der Romantik.* Jena, 1906.

Kroner, R. *Von Kant bis Hegel.* 2 vols. Tübingen, 1921–4.
(This work and that of N. Hartmann are classical treatments of the subject, from different points of view.)

Lutgert, W. *Die Religion des deutschen Idealismus und ihr
Ende.* Gütersloh, 1923.

Maréchal, J., S.J. *Le point de départ de la métaphysique.*

Cahier IV: *Le système idéaliste chez Kant et les post-kantiens*. Paris, 1947.

Michelet, C. L. *Geschichte der letzten Systeme der Philosophie in Deutschland von Kant bis Hegel*. 2 vols. Berlin, 1837–8.

Entwicklungsgeschichte der neuesten deutschen Philosophie. Berlin, 1843.

Chapters II–IV: Fichte

Texts

Sämmtliche Werke, edited by I. H. Fichte. 8 vols. Berlin, 1845–6.

Nachgelassene Werke, edited by I. H. Fichte. 3 vols. Bonn, 1834–5.

Werke, edited by F. Medicus. 6 vols. Leipzig, 1908–12. (This edition does not contain all Fichte's works.)

Fichtes Briefwechsel, edited by H. Schulz. 2 vols. Leipzig, 1925.

Die Schriften zu J. G. Fichte's Atheismus-streit, edited by H. Lindau. Munich, 1912.

Fichte und Forberg. Die philosophischen Scriften zum Atheismus-streit, edited by F. Medicus. Leipzig, 1910.

The Science of Knowledge, translated by A. E. Kroeger. Philadelphia, 1868; London, 1889.

New Exposition of the Science of Knowledge, translated by A. E. Kroeger. St. Louis, 1869.

The Science of Rights, translated by A. E. Kroeger. Philadelphia, 1869; London, 1889.

The Science of Ethics, translated by A. E. Kroeger. London, 1907.

Fichte's Popular Works, translated, with a memoir of Fichte, by W. Smith. 2 vols. London, 1889 (4th edition).

Addresses to the German Nation, translated by R. F. Jones and G. H. Turnbull. Chicago, 1922.

J. G. Fichtes Leben und literarischer Briefwechsel, by I. H. Fichte. Leipzig, 1862 (2nd edition).

Studies

Adamson, R. *Fichte*. Edinburgh and London, 1881.

Bergmann, E. *Fichte der Erzieher*. Leipzig, 1928 (2nd edition).

Engelbrecht, H. C. J. G. *Fichte: A Study of His Political Writings with special Reference to His Nationalism*. New York, 1933.

Fischer, K. *Fichtes Leben, Werke und Lehre*. Heidelberg, 1914 (4th edition).

Gogarten, F. *Fichte als religiöser Denker*. Jena, 1914.

Gueroult, M. *L'évolution et la structure de la doctrine de la science chez Fichte*. 2 vols. Paris, 1930.

Heimsoeth, H. *Fichte*. Munich, 1923.

Hirsch, E. *Fichtes Religionsphilosophie*. Göttingen, 1914.
  Christentum und Geschichte in Fichtes Philosophie. Göttingen, 1920.

Léon, X. *La philosophie de Fichte*. Paris, 1902.
  Fichte et son temps. 2 vols. (in 3). Paris, 1922–7.

Pareyson, L. *Fichte*. Turin, 1950.

Rickert, H. *Fichtes Atheismusstreit und die kantische Philosophie*. Berlin, 1899.

Ritzel, W. *Fichtes Religionsphilosophie*. Stuttgart, 1956.

Stine, R. W. *The Doctrine of God in the Philosophy of Fichte*. Philadelphia, 1945 (dissertation).

Thompson, A. B. *The Unity of Fichte's Doctrine of Knowledge*. Boston, 1896.

Turnbull, G. H. *The Educational Theory of Fichte*. London, 1926.

Wallner, F. *Fichte als politischer Denker*. Halle, 1926.

Wundt, M. *Fichte*. Stuttgart, 1937 (2nd edition).

Chapters V–VII: Schelling

Texts

Sämmtliche Werke, edited by K. F. A. Schelling. *Erste Abteilung*, 10 vols., 1856–61; *Zweite Abteilung*, 4 vols., 1856–8. Stuttgart and Augsburg.

Werke, edited by M. Schröter. 6 vols. Munich, 1927–8; 2 supplementary vols. Munich, 1943–56.

Of Human Freedom, translated by J. Gutman. Chicago, 1936.

The Ages of the World, translated by F. Bolman, Jr. New York, 1942.

The Philosophy of Art: An Oration on the Relation between the Plastic Arts and Nature, translated by A. Johnson. London, 1845.

Essais, translated by S. Jankélévitch. Paris, 1946.

Introduction à la philosophie de la mythologie, translated by S. Jankélévitch. Paris, 1945.

Studies

Bausola, A. *Saggi sulla filosofia di Schelling*. Milan, 1960.

Benz, E. *Schelling, Werden und Wirkung seines Denkens*. Zürich and Stuttgart, 1955.

Bréhier, E. *Schelling*. Paris, 1912.

Dekker, G. *Die Rückwendung zum Mythos. Schellings letzte Wandlung*. Munich and Berlin, 1930.

Drago del Boca, S. *La filosofia di Schelling*. Florence, 1943.

Fischer, K. *Schellings Leben, Werke und Lehre*. Heidelberg, 1902 (3rd edition).

Fuhrmans, H. *Schellings letzte Philosophie. Die negative und positive Philosophie im Einsatz des Spätidealismus*. Berlin, 1940.

Schellings Philosophie der Weltalter. Düsseldorf, 1954.

Gibelin, J. *L'ésthetique de Schelling d'après la philosophie de l'art*. Paris, 1934.

Gray-Smith, R. *God in the Philosophy of Schelling*. Philadelphia, 1933 (dissertation).

Hirsch, E. D., Jr. *Wordsworth and Schelling*. London, 1960.

Jankélévitch, V. *L'odysée de la conscience dans la dernière philosophie de Schelling*. Paris, 1933.

Jaspers, K. *Schelling: Grösse und Verhängnis*. Munich, 1955.

Knittermeyer, H. *Schelling und die romantische Schule*. Munich, 1929.

Koehler, E. *Schellings Wendung zum Theismus*. Leipzig, 1932 (dissertation).

Massolo, A. *Il primo Schelling*. Florence, 1953.

Mazzei, V. *Il pensiero etico-politico di Friedrich Schelling*. Rome, 1938.

Noack, L. *Schelling und die Philosophie der Romantik*. Berlin, 1859.

Schulz, W. *Die Vollendung des deutschen Idealismus in der Spätphilosophie Schellings*. Stuttgart and Cologne, 1955.

Watson, J. *Schelling's Transcendental Idealism*. Chicago, 1892 (2nd edition).

For a further bibliography see: *Friedrich Wilhelm Joseph von Schelling. Eine Bibliographie*, by G. Schneeberger. Bern, 1954.

Chapter VIII: Schleiermacher

Texts

Werke, Berlin, 1835–64. (Section I, theology, 13 vols.; Section II, sermons, 10 vols.; Section III, philosophy, 9 vols.)

Werke (selections), edited by O. Braun. 4 vols. Leipzig, 1910–13.

Addresses on Religion, translated by J. Oman. London, 1894.

The Theology of Schleiermacher, a Condensed Presentation of His Chief Work 'The Christian Faith', by G. Cross. Chicago, 1911.

Studies

Baxmann, R. *Schleiermacher, sein Leben und Wirken*. Elberfeld, 1868.

Brandt, R. B. *The Philosophy of Schleiermacher*. New York, 1941.

Dilthey, W. *Leben Schleiermachers*. Berlin, 1920 (2nd edition).

Fluckinger, F. *Philosophie und Theologie bei Schleiermacher*. Zürich, 1947.

Keppstein, T. *Schleiermachers Weltbild und Lebensanschauung.* Munich, 1921.

Neglia, F. *La filosofia della religione di Schleiermacher.* Turin, 1952.

Neumann, J. *Schleiermacher.* Berlin, 1936.

Reble, A. *Schleiermachers Kulturphilosophie.* Erfurt, 1935.

Schultz, L. W. *Das Verhältnis von Ich und Wirklichkeit in der religiösen Antropologie Schleiermachers.* Göttingen, 1935.

Schutz, W. *Schleiermacher und der Protestantismus.* Hamburg, 1957.

Visconti, L. *La dottrina educativa di F. D. Schleiermacher.* Florence, 1920.

Wendland, I. *Die religiöse Entwicklung Schleiermachers.* Tübingen, 1915.

Chapters IX–XI: Hegel

Texts

Werke, Jubiläumsausgabe, edited by H. G. Glockner. 26 vols. Stuttgart, 1927–39. The first 20 vols., containing Hegel's writings, are a reprint of the 1832–87 edition (19 vols.). Vols. 21–2 contain Glockner's *Hegel* and Vols. 23–6 his *Hegel-Lexikon.*

Sämmtliche Werke, kritische Ausgabe, edited by G. Lasson and J. Hoffmeister. This critical edition, originally published at Leipzig (F. Meiner), was begun by G. Lasson (1862–1932) in 1905. On Lasson's death it was continued by J. Hoffmeister, and from 1949 it was published at Hamburg (F. Meiner). It was planned to contain 24 (later 26 and then 27) vols. Some of the vols. went through several editions. For example, a third edition of Vol. 2 (*Die Phänomenologie des Geistes*) appeared in 1929 and a third edition of Vol. 6 (*Grundlinien der Philosophie des Rechts*) in 1930. The total work remains unfinished.

Sämmtliche Werke, neue kritische Ausgabe, edited by J. Hoffmeister. This edition, planned to contain 32 vols., is published at Hamburg (F. Meiner) and is designed both to complete and to supersede the Lasson-Hoffmeister edition, now known as the *Erste kritische Ausgabe*. The situation is somewhat complicated as some of the volumes of the Lasson-Hoffmeister edition are being taken over by the new critical edition. For instance, the first part of Hoffmeister's edition of Hegel's *Vorlesungen über die Geschichte der Philosophie,* which was published in 1940 as Vol. 15a in the *Kritische Ausgabe,* becomes Vol. 20 in the *Neue kritische Ausgabe.* Again, the first volume of Hoffmeister's edition of letters written by and to Hegel (1952) bore the title *Kritische Ausgabe* and mention was made of Lasson as the original editor, whereas the second volume (1953) bore the title *Neue kritische Ausgabe* and no mention was made of Lasson. (The *Briefe von und an Hegel* form Vols. 27–30 in the new critical edition.)

Hegels theologische Jugendschriften, edited by H. Nohl. Tübingen, 1907.

Dokumente zu Hegels Entwicklung, edited by J. Hoffmeister. Stuttgart, 1936.

G. W. F. Hegel: Early Theological Writings, translated by T. M. Knox with an introduction by R. Kroner. Chicago, 1948.

The Phenomenology of Mind, translated by J. Baillie. London, 1931 (2nd edition).

Encyclopaedia of Philosophy, translated and annotated by G. E. Mueller. New York, 1959.

Science of Logic, translated by W. H. Johnston and L. G. Struthers. 2 vols. London, 1929. (This is the so-called 'Greater Logic' of Hegel.)

The Logic of Hegel, translated from the Encyclopaedia of the Philosophical Sciences, translated by W. Wallace. Oxford, 1892 (2nd edition). (This is the so-called 'Lesser Logic'.)

Hegel's Philosophy of Mind, translated from the Encyclopaedia of the Philosophical Sciences, translated by W. Wallace. Oxford, 1894.

The Philosophy of Right, translated and annotated by T. M. Knox. Oxford, 1942.

Philosophy of History, translated by J. Sibree. London, 1861.

The Philosophy of Fine Art, translated by F. P. B. Osmaston. 4 vols. London, 1920.

Lectures on the Philosophy of Religion, together with a Work on the Proofs of the Existence of God, translated by E. B. Speirs and J. B. Sanderson. 3 vols. London, 1895 (reprint 1962).

Lectures on the History of Philosophy, translated by E. S. Haldane and F. H. Simpson. 3 vols. London, 1892–6.

Studies

Adams, G. P. *The Mystical Element in Hegel's Early Theological Writings*. Berkeley, 1910.

Aspelin, G. *Hegels Tübinger Fragment*. Lund, 1933.

Asveld, P. *La pensée religieuse du jeune Hegel. Liberté et aliénation*. Louvain, 1953.

Baillie, J. *The Origin and Significance of Hegel's Logic*. London, 1901.

Balbino, G. *Der Grundirrtum Hegels*. Graz, 1914.

Brie, S. *Der Volksgeist bei Hegel und die historische Rechtsschule*. Berlin, 1909.

Bullinger, A. *Hegelsche Logik und gegenwärtig herrschender antihegelische Unverstand*. Munich, 1901.

Bülow, F. *Die Entwicklung der Hegelschen Sozialphilosophie*. Leipzig, 1920.

Caird, E. *Hegel*. London and Edinburgh, 1883. (This is still an excellent introduction to Hegel.)

Cairns, H. *Legal Philosophy from Plato to Hegel*. Baltimore, 1949.

Coreth, E., S.J. *Das dialektische Sein in Hegels Logik*. Vienna, 1952.

Cresson, A. *Hegel, sa vie, son œuvre*. Paris, 1949.

Croce, B. *What Is Living and What Is Dead in the Philosophy of Hegel*, translated by D. Ainslie. London, 1915.

Cunningham, G. W. *Thought and Reality in Hegel's System*. New York, 1910.

De Ruggiero, G. *Hegel*. Bari, 1948.

Dilthey, W. *Die Jugendgeschichte Hegels*. Berlin, 1905. (Contained in Dilthey's *Gesammelte Schriften*, IV; Berlin, 1921.)

Dulckeit, G. *Die Idee Gottes im Geiste der Philosophie Hegels*. Munich, 1947.

Emge, C. A. *Hegels Logik und die Gegenwart*. Karlsruhe, 1927.

Findlay, J. N. *Hegel. A Re-Examination*. London, 1958. (A sympathetic and systematic account of Hegel's philosophy, in which the metaphysical aspect is minimized.)

Fischer, K. *Hegels Leben, Werke und Lehre*. 2 vols. Heidelberg, 1911 (2nd edition).

Foster, M. B. *The Political Philosophies of Plato and Hegel*. Oxford, 1935.

Glockner, H. *Hegel*. 2 vols. Stuttgart. (Vols. 21 and 22 in Glockner's edition of Hegel's *Works* mentioned above.)

Grégoire, F. *Aux sources de la pensée de Marx: Hegel, Feuerbach*. Louvain, 1947.

   Études hégéliennes. Louvain, 1958.

Häring, T. *Hegel, sein Wollen und sein Werk*. 2 vols. Leipzig, 1929–38.

Haym, R. *Hegel und seine Zeit*. Leipzig, 1927 (2nd edition).

Heimann, B. *System und Methode in Hegels Philosophie*. Leipzig, 1927.

Hoffmeister, J. *Hölderlin und Hegel*. Tübingen, 1931.

   Goethe und der deutsche Idealismus. Eine Einführung zu Hegels Realphilosophie. Leipzig, 1932.

   Die Problematik des Völkerbundes bei Kant und Hegel. Tübingen, 1934.

Hyppolite, J. *Genèse et structure de la Phénoménologie de l'Esprit de Hegel*. Paris, 1946. (A very valuable commentary.)

   Introduction à la philosophie de l'histoire de Hegel. Paris, 1948.

   Logique et existence: Essai sur la logique de Hegel. Paris, 1953.

Iljin, I. *Die Philosophie Hegels als kontemplative Gotteslehre*. Bern, 1946.

Kojève, A. *Introduction à la lecture de Hegel.* Paris, 1947 (2nd edition). (The author gives an atheistic interpretation of Hegel.)

Lakebrink, B. *Hegels dialektische Ontologie und die thomistiche Analektik.* Cologne, 1955.

Lasson, G. *Was heisst Hegelianismus?* Berlin, 1916.

  Einführung in Hegels Religionsphilosophie. Leipzig, 1930. (This book constitutes an introduction to Vol. 12 of Lasson's critical edition of Hegel's *Works,* mentioned above. There are similar introductions by Lasson; for example, *Hegel als Geschichtsphilosoph,* Leipzig, 1920.)

Litt, T. *Hegel. Versuch einer kritischen Erneuerung.* Heidelberg, 1953.

Lukács, G. *Der junge Hegel. Ueber die Beziehungen von Dialektik und Oekonomie.* Berlin, 1954 (2nd edition). (The author writes from the Marxist point of view.)

Maggiore, G. *Hegel.* Milan, 1924.

Maier, J. *On Hegel's Critique of Kant.* New York, 1939.

Marcuse, M. *Reason and Revolution: Hegel and the Rise of Social Theory.* New York, 1954 (2nd edition).

McTaggart, J. McT. E. *Commentary on Hegel's Logic.* Cambridge, 1910.

  Studies in the Hegelian Dialectic. Cambridge, 1922 (2nd edition).

  Studies in Hegelian Cosmology. Cambridge, 1918 (2nd edition).

Moog, W. *Hegel und die Hegelsche Schule.* Munich, 1930.

Mure, G. R. G. *An Introduction to Hegel.* Oxford, 1940. (Stresses Hegel's relation to Aristotle.)

  A Study of Hegel's Logic. Oxford, 1950.

Negri, A. *La presenza di Hegel.* Florence, 1961.

Niel, H., S.J. *De la médiation dans la philosophie de Hegel.* Paris, 1945. (A study of Hegel's philosophy in the light of the pervading concept of mediation.)

Nink, C., S.J. *Kommentar zu den grundlegenden Abschnitten von Hegels Phänomenologie des Geistes.* Regensburg, 1931.

Ogiermann, H. A., S.J. *Hegels Gottesbeweise.* Rome, 1948.

Olgiati, F. *Il panlogismo hegeliano.* Milan, 1946.

Pelloux, L. *La logica di Hegel*. Milan, 1938.

Peperzak, A. T. B. *Le jeune Hegel et la vision morale du monde*. The Hague, 1960.

Pringle-Pattison, A. S. (=A. Seth). *Hegelianism and Personality*. London, 1893 (2nd edition).

Reyburn, H. A. *The Ethical Theory of Hegel: A Study of the Philosophy of Right*. Oxford, 1921.

Roques, P. *Hegel, sa vie et ses œuvres*. Paris, 1912.

Rosenkranz, K. G. W. F. *Hegels Leben*. Berlin, 1844.

Erläuterungen zu Hegels Enzyklopädie der Philosophie. Berlin, 1870.

Rosenzweig, F. *Hegel und der Staat*. 2 vols. Oldenburg, 1920.

Schmidt, E. *Hegels Lehre von Gott*. Gütersloh, 1952.

Schneider, R. *Schellings und Hegels schwäbische Geistesahnen*. Würzburg, 1938.

Schwarz, J. *Die anthropologische Metaphysik des jungen Hegel*. Hildesheim, 1931.

Hegels philosophische Entwicklung. Frankfurt a. M., 1938.

Specht, E. K. *Der Analogiebegriff bei Kant und Hegel*. Cologne, 1952.

Stace, W. T. *The Philosophy of Hegel*. London, 1924 (new edition, New York, 1955). (A systematic and clear account.)

Steinbüchel, T. *Das Grundproblem der Hegelschen Philosophie*. Vol. 1. Bonn, 1933. (The author, a Catholic priest, died before the completion of the work.)

Stirling, J. H. *The Secret of Hegel*. London, 1865.

Teyssedre, B. *L'ésthetique de Hegel*. Paris, 1958.

Vanni Rovighi, S. *La concezione hegeliana della Storia*. Milan, 1942.

Wacher, H. *Das Verhältnis des jungen Hegel zu Kant*. Berlin, 1932.

Wahl, J. *Le malheur de la conscience dans la philosophie de Hegel*. Paris, 1951 (2nd edition). (A valuable study.)

Wallace, W. *Prolegomena to the Study of Hegel's Philosophy and especially of his Logic*. Oxford, 1894 (2nd edition).

Weil, E. *Hegel et l'état*. Paris, 1950.

NOTES

[1] The fact that there were later idealist movements in Britain, America, Italy and elsewhere does not alter the fact that after Hegel metaphysical idealism in Germany suffered an eclipse.

[2] I say 'could develop' because reflection on Kant's philosophy can lead to different lines of thought, according to the aspects which one emphasizes. See Vol. VI, Part II, pp. 223

[3] See Vol. VI, Part II, pp. 62–6, 175–7.

[4] See Vol. IV, pp. 70–5 and Vol. VI, Part II, pp. 28–9.

[5] Vol. IV, p. 71.

[6] Necessity and causality are for Kant a priori categories. But he does not deny, indeed he affirms, that the world of science is 'phenomenally real'.

[7] This is true at least if we refrain from pressing Kant's doctrine of the restricted field of application of the categories to an extent which would exclude any meaningful talk about supersensuous reality, even in the context of moral faith.

[8] See Vol. 6, Part II, ch. 15.

[9] Hegel admits the idea of free creation on the level of the language of the religious consciousness. But this language is for him pictorial or figurative.

[10] See Vol. VI, Part I, pp. 210–1, 214–6.

[11] According to Rudolf Carnap, metaphysical systems express a feeling for or attitude towards life. But such terms are much more applicable to the romantic spirit than, say, to Hegel's dialectical system.

[12] Two comments are appropriate here. First, I do not mean to imply that the romantic movement proper followed immediately upon the Enlightenment. But I pass over the intervening phases. Secondly, the generalization in the text should not be interpreted as meaning that the men of the Enlightenment had no understanding at all of the importance of feeling in human life. See, for example, Vol. VI, Part I, pp. 38–41.

[13] It is a mistake to suppose that Hölderlin's attachment to Greece necessarily makes of him a classicist as opposed to a romantic.

[14] See Vol. VI, Part I, pp. 160–8, 198–205.

[15] Schlegel's view can be compared with the view advanced by some modern writers on metaphysics, that what really matters in a metaphysical system is the 'vision' and that arguments are persuasive devices to commend or put across a vision.

16 *Appearance and Reality* (2nd edition), p. 447.

17 *Speculum Mentis*, p. 151.

18 The adequacy of this interpretation of Hegel is highly disputable. But this is a question which need not detain us here.

CHAPTER TWO

1 From about 1797 Reinhold accepted and defended the philosophy of Fichte. But he was a restless spirit, and after a few years he turned to other lines of thought.

2 It is perhaps needless to say that the word 'science' must be understood in the sense of 'knowledge' rather than according to the narrower modern use of the term.

3 A. G. Schlegel had already spoken in a not dissimilar vein of Germany's cultural mission in a course of lectures given in 1803–4.

4 *F*, I, pp. 41–2; *M*, I, p. 170. In this and similar references to Fichte's writings *F* and *M* signify respectively the editions of his *Works* by his son, I. H. Fichte, and F. Medicus.

5 *F*, I, p. 48; *M*, I, p. 177.

6 *F*, I, p. 423; *M*, III, p. 7.

7 *Ibid.*

8 *F*, I, p. 433; *M*, III, p. 17.

9 *F*, I, p. 463; *M*, III, p. 47.

10 *Ibid.*

11 *F*, I, p. 440; *M*, III, p. 24.

12 See Vol. VI, Part II, pp. 47–50, 75–9, 181–3.

13 *F*, I, p. 466; *M*, III, p. 50.

14 See Vol. V, Part II, pp. 104–9.

15 *F*, II, p. 607 (not included in *M*).

16 *F*, I, p. 459; *M*, III, p. 43.

17 *F*, I, p. 98; *M*, I, p. 292.

18 *Ibid.*

19 *Durch ein Handeln auf ein Handeln*. The philosopher's reflection is an activity, a doing. It makes the spontaneous activity of the pure ego relive itself, so to speak, for consciousness.

20 *F*, I, p. 104; *M*, I, p. 298.

21 *F*, I, p. 110; *M*, I, p. 305.

22 We can notice again the distinction between phenomenology and idealist metaphysics. It is one thing to say that the positing (recognition) of the non-ego is a condition of human consciousness. It is another thing to say that the non-ego is posited (produced or created) by the pure or absolute ego.

23 On the hint of a dialectical method in the philosophy of Kant see Vol. VI, Part II, pp. 45–6. Kant's antithetical development of the antinomies (Part II, pp. 80) is also relevant.

24 *F*, I, p. 255; *M*, I, p. 448.

25 *Ibid.*

26 We have noted Fichte's frank admission that no purely theoretical deduction of the second basic proposition is possible.

27 *F*, I, p. 95; *M*, I, p. 289.

28 *F*, I, p. 99; *M*, I, p. 293.

29 See Vol. VI, Part II, pp. 50.

30 This is given in the *Basis of the Entire Theory of Science*. A more detailed analysis of some of the stages is given in the *Outline of the Essence of the Theory of Science*.

[31] F, I, p. 242; M, I, p. 435.
[32] F, I, p. 244; M, I, p. 437.
[33] F, I, p. 291; M, I, p. 483.
[34] F, I, p. 301; M, I, p. 492.
[35] F, II, p. 614 (not included in M).

CHAPTER THREE

[1] F, IV, p. 122; M, II, p. 516.
[2] F, IV, p. 13; M, II, p. 407.
[3] F, IV, p. 122; M, II, p. 516.
[4] F, IV, p. 124; M, II, p. 518.
[5] F, IV, p. 130; M, II, p. 524.
[6] There are activities in man, the circulation of the blood for example, of which he is not immediately, but only mediately, conscious. And he cannot be said to control them. But when I am immediately conscious of an impulse or desire, I am free, Fichte takes it, to satisfy or not to satisfy it.
[7] F, IV, p. 29; M, II, p. 423.
[8] F, IV, p. 53; M, II, p. 447. Kant, Fichte remarks, did not mean that the *thought* of freedom is derived from the thought of law. He meant that faith in the objective validity of the thought of freedom is derived from consciousness of the moral law.
[9] F, IV, p. 59; M, II, p. 453.
[10] F, IV, p. 173; M, II, p. 567.
[11] F, IV, pp. 173-4; M, II, pp. 567-8.
[12] F, IV, p. 169; M, II, p. 563.
[13] F, IV, p. 191; M, II, p. 585.
[14] F, IV, p. 193; M, II, p. 587.
[15] This happens, for example, if I do not really size up the situation but look exclusively at one partial aspect.
[16] F, IV, p. 194; M, II, p. 588.
[17] F, IV, p. 300; M, II, p. 694.
[18] F, IV, p. 150; M, II, p. 544.
[19] F, II, p. 143; M, IV, p. 143.
[20] *Ibid.*
[21] F, III, p. 8; M, II, p. 12.
[22] F, III, p. 10; M, II, p. 14.
[23] F, III, p. 106; M, II, p. 110.
[24] It is worth noting that for Fichte rightful ownership of a thing is really the exclusive right to perform certain actions in regard to it. For instance, a farmer's property right in regard to a field is an exclusive right to sow it, plough it, graze cattle on it, and so on.
[25] F, III, p. 129; M, II, p. 133.
[26] Fichte distinguishes various stages of the social contract, culminating in what he calls the union-compact, whereby the members of political society become an organized totality.
[27] See Vol. 6, Part I, chapters 3 and 4.
[28] F, III, p. 160; M, II, p. 164.
[29] Fichte assumes that there will be three main economic classes. First, the producers of the raw materials required for human life. Secondly, those who transform these raw materials into goods such as clothes, shoes, flour and so on. Thirdly, the merchants.

30 F, III, p. 421; M, III, p. 451.

31 Fichte's advocacy of a 'closed' commercial State is not based entirely on economic reasons. Like Plato before him, he believes that unrestricted intercourse with foreign countries would hamper the education of the citizens according to the principles of the true philosophy.

CHAPTER FOUR

1 F, v, p. 5 (not contained in M).

2 F, v, p. 8.

3 F, v, p. 43; M, I, p. 12.

4 F, I, p. 254; M, I, p. 448.

5 F, v, p. 179; M, III, p. 123.

6 F, v, p. 185; M, III, p. 129.

7 F, v, p. 186; M, III, p. 130.

8 F, v, p. 185; M, III, p. 129. It is important to notice the original German text: *Dies ist der wahre Glaube; diese moralische Ordnung ist das Göttliche, das wir annehmen. Er wird construirt durch das Rechtthun.* Grammatically, *Er* (It) should refer to *der wahre Glaube* (the true faith) and cannot refer to *diese moralische Ordnung* (this moral order). Unless, therefore, we are prepared to say that Fichte has simply neglected grammatical propriety, we must recognize that he is *not* saying that God, identified with the moral order, is no more than a creation or construction of man.

9 F, v, p. 261. (Fichte's *Gerichtliche Verantwortungsschrift* is not printed in M.)

10 F, v, p. 382; M, III, p. 246.

11 F, v, p. 261.

12 F, III, p. 39; M, II, p. 43.

13 F, v, pp. 394–5; M, III, p. 258.

14 F, II, p. 299; M, III, p. 395.

15 F, II, p. 303; M, III, p. 399.

16 F, II, p. 245; M, III, p. 341.

17 F, II, p. 303; M, III, p. 399.

18 *Ibid.*

19 *Darstellung der Wissenschaftslehre.*

20 F, II, p. 68; M, IV, p. 68.

21 F, II, p. 19; M, IV, p. 19.

22 *Ibid.*

23 This idea had already been mentioned in the *Wissenschaftslehre* of 1801.

24 F, x, p. 117; M, IV, p. 195.

25 F, x, p. 206; M, IV, p. 284.

26 F, VI, p. 362; M, v, p. 17.

27 F, VI, p. 367; M, v, p. 22.

28 F, VI, p. 361; M, v, p. 15.

29 F, v, p. 403; M, v, p. 115.

30 F, v, p. 539; M, v, p. 251.

31 F, v, p. 457; M, v, p. 169.

32 F, v, p. 407; M, v, p. 119.

33 In what Fichte calls the higher morality man is creative, seeking actively to realize ideal values. He does not content himself, as in the lower morality, with the mere fulfilment of the successive duties of his state of life. Religion adds belief in God as the one reality and a sense of divine vocation. The life of higher morality is seen as the expression of the one infinite divine Life.

[34] *F*, II, p. 685 (not included in *M*).

[35] *Ibid.*

[36] *F*, II, p. 696; *M*, V, p. 615.

[37] *Ibid.*

[38] *F*, XI, p. 5; *M*, VI, p. 5.

[39] *F*, XI, p. 7; *M*, VI, p. 7.

[40] *F*, XI, p. 4; *M*, VI, p. 4.

CHAPTER FIVE

[1] For Jakob Boehme (1575–1624) see Vol. III, Part II, pp. 80–3.

[2] Hegel himself does not seem to have been much concerned with personal rivalries as such; he was absorbed in ideas and in the exposition of what he believed to be the truth. But Schelling took Hegel's criticism of his own ideas as a personal affront.

[3] *W*, I, p. 57. References to Schelling's writings are given according to volume and page of the edition of his *Works* by Manfred Schröter (Munich, 1927–8).

Schelling prefers '*I is I*' (*Ich ist Ich*) to 'the ego is the ego' (*das Ich ist das Ich*) on the ground that the ego is given only as *I*.

[4] *W*, I, p. 103.

[5] *W*, I, p. 100.

[6] *W*, I, p. 237. This work will be referred to in future simply as *Philosophical Letters*.

[7] *W*, I, p. 208.

[8] *W*, I, p. 214.

[9] *W*, I, p. 220. The reference is, of course, to Fichte's idealism.

[10] *W*, I, p. 238.

[11] *W*, I, p. 259.

[12] *W*, I, p. 263.

[13] Fichte himself came to assert that the absolute ego is the identity of subject and object. But he did so partly under the influence of Schelling's criticism. And in any case Fichte's idealism was always characterized, in Schelling's opinion, by an overemphasis on the subject and on subjectivity.

CHAPTER SIX

[1] *W*, I, p. 663.

[2] *W*, I, p. 706.

[3] *W*, I, p. 708.

[4] *W*, I, p. 712.

[5] *W*, I, p. 714. I have used 'absoluteness' to render *Absoluthheit*.

[6] *W*, I, p. 717.

[7] Schelling's picture of the metaphysical basis of a philosophy of Nature exercised a powerful influence on the thought of Hegel. But it would be inappropriate to discuss this matter here.

[8] *W*, II, p. 283.

[9] *Ibid.*

[10] *W*, I, p. 416.

[11] *Der allgemeine Weltbau und die Körperreihe*; *W*, I, p. 718.

[12] *W*, II, p. 320.

[13] *W*, I, p. 449.

[14] *W*, I, p. 413.

[15] *W*, I, p. 417.

[16] The details of Schelling's construction of Nature vary somewhat in his different writings on the subject.

[17] *W*, II, p. 331.

[18] *W*, II, p. 374.

[19] *W*, II, p. 388.

[20] *W*, II, p. 370.

[21] *Ibid.*

22 W, II, p. 369.
23 W, II, pp. 573-4.
24 W, II, p. 586.
25 W, II, p. 587.
26 W, II, p. 592.
27 W, II, p. 603.
28 We can call this a doctrine of divine providence if we like. But at this stage at any rate of Schelling's thought we should not think of the Absolute as a personal Deity. The working out of the absolute synthesis is the necessary expression of the Absolute's nature as pure identity of the ideal and the real.
29 W, II, p. 349.
30 W, II, p. 351.
31 W, II, p. 615.
32 Ibid.
33 Similarly, the philosophy of Nature starts with the postulated infinite activity which manifests itself in Nature.
34 W, III, p. 400.
35 W, III, p. 402.
36 The reference is obviously to what the Scholastics called ontological truth, as distinct from logical truth.
37 W, III, p. 419.
38 W, III, p. 425.
39 The reader who is interested in this subject can consult the third part of Schelling's *Philosophy of Art* or, for example, Bernard Bosanquet's *History of Aesthetic*.
40 W, III, p. 9.
41 W, III, p. 11.
42 W, III, p. 10.
43 W, III, p. 25.
44 W, III, p. 21.
45 W, III, p. 16.
46 W, III, p. 23.

47 Ibid.
48 W, III, p. 155.

CHAPTER SEVEN

1 W, IV, pp. 15-16.
2 W, IV, pp. 23-4.
3 W, IV, p. 21.
4 W, IV, p. 28.
5 W, IV, p. 31.
6 W, IV, p. 32.
7 W, IV, p. 30.
8 W, IV, p. 31.
9 W, IV, p. 30.
10 W, IV, p. 32.
11 W, IV, p. 47.
12 The revised system is also expounded in the Stuttgart lectures (1810), which are printed together with *Philosophical Inquiries* in the fourth volume of his *Works*.
13 W, IV, p. 234.
14 W, IV, p. 244.
15 W, IV, p. 252.
16 It should be noted that the divine Being is now for Schelling a personal Deity and no longer an impersonal Absolute.
17 W, IV, p. 251.
18 W, IV, p. 330.
19 W, IV, p. 331.
20 W, IV, p. 316.
21 W, IV, p. 324.
22 W, IV, p. 326.
23 W, IV, p. 267.
24 W, IV, p. 256.
25 W, IV, p. 274.
26 W, IV, p. 277.
27 W, IV, p. 278.
28 W, IV, p. 295.
29 W, IV, p. 296.
30 Ibid.
31 W, V, p. 558.
32 *als reines Dass*; W, V, p. 746.

[33] *Ibid.*

[34] *Ibid.*

[35] W, v, p. 746.

[36] Schelling's distinction is similar in certain respects to the distinction made by some modern writers, notably Professor Gilson, between essentialist and existential philosophy, the latter term meaning, not 'existentialism', but philosophy which lays its fundamental emphasis on being in the sense of existence (*esse*) rather than on being in the sense of essence. But the extent of the similarity is limited.

[37] W, v, p. 746.

[38] W, v, p. 748.

[39] *Ibid.*

[40] W, v, p. 750.

[41] W, v, p. 753.

[42] W, v, p. 729.

[43] W, v, p. 437.

[44] W, vi, p. 396.

[45] *Ibid.*

[46] W, vi, p. 395.

[47] The reference is to the logically distinguishable 'potencies' in God's inner life.

[48] W, v, p. 437.

[49] W, v, p. 440.

[50] Schelling's theory of the Absolute as pure identity can be regarded as a continuation of Bruno's idea of the infinite as the *coincidentia oppositorum*, an idea which was itself derived from Nicholas of Cusa.

[51] Schelling's influence was felt in southern rather than in northern Germany.

[52] Soloviev made great play with the idea of Wisdom or *Sophia*, as found in the Bible and also, for instance, in the writings of Boehme.

CHAPTER EIGHT

[1] As was mentioned in the account of Fichte's philosophy, the strength of this tendency was considerably weaker in his later thought.

[2] W, iii, p. 59. References to Schleiermacher's writing are given according to volume and page of the edition of his *Works* by O. Braun and J. Bauer (4 vols., Leipzig, 1911–13). This edition consists of selections.

[3] W, iii, p. 71.

[4] W, iii, p. 72.

[5] *Ibid.*

[6] W, iv, p. 240.

[7] W, iv, p. 235.

[8] W, iv, p. 236.

[9] *Ibid.*

[10] W, iv, p. 243.

[11] W, iv, p. 242.

[12] W, iv, p. 243.

[13] W, iii, p. 81.

[14] W, iii, p. 86.

[15] W, ii, p. 92.

[16] W, iii, p. 128.

CHAPTER NINE

[1] This was the year of Kant's inaugural dissertation. It was also the year of birth of Hölderlin in Germany and of Bentham and Wordsworth in England.

[2] W, i, p. 44. Unless otherwise stated, references to Hegel's writings will be given according to volume and page of the jubilee edition of his *Works* by Hermann Glockner (26 vols., Stuttgart, 1928).

[3] W, i, p. 50.

[4] W, i, pp. 69.

[5] W, i, pp. 143–4.

[6] W, I, p. 122.

[7] Ibid.

[8] Needless to say, the reference is to Schelling's philosophical ideas in the first years of the nineteenth century.

[9] W, II, p. 21; B, p. 79. In references, as here, to *The Phenomenology of Spirit* B signifies the English translation of this work by J. B. Baillie. But it does not necessarily follow that the present writer has followed this translation. The like holds good of other such references to standard English translations, which are included for the convenience of readers.

[10] W, II, p. 22; B, p. 79.

[11] W, II, p. 24; B, p. 81.

[12] W, II, p. 23; B, p. 81.

[13] W, II, p. 24; B, p. 81.

[14] W, II, p. 14; B, p. 70.

[15] W, II, p. 22; B, p. 80.

[16] Hegel frequently speaks of the Absolute as 'God'. But it does not necessarily follow from his use of religious language that he looks on the Absolute as a personal Deity in the theistic sense. This question will be discussed later.

[17] The word 'Idea' can have different shades of meaning with Hegel. It may refer to the logical Idea, otherwise called the Concept (*Begriff*) or Notion. It may refer to the whole process of reality, as the actualization of the Idea. Or it may refer primarily to the term of the process.

[18] The terms 'understanding' and 'reason' are not used in precisely the same ways by Kant and Hegel. This fact apart, however, the contrast between Kant's mistrust of the flights of reason, coupled with his admission of its practical function, and Hegel's depreciation of understanding, coupled with a recognition of its practical use, well illustrates their respective attitudes to speculative metaphysics.

[19] I do not mean to imply that for Hegel philosophy is the only way of apprehending the Absolute. There are also art and religion. But in the present context we are concerned only with philosophy.

[20] For obvious reasons Hegel's profound analysis of the master-slave relationship contained lines of reflection which found favour with Karl Marx.

[21] Hegel, the Lutheran, tended to associate the unhappy or divided consciousness, in a somewhat polemical way, with mediaeval Catholicism, especially with its ascetic ideals.

[22] W, II, p. 610; B, p. 798.

CHAPTER TEN

[1] W, IV, p. 46; J-S, I, p. 60. The letters J-S signify the English translation of the *Science of Logic* by W. H. Johnston and L. G. Struthers.

[2] W, IV, p. 89; J-S, I, p. 95.

[3] This statement does not contradict what has been said about the non-temporal nature of the logical Absolute. For we are not concerned here with the actual process of the Absolute's self-actualization.

[4] W, IV, p. 662; J-S, II, p. 160.

[5] As the word 'concept' has too restricted a meaning in English, Hegel's *Begriff* is frequently rendered as 'Notion'.

[6] W, v, p. 328; *J-S*, ii, p. 466.

[7] The *Logic* contained in the *Encyclopaedia* is known as the *Lesser* or *Shorter Logic*, in distinction from the *Greater Logic*, that is, Hegel's *Science of Logic*. Quotations in the last section were from the latter work.

[8] W, vi, p. 144; E, 191. The letter E stands for *Encyclopaedia*. As this work is divided into numbered sections, no reference to particular translations is required. A glance at the number of the relevant volume in the reference to W will show whether it is the Heidelberg edition (W, vi) or the Berlin edition (W, viii–x) which is being referred to.

[9] Cf., for example, W, ix, pp. 51–4; E, 247.

[10] The theistic view is certainly admitted by Hegel as far as the religious consciousness and its own characteristic expression are concerned. But we are treating here of the strictly philosophical point of view.

[11] W, vi, p. 147; E, 193.

[12] W, ix, pp. 63–4; E, 250.

[13] W, vi, p. 147; E, 193.

[14] W, vi, p. 149; E, 194.

[15] W, ix, pp. 59–62; E, 249.

[16] W, vi, p. 228; E, 302.

[17] The logical Idea, considered precisely as such, is the category of Spirit, of self-thinking Thought, rather than potential Spirit.

[18] W, ix, p. 50; E, 247.

[19] W, vi, p. 229; E, 305.

[20] W, vi, p. 232; E, 309.

[21] W, x, p. 379; E, 481.

[22] *Ibid.*

[23] W, x, p. 380; E, 482.

[24] W, vii, p. 94; R, 41. The letter R signifies *The Philosophy of Right*. The following number refers to the section. In references to R the word 'addition' refers to the additions made by Hegel to the original text. In Professor T. M. Knox's translation these additions are printed after the version of the original text.

[25] Hegel is speaking of the right of property in the abstract. Needless to say, once the concept of society has been introduced the range of legitimate appropriation is restricted.

[26] This refers to religion as something internal. In a state of organized society a man cannot claim inviolability for the external expression of his religious beliefs when such expression is socially harmful.

[27] W, x, p. 392; E, 503.

[28] W, vii, p. 164; R, 105.

[29] W, vii, p. 188; R, 129.

[30] W, vii, pp. 196–7; R, 137.

[31] W, vii, p. 237; R, 157.

[32] Obviously, Hegel is not so foolish as to maintain that as a matter of empirical fact every family is united by love. He is talking about the concept or ideal essence of the family, what it ought to be.

[33] W, x, p. 401; E, 523.

[34] To speak of civil society as representing 'sheer particularity' is from one point of view to be guilty of exaggeration. For

within civil society itself the antagonisms consequent on the emergence and self-assertion of the particulars are partly overcome through the corporations on which Hegel lays stress. But the union of wills among members of a corporation in seeking a common end has also a limited universality and prepares the way for the transition to the concept of the State.

35 W, x, p. 409; E, 535.

36 W, vii, p. 328; R, 257.

37 W, vii, p. 336; R, 258, addition.

38 Ibid.

39 It should be remembered that Hegel was partly concerned with educating the Germans to political self-consciousness.

40 Cf. W, vii, p. 344; R, 265, addition.

41 W, x, p. 416; E, 540.

42 W, vii, p. 376; R, 274, addition.

43 W, vii, p. 376; R, 273, addition.

44 W, vii, pp. 36–7; R, preface. Marx's equally famous retort was that it is the philosopher's business to change the world, not simply to understand it.

45 W, vii, p. 33; R, preface.

46 W, vii, p. 35; R, preface.

47 W, vii, p. 33; R, preface.

48 W, vii, p. 36; R, preface.

49 W, vii, p. 434; R, 324.

50 Ibid.

51 Ibid.

52 See Vol. VI, Part I, pp. 214 and 240.

53 In justice to Hegel we can recall that he himself had felt the effect of war, its exhibition of the transitoriness of the finite, when he lost his position and belongings at Jena as a result of Napoleon's victorious campaign.

54 W, xi, p. 34; S, p. 8. The letter S signifies J. Sibree's translation of Hegel's lectures on the philosophy of history.

55 W, xi, p. 34; S, p. 9.

56 W, xi, p. 36; S, p. 10.

57 W, xi, p. 46; S, p. 19.

58 W, xi, p. 40; S, p. 14.

59 W, viii, p. 446; R, 340.

60 W, vii, p. 449; R, 347.

61 W, xi, p. 45; S, p. 18.

62 Hegel's answer to any theologically-minded critic is that the theory of the cunning of Reason is in accord with Christianity. For Christianity maintains that God brings good out of evil, using, for instance, Judas's betrayal of Christ in the accomplishment of the Redemption.

63 See Vol. VI, Part I, pp. 244–6.

CHAPTER ELEVEN

1 W, xii, p. 160; O, i, p. 154. In references to Hegel's lectures on The Philosophy of Fine Art the letter O signifies the English translation by F. P. B. Osmaston.

2 W, xii, p. 110; O, i, p. 98.

3 W, xii, p. 472; O, ii, p. 74.

4 W, xii, p. 480; O, ii, p. 83.

5 Ibid.

6 W, xiii, p. 14; O, ii, p. 180. Note that Hegel here associates a particular type of art with a particular type of religion.

7 W, xiii, p. 334; O, iii, p. 91.

8 To repeat, this transition is

dialectical rather than temporal. The Egyptians and the Hindus, for instance, had their own religions as well as their own forms of art.

[9] W, xii, p. 151; O, i, p. 142.

[10] W, xvi, p. 361; SS, iii, p. 156. In references to Hegel's *Lectures on The Philosophy of Religion SS* signifies the English translation by E. B. Speirs and J. Burdon Sanderson.

[11] W, xvi, p. 361; SS, iii, p. 157.

[12] W, xvi, p. 457; SS, iii, p. 259.

[13] W, xvi, p. 456; SS, iii, p. 259.

[14] Evidently, the third member of the triad, the religion of utility, is from one point of view a degradation of religion. For it practically reduces God to an instrument. At the same time it demands the transition to a higher form of religion. For example, the admission by Rome of all deities into its pantheon reduces polytheism to an absurdity and demands the transition to monotheism.

[15] W, xv, p. 37; SS, i, p. 19.

[16] W, xv, p. 37; SS, i, p. 20.

[17] W, xv, p. 37; SS, i, p. 19.

[18] W, xv, p. 38; SS, i, p. 20.

[19] *Ibid.*

[20] W, xv, p. 35; SS, i, p. 17.

[21] *Studies in Hegelian Cosmology* (1901 edition), p. 250.

[22] W, xix, p. 685; HS, iii, p. 546. In references to Hegel's *Lectures on the History of Philosophy HS* signifies the English translation by E. S. Haldane and F. H. Simson.

[23] W, xix, pp. 690–1; HS, iii, pp. 552–3.

[24] W, xvii, p. 65; HS, i, p. 35.

[25] W, xvii, p. 66; HS, i, p. 36.

[26] W, xix, pp. 689–90; HS, iii, p. 551.

[27] W, xix, p. 690; HS, iii, p. 551.

[28] W, vii, p. 35; R, preface.

[29] *Das Erbrecht in weltgeschichtlicher Entwicklung* (1824–35).

A pair of masked robbers was ripping off the most exclusive restaurants in L.A., leaving no clues behind, but leaving the cash registers bereft of thousands of dollars.

A wealthy widow was viciously slain in her respectable apartment, a broken string of love beads under her battered body.

Two junkies were shot dead in an old car after leaving their baby at home—doped with marijuana.

Mrs. Ida Moffat was found dead of a skull fracture in her dingy, not-too-clean apartment. She wasn't too well kept herself, though she was well stocked with cheap muscatel.

All the stupidity and cupidity in the world seemed to be centered in Los Angeles, giving Lt. Mendoza and his men the infernal task of catching faceless criminals—and giving the reader another incomparable police procedural novel to celebrate Lt. Mendoza's twenty-fifth appearance on the mystery scene.

CRIME FILE
was originally published by
William Morrow & Company, Inc.

Dell Shannon

CRIME FILE

 A POCKET BOOK EDITION published by
Simon & Schuster of Canada, Ltd. • Markham, Ontario, Canada
Registered User of the Trademark

CRIME FILE

William Morrow edition published 1974

POCKET BOOK edition published January, 1976
2nd printing .... November, 1975

Standard Book Number: 671-80255-0.
Library of Congress Catalog Card Number: 74-7374.

"What do you think of it, Moon,
As you go?
Is life much or no?"

"Oh, I think of it, often think of it,
As a show
God ought surely to shut up soon,
As I go."

—THOMAS HARDY

CRIME FILE

- 1 -

"I didn't mean to hurt her none," said the stocky bald fellow, blinking up at them. He was slumped over the little table in the interrogation room, frightened and sullen in turn, and also still surprised. "Don't seem possible I *coulda*. I didn't hit her hard, and I never hit her before, ever, she could tell you that——"

"Only she's dead, Mr. Parsons," said Hackett. He exchanged a look with Mendoza.

"I know. Don't seem possible." Parsons shook his head. "I never meant to hurt her—I wouldn't hurt Myra. It was just, I had enough o' her complainin'. Squawking about not enough money alla time. I supported myself ever since I was twelve years old. I'm a good worker, I don't sit around takin' the welfare like a bum. I haven't got much learning, so what's that say? On what a trucker earns, she's gonna starve? But she's got to have a new color TV, got to have—But I didn't go to hurt her. I'm sorry—I'm sorry." His head sank to the table.

Hackett sighed and followed Mendoza out to the anteroom of Robbery-Homicide, where Sergeant Lake sat at the switchboard reading a paperback. The office was quiet; only the subdued busy click of Policewoman Wanda Larsen's typewriter sounded as she typed up somebody's report. The men at Robbery-Homicide were still feeling appreciative about their unexpected secretary.

"And they make TV shows about the glamorous, exciting job of being a cop," said Hackett.

"Occasionally it can be exciting," said Mendoza. "Just occasionally. There's nothing to that but a report. The D.A.'ll call it manslaughter and he'll get one-to-three."

"And serve half of it," said Hackett. "The way these damn judges are letting them loose these days——"

9

"Don't raise my blood pressure," said Mendoza. He lit a cigarette; as usual he was dapper in silver-gray Italian silk, snowy shirt, discreet tie. "Anything new down, Jimmy?"

Lake looked up. "Dead body reported over on Stanford Avenue. George and John went out on it. Jase and Tom are out talking to witnesses on that heist, and Matt just came back. I don't know what he got—"

"Nada absolutamente," said Mendoza, "probably. A very anonymous thing, a take of forty-two bucks, no M.O. to speak of. It'll go into Pending tomorrow. I do get tired, Arturo."

"You can always resign. You don't have to work for a living."

"Comes the crash, I might. Take him over to jail and give the gist to Wanda for a report."

"Oh, you've got a memo from the D.A.'s office," said Lake. "On your desk. Something about those floozies last April."

"¿Qué?" Mendoza went into his office, noting Wanda typing at her desk in the sergeants' office, and Matt Piggott on the phone looking earnest, and found the memo. A minute later Lake heard him swearing comprehensively in Spanish. "More equal than others, isn't it the truth. *Dios,* does he think we can make bricks without straw?" But the D.A.'s note was apologetic; the D.A. was being pressured —read hounded, thought Mendoza—by some civil-rights group: why hadn't the police found and arrested the foul racist dog who had murdered those innocent black girls two months ago?

On that one there'd simply been no leads at all, and it had been filed in Pending at the first of this month. Innocent was an ambivalent word: they hadn't deserved to be murdered maybe, but they'd all had long rap-sheets as casual prostitutes. It had been a queer one, and without much doubt the X on that was a nut, poisoning the floozies with cyanide in their liquor, but after the fourth one there hadn't been another, and all the men at Robbery-Homicide were inclined to think he'd left town. Mendoza had passed on the relevant facts to NCIC; if X showed up anywhere else murdering Negro prostitutes they could guess it was the same boy. That was about all they could do, with the dearth of physical evidence.

Resignedly Mendoza picked up his phone and told Lake to get him the D.A.'s office. If the D.A. wanted a nice apologetic letter to show the civil-righters, that was about all Mendoza could do for him. While he waited for the D.A.'s secretary to locate him, he looked out the window to the clear line of the Hollywood hills in the distance. They hadn't yet had their usual first heat wave in June; the weather was for once being reasonable in southern California—warmish, with a breeze most of the day, blue skies and sun.

And Robbery-Homicide had been busier; on the downtown Central beat, LAPD, there was always enough business, but they weren't feeling harried. They had four separate heist jobs, with no leads on any of them. There was still some paper work to clean up on a suicide, there were two unidentified bodies in the morgue, one dead of knife wounds, one of an overdose. There had been a bank heist last week, but the Feds were definitely sure who that pair was—ex-cons from the Midwest, one wanted for P.A. violation; the A.P.B.'s were out and maybe one of their pigeons would finger them.

The phone hummed emptily at him, and through the two open doors he heard Wanda's practiced typing and Piggott's voice. Piggott was saying something about dishpans and screens, and Mendoza was still wondering about the combination when the D.A. came on the line.

"Listen, damn it," he said, "look, Lieutenant, I know you worked that into the ground, there just wasn't anything to get. But these damned—"

"Racists in reverse," supplied Mendoza. "Yes, I know. Shall I write a nice letter of apology?"

"Not that it'll satisfy 'em, we both will," said the D.A.

"I'll get some screening at the hardware store on my way home," said Piggott into the phone. He sounded resigned too. It was now three months since he'd been bitten

11

by the unlikely fascination for the pretty little tropical fish.
But, he was reflecting now, it was Mammon which had
prompted him to try the breeding, when that female head-
and-taillight tetra proved to be full of eggs. Mr. Duff at the
Scales 'n' Fins shop saying he'd pay twenty cents for every
one they raised to three months. Piggott and Prudence had
spent the last seven weeks frantically rescuing the smaller
tetras from their bigger siblings, and at the moment had
seven dishpans standing about full of baby tetras, carefully
graded as to size. There had been over three hundred to
start with, but the ranks had been considerably thinned.

"Well, if you would," said Prudence. She sounded dis-
tracted. "The bigger ones jump so—I've caught six of
them getting clear out this afternoon. You'd better pick
up another dishpan, Matt. It's funny how they grow at
such different rates—and if we'd known they were cannibals—"

"Only until they grow up, Duff says. All right," said
Piggott. He reflected gloomily that he should have known
better than to succumb to greed: the love of money . . .
By the time the baby tetras were three months old, he'd
be lucky to break even on the deal. Just last Sunday the
sermon had been about covetousness.

He hadn't any report for Wanda to type. All of these
heists were likely going to stay anonymous. He wandered
out to the anteroom and asked Lake if anything new had
gone down.

"Body over on Stanford. George and John went out on
it."

Wanda came out of the sergeants' office with a page
in her hand and said briskly, "This just came over the
telex—we'll be putting it out countywide."

Lake looked at it and buzzed the lieutenant's office.
"A.P.B. from Folsom. A mean one. He went over the wall
last night and they think he'll probably head here—"

Mendoza scanned the teletype rapidly. One Terry Conover, twenty-four, Caucasian, six one, a hundred and
ninety, black and blue, no marks, a long pedigree of much
violence, in on a five-to-ten for murder two. He had a

12

mother and a girl and pals in L.A., and probably would be heading here: addresses were appended for the mother and girl friend. Folsom wasn't so far away; if he'd got hold of a car, he could be here by now.

"Well, we'll have to look," said Mendoza. Jason Grace and Tom Landers came in, and he added, *"Por fortuna,* just as we need you. Do any good?"

"Are you kidding?" said Landers. "Nobody could give us a description, him in that ski mask. Not even an approximate height and weight—you know people. It might have been any hood in L.A., we'll never drop on him. I guess Rich is still out asking futile questions." He and Rich Conway, inherited from the old Robbery office when the two had been merged, had taken to each other at once; and they'd both just come off night watch a month ago.

"So, we've got a new one?" asked Grace. He read the teletype interestedly, brushing his neat moustache in unconscious imitation of Mendoza, and his chocolate-brown face wore a sardonic grin. "Yeah, in case Terry has made for home and mother, we'd better go and ask—more than one of us. Consider armed and dangerous. I wonder if he had help in getting over the wall—if he did, there was probably transportation waiting, and more than likely a gun. With his pedigree of armed robbery."

"That's the general idea," agreed Mendoza. His senior sergeant, bulky and burly Art Hackett, came in from escorting Parsons over to the jail, and Grace handed on the teletype. "Suppose you and Matt go have a look at his mother's place, and Art and Tom can look at the girl."

Hackett reached up to adjust the Police Positive in the shoulder holster and copied down addresses noncommittally. "That should take us to the end of shift just nicely. Come on, Tom. You getting anywhere with that cute blonde down in R. and I.?" They went out, with Grace and Piggott after them. It was three o'clock.

Mendoza asked Lake, "What was the body?"

"By what the uniformed men said, homicide of some kind."

"Maybe business is picking up a little." Mendoza

yawned. "I do get tired, Jimmy. Ninety-eight percent of what we see is just—the damned foolishness."

"As Matt would say, the devil going about," said Lake.

At a tired-looking old eight-family apartment out on Stanford Avenue, Sergeants Higgins and Palliser were talking to a scrawny, scraggly middle-aged woman in the upper hallway. The uniformed men had gone back on tour; Scarne and Duke had arrived with a mobile lab unit and were busy in the rear apartment to the left, past the open door behind the two detectives.

"You hadn't heard anything from Mrs. Moffat's apartment before that, Mrs. Kiefer?"

"Not a thing." She kept trying to see into the apartment, what the lab men were doing, past Higgins' broad shoulders. "Not that I would. I mean I wasn't listening, why should I? I'm not anybody's keeper." She was sloppily dressed in old jeans and a white T-shirt, and her graying hair was in big fat pink curlers, with no scarf over it. "Well, I mean, I hope we're respectable—"

"And Mrs. Moffat wasn't?" asked Palliser in his pleasant voice. She looked at him with slightly more approval, at his regular lean features and neat tailoring; Higgins, of course, in his bulk and cragginess, had COP written all over him.

"Well, I—well, she wasn't a lady, is all I can say. I didn't *know* her. Just to know her name, is all. But to think of anybody getting murdered, here? It's enough to scare you to death! Like I told you, and believe me it's all I can tell you, I had a phone call from Miss Callway's sister—Miss Callway lives in Seven, right there"—the door across the hall—"and she can't afford a phone, but she's a nice woman and I don't mind taking messages for her—and I come up here to pass it on, only she's not home, and there's Mrs. Moffat's door open and her laying in there all over blood, and I screamed, but I didn't go in, no, sir, I went right down and called police—but to think of it, a murder, even Mrs. Moffat, her getting murdered right here—"

"Well, if that's all you can tell us," said Palliser, "we'll want a statement from you later on, but for now you can go back to your own apartment. Thank you, Mrs. Kiefer."

"What are they doing in there, anyways? Aren't you going to take her away?"

"After a while," said Higgins. They got rid of her finally and went back into the apartment to watch Duke and Scarne dusting for prints and taking pictures. It was a shabby place, barely filled with ancient furniture, and whatever else she had been, Mrs. Ida Moffat hadn't been a very good housekeeper; there was dust everywhere, a pile of dirty dishes in the kitchen, the windows filmed with dirt. Mrs. Moffat herself didn't look too clean, flat on her back on the living-room floor: she was wearing a faded pink kimono and it had come open to show her only underwear, panties and a bra both once white but now grime-gray. She couldn't have been less than fifty or so but she hadn't had a bad figure; the blue-mottled veins in her legs, her worn, uncared-for hands, told her age better.

"You pick up anything?" asked Higgins.

"No idea," said Duke. "Plenty of latents around, but may be mostly hers."

"Even Mrs. Moffat," said Palliser. "What do you suppose she meant by that?"

"Not a lady," grunted Higgins. "By what else she could tell us, perfectly ordinary woman."

Palliser scratched his admirably straight nose and said, "I wonder." All Mrs. Kiefer could tell them about Ida Moffat was that she took jobs housecleaning for people; she had several regular jobs up in Hollywood, one place twice a week and helping out at parties. She didn't know if Mr. Moffat was dead or divorced, or about any family. "Well, have a look around when you boys are finished."

"Just about," said Scarne. "You can read it—probably all the action was right here." She had fallen, or been knocked down, against the fake stucco hearth, where there was blood, and more blood on top of the electric heater below; she had lived long enough to crawl a few feet

15

toward the door. "Skull fracture for a bet. A fight with somebody."

"Over something," said Palliser.

"Her handbag's in the bedroom, on the bed. Money still in it. Place hasn't been ransacked."

"So, not a burglar. She let him in," said Higgins, looking at the apartment door. It had a lock minus a deadbolt, an easy lock for a burglar to break in, but it wasn't broken; there was a stout chain fastened to door and wall, the catch now neatly reposing in its slot. In this area, it was a good bet that a woman living alone would keep that chain fastened when she was home, even during the day. "Did you print this, Bill?" Scarne looked at him reproachfully. "All right, all right, just asking."

When the lab men had gone, they had a look through the apartment. They found a few interesting things. There were nine bottles of cheap muscatel on a kitchen shelf. "How anybody can drink that sweet stuff is beyond me," said Higgins. "Think it'd make you sick before you got tight." Her handbag, a shabby black plastic one, was open on the bed; it contained a billfold with eighteen dollars in it, some loose change, and a check for thirty-five dollars signed by Winifred Bloomfield of an address in Hollywood; two soiled handkerchieves, three used lipsticks, half a pack of Camels, a very dirty powder puff, a bunch of keys, and a little plastic book with slots for snapshots. That was full; and the twenty snapshots in it obviously dated from disparate periods, all showing Ida Moffat at various ages from the twenties on up. All the snapshots showed her with men, all different men.

"My God," said Higgins mildly. "What a gal." The men were all different shapes, sizes, and ages; one, smiling at an Ida of perhaps twenty years ago, was in Army uniform, and another—a hairy-chested fellow with a mop of dark hair—was in swimming trunks, with a plastic tag around his neck that said *Life Guard,* but aside from that there was no clue to their identities, no writing on the back of the snapshots.

"Not a lady," quoted Palliser. "I wonder if we'd get anything in the local bars. She didn't have a car, that we do know. If she—"

"By that collection, she stayed home to do her drinking," said Higgins. They began opening drawers, looking for an address book, but there didn't seem to be one. Beside the wall telephone in the kitchen was a dime-store tablet hung on a string by a nail, and on several pages were scrawled notes—*Call Al at home bef. 9—new no. Bruce CA-1498—Jean 421-4243* . . . They took that to go through at leisure. Without discussing it, they were in tacit agreement that the world was probably not going to miss Ida Moffat, and it was going to be a tedious little job, probably, to find out who had had a fight with her, knocked her down and killed her, but it was the job they were paid to do and they'd do it to the best of their ability.

The morgue attendants came for the body.

It was twenty minutes to six. They found the key to the door and locked it after themselves. They'd driven over in Higgins' Pontiac, and now went back to Parker Center where Palliser reclaimed his Rambler from the lot. By then, Wanda would be gone; dictate a first report on it to her in the morning, and go on from there. This wasn't one where they'd be asking Luis if he had a hunch, thought Higgins. A tiresome routine job.

On the way home, through end-of-workday traffic, his mind switched from the job to his family: even after this while, he wasn't taking a family for granted, he'd been without one so long. His darling Mary, and Bert Dwyer's good kids, Steve and Laura, and now the baby, Margaret Emily, who unbelievably was nearly ten months old—and Mary was just kidding when she said he and Steve would spoil her rotten. . . .

And on the way home, Palliser thought fondly of Robin and their almost-brand-new David Andrew, not quite three months old; but that made him remember that very minor little thing last January, that accident on the freeway, and Miss Madge Borman of Tempe, Arizona—and her dog. He frowned. He had hoped at the time that Miss Borman

might forget her promise, but he had the uneasy feeling
that Miss Borman was not a woman who forgot promises.
Never forget how kind you've been, she'd said, don't
know what I'd have done—and when he just happened
to mention Robin talking about a dog after the baby was
born. Not another word, Sergeant, you shall have one of
Azzie's pups . . . Damnedest name for a dog he'd ever
heard, and it took Matt to unravel that: Dark Angel of
Langlet, Azrael for short. And, I'm breeding Marla to
him next month—and that was the biggest German shepherd he'd ever seen, he hadn't said a word about it to
Robin, and she'd have a fit—nice dogs but too big for the
city. And no fence around the backyard, and what it
might cost to put one up. He also wondered just how long
it took for dogs . . .

He'd asked the lieutenant, who would know, and Mendoza had said absently, "Sixty-three days. Don't tell me
you're going in for dog breeding? Matt and his fish are
bad enough—"

"No, no," said Palliser hastily. But if that creature had
been bred to Marla, presumably one like him, in February,
the resultant pups would be about ready to leave home
and mother some time this month. And how he would ever
explain it to Robin . . .

He just hoped Miss Borman had forgotten all about it.

Robin had dinner ready when he came in, and the baby
—such a good baby, who seldom cried or fussed—was
asleep. Palliser kissed her and she asked, "Busy day?"

"The usual," said Palliser.

Higgins pulled into the drive of the house on Silverlake
Boulevard to find Steve Dwyer industriously oiling his
bicycle in front of the garage, with the little black Scottie
Brucie watching.

"Hi, George! Say, I just developed this last roll of negs
and I've got some great shots—wait till you see! They're
almost dry now . . ." Steve, going in heavily for the art-
composition black-and-white photography, these days was
processing it all himself, proudly, in the little darkroom

18

CRIME FILE

Higgins had put up in the garage, with the help of Henry
Glasser on the electric lines.

Higgins went obediently to look at the roll of negatives
before he went into the house. Steve thought it was lucky
that Higgins had been there, to take care of them all, when
Bert got shot by that bank robber. Higgins reckoned he'd
been pretty lucky too.

"You'd better believe I'd call you quick enough if I'd
heard from Terry!" She looked from Grace to Piggott,
troubled. She was a little woman, slim and good-looking,
dark and vivacious. This was a modest but well-maintained
single house in Hollywood, on Berendo; the name on the
mailbox was Fitzpatrick. She had asked them into a neat,
nicely furnished living room, and a boy about ten and a
girl a little older had looked at them curiously and obediently vanished at her quick word.

"Do you think he might try to contact you, ma'am?"
asked Grace.

"I don't know. I don't think so, but—" She bit her lip.
"Nobody could know, with Terry." She ran a hand through
her thick short hair, distractedly. "I was a fool—well, I
was sixteen. I guess that says it all. He was a wild one,
Jim Conover. I was crazy in love with him, and we ran
away to Vegas to get married and my mother about had
a fit—and of course it wasn't three months later I knew
what a fool I'd been. Jim knocking me around when he
felt like it—and I guess I was lucky at that, you know—
him getting killed in that accident just before Terry was
born. But Terry's just like him—a wild one, and nobody
could do anything with him. He got into trouble—stealing
—when he was only seven. I tried, but having to work—"

"Well, if he does contact you," said Piggott, "we'd like
to know."

She nodded. "Before he got sent up this last time, he
used to come once in a while when he was broke. Asking
for money. The last time, he threatened to—to hurt the
children if we didn't—but I'm really lucky now." She
smiled at them. "My husband's a good man, and he—got

19

it across to Terry all right. He knocked him down and threw him out, told him just what he'd get if he tried anything. I don't think Terry'd come here—anymore. But I've got to say I don't know. But believe me, if he does we'll call you right away."

"We have information that he has a girl here," said Grace. "A Betty Suttner—they lived together a while, a few years back."

"Oh," she said. "I wouldn't know. You mean he might try to contact her?" She laughed. "He might or he might not—when it comes to girls, it's out of sight out of mind with Terry. I suppose it's possible."

"Well, thanks very much," said Piggott.

"People, people," said Grace, sliding under the wheel of the little blue racing Elva. "It's getting on for end of shift. I'll take you back to your car."

"No snapshots today." Piggott yawned.

Grace grinned. "I guess we're getting used to having a family, after six months." And his father (who should know, chief of gynecology at the General Hospital) still saying probably now after adopting little Celia Ann, they'd be producing one of their own. . . .

Piggott stopped at a hardware store on the way home and bought four feet of screening and a dishpan. In the apartment, his russet-haired Prudence was fishing for medium-sized baby tetras to transfer to a dishpan of their own. Even as he came in, one of the larger babies neatly swallowed a smaller sibling an inch from her little net, and Prudence said crossly, "Oh, *damn!* I don't care, Matt, I know I shouldn't swear, but it's perfectly maddening! There must have been over three hundred to start with, and I can't understand why some grow so fast and others don't—"

They got about twenty-five of the middle-sized ones into the new dishpan and covered with screening before dinner.

Landers, getting into Hackett's scarlet Barracuda, had said he hoped he was getting somewhere with that blonde.

Little blond Phil O'Neill, down in R. and I.—Phillipa Rosemary, only not for a lady cop, as she said—was a very sensible sort of girl, and kept telling him they hadn't known each other long enough. She didn't, she said, believe in hasty marriages—or divorce. Well, they'd known each other over a year now, and Landers knew all he wanted to know about Phil. But women—

The address Folsom had given them for Terry Conover's girl friend Betty Suttner (and apparently he'd written her letters or Folsom wouldn't have had it) was on Barton Avenue in Hollywood. It was one of the bright-painted jerry-built new apartments, about twenty units, and at number four a thin elderly man answered the door and said he'd never heard of her. "Maybe she used to live here."

There wasn't a manager on the premises. Rent was paid to a big realty company out on Santa Monica. They went up there to ask. Betty Suttner had moved three months ago and left no forwarding address. "Are you *cops?*" asked the young woman they talked to. She looked at Landers curiously. "You don't look old enough to be a *detective*—"

That one Landers was used to hearing. It used to make him mad. Phil said that funny affair last year when he'd got suspended by Internal Affairs had aged him, apparently not all that much.

"I wonder if a moustache would make any difference, Tom," said Hackett, back in the car. "Just an idea."

"Phil doesn't like moustaches. I asked her. Funny," said Landers, "a lot of women do. The lieutenant—well—"

"Man about town. Yes," said Hackett. "Until he got caught, if belatedly. I wonder if we could trace this Suttner girl through her job. If anybody at that apartment remembers where she worked—"

"In case Conover contacts her. I have had a further thought," said Landers. "He probably hasn't much money. Even if the escape was set up by some of his pals. We may hear of him first when he pulls a heist somewhere."

"Which is also an idea," said Hackett.

It was a quarter to six. They went back to headquarters.

Mendoza had already left, and Lake. Hackett left the telex message about Conover pinned down by an ashtray on Shogart's desk. This was Wednesday, Henry Glasser's day off, so the night watch would be short one man. He followed Landers' Corvair out of the lot and got on the Pasadena freeway.

At the house in Highland Park, he found all serene: his inspired cook Angel busy over the stove, her brown hair in disarray from the hot oven, nearly-five Mark absorbed in the McGuffey First Reader, two-year-old Sheila (and her hair was really going to be reddish, like his mother's) coaxing the dignified silver Persian to play— Luis, wishing that cat on them, remembered Hackett amusedly, suffering Sheila's strangling hug and patting Silver Boy.

"Busy day, darling?"

"The usual," said Hackett. And to her further automatic question, "No, I haven't weighed. The hell with it. And all the diets. After all, I am six three and a half—"

Rich Conway had been wandering around all alone since noon, questioning the various witnesses on the four heist jobs. He hadn't got a thing. He felt frustrated and lonesome. He'd rather looked forward, getting off night watch on to days, to seeing more of Lieutenant Mendoza, that rather legendary character, now Robbery and Homicide were merged; but in this last month he hadn't had occasion to, much; they'd had a lot of tiresome routine, the legwork.

He went home and put a frozen dinner in the oven, and phoned Landers, who had just got home. "What about setting up another double date on Tuesday?" They were both off on Tuesday, and Conway was dating a policewoman too, Margot Swain, who was working out of Wilcox Street in Hollywood.

"I'll ask Phil," said Landers amiably. The girls liked each other.

*　　*　　*

Mendoza, who had walked alone so long, these days came home to a crowded house on Rayo Grande Avenue up in Hollywood. As he slid the Ferrari into the garage beside Alison's Facel-Vega, he wasn't worried or much interested in any of the various cases they had on hand. He didn't like to stash cases away in Pending but sometimes it was unavoidable. He'd hear about the body on Stanford Avenue in the morning; they'd probably pick up Terry Conover somewhere, sometime; the heist jobs were anonymous, like so many of the casual robberies, burglaries; it was to be hoped those two bodies would get identified eventually, to get buried under the right names.

He got a little tired sometimes, of the eternal damned foolishness, wanton violence, random stupidity. He had put in, for his sins, twenty-five years of watching it, on this top police force, and he got a little tired. Seeing that he didn't have to go on with it—the old man having been that rare bird, a lucky gambler—he sometimes wondered why he stayed on down at headquarters.

But at home in the big Spanish house was red-haired Alison, who had so belatedly domesticated Luis Mendoza, and Mairí MacTaggart busy over her special scones, and the livestock—the Old English sheepdog Cedric offering a solemn paw, somewhere the four cats, Bast, Nefertite, Sheba and the wicked El Señor; and, of course, the twins.

Mendoza, these days, had the vague thought that parenthood should be entered into young. The twins, such an uncanny combination of himself and his Scots-Irish girl, sometimes confounded him.

"*Amador,*" said Alison briskly, returning his kiss. "Blue cheese or Roquefort dressing? It's just salad, steak and Mairí's scones. Do you want a drink before dinner? And they have really related to Lesson Twenty-four in the first reader."

"*¿Por qué?*" said Mendoza. "Why do I stay at this thankless job?"

"I often wonder," said Alison. "It's the goat. Lesson Twenty-four."

"*¡No me diga!*" said Mendoza.

"Well, go and hear."

In the nursery, a term the twins objected to, he was greeted by loud demands. The twins were not quite four; at least, mercifully, the McGuffey Readers had them talking mostly English now. "See, Daddy, a *nice* goat—named Jip—he pulls the cart— A goat, he'd be fun to have, we be all *bueno* to him—" Master Johnny was excited at the thought.

"Want a goat!" said Miss Terry simply.

"*¡Dios me libre!*" said Mendoza. He wondered how you could explain zoning laws to a nearly-four-year-old. He wondered how he'd ever got into all this.

The night watch, minus Glasser tonight, came on—Shogart the plodder, Galeano, Schenke. It was a quiet night; nothing turned up for them until nine-thirty, when they had a call from the black-and-white chased out on a call. Another heist, at—of all places—Chasen's new downtown restaurant. That was a very class place, one of the few good restaurants on Central's beat. Shogart and Galeano went out on it.

"We were just about to close," said the maître d' agitatedly. "The last customers were just out, I'd already put up the sign, most of the girls already gone—"

The manager was moaning, "Never had such a thing happen—I couldn't believe it, and for a Wednesday it'd been a good night—all the receipts—I hadn't counted it, I don't know—"

Two men, they both said: one chef had still been here, but back in the kitchen, and hadn't seen them. The restaurants which offered live entertainment, a combo, a pianist, would stay open till past midnight; but Chasen's just offered good food and a quiet atmosphere, and closed between nine and nine-thirty. Two men, and all the manager and maître d' could say was, middle-sized, stocking masks over their faces, two guns. "I don't know anything about guns," said the manager, "I don't know what kind. All the receipts—it was a busy night—and I always go straight to the night-deposit box at the bank—"

"That's kind of a smart job," said Galeano thoughtfully. "Somebody thought about this, E.M. Figured somebody'd be taking all the nice cash to a night-deposit box—get in first, just at closing time." But there wasn't much to go on. Tomorrow, the day men could ask the computers who might have records of having held up restaurants before. The only definite thing that emerged was that the heisters hadn't touched anything here, and might have been wearing gloves anyway. It'd be no use to call out the lab on it.

Thursday morning, and Hackett and Higgins off. Mendoza, coming in at eight sharp, was reading the report Galeano had left him on the job at Chasen's when the day men came drifting in, Piggott, Palliser, Landers, Conway, Grace.

"This Moffat thing," said Grace, following the rest of them into Mendoza's office. Palliser, seeing Wanda come in, had cornered her and was starting to dictate a report about that. Having the gist of it from him, Grace passed on to Mendoza what they had so far. "We're going to nose around that apartment, see what gossip we can pick up. She doesn't seem to have been exactly the shrinking violet. Could be somebody'll know the names of a few current boyfriends."

"It's a place to start," agreed Mendoza absently. "Now, this slick little heist last night—" He looked at Galeano's report meditatively. "If we ever pick up the X's on those other jobs, it'll be pure luck— Tom, you and Conway might as well do a little routine on this. I've got the manager and the maître d' coming in at ten to make statements. When you come to think of it, it's a wonder nobody had that thought before—the genteel restaurants, at closing times. At least I don't remember any such caper."

"There'd be quite a take, I suppose," said Conway, "if half of it wasn't credit-card records, but they couldn't be sure—"

"Ah, but they could. Nearly," said Mendoza. "The place with a floor show, a band, dancing, there'd be a good many people around at closing time. The nice quiet restaurant, no. By the time the manager or whoever was ready to take off for the night-deposit box, the waitresses gone, chefs gone. An ideal setup really. I wonder what the take was."

As they went out Conway said to Landers, "That aspect of it never occurred to me. He does see things. But what do you bet that this turns out just as anonymous as the other ones?"

"No bets, with the violent-crime rate up. We can make the gestures at it." They went down to R. and I. and consulted with Phil O'Neil. She really was a very cute blonde, neat and trim in her navy uniform, with the dusting of freckles on her upturned nose, and Landers looked at her fondly. "Do we have any records of anybody heisting restaurants, lady?"

"See what the computer says," said Phil. Rather surprisingly, the computer gave them two names. One Albert Pritchard, one Sam Olinski had held up the Tail o' the Cock, three years ago. Olinski had a mild record of common theft and burglary prior to that; Pritchard only a count of drunk driving. They'd both got a one-to-three and would probably be out now. The addresses would be up-to-date if they were both on parole. Reluctantly Landers followed Conway out— Phil had agreed to the date Tuesday if it was all right with Margot—and they took the Corvair to check out the address on Olinski, which was over in Glendale.

It was an old frame house on a quiet residential street, and they found Olinski sitting in a rocker on the front porch. By his pedigree he was fifty-one, but he looked older: white-haired and rather feeble. He looked at the badges and peered at Landers. "Seems you cops look younger to me every time I see one—but so does everybody, come to that. You ain't tryin' to pin anything on me, are you?"

"Depends if there's anything to pin, Mr. Olinski," said Conway, his cynical gray eyes amused. "Can you tell us where you were last night at about nine-thirty?"

"Sure. Right here. That is, in the house. Watchin' TV. With my daughter Eleanor and her husband Jim. Did you think I was up to something?" He laughed shortly. "I guess

27

you picked me up the last time, boys. Can't do much of nothin' these days. I had me a big old heart attack while I was still in the joint, last year."

The daughter was there, and indignantly confirmed that. "So somebody else had the bright idea," said Landers. Olinski said he didn't know where Pritchard was; he didn't know him very well, they'd only pulled that one job together and Pritchard had got paroled before he had.

The address they had for Pritchard was in West L.A., and when they found it, he had moved away last week. A phone call downtown confirmed that Pritchard had got off parole about the same time he moved. He still could be one of the boys they were after, so they went back to the office to sit in on the interview with the manager and maître d'.

They got there as the two men were arriving.

The manager, Dave Woodward, was still shaken. "We'd never had it happen before, Lieutenant—you don't think of a good restaurant as a place that gets held up, if you take me—and I was so surprised—I'm afraid neither of us can be of any help to you, we couldn't possibly identify anybody, they had these stocking masks on, pulled right down over their faces, and they couldn't have been there five minutes—"

"Less," said the other man, Chester Hunter. He looked very unlike a suave maître d', in a tweed suit and loud tie: he was very tall and thin, Woodward short and stocky, but they both wore mournful expressions. "Mr. Woodward had all the receipts in his briefcase, all ready to leave. They took it and went."

"¿Qué?" Mendoza sat up. "As if they knew the routine?"

"We thought about that," said Woodward, "but anybody could figure the day's receipts would be taken to a night-deposit box after we closed, and it was a good time to hit us. I scarcely think it was—er—what you'd call an inside job, Lieutenant." He smiled faintly. "Every restaurant I've ever worked in had more or less the same routine on that."

28

"What about the briefcase?" asked Landers, thinking about latent prints.

"Oh, they took it. Just looked to be sure what was in it, and—and went," said Woodward. "Fortunately, of course, I've got the figures. For what it's worth. Six thousand eight hundred and forty-two dollars in cash. The credit-card records—"

"They'll dump those," said Conway. "My God, would that be an average take for one day?"

"Slightly under—it was Wednesday, it's usually slower in the middle of the week," said Woodward. "But really, I was so surprised—and with the masks—I couldn't possibly describe—"

"Well, you can give us some idea about sizes—clothes," said Landers.

They consulted with each other mutely. "Both young, I'd say," said Hunter. "One about maybe five ten, other one shorter. Just dark clothes—pants and jackets. Black or dark gray." Woodward agreed. "Neither of 'em fat or thin, just ordinary."

That left Pritchard in, just about. He was thirty-three, five ten, a hundred and fifty.

Only they didn't know where to look for him. They'd get word out to the pigeons; maybe somebody knew where he was.

Grace and Palliser, at the Stanford Avenue apartment, were feeling frustrated and getting nowhere.

Miss Callway, who lived across the hall from Ida Moffat's apartment, said primly that she hadn't known her at all. "Not even to speak to. I hope I know how to mind my own business."

Mrs. Licci in the front left upstairs apartment told them she really didn't know anything about Mrs. Moffat, and hadn't wanted to know anything, but she wasn't surprised she'd got herself murdered though it was a terrible thing to have happen right here. She'd get her husband to move except that they probably couldn't find anything so cheap so close in to town. "Why weren't you surprised?" asked Grace in his soft voice. "If you didn't know her?"

Well, said Mrs. Licci darkly, she didn't *know* but there were feelings to these things. Pressed, she added that she was very busy cleaning and really couldn't spare any more time.

The three couples in the other apartments upstairs and downstairs rear all worked and weren't home. In the downstairs right front apartment Mrs. Schultz shied back from the badges and said she didn't know anything. Mrs. Kiefer was the manager, she said, if anybody knew anything about Mrs. Moffat it'd be her.

Mrs. Kiefer was just leaving for the market, and said she was in a hurry. "I told you all I know yesterday, anyway," she said to Palliser. "I mind my own business, and I don't like gossip. I told you—"

"Mrs. Kiefer," said Grace gently, "does your husband work around here?"

"Now what in time that's got to do with anything—! Yes, he's got the Shell station at Vermont and Olympic. But what you're asking for—"

"What were you asking for?" asked Palliser as they started back to the car. They'd taken his Rambler; he refused to squeeze his six feet into the little blue Elva.

"Well, I've got a simple mind, John," said Grace, "as we all know. And for all Matt's right about being back to Sodom and Gomorrah, and the devil converting all too many people, it occurs to me that there are still some— mmh—skittishly respectable females left among us. I think we've been talking to some of them. And I'd take a bet the Lieutenant'd say that when Mrs. Kiefer tells us she doesn't like gossip, that's the warning rattle."

"I believe you," said Palliser.

"I'll bet all the women in that apartment exchanged a lot of gossip about this Moffat female, but they're not about to come out plain and talk about anything with *s*-blank-*x* in it, to a couple of strange cops. Just occurred to me that one of the men living there might not be so prudish."

"You've got a simple mind," said Palliser, switching on the ignition. "Let's go and see."

At the Shell station he pulled the Rambler off to one side of the pumps; they got out and asked a dirty-looking kid with long hair and sideburns for Kiefer. "That's him there—" He pointed incuriously. Kiefer was big and blond, balding, and friendly by the grin he was giving a customer as he polished the windshield. They went up and introduced themselves as the car pulled out, and Kiefer was more than friendly; he was pleased as punch to see them.

"I wondered if any of you fellows'd want to talk to me— I'll take a break—hey, Benny, you take over, hah? Now what about that, a murder right in our building! You'd took the body away, time I got home last night, but the wife told me all about it—I can't get over her bein' the one to find the body! A body—my God. So, what you want to ask me? Anything I can tell you—"

"About Mrs. Moffat," said Grace. "We've been talking to the women at the apartment, and—"

"And they was all nervous as hell about it and too mealymouthed to tell you anything, hah?" Kiefer laughed and lit a long black cigar, after politely offering the box. "Women, my God! That old biddy was about all they talked about since she lived there. My God, it makes you wonder what gets into some women, fellows. That one, she'd been around but good. Man crazy—anything in pants, I give you my word. Made a pass at me once, shows you she'd go for anything." He chuckled comfortably. "And I don't say, if she'd been twenty years younger and sober at the time, I wouldn't 'a took her up on it, but I'm a little more particular, you might say."

Palliser grinned. "We did gather, from this and that in the apartment—"

"Man crazy," repeated Kiefer. "The wife's told me, many's the time she'd see Mrs. Moffat bring men home. Never any noisy parties, nothin' to complain about, you see, but anybody can add two and two knew what was goin' on."

"Did she have a regular boyfriend?" asked Grace.

"I wouldn't think so. The wife says she never saw the same man with her twice. I wouldn't know where she picked 'em up. I don't think she hung around local bars, not by the hours she'd be in and out, what the wife says. She worked pretty regular every day, and then she'd go out early in the evening, see." But he couldn't offer them any descriptions, any names. "And tell you the truth, I don't think the wife or any of the other women could either. See, take this latest time it happened—last Monday night. I'm sittin' there readin' the paper, the wife says there's that woman comin' in, and opens the door a crack mighty careful to do some snoopin', see. Says she saw Mrs. Moffat in the front hall, man with her, just saw his back, but she didn't think it was the same man come home with her Saturday night anyway. It was like that. The hall's dark, and for all the women's snoopin' I don't suppose they spotted her every time she brought a man home."

"So it could just as well be she did have a regular boyfriend," said Palliser. "Or several."

Kiefer thought that over and agreed. "I guess so."

"Mr. Kiefer," said Grace, "I understand your wife manages the apartment. Collects the rents and so on. Why didn't she ask Mrs. Moffat to move, if—"

"My God, man," said Kiefer, "them women wouldn't 'a had anything nearly so damn juicy to gossip about, hadn't been for Ida Moffat! Women ain't logical, Mr. Grace. I asked her the same thing once and she just says there's no technical reason, woman don't make any disturbance."

Grace laughed. "And I ought to know human nature better by this time."

But as far as tracking down any of the men Ida Moffat had known, that was a handful of nothing. Back in the Rambler, Palliser said, "There was a check. Evidently somebody she'd worked for. I don't suppose the woman could tell us anything, but we'd better give it a try. I've got the address—Briarcliff Road in Hollywood."

* * *

Just after Woodward and Hunter left, a black-and-white called in to report two new bodies, in a car on the street. A citizen had come in ten minutes before, asking to see one of the unidentified bodies; he'd reported his son missing and Lieutenant Cary of Missing Persons had sent him up here. Piggott had taken him to the morgue. Landers and Conway had just come back from another visit to R. and I. with a list of common-garden-variety heist men to chase down, with nothing at all to say that any of them had been the X's at Chasen's last night or on the other jobs; Mendoza chased them out on the new homicides.

Fifteen minutes later he was methodically stacking the deck, practicing the crooked poker deal, when Sergeant Lake buzzed him and said business was picking up. "You've got another new body, at the Clark Hotel."

"Caray," said Mendoza. "So I'll go and look at it." He reached for the perennial black Homburg.

"There's an ambulance on the way and I'll get the lab out. The black-and-white's still there."

The Clark Hotel on Hill Street, like some other hotels in downtown L.A., had once been a good hotel, a quiet middle-class place with no pretension to elegance, but eminently respectable, offering good service and comfort. It was still respectable, but with the inevitable decrease of respectable transients staying in the inner-city area, when classier hotels in cleaner areas were available, the Clark looked somewhat down-at-heel and poverty-stricken now. Its brown brick front was grimy, and inside the lobby the carpet was wearing thin. One of the uniformed men, Fred Ware, was standing by the desk; recognizing Mendoza, he came forward.

"It's the fifth floor, Lieutenant. Quigley—he's the manager—is having kittens about keeping it quiet. Seems they don't have all that many customers anymore and maybe news of a murder'd drive everybody out they've got. He's up there with my partner."

"What's it look like?" Mendoza buried his cigarette in a sand tub.

"Well, it's murder one all right." Ware was a big dark

young fellow, and he'd been a cop for some time, but he looked shaken for a moment. "An old lady—Mrs. Harriet Branch. She lived here—they've got more permanent tenants than people passing through, I think. She's been beaten up—it's a mess. Place ransacked. The daughter called in when she couldn't get her on the phone, they usually talked to each other the same time every day. Quigley thought she might have had a heart attack or something, and went up and found her."

"Así," said Mendoza. "Funny place for a break-in. Or was it?"

"The door wasn't broken in. Looks as if she let in whoever it was herself. Which is also funny," said Ware.

"The lab team'll be along—send them up."

"It's five-fourteen, Lieutenant."

Up on the fifth floor the other uniformed man was trying to calm down Quigley—a little plump man in a tight brown suit—and an agitated Negro maid in a white uniform. He greeted Mendoza in some relief. Mendoza said, "You can get back on tour as soon as the lab shows up."

"We've preserved it tight for you, sir. Nobody in since Mr. Quigley called in."

"Bueno," Mendoza introduced himself to the other two. The maid was Agnes Harvey, and even in her agitation her mind was moving faster than Quigley's.

"I just hope you won't think I had anything to do with it, Lieutenant—I can see the lock's not broken, and of course I've got a key, but you've got to believe me, she always kept the bolt up too and when I came to clean I'd have to call out who I was before she'd let me in—I wouldn't have hurt Mrs. Branch, she was a nice old lady —and to see her laying there like that—"

"I'm sure they wouldn't think that, Agnes," said Quigley, shocked all over again. "Such a terrible, terrible thing —we've never had such a thing happen—"

"We'll want a statement from you, Mr. Quigley—can you wait a little while, please? There'll be some men out from the lab, and then I'll want to talk to you." Quigley

34

stuttered obedience. Mendoza shoved the door of five-fourteen wider with a cautious toe, and went in.

The center light was on, and showed him an old-fashioned hotel suite, what used to be called a bachelor apartment. The living room was about twelve by fifteen, furnished with shabby, nondescript, comfortable furniture, an overstuffed couch, a matching chair, a little desk with a straight chair, a thin flowered carpet; there were sheer lace curtains at the windows. A door to the left gave a glimpse of a tiny kitchenette, an apartment-sized stove, a small table. A door to the right led into a small square bedroom just big enough for a single bed, a double chest of drawers, another straight chair. There was a walk-in closet, and a postage-stamp-sized bathroom beside it.

The body of the old woman was in the middle of the living-room floor. She lay on her side, arms over her head as if she were still trying to protect herself from the blows rained on her. Mendoza bent and felt one arm; it was stiff. He thought, looking at his watch, sometime yesterday evening. There was a good deal of blood; her mouth was open in a silent scream. She'd been a thin, frail old lady; she was wearing an old-fashioned cotton nightgown with a high neck, and a fleecy pink housecoat over it, both torn and bloody. One flaccid limp breast spilled out on the carpet.

The whole place had been ruthlessly ransacked—drawers yanked out and dumped, clothes pulled off the rod in the closet, the medicine chest in the bathroom swept clean; a bottle of aspirin, toothpaste, eye lotion, and mouthwash bottles dumped to the tile floor, smashed. Near the body lay an old-fashioned black handbag, open, with a generous-sized coin purse beside it, empty. An ink bottle was overturned on the desk, and a pool of ink stained the carpet. The standard reading lamp by the upholstered chair had been knocked flat, its bulb broken.

Mendoza said to himself ruefully, *"A su tiempo maduran las uvas.* And what a harvest do we reap." The statistics every cop knew, but that was figures on a sheet of paper: Mrs. Branch, horridly and cruelly dead in this quiet room, made the figures come to life: the crimes of violence up by 622 percent in the last twelve years.

He went back to the living room for another look at the body, and this time spotted something else; he bent closer. There was a noise at the door and Duke and Scarne came in loaded down with the usual equipment. "That's pretty," commented Duke. "I wish you'd find a nice neat corpse for us some time, Lieutenant."

"Few and far between," said Mendoza. "Look, Bill—there's something under the body—I'd like a look at it."

"Wait till I get some pictures." Five minutes later Scarne put down the Speed Graphic, bent over the body and grunted, "I see it." He lifted the body slightly and with the handle of a dusting brush hooked something out to slither into full sight on the carpet. "And isn't that pretty."

"No," said Mendoza. "It's an ugly little joke, Bill." He brushed his moustache back and forth. And in one way he liked it a little, and in another he didn't. Symbols, he thought.

The object that had fallen under the body—he had a vision of the old lady trying to put up a fight, grabbing and holding—was a long string of violently colored plastic love beads, the kind worn by both sexes of the Now generation. It was broken, and several beads had slid off the thin wire that had held them. At one end of it was a crudely made bright brass circle-and-cross, the Egyptian *ankh* that was the symbol of Life.

"It's all yours," said Mendoza, and went out to talk to Quigley. The maid had disappeared; Quigley, hovering in the hall, was only slightly calmer. "Could we go to your office, Mr. Quigley? I'll want to know everything you can tell me about Mrs. Branch."

"Oh, yes, certainly, certainly." But downstairs they were intercepted by the desk clerk.

"Mrs. Whitlow's been calling every five minutes, Mr. Quigley, and I didn't know what to do—I didn't like, over the phone—but I suppose she ought to know—"

"Oh, my God," said Quigley. "I forgot all about her! I ought to have called her! Mrs. Branch's daughter! My

God, how can I tell her over the phone her mother's been murdered? My God, I need a drink."

"You'd better let me do it," said Mendoza. It was another unpleasant job cops got used to. The clerk put the call through to Mr. Quigley's little cubbyhole of an office; economically Mendoza introduced himself and broke the news to Mrs. Whitlow, who sounded level-headed even in crisis. He would probably want to talk to her later, today or tomorrow; the body would have to be formally identified. She said yes, and she'd call her husband right away; she gave him the address and remembered to thank him before she began to cry and hung up.

Quigley was apologizing, recapping a bottle of Scotch. "Really, I'm not a drinking man, Lieutenant, but this has upset me so—we've never had such a thing happen—Mrs. Branch! Such a nice old lady, and a real lady too—she'd lived here for over twenty years, and the last few years with her arthritis so bad she hardly went out at all, except when her daughter came for her—she had Sunday dinner with them every week—Mrs. Whitlow's a nice woman too, and I must say I can hardly blame her for trying to get Mrs. Branch to move away, go to live with them. There's no denying that this area isn't as safe or—or pleasant as it used to be, when Mrs. Branch first lived here—it was so convenient, she used to say, just a couple of blocks up to Bullock's, The Broadway practically next door, all the shops—and we'd have missed the old lady, but I did see why Mrs. Whitlow—"

Mendoza started to get him calmed down to answer questions.

"We noticed the old heap when we came on at six," said the uniformed man to Landers and Conway. "This couple asleep or passed out. No reason to check 'em out—along here you get that sometimes." The car was an old Dodge sedan, much dented. "But when we swung round here again, half an hour ago, they were still here, so Jack said we'd better check to see if they're high on something.

And they're cold. I think they were shot—there's blood. Didn't want to mess up any latents for the lab."

Landers and Conway peered into the car, which had its windows down. The bodies were a man and a woman, both young. There was blood all right. "Have to tow it in before we can get at 'em," said Conway. "There could be prints on the car." And it would be just as well anyway; this was a sleazy backwater, Naud Street down below the Southern Pacific railroad yards, and already a little crowd of noisy youngsters had collected across the street and were yelling the usual names at the uniform.

"Everybody," said Landers, straightening his slim height from the car, "has got civil rights but us. Give the garage a call." In fifteen minutes a tow truck came up; the black-and-white went back on tour and Landers and Conway followed the truck back to the garage.

When the lab men had dusted the outside of the Dodge, they got pictures of the corpses *in situ* and then opened the door and got them out. The man looked to be in his early twenties, a weedy little fellow with shoulder-length blond hair and sideburns, a straggly moustache; he was wearing old jeans and a sleeveless shirt embellished with colorful flowers. He'd been shot at least once in the body. The woman was about the same age, with long dark hair, in jeans and a dirty T-shirt; she'd been shot in the head.

The Dodge was registered to a Godfrey Booth at an address on St. Andrews Place. There was a billfold on the man, empty of money but containing an I.D. card filled out: Godfrey Booth, the same address. There was a woman's handbag, no money in it but a lot of miscellany: lipsticks, powder puffs, Kleenex, matches, a bunch of keys, an address book, a paperback book entitled *How to Become a Witch*.

"Drifters," said Conway. "The mod squad."

"And no money. Just the casual violence for what they had on them?" wondered Landers. The morgue attendants came for the bodies; maybe the autopsies would tell them something more. And there were rules and regulations; if possible they had to get the bodies identified. They drove out to St. Andrews Place to see if anybody there had known Godfrey Booth and who the girl might have been.

It was an old run-down four-family place. When they stepped into the lobby they could hear a baby crying somewhere. Landers punched the bell of the apartment on the left and presently a mountainously fat woman in a bright-red cotton pantsuit opened the door. "Excuse me," said Landers politely, "do you know a Godfrey Booth who lives here?"

She stared at them, shifting a wad of chewing gum in her mouth. "Sure, I know God and Sue. Why? They're gone some place."

"Sue?" said Conway.

"Sue's God's wife. It's kind of a joke, call him God. I dunno where they went. They got the left back upstairs." Landers opened his mouth to tell her they were dead, and she added resentfully, "Went off and left their brat on my hands. I got no time to tend to him—that's him yelling." In spite of which, when they did tell her, she went into hysterics and they had to call an ambulance.

"And I tell you something, Rich," said Landers when she'd passed out and they were waiting for the ambulance, "there's something wrong with that baby."

Neither of them, as ignorant bachelors, knew much about babies; they couldn't have a guess about this one, except that it was extremely dirty; but it was crying intermittently and jerking its arms and legs around as if it were about to have a fit. They eyed it nervously. When the ambulance came, the attendants said it might be epileptic, and took it along too.

Nobody else was at home in the apartment house. It was getting on toward twelve-thirty, so they went up to Federico's on North Broadway for lunch. Palliser and Grace were already there, and Piggott came in five minutes later.

"We've got the overdose identified," he said. "Douglas Horne. Nineteen. I heard all the usual tale from the father." He didn't have to go into detail; they'd all heard that, *ad infinitum.* "The devil getting around." And maybe once they'd regarded Matt Piggott the earnest Christian a little amusedly, but these days they didn't. The devil was surely covering ground in this year of our Lord.

When they got back to the office, Landers asked Lake to start the machinery on a search warrant for the St. Andrews Place apartment. Palliser and Grace wanted to bring Mendoza up-to-date on Ida Moffat—he might have a hunch where to go looking. They found him sitting on the edge of his spine in his desk chair contemplating a broken string of plastic love beads. A cigarette smoldered on his lower lip; his normally sleek, thick black hair was ruffled where he'd run fingers through it.

"We've got to a dead end," said Grace. "You're thinking of joining the love generation?"

Mendoza laughed. *"Tal cosa, no.* Symbols. What's your dead end? . . . Oh. Well, all that occurs to me is that the woman must have had some friends somewhere. Female friends. The same kind as herself, she might have talked to about boyfriends."

"I suppose so. But would she have mentioned their names to people she worked for?" said Palliser doubtfully.

"And if it ends up in Pending, not much loss," said Mendoza. He sat up abruptly. "I'm feeling a little more concerned about Mrs. Harriet Branch. Although—*¡singular!*—they both opened their doors to murder. That bolt —Quigley said she asked permission to have it put on—" His voice trailed off; he got up. "Her daughter sounded like a sensible woman. I'd better go and talk to her."

They had called Mrs. Bloomfield at the Hollywood address, and got no answer. Now they'd try her again. "And you know she won't be able to tell us anything," said Palliser.

"No harm in asking," said Grace.

Landers and Conway were driven back to the list of possible heisters from Records, but just as they were leaving the office Lake hailed them. "It's Hollywood Receiving—a Dr. Schiller."

40

"Detective Landers, Robbery-Homicide, Doctor. What—"

"What kind of devilry you boys are sending us these days," said Dr. Schiller coldly, "really has to be seen to be believed. I understand it was your office sent over this baby—I don't know the circumstances—male, approximately ten months old, some malnutrition and a respiratory infection."

"Well, yes?" said Landers.

"What kind of *mentality*—" said Schiller. "Well, of course the normal sane individual simply cannot grasp the enormities possible to the addicts—but—! The baby, Detective Landers, has been subjected to probably repetitive doses of marijuana. He is in a dangerously comatose state at the moment, but I think we can stabilize him with care. What brain damage or chromosome damage may have been done is something else. I suppose ycu have to—"

"What?" said Landers incredulously. "The baby—*marijuana?*"

"Almighty God," said Conway mildly.

"—know something about the latest research on narcotic drugs," said Dr. Schiller sardonically. "So possibly you are aware that the new findings are that many of the effects, such as chromosome changes and the probability of deformed genes, as well as simpler brain damage, which we once attributed to LSD, have now been determined to be in fact a result of marijuana ingestion."

"My God," said Landers. "My God. Look, Doctor, we didn't feed the baby the marijuana. But, my God, yes, I saw that release—but who would—a *baby*—"

"I only thought you'd like to know," said Schiller.

Landers put the phone down and passed that on. All of them but Piggott swore, and Piggott simply said, "And if that isn't diabolical, I don't know what is. A baby."

And Conway said thoughtfully, "The Mary Jane. You know, Tom—that's kind of basic, isn't it?"

"What do you mean?"

"Well, who had access to the baby, to feed it the marijuana? The parents. Godfrey and Sue Booth. I think—"

Kind of a joke, call him God. Landers thought, perhaps irrelevantly, of a bumper sticker that had given him a chuckle on the way home the other day: *God is back—and is He mad!*

"I think," said Conway, "we go up to Narco and ask if anybody there knows anything about Godfrey and Sue."

"I think so too," said Landers purposefully.

The address Mrs. Whitlow had given Mendoza was on Creston Drive in the hills above Hollywood. It was a sprawling old Spanish house; this was an old residential area redolent of substance rather than new money. She opened the door to him herself, acknowledged the badge and introduction with a silent nod.

"I've been trying to reach Walter—my husband. He had to go up to San Francisco to a sales convention. The hotel promised to pass on a message as soon as he comes in. I've tried to keep my head, but—Mother! To think of— Please, won't you sit down." She was tall, fair, good-looking in a broad Scandinavian way, her face now drawn with grief. The room was a little untidy, pleasantly furnished for comfort rather than show. "I know there are things you want to ask—but I don't understand how it could have happened, some criminal getting in—"

"Well, we'd like to find out too, Mrs. Whitlow," said Mendoza. He offered her a cigarette, lit it for her, lit his own. "Mr. Quigley told me you wanted your mother to move."

"Oh, good heavens, yes," she said. "When she first went to the Clark, it was nice. And convenient, right downtown. But now, it wasn't even safe—not that Mother went out much down there, since her arthritis had been worse. I used to change her library books for her once a week, and bring her here to dinner on Sunday— But she'd lived there so long, since Dad died, and she knew all the people at the hotel, it was home to her."

"Did she have any friends living there too?"

She nodded. "Especially Mrs. Davies, she was about Mother's age—she died last month. I know Mother said she was going to miss her—they used to spend afternoons together, Mother's apartment or hers. Most of the permanent tenants there are older people, but a lot of them have moved away in the last few years. But I just can't understand how a thing like this could happen, right in the hotel—Mother always kept her door bolted, Walter put that on for her—"

"Mrs. Whitlow, can you give us any idea how much money your mother might have had in the apartment?"

She nodded. "It's only the second week of the month. She'd have had her check about the third or fourth— I shopped for her, just a few groceries, last Saturday, and it came to twelve something, she'd given me a twenty. Her annuity check. Dad took it out for her when he made that killing in the market, and the agent said he was crazy—"

"How much would she have had left?"

"Well, that's it. Heavens," she said, smoking quickly, staring past his shoulder into space, "I remember Dad saying that often enough—how he knew when Roosevelt took us off the gold standard the dollar was eventually doomed—just a question of time—and when he made that killing, it was during the war, he sank a lot of it into the annuity for Mother. He thought the currency might just hold for her lifetime, more and more inflated, of course. The agent said he was crazy, the monthly payment he wanted set up, but"—she smiled wryly—"I guess Dad knew what he was doing." She stubbed out her cigarette.

"And possibly a little something about basic economics," said Mendoza dryly. "How much?"

"It was fifteen hundred a month. Usually she took just what she needed for groceries and so on—I shopped for her once a week usually, if she didn't feel like going out— but I know last week she'd said she was going to take her fur coat in for storage, and it needed some repairs—and she probably took out enough for Walter's birthday present too, she wanted to get him a nice sports jacket, I was going to take her shopping— There might have been four or five hundred dollars there."

"What bank did she use?"

44

"The Security Pacific just down in the next block. Oh, I should have been firmer!" she said wretchedly. "I should have made her move away from there. But it's difficult with old people, if you—if you *manage* them they think you think they're not capable anymore—and it wasn't that, but—"

"Would you say your mother was—mmh—gullible, easily taken in? Would she have, say, got talking to a stranger, someone who seemed friendly, a woman especially—asked her to her apartment?"

"Oh, I don't think so—no, Mother was pretty shrewd, she had all her faculties all right. Strangers—but where would she meet any? She didn't get out much any more. Years ago she used to go up to Echo Park, MacArthur, on the bus, on nice days. But her arthritis the last few years—she was eighty-one, you know— And she'd have told me about anybody like that—"

"Did she know any young people?" asked Mendoza.

"*Young* people?" She stared at him. "Why, what do you —down there, do you mean? Oh, I don't see how—she never said anything about— Why?"

Mendoza looked at his cigarette. "You said she kept her door bolted. But suppose someone knocked and said there was a telegram, a special delivery letter. I suppose the hotel staff changes occasionally. Would she have opened her door, you think?"

"Oh, dear," she said inadequately, "I suppose so. Do you think that was how—? Oh, she would have. If they said they were from the desk. Right there in the hotel, feeling safe—" She sobbed once, and the phone rang in the hall. "Oh, thank God, that's Walter—" She ran. He listened to her murmuring voice out there for less than five minutes; when she came back she said, "He's flying right down, as soon as he can get a plane. He said something about—probably you have to have a formal identification."

"That's right," said Mendoza. "He can come to my office, take care of that tomorrow. Thanks very much, Mrs. Whitlow—if I think of anything else, we'll be in touch." He was thinking now, with this much background,

45

it could very easily be as simple as that: probably was. The old lady a fixture in the hotel, and all too probably chatting idly with the maids, Quigley, other people: the bit about the annuity, possibly even the amount, getting around by word of mouth. Getting to the ears eventually of some of the Now generation, too many of whom seemed determined to evade working for a living. The violence in that apartment, given one frail old lady as victim, could have been the work of one adult male. And in that big lobby, one adult male might not have been noticed, or noticed idly, passing through. But it'd do no harm to ask the night clerk if he remembered the love beads. As a rule, the love beads went with a few other rather bizarre items of apparel: but even that might be no help: a lot of that generation affected those.

Mendoza went back to the office and heard about the baby from Sergeant Lake, who was talking about it with a horrified Wanda. "¡Porvida! ¿Donde irá a parar todo esto? Where's all this going to end indeed?"

"Just what I said," said Wanda. "Sometimes I agree with Matt Piggott. A *baby*—"

"Oh, well, you just can't get decent servants nowadays," said Winifred Bloomfield to Palliser and Grace. She had looked a little undecided about letting a black man into her nice clean house, even when he wasn't very black and had on a sharp-tailored suit and white shirt; she talked mostly in Palliser's direction. She was a rawboned woman about sixty, overdressed and over-made-up, and her ultra-refined accent made both of them suspect strongly that she'd once been little Winnie Whatshername from the wrong side of the tracks.

"Had Mrs. Moffat worked for you long, Mrs. Bloomfield?" asked Palliser.

"Oh, a couple of years," she said vaguely. "Two days a week. Sometimes she helped out in the kitchen when we were entertaining. I didn't know her—I really couldn't tell you anything about her." And by her expression of delighted horror when they'd told her the woman had been murdered, thought Palliser, she'd be dying to ask questions, nobly restraining herself. "At least she didn't steal my husband's liquor the way some of the others did."

"Do you remember her ever mentioning the names of any friends?" asked Grace.

"Oh, dear me, I never exchanged any *conversation* with the woman." Of course, her tone implied, he wouldn't have understood that. "Oh, I believe she did have a friend called May or Maisie or—I'm afraid I don't recall. What? Oh, she was here last Tuesday, she left about five, I think. I'm afraid I really couldn't tell you a thing about her." She graciously identified the check as the one she'd given Ida Moffat that day, payment for two days' work.

"Doesn't mix with commoners," said Palliser in the Rambler. "You annoyed her, implying she gossiped with the hired help, Jase."

"What do I know about hired help?" said Grace. "So what do we fall back on? That dime-store tablet might need a code expert."

"There were a few phone numbers. See what they turn up." They drove back downtown and upstairs in the office heard about the baby. "My God," said Palliser.

Grace just shook his head, inevitably thinking of plump brown Celia Ann at home, as Palliser thought of David Andrew.

They sat down at their desks in the original communal sergeants' office and pored over Ida Moffat's personal memo-minder, sorting out decipherable phone numbers. They divided them up and started calling.

Palliser contacted four people who denied ever hearing of Ida Moffat; all four numbers belonged to rooming houses where the rate of transience would be high. On his fifth call he got a cautious male voice saying, "Yeah, I know Ida. Who's this?"

"I'm sorry to tell you she's dead, Mr.—"

"Molnar, Al Molnar—Ida's *dead?* For God's sake, what happened?"

"She was killed, Mr. Molnar, probably Tuesday night.

47

This is Sergeant Palliser, LAPD. We'd like to talk to you, whatever you can tell us about Mrs. Moffat—"

"Me? *Killed?* You mean *murdered?* Ida? Well, for Christ's sake!" Naked astonishment in his voice. "I don't know nothing about it—last time I seen Ida was Saturday—"

"We aren't suspecting you," said Palliser. "We'd just like to hear what you could tell us about Mrs. Moffat's friends. If you'll give me your address—"

"Well, my God, if that's so, Ida *murdered,* my God, what a thing, you knocked me all of a heap— I'd sure be glad to help you find whoever—but my God, nobody Ida knew 'd do a thing like that— How'd you find me, anyways? Oh, the phone number. Yeah, well, look, I'm at work—this is where I work, Mac's garage down on Vermont—but it's O.K., you can come here, the boss is gone for the day. My God, Ida murdered—"

They went out to talk to him. He was a big burly fellow in his fifties, fairly stupid, probably honest. He didn't mind telling them that he knew Ida went with other guys. She was good fun to be with, you had to have people to have fun with, going out and all, and he'd never got round to getting married. "What the hell?" he said simply. "It wasn't no skin off anybody's nose. I didn't own Ida or she me." He'd known her maybe five years or so. "She'd never been hitched either, just thought it sounded better, get called missus." She'd told him once she'd had a baby when she was just a kid, but she'd given it out for adoption, didn't even know if it was girl or boy.

"Could you tell us about any of her other friends?" asked Grace.

"Well, there's May. May McGraw, she was about Ida's best pal, I guess. She works at a place out on Union, the Tuxedo Bar n' Grill. I guess she'd know most of Ida's friends. Matter o' fact that's where I met Ida first—she useta like to go there for dinner sometimes, sit and talk to people, it's a nice little place." He asked eager questions about the murder; they were vague. "My sweet Jesus, I can't get over it, Ida murdered! Don't seem possible—I sure hope you get whoever it was!"

It was four-fifteen. They looked up the address of that bar and grill and drove down there. It was May's day off; the bartender obligingly gave them her address, Pennsylvania Street in Boyle Heights, and they tried there, at an old apartment house, but she wasn't home.

"One like Ida," said Grace, "out sitting talking to people in some nice little bar. Picking up the men."

"So maybe we'll get to talk to her tomorrow," said Palliser.

Piggott, said Lake when they got back, had gone out to untangle a freeway accident with two dead. Palliser thought again about that accident last January, and that enormous dog, and felt uneasy.

"Where's everybody else?"

"I haven't seen hide nor hair of Tom or Rich since that doctor called," said Lake.

Landers and Conway had gone up to the Narco office, presided over these days not only by Captain Patrick Callaghan but Lieutenant Saul Goldberg struggling with his perennial allergies. The sergeant at the switchboard said Callaghan was out, but he thought Goldberg was available. They went into the sergeants' office and found Detective Steve Benedittino talking to one of the mod squad—a tall young fellow with all the expectable accoutrements, tight black pants, leather jacket, boots, a T-shirt bearing the so-called peace symbol; he sported a thick blond handlebar moustache, curly hair down to his shoulders, and sideburns.

"Hi, fellows, what can I do for you?" asked Benedittino.

"Goldberg in?" Landers cast a glance at the flower child, who gave him the usual belligerent glare.

"Are we overlapping with Robbery-Homicide again? It will happen. He was on the phone to Sacramento a minute ago; maybe I'll do. What's the problem?"

Conway said, "No hurry—you were prodding at the junkie." His tone was low enough not to reach that one, but he scowled at them all the more. "I see he doesn't think much of our nice expensive plant."

Benedittino burst out laughing. "He doesn't think a hell of a lot of the job he's on, that's for sure. Hey, *paisano,* come and meet some Homicide dicks. Bob Miliani—Landers and Conway. Bob graduated top of his class at the Academy back in February."

"And I thought, damn it, I'd be wearing a uniform," said the flower child angrily. "My wife just moans every time she looks at me. If I'd known the brass was going to send me underground—my God!" He shook his luxuriant locks, disgusted.

"Never mind, we're letting you loose as soon as we get the works on that supplier," soothed Benedittino, "and by what's opening up, that could be any day."

"And I'll put in a voucher for what the haircut costs," said Miliani. "All I can say is, I think they're all nuts— it's the biggest Goddamned nuisance, falling all over the place—and the damn moustache getting in my coffee— gah! Well, I'd better get back to it and try to think of some new cusswords about the pigs picking me up on suspicion." Hunching his shoulders, he strode out.

"He'll be a good man," said Benedittino after him. "We pick the rookies—new faces, not so apt to be spotted even in costume, so to speak. He's given us quite a lot. So, what can we do for you?"

"Does the name of Godfrey Booth ring any bells?" asked Landers.

"It does. A faint one. A small-timer—the grass only, so far as I know. Sometimes a seller. He's served little stretches—got let off oftener. Why?"

"A user you can say," said Conway. "He and his wife—"

"Susan. Common-law."

"—were feeding it to their baby."

"My God in heaven," said Benedittino. "And that latest report, I suppose you saw it—the research boys have decided it's worse than the acid— My God. How'd you turn that up?"

They told him. "Would you have a guess about who they

were running with? It could have been the casual thing, for what they had on them," said Landers, "but a gun— and in Booth's own car—it could also be a personal kill."

"I'll agree with you. Lessee, I can tell you something. I picked Booth up for possession about six months ago— he's got a pedigree back to age sixteen. Right off I'll say two of his best pals are Randy Wyler and Bud Packer. They've got about the same pedigrees only not as sellers. We've probably got some addresses, not guaranteed recent."

"Anything you can give us," said Conway.

Goldberg, by the sounds from his office, was still on the phone, irately. In the end, Benedittino turned up six names for them, five men and a girl all about the Booths' age, who had been picked up with them before or were known associates. There were addresses appended, but these people tended to move around. "Good luck on finding them," said Benedittino. "Not that the Booths are any loss. The baby, my God. The things we do see."

Before they went out looking, Landers called Bainbridge's office to find out if any doctor had got to the corpses. One of Bainbridge's young surgeons told him that they wouldn't get to autopsies right away but he had probed for the slugs. Only one was intact, out of Booth, and he had sent it up to the lab, to Ballistics. Eventually they would hear what Ballistics could tell them about that.

They went out looking for the Booths' pals; they'd got side-tracked off the heisters. They drew blanks at four addresses, the pals moved on somewhere; but at four forty-five they found Randy Wyler and Bud Packer at a ramshackle rooming house on Magdalena Street the other side of the railroad yards, one step short of Skid Row.

Wyler and Packer had little records of possession, mostly suspended sentences; they took cops as a natural hazard of life and while they weren't exactly eager to answer questions, this and that emerged, back at an interrogation room at headquarters. The news that Godfrey and Sue had been shot opened them up a little farther.

"Gee, that's terrible," said Wyler. He was short and thin,

51

pockmarked with old acne, and looked as if he hadn't been eating regularly. "That's real bad, man. They were all-right people, God and Sue. Say, what about the baby? Did you know they had a kid?"

"That's right," said Conway. "Did you know they'd been giving the baby grass?"

Packer brayed a hoarse laugh, and sobered. He was about Conway's size, not tall, a stockier fellow with stringy long hair and a silly little wispy moustache. "Yeah, God thought it was a real kick, give the kid a high with its bottle. Like a fun thing. But, geesiz, who'd want to go and kill God and Sue? They wasn't doing nobody any harm."

Landers and Conway looked at each other. It would be a complete waste of time to try to reach this pair.

"It'll get to be legal pretty soon anyways," said Wyler.

"All right," said Conway, sounding tired, "did the Booths have any to sell recently? Do you know any of the people they'd been running with the last month? When did you see them last?"

Wyler and Packer exchanged glances. "Well, uh, last Saturday night, I guess," said Wyler. "There was a kind of party at their place. I dunno everybody was there—different people dropped in, like, you know—"

"Was there any grass floating around?" asked Landers.

Again the glances. "Well—some," said Packer. "Neither of us holding now," he added hastily.

"All right. Did you buy any?"

"It was a party—we were God's pals. He wouldn't make me or Randy hand out—I guess some of the rest of 'em, though. I don't know. No, I don't know where he got it—but it was no damn good, and I told him so—told him he got cheated on—"

"Bud, shut up."

"You said so yourself, damn it—it was just cut dust, it dint have no kick at all—" Packer subsided sullenly, and Landers raised his eyebrows at Conway. That was interesting.

"So, see if you can remember who was at the party," said Conway. They went on prodding at them, and came up with half a dozen reluctantly yielded names, two girls and four men. No, they hadn't seen any money handed over. They didn't know anything about Booth's supplier. Sometimes he had the stuff to sell and sometimes he was in the market—they didn't know any more, period.

It was getting on toward six o'clock; they let Wyler and Packer go.

"Say, has anything showed on that escaped con?" Landers asked Lake. "That Conover."

"Nary a thing. A.P.B.'s out statewide, but he seems to have crawled into the woodwork."

"Nobody ever did find that Betty Suttner," remembered Conway. "Well, so we go looking for these boys and girls tomorrow."

"Unless something new turns up," said Landers. "There's that list of heisters too."

"We were shorthanded today."

Wanda Larsen came past with a brisk Good Night; Lake went out. Mendoza's office was empty: eloquently, in the middle of his desk blotter was a long string of plastic love beads with a brass *ankh* at one end. "I wonder what that's all about," said Landers, yawning.

Mendoza came home looking preoccupied to find his household much as usual. With daylight saving on, the twins were out in the backyard chasing Cedric in circles, Cedric barking joyously. Their mockingbird, at least, had vanished again—doubtless temporarily; having raised a family in March, he and his wife would be back later this month to start another. The twins flung themselves on Mendoza; away from the reminding pictures in the McGuffey Reader they seemed to have forgotten the goat.

He went on into the house and found Alison and Mrs. MacTaggart busy over dinner. "And I need a drink," he said, kissing Alison. "The dirty job gets dirtier all the time, *cara.*" He told them about the baby.

"Guidness to mercy!" said Mrs. MacTaggart. "The puir wee mite! It's enough to make a body believe Satan's got

53

the upper hand, the way Holy Scripture says he will, whiles."

"But, Luis, that's—well, incredible is hardly the word," said Alison, horrified. "The things that go on—"

"And ninety-eight percent of it the damn random idiocy," said Mendoza rather savagely. "Doing what comes naturally—consequences five minutes ahead just not there for the idiots. I need a drink," and he reached for the bottle of rye in the cupboard.

El Señor the wicked, of the blond-in-reverse Siamese markings, heard him and came at a gallop from the front of the house. Automatically Mendoza poured him an ounce in a saucer, and Alison and Mrs. MacTaggart, still thinking about the baby, said never a word about alcoholic cats.

Hackett, as usual, had used his day off to get the lawn mowed and a little trimming and weeding done. Angel took the children to a nearby playground in the afternoon, warning him not to touch the angel food cake just out of the oven. But he was still feeling what-the-hell about the diet, and had a piece anyway.

Higgins, at loose ends, mowed the lawn front and back; Steve was good about doing it, but Higgins didn't mind. School would be out next week, and Steve would have more time.

The night watch came on—all of it but Glasser: stocky dark Nick Galeano, sandy slim Bob Schenke, the stolid plodder Shogart. "What's happened to Henry?" wondered Galeano. Anybody could get rammed by a drunk on the freeway.

Mendoza had left them a note on a homicide at the Clark Hotel: somebody to see the night desk clerk. Galeano said he'd go.

At the hotel, he talked to a friendly elderly man named Perkins, who was genuinely distressed at the old lady's death. A terrible thing, he said, didn't seem possible, right here in the hotel. She'd been such a nice old lady, it didn't bear thinking about.

There hadn't been an autopsy yet but Mendoza thought she'd been killed last night. Galeano asked questions. A young man, maybe a couple of young men dressed the way some young people did—the wild colors, the headbands and beads?

"We don't see any of them in the hotel," said Perkins. "I know the kind you mean. Why? You see them in the street, but not in here. Most of the people living here now—we've got mostly permanent tenants, not so much real hotel patrons like we used to have—are older people, Mr. Galeano. Oh, they'll have the younger people come visiting, family-like, but I can't recall I've ever seen one of the kind you're talking about, the funny clothes and all, right in here. Last night? No, sir. Yes, sir, I was here all evening, I came on at six and I was here till midnight when we lock up. We didn't used to do that, you know, a hotel is a kind of public place, open so people can come and go, but the last few years we do. In this area, the crime rate up—"

"You'd see anybody who came in the front door." The elevators were at the back of the lobby; anyone would have to pass the desk to reach elevators or the stairs beside them. "What about another way in? Is there a back door, to the kitchens or—"

"Oh, we don't have a dining room anymore," said Perkins sadly. "It got so there wasn't any call for it. The kitchens are all shut up. I can't recall when the back door, out to the alley, 's been used—it's always locked now. There's another front door, of course—it used to be the street entrance to the restaurant, but it's locked now too—"

"Are you sure it was, last night?"

"Oh, I'm positive," said Perkins. "Nobody uses it now."

"Are you sure," persisted Galeano, "that you were here at the desk from six to midnight?"

"Well," said Perkins with dignity, "I did once visit the lavatory adjoining Mr. Quigley's office. There wasn't a soul here. It was about nine o'clock, I suppose. I wasn't gone three minutes."

But maybe long enough. Galeano thanked him and went

back to the office. Glasser still hadn't come in. "I tried his apartment," said Schenke. "He's not there. Should we start calling hospitals?"

Five minutes later Glasser came in. As a rule Henry Glasser was an amiable man, a middle-sized sandy fellow with an unblemished record as an LAPD officer; but now he looked mad enough to breathe fire. "What happened to you?" asked Schenke.

"That Goddamned car!" said Glasser forcefully. "I swear to God, I try to be a good citizen and a good cop— what God had against my car I'll never know!" Glasser, figuring his budget last August, like a lot of other citizens hadn't reckoned on an earthquake. The earthquake had demolished his perfectly good car, and he'd been forced to buy new transportation. Being a cautious man with an instinctive distrust of installment buying, he'd got what he could pay for without interest.

"I told you then, it's false economy to buy cheap," said Schenke. "What happened?"

"That Goddamned thing lay down and died on the Pasadena freeway," said Glasser. "I couldn't even get it over on the shoulder. Traffic piled up and the Goddamned Highway Patrol came along and—it would be the Highway Patrol—"

"Brother officers," said Shogart.

"—be damned," said Glasser. "It was forty-five minutes before the tow truck showed and I thought I'd better go along to find out if it's worth the damn repair bill to fix it up. I'm still trying to decide. There's a crack in the radiator and it needs new plugs and a lube job. They said they can fix it to run, but they didn't look enthusiastic."

"So you'd better go looking for something better," said Shogart. "City employees always reckoned a good risk—"

"I don't like being in debt, damn it," said Glasser. "So all right, I'm old-fashioned. Damn it, what I don't need is another bill to pay every month."

He was still muttering about it at ten minutes to midnight when a black-and-white on routine tour called in about a probable assault: a man down and unconscious on the sidewalk alongside Pershing Square, obviously assaulted and robbed. There was an ambulance on the way.

Glasser still grumbling, he and Galeano went out on it; by the time they got there, the ambulance had been and gone, so they went on up to Hollywood Receiving Hospital. The doctor in Emergency said it was touch and go: skull fracture, a severe beating; they were still running X rays. He handed over the personal effects found on him.

There was a wallet, found beside him: empty of money. Everything else had been in his pockets, handkerchief, cigarettes, a little loose change. The suit, even bloodied and dirty, looked like a good one; it had a tailor's label in it, *Simpson, D Street, Sacramento*. In the wallet's little plastic slots was an I.D. card, photographs of a nice-looking dark-haired woman and two children, a membership card in the California Medical Association, a gasoline credit card. The I.D. was for a Dr. Bernard Ducharme, an address in Sacramento, notify wife in case of emergency.

"Well, well, a visitor to our fair city who fell among thieves," said Galeano. "I think we pass this on to the day watch, Henry. It's a little late to disturb the doctor's wife, and maybe by morning they'll know whether he'll make it or not."

"I suppose so," said Glasser morosely. He wasn't about to let the other boys know about another difficulty his suddenly carless state posed: he had a date to take Wanda Larsen to a horse show on Sunday—it seemed she was crazy about horses—and just what he was going to do now he didn't know. Well, they could use her car, but that seemed a little cheap.

Piggott was off on Friday. Before breakfast he had a look at the baby tetras swimming around in all the dishpans, and thought there were just a few less than there had been last night. It was an unexpected complication, the baby tetras—such pretty little colorful things, only a couple of inches long as adults—turning out to be cannibals in youth. He said, "I think we'd better take some of the bigger ones out of this pan, Pru."

"Honestly!" said Prudence. "Talk about, had I but known!" She looked at the array of dishpans in despair. "Honestly, what anybody would think, to see this place—"

Mendoza came in early on Friday morning, dapper as usual in gray Dacron, black Homburg in hand. He looked at the report Galeano had left and said, "Wide open. *Pues sí.* A little rudimentary planning—wait till the clerk left for a minute, which he was bound to do in six hours, and walk in. But— And business picking up as usual. Pity about Henry's car." Beyond his open office door he heard the rest of the men coming in—only short one man to-day—and picked up the phone. "Jimmy, get me a Mrs. Bernard Ducharme in Sacramento, this address—person to person. Wait a minute, on second thought I'd better talk to the hospital first—"

When he got her, Mrs. Ducharme had a charming contralto voice that reminded him of Alison's. She was alarmed at a call from an LAPD officer. Her husband was in Los Angeles, yes, over the weekend, for a convention of the California Medical Association. He was staying at the Biltmore Hotel. What concern was it of the LAPD?

Mendoza told her, gently. The hospital was now saying that Dr. Ducharme would make it, he was in much better condition.

"But, my God," she cried wildly, "what could have— how could he—oh, my God, but he only left a day early so he could work on that paper—Ruth's piano practice annoyed him so—oh, my God! Yes, I'll come—have to call Mother, look after the ch— But how could it have happened? I don't—oh, thank you for calling—I'll come as soon as—but I don't understand how—"

Mendoza went out to the hall. Hackett and Higgins were back, dwarfing everybody else: Landers talking to Conway and Grace; Palliser looking worried about something. "So, somebody chase over to the Biltmore and ask what they know about Dr. Ducharme," said Mendoza, and passed on Galeano's note.

"Did somebody say women's work is never done?" said Grace. "You can go hunting May McGraw alone, John."

"And Henry's feeling annoyed, you can see."

"I told him it was false economy," said Landers. "Now he finds out. Come on, Rich. We've got all these party-goers to find."

"And then the heisters." Who were just possibles, but you never knew where you'd hit pay dirt.

Grace went over to the Biltmore. The Biltmore had Dr. Ducharme registered. "Yesterday afternoon, one-thirty," said the desk clerk. "We're hosting this convention, of course."

Grace asked questions. Did the clerk remember when Dr. Ducharme had turned in his key? It hadn't been on him. If it had been the night clerk on duty, he'd have to chase him down. But it had been this one, on up to 6 P.M.

"But—did you say, a police officer? Has anything happened to the doctor? Yes, I can tell you that—it was just before I went off duty at six, the doctor turned in his key—of course we have a great many doctors registered here for the convention, but I happen to recall Dr. Ducharme because of the name—very peculiar, my grandmother's maiden name was Ducharme and we wondered if there was any connection—"

"Did he say anything about where he was going?" Grace had a simple mind. Sometimes people did.

"Oh, he said—yes, I remember that—he said something about deserving a little holiday—a night on the town, he said. He asked me to recommend a place around here, maybe with a good piano bar—I suggested The Wild Goose over on Spring, but I did warn him to take a cab—the way the crime rate's going—"

A night on the town. Grace thought a little sadly about the phrase Hackett had coined: the stupidity and cupidity.

"So I suppose we'd better go and ask if he ever got there," said Grace. "It won't be open yet."

"That place," said Mendoza. "It came into a case before. And if he got there after six, the same bartender and waiters won't be there till around five. He was found along Pershing Square. He could have been on his way to Spring or back to the hotel—walking like a damn fool." He had slid down in his desk chair, smoking lazily, and was fiddling with the love beads. "I'm waiting for Walter Whitlow to show up for the formal identification—he called in."

"You think those things point to one of the street kids."

"Kids and kids," said Mendoza. "Enough of them, and not kids either, in the twenties—drifters, irresponsible, on the grass or the hard stuff. I've been exercising my imagination, Jase. The old lady had lived at the Clark a long time. I've got no doubt that Quigley, Perkins, some of the maids knew about that annuity. All perfectly honest people. So, the maid Agnes, off duty, says something casual to her sister—and the sister mentions it to a boyfriend who works at a gas station on Hill—and he mentions it to a pal who knows somebody who works at The Broadway, right next to the Clark—And then again you never know, it could be even simpler than that. Violence is usually damn simple, *de veras*. Just as we've heard, there are a number of elderly people living at that hotel—the pensions, Social Security. And in most places like that the permanent apartments will be on the upper floors. It could be that X just meant to get into any one of those apartments, where there'd be the frail old people and hopefully some cash."

"I suppose you did have the lab print those beads?"

Mendoza cocked an eyebrow at him. "Teach your grandfather, Jase. *Nada* . . . I'm also expecting the doctor's wife later this morning. When and if he comes to, he can probably tell us what happened to him—not very likely who did it."

They were still sitting there talking about the various things on hand when Palliser and Higgins came back.

This time May McGraw had been at home. May McGraw was what some people might call the salt of the earth, if not exactly the most virtuous female walking around. She'd seen a lot of life and seen it hard, if a lot of trouble was her own making, and she'd preserved in a rough sort of way her sense of humor and courage. She'd looked suspiciously at craggy-faced Higgins, narrowly at the badges, and when they told her about Ida Moffat she burst into floods of tears, asked them in, wept for five minutes, dried her eyes, and said, "Well, I will be damned. Just about the last person in the world—getting murdered! My God. I tried to call her yesterday afternoon, but I just figured she was out. My God, a person just doesn't expect to have her friends murdered, for God's sake." She blew her nose and reached for a cigarette with a hand that shook a little. Palliser lit it for her. "You don't know who?"

"No, Mrs. McGraw—is it Mrs.?"

"He was a bum, I divorced him a long time ago, but I guess McGraw's better than Stepanowsky." She was a little plump woman in the fifties, with hennaed hair and a round face raddled with years of careless makeup. She had big dark eyes and a stubborn chin.

"We'd like you to tell us about other people Mrs. Moffat knew," said Palliser. "It looks as if she had a fight with somebody—"

"But, my God, nobody knew Ida 'd go to murder her! Sure, I can tell you people she knew, but it wouldn't be any of them, how could it be? Look, Ida, she was—you know—good-natured. Easygoing. She didn't have fights with anybody. I guess—you're thinking about men." She stopped, looking at them warily.

"We know she knew quite a few men," said Higgins

diplomatically. "We aren't here to judge anybody, Mrs. McGraw—we'd just like to find out who killed her."

"Oh, what the hell," she said drearily. "Life's a drag, here we are getting older every day and no money to count much, and nobody to care much—you got to take any little fun and good company where you find it, no? What's it to anybody if Ida slept around a little? Her own business. But none of them 'd have gone to murder her. Al Molnar—"

"We've met him," said Palliser.

"Well, he wouldn't—I don't want to get anybody in trouble, none of the guys I knew about would've—"

"Well, we don't know, do we? For instance, sometimes liquor makes a man belligerent for no reason, and if—" But there hadn't, of course, been any evidence that there'd been drinking going on.

"Oh, hell," she said miserably. "I knew she'd been with Al, and Eddy Weinbeck, he's the bartender at the Tuxedo, and lemme think, that railroad man comes in—"

"Where did she—that is," said Palliser, "did she—er—drop into bars near where she—or—"

"Say, mister, Ida wasn't a pro," she said indignantly. "She was just out for a good time when she could get it. She worked hard, you better believe, cleaning houses for people for a lousy three bucks an hour. She'd come in the Tuxedo three, four times a week, to see me, have her dinner, sit around over a few beers. Maybe she'd get talking to some guy, maybe not, whose business was it? It was just"—she groped for a word and found one sounding foreign to her vocabulary—"casual. Like that. Casual. Listen, who's going to arrange about a funeral? There's got to be a funeral. She didn't have any family. Listen, I know Al 'd want to help—I don't s'pose she had much dough—and I'll ask Eddy—"

"We can let you know when the body will be released."

"Yeah, I'd be obliged. It just—isn't anything that happens to somebody you know," said May forlornly.

"Can you give us any more names?" asked Palliser.

And now, back at the office, Higgins was saying, "But listen, Luis. A woman like that—just as Molnar said, it didn't bother him that she went with other men. No great romance with any of them. There wouldn't be that much emotion involved, for anybody to be jealous of her, or get into a fight with her—over what?"

"*¿Quién sabe?*" said Mendoza. "I'll give you that, George. But why should a stranger get into a fight with her either? We have to start with what we have. How many names did she give you?"

Palliser laughed. "A dozen. She said she couldn't be sure just who Ida might have got acquainted with, this week, last week, but these she's pretty sure of. There were some others whose names she didn't know."

"It just occurs to me," said Grace, "that with those respectable females at that apartment house watching Ida so close, didn't you ask them if a strange man was seen coming in that night? With or without Ida?"

"You've had some," said Palliser. "Go and try asking 'em, Jase."

"Well, I might," said Grace thoughtfully.

"And I tell you," said Higgins, "it'll be a waste of time to talk to any of these—these imitation playboys, Luis. What kind of boyfriends would one like that pick up? The old bachelors, the winos, the—"

"Statistics tell us that murder victims are usually murdered by people they know, if not relatives," said Mendoza. "Go and start looking." Higgins uttered a rude word, and Sergeant Lake looked in and said that Mr. Whitlow was here.

Higgins, Grace and Palliser went out. Wanda, with no reports to type, was straightening out a filing cabinet. Hackett had left with Landers and Conway, presumably to chase down the erstwhile pals of the Booths or the list of heisters.

"A damned waste of time," repeated Higgins. "But we have to go by the rules."

"You can go look for the playboys," said Grace. "I want to ask Mrs. Kiefer a couple of questions."

*   *   *

Walter Whitlow was a tall, dark, nice-looking fellow, right now a little haggard. He said all the expectable things; taken to the morgue, he formally identified the body of Harriet Branch, and when Mendoza explained that an autopsy was mandatory, just nodded.

"It seems—I don't know," he said, "well, strange, that she should have lived to be over eighty and then—end like that. Strange." He looked down the bare empty corridor, outside the cold room at the morgue. "Of course a thing like this is always a shock. Edna—my wife—it was just bad luck I happened to be away when— She bore up pretty well, but she's gone to pieces now. What—should we do about funeral arrangements?"

"We'll let you know when an undertaker can have the body."

"What—who do you think—could have done it? Or should I ask you that? I'm sorry, I don't know much about—how you operate, Lieutenant."

"Well, we're thinking now that someone, or a couple, of the young street thugs down here slipped into the hotel on the chance of easy pickings—con their way into an apartment, strong-arm the tenant. God knows there are enough of that kind with the habit to support."

"And—it just happened to be Mother's apartment they picked? The dope," said Whitlow. He looked suddenly more haggard and worried than when he'd come in. "Why a young one? Some reason you—"

Mendoza told him about the love beads absently, and was startled at the response that got. "Love!" said Whitlow in an almost savage tone. "Love! My God, what stupidities and madness are committed in that name! These stupid, criminal, suicidal *kids*—not dry behind the ears and they think they're so Goddamned smart—! Just tell me something, Lieutenant Mendoza. Just tell me what the hell's going to happen to this world when these brainwashed kids with their stupid ideas about peace and brotherly love and their immoral relative morality and do-your-own-thing-with-the-dope bit take over?"

Mendoza laughed. "There's a saying in Spanish, Mr.

Whitlow—*A su tiempo maduran las uvas*. In their own time the grapes ripen. Fortunately the youngsters do get older, and some of them a little wiser. And it's still the minority running around making all the noise and devilry."

"Sense of objectivity," said Whitlow a little wearily. "I daresay. Disraeli said it better."

"*¿Cómo?*"

Whitlow's expression turned sardonic. "That anybody who isn't a Socialist by the age of twenty lacks a heart, and anybody who isn't a Tory by the age of thirty lacks a head."

Mendoza threw back his head and laughed. " 'The Gods of the Copybook Headings.' Mr. Kipling said it even better than that."

"Oh, you're a Kipling man too? I've often wondered," said Whitlow, "whether it'd do any good to make it mandatory for all politicians to read that poem over once a month."

Mendoza was still chuckling over that when he got back to his office. But the love beads on his desk sobered his expression. That frail old body in the cold tray at the morgue—

Somebody had said that at least one slug out of the Booths had been sent to Ballistics. He got on the phone to the lab and asked if they'd looked at it yet.

"Oh, that," said Thomsen. "Yeah. It's out of a beat-up old S. and W. .22. Revolver. If you ever pick up the gun, we can make it easy enough."

"*Gracias,*" said Mendoza. It was a quarter to eleven; he wondered when the doctor's wife would show up. He also wondered if anything new would break today.

Of the six names Wyler and Packer had given them yesterday, Landers and Conway only found two: Ron Cook and Cheryl Perry. The other four, three men and a girl, had evidently drifted on from temporary addresses, nobody knew where or nobody was saying.

Wyler had told them Cook and the Perry girl had been living together. They found them at a trailer park out toward Monterey Park, off the Pomona freeway, where Wyler said they'd be. All the trailers were old and tired-looking, and the ground overgrown with weeds, cluttered with rubbish. The old trailers sat around at odd angles, half of them obviously empty; it was a far cry from the smart modern parks of mobile homes elsewhere. This pair looked like the counterparts of the Booths, scruffy and aimless and sloppily dressed. The girl was a natural blonde, the man dark with the usual wild long hair, moustache and sideburns. They looked at the badge in Landers' hand with automatic suspicion, and at the two LAPD men with resentment—perhaps a vague resentment at two clean-shaven, good-looking young men in suits and white shirts and ties, reminder that the majority of the world still hadn't collapsed to their own low standards.

They answered questions reluctantly until Landers told them about the Booths. "Jesus, who could've done that?" said Cook. "That's real sad, man." The girl just sighed.

"So, we understand you were at a party at their place last Saturday night," said Conway. "With some grass floating around. Did you buy any?"

"You got a search warrant?" asked Cook warily.

"Not yet," said Landers. "Look, we can take you down-town to ask questions." They hadn't been invited into the trailer; they stood around the door, in the weed-grown lot.

"We're not holding. We don't know anything about who did that. We liked God and Sue O.K., man, you can't prove any different."

"We weren't going to try," said Landers, "if you can tell us about somebody who didn't. That wasn't very good grass Booth was passing out that night, was it? Cut stuff—dust."

Cook licked his lips. "I wouldn't know."

"Was he selling, or just handing it out for the party?" Cook was silent. "Let's go downtown," said Conway.

"I wouldn't know," said Cook.

"Can you tell us who else was there?"

"I didn't know everybody else there. I'm not about to get anybody in bad with the fuzz."

"You said you liked the Booths—don't you want us to pick up whoever took them off? Come on," said Landers. Cook opened his mouth and shut it. The girl was staring away from all of them, dreamily; Landers wondered if she was riding a little high. "Who was there, Cook?"

"You better tell them, Ron," said the girl in a thin voice, without looking at any of them. "What happened to the baby? They had a baby."

"That's right," said Conway. "A baby they'd been feeding the grass. It's in the hospital. Being looked after."

"Oh, was he sick? He's a cute baby."

"Come on, Ron—what's she want you to tell?" asked Landers.

"You just shut up," he said to the girl. "You just—"

"But I bet it was them," she said. She turned suddenly and climbed into the trailer, came out a minute later with a hairbrush, and sat on the trailer step and began to brush her hair with long slow sweeps of the brush.

"Who, Miss Perry?"

She giggled. "That sounds funny. Everybody calls me Sherry. Sherry Perry. I bet it was Sid and Janie. Or Sid, anyway. Because he was awfully mad at God. About that grass. It was real nothing stuff, no kick at all—God got crossed on that, wherever he got it. Ronnie was mad too—"

"Listen, *shut up!* I'm not about to get mixed in—"

"—only he didn't pay God for it so it wasn't a big thing. We went over to Sugar's and he had some pretty good—"

"Shut up!" Cook slapped her across the face and Landers pulled him back from her.

"That's enough of that. Who are Sid and Janie?" It could be that the Narco office could tell them.

"I don't like Sid," she said. She retrieved the hairbrush from where it had fallen and went on brushing her hair.

"Sid who?" asked Conway gently.

"Oh, it's a funny name. I don't know. What an awful

name for a person to have. I used to live in Beverly Hills,
you know. My mother and father have an awful lot of
money—I was brought up to be a lady. That's right. I
shouldn't think any girl would ever want to marry a man
with a terrible name like that." She laughed and went on
laughing, and Landers felt Cook's arm muscles tense with
fury, and then she gasped, *"Belcher!* Isn't that perfectly
awful?"

"You bitch," said Cook, "tying us in—"

"I think as material witnesses anyway," said Landers.
And neither he nor Conway mentioned it, but they both
wondered whether this precious pair would be out on bail
within twenty-four hours, and promptly vanish. Some of
the softheaded judges—

They ferried them back downtown, to the jail on
Alameda, thinking of lunch afterward. In the lobby they
found Mendoza delivering a lecture to the chief jailer.
He was looking annoyed.

"What's up?" asked Landers.

Mendoza had just finished talking to Mrs. Ducharme at
eleven-thirty; she had phoned from the hotel, having taken
over her husband's room at the Biltmore. He told her the
hospital expected her husband to be conscious sometime
today; he told her the name of the hospital, and she said
crisply he'd find her there if he wanted to talk to her.
He was thinking of going out for an early lunch when
Sergeant Lake buzzed him and said they had a new
homicide. At the Alameda jail.

"At the *jail?*" said Mendoza. *"¡Parece mentira!"* He
took up his hat and went out. "Nobody else here?"

"Art just fetched in one of the possibles off that list of
heisters—first interrogation room."

Mendoza said, "Women's work!" and marched out to
the elevators. He was curious enough that he used the
siren on the Ferrari out to Alameda Street. At the jail,
he met an ambulance just arriving.

The chief jailer and three of his underlings were arguing

together in the lobby. On Mendoza's arrival they suddenly banded together defensively and began to explain.

"Listen," said the chief jailer, "things materialize out of the blue! My God, Lieutenant, we could search every cell once a day and things would still turn up! Do I know how? Things turn up in books in the library, lawyers I got to let in to see clients and not all lawyers are so damn law-abiding, the short-term birds work in the shop and make things—we do our best, but—"

"So what turned up this time and what happened?"

"My God," said one of the jailers, "is it a major operation, smuggle in a pair of dice? They were shooting craps—I didn't know it till the row broke out—"

"A pair of dice. What else?"

The jailer moaned. "A straight razor. I didn't know a damn thing about it till the argument started—he claimed they were loaded dice, and—"

There hadn't been much to choose between the prisoners: Willy Brisbane and Charles Ferguson, both Negro, both with long rap-sheets, both awaiting trial—Brisbane for rape, Ferguson for grand theft. It was Ferguson who had ended up with a cut throat.

Mendoza was annoyed. This kind of careless and unnecessary thing made paper work; it was a nuisance, when they had quite enough to cope with from people still outside jail. He told them so. The ambulance attendants took away the corpse. Mendoza was still expressing himself to the jailers when Landers and Conway walked in and heard about it.

They booked Cook and the girl in, and went up to Federico's for lunch, where Mendoza heard about Sid Belcher. "We'll ask Narco if they know him," said Landers.

"That's the first place to ask," said Mendoza. "I wonder what the other boys are getting."

"That Moffat thing is—shapeless," said Landers, when they'd been brought up-to-date on that. "But that's not what you're annoyed about—or all the paper work on Ferguson." He eyed Mendoza shrewdly.

69

"I am really not so much interested in how that silly female came to get a knock on the head," said Mendoza, swallowing black coffee. "What I am feeling damned annoyed about, boys, is that there isn't one single damned lead on whatever mindless street thug walked into the Clark and beat Harriet Branch to death for whatever cash she had."

"It might have been any hood on the beat," agreed Conway sadly. "There's nothing to say, unless the lab picked up some latents there. I don't suppose you've had a report. Slow but sure, the lab."

"It's possible, but I wouldn't take a bet on it," said Mendoza.

Henry Glasser, after debate, had called the garage when he got up at noon and told them to go ahead and fix up that heap. They gave him an estimate of three-fifty plus, which at that was less than he'd have to pay for anything worth buying, and also said they'd let him have a loaner meanwhile. Glasser closed with this offer, and took the bus downtown to pick up the loaner. It turned out to be an old Plymouth two-door, banged up somewhat, but in running condition—about all you could say.

Driving back to his Hollywood apartment, he stopped at the nearest supermart for a couple of frozen dinners, a loaf of bread, and had to wait at the checkstand. When the checker handed him his change, she thrust a slip of paper into his hand with it. "Be sure and fill this out, sir, and drop it in the box over there. We're having a big drawing next week, you might be one of the lucky ones!"

"You'll never know how unlucky I feel," said Glasser. But he did fill out the slip with his name and address, and dropped it into the box. Fate hadn't been kind to him lately; but she was apt to be a changeable lady and you never knew.

Palliser and Higgins had spent the entire morning, to Higgins' disgust, in a very abortive hunt for Ida Moffat's recent or not-so-recent boyfriends. Only one of them they'd heard about from May McGraw was in a regular job, and he was a railroad engineer presently riding a locomotive back in the Midwest on a regular run to Chicago. May had been able to give them only one address, a regular patron of the Tuxedo, Jim Waggoner who lived at a rooming house on Shatto Street around the corner from the bar.

Him they found home, a fat man with an artificial leg and a pension from the government. He was sorry to hear about Ida, she was a real fun gal, he said, and who would have wanted to hurt Ida anyways? All these criminals around, what the world was coming to— But he also had an alibi, it transpired. He was a widower, and last Tuesday night he'd been at his daughter's place in Montebello because it was his birthday. It didn't cross his mind that they might have suspected him of the murder; that came out in the course of the conversation, and when they left he thanked them for coming to let him know about Ida. Poor Ida.

They resorted to the telephone book for the other names, but only one was listed, Peter Conroy, and he lived over in Glendale so they doubted he was the one who'd known Ida.

The Tuxedo Bar and Grill opened at eleven, and they went up there to talk to May again and hoped maybe to find a couple of the boyfriends dropping in. Higgins was still saying it was a damfool waste of time. But they hadn't been talking with May, still subdued, five minutes before she pointed out a nondescript fellow in his fifties who'd just come in and said Ida'd known him, she'd seen her talking to him one night. She didn't know his name.

It was Jack Smith. He looked at the badges in surprise, and he was shocked to hear about Ida. He was on Welfare —he had a bad back, he said, couldn't work at all—and he just couldn't think who might have wanted to hurt Ida. Tuesday night? Say, they didn't think he'd hurt Ida, did they? He'd liked Ida—a real nice girl, and accommodating. Palliser stored the word up to pass on to Robin. Tuesday night Jack Smith had spent playing cards with some other fellows at his apartment. He gave them names. He was indignant at the implied suspicion.

"Look, didn't I say it?" said Higgins. "The casual thing —for everybody, her included. Nobody felt strongly enough about the woman to care if she lived or died, John."

"But she got killed. Somehow." They knocked off for lunch, not at the Tuxedo but a coffee shop downtown, and afterward checked back with the office to see if anything new had gone down.

It was one o'clock and nobody else was there, said Lake, sounding relieved at Palliser's voice. "I just got a call from a black-and-white—a new body. It's Park View, over by MacArthur. I don't know what it is."

"Well, we might have known," said Palliser.

"And Pasadena called just before. They had a heist pulled over there last night, and they think by what the witnesses said it might have been that Conover. They didn't have a mug shot. I sent one over."

"O.K. We'll get on the new one."

When he told Higgins about it, Higgins said, "Thank God. Bricks without straw. Ida'll go into Pending."

They were using his Pontiac. They drove over to Park View Street. The black-and-white was still there and the uniformed men greeted them with relief. "We were wondering if you'd forgotten about us," said one of them. It was an ugly little square cracker-box stucco duplex in the middle of the block, painted dirty tan, and a fat middle-aged woman in a pink dress was standing on the front steps of the right side of it, watching them.

"What's it look like?"

"Another husband losing his temper," said the uniformed man. "But she's been dead awhile. Few days, maybe. Good thing we're not in the middle of a heat wave. That's Mrs. Cohen," he added, nodding at the fat woman. "She called in. Got worried because she hadn't seen this Mrs. Upton in a few days, and then there was"—he sighed —"the smell."

"One of those," said Palliser. "We'll want the full

treatment." He used the radio in the car to ask for a lab truck and the morgue wagon, and sent the squad back on tour. Higgins was already talking to Mrs. Cohen.

"She was a nice girl," she was saying, shocked and a little grieved and also excited—the inevitable human reaction—at being in the middle of a murder case, Authority consulting her. "Cicely her name was, Cicely Upton. I liked her right from the time they moved in— I own this place, you see, rent out the other side. Not him, but her I liked. She was nice, a real ladylike girl. A homebody too. She asked for my recipe for molasses cookies. Over a year they'd lived here, but it wasn't till about a month ago she broke down and told me about him—like I say she was a nice girl, loyal to her husband and all, but we'd been neighborly back and forth, and after they had that argument, poor girl, I guess she had to have somebody to talk to. She didn't believe in divorce, but there'd been trouble—"

"Yes, Mrs. Cohen, we'll want to talk to you later, but right now, if you'd let us look around—"

"Anything you say. I've got nothing else to do. I just wish I'd called the police sooner, but how was I to know— The other men had to break in the door—"

There was a rickety screen door; the front-door lock had been splintered by the uniformed men. Before they went past the open door, they received the sickish-sweet message of death inside.

It was a bare little place, sparsely furnished, but a good-sized color TV sat in a corner of the living room; the few pieces of furniture were violently modern in style, vinyl upholstered. The body was in the front bedroom, where there was just space for a double bed, a couple of chests of drawers; one wall there contained a wardrobe with sliding doors. There was no closet.

"The surgeon will say how long," said Higgins, grimacing. She lay quietly on the bed, just one leg dangling off it; she had been dead long enough for her face to be a little bloated, but she might have been a pretty girl. Not very old, maybe in her twenties. She was wearing an ankle-length blue nylon housecoat, and one worn white satin slipper had fallen from the foot dangling off the bed. Her dark-brown hair was matted with a little blood, old and dry, at the left temple, but otherwise she looked quite natural lying there on the bed, as if she'd dropped down for a nap.

Palliser spotted the framed photograph on one of the chests: a glossy five by seven in a dime-store frame. It showed a smiling couple, the girl pretty with curly dark hair shorter than she had worn it now; she was clinging to the arm of a big-chested young man with crew-cut blond hair. They were obviously dressed up, he in a dark suit, she in a light-colored summer dress. "Wedding picture?" said Palliser a little sadly.

But Higgins had spotted something else. "I've seen a few," he said laconically. "Give you odds, she was knocked down and fractured her skull on that." He pointed. The bedstead was an old white-painted one, head and footboards rather high. On the top of the footboard was a little brown smear of what would probably turn out to be blood. There wasn't any carpet in here, and the small cottonterry scatter rug at the side of the bed was wadded up in a bunch.

"You can read it," agreed Palliser. "Another one like Ida. She was knocked down, or fell, tripped on the rug—"

"Argue ahead of evidence. But there's friend hubby. If it was accidental, why was she left? Well, we'd better hear what Mrs. Cohen has to say. Leave this to the lab boys and Bainbridge."

They went back to the front step. Mrs. Cohen was still there, waiting. A few curious neighbors were out, staring and muttering. "Can we go into your place, Mrs. Cohen? We're waiting for more men, and we'd like to hear whatever you can tell us."

"Sure," she said. She turned and led them into a duplicate of the living room next door, but vastly different, with old-fashioned velour-upholstered furniture, a Boston fern in a wrought-iron stand. "It's just an awful thing, but it was him. He's gone, you know, his car and all. So it was him. Like I started to tell you, she never said a word against him—a good wife she was—till that time, about a month ago it was, they had a terrible argument one night, I heard him swearing and all, and next day—she had to have somebody to talk to—she sort of confided in me. We'd been neighborly, back and forth, and it was always her paid the rent. I took her my cookies, and she give me her mother's recipe for apple strudel. Her mother was dead —she hadn't any family left, she said. She cried and said how they'd been making a new start, Johnny'd promised to try and be a better husband. She was a good Christian girl," said Mrs. Cohen. "Oh, I suppose you'll think that's funny for me to say, but I'm Congregationalist myself— and a better man than my Joel never lived, God rest him. They'd been married five years, she was twenty-six, and there'd been trouble—he's the kind has a temper goes off like a rocket, and she said he'd beat her up once before, but he was sorry afterward. A lot of good that was! But she said he'd promised, he'd try to do better, and they came down here—they were living in Fresno then—and he got a better job, working for the city—the gas company."

"When did you see her last?" asked Palliser.

"That was it. Monday and Wednesday she usually had a wash on the line, and there wasn't any. He didn't want her to work, you see, and she was a real homebody. She told me she'd hoped to start a baby, but no luck. And I hadn't seen him—or his car—since Monday. Monday night he came home, like always, about six-thirty. And it's not once in a blue moon I'm out at night but I was that night, I went out with my friend Mrs. Rogers from down the street, to a movie. But now I look back, I'm up early as a rule, and I didn't see him leave for work on Tuesday. Unless he left earlier than usual." Her thin lips clamped shut for a moment, worked nervously.

"His name's John Upton? He's got a car—would you be able to tell us what make?" asked Palliser.

"It's a Plymouth Valiant," she said. "White. About a sixty-four. I've got to say I didn't hear any more arguing and swearing that night, before I went out, but there

75

might've been later. But he hasn't been back since. I knocked on her door yesterday—him not coming home like that I thought maybe they'd had a fight and he'd left her, maybe she'd want to talk—but I never thought of anything so awful as this. Until—" She was silent.

Until she noticed the smell.

A car door slammed outside; there were voices and footsteps. The lab boys had arrived.

"Well, thank you, Mrs. Cohen," said Higgins. "We'll want to get a statement from you later."

"She was a nice girl," said Mrs. Cohen.

Mendoza came back from a belated lunch; Landers and Conway had gone back to looking for the just-possibles, on their several heist jobs (a dairy store, a neighborhood market, a liquor store—and of course the job at Chasen's). Hackett came in and said he was getting nowhere.

"You know how the damn routine goes. The one I found—he's still on P.A. so we had his address—had an alibi for all four jobs. He's just, for God's sake, had a grand reconciliation with his wife and they're being all lovey-dovey. The landlord can also say, and assorted neighbors."

"¡Vaya despacio!" said Mendoza, and Jason Grace wandered in looking pleased with himself.

"Good—somebody here," he said. "To come and be a witness. When I'd got just so far, I thought I'd better take a witness along. Just in case. I don't know that it's anything important, I've just got a kind of hunch."

"I'm the only one allowed hunches around here," said Mendoza. "About what, Jase?"

"Oh, Ida," said Grace. "I went and annoyed Mrs. Kiefer, and she finally got what I was driving at and said she didn't know we were interested in honest respectable people, and why were we, because Mr. Stanhope was a very nice man. And as it turned out, the pharmacy—Mr. Stanhope's pharmacy on Olympic—was closed because Mr. Stanhope's mother-in-law just died and the funeral was this morning. But he opened at noon—"

"Stanhope? *¿Qué es esto?*"

"Well, I think maybe," said Grace, "we ought to go and talk to this William Linblad. I was just following my nose, you know."

"Well, you know what we had before from the women at that apartment," said Grace to Mendoza's question. He sat down and lit a cigarette; his brown face was gravely amused. "We couldn't even get any of 'em to say whether or not they saw Ida come home that night, alone or not. But I got to thinking, after we'd talked to Kiefer, and the first thought I had was, those nosy females keeping tabs on Ida pretty close, if she had had a man with her when she came home, we'd likely have heard. One of the women would have just happened to be out in the hall or something."

"So she didn't," said Mendoza. "You think one of them saw her come in?"

"I'd have laid a bet," said Grace. "Have we had the autopsy report yet? Well, that should tell us something. And then I thought, maybe our Ida had noticed the snooping and didn't like it. Maybe she told a boyfriend to sneak in after her. Anyway, I went back to talk to Mrs. Kiefer. I figured by then her husband would have told her we'd talked to him, and maybe she'd be a little less unforthcoming. She was. I pressed her, did she or anybody else see Ida Moffat come in that night? By chance or otherwise? And she finally said, well, she just happened to remember she hadn't looked in the mailbox and she'd been in the lobby and saw her come in. It was about six o'clock. And she'd been thinking it over, and Mrs. Licci felt the same way, it all went to show that we didn't know what we're doing, saying the woman was murdered."

"*¿Qué es esto?*" said Mendoza.

"Because it wasn't a very nice thing to have to say, but Mrs. Moffat was drunk. Staggering, and jolly. Not my words—hers. I deduce that Ida 'd had a few and was just feeling happy, not falling-down-drunk. I was grateful for the news, and Mrs. Kiefer went on to say that they'd decided she must have just fallen down and hit her head and killed herself. And you know, I suppose she could have—if she'd started to hit the drink hard, but we didn't gather she had. Because, said Mrs. Kiefer, she didn't have anybody with her—she was alone. Was she sure, I asked. What with the rise in crime, and her being the manager of the apartment, I supposed she took note of the people coming into the building. She did. She said nobody had come in later. What about the people who lived there, I said, and she said oh, well, of course Mrs. Licci and her husband had come home. Nobody else, I said, and she said nobody she'd ever seen with Ida. Nobody at all, I asked, and that was when she said she didn't know I meant respectable people, but aside from the Liccis there'd only been the boy from the pharmacy she knew of."

"¡Maravilloso!" said Mendoza encouragingly.

Hackett got up. "If you two soul mates are making head or tail of this, I'm not. I've got more legwork to do. Have fun with your gossips," and he went out.

"¡Siga adelante!" said Mendoza.

"Well, that's what we'd better do," said Grace, "if you'd like to come along as a witness." Mendoza got his hat without a word and they started for the elevators. "After I'd talked to Stanhope—the pharmacist—I thought you'd better hear about it so far. It's an independent pharmacy round the corner on San Pedro. He delivers, and he hires this high-school kid, William Linblad, to do it—and clean up the place and do odd jobs. Three of the people at that apartment house have regular prescriptions lodged with him—Mrs. Licci, Miss Callway, and Ida Moffat. She was taking pills for high blood pressure. And she'd been in that day. I deduce she got home on the bus, that is to that area, about four, and after she stopped at the pharmacy she went somewhere and had the drinks. Stanhope said she usually waited for the prescription and took it with her, but that day she asked for it to be delivered.

There were seven or eight deliveries, and the boy left about six."

"And it never occurred to either of them that we'd be interested, after she was found dead?"

"Not to Stanhope," said Grace. They'd taken the Ferrari, and now Mendoza asked where they were going. "That public high school out on Ninth. Stanhope's a vague old fellow about seventy, I'd say no interests outside the store. He might not even know she's dead. But I thought this Linblad—"

"*Pues sí.* It might be interesting to hear what he has to say."

When they got to the school, there were four black-and-whites and seven men in uniform with riot guns standing around. "What the devil—" said Mendoza, and edged the Ferrari up beside the group and produced his badge. "Has war been declared?"

"We didn't ask for detectives, sir." The Traffic man was surprised. "We had a tip that there's a gang rumble called for sometime this afternoon. Just thought a little show of force might make 'em think twice."

"*Dios,*" said Mendoza as they got out of the car, "I may be sorry I didn't bring any hardware along. Schools are dangerous places these days," and he wasn't kidding.

They were let in to see the boys' vice-principal and asked for Linblad to be fetched out of class. The vice-principal didn't seem to recognize the name, had his secretary look in the files for where he'd be. Five minutes later a tall boy came shambling in, looking nervous, and stood waiting silently. "Er—" said the vice-principal, " I suppose you'd prefer—? Just so. I'll just go along to the lounge." He was a tired, worried man; he didn't want any more bad news. "Er—these are police officers. They'd like to talk to you." He went out quickly.

The boy looked up fleetingly. He was a big boy, not bad looking, with darkish blond hair not too long and childlike blue eyes, round and sandy-lashed. He looked immature, shy and awkward. "What—do the police want with me?" he asked in a high voice, and swallowed.

"Lieutenant Mendoza—Detective Grace. You work at Mr. Stanhope's pharmacy after school, don't you?" asked Grace. "Sit down, William—we don't bite. You remember last Tuesday night?"

The boy nodded. He sat down on the edge of a straight chair suddenly, as if his knees had given way, and stared at them dumbly. "You had some deliveries to make for the store—one to a Mrs. Moffat at that apartment on Stanford?" Another nod. "Well, when you got there, could you tell us if she was alone? Did she—"

"I never meant to do it!" said Linblad in a kind of wild croak. "I never meant nothing! But it was so awful—she scared me!" He was scared now: a senior here, turned eighteen, but very immature eighteen, even with all his growth. "I never—I never—"

"Take it easy," said Mendoza, interested. "Just tell us what happened. But maybe we'd better give him his rights first, Jase."

Linblad hardly listened to that little set piece, nodded again when Grace asked if he understood it. "I—I been scared ever since, I guess— I wanted to tell somebody but I didn't—I didn't know—what you might do to me. I—I —when I heard about it, couple of women in the store saying how she's dead, I didn't believe it—I thought, maybe she just—sort of died—later. I—I—"

"What time did you get there?" asked Grace.

"It was the last delivery. I'd never been there before, I had to look at the mailboxes—it was about eight, maybe. Just getting dark." And suddenly he began to gabble it out at them fast, as if to get rid of it once and for all. "It was —just awful—when she opened the door, she—I mean, she was an old lady, all this gucky makeup all over her face, and she was sort of drunk—not awful drunk but some—and she—and she—started to call me lovey-dovey names and nice boy and she t-t-tried to kiss me, she said didn't I want her to be nice to me—and it was just awful, I tried to get loose from her, and I just gave her a shove like and she started to cry, and I just sort of pushed her away—she hadn't paid me yet but I just wanted to get

away—" Suddenly she began to cry just a little. "I mean—
I mean," he said, ashamed, getting out a handkerchief,
"I'm not a *kid*, if it had been a pretty girl—but *her!* It
was—like to make me sick—"

Mendoza looked at Grace. "You wanted a witness. A
real hunch."

"It just crossed my mind as a possibility," said Grace.
"Given what we knew about Ida."

"What—what are you going to do?" asked the boy. "It
wasn't—it couldn't've been—just that little shove I gave
her—was it?"

Palliser took Higgins back to the office, to dictate the
initial report on Cicely Upton and fill Mendoza in, and
then drove down to the gas company offices. Personnel
there told him that John Upton was working on repair
crews out of a station on Santa Barbara. Out there, Palliser talked to the dispatcher, Stan Rodman, who listened
to him with various expletives and before he said anything else picked up the phone and told someone to send
up Dickey and Collins if they were in. He leaned back in
his chair and regarded Palliser with interest, a lean rawboned man in olive-green uniform.

"Well, you never know what's going to happen, isn't
it the truth," he said heavily. "You think he killed his
wife? I will be damned. He seemed like a good enough
young fellow—good worker, I will say. But I wasn't working that close to him, say what kind he was. He hasn't
showed up since Monday, or called in sick, so that fits
right in, don't it? I will be damned."

"He worked last Monday?"

"Same as usual—eight to five. Reason I called up Chet
and Bill, they made up a crew with Upton, they'd know
him better. If this isn't the damnedest thing—but like I
say, you never do know what's going to happen the next
minute. I often thought it must be an interesting job, being
a cop. You like it?"

"It can be interesting—and damn boring sometimes,"
said Palliser.

"I suppose. Here's Chet and Bill. Say, what do you know, fellows? This is a cop, Sergeant Palliser—and he says Johnny Upton's murdered his wife and skipped town. You ever hear the like?"

The two men just entering the office were both wearing olive-green uniforms with the little insignia on the left pocket—*Southern California Gas Company*. Dickey was short and stocky and very dark, Collins taller and thinner and younger. They both said they'd be damned, and Chet Dickey said, "When did it happen? He hasn't been to work since Monday—"

"I just told him," said Rodman.

"It could have been Monday night," said Palliser. "We won't know until there's been an autopsy."

"That's a real shame," said Dickey, and he looked as if he meant it. "Cicely was an awfully nice girl."

"Did you know her?" Palliser was surprised.

"Well, see, we're all—I mean me and Bill and Johnny —we were all on the company bowling team. I live up on Bonnie Brae, not so far from Johnny, and we used to take turns to drive, on practice nights."

"That's right," confirmed Collins. "And come to think, Chet, last Monday you said—"

Dickey nodded. He looked solemn. "I didn't think too much about it," he said. "Johnny's pretty good, he could skip practice. He called me up about seven that night, said he wasn't feeling too good, I shouldn't stop by for him. I thought it was a little funny he hadn't said something before he left work, but he said he had a headache come on sudden. I bet that was when he— My God, to think of a guy you know doing something like that—I only knew her from stopping by for him that way, but—"

"Well, it looks as if it was that night," said Palliser. "That just fills in some more, thanks."

"And I'll tell you something," said Collins suddenly. "One thing about Johnny, he's got a temper goes off real hot. Remember that time, Chet, one of us left a hammer or something alongside a trench and he tripped over it? For a minute there, way he was cussing and all, his expression, he looked ready to do murder—" He stopped, and added, "Not but what he got over it in a minute, but—you see what I mean."

And murder could be done in a minute, or less, thought Palliser, and a man sorry afterward, but it couldn't be undone. He said, "We'll probably want statements from you," nodding at Dickey and Rodman.

"Sure—whatever we can do." Dickey shook his head. "That's a real bad deal for Johnny. I'm sorry to hear about it. What'll you do to find him?"

"There are things to do on it—just hope we'll pick him up."

"Did he take his car?" asked Collins.

"It's missing."

"Well, I just might mention that he'd been having trouble with it, it needed a lot of work. Maybe he might not get far in it."

"Thanks very much," said Palliser. "That might help."

When he got back to the office, Higgins had filled Mendoza in and heard about William Linblad; Grace had taken Linblad over to jail and gone to see his parents. The D.A. would probably call it involuntary manslaughter; and of course, as Palliser conceded, the thing had its humorous aspects.

"Our Ida was feeling amorous just once too often," said Mendoza sardonically. "And that poor innocent teen-ager—"

"My, what big teeth you have, Grandmother," grinned Higgins. "In ten years he'd react different. As it is, he'll get a year or so and serve half of it."

"So you've been sitting here chatting about Ida," said Palliser. "What have you done on Upton?"

"What there was to do. Gave the gist to NCIC and put out a statewide A.P.B. on him and the car. I got the plate number from Sacramento. What'd you hear at the gas company?"

Palliser told them. "Nothing very abstruse about it—how many times has it happened, husband losing his temper, wife dead. Maybe he's sorry but he's not going to come begging to be put in jail. But if that car's in bad shape, he may drop it somewhere and pick up another—though come to think, so far as we know he hasn't got a record, he might not know how to hot-wire a car."

"We know," said Higgins. "At least as far as we're concerned, he's got no record. Mrs. Cohen said they came from Fresno, I sent a telex up there to ask."

"So we wait and hope we pick him up. What's the status quo otherwise?"

Mendoza flicked a report on his desk. "Autopsy report on Ida. She wasn't legally drunk—just happy, as Jase said. Fractured skull. The more I think of that one—" he laughed. *"Se lo digo,* no happy medium with the kids! Either the smart-aleck sophisticates who know it all, or—the ones like Linblad. Yes. The ones like—*Dios,* I hope to hell the lab picked up something useful in that Clark Hotel apartment."

"Mrs. Branch. If they didn't, we're fresh out of leads—except for your love beads, a dime a dozen at any of the freaky shops for the flower children."

"Damn it, they've had two days," said Mendoza, and reached for the phone; it buzzed at him and he picked it up. "Yes, Jimmy?"

"Your assaulted doctor is now conscious and can be talked to," said Lake.

"Oh, thanks so much." Mendoza got up, reaching for his hat. As he passed Lake's desk outside, he said, "You look happier these days, Jimmy. Forgotten the diet?"

"Like hell," said Lake gloomily. "I can hardly get into this uniform, and I'll be damned if I lay out for a new wardrobe. Caroline found one that's all low protein, I'll start on it tomorrow." He sighed.

At Hollywood Receiving Hospital Mendoza was told he could talk to Dr. Ducharme just ten minutes. His wife was with him. When Mendoza came into the little room, with only one of the single beds occupied, Mrs. Ducharme was looking rather glamorous, her color high and eyes bright.

"And here," she said to her husband, "is a police officer, and you'd better tell him all about it. Oh, I'm sorry, Bernie, but of all the crazy stupid things to do! I really thought you had better sense than that, and you're just lucky—we're all lucky—you didn't end up getting killed!" She turned away to the window. "His name's Lieutenant Mendoza," she added a little crossly.

"Mea culpa," said the man in the hospital bed in a faint voice. "I'll admit it was stupid. We all do the stupid things sometimes." His head was bandaged, and he needed a shave, his beard as thick and black as Mendoza's. He was nearly handsome, a strong nose and chin, olive skin and dark eyes.

"And now I know you'll be all right—honestly, Bernie, I'm mad at you! Risking your life like that, with me and the children—"

"So what happened, Doctor?" asked Mendoza.

Ducharme said fretfully, "I've got a hell of a headache. Deserve it, I suppose. They wanted to give me some more Demerol, but I'm leery of that stuff. Might start up that damned allergy again. Well, I was stupid, Lieutenant. I was alone, in a strange town, and I guess for a while I was feeling like a young blade again." An intern came in and told him not to talk too much or exert himself. "You run along—I'm a doctor, too, you know. I left the hotel, and I meant to find that place the desk clerk recommended, but I didn't, I went into a bar up the street, something like Romero's—Moreno's. I had a few drinks—which I don't as a rule, I'm not used to more than a couple—and I got talking to a man there. He seemed like a nice fellow—"

"With all the drinks addling your brains," she said, but then she laughed.

"Well—and I'm afraid all I recall after that is being outside again and trying to fight them—it was two men, I'm pretty sure of that, they were hitting me with something—"

"Mmh," said Mendoza. "Don't be too hard on him, Mrs. Ducharme. That's not too safe an area around

86

there—reason the clerk advised you to take a cab. And we used to think of the B-girls as the ones who slipped the customer a Mickey Finn to roll him outside, but there are men who go in for it too. You were wearing good clothes, Doctor, you looked prosperous—you might offer good pickings. I'd have a bet the one in the bar slipped a small dose of chloral hydrate into your drink, eased you out to where his pal was waiting. Then you woke up when they were stripping you and began to fight them, so they had to put you out a quicker way."

"I'll be damned," said Ducharme.

"What did they get?"

"My watch—Longines wristwatch—and my diamond ring. About forty dollars in cash. I'd had the sense to put the rest in the hotel safe."

"Could you describe the man in the bar?"

Ducharme shook his head and groaned involuntarily. "Not much—young, medium coloring, middle height—pretty sharp sports clothes."

"Well, we've got some mug shots of men who've pulled that kind of caper. When you're feeling better you might like to take a look. Meanwhile, if we can have a description of the jewelry we'll get it on the pawnbrokers' hot list."

"I can give you that," she said. "Honestly, Bernie—of all things to happen."

Landers had said why bother Narco again, they had their own business, and if Sid Belcher had a pedigree R. and I. would turn it up faster. Conway's cynical gray eyes were amused, but he went along with that. Down in Records, Landers looked at his girl fondly, neat little Phil O'Neill, and said, "What about Tuesday night, The Castaway again?"

"Fine with me," said Phil. "I just hope Rich realizes what he's getting into with that Margot. Did you know she's taking night classes in karate?"

"I had heard," said Conway, his lips twitching. "That's the way to keep a man from getting fresh all right."

"So what are you after now?"

"Sid Belcher. I don't know if that's his real name—"

"It'd almost have to be," said Phil. "Nobody would deliberately adopt a name like that, Tom. I'll have a look."

She brought the package to them five minutes later. Sidney Charles Belcher was described as Caucasian, twenty-four now, six feet, one ninety, brown and blue, no marks. He had a pedigree of possession, one count of assault, one of rape. He'd been off parole for six months. The last known address was Cahuenga Boulevard in Hollywood.

"Well, we can start there," said Landers. He was disposed to linger chatting with Phil, but Conway reminded him what he was getting paid for and reluctantly Landers followed him out. They took Conway's Dodge.

That was an old section of Hollywood; these days some old buildings were getting knocked down and new ones put up, and along the block they wanted the contrast was glaring: the old apartment buildings dirty white or tan stucco, square and solid and plain, the new ones sprawling with sun decks, colored plastic patio shelters and bright colors that would fade quickly in the hot sun. The one they wanted was one of the old ones. There wasn't a parking slot for a block and a half; they walked back.

"Past time we're due for a heat wave," said Conway.

"Don't call it down—it'll be coming." It was a three-story place, with steep steps up to a square-roofed porch, where the rows of mailboxes were lined. *Belcher* was listed at apartment eight. "Still here, anyway."

They went in and climbed uncarpeted stairs. Upstairs the hall was narrow, and there was a faint smell of frying onions somewhere and another of a cloying room freshener. The place was very quiet. At the door numbered eight Landers pushed the bell, and there was a shrill high buzz beyond the door. They waited. Unconsciously Landers reached up to adjust the shoulder holster.

The door opened; their eyes, adjusted for six-feet-high Sid Belcher, met space. They looked down. "Yes?" she said brightly. "What was it?"

88

"We're looking for a Sidney Belcher," said Conway. "Does he still live here?"

"When he's home, boys. Which is sometimes," she said airily. "Come on in. You friends of Sid's? Haven't seen you here before. I'm Sid's mother, in case you didn't know." She blinked and simpered at them.

She was a little woman, bleached blonde and skinny as a plucked chicken. She had on a purple nylon housecoat, and her fingernails matched it. She was in her bare feet; on the coffee table in front of a sagging couch was evidence of what she'd been doing—painting her toenails to match both. There was also a cocktail shaker half full and a lone cocktail glass, empty.

"You like a drink?" she asked hospitably.

"No, thanks, Mrs. Belcher," said Landers. "Do you know when Sid might be home?"

"No idea," she said. She sat down and refilled her glass from the shaker. She was facing the light and the merciless afternoon sun showed the telltale broken red veins in her nose, the splotchy skin covered with makeup. "He comes and goes, comes and goes. Come to think, he's gone. I just remembered he took a suitcase with him. He said where he was going, but I just don't call it to mind—my memory's getting terrible." She drank.

"Where does he usually go?" asked Conway somewhat inanely.

"Now there's a good question, mister," she said. "A very good question. Where does he? He was in a hurry, that I do remember. And he asked me to do something for him while he was gone. I was sitting here just now doing my toenails, and I said to myself, Bella, I said, what was it that Sid asked you to do? He said it was important, and I'd better do it right away. He used to like Disneyland, but I don't suppose he'd be going there now."

"When did he leave?" asked Landers.

"Oh, a while ago," she said vaguely. "Probably he owed somebody some money. That's always a good reason for leaving, isn't it? Are you sure you won't have a drink?"

"No, thanks," said Conway. "Was Janie with him?"

"Which Janie you mean? Oh, *that* Janie. I'm sure I don't know," she said, and hiccupped and added, "Parm me. Does Sid owe you any money? Because if he does, you're out of luck, I couldn't oblige him—not this month. The alimony was late again, and it's what they call—vicious circle, y'know. Got you comin' and goin'. You don't get the alimony, you can't pay a lawyer to get it for you. Lawyers are all crooks anyway. Are you lookin' for somethin'?" she added to Conway in mild curiosity. "The john's off the hall."

"I was just noticing this," said Conway casually. "Does it belong to Sid?" He jerked his head at Landers, who came to look. It was lying there in full view on a pile of old *True Romance* magazines, a rather rusty old Smith and Wesson .22.

"What?" She padded over to look, and sudden enlightenment came into her eyes, focused on it with some difficulty. "Oh, *now* I remember what it was Sid told me to do! I was s'posed to get rid of that some way, throw it out in the trash. 'S lucky you happened to notice it—" She swayed a little, peering up at them, and suddenly she said, "Say, just who are you guys, anyway?"

"It's the plain stupidity that gets you," said Landers disgustedly. "Him relying on that lush to get rid of the gun—"

"And shooting the Booths in the first place."

"Over the no-good pot. As Jase says, people."

They turned the gun over to the lab; they'd given her a receipt for it but she probably hadn't known what it was. Landers gave Wanda the gist of it to type into a proper report, and they put out a statewide A.P.B. for Sid Belcher and flashed the word to NCIC in case he'd gone farther. They queried the D.M.V. in Sacramento and learned that he had a car registered, a VW, and added the plate number to the A.P.B. They heard about William Linblad from Lake, and agreed that it was a funny one. You did still, in the midst of a renewed Sodom and Gomorrah, find the innocents.

They went home. Landers was feeling rather ambivalent about the double date on Tuesday night. He and Rich had taken to each other right away, and he liked Rich's girl all right, but he'd rather have Phil to himself. They'd known each other over a year now, and if she'd ever think about marrying him—

Grace told Virginia about William Linblad as he watched her giving Celia Ann her bath. "Maybe I'm growing the faculty for hunches too. But you could sympathize with the kid at that, funny as it was."

"Not funny," said Virginia. Celia Ann splashed and gurgled and they smiled at her; even after six months they hadn't quite got used to having their own baby. "What a woman, Jase. Maybe she got what she deserved."

"Not the nicest person in the world, Ginny, but maybe she didn't want to die."

Just before Mendoza left the office, the autopsy report came up on Harriet Branch. He was annoyed all over again, reading it. She had actually died of manual strangulation, though she'd been knocked around; there were bruises. Estimated time of death, between 8 and 10 P.M. Wednesday. Otherwise she had been a fairly healthy old lady, for her age: the heart slightly enlarged, the arthritis, but she might have had some years to go, living quietly there with her little amusements, an attentive family.

The victims like Harriet Branch always annoyed Mendoza. A good many victims of murder had invited it, by being stupid, or greedy, or careless. But Mrs. Branch, the harmless nice old lady, hadn't deserved to die that kind of death: and it didn't look as if there'd be any way for them to track down who'd brought it on her. Those damned love beads—

He drove home, consciously shelving the dirt and idiocy and brutality he dealt with on the thankless job. The house on Rayo Grande Avenue was a stark contrast, and his red-haired girl trying to cope with the twins bouncing on their beds. Mairí MacTaggart's sister was having a birthday party, and their treasure had deserted them temporarily.

Terry and Johnny abandoned persecution of their mother to fling themselves at Mendoza. "Show you how good I read!" said Johnny peremptorily. "I show you better!" said Terry instantly. "But, *Padre*, what's a pond?"

"That is a marvelous book," said Alison as they scrambled to fetch their McGuffey Readers. "They hardly ever get confused with Spanish now—but raising children in the city, there are a few things—"

"What's a pond, Papa?" Johnny pulled at him. "It says they went there. *Mamacita* says water but water's in the faucet."

"Yes, I do see what you mean," said Mendoza. Occasionally he felt his years. Automatically patting all four cats curled in a heap at the foot of Terry's bed, he added, "Parenthood is for the young."

"Speak for yourself, *amador*. Statistics say children of elderly parents are more intelligent."

"I'm not feeling quite elderly yet, my love."

"Oh, you needn't tell me *that*," said Alison.

The night watch drifted in. Glasser told the rest of them about the car. "Lesser of two evils," he said.

"I don't see it," said Schenke. "You'd be better off to buy a good used job. I could recommend a lot—"

The first thing turned up at nine forty-five, and maybe they should have expected it. Another heist at a restaurant just closing. This time it was that place so improbably popular, Le Renard Bleu, the unpretentious French family restaurant over past New Chinatown. It offered nothing but good food and good service, and you always had to make reservations. Glasser and Shogart went out on that, and heard very much what they'd heard about the Chasen job.

The shaken proprietor, Monsieur Robineau, was comforting a more shaken cashier, who turned out to be his niece, Mademoiselle Guillaume.

"We had only just closed—nearly everyone is gone, the

chefs, the waitresses, and we are just counting up the
money, it was a good night, when they came in—" Robineau gestured dramatically. "I am careless, there was a
last couple lingered, and they had just left, I should have
locked the door then—"

"Such big, big guns!" said the pretty, dark cashier.

It sounded like the same pair, stocking masks, the big
guns, in and out fast. "I do not have to figure to tell
you," said Robineau. "They stole five thousand eight hundred and thirteen dollars and thirteen cents. In the little
canvas bag I use to carry money home. But I saw something. I would not know their faces, no. But one of them,
he has on his right hand—I am sure!—a great long scar,
like from a knife, on the back of the hand. Perhaps the
police know a criminal with such a scar, eh?"

It wouldn't be much help. They'd want formal statements
on it, but it looked, as Glasser said, as if that pair had
realized they'd stumbled on a very nice M.O., and were
bent on building up a good take. None of them had
grasped before what kind of cash money the good restaurant would have on hand at closing time. "I wonder,"
said Glasser thoughtfully, "if one or both of them have
worked in places like that?" It was an idea; it wouldn't
take them any further in finding them.

At eleven forty-five they had a call from a Traffic unit.
"You desk boys will be taking a lot of statements on this,"
said the squad-car man tersely. "And there's an assault
with intent at least—it looked touch and go, may turn
into homicide."

Galeano and Schenke went out on that, and heard about
it at length from Patrolman Bill Moss and his partner,
Frank Chedorov. "We've practically been chasing this
guy all night," said Moss. "We haven't laid eyes on him,
but plenty of people have. I wouldn't have a guess whether
he's drunk or high on something else." They were in front
of a single frame house on Diana Street. "The first call we
got about two hours ago, a prowler over on Westmoreland.
I've got all the names for you—you'll be taking statements
like I said." He leaned against the squad car, a very tough,

93

competent LAPD man, tall, dark, grim-faced, a good-looking young man. "Householder heard him trying to break in the back door, and scared him off with a light. Got a look at him as he ran—best he could give us, a tall thin guy, Negro, ran fast, no make on his clothes. About half an hour later we got sent over on Geneva, just around the corner. Two girls, nice girls, sharing an apartment there—man broke into the place, one of these flimsy back-door locks, and they had quite a little fight with him, he mauled them both around some—we called an ambulance, but neither of 'em's seriously hurt, just bruised. Good girls, they put up a fight, banged him over the head with a flashlight, and he got away and ran. They told us, a tall thin Negro in a tan jumpsuit." Moss lit a cigarette.

"By this time," said Chedorov, "we were cruising the neighborhood on the lookout for him. And not fifteen minutes later we got a call to Diana Street here—another prowler call—half a block up, that way. Another attempted break-in, but the householder had a gun, turned a light on and showed it, and the prowler ran through the backyard and got away. But the householder got a good look, in the floodlight at the back. Tall thin Negro in a tan jumpsuit. We were just behind him all the way."

"So then we get a call, prowler, right here," said Moss. "We came up in a hurry, it's got to be him, but we're just too late. We heard about it from the neighbors." He gestured.

This block was in a mild uproar, lights on and people out in the street with flashlights, clustering, talking excitedly. The ambulance had just taken off as Galeano and Schenke arrived.

"It's a Mrs. Elsa Short. Widow, lives alone in this place. The Leemings live next door," said Moss. "That's Mr. Leeming with the shotgun. Mrs. Short, by what we can figure, called in when she heard this guy at her back door, but we hadn't got here when Leeming heard her screaming. He got his gun and came out, saw the guy come out the back door running—across the backyard. He said he didn't take a shot at him because the neighbors on the other side were coming out then and he didn't want to kill an innocent bystander. But it was a tall thin Negro in a tan jumpsuit."

"Thank you so much for nothing," said Galeano. "What about the widow?"

Moss stepped on his cigarette. "Not so good. He'd got in, and he had a knife. By what Leeming said he probably didn't have time to grab anything. Putting it all together, he's probably drunk or hopped up. A real stupid deal."

"Which so many of them are," said Galeano.

Sergeant Lake was off on Saturday, and Sergeant Rory Farrell sitting on the switchboard. Mendoza came in at ten past eight and looked at the reports the night watch had left, swore over the heist at the Blue Fox—"Do you remember that funny case, Art?"—and regarded the reported trail of the prowler with resignation. "Rory, check with the receiving hospital—Mrs. Elsa Short."

There was nothing in from the lab on Harriet Branch's apartment. *"¡Mil rayos!"* said Mendoza, Farrell buzzed him.

"Mrs. Short died about three A.M. Multiple knife wounds and shock."

"Gracias for nothing," said Mendoza. Something else to work, and no handle. The men were coming in— Landers, Conway, Piggott, Hackett and Higgins, Palliser, Grace. "We've got something new," said Mendoza.

At five minutes of nine, Farrell buzzed him again. The rest of them had drifted out on the endless routine legwork. "There's a Mr. Perkins here," said Farrell.

"Perkins? Oh. Well, show him in." And what he might want—Mendoza sat back and lit a cigarette, and the little desk clerk came in and sat down in front of the desk.

"We thought someone ought to tell you," he said earnestly. "Mr. Quigley and I talked it over, you see. Putting together what the other officers said, and that detective who talked to me. How you thought some—some person had got into the hotel while I was in the lavatory. Well, Lieutenant, I don't mean to tell you your business, you're an experienced officer, but it just occurred to both of us, you know—if that was so, how did he get out?"

Mendoza stared at him. *"¿Qué?"*

"I wasn't gone five minutes," said Perkins. "And after midnight the door was locked. And nobody came out past me after I'd been to the lavatory."

Mendoza sat up abruptly. *"¡Diez millones de demonios negros desde el infierno!"*

"Oh, Luis—" Hackett came in. "Sorry, I didn't—"

"Come in and listen to this, Art. Sergeant Hackett, Mr. Perkins. Night clerk at the Clark. Go on, Mr. Perkins."

"Well, that's just it," said Perkins, his nearsighted eyes behind rimless glasses a little anxious. "It's the kind of lock, you have to use the key on either side, to lock or unlock it. It's not a question of pushing a button or anything like that, and besides the door *was* locked that next morning. Anybody going out would have had to have a key."

"Now let me get this straight." Mendoza sat up and lit a cigarette. "You lock the front door at midnight. It's the only door used any more—others are all locked." Perkins nodded. "What about the permanent tenants? Suppose they're out after midnight?"

"Oh, they've all got keys."

"I see. And the ordinary hotel guests? You do have—"

"Oh, yes, sir. Not nearly so many as we used to have, but we get quite a lot of salesmen and business people passing through, who like to be in the downtown area, or are on tight expense accounts, don't care about the fancy places. People on vacation, just out for a good time, they want to stay somewhere fashionable, one of the Hiltons or the Century-Plaza. Mostly the people we get are quiet people on business, in before midnight, but there's a notice posted and if any of them are going to be late, they can borrow a key. But Mr. Quigley's very punctilious about keeping track of the extra keys—they're always locked in his desk. As it happens, I can tell you that nobody had an extra key that night—last Wednesday night."

"And you didn't see anybody in the freaky clothes, the love beads, come in."

"Oh, no, sir. Just as I told the other detective. All the guests were in by ten—they'd all gone out at various times for dinner. It's a shame to think how the hotel's gone down," said Perkins. "Really a skeleton staff these days. No room service, no dining room—it's just a glorified rooming house now—but our charges are according, and we do offer clean quiet rooms. I—"

"You went to the lavatory at nine o'clock."

"Somebody—of the kind you mean—could have slipped in then, yes, sir. But there was only one guest came and got his key after that, about ten o'clock. I was sitting there reading, but I'd have seen anyone go across the lobby and out. I—"

"Look here," said Hackett, "how about the fire department regulations? Aren't you supposed to have an emergency exit open at all times?"

"Certainly," said Perkins. "It's in Mr. Quigley's office off the lobby, out to Hill Street. There are three signs about it in the lobby. The door only opens out, of course." He looked uneasy. "Or it's supposed to. The fact is, it's out of order. That's actually what got Mr. Quigley and me talking about this. It's stuck. Mr. Quigley's been calling all around trying to get somebody to come and fix it, or if necessary put in a new door, but"—he sighed—"you know how it is, try to get a workman to come. Ordinarily, anybody could have come downstairs after midnight and gone out that way, and nobody the wiser. But now, no. They'd have to have a key to unlock the front door. Well, to go on. I locked up at midnight and went to bed. I have an apartment on the fifth floor. Mr. Quigley is on the sixth. He tells me when he came down to unlock the door next morning it was just as usual, locked up just as I'd left it. So whoever it was did that terrible thing to Mrs. Branch, he must have got hold of a key somehow, and it occurred to us to wonder—"

"*¡Por Dios!*" said Mendoza. He got up. "Come on—I want you to take a look at something." Hackett trailing them, he took Perkins out to the elevator and down to the lab. "You haven't sent up a report on the Clark Hotel job," he said to Scarne, the first man they ran into, "but right now I want a look at what you brought in to process. Any keys?"

"Sure." Scarne looked a little surprised. "We didn't fetch in all the personal effects, but anything standing out that might've collected latents— And you never do know where you'll pick some up. We took her handbag, naturally, and there was a bunch of keys in that. They're clean—smudged, but nothing liftable."

"Show, show," said Mendoza impatiently. Perkins was looking around this big, bare room with its wall benches and sophisticated mysterious equipment with interest. Scarne rummaged and came up with a brown leather handbag, a little worn, still bearing a few marks from the dusting powder. "We'll clean it up before we hand it over to the relatives. Sorry, just smudges on this too. We put everything back—you can handle it."

Mendoza upended it unceremoniously on a table. A clean handkerchief, a gold-colored compact for loose powder, a pale pink lipstick, a coin purse, a new-looking blue vinyl folder for bills, empty, fell in a heap with a bunch of keys. Mendoza pushed those away from the rest with a long forefinger. There were several keys on an old-fashioned steel ring. "What about it, Mr. Perkins? Is the front-door key here? You'd know it?"

"Oh, dear, yes. I've been at the Clark for twelve years, Lieutenant. No, it's not," he said after a minute. "It's gone."

"*Un momento.* I don't suppose she used it often—the Whitlows said she didn't go out much anymore, she wouldn't be out after midnight. It could be she didn't keep that key with the rest." Mendoza was sorting them out: a Yale key, could be the key to the apartment, a long thin key that would fit a safe-deposit box, another Yale key—possibly the Whitlow house?—a couple of old ones he wouldn't have a guess about.

"Oh, but she did," said Perkins unexpectedly, "and I'll tell you how I happen to know. Let's see, this is June. It was back in February, there was a series of musicals at the Music Center, and Mr. and Mrs. Whitlow took her to see *The Mikado*. Gilbert and Sullivan, you know. She did look forward to it, and as luck had it that was one of her better days, when her arthritis wasn't so troublesome. They picked her up just as I was coming on duty, and I reminded her about the door, if she'd be late coming in—and she smiled at me and said she had her key, she took that ring out of her purse and showed it to me. And as a matter of fact they brought her home after midnight, and the next time she saw me she said how Mr. Whitlow had unlocked the door for her and taken her up to her apartment."

"*Así*," said Mendoza absently. "But that's— What it comes down to is that X knew. I will be damned. I will be—he knew you'd be on the desk till midnight, and then locking up. He thought he'd get out the emergency door, but when he found it was stuck, he knew about the keys—that Mrs. Branch would have one. And, by God, he knew the right key—if he hadn't, he'd have taken the whole bunch. But instead, he simply takes that key off her ring—"

"Like a damned fool," said Hackett, hunching his bulky shoulders. Perkins was looking from one to the other. "Because you know where that takes us. Somebody from the hotel."

"Oh, no, I'm quite sure you're wrong there!" said Perkins agitatedly. "That's quite impossible. We're reduced to a much smaller staff than we used to have, but all respectable, decent people—I'm quite sure—"

"I want to get these keys sorted out!" said Mendoza forcefully. "Bill, if you don't send me a report on all this by tomorrow I'll report you to I.A. Come on, we're going over to the hotel to go into this in depth. Did you park in the lot?"

"Oh, I came on the bus—"

Mendoza led them down to the lot; they squeezed Perkins into the jump seat of the Ferrari and had a quick ride up to Hill. There are a few advantages to being a cop;

Mendoza left the Ferrari in a loading zone and they went in.

Mendoza and Hackett went first to look at the emergency door. It was firmly stuck on dead center: Hackett exerted all his strength and couldn't move it. Nobody had got out that way.

Quigley was also agitated at the implication; but both he and Perkins were experienced in the ways of hotels, and a wealth of facts was disclosed in rapid order, on consultation of the register. On Wednesday night there had been forty-nine transient guests at the hotel, all but four of them men, all probably business people, sales representatives—that type, by what both men said. Quigley said at once that he had ten duplicate keys to the front door, always kept in a locked drawer in his desk, and all ten were there now; they looked. There was his key, and Perkins' key. There were thirty single apartments on the fifth and sixth floors of the building, with twenty rented: two more were occupied by Perkins and Quigley.

On Thursday, it hadn't seemed worth the while to talk to any of the other tenants on the fifth floor. Mrs. Branch's apartment was at the end of a short corridor down from the elevators; there were only two others in that little wing. The one across the hall was empty; the one on the same side, its front door twenty feet away from Mrs. Branch's, had been occupied by Mrs. Davies until her death last month. This was an old building, very solidly built, and it was not very likely that any of the tenants farther away—ten more small apartments on that floor— had heard any little struggle and outcry from Mrs. Branch's apartment.

Now, Mendoza wanted the full treatment. He called the office and asked who was there. "John and Jase went out to get statements from all that rumpus last night," said Farrell. "On the Short woman. Henry had a little idea about the restaurant heisters and it paid off, Piggott's out on that. Tom and Rich Conway were just leaving—"

"Hold it. Send them over. We've got some questions to ask here too."

"Will do," said Farrell. "I'll just catch 'em."

"Now, I want to hear all about your employees," said Mendoza to Quigley.

"I'm sure you're wrong about that, Lieutenant. Most of them have been with us a long time, all reliable people. But of course, anything I can tell you—"

There were four maids for the first four floors, where the single hotel rooms were located. Three of them had worked there for five, six, ten years: all middle-aged women, said Quigley, never any trouble, hard workers. The fourth had only been there a month, a Laura Schoonover: she seemed like a nice quiet girl, said Quigley, about thirty. Got along with the others all right. For the two top floors, where the apartments were, there were two maids: Agnes Harvey and Louise Wilding. Not all the permanent tenants wanted to pay extra for maid service: Mr. and Mrs. Bolt didn't, or Miss Trucker, or Mr. Yates; with him it wasn't the money, he was a secretive old chap who didn't like strange women fussing about his quarters. The other seventeen apartments occupied were cleaned by the maids once a week. Usually Agnes Harvey did the fifth floor and Louise Wilding the sixth, but there wasn't any rule about it.

Landers and Conway arrived. "We're going to talk to everybody who lives here," said Mendoza. "And we're going to make sure where their front door keys are, all accounted for. This might give us some very useful ideas where to look. Art, you go and talk to the maids. Especially Harvey and Wilding."

"Yes, I think this may be it," said Hackett. "See what I turn up." He might not have the built-in radar like Mendoza, but he'd been a cop a long time and any cop got feelings about people.

By one o'clock they had talked to everybody but Mr. Yates. Miss Trucker was a sales clerk at Bullock's, and Conway had gone up there to see her, had seen her key. Everybody else living at the Clark was elderly, retired, and at home. The Bolts were the only married couple; there were two spinster sisters, the Misses Catton; everyone else lived alone. They all had their front-door keys to show; few of them ever used them. When Landers tried to talk to Mr. Yates, the door was opened a cautious few inches on a chain, and Mr. Yates said, "Don't know anything about it," to Landers' questions. "A murder? Murders all over. Dangerous. I don't go out. Get the drugstore to send up my breakfast and dinner. What say? What key? Oh, that key. I never use it."

"Have you still got it? I'd like to see it, sir." And presently, grumbling, Mr. Yates held up to the crack a single bright Yale key. Landers could recognize it by then, having looked at a dozen others.

All the front-door keys were accounted for except Harriet Branch's. Nobody who lived on the fifth floor had heard any kind of disturbance on Wednesday evening, between eight and ten. All of them had been home; most of them had been watching TV.

"*¿Cuánto apuestas?*" said Mendoza. He stood in front of the desk in the lobby, smoking and rocking gently heel to toe. "That puts it right here. Right here at the hotel."

"And what a damn fool thing to do," said Landers. "Anybody could figure that. Who else would know that key by sight, to take just that one?"

"He hadn't any choice about the key," said Mendoza. "Not after he found that emergency door blocked. But he'd have been smarter to take the whole bunch."

"The maids don't have occasion to use the key," said Quigley behind the desk.

"No, but they've seen it—they're familiar with it. There's the one in your office. I noticed you've got it hanging there on the wall all by itself. Why?" asked Mendoza suddenly. "Why don't you keep it with your others?"

Quigley looked distressed. "I used to. It's only there during the day—I take it with me when I go off duty. The only time I use it as a rule is when I open up in the morning. But—at the time of the Watts riots, there were several incidents—looters coming in off the street—oh, nothing like what it was down there, but we did finally lock the door when a noisy gang came by, and Mr. Perkins said then perhaps we should keep a key handy for—emergencies. If I was away from the desk, or—"

"The maids go in there, they'd know the key."

Quigley admitted it. "But really, to think that one of them could—"

"They've got personal lives," said Mendoza "Relatives, and probably troubles. What did you get from them, Art?"

"I'll tell you over food," said Hackett. "I'm starving."

Glasser's little idea last night, expressed in a note to Piggott, had rather surprisingly paid off. Landers had said it was brilliant, and chased down enthusiastically to R. and I. to see what Phil could turn up from the computer. The criminal records of the LAPD were quite extensive; fed the proper questions, the computer turned up eighteen men with records of armed robbery who had at one time or another been employed at restaurants. Landers stared at the list, aghast.

"Well, you're setting up some legwork for yourself," said Phil, surprised too.

But as soon as Landers got back, he and Conway were chased over to the hotel. Palliser and Grace, looking without enthusiasm at the list, were just as pleased there was another job than that one to work. Piggott had started out with the first few names.

At least it was Saturday, and most people would be home. They had the names and addresses from the night watch, of the trail of the prowler last night in that neighborhood.

Alberto Perez, on Westmoreland Avenue, said he'd been in bed when he heard the prowler. His wife was visiting her mother in Bakersfield; he was alone in the house. He had got up and turned on the backyard lights, two floodlights, and scared the prowler away, having called the police first; but when they came the man had run off. He gave them a fairly good description.

Palliser thanked him; he'd taken notes for Wanda to type up into a statement, and he explained about coming in to sign it tomorrow.

"Sure," said Perez. "I heard he ended up killing a lady. My God. Sure, you got to be a good citizen."

From there they went on to the apartment on Geneva Street, which Kathy Bryan and Linda Poling shared. The girls were there, willing and anxious to talk about it, and pleased at the attention. They were both young and good-looking, Linda a diminutive blonde and Kathy a statuesque brunette. The apartment was on the ground floor; this had been a big single house, now cut up into four apartments, and someone had done some remodeling: in this ground-floor unit, a former side door had been replaced with a sliding glass panel.

"I tell you, I've always been a little nervous about it," said Kathy. "We got that special lock for sliding doors, and I know it's awfully thick glass, but still it is glass—and of course that was where he tried first. We were both in bed, and we heard him at the same time, and I peeked around a corner of the bedroom and saw him—it was moonlight, you know." The glass door was in their living room. "It's lucky the phone's in the bedroom. I called the police as quietly as I could, and then I grabbed up this flashlight—" It was a good hefty one, metal and at least a foot long.

Linda chuckled. "I sneaked out to the kitchen and got that big cast-iron skillet. I always said it'd make a good weapon."

"And he didn't get in the glass door, so he came round and tried the kitchen door, and I think he kicked it in," said Kathy. "It made an awful noise. The lock's broken, and Mr. Winter said he'd see it was fixed today—I hope! Anyway, there he was—the man, and I was terrified but I banged him on the head with the flashlight as soon as he got in—"

"Do you think he was drunk?" asked Grace.

"There wasn't any liquor smell, but I think he might have been doped up on something, he acted so sort of wild—and he was awfully strong, I can testify to that! He grabbed the flashlight away from me—"

"This flashlight?"

"Yes, he just threw it across the room, I found it later—"

"Don't touch it!" said Palliser sharply as she reached for it again. "Just hope, if he left any prints on it—"

"I haven't messed them up already—oh, dear," she said, "I *am* sorry, I just never thought. Yes, you can have it—as long as I get it back. Anyway, he grabbed me and knocked me right down across the kitchen table—you should see my bruises—"

"And about then I tried to hit him with the skillet," said Linda, "but the darned thing's so heavy, I couldn't aim it very well—and he came at me and knocked me down, right on the floor, and I'll never forget it—there was the moonlight coming in, and he had a knife in his hand, the light hit the blade and it looked three feet long, I could feel it coming right for my middle—" She shuddered.

"And then—I guess we'd both been screaming blue murder," said Kathy, "Mr. Winter got there, yelling what was the matter—he's the landlord, he lives in front—and the man just turned and ran out. Boo! That was a real experience! It's convenient, living pretty close to work here"—they both worked at a big travel agency downtown—"but I don't know, maybe safer away from what they call the inner city." They both said they'd be glad to sign statements.

Palliser and Grace went on to the first householder on Diana Street, Rupert Lutz. He said he had his house up for sale. On account of the crime rate. "I got four years to retirement, boys," he said, "but I'm not takin' the gamble. Not here. Me and my wife are getting out, goin' up to Montgomery Creek way up north. Wide place in the road. We got a trailer house there, and an acre and a half. Grow some food, maybe have a cow." He'd gone for his gun right off, hearing the prowler, saw him at the back door; his wife had called the police, but as soon as he'd turned on the outside lights and yelled out a window that he'd shoot, the prowler had taken off. "I heard that woman down the street died—is that right? He cut her up?" Lutz shook his head. "That's awful. I sure hope we sell this place soon."

They went on to Mr. Leeming, next door to Mrs. Short's house. Mendoza had routed out the lab, and the truck was still in the drive, Marx and Horder busy packing away cameras and equipment. Palliser handed over the flashlight in its plastic evidence bag. "Think you picked up anything?"

"Anybody's guess," said Marx. "There was quite a lot of blood—looks as if all the action was in the kitchen. You'll like one thing we got—but no telling whether it'll be any use. He stepped in some of the blood. He was in his bare feet."

"What?" said Grace. "I'll be damned. Good print?"

"Fair. I'd make it about a size eleven, a wide splayed foot—he's used to going barefoot."

"Which might say this and that," said Palliser. "You'll send us a report."

"When we've looked at everything." Marx climbed behind the wheel and Horder got in beside him.

They had put a police department seal on the doors. Palliser and Grace walked around the little frame house and looked at the back door. A rather flimsy screen door had been wrenched off its hinges entirely, lay on the dry grass below the back step. But the inner door was a stout one, now crudely jimmied around the lock, splinters broken off. Grace said thoughtfully, "The girls said he was pretty strong. I'd say he had to be, to pry that open." Palliser agreed.

They went next door to talk to Leeming. He gave them the best description; he'd had a clear look at the prowler in moonlight as he ran out of the kitchen. "We heard about Mrs. Short," he said soberly. "We'd been neighbors a long time, I went out and asked the hospital to let us know. This is a hell of a thing—just a hell of a thing. He must've been drunk or doped—he didn't steal a thing, didn't have time—and there wasn't anything there to steal anyway. Mrs. Short just had the pension from her husband, he was a railroad man. There wouldn't be ten bucks in the house likely, she was careful about keeping cash around. Poor woman, not a soul of her own, they never had any kids. I don't believe there's anybody to see about a funeral, even cousins or anything. I guess she probably had enough in the bank to bury her, and she owned the house —my wife and I could do that much anyway, see to the funeral." They told him about the mandatory autopsy, the statement, and he nodded. "That's O.K., I'll be glad to."

It was getting on toward one o'clock then, so they handed all the notes to Wanda, and both of them starved, didn't waste time going out but went up to the canteen on the top floor for sandwiches.

Higgins and Piggott had been left with the new list of heisters with restaurant experience. They didn't feel enthusiastic about it, but the legwork was always there to be done. They went out looking, and found a few of them at the addresses from Records, brought them in to lean on. It was all up in the air; one had a solid alibi, the others were possible, with nothing to say yes or no.

They had just, after a lunch break, found another and were about to start talking to him when a cheerful-looking young man came in and said to Farrell, "Just checking into your nice inner-city beat. I'm from Wilcox Street—Bob Laird. Somebody like to help me make an arrest?"

"Sure," said Higgins. "Who're you after?"

"A fag by the name of Melvin Wenfer. I've got a warrant—assault with intent. He's supposed to be at a rooming house down on Temple—no guarantee he's still there. He's been living the high life up in Hollywood, little affair with one of the teachers at a public high school—"

"My God," said Higgins. "The innocent parents sending kids to those places. The teacher a fag—"

"As I'm always saying," said Piggott sadly, "right back to Sodom and Gomorrah. The love affair broke up?"

"Yep. Teacher decided Melvin was too expensive— caught him rifling his pockets and threw him out," said Laird. "Melvin missed the goodies, kept at him to start over, but finally a couple of days ago he got in a snit

108

and attacked teacher with a knife. Teacher ran to us—he had this address from when Melvin was still begging him to forgive and forget."

"They will do it," said Higgins. "You can talk to this bird, Matt. I don't suppose anything'll come of it." The heister was a morose-looking man still on parole.

Higgins and Laird went down to the lot, to Laird's car. "And in a way," said Laird as they climbed in, "it might have been better the other way round, Sergeant."

"How do you mean?"

"Well, that Piggott's a nice mild-looking fellow, you know. I just hope you won't scare little Melvin half to death."

Higgins grinned. "Never believe I've got a beautiful wife, would you? I hope the baby takes after her."

"Boy or girl?"

"Oh, a girl—Margaret Emily, nine months," said Higgins proudly.

Laird cast a thoughtful glance at him as he started the engine. "Let's hope the baby takes after your wife, Sergeant."

At the address on Temple, they surprised Melvin Wenfer considerably. "I didn't think Eugene 'd do a thing like that—swear out a warrant for me! He's just being mean! A lousy five bucks I borrow from him—he'd have given it to me if I asked!—" He was petulant. "You damn fuzz always down on us—just because we're different—" But Higgins, with COP emblazoned on his forehead, he didn't like; he didn't give them any trouble. They put him in cuffs just to make sure and Laird dropped Higgins off at headquarters.

The possible heister had come up with an alibi for last night, checked out. "I can't understand it," said Piggott. "How there could be so many."

"Well, you think about it," said Higgins, "it's natural maybe. The thugs getting out on P.A., they'll hold a job as long as they have to, and that's the kind of job that kind can get—dishwashers, bus boys."

"That's so. But it makes the legwork." However, about

then they got Landers and Conway back, from their morning at the hotel and a belated lunch.

Landers looked at the list, somewhat shortened, and said, "I suppose the quicker we get to it, the quicker we'll clean it up."

But as they came past the switchboard, an excited-looking woman came in and said, "Is this where I'm supposed to be? The man downstairs said I should come and ask to see the body—Holy Mother, a body he says—but it could be Carlos and no telling how long he'd been gone because I've been away since last Saturday, I've been on a trip with my sister—and I come home at noon today off the bus and Carlos isn't there! We live together, I'm a widow, and Carlos, he never got married after that girl jilted him—he's my brother—"

They got her calmed down a little. Her name was Vera Montoya, and she lived in a house on Miramar Street. She worked at a Manning's coffee shop, and Carlos was a checker at a Thriftimart market on Western, she said. He was off Saturdays, he always puttered around his garden, a fine garden he had in the backyard, but he hadn't been there and the neighbors hadn't seen him since last Saturday, thought maybe he'd gone off on the trip with Vera. Carlos, you could set your clock by him, a great one for routine and he'd never done such a thing— So she'd come to tell the police he was missing—

Apprehensively Higgins took her down to the morgue to look at the unidentified body dead of knife wounds. She gave one look and screamed, called on the Virgin and all the archangels, and said it was Carlos.

"That never harmed anybody his whole life, innocent as the babe unborn, how could such a thing happen to Carlos? When did you find him, how long is it? But how could such a thing—Carlos, he's the best man walking around, good, kind, everybody likes Carlos—"

Higgins took her back to the office and started to ask questions. The body had been found by Traffic just a week ago tonight, lying in the street along Loma Drive. He'd been stripped, nothing on him but cigarettes. She filled in a little, between exclamations and eulogy of Carlos. He'd been fifty-two, an old bachelor, a quiet man, Carlos Masada. He worked at his job, came home to work in his garden. No enemies. A man didn't need enemies, thought Higgins, when there were so many wild ones roaming around, to attack and maybe kill for what cash was in a pocket. Those were dark streets down there.

"Did he go out much at night, Mrs. Montoya? To a local bar maybe, or—"

"Never, never! He'd have a glass of wine before dinner, in the evening, but he never went out to sit in bars like some men, no. Go out, he would—he was crazy about the old movies, always when he saw there's an old movie playing some place, he'd go—the ones twenty, thirty years old, he remembers from when he was a young man—"

He'd probably been out to a movie, maybe up on Beverly Boulevard, close enough that he could walk there and back. And been jumped by one of the wild ones. It made more paper work; it was unlikely that they'd ever find out who it had been.

Mendoza sat at his desk chain-smoking and looking at the notes Hackett had taken on the employees at the Clark Hotel.

Those damned keys put it right back there—not, probably, to the actual maids themselves, though even that might be. But—connections. And a rudimentary plan— very rudimentary. He had a vague idea that possibly X had intended to get into more than one apartment there, quickly silencing the old people, ransacking; and then more loot than he'd expected showed up at Mrs. Branch's, and he'd stopped with that one. Or got scared when he saw he'd killed her. Because that at least they knew: he hadn't got out till after midnight, when Perkins locked up.

The two top-floor maids. Indignant and frightened, said Hackett, at being questioned—suspected. Conceivably the maids all quite innocent, just somebody taking in the casual talk?

111

No. The casual talk, damn it, wouldn't have told any-body what that key looked like.

Agnes Harvey was forty-two, had worked there for ten years. She was married; her husband drove a truck for Sears, Roebuck. Two children, a boy sixteen, a girl four-teen. They were buying a house on Fifty-second Street. They went to the Baptist Church regularly. Which said damn all, reflected Mendoza sardonically.

Louise Wilding was thirty, had worked there four years. She was divorced, lived with her widowed mother in the house her mother owned on Woodlawn Avenue. She had two children, a girl nine, a girl six. She went out with a man sometimes but she said she wasn't interested in marrying again. She had refused to give any names of the men to Hackett, said it was private business.

The other maids were all married: a couple of them had teen-age children. The first thing Mendoza had done on getting back to the office was to send Wanda down to R. and I. to check all of those kids. None had showed up in the j.d. records. Which again said nothing. There was always a first time.

Once a month an outside cleaning service came in to vacuum the lobby. Quigley's office, the elevators, the stairs, wash the front windows. Mendoza had just had a talk with the manager there, on the phone, and he was thinking about the cleaners as a distinct possibility, now. It was one of the big companies that took contracts for the routine cleaning of office buildings, hotels, public build-ings. The manager, somewhat puzzled to be consulted by the police, had been anxious to be helpful.

"Well, if you get me—did you say Lieutenant?—it's not so easy to get good workers, in this business. We pay a good rate, but it's hard work—no denying that, and we got a reputation to keep, got to do the work right. When it's so easy to go on the welfare, and you know with all the bureaucratic red tape a lot of cheats are really taking it on seven kinds of welfare, it's not just so easy to find men willing to put in a good day's work. But I don't get why you're asking, you don't think one of our men pulled something? A—a crime? Look, I don't think any of 'em 'd do that—we got a pretty good bunch of men here now—"

And, to another question, he was uneasy and apologetic. "Well, if you get me, we're taking who we can get, Lieutenant. I got to say—we used to ask men for references, we used to check, just like we used to say no long hair and like that—and see if they got a police record, or were drunks or whatever. But we got commitments, we got the jobs to do, and these days we take about anybody shows up to apply."

The cleaners? There half a day, most of a day, cleaning? Hearing the talk from the maids, from Quigley? In Quigley's office, seeing that key hanging there.

Those damned keys. It was a tricky little point, but it did say something. And rather often, these days, Luis Rodolfo Vicente Mendoza was wondering why he stayed on at the thankless job, but admit it: Mendoza the egotist always enjoyed getting his teeth into the little puzzle like this one, ferreting out the truth.

He got up. It was four o'clock. He reached for his hat and said to Farrell absently, "I may not be back."

"Tom and Matt just brought in another one off that list. It's all up in the air—nothing to say yes or no."

"Sometimes it goes like that, Rory." Downstairs, he headed the Ferrari for the Hollywood freeway. It could be that the Whitlows—more likely Mrs. Whitlow—could tell him this and that about how Mrs. Branch had felt about the staff at the Clark Hotel, where she'd lived so long.

The maids. The cleaners. But, those damned love beads? "¿Qué sé yo?" he said to himself, annoyed. "¿Qué significa eso?"

Higgins had just brought in another man to question, at a quarter to five, and Conway had resignedly joined him in the second interrogation room, when the outside line flashed and Farrell plugged in. "Robbery-Homicide, Sergeant Farrell."

"We just got a call to a place on Ocean View. Szorbic,

113

Traffic," said a hard young voice. "There's a body here, sir. At a house for sale—it was the realtor called us, he just found it."

"O.K.," said Farrell. "We'll be on it. Let me have the address." The only men in were Higgins and Conway; he went down to that interrogation room and passed on the news.

"Business picking up," said Higgins. "I suppose we'd better go look at it."

At the sprawling old house on Creston Drive in Hollywood, Walter Whitlow opened the door to Mendoza. "Oh —Come in. Have you—found out anything yet?"

"I've got a few more questions, Mr. Whitlow, if your wife doesn't mind."

"Well, come in. Edna hasn't been so well—she's lying down. I wanted to thank you—your office called to tell us we could have the body, and the funeral's arranged for Tuesday. I don't know, maybe I could help you?"

"I think your wife would be more apt to know about this. Something's showed that seems to put it right there at the hotel—the staff at the Clark—and I'd like to know anything she can tell me about Mrs. Branch's relationships with them. The maids—"

"Oh. The staff?" Whitlow looked surprised. "That seems impossible. Why should you think that?"

Mendoza sat down opposite him in the pleasant living room, lit a cigarette, and explained about the front-door key. Whitlow listened in silence, grasping the implications quickly, nodding. "Yes, I see. It still seems incredible. I don't know, Mother always seemed to feel the people there were—nice and obliging. I don't know about disturbing Edna, but she probably would— But, Lieutenant, you said before—how those damned love beads—a young person, a—one of these hippie kids?"

"We work with what we've got," said Mendoza. "This is a more important lead. It could be both—the kid connected with one of the maids some way—or somebody working for that cleaning service. We just go looking where it's indicated."

"Yes, I see that. I see that this key business does take
115

you right back to the hotel. I'll see if Edna feels up to—"
He got up.

"It's all right, Walter," she said from the door, "I've
been listening. Of course I want to help any way I can.
The people at the hotel—" She came in, sat down beside
her husband on the couch. She looked tired and worried,
her very fair skin a little blotchy, and her hands trembled
slightly. She was wearing a plain black dress. "I don't see
how that could be, Lieutenant. Mother liked everybody
there—they were good to her. She liked Agnes, the maid
who usually did her apartment, she used to look forward
to those days, somebody to talk to. Agnes used to tell her
all about her children and so on, it gave Mother an interest.
She always gave Agnes some money on her birthday. She
didn't know the other maid as well, it was just once in a
while she and Agnes changed, but Mother said she was
quite nice too. I just don't see how it could be—anything
to do with anyone at the hotel."

"There'd never been any trouble about any of the
maids, suspicion of theft or—"

"Never," she said firmly. "When Mother first went to
live there, there were different maids nearly every week—
well, I suppose the hotel was busier and had more employees—and some she liked better than others, but there
was never anything like that. I think she was—quite attached to Agnes."

"Yes," said Whitlow restlessly. "By the way, I checked
with the bank yesterday—we're both authorized to sign on
Mother's account—and she'd taken out five hundred in
cash when she paid in the annuity check. The rent would
have been due on the fifteenth but she'd have paid that by
check."

"Thanks very much," said Mendoza. "The lab's finished
with the apartment now, you can go in whenever you like,
by the way. I should have asked you, Mrs. Whitlow—we
didn't see a jewelry case, any jewelry boxes, around—
would there have been anything of value, outside the
cash?"

Edna Whitlow shook her head slowly. "Mother wasn't a

great one for jewelry. She didn't have anything but costume stuff—besides her wedding ring, and she couldn't get that off anymore." The corpse was still wearing it: a plain thin gold band.

Mendoza got up, feeling dissatisfied. "Well, thanks very much, but I'd hoped you could recall something more about—"

"Any trouble, but there never was any. As far as that goes," she said, a tinge of color in her cheeks, "when I say Mother was attached to Agnes, I think it worked the other way too. Really. I know about Agnes too, you know—she's worked there a long time—and I think she's a fine honest woman. A nice woman."

The trouble was, in the one brief encounter he'd had with Agnes, Mendoza was inclined to think so too.

"I don't understand all you said about that key," she told him. She looked troubled.

"Nothing much," said Whitlow soothingly. "It's just missing—but we won't be needing it, so it doesn't matter."

Mendoza got back into the Ferrari feeling as if he'd overlooked something: something had slipped past him somehow, that he should have grasped. He switched on the ignition. There was no sense going back to the office; he headed for home.

Higgins and Conway, at that end of the day, went out to look at the new corpse. At least the caustic comments of all the other men had weaned Conway from his little black cigars and he was back to cigarettes; he lit the last one in the pack as he got in the car beside Higgins.

Ocean View Avenue, so optimistically named, along here was a block of tired old frame and stucco houses dating from the twenties. There was a black-and-white and a bright new green Ford outside one about the middle of the block. Higgins parked behind the Ford and they got out; the two uniformed men were talking with a civilian on the front porch.

As they went up the front walk, the strip of uncared-for lawn on either side, they noticed the sign posted on the

right side: FOR SALE, HUNTINGDON REALTY COM-
PANY, and across it slapped diagonally a SOLD poster.

Fred Ware was one of the Traffic men. "This is Mr.
Odum," he said. "Sergeant Higgins, Detective Conway.
Mr. Odum just found the body."

"Damnedest thing," said Odum, who was big and bald,
with a paunch. "He was supposed to be out tomorrow, I
just stopped by to confirm that. I suppose the poor old
guy had a stroke or something—there's blood—damned
shame."

"What's his name, Mr. Odum?"

"James Blackwood. He's a widower, about seventy-five,
and it was getting to be too much for him to live here
alone, he put the place up for sale and he was going into
some rest home run by the church he went to. I was sorry
for the old guy, he kind of resented it that his daughter
didn't ask him to come live with her. Families ought to
stay together."

"Yes, well, if you'd wait a few minutes," said Higgins.
They went in; the front door was open.

Odum called after them, "The place was sold furnished
—he'd been getting his own things packed up ready to go,
poor old bastard—in the back porch."

It was a shabby little house, not very well taken care of:
the furniture dusty, the couple of pictures crooked. But
there was no evidence of violence until they looked into
the first bedroom. There, all the empty drawers in bureau
and chest had been pulled out. The second bedroom contained only a single chest, its empty drawers on the floor.
The bathroom medicine chest was open on emptiness.

The body was in the kitchen. Blackwood had been a fat
old man, bald and jowly. He was wearing black pants and
an old-fashioned silk undershirt, black slippers on bare
feet. There was blood in a pool under his head. Higgins
bent and felt one wrist. "Last night," he said.

"They had a look here too," said Conway. "And in his
suitcases." Cupboard drawers were open here on emptiness. The suitcases were in the service porch, two of them,
lying open and ransacked; they might have been packed

up, standing ready by the back door, and rifled hastily right there. There were piles of shabby clothing, one good dark suit, shirts, two pairs of shoes, handkerchieves, an old worn leather Bible, and that was all.

"As Luis says," said Higgins, "the jungle getting junglier, Rich. A poor old fellow like this, anybody could see there'd be nothing here to steal. But—"

Conway had discovered that the back door was unlocked. He poked it open with his pen and stepped out onto the back porch. "Oh, very nice," he said. Higgins came to look.

Just at the foot of the rickety back steps was a length of wood about two feet long, part of a two-by-four. One end of it bore a few dark stains. "And as Luis also says, I do get tired," said Higgins. He went back to the front porch. "Somebody got in and beat him over the head," he told the Traffic men. "We'll want the lab."

"What?" said Odum. "You mean he was *killed?* Well, for God's sake—"

Higgins used the radio in the Traffic unit to call the lab. They wouldn't do much here tonight but take photographs of the body and weapon so both could be moved. He took Odum's address, told him they'd want a statement, asked if he knew the daughter's address. "I don't," said Odum, "but I know her name's Mackey, Mrs. Clifford, and it's on Baxter Avenue. My God, what a damned senseless thing! What a—when all the arrangements were made and all—"

"About a rest home?"

"Yeah, yeah. He just had some equity in this place, didn't own it clear, and all he got out of the sale was turned right over to the church home to pay his way there from now on. Poor old bastard," said Odum.

Higgins and Conway waited for the lab team, who said they'd take the pictures, seal the place and come back in the morning. They went back downtown and Higgins dropped Conway in the lot; it was after six. "I'll look up the daughter," he said. "It's on my way home." Baxter Avenue was in the general direction of Silver Lake; he looked up the daughter in the phone book, after calling Mary to say he'd be late.

When he found the place, it was a neat colonial house, newly painted and smart-looking. The woman who answered the door didn't match it; she was fat, red-faced, with gray hair pulled back to a tight knob, suspicious eyes, and a sharp voice. "Yes?" she said impatiently. Higgins showed her the badge and said apologetically that he had some bad news for her, about her father. "Don't tell me he's in trouble with the police now?" she said.

Higgins told her what they had found. "It looked as if he was killed instantly, Mrs. Mackey. The place was ransacked, but Mr. Odum didn't think there'd have been anything of value to—"

"Oh," she said. "Oh. Well, poor old Dad." It was entirely perfunctory. "Shame it had to happen that way, but I guess he's better off at that. He was pretty old, you know, and getting forgetful and all—real nuisance to take care of. But thanks for letting me know."

"There'll have to be an autopsy," said Higgins, "but we'll let you know when you can claim the body."

"Oh, sure," she said. Suddenly she thought of something and her face got redder. "And my God, I bet we have to get a lawyer to get back all the money he paid that church home! I just bet."

"I wouldn't know about that," said Higgins.

"Well, thanks anyway," she said, and shut the front door.

When Higgins got home he felt grateful for the warm smell of cooking in the kitchen, and the sound of Laura practicing at the piano, and his lovely Mary a little flushed over the stove. He kissed her soundly. "It's always nice to come home, but especially tonight. I just ran into a hell of a female," and he told her about Mrs. Mackey. Mary laughed.

"People—they do come all sorts. But did it occur to you, George, that maybe Mr. Blackwood hadn't been the best father in the world, so she isn't the best daughter?"

"It hadn't, till you said so. Could be. Where's Steve?"
"Studying for exams. And the baby's asleep."

Hackett had had a small idea, which he'd mention to
Luis tomorrow, and he thought about it on the way home.
Now that this business about the key had turned up, on
the Clark Hotel case, could it just be that those love beads
were a fake clue? Dropped deliberately to point to the
hippie type, the younger generation—and away from, say,
some boyfriend of one of the maids? It was just an idea.

When he got home, Angel had dinner nearly ready, and
the kids were busy over coloring books, the big silver
Persian asleep in his basket. "And before you sit down,"
said Angel severely, "you're going to get weighed. You
know what the doctor said when you had your last physical, and I know you've gained."

"Oh, hell," said Hackett. "I know it too. I can hardly
get into these pants."

He was up to two twenty-nine. "So back on the diet you
go," said Angel. "And don't swear, Art. After all, you
don't want to develop high blood pressure at your age."
The trouble was, of course, that she didn't have to worry
about gaining, she was a good cook, and while he gloomily
ate lean hamburger and drank black coffee, she had the
Roquefort dressing, the baked potato, the angel food cake.
It wasn't fair, thought Hackett.

When Palliser got home that night, he was thinking
about the prowler and Mrs. Short. Of course Hillside
Avenue in Hollywood was a different place than that area
downtown, but crime was up—violent crime—anywhere
these days. He'd had good new locks installed on the
doors, and iron grilles across the back windows. But,
driving up to the open garage at the rear and finding
Roberta placidly weeding a bed while David Andrew
kicked and gurgled on a blanket nearby, Palliser suddenly
felt that it wouldn't be a bad idea at all to have a big alert
dog right beside those two. Behind a fence and a gate. A
gate with a lock.

121

He locked the garage and came to lift her to her feet and kiss her. "Listen, Robin, I think we'd better figure on getting a fence around the yard."

"I know we should—on account of the baby, later on when he's walking. With everything going up, maybe we had better do it now. Of course it wouldn't need to be much of a fence—wooden pickets or something, about three feet high."

Thinking about that great big German shepherd, Palliser said, "Higher. Say six."

Roberta laughed. "You cops—you get nervous on account of all the violence you see. We can get some estimates."

Saturday night was sometimes eventful for the night watch, but this one wasn't. There was only one accident with one killed, and the only other thing turned up at midnight when they had a call from a bar on Second. Galeano and Schenke went out to see what it was.

"I wasn't never so surprised in all my life," the bartender told them. He was a little fellow with a great black handlebar moustache. "I thought he was just passed out, like always. He comes in here four-five times a week, usually he's only got money for the wine, see. He's on a pension some kind, I think. I know him—he lives around the corner on Columbia, his name's Howard. He's got a wife won't let him drink at home. I don't mind him—he never makes no trouble, sits there quiet in the corner and usually just falls asleep across the table. Most of the guys come in here don't mind him. Only, time I come to close up just now, I try to wake him up and, my God, he's deader than a mackerel!"

They looked at the corpse. He looked to be in his seventies; it was probably a natural death. They called the morgue, and went around to the address the bartender supplied and told his wife, who was annoyed at being waked up and didn't go into any hysterics.

It was, for Saturday night in Los Angeles, quiet.

*   *   *

Sunday morning, and Wanda Larsen off. They wouldn't see Piggott until after church. Mendoza wandered in at eight-thirty, and listened to Higgins and Conway tell him about the prowler and Blackwood while he glanced at the brief report the night watch had left.

"There weren't any neighbors home yesterday—in a neighborhood like that, they probably all work," said Higgins. "It's a funny one, Luis—one look at the place would tell anybody there wasn't any loot there. Let's hope the lab gets something."

There were still some names left on that list of heisters to find; let the rest of the men go out on that legwork. When it got to be nine o'clock and a reasonable time to expect people to be up on Sunday morning, Higgins and Conway went back to Ocean View Avenue.

At the house on the left of the late Mr. Blackwood's, the door was opened by a middle-aged man in a violently striped bathrobe. He looked at the badges, looked excited, and said, "So something did happen next door! When we got home last night, Mrs. Wells across the street came and said about a police car, and then an ambulance— What happened? Is Mr. Blackwood all right?" They told him what had happened; his wife, hair in curlers and wearing a housecoat, came to listen with exclamations.

"That poor old man! He was kind of grouchy, didn't like the kids coming in his yard, but I guess he didn't deserve anything like that! Say, Joe, I wonder—"

He nodded vigorously. "So do I, Martha. Those people."

"Well, what we wanted to ask you, Mr.—"

"Pugh."

"What?" said Conway.

"Pugh, Pugh. My name's Pugh."

"Oh, yes, sir. It seems to have happened sometime on Friday evening. The autopsy will tell us more but right now that's what we're assuming. Did you happen to see anyone around the house next door about then?"

"We sure did," said Pugh. "See, these are kind of narrow lots, houses close together, and us and the people on

the other side of Mr. Blackwood's, we been interested to
see what kind of people bought the house. Find out what
they're like, you know, are they going to leave the radio
on all day, or keep the yard up, and like that. And when
we saw those freaks, my God, I was out workin' in the
yard, it was about eight o'clock Friday night, still light,
you know, and I come in and said to Martha, my God, I
said, I sure hope I haven't just seen our new neighbors—"

"And of course I went to look, and in a while I saw
them all come out in the backyard and then go right in
again, and it wasn't till after dark—I was watching—they
left. We sure wondered if they was the ones bought the
house, but now you tell us about this, I just bet it was
them. Did it. They was sure freaks."

"Can you describe them? How many were there?"

"Two men and two women," said Pugh. "More or less,
you might say. You know how these freaks look! One of
the men was black, rest of 'em white. They all looked, oh,
early twenties maybe. The black one had a real bushy
Afro hairdo—other man had the hair down to here, dark-
brown like, and a beard and sideburns. Like they do, you
know. The two girls, just long hair—both kind of dark
colored. And they all looked dirty, sloppy, well, like hippies. The jeans and T-shirts."

"Did they come in a car?"

"Sure did. Drove right up in front. I got a look at that
out the front window. It was a beat-up old Chevy, brown."

"Well, that's a funny one," said Higgins. "I suppose
we'd better check that they aren't the new owners. Thanks
very much, Mr. Pugh. We may want you to make a statement about this."

"Sure, have to help out the law. We didn't know him
very good, but I sure hope you catch whoever did that. An
awful thing," said Pugh.

The people on the other side were named Bowerbank,
a younger couple, but they said much the same things.
Noticing the freaks, they had devoutly hoped they weren't
the new neighbors. They added to the description that the
black one had been wearing a yellow shirt with so-called

peace symbols all over it. Mr. Bowerbank said regretfully, "If it was them did that to Mr. Blackwood, my God, I coulda got their license plate for you easy, I was out in the parking trimming the edge, but I never thought. If I'd just known—well, hindsight like they say—"

Higgins and Conway went back to the office and tried to reach Odum on the phone. Sunday would be a busy day for real-estate salesmen; but after a few tries, they finally found him in the office and asked about who had bought the house, described the freaks.

"Listen, are you nuts?" said Odum. "The ones like that go around buying houses? A Mrs. Widdemer bought the house. She's a nice quiet lady, divorcée I think, and she's got a little girl about ten and a poodle."

So that drew a picture for them. And a funny sort of picture it was.

Mendoza was brooding over the cards on his desk. He still thought better with the cards in his hands. Methodically he stacked the deck for a crooked deal, and found he was still in practice.

Those love beads. He felt ambivalent about Hackett's little idea; it could be, it mightn't be. But he couldn't read anything else into the key business but that it linked X to the hotel.

There'd be people coming in today to sign statements. Mrs. Cohen, on Cicely Upton. The A.P.B. hadn't turned up John Upton or his car. The other one hadn't turned up Sid Belcher. People to sign statements about the prowler who'd killed Elsa Short—and it was to be hoped the lab would give them some lead on him. Robineau and his niece, on the second restaurant heist . . . that had been a queer little case, where that restaurant had cropped up before.

There'd be arraignments coming up next week—William Linblad, that Parsons who hadn't meant to kill his wife.

The outside phone buzzed at him and he picked it up. "Lieutenant Mendoza, Robbery-Homicide."

"Captain Kettler, Pasadena. Say, Lieutenant, we asked

for a mug shot of that escaped con, Terry Conover. We've now got a witness—he just came to in the hospital—who says it was Conover who pulled a heist here last Thursday night. Liquor store—he got away with about five C's."

"Was he alone?"

"All alone, with a .45 of some kind. The witness is ex-Army and ought to know."

"*Interesante.* And nothing to do about it, but it's nice to know."

"Well, we thought you'd be interested. No make on any car, of course. Any good to get the press to run his picture, you think?"

"If you've been at this thankless job long, Captain, you'll know about the citizenry—*they have eyes and see not.* We can try. You never know."

"What I thought."

"I'll see the papers are called and send over copies. Maybe they'll run them tomorrow. You never know, with the press."

As he put the phone down, Sergeant Lake came in and said, "Mr. and Mrs. Linblad are here, want to see you. They're nice people, just scared and confused."

Mendoza sighed. "Shove them in, I'll talk to them."

Glasser picked up Wanda Larsen at her apartment at noon, and took her to the horse show out at a big fairgrounds. It was her idea; he didn't know anything about horses. But he got interested after a while, the horses were so beautiful, sleek and proud with arched necks. Wanda had brought a picnic lunch. Some of the horses had riders, and some drivers in carts, and some of them jumped fences, and there was judging with colored ribbons.

"I suppose there are different kinds of horses for the different things they're supposed to do," said Glasser, though they all just looked like horses to him.

Wanda looked at him, pink-cheeked and excited. "Oh, Henry. I see I'll have to educate you. I wouldn't go across the street to see the usual horse show—thoroughbreds." She didn't like thoroughbreds, whatever they were. "These are *Morgans,* Henry. The only American breed there is. Morgans do everything—the most versatile horse there is, and the very nicest."

"Oh," said Glasser.

"Before my father died, we lived on a ranch, you know. Right next to the Bluebell Morgan Farm up in Marysville. I've always loved Morgans. If I could ever own a Morgan, I'd be in heaven," said Wanda wistfully.

Hackett and Higgins had just finished talking to another one off the list of heisters—he had an alibi for Friday night—when a telex came through from the chief of police in Fresno. John Upton had once been charged with assault when he was living there, but the charge was later withdrawn; he'd accused a used-car salesman of palming off a lemon on him, and given him a beating.

"Not much of a charge," said Hackett, grinning. "A lot of people must have had the impulse to do that." There wasn't any other record on him there; he had been employed by a local garage, had a good work-record. The A.P.B. was acknowledged; he had a sister living in the area and she'd be contacted.

A report came up from Ballistics: the S. and W. .22 Landers had handed over yesterday was the gun that had killed the Booths. Hackett told Lake to start the machinery for a warrant on Sid Belcher; that would come through tomorrow.

At one o'clock Dr. Ducharme and his wife turned up; the hospital had released him and they were going home tomorrow, but he'd look at some mug shots now. Landers and Conway had just come back empty-handed from the hunt for the heisters, and Landers took the Ducharmes down to R. and I., lingered talking to Phil until the captain chased him away.

At three o'clock a Traffic unit called in; they had come across a body. It was a wonder, said the Traffic man, it hadn't been spotted before, and maybe it had been and the citizens just not bothered to do anything. It was in the parking lot of the Convention Center at Pico and Figueroa, a young girl, looked as if she'd been raped.

"It always happens," said Hackett. "I told you, George. Eighty-six on Friday, eighty-eight yesterday, and touching ninety today—the heat wave building up, and it always means more business for us." They looked into Mendoza's office to tell him about it; he was re-reading the autopsy report on Mrs. Branch and just grunted.

At the Convention Center, the black-and-white was parked along Pico; Hackett pulled up behind it and they got out.

"Looks as if she was dumped from a car," said one of the men. She was sprawled out there, just beyond the low planting marking off the sidewalk from the parking lot. She was half-naked—a pair of panties pulled down around her ankles, a knitted sleeveless tunic still on her upper body, sandals on her feet; her long brown hair was tangled, and you couldn't tell if she'd been pretty because she'd been strangled and her face was suffused and dark, with a tongue-tip protruding. Beside her, as if it had been just dropped there as an afterthought, was a cheap white shoulder bag.

There'd be nothing here for the lab; obviously, she'd been killed elsewhere and dumped. They called an ambulance, nudged the purse into a plastic evidence bag and went back to the lab to get it printed. There were a lot of latents on it—it was patent leather—and when Duke had finished lifting them, they opened it and looked at the contents. They were expectable: lipsticks, powder puff, a billfold of imitation ostrich, Kleenex, all the usual miscellany. In the billfold was a single dollar bill, and some I.D. in the little plastic slots.

She'd been, if this was her bag, Stephanie Midkiff, an address on Leeward Avenue. There was a school library card from the same high school the Linblad kid had attended. Snapshots, probably friends, family. "Why hasn't she been reported missing?" said Higgins. "Rigor had set in. I'd have a guess she was killed last night sometime."

"Maybe she has been," said Hackett. "We'd better go and ask."

The address on Leeward was a single house, a big old two-story house that had probably been here longer than any house around. When the front door finally opened to repeated ringing at the bell, a teen-age girl faced them. "We'd like to talk to Mrs. Midkiff," said Higgins.

"Well, I'll see if she'll come—the baby's got colic," she said. "What do you want?" They waited, and she said, "Ma! It's two men want to see you—"

"Tell her it's about Stephanie," said Hackett.

"Do you know where she *is*? I been worried, but I couldn't get Ma to pay attention— Ma! Please come!"

Mrs. Midkiff, when she finally came, looked tired and cross and worried. "I never buy at the door," she said, and Hackett showed her the badge.

"I'm afraid we've got some bad news for you about Stephanie. Is she your daughter?"

"Sure, that's right. You *police*?" She looked at Higgins. "Yeah, I guess so. What about Stephanie?"

"I'm afraid she's dead," said Hackett. There was a good deal of noise coming from inside the house; he had to raise his voice.

"Stephanie? What you mean, she's—"

The girl burst into tears. "Oh, I knew something was wrong! I tried to tell you, Ma, but with the baby fussing and the kids acting up—we should've *done* something when she didn't come home!"

The woman looked at the two big men, stunned, not taking it in yet. She had been a pretty woman once, dark hair and dark eyes. She said, "Stephanie—she'll be at Ruthie's, Linda. You know how often she stays over— she's all right, I don't mind—she just didn't think to say she was, is all. What do you m—" She stopped and went a curious muddy white. "My Stephanie—*dead*? What are you telling me? Oh, my God, how? Was it an accident or—"

"Can we come in?" asked Hackett.

Inside was confusion. There seemed to be twenty kids in

the big living room, all ages and all noisy; in the midst of all the other noise a baby howled steadily. The girl, who was about fourteen and seemed to be more on the ball than her mother at the moment—she'd probably been up nights with the baby, both Hackett and Higgins thought from experience—chased the kids out and got her mother settled in a chair. It was an untidy big room, but it felt, indescribably, like a family place.

Mrs. Midkiff listened to them silently, tears coursing down her cheeks. When they'd told her all they knew, she said heavily, "Linda, I'm not up to it—you got to call your father." The girl nodded and went out. "I thought she was at Ruthie's—they've been best friends all through school. I never thought a thing about it—she stays over at the Runnells' now 'n' then, and they're nice decent people, go to our church, it was all right. I thought that's where she was. Now you come and tell me— But she's only sixteen. My oldest, Stephanie. We got eleven, and it's a job, keep food on the table, but I'm a good manager and Steve takes extra jobs—and it don't matter how many you got, every child's as dear to you as if it was the only one—you telling me Stephanie's dead—like *that*—"

The girl came back. She was a skinny little thing with big dark eyes. "He's coming," she said. "He was crying. He said we should help the police any way, and he'd bring Father Michael."

She nodded. "But she was a good girl, my Stephanie," she said to Hackett and Higgins. "She didn't go racketing around—she was raised decent—how could such a thing happen?"

"We don't know yet, Mrs. Midkiff," said Hackett. "This Ruthie—they were best friends? Where was Stephanie yesterday, do you know? Did she go to see Ruthie?"

She looked at the girl. "I been so bothered with the baby—"

"She went out about three o'clock," said Linda. "She was going over to Ruthie's. And she never said about staying over, and she always did if she was going to—I was worried—" Her chin quivered but she'd stopped crying.

"Ruthie Runnells. Where?" asked Higgins.

"On W-W-Wilshire Place, half a block down. Three thirty-seven."

They didn't try to explain about the autopsy, the necessary statements; that could come later. They walked down the block and found the Runnells' house on Wilshire Place.

Ruthie Runnells was sixteen, the same age as Stephanie, and she was a fat blond girl, a flawless pink-and-white complexion her one asset. Her mother was fat too, and blond, and she burst into tears along with Ruthie when they told her about Stephanie.

"And—I—was—mad at her!" sobbed Ruthie. "I knew —it wasn't—her fault—but I was mad! I can't help— b-b-being fat!"

"You saw her yesterday, Ruthie?" asked Hackett. "Do you know where she—"

"I was the one made her!" sobbed Ruthie. "Oh, I deserve to get killed too—it was all my fault! A lot of the girls do it—everybody *says*—and it was—it was—sort of an *adventure!* She didn't want to—it was me made her— and I been scared to tell anybody!"

"Do what?" asked Hackett.

"Darling, if you know anything to help the police—"

Ruthie flung herself into her mother's arms. "Oh, I should've told you! I should've told somebody—but how could I know— It was all my fault! I'm sorry— I'm sorry! Everybody does it—the new fun thing, Rita Marks said and she's a *senior*—it was like an adventure!" She sat up and sobbed and hiccupped. "The boys put their phone numbers in library books at school—like, Tom, and a number—and you call and talk and maybe make a date—"

"Ruthie!" Her mother was shocked. "You know you're not allowed to date boys we don't know! I never heard of—"

"I *know!*" she said passionately. "That was—was why!
131

And—it—all—turned out— I was mad at her, and it wasn't her fault, and now—it was *him,* the one with the little moustache—*he killed her!*"

"Look, Ruthie," said Hackett gently, "if you'd just tell us what did happen, that you know about—" Mrs. Runnells was making shocked noises, incoherent as the girl.

She sat there, a fat kid hiccupping and crying, and she should have looked ridiculous but she said with incongruous dignity, "I *am* on a diet. That the doctor gave me, with the thyroid pills. I've got to sick to it. But—I egged her on, and we called that number, in the biology textbook. It said Rex, and a number. And he sounded sort of nice. Over the phone. He said, meet him at five yesterday —that place a lot of kids go—the Hangout, on Seventh— he'd have a pal along for me—"

"And did he?" asked Hackett.

"He—he—said go take a walk, kid, you're too fat! It was after Stephanie got in his car—and— There was another boy, he didn't say anything—"

"Can you describe them? What about the car?" asked Higgins.

"He was about twenty, I guess. He had a moustache. The other one, I don't know, he wasn't as old. Sixteen maybe. The car—it was new, it smelled new—and it was bright yellow."

Mendoza had just got up to leave, thinking dire thoughts about Scientific Investigation, when Sergeant Lake came in. "They finally got round to sending you a lab report on Branch."

"So I may not complain to I.A. after all." Mendoza sat down again and opened the manila envelope. Scarne had appended a note: "Sorry for the delay but we were waiting on the Feds. Hope it was worth the delay."

In a way, it was. It was interesting, and Mendoza's eyebrows climbed as he read, but there wasn't any real reason for surprise.

There had been a number of latent prints in Mrs. Branch's apartment, most of them hers; another set had been identified as belonging to the maid, Agnes Harvey, when she'd let them take her prints. That, reflected Mendoza, was neither here nor there; Agnes had a legitimate reason for being there. There were two other sets of prints at various places in the apartment; nine fairly good ones lifted from drawers, cupboards, and a china saucer: probably male prints. There were five others, possibly female, also picked up from drawers and in the bathroom.

The saucer, one of the regular set in the kitchen, had been used as an ashtray on the kitchen table. Somebody had smoked about three marijuana cigarettes there; the ashes had been analyzed. Good quality marijuana, if there was such a thing. There hadn't been any hard liquor in the apartment, but there'd been a bottle of sherry wine, and somebody had drunk some of it out of a teacup. The lab had lip prints from that.

"*Caray*," said Mendoza to himself, "and that was after he found he had to wait for Perkins to leave the desk." With the body in the next room—

All the prints were unknown to the LAPD files, so they'd been sent to Washington. The kickback had just come through. The possibly female prints were not known, but the others, probably male, had been on file. They belonged to one Alan Keel, who'd been picked up for possession in the company of a twice-convicted seller, three years back, in Seymour, Connecticut. It didn't sound like a very big town, and possibly it hadn't many police officers; at any rate, the prisoners had been brought in and were in the process of being booked in when the other man seized a gun from the booking officer and they escaped the building and eventually the town, in a stolen car. The other man, Webster Niles, had a record elsewhere and had since been arrested, tried and sentenced to prison in Illinois for selling heroin, but Keel had not been heard of again. Nobody knew if that was his real name; but at least the F.B.I. cross-indexed system could assure S.I.D., LAPD, that his prints were not on record with them under another name. The pair had got away before a mug shot had been taken of Keel, so none was available. He was generally described from that one abortive arrest as Caucasian, middle height and weight, brown hair, eyes blue, about twenty-three.

"¡Santa María!" said Mendoza, annoyed. Fingerprints could be very useful sometimes, but at others, he had thought before, the scientific investigation was only tantalizing. Here were some nice fingerprints, and they were no damned help at all. Well, some: identified as belonging to a probable user, as the X who smoked the grass in Mrs. Branch's apartment, waiting a safe time to get out of the hotel. And, appended Mendoza to that, possibly the grass was the reason—aside from getting stuck with a body— he hadn't gone on to more robbery in other apartments there.

He felt frustrated. He clapped on his hat and went home. There he found most of his household out in the backyard staring up at the alder tree. Cedric was barking, and the cats lined up on the back porch silently reminding everybody it was time for their dinner.

"He's back," said Alison unnecessarily as Mendoza came down from the garage. "Our little feathered friend. Him and the missus both, all ready to raise another family."

"*¡El Pájaro!*" the twins were shouting excitedly, and the mockingbird, with a flash of gray and white wings, uttered his all-too-familiar war cry, the first four bars of "Yankee Doodle."

"If you want a project for the month," said Mendoza, "why don't you put a phonograph out here and teach that damned bird the rest of it?"

"I wonder if he would pick it up," said Alison meditatively, and Mendoza regarded her with alarm.

Palliser was off on Mondays. He consulted the yellow pages over breakfast and called three contractors to get estimates on the fence. Only one man offered to come and look at the job today.

When Mendoza got to the office, Hackett and Higgins were waiting to give him a verbal report on Stephanie. Wanda was typing up a formal one for the files. "Another stupid thing," said Mendoza. "We seem to see more of it every day. The kids, I know, they haven't the experience, but— So where do you go on it first?"

"I hope," said Hackett, "we may get some news of Rex and his yellow car at that Hangout. If we have to hunt for that book—" He groaned. "Ruthie told us what it was—a biology textbook, *Life in Our World,* and it's a supplementary text to first year biology so God knows how many copies the school library might have. Stephanie copied the phone number—at Ruthie's urging— and took the book back to the library on Thursday."

"So, *buena suerte,*" said Mendoza.

"There was another break-in last night—market owner just called in, and Matt and Tom went out to look at it. If we're going to get with this, George, let's do it."

"And I," said Mendoza, "will be back at the Clark Hotel awhile." But as they came out to the anteroom, Lake was on the phone and beckoning at Grace and Conway at the door. Presently he put the phone down and scribbled. "What's up, Jimmy?"

"That was one of our pigeons," said Lake. "It just came to his notice that there's a reward on those bank heisters. The Feds made them for sure—that teller identified their mug shots. A couple of ex-cons from Chicago, Denton and Walker. This pigeon says they've got a room at the Ambassador Hotel."

"Oh, now, really," said Hackett. "Right under our noses?"

"Well, they don't know they've been identified, I suppose it's possible."

"Anything's possible," said Grace. "We'd better check it out anyway."

"That is indicated," said Mendoza. "We had some mug shots—the Feds sent them over at the time—" The bank job was two weeks old.

Wanda found them and Grace tucked them into his breast pocket. He and Conway took off for the Ambassador, Hackett and Higgins went out, and Mendoza was about to follow them when a big sorrowful-looking man came in slowly, his shoulders stooped, shabby in an old gray suit, and said his name was Steve Midkiff.

"When the police officers talked to me yesterday, they said about—identifying the body. My Stephanie."

"Oh, yes, Mr. Midkiff. I'll take you down." At the morgue, the attendants had cleaned up the body, and looking at Stephanie, Mendoza saw that she'd been a pretty girl, brown-haired, brown eyes, nice skin. She looked very young.

"I don't understand how this happened," said Midkiff. "Oh, I know about it—the kids and the phone numbers —but it don't make sense. Stephanie knew better than to do a fool trick like that. But the kids—" He made a defeated gesture. "Try to raise them right, and just one minute they forget everything they've been taught—and that's just enough. What—happens now? Do you think you can catch the one did it?"

"We hope so, Mr. Midkiff. We've got a couple of good ideas where to look."

"Well, that's good," said Midkiff heavily. "But then what? You put him on trial for murder and even if he's found guilty, the judge gives him maybe a couple years, and then he's out on parole ready to kill somebody else's girl."

"We're only paid to catch them," said Mendoza. "I know, Mr. Midkiff."

"You got a daughter?" he asked dully.

"One of each—twins."

"Oh. Well, you worry. You try your best, but you can't help worrying. But you know, it's funny—this is one thing I just never worried about, with Stephanie. She was a good girl. Sensible—I thought she was sensible."

"Just as you said—the moment's impulse."

"Yeah," said Midkiff. "Yeah. I guess so. People say damn fool things. Our neighbor lady, she come over last night to say she's sorry. She said, but we got ten left. As if— When can we have her?"

"We'll let you know. You understand there has to be an autopsy?"

"Yeah." Midkiff sighed.

On his way over to the Clark Hotel Mendoza thought about that; you worried, all right. About what world Terry and Johnny would grow up to, ten years from now. But there was a saying, the things you worry about never happen. Like hell, said Mendoza to himself.

At the hotel, he started out briskly with Quigley. Quigley had never, he said, heard the name of Alan Keel before. It was no use repeating the description to him, it was too general. "Mr. Whitlow's here," he told Mendoza. "I suppose it's all right? To—clear out the apartment, I mean."

Mendoza reassured him and sought out all the maids. He got no reaction from any of them to the name, and if any of them had recognized it he thought he would have. He went up to the fifth floor and looked for Agnes Harvey.

137

He found her past the open door of Mrs. Branch's apartment. She was saying, "Oh, I couldn't, sir. It's too much."

"No, really, we'd like you to have it," said Walter Whitlow. "Mrs. Branch thought a lot of you, you know, and we appreciate it that you—took good care of her here." He was a little embarrassed. They both looked round at Mendoza. Whitlow had a long brown mink coat in his hands.

Agnes Harvey's lips tightened a little as she recognized Mendoza. She was a good-looking woman, dark brown, with regular straight features, a fine deep-bosomed figure. She said quickly, "I hope it's all right, Lieutenant—the police are finished here?"

"It's all right."

She looked away from him. "I really couldn't, Mr. Whitlow. It's worth a lot of money, and you've given me so much already—all her nice dresses and good underclothes—"

"You know she thought a lot of you, Agnes, she'd like you to have it."

"Well, I thought a lot of her," she said. There were tears in her eyes; she dabbed at them with one hand. There was a neat pile of clothing on the couch, two suitcases standing beside the door. "If you really think so, Mr. Whitlow—"

"You take it," he said, heaping it into her arms. "Have you—got any further, Lieutenant?"

"We've got a name," said Mendoza, leaning on the doorpost. "Just a name. Alan Keel. Have either of you ever heard it before?" He watched them.

Both of them looked completely blank. "Never," said Whitlow. "Is he the one who—?"

"Possibly," said Mendoza.

"I never heard that name," said Agnes. "I just hope you don't think any of us had anything to do with it now. Coming asking for my fingerprints—"

Mendoza thanked them, asked if Louise Wilding was upstairs. When he retreated down the corridor, Agnes was still thanking Whitlow; and something was teasing at the back of Mendoza's mind. Something about Whitlow— a very brief expression in his eyes—

Upstairs he found Louise Wilding busy in the Bolts' apartment, and got her out in the hall a moment. She was nice-looking too, lighter than Agnes and with a slighter figure. She said she'd never heard the name of Alan Keel. "I understand you refused to tell Sergeant Hackett about any of the men you've dated, Mrs. Wilding."

"Why should I? I'm an honest woman, Lieutenant." She faced him squarely. "It's my private business, and if you think one of them might be a criminal, or even know somebody who'd do a thing like this, you can think again. I like to think I'm respectable. I've had one husband desert me, and I'm not about to rush into marriage again with the first man comes looking. I go out now and then, but you can be sure it's with men who know how to be gentlemen, and not common criminals."

Mendoza grinned at her. "So, stand up for yourself. I'll believe you." But all this was getting nowhere. He hadn't got any reaction to the name; if the man who owned those prints was connected to the hotel in any way, it wasn't under that name.

But as he got back into the Ferrari, it suddenly came to him what that faint expression in Whitlow's eyes had been.

Relief.

"¿Cómo no?" said Mendoza to himself thoughtfully. And what did that say?

Landers and Piggott, having looked at the break-in, explained to the market owner that there wasn't much to go on. They could call out a man to dust the door, places where stolen items had been, but it wasn't likely there'd be any evidence. This was a little neighborhood market, and the back door on the alley had been forced; as far as the owner could tell them, what was missing was cigarettes, a few bottles of wine. He said apologetically, "There's a burglar alarm, but it's just to hope I scare robbers off with the noise—it's not hooked up to the police station, it costs too much. I had new locks put on and that cost a fortune. I been thinking of quitting, just go to work for somebody, no responsibility."

"But you know, Matt," said Landers, "that sort of rings a bell with me. I know, the little overnight break-ins, a dime a dozen, how many have we had—but just now, looking at that place, I had the thought—very roughly, it's the same M.O. If you can say there is any."

"As what?" asked Piggott.

"As a spate of little jobs like that we've had the last couple of months. I didn't go out on all of them, but— there've been drugstores, other markets, a gift shop, and that place—I was on that one—that sells all the magic tricks and unfunny practical jokes— If I remember right, there were seven or eight, maybe more, all broken into by the back door and all with a pry-bar. Just the brute strength."

"Not much M.O. about that," said Piggott.

"No, I know, but I just wonder if all those haven't been the same joker." When they got back to the office Landers asked Wanda to look up those files, and studied them. There'd been other break-ins in that time, but there were fourteen that bore vaguely the same earmarks. All small jobs; the loot would add up, but it was penny ante. There were four drugstores (barbiturates taken there), three markets, the gift shop with some expensive costume jewelry taken, the magic shop, and five coin-operated Laundromats with the coin meters emptied. All of those had had their rear doors pried open; not surprisingly, in the downtown area, all of the rear doors had been on alleys. It just said to Landers that it could be the same one, or more than one, who had pulled all those jobs.

And whether it was or wasn't, it didn't much matter because there was no lead on it at all.

The desk clerk at the Ambassador Hotel looked at Grace and Conway in alarm and said, "Some of our guests? Here? Criminals?"

"Well, we had a tip," said Grace, and produced the mug shots of Denton and Walker. The clerk looked at them and turned paler; he was a willowy young man in a gray plaid suit.

"Oh, dear," he said. "Yes, I think— I mean, in these pictures they're not dressed up, and one of them needs a shave, but I think—oh, dear, I'd better call Mr. Montague, he's the manager—"

Montague was an older man, competent and brisk. He studied the mug shots seriously and said, "I've seen them around. I think they've been here about ten days, two weeks. I didn't register them in, but—" He thought. "I saw this man over at the travel-agency counter sometime last week." He trailed them over there curiously.

The pug-nosed young man at the travel-agency counter said, "Oh, I remember this one, yes. He bought two tickets on a guided tour—wait a minute, now, it's come to me—a three-day bus tour to the Hearst castle, it was, with a side trip to Sequoia National Park."

"Do tell," said Grace. "Well, so far as we know, they're new to California, evidently they want to see some of it. What name did he give, if any?"

"It was a traveler's check made out to John Dalton—" Conway yelped in pleased mirth and the hotel men stared at him. "He had identification—"

But that covered so many things, so easily falsified: easy to get a driver's license under any name, the bank-account number, whatever. They looked at the register; the man calling himself John Dalton was registered in a double room with a James Kelly, on the fifth floor. "You don't want me to go with you, do you?" asked Montague.

"No, no," said Grace. At this hour the big hotel was very quiet. They rode up in the elevator and had a little hunt for the room number, down several corridors. When they finally found it, Grace knocked gently on the door, waited and knocked again.

There was a stir and mumble beyond the door. "Who's it?" asked a thick voice.

"Western Union, sir," said Grace.

Another stir, another sleepy voice. "What is it, Dick? Mus' be middle o' the night—"

"What the hell, telegram for me, who the hell'd be sendin' me a telegram? Just a minute—" It sounded as if they both had hangovers.

The door was pulled open cautiously. Both Conway and Grace had their guns out. "Surprise, surprise," said Conway. "You're both under arrest. Mr. Denton and Mr. Walker, just as our pigeon said."

"Oh, for Christ's sake!" said Denton disgustedly. Walker was still in bed, and neither of them in any state to put up a fight. They got dressed under the guns, and were put into cuffs, and then Grace and Conway had a look around. They found a good deal of the bank loot, two Colt .45's, and a lot of fancy new clothes Denton and Walker had bought.

"You ain't give us our rights," said Denton on the way to the elevator. "You got to tell us our rights." He probably knew that set piece as well as any cop, but it seemed to give him some satisfaction to hear it.

Back at Parker Center they called the Feds to tell them about the capture. The Feds had a warrant on the heisters and came over posthaste to pick them up, and what remained of the loot. The pigeon, who had a long pedigree of petty counts, was at the moment clear of the law, and had spelled out his name carefully; he had a job as bus boy at the Ambassador Hotel.

Hackett and Higgins were a little surprised to find the place known as the Hangout open at this hour. It was hard to say what turned a place into the home-away-from-home of the teen-age kids, but evidently this was one of them. It was a long narrow storefront in the middle of a block on Seventh, not attractive at first glance, the ordinary quick-lunch place. But inside there were little booths with red-checked plastic tablecloths, a long counter with padded stools, a handwritten menu up on the wall behind that. Beyond the space behind the counter, through a square doorless opening, was visible a little kitchen with a grill, stove, refrigerator.

Only two people were there, sitting in one of the booths, a fat motherly looking woman drinking coffee and a fat bald man reading a newspaper. The woman looked up as Hackett and Higgins came in and said instantly, "Here are a couple of cops, Harry."

The man looked up. He was older than they'd thought at first, perhaps seventy. He had a genial round face and a fine even set of store teeth. He got up with great cordiality and said, "So they are, Millie. Morning, what can we do for you? We never had the law visit us before. Excuse me, I'm Harry Hart, late of the Dubuque, Iowa, force. Not that we can claim to be as good as you big-city boys, still we try to run a tight little force there. Sit down. Like some coffee?" He got them settled in a booth and supplied with thick mugs.

"Well, nice to meet you, Mr. Hart. We understand your place is pretty popular with the kids, the teen-agers around here." Hackett manfully drank black coffee minus sugar.

"That we are," said Hart, looking rather amused. "Came out here after I retired, tired of the winters back there, and opened up this place mainly to give us something to do, but I must admit we've kind of enjoyed it." He fetched himself more coffee and sat down opposite them, and the woman came to squeeze in beside him. "It's funny, how we got all the kids coming."

"It's natural," said his wife firmly. "We raised six of our own, I guess we ought to know something about kids. I'll tell you how it was—the first bunches of them came in, I can't say I liked it. All their noisy transistor radios and so on—and it didn't matter to us, maybe losing their business. We set up the rules and regulations, see—they want to come in here, no radios playing, no loud talk, no swearing, no dirty jokes, and they've got to behave decent, not leave the tables in a mess. And you know, kids like the rules and regulations. And so many kids these days, the silly way parents act, afraid to say no, you can't do that—a lot of kids, they've never had to keep to any rules

and regulations, it's a kind of novelty, and they like it."
She smiled. "Before we knew it, we had the kids around
all the time, after school, weekends. But mainly we get
the good ones—the really wild ones, they go someplace
else. But our kids, our regulars, I like to feel maybe we've
done some good here. Why, that Whitney girl came to me
before she went to her own mother, and I know most of
them, boys and girls alike, they've got different ideas about
police from listening to Harry."

"That's good, Mrs. Hart," said Higgins. In a quiet way
here, the Harts were making influences felt.

"But what brings you here?" asked Hart. "None of the
kids in trouble with the law?"

"We don't know—maybe you can help us, maybe you
know this one we're after." Hackett told them about
Stephanie. They hadn't known her, she hadn't been one
of their regulars, but they were shocked and sobered.

"In a way, it's worse than if she'd been a wild one running with any boy she could pick up," said Millie. "A nice
girl, and doing a fool thing like that, but kids— He told
her to meet him *here?* Rex— I can't call any Rex to mind."

"No," agreed Hart. "But come to think, boys, if she was
a nice girl—and he'd get that, talking to her on the phone
—he might've said that to make her think he was O.K.,
if she'd know what kind of place this is."

"That could be," said Hackett. "He's said to have a
new bright yellow car. No idea what make."

"Doesn't ring a bell," said Hart. "She met him here
on Saturday? About five o'clock?"

"The other girl said they didn't come in," said Higgins.
"He was waiting outside on the sidewalk with this other
boy. He'd told the girls to carry flowers so he'd know
them—they'd picked some roses from the Runnells' yard."
Millie snorted.

"Now I tell you, you might go and see Eddy," said
Hart ruminatively. "Eddy's a great one for cars—an expert, you might say. He's going to be an engineer. He
comes in here afternoons and Saturdays, to help out. It's
a job keeping the dishes washed up, and Eddy's a good

worker. Bright boy. He might remember seeing that car —not likely there'd be two like it around at the same time. Not many of the kids come here got cars, it's not like out in the suburbs. And if this Rex was here Saturday afternoon with his yellow car, ten to one it'd be parked in the public lot next door. Not often a place in the street."

"Which is a thought," agreed Hackett. Teen-age boys and cars— "Where do we find Eddy?"

"High school up on Ninth. Eddy Gamino. He's a senior."

"Well, thanks very much," said Higgins. They were both pleased with the Harts: nice people, doing a good job here.

"Any time, boys. Good luck on it."

When they got up to the high school on Ninth there were three black-and-whites outside and a uniformed sergeant with a riot gun on the front steps. "What the hell's going on?" asked Hackett.

The sergeant, taking them in comprehensively as fellow cops, said, "Sodom and Gomorrah. One of the teachers just got raped in her classroom. The other boys are inside chasing him—he's got a knife."

"They can probably use some help—" But as they started in, a crowd of uniformed Traffic men came out with a hulking big black boy yelling obscenities at them. They already had him in cuffs, and took him away in a hurry. An ambulance purred up and the attendants hurried in with a stretcher. The sergeant put the riot gun in the back of one of the cars and drove away.

"A fellow said to me the other day," remarked Higgins, "these are interesting times to live in. Interesting! I could do with a lot less interest."

They saw the boys' vice-principal and asked for Eddy Gamino. He just looked resigned, told his secretary to have the boy brought in. Five minutes later, where they waited in the outer office with its inevitable golden-oak furniture, the secretary busy over her typewriter, a boy came in. He was a sharp-faced, thin, dark boy about eighteen, neatly if shabbily dressed; he had a long nose like Mendoza's, and like Mendoza's it twitched curiously when he saw the badges.

"Say," he said, "is it about Miss Beal? I just heard about it, I've been in the chemistry lab, I don't know anything to—"

"Something else. Mr. Hart thought you might be able to help us," said Hackett.

"Oh, Harry." The boy smiled. "He is the world's greatest, Harry. Did he say how? Anything I can do, Sergeant." Hackett was surprised; he'd only flashed the badge for a second. Eddy grinned. "I've got a photographic memory. It comes in handy."

"I'll bet," said Higgins. Thinking of Steve Dwyer, he looked at Eddy approvingly. Even in the midst of this mess and madness, the chaos of the inner-city schools, there remained the sane ones like Eddy, somehow getting an education. The smart ones you found anywhere, but all too often, here and now, they turned the smartness toward the wrong goals. It was encouraging to find the ones like Eddy still around.

Hackett was explaining about Stephanie, Saturday afternoon, Rex and the yellow car. "Gee, that's bad, if she was a nice girl," said Eddy. "She went here? I didn't know her. At Harry's, about five o'clock, he told her? Well, I was there from about two on, helping out in the kitchen. We're usually pretty busy Saturdays, and the only time I'd get a look at that public lot is when I go out back to empty the garbage, the wastebasket—"

"All we know about the car is, it's yellow and the other girl said it smelled new," said Hackett.

"Along about that time, I probably would be going out to empty the cans— We were busy. Let me take a look back," said Eddy. He'd sat down on the built-in bench along the wall, long legs sprawling, and now he shut his eyes. "There's four aisles of parking, about twelve slots to an aisle. Yeah— I can't pin the time down for you closer than between four-thirty and five, but—yeah," he said, eyes still shut. "I saw it. There were a couple of light

146

cream-yellow heaps—a Corvair, a Rambler—but just the one chrome yellow, real bright. I got it." He opened his eyes. "It was parked on the second aisle over from the back door of Harry's place. It was a Ford Mustang— chrome yellow all over—and sure enough brand new. It still had the price tag on the side window, and it was wearing a temporary license—paper strip on the back bumper. I'm sorry I can't give you that, I didn't look at it, to have it register—just saw that it was a temporary license. But that's probably the car you want."

"You've helped a lot, Eddy." Hackett didn't feel it was enough to say; he wished there were better words.

"Just glad I could help you, Sergeant. I hope you get him."

As they watched him out, Higgins said, "It's kind of encouraging, Art."

"Oh, it is," agreed Hackett. Thank God for the Eddys, still there among the chaos.

They went up to the school library and talked to the head librarian, a thin, dark young woman with owlish spectacles, Frances Giffard. On the library shelves were four copies of *Life In Our World,* and those they commandeered. With Miss Giffard's help, they had a look at every page of all four books in the next hour: among the various marginal notations, including names and phone numbers, they found no Rex.

By the files, the library owned thirty-four copies of that book. The rest of them would be checked out by students. "I could send an announcement around asking them to be turned in," said Miss Giffard, "but whether it'd do any good—"

"Well, you'd better do that," said Hackett. "And as the copies do get returned, you'll hang on to them for us, let us know."

"Oh, I will. That's terrible, about that poor girl— A person gets frightened," she said. "All the violence, all over. Yes, I will, Sergeant."

*   *   *

Landers and Piggott, back to looking for the heisters and bringing in the last one on that list, at two o'clock on Monday afternoon, were greeted by Lake with a telex from San Diego. They had Sid Belcher. He'd been stopped for an illegal left turn, and the Traffic men had spotted the plate number from the A.P.B. There was a girl with him, Jane Alice Adams; the A.P.B. hadn't said anything about her so they let her go. He'd tried to put up a fight, but was presently tucked away in the city jail. Would L.A. send somebody to pick him up?

Mendoza, coming in from a belated lunch to hear that, said, "You'd better go down and ferry him back, Tom. The warrant came through this morning."

"Oh, hell," said Landers. "All right. I'm not at all sure we shouldn't have included that girl on it, you know. She might have been with him when he shot the Booths."

"If so, we may hear about it, when we talk to him."

Landers got out the phone book and called the Hollywood airport to find out about flights down there; it only took thirty minutes.

Most of the papers had run the official mug shot of Terry Conover today.

Poring over all the official mug shots down in R. and I. yesterday, Dr. Ducharme hadn't made any of them as the nice young fellow in the bar.

Hackett and Higgins had just come in from lunch and were telling Mendoza about Eddy Gamino when Sergeant Lake brought in a lab report.

"¡Qué caso tan singular!" said Mendoza, glancing over it. "So here they are, amigos—your freaks on Blackwood. Now you just have to find them." He handed it over.

"I'll be damned!" said Hackett. The lab had picked up some latents—quite a lot of them—in the Blackwood house. They were all in LAPD records. They belonged to Gilbert Deleavey, Roselle Kruger and William Siebert, all of whom had records of possession, burglary, petty theft; the girl had done a little stretch for soliciting. The lab had considerably requisitioned their packages from

R. and I. and sent those along too. By their descriptions and mug shots, three of the four freaky hippies were seen at the Blackwood house on Friday night.

"But that's crazy," said Hackett. "A murder? These small-timers? It doesn't make sense, Luis."

"The lab doesn't make mistakes, *compadre*. You may have some trouble finding them, these addresses aren't very recent—but you'd better go and look. At least we know, whatever the reason, they were there . . . And I do wonder, about Whitlow—but *casi no es posible*—they were fond of Mother—" Mendoza was sitting on the end of his spine, cigarette smoldering on his lower lip, fiddling with those love beads.

"At least nothing new's gone down," said Higgins, looking at the lab report. "This is a very funny damned thing, Art—"

"Famous last words," said Mendoza.

"—these little drifters, turning up on a murder. But they were there, so I suppose we go have a look for them."

And three minutes later Mendoza's casual warning came true. Robbery-Homicide, on the Central beat in L.A., seldom lacked for business. Usually humdrum business. But this was the day they were presented with that unprecedented thing, the locked-room puzzle. It happened in fiction. And in fiction it was more entertaining.

Sergeant Lake put through the call from Lieutenant Carey at two twenty-eight. "Look," said Carey, "I've got a thing, Mendoza. I think—I'm afraid it'll belong to you eventually. It is a hell of a thing, and so far we can't make head or tail of it, but it could be something nasty. I feel it in my bones. It's a four-year-old missing—apartment on Hooper Avenue—all colored, good middle class, these are all a good type of people—and we've found some blood in the hall. I want to search the building, because she never came out, by what all the witnesses say—"

A four-year-old. You worried, of course. About the hostages to fortune. "Business for Homicide, Carey?"

"I'd lay a bet on it," said Carey. "Damn it to hell—"

When Mendoza slid the Ferrari into a loading zone along that block of Hooper Avenue, there was a little crowd in front of the apartment house in the middle of the block. He walked back there. Three black-and-whites were around, one in the drive of the apartment, two on the street; two uniformed men stood on the top step of the entrance to the apartment, and Carey was talking to a couple in the drive. The squad cars had attracted the usual attention of the neighborhood, but along here it made no difference that most faces were black; it was a neighborhood of ordinary working people and they were interested, concerned; nobody was calling any names.

A city crew had been putting in a new sidewalk right in front of the apartment, half of the cement poured, the forms all in for the rest of it. The crew was standing around desultorily, watching the police.

Carey had spotted Mendoza, and started to meet him. The city crew, the couple Carey'd been talking with, all the little crowd around, eyed Mendoza's dapper tailoring and black Homburg with deep and passionate interest. Carey drew him over to one of the squad cars and they got in. "What's all the excitement?" asked Mendoza.

"Plenty." Carey's pug-nosed round face was grim. "I'll give it to you short and sweet. Mrs. Blaine, apartment thirty-four on the fifth floor. She missed the four-year-old, Katie May, about eleven-thirty. Says she always keeps a close eye on her, the way you do a four-year-old. Katie isn't allowed out of the building alone, and all the neighbors that are home say so too— Mrs. Blaine a good, careful mother. As I told you, you can see this is a good neighborhood, place kept up, they're all good people. She didn't think too much about it at first, went out in the hall looking, sometimes Katie May dropped into one of the other apartments, everybody likes Katie and she's a good little girl— I've seen her picture and she's a cute one, anyway. But, no Katie May. Some of the neighbor women started helping her look, and then they turned up the fact —when it seemed she wasn't anywhere in the apartment house—that she hadn't come out either. Because there were witnesses front and back, and nobody saw her."

"Elucidate," said Mendoza.

"It's—damn it, it's like one of those mysteries where the room was locked and the murderer got out by magic," said Carey. "Look at it. This is a big apartment house but there's only one front door and one back door. You can see the front. Ever since ten o'clock this morning that city crew's been there, working on the sidewalk. Six of 'em. Right up next to the apartment steps. And they all swear that no little four-year-old ever came out that door, alone or with anybody. They've all seen her picture too and they go on saying it. And the back door, at the end of the front hall, leads out to an alley that runs east-west along this whole block. The garages for the apartment are across the alley. And out in the alley, directly across from the back door, one of the tenants, Sam Appleby, and his sixteen-year-old son have been working on a car since eleven o'clock. Also, about twelve o'clock his wife came out and asked him to keep an eye on their five-year-old while she went to market. So he and the son both weren't too absorbed in the car that they had their eyes off the door where the five-year-old was sitting playing. They both swear on a stack of Bibles Katie May never came out that door, and they know her. For what it's worth, the five-year-old, sitting smack in the doorway, says so too."

"¡Cómo no!" said Mendoza.

"Well, to go back. The women were all alarmed by this time and Mrs. Blaine called the police. The Traffic men got interested when they heard the witnesses, and started to go through the apartment, and then they got to thinking maybe it wasn't such a hot idea without a warrant, and they called my office. I got interested when I heard the story, and came down to look at it for myself. The manager's out, nobody knows where, and all we're doing right now is marking time. I've got a Traffic man at back and front and on every floor, and there's no sign of her."

"You mentioned some blood."

Carey gestured, back and forth. "It says nothing. A little smear of it on the wall up on the fifth floor, but it could be where somebody had a cut finger. Only it looks fairly fresh." Carey reached into his pocket and produced a snapshot. Mendoza looked at it. Maybe it had been taken on a birthday or when she was dressed up for Sunday: in it Katie May Blaine was wearing a little pink dress with bows, and white socks and white slippers. She had faced the camera solemnly, a round-faced brown little girl, her hair in two neat pigtails tied with pink ribbon. "A cute one," said Carey. "I'll tell you what it comes down to, Mendoza. It doesn't look as if she came out of the building —but if she's still in there somewhere, she's being held in some way, or she's unconscious, or she's dead."

"I could think of alternatives."

"I have," said Carey. "There's no refuse chute to a basement—the apartments all have garbage disposals. I've been through the place and I can't spot anything that might pose any danger to a child. The neighbors, Mrs. Blaine, her husband—she called him about an hour ago and he came home, he's a dental technician—have been on every floor, calling her—so have all of us. Nothing. And the witnesses go on insisting she never came out. I tell you, Mendoza, I hope to God they're wrong— I hope she got out and is around somewhere. But—"

"Has everybody been hypnotized by the witnesses? Haven't you—"

"Not likely," said Carey. "We've looked elsewhere too. Up at the north corner there's a fellow with a little magazine and newspaper stand. He knows Katie May from seeing her go by with her mother. He hasn't seen her today. Down the other way are people who knew her by sight and say they'd have seen her if she went by, especially alone. Woman at the dress shop who's been redecorating the window, fellow at the drugstore on the corner putting up sales notices outside, down at the smaller apartment building two men washing the front windows."

"¡Porvida!" said Mendoza. He looked at the snapshot.

"Moreover, the mother says she's an obedient child, not exactly timid, friendly to people she knows, but a little shy. Nobody thinks she'd have tried to go out of the building by herself. And there wasn't any reason for her to run away, she hadn't been punished, nothing out of the ordinary had happened. She's just—gone."

In spite of himself Mendoza was caught by the puzzle. Carey seemed to have covered all angles. This was a crowded street, not a main drag but a busy street, and somebody should have seen Katie—known in the neighborhood—if she had passed anywhere along this block. "You want to go over that building foot by foot," he said.

"I do. I'm waiting for more men. Traffic wouldn't detail me any more, and while all the tenants at home have said a search warrant doesn't matter, I'd like to talk to the manager."

"I'll lend you some men." Mendoza went back to the Ferrari and used the phone in it to call his office. "Who's in, Jimmy?—well, chase them all down here—this might be a thing."

When he walked back to the apartment Carey was talking again to the Blaines. He introduced Mendoza casually; nobody was going to mention Homicide here until they knew a lot more. "There'll be some more men here in a few minutes," said Mendoza. "We want to search the building."

"But how could she be—I've called and called, we all did—" Mrs. Blaine stopped with a little gasp. She was a pretty woman, neatly dressed in a plaid cotton housedress, and her hands twisted together like separate frightened little animals. Her husband, a tall serious-faced man in a dark suit, had his arm around her. People from the apartment were standing close around, with concerned expressions, muttering speculations.

"We haven't got a search warrant," Carey was explaining to Blaine, "but it would take time—if we could reach the manager—"

A subdued clamor rose from the little crowd. "You can look in my place—" "You don't need a warrant, officer, you just find that baby if she's anywhere here—"

Mendoza went down the drive to the alley. One comprehensive glance showed him the back door—a narrow one, with a single step—and the old car up on blocks just outside the garage opposite, with just enough room for a car to pass between it and the apartment building. It was a narrow alley: the garages in a long row on the other side were mostly open, but three of the doors were closed. "What about these garages?" he asked the Traffic man posted at the back door.

"They weren't locked. We've had 'em all open. This is the damnedest thing I ever—I mean, where the hell can the kid be?"

Mendoza went back to the street just as the little blue Elva pulled up; Grace and Conway got out of it, and a minute later Hackett's scarlet Barracuda came up with Higgins beside him. They all huddled with Carey, hearing the story. Without discussing it, they stood back to let Grace talk to the parents; but all the obvious questions, Carey would have asked.

The parents looked blindly at Grace, slim and dapper as Mendoza, and told him all the things they'd told Carey. Katie May had never tried to run away; she was a good girl. A little shy. She knew she wasn't allowed out of the building alone. She always came when she was called. And she couldn't have got far, and everybody had been good, coming out to help, but when they hadn't found her by now, where could she have— "But she can't be anywhere in there!" said Mrs. Blaine with a frightened sob. "She'd have heard us calling— Oh, Dick!" She grasped her husband's jacket and wept. He looked steadily at Grace.

"You mean—if she's somewhere in there—"

"Now we don't know anything yet, Mr. Blaine. She could have fallen and hurt herself some way. Maybe in somebody's apartment, and nobody there— Now, I know how you feel," said Grace. "I've got a little girl at home too. We'll be looking."

Traffic had spared them six men. They left two at front and back, and were just deploying the rest to cover every foot of the building they could reach, when an agitated black man came pushing through the crowd demanding to know what was happening. Relieved cries went up on all sides—"Mr. Smiley, it's Mr. Smiley—" "You tell the officers it's all right, Mr. Smiley, we got to find her—"

Smiley was the manager. Apprised of the situation, he said instantly, "You got my full permission, search wherever you want, gentlemen! I got master keys to all the apartments where nobody's home, I'll be right behind you. We just got to find that poor mite, whatever's happened to her—and don't you worry none about it being legal, this place's owned by a big bank and they're not goin' make any trouble over police hunting a little girl lost. Come on, let's cover it and find her!"

They covered it. There were five floors, with eight apartments on each floor. On a week day, most of the tenants at home were women; most of them had been on the hunt with Mrs. Blaine the last couple of hours. There were, it developed, only five men at home in the building; they were all night workers, and they were all cooperative.

The men covered each floor systematically, taking note of the places where they got no answer. They went, in teams, into every room of every apartment, floor by floor, and then they used Smiley's master keys to investigate the places where nobody was home.

And they didn't find her.

At five-forty Mendoza and Carey were talking to the crew again; the crew was slightly annoyed at being kept hanging around, but they were concerned and interested in Katie May too. The boss was white, the rest Negro. They were all firmly positive that she hadn't come out the front door.

"Look," said the boss. "We sat right out here, had lunch

on the job. Sitting in the parking there, facing the front door. No kid came out."

Sam Appleby was trailing the detectives, to hear that. "And she never come out the back either," he said mournfully. He was a tall, broad, very black fellow, his old slacks still oil-stained from his work on the car. "I know Katie May—so does my boy Arthur—and we were on opposite sides o' the car, he'd have seen her, him facin' the back door, if I didn't—and I was glancin' up every so often, be sure Jackie was still there playin'—"

The Traffic men went off shift. There wasn't any reason to maintain a guard on the doors; there wasn't anything to guard. The detectives were talking among themselves.

"All right," said Hackett to Higgins, "what are we all thinking about? Five men alone at home here today. Just five."

"But they're all good types," said Higgins. "And if any of them had done anything to her, where the hell *is* she? Oh, I know, appearances—"

They went to see those men again; they all lived in the single apartments with one bedroom.

Chester Felleman lived on the fourth floor. He was a trumpet player in a combo playing at a supper club in Hollywood, and he was a friendly young fellow. He had let them look through the apartment willingly; he said now, "She must've got out and run off, though it don't seem likely—poor little kid." He said he'd been asleep when all the uproar started.

William Reed lived on the fifth floor. He greeted Hackett's reappearance with a silent nod; he was a man about forty, broad and brown and stolid. He was a waiter in a restaurant out on La Cienega, and he was getting ready to go to work now. "I suppose it's all right for me to leave?" he said. They'd searched that apartment too; he shared it with two other men who worked days.

Robert Wagstaff, in an apartment on the third floor, was a night security guard at a manufacturing plant, as was the fourth man, Nelson Procter, in an apartment down the hall. Both the men were young, and seemed concerned about Katie May; the apartments were clean.

Edward Mawson, on the second floor, worked at a twenty-four-hour tow-truck service garage, and he too was due on the job, he said, and he too looked perfectly straightforward, a quiet man about forty, his apartment very neat.

Mendoza hadn't called the lab to come and take a sample of that minute bloodstain for analysis, because it wouldn't be any use. The Blaines didn't know what type Katie May's was; they were Christian Scientists and didn't go to doctors unless it was absolutely necessary.

"*¡Diez millones de demonios desde el infierno!*" said Mendoza violently. They were standing out on the sidewalk beside the Ferrari, at ten minutes past six. "She didn't vanish into air, damn it! Now what the hell happened here?"

"I don't know," said Carey, sounding subdued, "but I'll make a prediction. I think she's dead. I think she ran into a pervert. Maybe, in spite of all the witnesses, she got out of the building, though I don't see how. But I feel in my bones something's happened to her, or we'd have picked up a trail."

The Blaines had gone back to their apartment, desolate; all the helpful neighbors had dispersed; with the squad cars gone, the little crowds passing didn't know that anything had happened here. "Well," said Carey, "no point hanging around. Tomorrow, we start hunting again. Unless—" He went back to his car and drove off.

"Is anybody taking any bets?" asked Mendoza. Nobody was. In unaccustomed silence they dispersed too, to go home. Wondering where Katie May was tonight.

Mendoza told Alison and Mrs. MacTaggart about it over a shot glass of rye, having inevitably poured an ounce in a saucer for El Señor. "But—the locked room you can say," said Alison. "I don't see how—Luis?"

"Well, *cara?*"

"Not to teach you your job, but—if the worst happened

and the poor child is dead, a four-year-old wouldn't— take up much space, as it were. I mean, I'm thinking of under beds, and the backs of closets, and even garment bags or big drawers—"

Mendoza said sardonically, "That we know too, my love. We looked at all those places. It's just a damned mystery, and locked rooms I prefer between book covers. I just hope to hell Carey isn't right."

"Och, the puir child," said Mrs. MacTaggart. "I'll be putting up a prayer for her." She regarded Mendoza's cynical glance severely. She was fond of her gallant Spanish man, up to a point. But if she'd despaired of immediately coaxing him back to Mother Church, she had, aware of her duty, seen to it that the twins were properly baptized. Long before they'd been of an age to babble Spanish or English, and no reason why their heathen parents need know anything about it, she reflected, warming up Mendoza's dinner.

Piggott, not knowing anything about Katie May, went home and frowned over the baby tetras. "Thank heaven," said Prudence, "they seem to have stopped eating each other. They're all about the same size now—but when I think of what we started with! And all the trouble it's been—"

"Yes, I guess we don't get rich raising exotic fish," said Piggott. Separated as they were in batches in the dishpans, they were a little easier to count; after some concentrating, he made it seventy-two. "That comes to fourteen-forty, at twenty cents apiece. What shall we blow it on?"

The heat was building up; it had gone to ninety-nine today, with the humidity soaring.

Landers called in at eight-fifteen to say there'd been a delay on the flight back from San Diego; he hadn't fetched Sid Belcher back till seven o'clock, and there hadn't been any food on the plane, it being a short hop, and he'd nearly starved to death. "I thought he could cool for a while— I didn't question him." They would leave that for the day watch.

But it wasn't a very busy shift for the night watch. They had an old wino found dead on the street, and a freeway accident with two D.O.A.'s. At ten-fifteen they had a call from Sergeant Barth at the Wilcox Street precinct in Hollywood.

"I saw in the paper that you'd had a couple of heists at the restaurants down there—the good restaurants. We just had one like that, I wondered if they matched up."

"Very possible," said Glasser. "They seem bent on building up a bundle, going at it every other night. What were your heisters like and where?"

"Two of them—descriptions nil except both medium-sized. Stocking masks. Two big guns. They came into a place called The Brass Pheasant on La Cienega, just as it was closing at nine-fifteen. Got away with about seven C's."

"That's our boys," said Glasser.

"I never stopped to think how much cash a nice restaurant would have on hand—"

"No, neither did we. It's a nice M.O.," said Glasser. "And nowhere to go on it."

Fifteen minutes later Traffic called in to report a brawl in a bar, with one man stabbed to death. Schenke went out on it with Glasser; it was Galeano's day off. They left reports for Wanda to type up.

At seven o'clock on Tuesday morning Alison was just getting out of bed when the phone rang. As usual, the livestock, including the twins, had been up for an hour, since Mrs. MacTaggart had padded down to the kitchen, and both Alison and Mendoza had been trying to ignore the happy shouts and barks from the backyard, interspersed with the mockingbird's various calls.

On the second ring, Mendoza bolted out of bed. "*Ahora veremos,*" he said alertly, "and that will be Carey. He felt it in his bones—and damn it, so did I—" He plunged out to the hall with Alison pursuing him with his dressing gown.

"Carey?" he said. "You knew it—so did I. What and when?"

"Damn it, how the *hell* could it happen— Yes, we've found her. Just as I knew we would. One of the tenants there, a Jim Rittenhouse, found her when he went to get his car at six-thirty. I just got here. The alley behind the apartment. Yes, she's dead."

"*¡Santa María y todos los arcángeles!*" said Mendoza. "All right, I'm on my way." He slammed the phone down, picked it up again and dialed. In sixty seconds he was talking to an outraged Dr. Bainbridge, who swore, listened, and said he'd be on the way.

Alison made him drink a cup of coffee. This morning he wasn't choosing a wardrobe with care, but automatically he put on the sharp-tailored dark Italian silk suit, the discreet tie.

It was seven-forty when he got to that block on Hooper Avenue, having used the siren. There were plenty of parking slots on the street. He went down the drive and found a little group just standing around: Carey, the two men from the squad car, Smiley, another black man in work clothes looking shaken and solemn.

"Mr. Rittenhouse, Lieutenant Mendoza," said Carey sadly. "Will you tell me how, Mendoza?"

"*No se.*" He went to look.

Katie May had vanished neatly dressed in a blue cotton dress, blue ribbons on her pigtails, white cotton socks and white shoes, white cotton panties. The dress was missing, and the panties; one bow was gone from a pigtail. The little body lay face down on the old scarred blacktop of the alley, mute and pathetic. There was dried blood on the legs. And the body looked curiously flattened, even smaller than it should have looked.

"I just didn't feel like goin' on to work," said Rittenhouse to nobody in particular.

"The Blaines?" said Mendoza.

"I told them," said Carey. "They came down—well,

you don't have to be told, all broken up, their only one. I couldn't let them touch her—anything that's here, we want to know. They're intelligent people, Blaine saw that. They're upstairs."

"There'll be a lab team here but I don't think there's anything to be got." Mendoza was smoking rapidly. "You know why. She was—somewhere—yesterday. After everything was quiet, she was brought here and left. How the hell—how the *flaming* hell—did we miss finding her, Carey? If she was in this building?"

"You tell me—I'm beyond wondering."

Paunchy little Dr. Bainbridge came trotting down the drive, carrying his bag. "Oh, yes," he said, looking. "Very nasty. I can't do much here."

"We'll want priority on the autopsy, Doctor. Can you give us an idea when?"

Bainbridge squatted, felt the body, took his time peering. "Approximately sixteen to eighteen hours."

"Hell!" said Carey loudly. "That puts it within an hour, two, of when she was missed—while all those women were roaming around that place hunting and calling for her! She must have heard them—if she was—"

"We don't know that," said Mendoza. "All right, the witnesses. They can be wrong. It could be she got half a block down and ran into the pervert. And there'll have been a lot of talk along this block about Katie May—could be he thought the safest place to leave her was right here, make us think we missed her here, put it right back to this building." Just as, he thought, that damned front-door key was the link between that X and the Clark Hotel.

"I want to take her in," said Bainbridge. "It's odd— I'd almost say she'd been run over, but there's not enough damage—" He stood up, pursing his lips. "Could have been a motorcycle, maybe along here in the dark without a light—or one of those little Honda cars, though even that'd be heavy enough to— Well, I'll have a look. These damned things make me feel I've lived too long, Luis. I'm getting tired of this place—it seems to be asking for another Flood to drown all the sinners, any day."

"The Lord promised He wouldn't do it that way again," said Carey.

Bainbridge snorted. "It seems to me He's trying to tell us something, with all these earthquakes and volcanic eruptions and tidal waves."

Two ambulance attendants came down the drive with a stretcher.

As the day watch came into the office, Mendoza briefed them on Katie May. They couldn't do much about it until they heard from Bainbridge. All of them felt a curious outrage about Katie May, not so much for the mere fact of death—as the tough Homicide cops they were used to the violence and death, though nobody ever got tough enough to look at the Katie Mays with equanimity—but because it was impossible that they could have missed her yesterday.

"Where in hell was she?" asked Hackett in frustrated rage. "We tore that place apart, Luis! We looked in closets and clothes hampers and bureau drawers! She wasn't there, that's all. Damn the witnesses, she got out of the building and got picked up somewhere else. Just as you say."

"Those witnesses were damn certain," said Higgins. And whenever a thing like this happened, inevitably they were thinking of their own hostages to fortune at home. Palliser, hearing about Katie May for the first time, looked angry.

"You must have missed her, and those witnesses—they couldn't be absolutely certain—"

"And," said Mendoza, lighting a new cigarette, "before I went home last night I came back to R. and I. and checked all five of those men out. The five lone night workers who were at home there yesterday. And they're all clean. No pedigrees anywhere at least under those names. I asked NCIC."

"Hell and damnation!" said Hackett.

And until they heard from Bainbridge, there was continued business. Somebody had to go over to the jail and talk to Belcher, not that there was much in that: the gun tied him to the Booths' killing. Parsons was being arraigned this morning. No pigeon had called in to finger Terry Conover, no excited citizen to say he'd been seen.

And Miss Frances Giffard, at the school library, had called late yesterday afternoon to say that three more copies of that biology textbook had been returned. If they were ever going to chase down Rex and his bright yellow Mustang, that would probably be the best bet, finding that marginal note.

And then there were the freaky hippies they were after on Blackwood. That autopsy report had been waiting on Mendoza's desk this morning: it said expectable things; he'd died of a fractured skull. The lab would be matching up the blood on that piece of two-by-four to the old man's type.

Gilbert Deleavey, Roselle Kruger and William Siebert—all in records. The addresses for the men had proved N.G. —they had moved on awhile ago. Yesterday, before being called up on the hunt for Katie May, Hackett and Higgins had found Roselle's sister Marjorie, who looked to be much the same type as Roselle, at an apartment on Virgil where Roselle had been living the last time she was picked up. Marjorie had peered at them through tangled brown hair and said, Oh, Roselle'd gone to live with Lorna a couple of months back. She couldn't remember Lorna's last name, but added vaguely that she used to go around with Billy Weber—or maybe his name was Holland—and they used to hang out at the psychedelic coffee shop up on Third. It did seem significant, as Hackett pointed out, that that was in the general neighborhood where the Blackwood house was.

That was as far as they'd got on it. Now Piggott and Palliser went out to the Ninth Street school to leaf through the biology textbooks, and Hackett and Higgins started for the psychedelic coffee shop to see if it was open.

Mendoza went out for some breakfast.

Sergeant Lake, knowing Grace would want to hear, called him at home and told him about Katie May. Grace said sadly he'd been afraid of that, but how the hell had they missed her? He added, "I'll come in. Nothing special to do, and you're shorthanded with Tom and Rich off."

The psychedelic coffee shop was open, surprisingly. There were only two people there, in the little room hung with the violent-colored posters, and the men from Robbery-Homicide looked twice to decide the sexes. Both of them had the shoulder-length hair, but the one with the sideburns and beard would be male. They were both wearing Hawaiian shirts and pink pants, and they were sitting at one of the tables drinking coffee and listening to very loud rock on a tape recorder. They looked up as Hackett and Higgins came up to the table, and the girl reached to turn the volume down.

"We're not open," she said, and took another look and said, "You're cops."

"That's right," said Higgins, and produced the badge. "And the door's open."

"Only," said the male, "to symbolize that our hearts are ever open to peace and love."

"Is that so?" said Hackett. "We're looking for Roselle Kruger, said to be a pal of Lorna, who comes in here with Billy Weber or possibly Holland."

"We have nothing to do with man persecuting man in the name of the law," said the male. "There is no such thing as a criminal, my dear fuzz—only differences of opinion on right action."

"Now that's an interesting theory," said Higgins. He reached down casually and picked up the lofty one's coffee cup. The reaction was instinctive and immediate.

"Hey, that's mine!"

Hackett laughed. But it would be a waste of time, trying to point the moral to them; maybe experience and age would give them a little common sense, or maybe not. "We're not after Lorna or Billy," he said. "Just Roselle, and they might know where she is."

"Oh," said the girl. "Roselle is a young soul. One mustn't hold grudges, but I must say—after she swiped that ring—I couldn't care less. I haven't seen Lorna, about the last month, but Billy—his name's Langendorf if it matters—is living with a lovely group of people right around on Burlington Street. It's called Indigo Meditation—some of them come to our Yoga classes every Monday and Wednesday."

"I suppose," said Higgins back in the Barracuda, "every generation has its rebels, Art, but this particular point in history seems to be turning out some funny ones."

"That you can say three times."

On Burlington, they idled along looking. On the corner of the third block down was a big ramshackle two-story house with a wide front porch. On the porch railing was hung a big hand-lettered cardboard sign with astrological symbols all over it and the legend *Indigo Meditation*.

Hackett parked in the first place he found and they walked back. They climbed old wooden steps to the front porch and faced two young men sitting on an old-fashioned porch swing drinking what looked to be iced coffee out of tall glasses.

It was going to be much hotter today; the humidity was still building.

"And what does the upstanding fuzz want here?" asked the blond one brightly.

"We're looking for Billy Langendorf," said Hackett.

"Oh, then you are in luck. I am he. In case you're interested, this other free soul is Howard Nutley. What can I do for the fuzz?" He was good-looking, or might have been without all the hair: handsome, rather girlish features, and at that he hadn't quite so much hair as the other one.

"Just a few questions," said Hackett, feeling rather tired of these people.

"Oh, shake not thy gory locks at me!" said Billy. "We are, in this little commune of kindred souls, in the jargon very clean. But clean. The Supreme Court has seen to that, bless their souls. Time was, you know, we free spirits had to resort to the shoplifting and all such undesirable methods of attaining the regular diet. But of late, life is much easier, all owing to these blessed judges. Those big bad reactionary Congressmen tried, oh, yes, indeedy, they thought up a law that anybody getting the food stamps at one address had to be related, but the Court clobbered that one. Unconstitutional! So we're but clean, police. Ask what you will."

"You talk too much," said the other one.

"Look, all we want to know," began Higgins, and was overridden.

"It's beautiful," said Billy. "But beautiful. You want to know how it works?—the lovely general welfare—so I tell you. I buy thirty-eight bucks' worth of food stamps for fifty cents, and I spend the stamps for thirty-seven bucks and fifty-one cents' worth of the groceries, and get the maximum change allowed—forty-nine cents. I put another penny to it and buy another fifty cents' worth of food stamps— Well, it's beautiful. It snowballs. The fourth week I sell the stamps for fifteen bucks—and what it works out to, in a month I get nearly a hundred bucks' worth of groceries and fifteen bucks cash, no sweat at all." He beamed at them. "Twenty of us free souls in this place, all doing the same, and we live high—very high, I tell you."

"You talk too much," said Nutley.

Hackett and Higgins, who had—what with the hostages to fortune—budgets to figure, stood there silent, because there was too much to say that this free spirit wasn't equipped to understand. Maybe the inevitable end to the free—and worthless—money would teach a lot of people a few basic lessons. Maybe not.

"Do you know," asked Higgins, "where Roselle Kruger is living?"

"Roselle—oh, that dear soul," said Billy. "She found communal life a trifle claustrophobic. She and Lorna made other arrangements—with a couple of kindred spirits I'm not acquainted with. I do recall she mentioned a name. Claude Sharp."

"Thank you so much," said Higgins.

– 10 –

By the time Palliser and Piggott got out to the school, Miss Giffard reported that two more of those books had been turned in. They all should be in by tomorrow, she said, because this was the last week of school; but so many children were so irresponsible these days, some of them might forget. She was busy checking files, getting ready for the closing of the library; they sat down at one of the empty tables and each started to leaf through a book. It was tedious work, deciphering all the marginal notes, quite a few of them pornographic; and when they'd finished this batch, it was nearly noon and they hadn't found Rex and his phone number.

They went back to the office to see if anything new had come in, just as Traffic called. Some kids playing in an empty lot down on Santa Barbara had just found a man's body. "The heat wave," said Palliser. "Business always picks up."

"No, by what they say it's been there awhile," said Lake.

Piggott said he'd go and look at it, and just then a lab report came up, so Palliser took it into Mendoza's office to hear if Bainbridge had called.

He hadn't. Mendoza was sitting there rapidly shuffling the cards, looking annoyed. Glancing up to see who it was, he said, "And I'll tell you something, business picking up or not, we're going to get a rundown on every soul employed at the Clark Hotel—relatives, boyfriends, financial status, personal problems and so on, however long it takes. That key is a direct connection—"

"We didn't find Rex," said Palliser. "If all those books don't get returned before school closes, we may never find him. Has Bainbridge called?"

167

"No." Mendoza opened the lab report. "So they finally get round to telling us," he said a moment later. "That flashlight the Bryan girl gave you—they picked up some latents on it. Enough. The prowler was Lester Watson, quite a pedigree. I had that autopsy report an hour ago—Elsa Short. She died of shock and multiple knife wounds. Here's his package—you name it, it's here, assault, D. and D., possession, pushing, assault with intent, resisting arrest."

Palliser took the package with some interest. Watson was tersely described as Negro, male, six one, one hundred fifty, black and brown, various scars, forty-two. Palliser didn't ask why he was walking around loose, with a record like this. "The address is fairly recent."

"And he's still on P.A.," said Mendoza. "Come on, let's justify our existence and go pick him up—clear one away at least." Mendoza stood up, yanking down his cuffs, reaching for his hat.

The address was one of the government-erected huge apartment complexes, down on Seventy-first. As with most of these places, where few of the tenants were earning the money to pay the rent, or had many personal standards, it had deteriorated rapidly in the couple of years it had been up, and there was garbage strewn around the halls, stains on the walls where plumbing had been wrecked, and various smells. They got no answer to a knock at the door of Watson's apartment, and when Palliser knocked again the door across the hall opened and a woman looked at them briefly. She was slatternly, ungracious, smelling of cheap wine.

"Either you gents Mr. Tucker? Mr. Watson he tole me to say, tell Mr. Tucker as he's out lookin' for a job does he come, 'n' he be back sometime. I was jus' to say." She shut the door.

"Tucker being his parole agent, I suppose," said Palliser. "What do you suppose he was doing uptown last Friday? All hopped up?"

Mendoza shrugged. "Met the supplier somewhere up

on our beat. Doing what comes naturally. I get tired, John. I also want some lunch."

Piggott looked at the new body, wondering just how it had got here. This wasn't an empty lot exactly; it was a huge bare plot of land on a corner of Santa Barbara Avenue, completely enclosed with a high board fence about twelve feet high. There were no signs on the fence to indicate ownership or intent to build; something had evidently been torn down here, but the earth was overgrown with weeds and wild mustard, and the tearing down had left mounds and hillocks and depressions here and there.

There was a gate in the fence, on the side street, with a padlock on it; but you could always trust the kids to find a way in to an intriguing off-limits playground. The two eight-year-old boys out there by the gate with the other Traffic man and a couple of mothers were scared now, but they'd been getting in here lots, they said, only they never noticed the body before.

By law there had to be an emergency number posted on all locked public premises. The Traffic men had called it. This lot was at present controlled by a realty company in Beverly Hills, and a very annoyed clerk had appeared just now to unlock the padlock. The Traffic men, young and trim, had climbed the fence where the boys had, at the rear where it adjoined an alley, but Piggott hadn't felt inclined for the exercise.

The body had been here awhile; he couldn't guess how long. It was male, good-sized, with dark-blond hair, and dressed in ordinary sports clothes: gray slacks, a dark jacket, striped shirt. There didn't seem to be any blood anywhere, or any bullet holes visible.

Piggott went out to talk to the boys. "How long have you been getting in here?" he asked mildly.

They looked defiant. "Since about last week, week before—we didn't hurt nothing. But we never went over to the front side before. We thought it was a bundle of ole

clothes or somethin' there. Wasn't till we got close enough
to see—"

The mothers were agog with interest. "A murder!" said
one of them to the other. "And my Bobby found it! Wait
till his dad hears—"

"Aren't you supposed to be in school?" said Piggott.

"Aw, it's only the last couple days, it don't matter."

There wasn't much to do about it but send it to the
morgue, have the doctors and lab look at it and take its
prints, and hope it would get identified. Piggott saw it off
in the ambulance, and stopped halfway back to the office
for lunch; from there he called Sergeant Lake. "You might
tell the lab to go get the prints. It's been dry and hot, and
I don't think he'd been there that long—they can get
some."

"Will do," said Lake.

Hackett and Higgins, following the routine that so often
breaks cases, went back to S.I.D. looking for some traces
of Claude Sharp. Surprisingly, he didn't show up in records.

"Maybe a newcomer to L.A. and hasn't been picked up
for anything yet," said Higgins. "So where next?"

"I can just hear what Jase would say," said Hackett.
"Him and his simple mind." He asked for a phone book
and looked in it, and there he was, on Savannah Street in
Boyle Heights.

"Oh, no," said Higgins. "It can't be the right one, Art.
Running with these drifters and dopies? In the phone
book?"

"Well, no harm checking it out," said Hackett. They
drove over there; the address was another of the old
apartment houses like so many in this downtown area,
and the mailbox numbered four bore the handwritten
name of Sharp.

They went down the hall and found it. "I still can't
figure this one, Art. These small-time junkies and a murder. It doesn't fit." Higgins pushed the bell. After a while
he pushed it again.

"Nobody home," said Hackett. But a moment later the door opened slowly and somebody asked sleepily, "Whatcha want?"

It was a girl. "We're looking for Roselle Kruger," said Hackett. The light was very dim, and they couldn't see her well enough to compare her mentally to the mug shot.

"Whaffor? Come around in the middle o' the night," she said, yawning.

"It's eleven o'clock," said Hackett.

"Who notices clocks? Whatcha want with Rosie?"

"Are you by any chance Lorna?" asked Hackett gently.

"Yeah, thass me, why?"

"Suppose we come in and tell you," said Higgins. She went back inside, leaving the door open, so they went in.

"Hey, Rosie, some guys want to see you. Maybe that dude promised to let you have the barbs——"

It was a bare, dirty little place, clothes strewn around, a portable TV in one corner, no carpet. In here it was much lighter, with the curtains pulled aside; one glimpse past the door at the left showed them a kitchenette in a wild clutter of dirty dishes and food standing around. In the other direction was the half-closed door to a bedroom, presumably.

Before they saw Roselle, a man came out of there, also yawning: William Siebert, one of those they wanted. He would be the black one among the hippies noticed so apprehensively by the neighbors. He was clad simply in a pair of white shorts, and he was scratching his chest lazily. He stopped short on noticing the two big men, and suddenly yelped shrilly, "They're cops! Lorna, you damn fool, they're cops!" He turned in panic to run and Higgins got hold of him.

"You just calm down——" They hadn't expected to find a bonus. The next minute, with Siebert flailing at Higgins, Gilbert Deleavey appeared from the bedroom and with one horrified look ran for the door. Hackett grabbed him and groped for the single pair of cuffs he had on him, but before he got them on, the two girls were there, screaming and trying to scratch his eyes out.

171

"Take it easy, damn it—" One of the girls raked his left cheek painfully, and Deleavey got loose and tried for the door again. Somebody out in the hall asked loudly what the hell was going on. Hackett got Deleavey pinned against the wall and fastened the cuffs on him. Like a horse in halter, he calmed right down. Hackett went to help Higgins and they got the cuffs on Siebert.

In the next few minutes, they wished they'd put them on the girls instead. The girls put up quite a fight, but eventually Hackett managed to get his gun out and pull the bigger girl off Higgins, who yanked his out too. The girls subsided sullenly onto the sagging couch and started to call them dirty names. The arrest warrant had come through this morning, with the nice lab evidence, and Hackett had just pulled it out and was about to recite the little piece about their rights when a hard hand snatched the gun away from him and a hard voice said, "What's going on here?"

One of the neighbors had called the police.

The uniformed men apologized. "All the screaming and yelling, you can understand— Say, you're both bleeding, did you know? You'd better get patched up when you take these birds in. You Narco?"

"Robbery-Homicide," said Hackett, feeling his cheek.

"No kidding? They don't look like killers, though they did a little job on you." The patrolmen were amused. They supplied extra cuffs and obligingly ferried the prisoners in.

Before they talked to them, Hackett and Higgins went down to First Aid where the nurse washed off the blood and said dryly stitches wouldn't be necessary.

They got Siebert and Deleavey into the second interrogation room and for openers asked them who Claude Sharp was. It seemed he was a fellow they'd met somewhere who was taking off, somebody after him, said Deleavey, and he'd let them have the key to his place. That was all they knew about him.

"And I heard what you said to the other fuzz. Like, homicide. That's murder, man. We never killed nobody."

"What about Mr. Blackwood?" asked Higgins.

"Who's he?"

"The old man," said Hackett patiently, "whose house you broke into last Friday night. It'd be interesting to hear why, almost anybody could have guessed there wasn't anything of value there, but we know it was you. About eight o'clock at night." Still broad daylight, and all those neighbors giving the accurate descriptions. Just how stupid the little punks could be—

Deleavey and Siebert looked at each other. "Oh. We never found a thing," said Siebert mournfully. "There wasn't nothing worth a buck even. That old man, he let us in, but I guess he was expectin' somebody else, when he saw us he kept sayin', get out—"

"It was all Rosie's notion," said Deleavey. "Might've known it'd turn out a real nothin', she's a know-nothin' chick all right."

"So you hit him with a piece of two-by-four," said Higgins. "You must have brought that with you just in case. You knocked him down and killed him, if you're interested."

They looked at each other. "Is he *dead*—that old man?" asked Deleavey incredulously. "Man, nobody meant him to be dead! It was just a li'l tap, stop his noise while we looked for the loot—"

"I dint do it," said Siebert hurriedly, "Gil did."

Deleavey turned on him wrathfully. "You damn liar, it was you hit him!"

"It wasn't my idea—"

Hackett and Higgins got tired of listening to that; they'd probably go on saying it all the way up to and including the trial. They went to talk to the girls in the next interrogation room. Lorna was sullen until she heard that Blackwood was dead, and then started to cry.

"So it was your idea?" said Hackett to Roselle. "Why? What gave you the idea Blackwood had a lot of loot there?"

She looked at them foggily, a mousy little thing with the usual stringy brown hair parted in the middle, tangled around her shoulders. "How'd you know it was us there, anyways?"

"You left some nice fingerprints all over the place," said Higgins.

"We did?" She looked at her hands. "I still don't get it. There shoulda been a lot of money there."

"What made you think that?" asked Higgins.

Insofar as her rather dull eyes showed any expression, she was surprised at the question. "Gee," she said, "we was all surprised there wasn't nothing there. Nothing! He'd just sold that house, it said so on the sign out front. Houses, they cost an awful lot of money—thousands of dollars. And he'd just sold it to somebody."

Hackett and Higgins looked at each other. "My God in heaven," said Hackett.

They called up another squad car, ferried the four of them down to the jail on Alameda, and drove up to Federico's for a belated lunch.

They found Mendoza and Palliser sitting at the big table in front drinking coffee and awaiting food. "You're not going to believe this, Luis," said Hackett, sitting down beside him. "I know a lot of the people we deal with are fairly stupid, but anybody that stupid—" He told them about the hippies.

"You coined the phrase, Art—the stupidity and cupidity," said Mendoza. "We've got the prowler identified, at least, if we ever find him home. And there was another telex in from the chief in Fresno. John Upton's sister hasn't seen or heard from him for a couple of weeks, since she had a letter from his wife. It's—mmh—a little *extraño* that A.P.B. hasn't turned up a trail. If he was a pro with a pedigree used to running, I wouldn't be surprised, but he's not."

"Has Bainbridge called yet? . . . And you know," said Higgins, "whatever he tells us, where do we go from here on that? However the hell we missed Katie May yesterday, there's only one way to go at it. Ask R. and I. for the records of all the perverts—and there are hundreds in the files—sort out the ones in this area, as well as we can pin them down, and go out to find them one by one."

"*Seguramente qué sí*," said Mendoza, putting out his cigarette as his steak arrived.

"And," added Hackett to that, contemplating his dieters' special sourly, "how many of them are around who haven't accumulated records, Luis? While we chase our tails at the routine, he could be somebody—in that apartment or somewhere on that block—looking upright as hell, and nothing to show."

"*Pues sí*. Frustrating," said Mendoza. "And I'm also feeling frustrated about Harriet Branch. Nobody knowing Alan Keel. As I told John, we're going back to take a long close look at all those hotel employees."

"With everything else on hand? There's also Rex," said Palliser, "and a new body—I haven't heard about that yet."

"Just an unidentified body," said Mendoza, who had called in while they waited for lunch. "Matt thought, a couple of weeks old." Even in the crowded city, there were places a body could stay unnoticed.

"Which reminds me of Carlos Masada," said Higgins. "Nothing to do on one like that."

"What we didn't tell you about," remembered Hackett suddenly, "was Billy. Billy and the food stamps—"

Mendoza, hearing about that, went on laughing for some time. "Is it that funny?" asked Hackett. "I thought it was pretty damn sad myself. Living on other people's money, the money forcibly taken away from people who work, and the damn fool doesn't even know that."

"It's funny, Arturo, in a sinister kind of way, and I use the word advisedly," said Mendoza. "Yes— Mrs. Whitlow's shrewd father, and the insurance agent thought he was crazy—but what's fifteen C's a month now? Don't worry, *compadres*. What this benighted country needs is a damn good depression, and— *¡Ay de todos políticos!*— are we going to get one! The ride on the merry-go-round comes to an end eventually, for all the Billys."

"Ancient Rome," muttered Higgins.

"Let's go back and try Bainbridge's office," said Palliser.

At the office, they found Jason Grace talking to Lester Watson's parole officer. Coming in to help out at the odd jobs, on his day off, Grace had heard about that from Lake and called around to find Tucker.

Tucker just made a defeated gesture to questions about Watson. "Look, it's impossible to do anything for that kind. What is there to do? Keep an eye on him while he's on P.A.—and the kind with any mind left, at least they'll mind their p's and q's while they're being checked on, but the Watsons can't even do that—as witness your evidence. He's been on the hard stuff since he was sixteen, and it's a wonder to me he's still alive. Now he's killed a woman, just for nothing. His mind blown by the H or whatever, running berserk. I hope now they'll tuck him away at Atascadero, but I take no bets. Did you hear about the proposal to close all the insane asylums? Nothing said about what to do with the inmates. I think most politicians are crazy themselves."

"Maybe we wouldn't notice," said Hackett wryly, "if they did just turn the lunatics loose. Enough walking around that way now. We'll try to pick Watson up before he goes berserk again."

Tucker just shook his head and went out.

Sergeant Lake was plugging in a call. "It's Bainbridge, Lieutenant." Mendoza fled into his office, with the rest of them on his heels, and put the phone in the newest gadget he'd acquired, the amplifier. "Yes, Doctor?"

"Well, she was raped," said Bainbridge abruptly. "The actual cause of death was manual strangulation, but she was knocked around a little—not enough to do any serious damage, before death. I pinned it down to between noon and two P.M. yesterday."

"But that's—damn it," said Hackett, "just when that hunt was under way—"

"In the apartment," Mendoza reminded him. "This might have been half a block away."

"Those witnesses—" muttered Grace.

"So, go on, Doctor."

"When you give me a chance. There's something rather funny, Luis, and I don't know what caused it. I said at first it looked as if she'd been run over—well, I suppose it could have been done that way, a motorcycle or— But the body, the torso that is, has been oddly compressed in some way, some of the internal organs bruised, as if she'd been—oh, damn it, all I can say, as if something heavy had been on top of her for— What? No, that was after death."

"¡Vaya por Dios!—¿Cómo dice?" Mendoza bounced upright in the desk chair. "Compressed? Listen, Bainbridge—could that have been done when the body was hidden somewhere, maybe pushed under a couch or— un momento, I've got an idea coming—behind a trunk in a garage or—"

"That's quite possible," said Bainbridge. "There's no evidence to say. I had Scarne and Horder here, a minute examination of all body surfaces and all the clothes. There's nothing. And no fingernail scrapings."

"But a four-year-old couldn't put up much of a fight," said Mendoza. "And the dress was missing. Is that it?"

"That's it. I could probably pin the time down closer with an analysis of stomach contents."

"I don't think that's necessary. Thanks very much." Mendoza replaced the phone and lit a cigarette.

"Right up in the air," said Hackett disgustedly. "Nothing! She could have been a block away from the apartment—"

"I don't think she was," said Grace slowly. "I think those witnesses knew what they were talking about."

"Then why the hell didn't we find her, Jase? My God— weren't we all thinking of those five men living there, at home in the daytime? I looked at two of those places— Reed's and Wagstaff's—and I mean looked," said Higgins. "In hampers and garment bags and bureau drawers and the back of the closet shelf—places not really big enough —she couldn't have been—"

"I think she must have got out of the building," said

177

Hackett. "Just as you said, Luis. Ran into the pervert down the street."

"And," said Mendoza, blowing smoke like a dragon, "was grabbed up off the street while nobody saw it or did anything? The people out who knew her?—or anybody else? I never said I thought that happened, Art—I said it could have."

"It's got to be the answer. And it puts us right back to Records and the Goddamned routine. There's no other way to go."

Suddenly Grace said, "The elevators— I know we looked, and there's no place to hide a mouse, but if the lab had a look for traces of—"

" ¡Media vuelta!" said Mendoza loudly. " ¡Pedazo del alcorno qué—! Me, the blockhead to end all— The roof! My God, the roof!"

They stared at him, and were all on their feet the next minute. With no wasted words they fled for cars in the parking lot. Grace tumbled into Palliser's Rambler with Higgins, and the siren on the Ferrari started to howl as they turned out to Los Angeles Street.

Twelve minutes later the Ferrari braked in the loading zone outside the apartment house, the Rambler behind it; they ran in to find Smiley. He was just coming out of his own front apartment on the ground floor.

"Gentlemen—" He looked a little surprised.

"The roof!" barked Mendoza. "Is there access and where? From inside?"

"My sweet Jesus Christ!" said Smiley. A look of horror came into his eyes. "We never thought about the roof—my God! That's where it must've—acourse there's access inside, got to be for the elevators and air conditioning. The housing's on the roof, they got to get up there to do any repairs. We had an elevator stuck"— they were hurrying along, he leading the way, toward the elevators—"about two months back, the men were here two days fixing it. It—"

"My God, what fools we were not to think of—but if there's a trapdoor, why didn't any of us notice—"

"It's pretty near invisible," said Smiley, pushing the button for the top floor. All of them crowded into the tiny space, they rode slowly upward, impatient. "It's one of those counterbalanced things," said Smiley. "Door's built in the ceiling and when you pull it the ladder unfolds right down. There's a space there for insulation, and a trap to the roof." The elevator landed and they all piled out and followed him down the hall.

"And at least the male tenants probably guessing that," said Mendoza.

"Lieutenant, everybody here'd know about that after the time we had gettin' that elevator fixed back in April," said Smiley.

"Q.E.D.," said Hackett.

"There you are." Smiley pointed. In the ceiling at this end of the hall, nearly invisible unless you knew it was there, was inset a square board painted the same off-white as the ceiling and walls. There was no visible handle, but Smiley reached to the ordinary red fire extinguisher hung on the wall there and produced from behind it—"It's kept right here handy"—a short steel rod something like a boathook. Reaching up, he engaged the hook in a tiny aperture in the board and pulled. Silently the board swung down and following it came a folding ladder just reaching to the floor.

"Wait a minute," said Hackett. "We don't want to ruin any lab evidence, Luis."

"We've got to see what's up there. Jase, take it easy and don't fall down and break a leg." Mendoza regarded the ladder dubiously.

"Straight up," said Smiley, "and right over your head's the other trap. You can only open it from inside. But that space's only about three feet high, be careful."

Grace went up the ladder with his own handkerchief in one hand and Hackett's in the other. He was excitedly convinced that this was the answer to the locked-room mystery, and why none of them had thought of it— Reaching the space above the ceiling and discovering that it was floored solidly, he had another thought. There wasn't an-

179

other building on this block over four stories high, and even in the unlikely event that anybody had been on another roof along here, they couldn't have seen—

Little Katie May, with her pigtails and solemn eyes, in this place—maybe with somebody she knew from the apartment, someone Mommy and Daddy knew—

He reached up and pushed cautiously, and the other trapdoor went up silently at about the level of his waist, and he straightened up through it. The hot sun struck glaring on his face after the air conditioning inside, and it was a moment before his vision cleared.

Three feet ahead of him was the housing for the elevators and air-conditioning mechanism, about seven feet by ten. And all around him, as he slowly swiveled to examine it closely, was the roof: the rough synthetic slate, in this dry summer climate, covered with the accumulation of thick dust untrammeled by any mark at all.

"Damnation," said Grace softly to himself. He reached out an arm's length and put his hand down on the roof. When he took it away, there was a distinct palm print in the dust. If anybody had been up here since the elevator had been repaired two months ago, they'd have left a plentiful trail of footmarks. But nobody had been. Nobody at all.

Resignedly, the rest of them went back to the office to get started on the routine. Grace said he wanted to talk to the Blaines, he'd get a cab back.

There wasn't, of course, much to say to them. They both looked haggard. Grace didn't know much about what Christian Scientists believed, he'd been raised an Episcopalian himself, but he supposed any religion taught that there wasn't such a thing as death being an end to a person. It wasn't logical, anyway. He figured that people on the other side were taking care of Katie May, but he didn't quite know how to say that to the Blaines.

"If only we could have bought that house," said Mrs. Blaine. "If we hadn't been living here—"

Blaine said heavily to Grace, "You see, I only just

graduated and started to work regular six months back. I was in school up to then, training. We haven't been able to save much. There was a house in Leimert Park we liked, but the down payment was pretty steep, we couldn't—"

"I can't have any more babies," she said. "Something went wrong. If only we hadn't been living here—"

"Have you—got any idea about how—?" asked Blaine.

"We'll be looking," said Grace. He thought there might be something he could do for the Blaines. He gave them his warm smile. He said, "You know, my wife can't have any either. At least, no luck yet. But we adopted one—her mother and father got shot by a lunatic when she was only three months old, and there wasn't anybody to take her. So Ginny and I pestered the County Adoption people and finally got her. She's just over a year now. Would you like to see her picture? Her name's Celia Ann."

"I'd like to, Mr. Grace." Mrs. Blaine looked at the snapshots of Celia Ann, in her bath and with the big furry gray cat the Lieutenant's wife had given her to celebrate signing the adoption papers, and cried a little, and said, "She's a darling."

"And I know you don't want to think about it now," said Grace, "but sometime later on, well, you know, there's always babies left with nobody to look after them. And they—get to be your own, however they come."

"Thank you, Mr. Grace," said Blaine. "We'll—sort of think about that."

Predictably, the computer turned up a large number of the known sex perverts from the LAPD files. And on one like this, as Mendoza said, there were no hard and fast rules: you could sensibly reckon that a pervert living, say, within a mile-square radius of the crime was more likely to be X, but a man might have wandered up from Santa Monica or the Valley, for whatever reason, and just have been there at the wrong time for Katie May.

It was going to make a lot of legwork.

Mendoza had had a long day, and was just starting

home at five o'clock, when Lake stopped him in the ante-room and indicated Horder.

"Here's a funny thing," said Horder. "This new body—the one in an empty lot somewhere. I went and got its prints—nice clear set. And I'd been looking at the other ones fairly recently, and I thought where had I seen that tented whorl before, and so I checked. The prints match a lot of the prints we picked up in that Park View Street place, Lieutenant. The Upton girl."

"*¿Cómo no?*" said Mendoza, astonished. "But—" The unidentified corpse, of course, could conceivably be a suicide, he thought suddenly. They didn't know how he had died. John Upton, that hot-tempered man, lashing out and feeling sorry afterward. "That's funny all right. But the A.P.B. hasn't turned up a smell of the husband. He had a little arrest record in Fresno—they probably printed him. You'd better check and see."

"O.K. I thought it was a very queer thing," said Horder.

"Which we do sometimes get," said Mendoza.

Landers and Conway took their girls out to The Casta-way, that nice restaurant in the hills above Burbank, where there was such a fabulous view out over the metropolitan area. And Landers enjoyed the evening, but taking his girl home, little blond Phil O'Neill, he felt vaguely dissatis-fied; he'd rather have had Phil to himself. He'd asked her to marry him twice, and she said she was still thinking about it. Maybe third time was lucky, but he felt this wasn't an auspicious occasion. She'd enjoyed Rich Con-way's jokes a little too much. And Margot Swain was a nice girl, but—

That night the restaurant heisters hit the Tick-Tock restaurant in Toluca Lake, and the night watch had the Burbank force calling to match the M.O. and descriptions. It looked like the same boys.

They had heard something about Katie May from the news on TV and the grapevine; the locked-room puzzle. It was an offbeat one, and they kicked it around a little.

Glasser was still driving the loaner, and feeling annoyed at the garage; they'd said he could have his own car back today, but it hadn't been ready and the old Plymouth had developed a noisy muffler.

At nine-thirty they got a call: two men attacked and robbed on the street by two j.d.'s, one seriously hurt. Glasser and Galeano went out to look at it, and found the squad-car men holding one suspect. The ambulance had come and gone.

"We were just on our way to the parking lot," said the uninjured citizen, dazed, talking compulsively. "We both work at the post office, Bob and I've known each other fifteen years—Bob Thatcher—we'd been overtime on account of everything piling up—the Goddamn standards lowered so much, you get all these illiterates can't read, the mail piling up, and— But some of us are still conscientious—we were just on the way to the lot, Bob talking about all the damn inflation and prices— Those two came running up behind us and knocked Bob down, grabbed me, they got my wallet, the one that got away— he had a knife—but I got hold of the other one, that one, and—"

His name was William Spears, a middle-aged man, lean and gray, ordinary looking. He had held on to the other one, and dragged him back into the post-office building and yelled for help and cops. The other one had got away.

They looked at the one they had. He wouldn't say anything, sullen; but surprisingly he had a Social Security card on him. His name was Raymond Halley, and he was about twenty. He wouldn't tell them about his pal. They stashed him in jail for the attention of the day watch.

The hospital said Thatcher was in serious condition. They had to notify his wife.

On Wednesday morning, with the office back to full strength, Mendoza came in late at eight-thirty and read the report Glasser had left on the assault with intent. At least they had one in jail. He might be persuaded to tell who the other one was.

Hackett had gone over to talk to him, said Lake.

At nine o'clock the lab called. "This is a queer one, Lieutenant," said Scarne. "This new body—Horder said he called you about it—we've made him. We asked Fresno for Upton's prints last night and they sent 'em right down, it was the first thing I looked at. It's Upton all right, the body."

"¡Cómo no!" said Mendoza. "You don't tell me." The body there, maybe, since the night he'd killed his wife. Maybe suiciding in remorse. But how the hell and why had he climbed over that fence to do it in such a funny place? "So, thanks very much." He told Lake to call Bainbridge's office, see if there'd been an autopsy yet; at least they might give him the cause of death.

Everybody was out on the inevitable dogged routine.

"Excuse me, Lieutenant," said Sergeant Lake formally, at the door ten minutes later. "Mr. and Mrs. Whitlow would like to see you."

Mendoza looked up, and what Mrs. MacTaggart said was his second sight fingered a little cold line up his spine. "Oh? Shoot them in, Jimmy."

The Whitlows came in rather hesitantly. Mendoza had stood up beside his desk, and greeted them with veiled curiosity. They both looked ghastly. Mrs. Whitlow was in a plain gray dress, her hair untidy, and no makeup on; Whitlow correct in a dark suit, but his eyes were tired.

Mendoza waited for them to open a conversation; the little cold finger was still edging up his spine. He asked them to sit down, and Whitlow guided his wife to one of the two chairs in front of the desk, took the other. He got out cigarettes and gave one to her, lit it, lit his own. Mendoza sat down again and picked up the gold desk lighter. "Have you thought of something you haven't told us?" he asked at last.

"Yes," said Whitlow flatly. "That's a way to put it. I'm sorry, this isn't easy. My wife—thought of it first, and we've talked—and I do see that it could possibly—might just possibly—have—something to—do with Mother. That we should tell you."

She raised her eyes from her cigarette. "It's hard for Walter to say it, Lieutenant, because he—we've cut all connections now. There wasn't anything else to do— I tried —we both tried so hard, for such a long time, but I came to see it—it was a waste of time."

"I can tell him, Edna. You see, our daughter—our daughter Harriet—"

"We'd been married ten years before she was born," said Edna Whitlow, "and you can imagine how we felt. She was such a pretty baby—we named her for Mother, you see. And maybe—it's a thing parents do—maybe we spoiled her, indulged her. Too much. Believed all the—the jargon about not punishing or—" She shook her head blindly. "And we thought afterward—if we'd sent her to the private schools instead—but I guess we'll never know about that." She put out her cigarette, took a tight grip on her handbag, and said, "And I suppose—the police— hear the same story from a lot of parents these days. Don't they? How could she, how did we go wrong, what can we do? Oh, God, the times we tried to reach her, the ways we tried— But you know what I'm telling you. We found she was taking drugs when she was still in high school. Then she dropped out, and we didn't know where she was for six months. Then she came home asking for money. We—"

"Call that a synopsis of the last eight years," said Whitlow, "and leave it at that. As my wife says, we tried. That psychiatrist, after I'd listened to him half an hour I thought he was on drugs too—another waste of time, we didn't send her there. She wouldn't have gone anyway. I don't know and after all this while I don't care all the places she'd lived, the men she's lived with, since she left—some of those communes, the cheap rooms, the— At first we didn't like to think of her going hungry, and when she came we gave her money—we thought as long as she came, it was a link, sometime we might reach her, might— But in the end I saw we never would. She's lost, she's gone. It's as if she'd died, Lieutenant—or been possessed by that—that slut of a drug-ridden—"

There was a long pause. "You see," she said painfully, "it was that key. I heard you talking about it that day, and I asked Walter about it, but he wouldn't tell me. Because —he'd already thought what it might—"

"Oh, my God," said Whitlow tiredly, "how far can a man rationalize? Yes, I'd seen it was no use—she can't be reclaimed. But to think of—anything worse—"

"I think," she said, "women are inclined to look at these things a little straighter. When he did tell me, I saw it right away, and I thought we'd better tell you. You know how long Mother'd lived at the Clark. I used to take Harriet with me, to see Grandma—she used to like that, especially all that time back when the hotel was busier, all the people. That's—when she was quite a baby, three, four. And Mother would come downstairs when we left, we'd talk to Mr. Quigley and— Well, that doesn't matter. But the first time Harriet came home—I thought it was going to be all right, she was going to do everything she promised, get off the drugs and straighten up. She stayed home three months that time. And Mother had been—so distressed over it—I took Harriet to see her, we were all so happy that she was home. And you see, that was the very day—that Mr. Quigley came to explain—how they were going to start locking up at midnight, and gave Mother that key to the front door. She put it on her ring right away."

"¡Ca!" said Mendoza softly.

"She'd—remember that," said Edna Whitlow. "You said to Walter, somebody knowing about that key, and the hotel being locked at midnight, made you sure it was one of the hotel people. But I never thought any of them would have—anything to do with—what happened to Mother. And I just saw how it could be. Mother 'd never given up hoping she'd come home. Be good. I—we never told her about some of the men we saw her with, coming asking— or the places she'd lived, we used to go begging her— But if she'd come—and asked Grandma for help—" She stopped.

"And doesn't that fall into place," said Mendoza, fitting jigsaw pieces in his mind. "Yes. I'll have to ask you if you know where she's living now."

"She's probably in your records, Lieutenant," said Whitlow. "I don't know if she's still at the address we had two months ago. It's on Howard Drive out in Monterey Park, I've never been there. I don't know if she was there alone or how she was getting money for the junk, for food. I said she needn't come to us again—we were finished. And she laughed at me." He got up. "So we've told you. Edna—"

"It's easy to say, isn't it," she said to Mendoza, "that I'll never forgive myself I didn't make Mother move away. If Harriet hadn't known—and about that monthly check too—"

187

"We don't *know*," he said. "It's just possible."

"Oh, I know," she said. "I've known ever since I heard about that key." She nodded to Mendoza; they went out quietly.

And the jigsaw pieces fitted better this way than the other. Mendoza got up and went out to the anteroom; Hackett was just coming in shepherding a man before him. "Who have you got?" asked Mendoza.

"One off the list of perverts, what else?"

"Stash him away," said Mendoza, "or let somebody else talk to him. We're going calling." He told Hackett about this on the way downstairs. They stopped at R. and I. to see if they had Harriet Whitlow in the files. She was there, from five years back: possession, soliciting, several counts. She'd served a single three-month sentence in the County Jail. The latest address in their records wasn't the same one Whitlow had given Mendoza.

"So we try there first."

They had a little hunt for the address, over in east L.A. When they found it, it was an old stucco four-family place looking ready to fall apart, and there was a sheriff's notice posted that it had been condemned. "*¡Condenación!*" said Mendoza, but they went in to see. They got no answer at the right-hand door on the ground floor; the place looked deserted, but they went to try the left one.

It was jerked open suddenly from inside as they got to it, and a man appeared talking over his shoulder loudly. "And you can damn well put up or shut up, you little bitch! When I get back with the john, you play up or I'll give you a working— Who the hell are you?" He brought up against Hackett's bulk solidly. Mendoza had the badge out. The man swore obscenely and expressively, but Hackett had a grip on him.

He was about twenty-eight, medium height and weight, dark-haired. "Now I wonder," said Mendoza, "if this could be Mr. Alan Keel."

The man went tense and quiet under Hackett's hand, and just as a precaution Hackett patted him down and

188

got his own gun out. Mendoza pushed the door farther open and they went in.

This was Harriet Whitlow; they'd seen her mug shot now. She was twenty-four, and she looked twenty years older. She'd been a pretty girl once, blond like her mother, but the years of drugs had blotched her skin and puffed bags under her bloodshot eyes and the hard living had marked her. She was dirty, and thin, and sloppily dressed in shorts and a filthy terry halter, and she stared at Mendoza and Hackett in dull surprise.

"Cops," she said wearily, eyeing the badge. "On account the building's gonna be torn down and we got to get out."

"Cops," said Mendoza, "on account of your having the little brainstorm about visiting Grandma a week ago tonight when you were short of the money for junk."

The drugs, of various types, did nothing at all for the user's brain; she was surprised, and hadn't any quick defense, even automatic denial. "How'd you know about that?" she asked stupidly.

"Oh, we generally get there," said Mendoza. "And I rather think this *hombrate* was with you. Have you got a name?"

"Go to hell," said the man.

"His name's Alan Lord."

"And you shut up!"

Mendoza glanced around at the bare dirty room where they'd been camping out. Odds and ends of clothes, packages of potato chips, cheese crackers, soft drink bottles. Among the miscellany on a rickety table was a woman's handbag, shabby white plastic. Mendoza eyed it; legally, he couldn't look inside it without a warrant unless they resisted arrest.

"You're both coming in," he said.

Suddenly she came out with a string of obscenities, as it reached her that she was going to be taken in, away from the drugs, whatever she was on at the moment. She grabbed up the bag, first thing to her hand, and threw it at Mendoza clumsily. Instinctively he ducked, and the bag flew open and scattered things around him on the floor—lipsticks, a compact, an aspirin bottle full of red barbs, a hypo in its own box, a shower of small coins—and a key.

"*¡Qué mono!*" said Mendoza. "Thank you so much, Miss Whitlow." It was the Yale key for the front door of the Clark Hotel.

"Goddamn you"—she turned on the man—"I bet you left some prints—you thinking you're so damned smart—"

"Shut up," he said automatically.

"You're both under arrest," said Hackett, and began to recite the set piece about rights.

The jungle, thought Mendoza, looking at the girl. "Grandma opened the door to you right away, did she? Quite possibly she'd have given you money if you asked nicely. Just why did she have to be killed?"

The girl's mouth was sullen; she jerked an indifferent shoulder at him. "This creep had to be along—she didn't like his face or something, started to raise a fuss. She was old and ready to die, what the hell? And then when that damn snotty little night clerk went off, the damn emergency door—"

"But you remembered the right key," said Mendoza. "Yes." He went out and used the phone in the Ferrari to call for a squad car. When it came, they handed them over to be ferried in. What the girl had said would make a statement of sorts if she'd sign it; but it had probably been the man who'd killed Mrs. Branch.

Mendoza was curious about him, and they questioned him at the jail; they got nothing out of him, not even a name. "Lord will do," he said flatly. When they processed him in, Mendoza asked for the prints to be sent to the lab, and eventually they were identified as those found in that apartment, tied to the name of Keel. Maybe neither was his right name, conceivably they'd never know.

Mendoza applied for the warrant; it would probably be called murder two and conspiracy.

Landers had gone over to the jail to talk to Raymond Halley on that assault last night. The second post-office employee, Bob Thatcher, was listed in critical condition at the receiving hospital; he'd been stabbed several times.

Halley was about twenty, and Landers felt that he'd talked to so many like him in the last few years, all the faces blended into one. First, Halley was sullen and silent. When Landers told him about Thatcher, he suddenly saw the light—he was in jail and his pal wasn't. "Listen," he said to Landers, "Pat had the knife, I didn't. I just knocked that one guy down and took his wallet—it was Pat—"

"Pat who?" asked Landers.

"Uh—Pat Norton. See, we been living in one of these communes, over in Hollywood, only Pat got fooling with some girl and her old man clobbered him— I tried to help him and we both got thrown out, and those Goddamned thieves stole all our food stamps!" said Halley indignantly. "We didn't have nothing but about thirty lousy bucks I got—" He stopped.

"Got where?" asked Landers.

"Well, uh, I grabbed a purse from a dame in the street —night before last, I guess. We got a room to sleep in and then that damn fool Pat hadda go and blow the rest of it on speed! So we—"

"Where's the room?" asked Landers. "Do you think he went back there?"

"How the hell would I know? All the clothes we got are there." He gave Landers the address; it was on Temple.

Landers went back to the office to give that to Wanda for typing. Higgins had gone out hunting Lester Watson again; everybody else was busy at the routine, hunting for the perverts off that list, when they found them bringing them in to question. Conway was just emerging from a session in an interrogation room, and Landers suggested that they go look for Norton together. He still had the knife, presumably, and if he'd been riding high on the Methedrine— They found the address, an old rooming house, and went in. An indifferent fat woman downstairs said there were two young fellows had rented her second back a couple days ago. They went upstairs.

They found Pat Norton sitting on the bed, taking off his

shoes. He was about Halley's age, with the long hair and a scruffy little beard, and he looked dazed and unwell, his eyes shot with red. "Cops?" he said. "What do the fuzz want? Where's Ray?" He looked around as if suddenly aware of something missing.

"In jail," said Landers. "You remember ripping off those two fellows last night? On the street? One of them grabbed Ray. He told us where to find you."

"Oh," said Norton. "Oh. What'd you say we did? I just found my way back here awhile ago— I don't know where I been." Absently he started to take things out of his pockets, and the first thing he brought out was the knife— about an eight-inch blade, still stained. Landers took it away from him. The second thing was a wallet, with a few bills in it, bulging otherwise with I.D., snapshots. Landers looked at that; it was Thatcher's wallet.

"Do you know that the man you stabbed is in critical condition, that he may die?" asked Conway.

Norton stared at them open-mouthed. "I don't remember stabbing anybody. But I don't know— I been on speed. A real high ride, man. I don't remember anything Ray and I did all yesterday. Like I say, I just got back here awhile ago—don't know where I been—"

They took him in, and would be applying for the warrant. As they handed him over to the jailer, he turned to Landers and said seriously, "Did I do that? Stab somebody? I honest to God don't remember. Say, you think if you give me one of those—you know—lie-detector tests, it'd say for sure?"

It was getting on toward one o'clock when Mendoza and Hackett got back, and found the office humming quietly. A piece of routine legwork like this was tiresome, but it kept them busy. In the natural course of events, the kind of men they were hunting were sometimes elusive, usually loners, often drifting around—they wouldn't find all of them on that list. Lake said Higgins hadn't found Watson yet, and was out on the other thing. Grace had just brought in another one to question; they were both interested to hear about Harriet Whitlow. Having talked to Landers, Grace passed on the news about Norton and Halley, and just about then the switchboard flashed and Lake plugged in. "Robbery-Homicide, Sergeant Lake . . . Thanks for letting us know. . . . The hospital. Thatcher just died."

"Well, convenient timing," said Mendoza cynically. "We were going to ask a warrant for assault with intent. Now it'll be murder two." He wondered if he ought to call the Whitlows, and decided against it: Edna Whitlow knew, and had it to live with.

"That's funny," said Wanda suddenly. The mail had just been delivered, and she'd been going through it. She held up a long envelope. "It's for Sergeant Palliser. A personal letter, and we're not supposed to get personal mail at the office—"

Mendoza took it and looked at it idly. In the upper left-hand corner of the envelope was a little black-and-white cut of a dog's head: a German shepherd. The return address was Langley Kennels, For the Finest Shepherds, M. Borman, Tempe, Arizona. It was addressed in typescript to Palliser at LAPD headquarters. "Now I wonder what that's about," said Mendoza. "Leave it on his desk. I guess you and I have lunch alone, Arturo."

Palliser, coming in at two-thirty with one Wilbur Sullivan from the list of perverts, took one look at the letter and groaned. He had known that Madge Borman, a nice woman, wouldn't forget that promise. Better know the worst: he slit the envelope and brought out a friendly effusion from the nice woman. —Don't know what I'd have done, so far from home and laid up in the hospital, so kind, seeing that Azzie was looked after. Marla's pups born on April first, ready for new homes at the end of June or first week in July. And, remembered what you said —watchdog for the baby—shall have one of the girls, a very nice little girl registered as Trina. And, you can pick her up at the airport, let you know when—

Palliser felt uneasy; that was so definite. Well, nothing

to be done immediately. If he found Robin in a good mood tonight, break the news gently.

Higgins had just come back after another abortive look for Lester Watson; they teamed up to talk to Sullivan.

And they complained about the endless routine: on other cases, reduced to finding the possibles out of Records and bringing them in to question, they had spent days at it only to come up with nothing. But sometimes the routine paid off right away.

All of a sudden, it looked as if that was going to happen here too, and Palliser and Higgins felt a little excited. If Sullivan was X on their locked-room puzzle, they might hear some answers in a minute.

He was a tubby man in his forties, going bald, and his eyes were furtive. He had a record of child molestation, one count of child rape that hadn't stuck; there'd been some legal hassle, as often happened, and with everybody knowing he was guilty he'd gone free. The third time he was picked up for molestation he'd been sent to Camarillo; he'd been out of there for a year. He was living with his mother at an apartment on Crocker Street, and he had a job in a men's store on Vernon Avenue, about three blocks up from Hooper.

And after forty minutes' session with him Higgins said, "I like him, John. I like him a lot, on Katie May. He's got the right record and all the wrong answers. Let's hear what Luis thinks."

Mendoza rather liked Sullivan too, just at first. Sometimes they got lucky and turned up an ace on almost the first draw.

Sullivan said he'd been at work all day Monday. He hadn't done anything bad like that, he was all cured of wanting to do like that since he'd been in the hospital. They asked if the store owner would back that up. He shuffled around and said Mr. Brown had been out about noon, to the bank, but he'd been in the store all the time. Higgins had gone out to see Brown, who said he'd been out of the store, leaving Sullivan there alone, from noon to one-thirty, and he was damned annoyed and about to fire him, because a good customer had come in just today and said he'd been there about one o'clock on Monday and the store was empty, no clerk there. Leaving the place open, said Brown, for shoplifters; just walking out—

That was definitely interesting, and Mendoza went back to the interrogation room where Sullivan was sitting huddled miserably in the little chair. "Mr. Brown's found out about your leaving the store open on Monday and just walking out," he said conversationally. "Where did you go, Sullivan?"

"Oh, hell, I was scared he would," said Sullivan. He was a mixture: a hint of some Oriental in his eyes, and he was a light saffron color. He said earnestly, "Honest, I don't— I don't want to do that to kids any longer. I never did that to that little kid. Honest."

"Where did you go on Monday?" asked Higgins.

"Oh, hell," said Sullivan. "If it isn't one thing it's another. Now I got to tell you and I get in more trouble. Oh, hell. I went out to put a bet on a horse. That's all."

"Where?" asked Palliser.

"Oh, hell," said Sullivan unhappily. "I don't see nothing wrong, put a bet on a horse. Don't see why it should be against the law. Now you close up that place, and everybody blames me. Oh, hell. It's Sam's Bar and Grill down the block. There's a racing board up in back."

"*Se comprende*," said Mendoza amusedly in the hall. "Out of the frying pan—"

"See if it checks out," said Higgins.

"And just how do we go about that?" asked Palliser.

"There are other specialists in the building," said Mendoza. He went into his office, told Lake to get him Vice, and laid the phone in the amplifier. The desk sergeant answered and he asked, "Is Perce there? Mendoza." In a minute he was talking to Lieutenant Andrews. "Perce, we've just heard there might be a horse parlor in the back of Sam's Bar and Grill out on Vernon."

"Is that place open again?" said Andrews. "Between you and me, Luis, I don't see that it's very logical it should be legal inside the fence and illegal out, but that's what the law says and we're paid to enforce it. Besides, those operations take quite a cut. The last time we closed that one up was six months ago, thanks for the tip."

"Well, we've got a rather important alibi hanging on what—mmh—Sam and his cohorts may have to say." Mendoza explained and Andrews laughed.

"Yes, I see—unlucky for Sullivan. Well, we're sort of at loose ends here, some of us may as well go down there and pull a raid. I'll get back to you, Luis."

"And until we do hear, we hold Sullivan," said Higgins. "Just in case."

"I think so. The neighborhood's suggestive, but I also think"—Mendoza leaned back smoking meditatively—"I have the feeling, George, that the answer isn't that easy. That simple. Sullivan is obvious—and incredible."

"You just lost me."

"He was so handy—right there, a known pervert, a couple of blocks away. Did he suddenly get the urge and wander off his job looking for any child? Did Katie May run away, something she'd never done before, get out of the building unseen by all those witnesses, and just fortuitously meet up with Sullivan two, three blocks away? How? And if it was that far away, how did he know where she'd come from, to put her back there? And—"

"All right, I'm caught up," said Higgins, rubbing his prognathous jaw. "But I still want to clear him out of the way."

"*Conforme.* We'll be hearing what Vice picks up."

At five o'clock Sergeant Lake, with an incoming call, glanced around the office for somebody to take it. Three interrogation rooms were in use, and nobody but Wanda visible, but as he turned back to the phone Palliser came in with a young Negro fellow who was protesting that he was clean, real clean. "Oh, John."

"Anything new?"

"It's that librarian—Miss Giffard."

"Oh." Palliser took the phone and said his name.

"There are only six more of those books have been returned, Sergeant," said Miss Giffard. "Really, the students are so irresponsible—and I doubt if there'll be any more, goodness knows where they'll be. It's the last day of school tomorrow, graduation exercises Friday night, and only a handful of them will be here tomorrow, probably none coming in here. And then we're closed till September— oh, summer school starts in two weeks but—"

"Yes," said Palliser. "Well—" That was another piece of routine, where the tedious work was the only answer. If they were ever going to identify Rex, it would probably be by finding his name and phone number in one copy of that damned book. Ruthie Runnells had said he was too old to be in school, and that chrome yellow Mustang with its temporary license plates might have been sold by any Ford agency in Greater Los Angeles; sometimes people shopped around. "I'll come over and get the books. We can return them to the school when it's open again."

He left the suspect—a rather unlikely one—under Lake's eye and went to pick up the books, giving Miss Giffard a receipt.

Lieutenant Andrews called back just as Mendoza was about to leave the office. He said that Sam's horse parlor had been closed down. Sam and three of his cohorts were under arrest, and had resignedly backed up Sullivan's story: Sullivan had been there from half-past twelve to half-past one on Monday.

"I knew it couldn't be that easy," said Higgins. They let Sullivan go; if Andrews wanted to pull him in, let him. Mendoza could never get excited about the gamblers, it was a human foible, and there were others who did a lot more harm.

The day watch was drifting out. The routine would go on, on Katie May. Maybe one of those biology texts was the one with Rex's name in it. And sometime they'd pick up Lester Watson; there was an A.P.B. out on him. The restaurant heisters hadn't hit in their territory again. And there'd be other things coming along.

At which point, hat in hand, cigarette snuffed out in the ashtray, Mendoza uttered a sharp yelp and said, *"¡Mil rayos! ¡Dios me libre,* I'm going senile! I'm—"

"What hit you?" asked Sergeant Lake, hand on the door.

"Upton!" said Mendoza. "John Upton! And it went out of my head completely, I never—" He manipulated the switchboard and called Bainbridge's office, but nobody was there. "Remind me in the morning to find out if he committed suicide or what."

However, they were to have other things to think about on Thursday morning.

On Wednesday, his day off, Glasser spent an hour or so solemnly reading a juvenile book Wanda had given him, *Justin Morgan Had a Horse*. She'd also given him a magazine all about Morgan horses, and the photographs were nice. Beautiful creatures, she said fondly. Glasser liked the Morgans all right—they were very handsome. But he liked Wanda better, and if she was interested in horses—

He could hear her saying, Not horses, *Morgans*.

Mendoza was just getting undressed at eleven-thirty, wandering around the bedroom and looking approvingly at Alison sitting up in the king-sized bed, red hair shining in the lamplight, doing her nails. "You look very fetching, *enamarada*. It's a pity you've got an idiot for a husband. Forgetting that entirely—but at least we know, on Mrs. Branch—and what a hell of a thing for the Whitlows." And the hostages to fortune—you never knew how they'd turn out. You tried, you hoped, but you didn't know.

Their particular hostages right now had progressed to the last lesson in the first McGuffey Reader and were demanding a hen so they could gather eggs "like *los niños* in the story."

"That stray tom was around again," said Alison, "and speaking of idiots, you know El Señor—he hasn't the least idea how to put up a fight, and he's too proud to run. The last time he got bitten there was an abscess the size of an orange and Dr. Douthit said—"

The phone rang in the hall. Mendoza, shirtless, went to

answer it. Two minutes later he came back and reached for his shirt. *"¿Qué occure, amado?"* asked Alison.

"I'll tell you when I've heard."

Bill Moss and Frank Chedorov, on routine tour, had come on shift at six o'clock. It had been a quiet night. They'd handed out a couple of traffic tickets and brought one drunk in to the tank. At nine they knocked off, Code Seven, for sandwiches and coffee at an all-night place on Broadway.

At ten-fifty they were cruising down Hope Street; there wasn't much traffic now, no freeway entry near. They were talking desultorily about politics—fortunately they both shared the same opinions—and rather looking forward to the end of shift. It had gone up to a hundred and two today, and only dropped to about ninety after dark. In June, the heat wouldn't last; it should start to cool off tomorrow or next day.

"Hold it," said Chedorov suddenly. Moss, who was driving, braked.

"What's up?"

"That drugstore on the corner—there were flashlights inside. Just as we passed."

Moss grunted and swung the squad car around to the side street, which was much darker. The drugstore backed up to an alley on the side street, as all that block of buildings would; they stopped at the mouth of the alley and peered, not wanting to use their own flashlights. "There's a car up there," said Chedorov. "Right up from the back door of the drugstore, Bill."

Moss grunted again. They were both experienced cops; they didn't have to discuss what to do. Moss took the squad car past the alley and parked it quietly along the curb; they both got out. They didn't take the shotgun until they knew what they had here. Flashlights in hand, they went down the alley to the rear door of the drugstore. Chedorov flashed a light briefly on the lock. It was an old building, and the door was a wooden one, not especially strong. There were pry marks all around the lock and the door was a couple of inches open. They listened and heard cautious voices from inside, shuffling steps.

Chedorov made a move toward the door, but Moss gestured him back savagely. "They're on the way out," he muttered, "wait till they come." They both fell back down the alley, guns out, ten feet apart.

The door creaked and two vague dark forms came out, down the step to the alley. Moss and Chedorov switched on their flashlights simultaneously and Moss shouted, "Police! Hold it! Freeze!"

The two ran instead, dropping a large bundle by the back door; in the split second the light had been on them, all Chedorov had taken in was dark clothes, two white faces. They ran up the alley toward the car parked there, and Moss shouted again, and fired the warning shot in the air. The flashlights roamed up the alley, an engine started to life with a great roar, and Chedorov fired straight at the sound. Then, in the glare of the two flashlights, he saw, as if the moment were frozen in time, the top of the hood, the car coming straight for them, he saw clearly the little circle and three lines inside, a Mercedes, it was a Mercedes—

He leaped to the side of the alley desperately, dropping the flashlight. Moss, nearer the center of the alley, didn't make it. The fender caught him as he jumped, and threw him between the wheels. The car roared by, and Chedorov swung with it and emptied his gun after it. Moss's flashlight, still switched on, had fallen pointing toward the mouth of the alley, and its beam just caught the fast-receding license plate and burned three figures into Chedorov's mind.

"It was a blue and gold plate," he said to Mendoza, at the hospital. "I know that. I saw it. I didn't get it all, just the first three numbers. It was zero-one-one. I'd swear to that."

"There's no way to check a partial," said Mendoza. "I don't have to tell you."

"No, sir. But they knew what they were doing—we'd

warned them. They saw us—Bill. Listen, we rode a squad together four years, Lieutenant. They don't come any better than Bill. Listen, he hasn't got any family—there's nobody. His folks got killed in an airplane crash last year, and he's not married. There's nobody to care." He sat there on the vinyl couch in the hospital corridor and looked at Mendoza dumbly, a young man with a square bulldog face, and he said, "I ought to—we had two hours to go, end of shift—"

"Forget that," said Mendoza. "And there are people to care, Frank. Because he is a cop." It would be assault with intent at least.

"Assault with intent," said Chedorov. "Unless— Look, they've had him in there hours, when the hell will they tell us—"

"Presently."

"It was a blue and gold plate. Zero-one-one," said Chedorov. To make matters a little more confusing, there were two kinds of California license plates now. Since last year, the drivers who wanted to pay extra could get plates in the state colors, gold on blue; if they wanted to pay more extra, they could buy the vanity plates like that, make up their own. The regular plates in the new colors had the three numbers first, three letters second. The old ones, still a lot around, orange on black, were just the opposite: letters first, numbers second.

"It was a Mercedes," said Chedorov. "I saw the insignia on the hood—you know it—sticking up from the hood, a circle with three lines."

And their treasure Mrs. MacTaggart, the Highland Scot only transplanted here a few years, had once presented Mendoza with the curious information that that insignia was the heraldic arms of the Isle of Man. He wondered how it had got transplanted to the Mercedes manufacturers.

And how many thousands of Mercedes, old and new, might be tooling around L.A.—

A doctor came out eventually. "Well, we've put him on the critical list. He's got both legs broken, a broken pelvis, one arm—compound fracture—internal injuries, fractured skull. He's lost a lot of blood—"

"Type O," said Chedorov. "I'm Type A. But a lot of the fellows would— I mean, they don't come any better than Bill."

"We're managing with plasma," said the doctor. "We won't know just yet. Say by sometime tomorrow. He's got a very sound constitution and everything on his side."

"Yeah," said Chedorov. "Yeah. That's it for now?" He got up, bulky in his uniform. "So we just put up the prayers, Doctor?"

"It's a factor," said the doctor. "It is indeed."

"Yeah," said Chedorov. He looked at Mendoza blindly. He said, "One thing, they close the Protestant churches at night. Ours, no. I guess you'll want a formal statement, Lieutenant. In case you ever get them—for a trial. It was a Mercedes—I saw the insignia. And the plate started zero-one-one. I better take the squad car back to the station—"

Before this all erupted, Mendoza had been reading Mr. Kipling. He liked Mr. Kipling—a sane voice in the wilderness. He thought now, wry and sardonic, *And there is no discharge in that war*. The ultimate war all cops saw so close, every day.

"We posted a couple of men there in case they came back for the loot, but it was a waste of time." Mendoza was briefing the men on Thursday morning; they had all come in more or less together. "The lab's got all the collection they dropped, and let's hope there may be some latents— and if so, that they're in our files. There'll be a team at the pharmacy now, it's an independent and we notified the owner, he'll be taking stock in case they didn't drop all they got."

"Moss?" asked Palliser.

"He's holding his own, we can hope he'll make it. I'll remind you all that Art Hackett was worse off once, and all of us doing the worrying, and look at him now."

"Back on the diet." Palliser grinned. "We can hope."

"And didn't I have a little idea about that," said Landers rather excitedly. "When we went out on that break-in the other day. Matt, remember? If a lot of those little break-ins haven't been pulled by the same ones—maybe this pair. Because if you can say there was an M.O., it was the same." He turned to Wanda, listening with a troubled expression. "Those files I asked you to pull— remember?" She nodded and went to get them again.

Mendoza looked them over interestedly. "And you could be right, Tom. But anonymous, *absolutamente*—just like the one last night. The same M.O. all right, the pry-bar to the back door overnight. These are small-timers, and if they were the same ones, I think they panicked last night. It'd be a charge of assault with intent, if we catch up, but I don't think it was, technically."

"And just what chance in hell have we got of catching up?" asked Conway savagely. "The first three numbers on a plate, and the make of the car? It's nothing to work on.

203

We can't check a partial, and how many Mercedes are there around?"

"So we hope there are some latents," said Mendoza. "Or something." And there was still a lot of the routine to get through—they hadn't got halfway down the list of perverts. The six biology textbooks Palliser had got from Miss Giffard yesterday were still unexamined. The A.P.B.'s hadn't turned up either Lester Watson or Terry Conover.

It would be a while before they heard from the lab. The hospital had been asked to call in any change. It was Frank Chedorov's day off; he came in to make a statement, and repeated all that about the plate and the car, for what it was worth, which wasn't much.

Lake had called Hackett and Higgins, who were off today, and they both came in about ten. Hackett had been going out to price a new suit, and Higgins to lay in some film and magnetic cubes to get pictures of Laura at the graduation ceremony tomorrow night; but with all the routine piling up, the office shorthanded, they came in.

Palliser and Grace sat down with the biology texts, and everybody else went out on the perverts. Mendoza, more on the ball this morning if somewhat short of sleep, called Bainbridge's office.

"That corpse"—from an empty lot somewhere?—he didn't remember seeing a report on that but there must be one—"that got identified as John Upton." He hoped somebody had remembered to cancel the A.P.B. "Have you looked at it yet? What's the cause of death?" He was talking to one of the young surgeons down there; Bainbridge wasn't in yet.

"Oh, that one. We haven't posted him yet, as a matter of fact I was just getting to it, but what he died of, without much doubt, was a bang on the head," said the surgeon. "A hefty bang on the back of the head—deep depressed skull fracture. I'd say he'd been dead about ten days. Call it a week last Monday or Tuesday."

"¿Cómo dice?" said Mendoza. "I'll be damned. That's very funny. You'll let me know more when you've looked." Now what the hell was this? Five minutes later Landers,

coming in with a likely looking prospect and finding nobody else there to help lean on him, looked in to find
Mendoza talking to himself. He told Landers what the
surgeon had said.

"It's funny enough that it should be Upton," said
Landers. "Do we deduce now that somebody murdered
both of them? But it looked like the perfectly straightforward thing—husband losing his. temper, knocking her
down, and running when he saw she was dead. When
Jimmy told me the lab had identified the corpse as Upton,
I thought he'd probably committed suicide."

"*Ya lo creo.* Where's the first report on the body?"
Mendoza searched the tray on his desk and found it,
where Wanda had carefully filed it and he hadn't, in the
press of business, bothered to read it. "Santa Barbara
Avenue. *¡Caray!*—a high board fence. And just how—
What the hell is this, Tom? If somebody killed both of
them at more or less the same time, why move Upton's
body?—and to such a peculiar place? I don't like this—
there's no sense in it."

"It's funny all right," said Landers. "I wasn't on that—
were there any other latents picked up in the house?"

"No. The wife's, that's all. And damn it, if there was any
lab evidence that anybody else had died there, or any
other evidence at all, we'd know it by now. I can't make
this out at all—there's no shape to it," said Mendoza.
Untidiness always annoyed him, and this funny business
was untidy all right. He couldn't think of anywhere to look
on it, any questions to ask anybody, but it nagged at him.
He told Landers to have fun with his prospect; the routine
had to be done, but he didn't think they were going to
find the X on Katie May by the routine. He got his hat,
went downstairs and drove down to Santa Barbara Avenue
to look at the place where Upton had been found.

He remembered absently, walking back from the parked
Ferrari, another body behind a high fence, awhile back.
But that one— He stared at the high board fence. What a
place to put a body, he thought. And why? Or had Upton
actually been killed on the spot—and how? The fence was

at least twelve feet high, and Upton hadn't been a small man. Why go to all the trouble?

The answer, of course, was that A.P.B. It had, as Landers said, looked straightforward; if Upton hadn't been found and identified, they'd still be thinking of him as on the run after killing his wife. Somebody else with a motive for killing Cicely Upton? Who?

And where was his car?

Mendoza, his long nose twitching, walked around the fence down the side street. The fence was just as high there, it enclosed this whole huge corner lot down along the next street running parallel to Santa Barbara. He turned down that. In the middle of the length of fence here, however, was something new. Piggott's report had said some kids had found the body, and here was how the kids had got over the fence—a tall mound of earth had been left outside the fence when the old building had been torn down, and the kids, or somebody, had laid a couple of planks from it to the fence top. Fastidiously, Mendoza tackled the climb and peered over the fence. On the other side another couple of boards had been laid, at a low angle to the ground: easy enough to slide down, or pull yourself up again. Kids? That, he'd take a bet on; but they'd have to find out. And somebody—the X on the Uptons—had known about it. How?

He found a public phone and called the office for the names of the kids who had found the body. They both lived on the other side of the street across from the back of the fence. He only found one to talk to, Bobby Starling, but that was enough. Sure, Bobby said, him and Tim had fixed those boards to get over the fence. Nothing over there they could hurt, he didn't know why the ole company had to put up a fence anyways. And of course now, thought Mendoza, hopeless to expect the lab to find any of X's latents on those boards, the fence.

"*¡Mil rayos!*" he said to himself. He couldn't make head or tail of this at all. He started back across the street, to head for the Ferrari, and was nearly cut down by a small olive-green truck whizzing round the corner. He wondered how Bill Moss was doing.

None of the biology textbooks was the one with Rex's name and phone number. "We find ourselves doing some pretty queer things in this job sometimes," said Grace, shutting the last one, "but this is about the queerest piece of detecting I ever did, John. Seems to be the only way we're going to locate him, though."

Palliser agreed. They sat there a moment, somnolent, after the tedious peering at pages; they could hear the office humming at work all around. Two interrogation rooms were in use; Hackett and Higgins had just turned a man loose after questioning him and were talking to Lake before starting out again.

The list of perverts being what it was, this routine hunt could go on for days. "I suppose," said Grace, "we'd better get back to the legwork on that list. The rest of these books aren't available, you said."

"Miss Giffard said. Irresponsible kids forgetting to turn them in. Summer school open in two weeks, a few may show up then."

Just as they got up, Lake gave them a hail. "I just had a pigeon call in on Lester Watson. He's said to have a job washing dishes at a short-order place on Jefferson. Here's the address."

"So let's go see if he's there," said Grace.

He wasn't. The owner of the place, a very black fellow even bigger than Hackett, with an amiable smile, said his name was Soames. He'd never seen Watson before he showed up two days ago in answer to the sign in the window offering a job. "But one day is enough," said Soames. "Man, that boy is so punch-drunk he's walking around in a dream. You can't trust him, carry a plate across the room, I tell you. I told him to get out, yesterday. Paid him five bucks, and it was worth it to get rid of him."

When they asked him to call in if he spotted Watson anywhere around, he asked. "What's he done, anyway?

I wouldn't think he'd have brains enough to shoplift a candy bar."

"Murder," said Grace.

"You got to be kidding," said Soames. "Him?"

"Him. He stabbed an old lady to death. He's punch-drunk on too many years of heroin," said Palliser.

"I will be Goddamned. Listen, gents, I sure call in, let you know, if I see him. I sure will."

They thanked him for the intention, and went on to lunch at Federico's. Palliser called the office; Lake had checked with the hospital, and Moss was holding his own, very slightly improved. "I hope he makes it," said Palliser.

He was still feeling uneasy about Madge Borman's letter, reposing in his breast pocket. When he'd got home last night, Roberta had been breathing fire; the third man had appeared to give an estimate on putting up the fence, and said the best he could do was three hundred and fifty dollars, it was a big yard. Outrageous, she had said, and why Palliser insisted on such a high one—three feet would be plenty. Palliser had held his peace, and offered to give the baby his bath while she got on with dinner. He'd see how she was feeling tonight, if it seemed auspicious to break the news to her about Trina.

"You know," said Grace thoughtfully, "Katie May's funeral is tomorrow. I was thinking I might go. Those are nice people, the Blaines."

At one-thirty, with Mendoza talking to himself about Upton and pacing his office, they had a harried call from Traffic. As if to celebrate the end of the school semester, there was quite a sizable gang rumble going on up on the playground of that Ninth Street high school. The gangs were Negro and Mexican respectively, and there were knives around, quite a few, and clubs, and chains; three Traffic men had been injured and one Negro boy was dead. There could be others. There were eight squad cars and a couple of uniformed sergeants with riot guns there.

"Happy, carefree school days," said Hackett. He and Higgins went out to look at that; by the time they got there the fighting was just about over, and the ringleaders in cuffs ready to take in. The dead boy was Sam Safford; the school supplied his name and an address for him. He'd been stabbed in the heart.

The Traffic men had confiscated seventeen knives, twenty-six improvised clubs and assorted lengths of chain. In all the confusion of the melée, it wasn't at all clear who had stabbed Safford, and probably never would be. The autopsy might pin down a particular blade.

They tried to talk to some of them at the jail, and got nowhere, of course. To this kind, confused aimless kids so easily stirred up by a good many real and some imagined grievances, police were the enemy, and they just growled sullenly and repeated all the familiar names.

They gave up after a while, and Hackett dropped Higgins back at the office to give Wanda a first report on it, and went down to Twenty-fourth Street to break the news to Safford's family, if any.

It was another old apartment building, the little strip of ground in front bare of grass. Hackett went in and looked at the mailboxes; Safford was the first floor left rear. He walked down the hall and pushed the bell. Nobody enjoyed bringing the bad news, but it was another job cops had to do.

The door was opened, but he didn't attempt to break the news. The man leaning on the door was incapably drunk, about ready to pass out. As Hackett hesitated, he folded to the floor; the little shabby old apartment was empty except for him. Hackett found the door marked *Manager* and a sharp-faced middle-aged Negro who said merely, "Sam drunk again? It beats me how that woman puts up with it. Her, she'll be at work—they couldn't meet the rent, wasn't for her. What'd you want?" Hackett told him. "Oh. Him. Well, his ma'll be sorry, but between us he was a worthless little bastard. Chip off the old block. Well, I'll tell her."

The legwork had turned up quite a few of the perverts now, and none of them had looked remotely possible, after

Sullivan, until Landers brought in the young fellow this morning. He worked for a furniture company on Jefferson, driving a delivery truck, and a little questioning revealed the fact that he'd made a delivery to the apartment on Hooper last week. There were two counts of child molestation on him; it was possible he'd seen Katie May there, marked her. Somehow enticed her out of the building?

With some elementary follow-up on that, it fell to pieces. He'd been on the job last Monday, and they placed him at a lunch counter way out on Atlantic between twelve and one, vouched for by four witnesses.

"Witnesses," said Grace, lighting a cigarette after the fellow had taken off in a hurry. "I don't get past those witnesses."

"They've got to be wrong," said Hackett, stretching and massaging his neck muscles. "There's no way it could have happened in that building, Jase. After we thought of the roof—"

"Well, we didn't think of it right off. I just wonder if there isn't something else we haven't thought of," said Grace.

"Reaching for the hunches—better leave it to Luis," said Higgins.

"He's trying for one on the Uptons." Hackett laughed. "You know, that is a hell of a funny thing—the Uptons. It looked so—basic. Simple. And then it turns out—but by all we heard, who could have wanted to kill both of them? Why? Except for his temper, Upton seems to have been well liked enough, and she was—as Mrs. Cohen said— quite the homebody, quiet young woman minding her own business." He yawned. "Say, I wonder if anybody remembered to tell Fresno about Upton. Somebody ought to tell his sister he's dead."

He went to ask, and found Mendoza sitting up at his desk shuffling cards, cigarette in one corner of his mouth. "This is the damnedest thing we've had to nag us in a while, Arturo. What? —yes, I thought of all that. And damn it, I've got a little feeling—just a vague little feeling *extraño*—that there's something I ought to remember,

210

just on the top of my mind—something about something—and it won't come. *Eso es lo peor.* Damn it— What?"

"His sister. Up in Fresno." Hackett regarded him rather amusedly. Mendoza in the throes of trying to have a hunch was never very coherent.

"Dios, no, I didn't—you'd better send a telex up to the chief."

Hackett saw to that. Conway and Landers had just brought in another man to question. It looked like the long way around to go, but as Shogart always said, it was so often the routine that broke cases. And the types they were after here were apt to be chancy characters, ill-balanced, and the guilty one might come apart as soon as they looked at him. And then they might get some answers to the locked-room puzzle.

Hackett, who was not frequently given to hunches, frowned suddenly as he thought that. Something vague just floated across the top of his mind—and floated away. Something—something about locked-room mysteries—no, it was gone. Whatever it had been. If it was anything important it would come to him eventually.

At five-thirty the hospital called. Moss had been conscious, and they were saying now he'd make it; there would be a while of convalescence, but he'd be quite all right. Everybody was pleased about that.

"And just what kind of a chance do we have of getting that pair?" said Palliser, coming in to hear that and joining in the general relief. "Has the lab got anything?"

"We don't know yet," said Mendoza. "They picked up a lot of latents off the loot—they'd gone in for the drugs mostly this time, cigarettes, some liquor. We don't know they belong to our pair, but it's a good chance, the places they were picked up. But they're not in our records."

"Didn't I say it," said Landers. "The small-timers—and on jobs like that, just as I said to that fellow the other day, hardly worth our time to look for prints, there's never any solid lead. They could be just starting out, never been picked up at all."

"And I wonder how many of the new plates start out zero-one-one," said Higgins.

"Well, you know," said Hackett, "I had a little thought on that—" And the switchboard flashed and Lake plugged in. A minute later he turned.

"Traffic's picked up Lester Watson," he said succinctly. "There's a unit in pursuit now."

"In pursuit? Watson hasn't got a car—"

"He has now, evidently," said Lake. Hackett ran into the sergeants' office and switched on the monitoring radio tuned to their frequency. In thirty seconds it came on— "All units, K-one-ninety is in pursuit of stolen car. K-one-ninety on Jefferson Boulevard approaching Central, all units—"

They listened, following the pursuit. There was carnage on the way: the stolen car, driven very erratically to say the least, by the terse descriptions of the men in the squad car after it, struck a group of pedestrians when it mounted the sidewalk along Central, somehow ploughed on back to the street, and hit ninety m.p.h in the next block.

The end came at Central and Ninety-second, where the car failed to negotiate a right-angle turn and went through the front window of a bar. After a brief hiatus, there was a call for an ambulance; a moment later, for another.

"His P.A. officer did say," commented Hackett, "that he hoped we'd pick him up before he did any more damage. We'd better go and find out just how much—leave a little work for the night watch for a change."

The two Traffic men said they'd spotted Watson along Jefferson, on the street, and when they left the car to take him he'd jumped into a car just starting up at the curb, shoved the driver out. The owner of the car, a respectable citizen who'd just stopped to buy a pack of cigarettes, was mad: the car, a year-old Impala, was a total loss.

Watson was dead of a severed artery from the broken glass; five people in the bar and four more in that group of pedestrians were seriously injured, and one baby was dead.

They left all the information for the night watch, but undoubtedly they'd come in for some of the statement taking too.

Mendoza went home, locked the garage and went across the backyard to the kitchen door, not even casting one baleful look at the happily yodeling mockingbird in the alder tree. In the back porch Cedric was slurping from his bowl; he looked up and offered a polite paw which Mendoza didn't see.

In the kitchen there was an appetizing smell of baked ham. It hadn't been quite as hot today but the air conditioning was on, gratefully cool after the still strong sun outside. Alison was shredding lettuce at the sink and Mrs. MacTaggart just opening the oven.

"Busy day, *amado*? How's that patrolman?"

Mendoza said, "What patrolman? Oh, Moss. He'll be all right." The four cats were weaving in and out between legs, reminding people that this was usually the time they had dinner. "I need a drink."

"You look as if you'd already had some. Something," said Alison unerringly, "is trying to come to you."

"I don't know," said Mendoza, his eyes unfocused. "Damn it, I can't put a finger on it. That is the most shapeless damned thing—it makes no sense. *Pues sí*. The hot temper—and how many people have? Other than that, the ordinary young couple—"

"You need a drink," said Alison, and got down the bottle of rye. El Señor, forgetting about dinner, floated up to the counter top and uttered indignant wails as Mendoza poured his own without getting out a saucer. Alison supplied him and El Señor lapped.

"Dinner in ten minutes. I hope it comes to you," she said. "You're really not *compos mentis* when a hunch is trying to come through."

Palliser, coming in the back door of the house on Hillside Avenue, found his household more serene than last night. Roberta looked quite peaceful, setting the table; the baby was asleep or at least silent, and the coffee was just perking. He told her about Moss, and the tiresome day at all the routine, and she said, "Poor darling. Just for once, how about a drink before dinner?"

"That's a good idea," said Palliser. And five minutes later, when they were sitting relaxed at the table and she'd had a sip or two of gin-and-tonic, he began cautiously, "You remember that thing last January—the freeway accident, and the dog?"

"Um, that's rather nice," said his Robin. "Oh—yes. The dog with the funny name. Azzie. A great big black German shepherd. What about it?"

"Well," said Palliser, "I didn't mention it at the time because—well, I just didn't. She might have forgotten all about it. But she didn't."

"Didn't what? You made these awfully strong, John," said Roberta.

"Well, she was so grateful for my getting the dog taken care of while she was in the hospital—it wasn't anything, but she was—and just as I suspected, she didn't forget. I had a letter from her yesterday, and the fact is, that dog— Azzie, you know—he's a show champion, she said—the fact is—"

"How many drinks have you already had?" she asked. "The fact is what about Azzie? And of all ridiculous names—"

"Well, you see, she breeds them. Little Azzies. Only it's a she."

"John Palliser," said Roberta dangerously, "you're trying to tell me something, so just go ahead and do it."

"Well, she's giving us one. Of Azzie's latest pups. At the end of the month. I've got to go to the airport to pick her up. Her name's Trina. Miss Borman says the females are better watchdogs," said Palliser baldly.

Roberta stared at him over her glass, aghast. "A—one of those? A—good heavens, John!"

"They're nice dogs, and good watchdogs," said Palliser. He gave her the letter.

Roberta read it and took another swallow. "You know," she said, "that's really very nice of her. She needn't do that. I know they're nice dogs. And people do—keep them in the city, I mean. And it's a big yard, once we get the fence built— And I suppose a pup from a good kennel like this would be terribly expensive."

"You don't mind? You said a dog, but— Well, after all," said Palliser, much relieved, "if we're going to have a dog, it might as well be a dog that is a dog, Robin. If you know what I mean—"

"I think we're both a little tight," said Roberta. "No, now I think it over, I think it'll be fine to have a real dog. Only we'd better get that fence up, if you have to build it yourself."

"That's too much like work. We'll find somebody to build it."

The night watch had heard about Moss, and were relieved to know he'd make it all right. They didn't get any calls until ten-thirty, which was just as well: Glasser and Galeano went out to see some of the witnesses on that spectacular pursuit and crash that afternoon; there'd be inquests, and the evidence had to be gathered, pointless as it might seem. The remains had to be legally tidied away.

"It just occurs to me," said Glasser, "any cop might have a few vices, Nick, but that's one thing none of us would take up—we see too much of what it does. The dope."

They took Galeano's car because the loaner Plymouth was now belching black smoke out of its tailpipe. "Haven't you got your own piece of junk back yet?"

"They say I can have it on Saturday," said Glasser gloomily.

At ten-thirty they had a call from a sheriff's detective out in County territory in Hollywood. He said one of the good restaurants along Sunset had just got hit by heisters as it was closing, and it sounded like the same pair Central had first sounded the alarm on. Medium size, stocking masks and big guns. They'd got away with nearly three thousand bucks. "I never realized how much an expensive restaurant might—"

"Have on hand at closing time," said Glasser. "That sounds like them. I don't know what we can do about it."

"Well, we thought you'd like to be kept up-to-date," said the sheriff's man.

Friday was Piggott's day off. After he'd had breakfast he got the extra tank, that they'd got to try the tetra-breeding in, all ready and heated to proper temperature, and with a net he fished all the baby tetras out of the dishpans and transferred them to it. Any amount of water was astonishingly heavy; he panted downstairs with it and got it into the back of the Nova and drove out to the shop called Scales 'n' Fins on Beverly Boulevard.

"Oh, my," said Mr. Duff who owned the shop, "you've done very well, Mr. Piggott. Especially for the first time. How many did you have to start with?"

"All I can say is, you might have warned me," said Piggott feelingly. "More than three hundred and fifty, I made it."

"Well, I did. I said you'd need to separate them as some grew faster."

"Grew faster by eating their brothers and sisters."

Mr. Duff dipped the baby tetras out with a net and transferred them to one of his tanks at the back of the store. There were seventy-three. "That's very good," he said. "Congratulations." He paid Piggott fourteen dollars and sixty cents out of the cash register.

When he got home, Prudence had the living room straightened up. "My heavens," she said, "isn't it peaceful, to be back just watching the pretty grown-up ones sailing around?" The original tank, full of the beautiful exotic fish, looked tranquil indeed, the lovely little fish in their bright colors wandering among the foliage. "But,

Matt, what on earth are we going to do with all those dish-pans and screens?"

When the day watch came in on Friday morning, they found a new one to make the paper work—not much of a thing. At five o'clock this morning, long after the night watch had gone home, a Highway Patrol unit had happened across an accident, with a D.O.A. in it, at the entrance to the Harbor freeway. The report said it looked as if the car had gone out of control and rammed the central divider. The D.O.A. had been a young woman, sent to the central morgue. Her handbag and personal effects would be there too, but the car had been registered to Ernesto Moreno at an address in Santa Monica, and in her handbag was identification: she was Loretta Moreno of the same address.

Mendoza, looking even sharper than usual in a new silver-gray Italian silk suit, had come in, looked at the overnight report, and got out the deck of cards. He sat there stacking the deck, to practice the crooked poker deals, and he said to Hackett, who had come in with the news that Moss was conscious and swearing a blue streak because there wasn't any lead on the pair in the Mercedes, "*Pues sí.* Mrs. Whitlow's shrewd father—the ride on the merry-go-round has to end sometime. *¿Para qué? Nada más.* Just in case, with the hostages to fortune—" He began to deal rapidly. "And somebody knew the way over that damned fence. How? And, for the love of God, who? And why?"

"The Uptons," said Hackett. "Who indeed. The hunch hasn't come through."

"The lab," said Mendoza, "sent those latents from the breaker-inners' loot to the F.B.I. and NCIC. Scarne just called. NCIC doesn't know them at least."

"Oh, great," said Hackett. "Just as Tom said, they've never been picked up. Small-timers. Well, at least Moss will make it. I noticed the restaurant heisters are still on the take."

"A very profitable M.O.," agreed Mendoza. He contemplated the dealt hands, gathered them all in and began to shuffle.

"There's a proverb in Spanish," said Hackett. " 'Patience, and shuffle the cards.' "

"I'm familiar with it," said Mendoza. "Damn it, there's something—some little thing—I can't put a finger on. What gets me, Arturo, is—why move one and not the other? And, *Dios*, where's Upton's car?"

"It's shapeless all right. He didn't give himself that bang on the head."

"*Obvio.*" Mendoza squared the deck. He cut it once, to the king of spades. Twice, to the king of diamonds. Three times, and turned the king of clubs. Four, and the king of hearts.

"That's very pretty," said Hackett, "but it butters no parsnips."

"Go away and do the legwork, Arturo." Mendoza lit a new cigarette. "I'm busy working." Suddenly he discovered those love beads on the far side of the ashtray, and without comment dropped them into the wastebasket.

The routine forever came up to be done. That morning, before setting out on the routine on the perverts, Landers looked up the number and called Ernesto Moreno to break the news about Loretta. As the citizens so often were on these occasions, Moreno was dazed and incredulous. "Dead?" he said. "Loretta's dead? An accident?"

Landers explained about the formal identification, about the accident. The car had been an old heap, a fourteen-year-old Chevy; possibly the brakes had failed. Moreno said in a fading voice that he understood. "You kinda knocked me for a loop," he said. "I been sitting in an all-night poker session with some fellas. I guess I'm not exactly— Where'd you say I should come?"

Landers repeated the address, and Moreno said he'd be down.

Grace went home to View Park at ten-thirty and picked up Virginia, and they went to Katie May Blaine's funeral. She was buried at the Rosedale Cemetery. Grace introduced Virginia to the Blaines afterward, and of course

Virginia found the right way to say things. "You don't want to worry," she told Mrs. Blaine simply. "She's being looked after, the other side. She'll be all right." And whether or not that was what Christian Scientists believed, the Blaines nodded and seemed grateful.

Ernesto Moreno showed up at ten o'clock, and Landers happened to be in so he took him down to the morgue. Moreno was a little man, dark and thin, about thirty, and he looked at the body in the cold tray and licked his lips and said, "Yeah, it's Loretta. My wife. I mean, it's such a *surprise*—when you called—"

"There'll have to be an autopsy, sir. And an inquest." All the tidying away in legal terms.

"What's that? Oh, yeah—whatever the laws says," said Moreno dully. "That's O.K."

"We'll let you know when you can have the body," said Landers. "It's just a formality, Mr. Moreno."

"Yeah, O.K.," said Moreno.

The five men from the list of perverts they had found and brought in that morning were all N.G. Two of them had alibis for Monday, and the other three were—as so many of them were—inconclusive. Possible, not very probable.

Sid Belcher was due to be arraigned in court at ten o'clock, and Palliser went to offer the brief police evidence on that. After they had worked a case, it was the necessary nuisance to take time off something new, to contribute to the legal machinery, often cumbersome and slow, occasionally venal, always there.

But Palliser was feeling relieved, and rather looking forward to meeting Trina, their very own real dog-that-was-a-dog, daughter of that quite imposing creature Dark Angel of Langley. The champion.

He got back to the office at twelve-ten, to find Hackett, Higgins, Conway and Landers just leaving for lunch, having just let the latest two go—more inconclusives.

Mendoza came out of his office looking preoccupied. Evidently the hunch hadn't jelled yet.

"We've been talking about all the pros and cons," Lake was saying to Higgins. "Everybody says electric stoves are cleaner, and last longer. Even now. But Caroline says about the energy shortage, maybe there'd be gas when there wasn't power. And they're cheaper."

"Well, we've got an electric one," said Higgins, "and Mary likes it better, she says. It doesn't get the walls as dirty. I don't think there'd be much difference in price now, Jimmy."

"Well, the other thing is, you call the city for service on the electric ones, and it isn't so expensive. The gas company—"

"¡Diez millones de demonios negros desde el infierno!" said Mendoza loudly. "¡Válgame Dios! By God, the gas company— And what the hell was his name, what the—"

"Don't tell me the hunch has finally arrived?" Hackett was interested.

"It nearly ran me down—a gas company truck— And he was supposed to go bowling that night— What the hell was his name?" Mendoza stared into space for thirty seconds and said, "Chet Dickey. At the gas company— And he said, take turns driving—and she was a nice girl— But why the hell should he—"

"Who?" asked Conway, muddled.

"Wait for it," said Higgins. "Something's coming through, anyway."

13

"Because that was the night—" said Mendoza. "But what possible reason— It was in George's report, I remember— On the other hand—" He was staring at the wall raptly. Slowly his eyes focused and he swung around. "But just in the event that I'm not seeing ghosts, it won't do any harm to go and ask a few questions. Let's go."

"I'll hear about the hunch later," said Higgins. "I'm starving and I'm going to have some lunch." But Hackett and Palliser, always interested to see the boss's second sight in operation, trailed along, and in the lot he said they'd take Palliser's car.

"We're bringing back a passenger?" said Hackett.

"*No sé.* Maybe."

Palliser said, "It's all right with me, but where are we going?"

Mendoza told him: that gas company station on Santa Barbara. He remembered the names from that report; when they got there he asked for Rodman. The dispatcher was on the phone, a stack of papers before him. He looked at the three men in faint surprise, at the badge with instant excitement, and put the phone down. Mendoza introduced himself. "Couple of different fellows. You were here the other day," said Rodman to Palliser. "Have you found Johnny Upton yet, Lieutenant? I haven't seen anything about it in the papers—"

"Yes, we have," said Mendoza. "Is Chet Dickey around? We'd like to talk to him."

"Chet? I'll check and see—he and Bill were out repairing a line but they ought to be back now—" Rodman was fired with curiosity, hesitant to ask questions. He used the phone and said, "He'll be right up, just got back. I didn't see anything in the papers about you arresting Johnny."

"So you didn't," said Mendoza. They waited, and a minute later Dickey came in. It was the first time Mendoza had laid eyes on him, and he remembered the terse opinion in Higgins' report: "Liked Upton, liked wife, ordinary casual friend." Like that, thought Mendoza; exactly what Dickey looked like. He was only middle height but stocky and heavy-shouldered, with a nondescript unhandsome face and rather cowlike brown eyes, short dark hair.

"More cops, Chet," said Rodman. "They want to talk to you."

Dim apprehension came into the brown eyes. "Oh." He stared at Mendoza, who introduced himself again.

"And Sergeant Hackett, Sergeant Palliser. We found John Upton, Mr. Dickey."

Dickey licked his lips. "You did."

"And identified him by his fingerprints."

"Oh," said Dickey, and looked ready to cry.

"Could you tell us anything about it? Because it was that Monday night, wasn't it? A week ago last Monday night."

Dickey looked around wildly and dropped the hard hat he was carrying; it rolled and bounced of a leg of Rodman's desk.

"It just occurred to me," said Mendoza, and his long nose was twitching, "that you told Sergeant Palliser Upton called you that night and said he wasn't going bowling, but did he really? You just said so."

"Oh, my God," said Dickey. "I—how'd you come to find him? I thought—"

Rodman was staring.

"Some kids climbed the fence."

"Well, that just shows you," said Dickey. He sounded faintly indignant. "I know the police got a lot to do, and not enough men, but I made sure that cop was going to stop that. One of the squad cars along there, I hailed him and told him, kids getting over there and it was dangerous, and he said he'd talk to 'em. I sure thought—" He bent and picked up his hat. "Oh, hell," he said miserably. "I guess I got to tell you all about it. I'd just as soon not—"

He looked around, avoiding Rodman's eyes, and now he looked merely embarrassed.

"Suppose you come back to headquarters with us," said Hackett. They left Rodman looking after them with an expression compounded of excitement and incredulity. He was reaching for the phone.

In an interrogation room at the office, Dickey sat on the straight chair looking forlorn and said, "I don't know— it's been on my conscience awful and maybe I'd've come to tell you even if you hadn't—because God knows I didn't do anything awful wrong—and way I was brought up, a person's supposed to have decent burial even if I come to think it's not so all that important—and God knows Johnny was a nice guy, except he had a temper, you know."

"We've heard," said Mendoza.

"Well—well—" He was stuck, and Hackett helped him get started.

"Upton didn't phone you that night?"

"No, he never. I went to pick him up—for the practice bowling—at seven o'clock. They lived in one side of this duplex, you know, and when I came up to the door I could hear they was having an argument. Now I guess we all got a few faults," said Dickey anxiously, "but I got to say, about Johnny, he wasn't mean. It wasn't that. I rang the bell, I thought maybe they'd stop when I came in, and Cicely did, but he didn't. Seemed she'd got a new dress and he thought it cost too much and told her to take it back, but she wouldn't. Like I say, Johnny wasn't mean, but he was worried about expenses—like everybody else— and he didn't like running charge accounts. Well—that was what it was about."

"So?" said Mendoza.

"Well, he was going on at her, time he got ready to go with me, see. She went in the bedroom, and he was banging around in a temper, like, all over that fool dress, and pretty soon I heard Cicely give a sort of little scream and there was a bang, or a thud like, and then Johnny says to her to get up, damn it. I went in there and she was lyin' half on the floor by the end of the bed, and Johnny picked her up and laid her in the bed and says she just been knocked out, she'd be O.K. Well, look"—Dickey looked around at them earnestly—"I didn't like that. Way I was brought up, a man just don't go hitting women, specially his wife, and I said to Johnny he shouldn't've done that, and he says to mind my own business, she'd be O.K., and were we going to bowl or weren't we. So we got in my car and went out to the bowling alley, out Beverly, but all the way I was thinking we ought to've made sure Cicely was all right. That was a terrible thing to do, knock her down like that. And when we got out in the parking lot—we were already late then—I said to Johnny, about that—maybe phone and see if she was O.K.—and he got mad at me. He said his wife was his own business and I said sure she was but he hadn't got no call to knock her around and I wanted to know was she all right. Well, that made him madder, and he landed one on me and knocked me down, and that made me mad."

"Very natural," said Palliser.

"You bet it was. I'm not as tall as him but I can hold my own all right, I got up and swung on him, and all I can figure is I musta caught him off balance. He went right over, back against the car, and folded. Look, I didn't believe it. I thought he was just knocked out. I tried to bring him to, must've been five minutes I worked on him, and God's mercy nobody else drove into that lot. I got a flashlight from the car, I—but my God, he was dead. He was dead! I never meant to kill Johnny! I couldn't believe it, but he was dead!"

That deep depressed skull fracture: a very accidental homicide.

"Well, my God, I didn't know what to do!" said Dickey. "I was scared as hell. I'm not a murderer! I didn't know how the law might look at it, I was mad at him when I hit him—well, I was scared. I just thought, have to cover up somehow. I—I got him in the trunk of my car, and I went in the bowling alley. I was awful late then, I had to tell the other guys I had trouble with the car. And I said how Johnny'd called me.

"And then when we was bowling, I thought, my God, Cicely knows that's not so. She'll say. And look"—he gestured helplessly—"they was really in love, even if they got mad at each other, Cicely'd be awful upset about Johnny being dead—and I wasn't bowling so good anyway that night—"

"I bet," said Hackett. Mendoza leaned on the wall smoking.

"So I just took off early, and I had a kind of idea about going and telling Cicely how it had happened, so I went back there. Only I couldn't get her to come to the door, and finally I found Johnny's keys and got in, and—my God—there she still was on the bed, and she was dead too! Look, I really got the shakes—I don't know anything about the law, about how cops do—I mean, I know you guys try to do things right, but my God, how did it *look?* I could see right off how anybody might think, my telling that story —and already told a lie to the other fellows—my God, you'd think for sure I'd been messing with Cicely and Johnny's found out and—maybe you'd think I killed them both! I could see that—"

"What made you think about that fence?" asked Mendoza curiously.

"I was scared just silly," said Dickey. "But after a while my brain started to think again and I thought if you just found her and not him, you'd think he killed her and run away. Which maybe he would've done, when he found out he killed her—I don't know. But I thought about that place —my God, Johnny and Bill and me 'd been workin' on a line on the street right behind it the last two days—and everybody knows about that lot where the old bank was. It's all tied up in the courts—some legal trouble about who really owns it, a couple of lawsuits and all—it might be years before it all got untangled and anybody come to build anything there. And we'd seen the kids getting over, with those boards. So I—so I just drove out there, it was late then and nobody around, and it was a hell of a job but I got him over that fence and way over across by the other side—the kids seemed mostly to play by the back there.

But I thought wouldn't be any harm, speak to that cop so he'd warn 'em off. Just in case. I—"

"What the hell did you do with his car?" asked Hackett.

"Oh—I thought about that when I was lugging him over the fence. There's a junkyard out on Third, and no fence around part of it. You never see anybody around there, and I figured who'd notice one more old heap."

"Shades of the Purloined Letter," said Palliser.

"I had his keys, I drove it out there and stripped it— make it look like just another pile o' junk," said Dickey simply. "I got to think it's lucky I'm not married, live alone —it was four A.M., time I walked back where I'd left my car, and went home. And I been scared ever since. I don't know if you believe me, but honest to God that's how it happened. Johnny didn't mean to but he killed her. And I didn't mean to, but I killed him. And—" His eyes were anxious.

"Accidental homicide, Mr. Dickey," said Mendoza, "and thank you for all the answers. Now all the pieces fall into place— Yes, I think we believe you all right. And if you'd just come and told us what had happened—"

"Well, but I knew how it looked—"

"Some of us have some imagination, and God knows experience of human nature," said Palliser; but he laughed.

Dickey relaxed a little. "What—what'll happen to me?"

"Well, I should think the D.A.'ll call it accidental homicide and let it go. There's a technical charge about concealing a corpse, but that won't come to anything. If I had to give an educated guess, you'll get a suspended sentence," said Mendoza, stabbing out his cigarette.

Dickey looked incredulous. "Is that a fact? I'll be damned—" Huge relief settled over his face. "I been so worried and scared about it—"

"We'll have to book you into jail right now. But you'll get a lawyer, and make bail. Don't worry about it. I'm just damned relieved," said Mendoza, "to have this little mystery off my mind."

They were all, they realized suddenly, also starving.

They ordered lunch for Dickey from the canteen and drove up to Federico's.

They could send a lab team out to that junkyard, to find Upton's car; there were probably more latents on it.

When Grace and Higgins let the latest pervert go, at four o'clock on Friday afternoon, Grace said it wasn't good enough. The time-tried routine, but he still thought, on Katie May, that those witnesses knew what they were talking about. There were all the other men at that apartment, he said, besides the five night workers: had they all really been at work that day? Vouched for? Could one of them— a single man, or even a married man whose wife was out— have been there at the apartment? A man known to Katie May?

Higgins was tired of hunting the perverts too; he shrugged and said he'd play along. They made a start on it then, collecting all the names of those male tenants, where they worked. They wouldn't get to check any of them today; that took them to the end of shift, and some of the places wouldn't be open tomorrow, but they'd check where they could.

At four-thirty Landers and Conway went out on a new call, and a new body. There had been a heist in broad daylight at a dairy store out on Wilshire, and a woman shot dead. The more they listened to the witnesses, the more they thought this was one they wanted to drop on fast.

"But he was just a kid!" said Howard Knisely, the manager of the store. He was still dazed, incredulous. "I couldn't believe—he didn't look a day over fifteen, and young for that! And there were other customers here—Mrs. Piper there, she must have thought he was kidding— *I* thought he was—and he said it's a stickup, and I saw the gun, Mrs. Piper tried to grab it from him, and he just—he just shot her! It was so fast—I didn't believe—but then I opened the register, and he—"

The woman, Evelyn Piper, who lived in the neighborhood, had been shot in the chest. They called up an ambulance, started to talk to the witnesses. Nobody could give

them a complete description, except that the heister was—
or looked—so young.

Mrs. Ellen Shaw said to Landers, "Like you, young man
—you don't look old enough to be a policeman. Not that
you look as young as *him*—not a day over fifteen like
Mr. Knisely said, and—I think he had on dark pants, a blue
shirt or maybe gray—"

Miss Jean Anderson said he had on jeans and a white
T-shirt. "But it was just a minute—don't seem possible,
that poor woman shot right before our eyes! I didn't believe it was real—"

Baby-face, as Landers and Conway were already calling
him mentally, had got away with a hundred and eleven
dollars. He'd been alone, and none of them had seen him
get into a car, hadn't in fact noticed which way he went,
taken up with Mrs. Piper—but with all the traffic passing,
he could have had a pal waiting in a car around the corner.
Nobody could say what kind of a gun it was: Ballistics
would tell them.

"I've got a feeling, Rich," said Landers, "that this is a
mean one—hair-trigger." And everybody had said he
hadn't touched anything in the place, so it wouldn't be any
use to call out the lab to dust for prints.

By then it was getting on to end of shift, and they went
back to the office and left notes for Wanda to type in
the morning, and for the night watch, in case Baby-face
showed up on something of theirs.

They went home, and Landers phoned Phil and asked
her to go to dinner with him on Tuesday night. "I'm a little
fed up with all these double dates," he said frankly. "Maybe Rich wants protection from the karate expert, but—"

Phil laughed. "As a matter of fact, maybe he does,
Tom. Margot says she's given him every hint she can
think of, in a ladylike way, but he's still shy of the marriage
license."

"How about you?"

"I'm thinking about it," said Phil with a smile in her
voice. Landers felt fine when he hung up; it was going to
be all right, eventually he'd get her. His mother and his

sister Jean kept asking him when they were getting married; they liked Phil, from when they'd met her last year, on that funny case where she'd done the detective work and got him off the hook with I.A. Darling Phil, thought Landers fondly. Everything would be fine.

"When you know what happened, how very simple," said Mendoza. "But the general effect left behind was so damned shapeless—"

"At least you're acting human again," said Alison. "And I think that stray tom has moved in with those new people down the street. He was sitting on their front porch this morning and I saw her patting him. I hope to goodness, if he has, they have him neutered." She was encumbered by Bast and Sheba; Mendoza had Nefertite, and El Señor was brooding on the credenza. Cedric was stretched out properly at his master's feet.

"*Pues sí*. And I do see what Jase means. Those witnesses on Katie May—we might turn up something— Most of what we see in the jungle is simple—if sordid—and follows a pattern, which is why routine pays off. But sometimes there's a wild card in the deck. And damn it, I'd like to get those small-timers who nearly killed Moss, but there's no possible lead—"

"Bringing the office home," said Alison.

That McGuffey Reader was really a wonderful book, said Angel. Hackett agreed with her. His darling Sheila wasn't of an age to take to the printed word, but their bright boy Mark was mastering it by leaps and bounds. Cunningly putting off bedtime, he sat in Hackett's lap and showed him how well he was learning.

"See, Daddy, it says O, O, John, the sun has just set. I can read it all. There are a lot of ooohs in this lesson," said Mark.

"A lot of what?"

"Ooohs, Daddy. Big round ones," and Mark pointed. "When they're together they make oooh, but all alone they're in front of one."

Hackett looked at Angel, nonplussed, and she laughed over her sewing. "It's that chart I got for his room, Art. With all the numbers on it, and a zero first."

"A—for God's *sake!*" said Hackett suddenly "For God's—now I will be damned eternally!"

"Art, you know how he picks up everything—"

But Hackett was staring at all the ooohs in the Mc-Guffey Reader.

On Saturday morning, with Lake off and Farrell at the switchboard, Hackett collected Higgins as he came in and marched him into Mendoza's office. Mendoza was sitting smoking over the night watch report; it had been a quiet night, two accidents at the Stack where all the freeways came together, another brawl in a bar.

"Look," said Hackett. He filched a sheet of paper from the left top drawer, took out his pen. "What does this say?" And he put down the three marks, large and plain. 0 1 1.

"The first three numbers of that damn plate," said Higgins, yawning. Last night had been a big one: the graduation ceremony with Laura Dwyer officially graduated from elementary school, and Higgins had shot up a good deal of film, she'd looked so pretty in the filmy pink dress—she was going to look a lot like Mary, with her mother's big gray eyes. Well, Steve said they were lucky Higgins had been there to look after them, when Bert was shot. Higgins hoped he was doing a good job by Bert's kids, and so far he thought he was.

"And also what?" said Hackett. "Letters too—*¿cómo no,* Luis? Oh-el-el."

Mendoza sat up. "Meaning? Oh—I do see, Art. Oh, yes. Isn't that pretty? If, of course, it was."

"Was what?" said Higgins.

"It took a little child to make me see it, so to speak. Look—" Hackett sat down, the chair creaking with his weight, and lit a cigarette. "It happened fast. It was dark. Chedorov's a trained man, used to noticing plate numbers too, riding a Traffic unit. But he'd just jumped clear of that

Mercedes himself, he'd seen Moss run down, and he wasn't thinking just so clearly as he might have been. The car lights weren't on—he caught a glimpse of that plate by Bill Moss's flashlight, he saw it was gold on blue—"

"So, knowing how the new plates read, numbers first, he registered it as the numbers oh-one-one," said Mendoza. "I like that very much, Arturo. *¡Qué mono!*"

"For God's sake!" said Higgins. "It's either one. Numbers or letters. And if it was letters—"

"If it was letters, it's a vanity plate," said Hackett. "Somebody's own private plate number."

"With a couple of small-time pros in the car?" said Higgins.

"Now don't throw cold water, George," said Mendoza. "It could be. There are the hell of a lot of them around."

"And some damn queer ones too," said Hackett. "You know how the rules read—no more than six letters, but any number up to six. A lot of people have used their initials, or a first name and a last initial, or vice versa. Or a company name, or—you name it. We've all seen them around. I passed GLORIA the other day, and one that said YLB 2. Funny ones—we've all seen them."

"And I'll tell you something else," said Mendoza, "and that is, if that was a vanity plate it had six letters. Because the first three were in the position where Chedorov expected to see them. Vanity plates with only three initials or something like that, the letters are centered."

"That I hadn't thought of, but you're right," said Hackett rather excitedly. "And I'll remind you how those are handed out. There aren't any duplicates. If you think up a combination you want on a vanity plate and somebody's already got it, nothing doing. And I'll bet you there wouldn't be many around that start out oh-el-el."

"That I wouldn't bet on," said Higgins, "with the number there are out. But I guess it'd do no harm to ask."

Mendoza was studying the three letters interestedly. "I'll agree, some damned funny ones," he said, flicking the desk lighter, "but oh-el-el— I don't know, it could be any damned thing. What about oh-el-i? Or oh-h, come to that—"

"Look, let's start out with what we have, not guesswork," said Hackett.

Among the marvelous machines they had to help them now was the direct hookup to the D.M.V. in Sacramento. A partial make on a regular plate number was no use to them; there were too many possible combinations on too many cars, in California. But a partial on a vanity plate could be fed into a computer.

They sent up the enquiry: any vanity plate starting out O L L. They waited; this would take a little time. "Where's everybody else?" asked Higgins.

"Checking out a brainstorm of Jase's. I rather like it," said Mendoza; but then he was not so constituted that he enjoyed the routine, either.

The first reports came back. There was a plate OLLY M registered to an Oliver Manning in San Francisco. A plate OLLOVE registered to an Olaf L. Love in Alhambra. A plate OLLY registered to an Oliver DuBois in Bakersfield. "Well, Alhambra," said Hackett. The machine clicked over slowly and spelled out another: OLLER, registered to Richard Oller in Santa Monica. That, it seemed, was all.

"Well, it's possible," said Hackett. "The one in Alhambra—"

"Let's just ask," said Mendoza, and sent up the enquiry: how about vanity plates starting out O L I? They waited.

"I mean, it was just an idea," said Hackett. Mark and his ooohs . . .

The machine clicked and spelled out an OLIVER registered to Oliver Goodis of San Mateo. And OLIFFY registered to an Osbert Liffy of an address in Boyle Heights.

"Take your pick, but I know which is likeliest," said Mendoza softly. "Alhambra, Boyle Heights—given Tom's little idea that this same pair has been out on a number of jobs like that, the same general M.O. They were all around that side of our beat—"

"Let's check it out," said Hackett energetically. "By God, I'd like to get these punks."

They tried the nearer one, Boyle Heights, first; as Mendoza said it was the likeliest. It was an address on Murchison, a block of single old houses. Hackett was driving, Higgins looking for house numbers, and as he said, "It's this side of the street, couple of houses down," they both saw it at the same time.

There was an old gray Mercedes sedan sitting in the drive.

"My God almighty!" said Higgins. "You called it, Art."

"Give the credit to Mark," said Hackett. He parked the Barracuda in front of the old frame house. As they went up the walk, they checked the plate: a vanity plate, gold on blue, OLIFFY.

The man who answered the bell was paunchy, nakedly bald, relaxing on a warm Saturday in shorts and white T-shirt. He looked at the badges and said, "Anything wrong?"

"Is that your car in the drive, sir?"

"Yeah, that's right. I'm Osbert Liffy." Suddenly he looked alarmed. "Now don't tell me that fool kid was in some mix-up with it and never told me! There isn't any damage to it—say, I thought twice about letting Jerry drive it, but that heap of his just died on him, and he's usually a careful driver. My old Merc there, it's near twenty years old, and still perkin' along just fine. I'm some proud of that car. Was there some trouble about—"

"Would you know who was driving it last Wednesday night?" asked Hackett.

"Wednesday—well, yeah, Jerry had it then. He and Jim wanted to see a show somewhere uptown, I let him—"

"Jerry who?" asked Higgins. "Jim who?"

"Say, what's this about? My boy Jerry and his best pal Jim Slayback. You want to see them? Cops? What for? They're out back in the garage workin' on Jerry's car, but I think that heap's laid down for the last time—"

*   *   *

They were too surprised—not quite pros as yet—to be dropped on, to put up much defense. On the ride back to the office, the pair was dumb. Jerry was about twenty, stocky and inclined to stoutness like his father, with a wild mop of dark hair; Jim was about the same age, wiry and blond.

The first time one of them opened his mouth was when Hackett and Higgins stood back for them to pass under the sign, Robbery-Homicide, into the office, Jerry turned to Hackett, wetting his lips. "Did—did that cop die?" he asked.

"Suppose you go on worrying about that a while longer," said Hackett.

Mendoza's cold dark gaze completely demoralized them. "So we catch up to this pair of little sneak thieves," he said, blowing smoke through his nostrils. "You've been on that lay for some while, haven't you?"—and he succinctly enumerated all the break-ins they'd tied together, on Landers' little idea. Jerry and Jim looked astonished.

"How'd you know—that was us did those?"

"Because you are a stupid pair of little louts," said Mendoza. They flushed.

Jim tried to bluster. "Say, you can't talk to us that way —we got rights, you got to—you can't—"

"Everybody's got rights but cops," said Hackett. "You knew that was a police officer you ran down last Wednesday night. You ran him down deliberately."

"It was an accident!" said Jerry, going green-white. "My God, my God, don't you lay a hand—I know how you big apes feel about anybody hurts a cop! Don't you— My God, why else was we doing like that, real careful about there not bein' anybody around, don't take any chance we have to hurt anybody, I always said to Jim—then even if we do get caught, it's nothing, no kind of charge, just little stuff—"

"We have taken the trouble to add up the value of all the little stuff you got away with," said Mendoza. "Whatever you got for it. It comes to some four thousand three hundred bucks' worth—"

"Jesus!" said Jim blankly. "I don't think altogether we got about seven hundred, sellin' it—"

"Of," said Mendoza, "private property. Somebody's private property. But they don't teach you—mmh—young inheritors of freedom about private property any more, do they?"

And Jerry said, a lesson learned and memorized, "Human rights come before property rights. Like they say—"

"Oh, you Goddamned stupid little bastards," said Mendoza. "I do get tired of looking at you. Too damned many of you. Take them out of my sight, Arturo, before I forget I've got a fairly clean record with this force."

They got a statement of sorts from both of them; they took them over to the jail. At the processing desk, the sergeant told them to empty their pockets, and confiscated a pocketknife from Jerry and a nail file from Jim, counted and put away the money on them.

"Hey, that's mine!" said Jerry and Jim simultaneously.

Hackett and Higgins just looked at each other.

On the way back to the car Higgins asked, "Have you read that thing, Art—very interesting—*Territorial Imperative?*"

"Oh, yes," said Hackett, grinning. "And it's slightly encouraging to reflect, George, that just like the old tag says, the truth is mighty and will ultimately prevail."

"I suppose so, eventually," said Higgins, "but sometimes I doubt if I'll live to see it, Art."

"Cheer up, *compadre*. At least we got them. Let's go tell Bill Moss how."

At the hospital, Moss was half sitting up, some color in his face, all tied up in traction but very much himself and complaining about the nurse who'd stolen his cigarettes. "She's one of these Goddamned idiots who think they're dangerous," he said crossly. "And my God, talk about a censored press—I saw that report in print just once, a couple of years back, all the research at some big hospital saying no proof it's got a damned thing to do with lung cancer, but all the scare tactics—" Grinning, Hackett and Higgins contributed the half packs on them, and he was duly grateful.

"We just thought you'd like to know we dropped on them," said Higgins. "The punks who ran you down." They told him how, and he was amused and resentful.

"So you give that boy of yours a pat on the head for me," he said to Hackett. "But damn it, I'll be here for six weeks and then a month at home before I go back on the job! Damn it, just a pair of small-time punks—"

They couldn't blame him for being annoyed.

They heard about Grace's project at lunch. Grace, Palliser, Conway and Landers had made some headway at it even on Saturday, leaving Piggott to get all the statements on Baby-face and that heist yesterday.

Some of those men, day workers, who lived at the apartment on Hooper, worked at places that were open on Saturdays. There were fifty-five men living there who worked regularly eight to five or some such hours. This morning they had checked fifteen of them, and all fifteen had been proven to have been at their regular jobs, all day last Monday.

"I just have the feeling," said Grace, "that it comes back to that apartment house."

"I won't say you're wrong, Jase," said Palliser thoughtfully. "But they're all such upright citizens. And from what you told me—if it does, where the hell *was* she? If she didn't get out of the building? You said you were all pretty thorough."

"Sherlock Holmes," said Grace, lighting a cigarette.

"What about him?" asked Higgins.

"I can't quote it exactly. About what's left after you've removed the impossible must be the answer, however improbable it looks. I just think we ought to rule out everything we can. Then what's left—"

"If those witnesses were right, the locked room," said Palliser.

But locked room or not, it wasn't exactly a puzzle on

paper to them. Because of that small corpse in the dirty alley—Katie May with her pigtails and solemn dark eyes.

That afternoon they traced down nine more men resident at that apartment. Some of the tenants were like Blaine, professional men just starting out, in five-day jobs; the ones they had checked today were delivery-truck drivers, barbers, one bartender, bus drivers, a clerk at a travel agency, market checkers, salesclerks. All nine men had been where they were supposed to be last Monday, vouched for, innocent.

"We'll clean them up on Monday," said Grace. "Know for sure."

Ballistics called in the middle of the afternoon. The slug from Evelyn Piper's body had come out of a Colt .45.

At five-thirty Saturday afternoon Glasser called Wanda Larsen and said, "You'll never guess what just happened."

"What?"

"I won a new car in a drawing," said Glasser. He still sounded surprised. "They just called to tell me. I don't have to buy anything or—there aren't any strings, I wasn't even there. They say I can pick it up tomorrow, at the agency."

"Oh, Henry!" said Wanda. "How exciting! And of course just what you need—what is it?"

"Well, it's one of those Gremlins—American Motors. I don't know anything about it," said Glasser. "But of all the damned lucky breaks—a new car is a new car. I never won anything before in my life!"

"Oh, Henry, you'll love it," said Wanda. "Phil O'Neill down in R. and I. has one, and she's crazy about it. She says it gets marvelous mileage, and it's fun to drive— what color is it?"

"I don't know, I haven't seen it. Is that so?" said Glasser. "Well, it's a damned lucky break, is all I can say. Look, I'm supposed to pick it up in the morning. I thought I'd come by about two and we can take it out on the freeway, see how she rides, and maybe out to dinner up the coast somewhere."

"Fine," said Wanda. "I'd love to, Henry." She was pleased about the good luck; she spread the news through the office.

Sunday morning saw Mendoza in late; the heat wave was departing and the smog level down. He read the statements on that heist and Baby-face. A big gun. *Dios,* this was one they'd like to pick up in a hurry, he thought, shooting from the hip like that—hair-trigger. They had had a formal identification from the husband.

Robbery-Homicide always had business on hand, and always more coming up. He wondered why he was still here.

The phone buzzed at him and he picked it up. "Mendoza."

"Bainbridge. I'm sorry, Luis, but your office tagged it a traffic accident. Why? I just came to look at it five minutes ago. This Loretta Moreno."

"What about her?" asked Mendoza.

"It wasn't an accident," said Bainbridge. "Whatever it looked like. She was stabbed in the chest. With a very thin knife."

"*¿Qué? ¡Por Dios!* And what the hell—stabbed? That was Landers' report—what the *hell?*" said Mendoza blankly. "Thanks very much for another mystery." He got up and went out to the hall. "Where's Tom?"

14

"Stabbed?" said Landers, startled. "It looked like a simple accident. I thought she'd probably been thrown against the dash. The husband came in and identified her. He didn't seem too bright, but I put it down to shock, you know."

"Well, we are going to ask Mr. Moreno some questions *pronto*," said Mendoza forcefully. "What's the address?"

"It was down in Venice somewhere, it'll be in the report." Landers found it, rummaging. They took the Ferrari, and Mendoza stayed on surface streets. At this hour on a warm June Sunday the freeways would be thronged with people heading for the beaches.

It was a poor section of that old beach town, when they found the address, the house a tiny old frame at the back of a narrow lot. As Mendoza and Landers walked up the cracked sidewalk to a low step, a minute sagging porch, they heard sounds of altercation inside, men's voices raised. Landers pushed the bell and the voices quieted at the loud buzz. In a minute, Moreno came to the door, the little man he remembered, dark, with slightly pockmarked skin, a rather stupid expression, dull eyes. He looked at the badge in Mendoza's hand. "Lieutenant Mendoza—Detective Landers. We'd like to talk to you, Mr. Moreno. We've just found out that your wife's death wasn't an accident. She was stabbed." Sometimes the shock value of direct talk was useful.

Moreno's expression didn't change. He said mournfully, "Yeah, I know. How'd you know?"

"The doctor—"

"Oh," said Moreno. "I never thoughta that. It wasn't my fault, it was that damn fool Joe."

"I think we'd better come in," said Mendoza, and

Moreno just nodded. He was a sad little man. He turned and went into the room ahead of them, a square and bare little room where two other men were standing. Both were bigger than Moreno, about his age, in the thirties, one Negro and one white.

"The cops found out," said Moreno.

The other two looked merely downhearted. "Gee," said the black one, "I guess we blew it. I'm awful sorry, Ernie. It was just—"

"Suppose we hear some names," said Mendoza. "And some answers to questions." His nose was twitching again.

"I guess I got to tell you," said Moreno. "Nothin' else to do. See, we been on the welfare since I got laid off. I useta work with Joe and Nat. That's Joe—" Sanchez, it transpired, the white one, and Nat Foster. "For the city, pickin' up garbage. But I got laid off and Loretta, she went and saw this movie." He sniffed dolefully. "About some guy pretended his wife got killed and there was a lot of money from a thing called insurance. She said we could do like that. And she looked up a place in the phone book, get it fixed so if she dies I get a lot of money. But nobody meant it to happen for real—Loretta and me, we got on just fine. I thought a hell of a lot of Loretta!" He was faintly indignant now. "I had to have the damn fool notion, get Joe and Nat help out on it."

Neither of them looked very bright either. Joe said, "Well, it just never come to me till we was there, Ernie. We was just helpin' Ernie and Loretta out," he explained to Mendoza, sounding helpless. "An' glad to, we was friends. Nat came along, drive Ernie's car, on account Loretta she can't drive."

"And you never noticed there wasn't a driver's license in her handbag?" said Mendoza to Landers.

"It wasn't me. The Highway Patrol."

"Ah, I might have known," said Mendoza darkly. "And?"

"And Ernie said, get a chicken or somethin' and put blood all over. Fix the car like there was a accident. See, Loretta was along because we was goin' to take her to her

240

mother's up in San Luis, so nobody'd know she wasn't dead," said Nat. "And I'm sorry, Ernie. Maybe I shouldn'ta said it. But it just come to me, after we got the car fixed against the fence and all—it was me said do it real late so nobody around—it just come to me, the cops wasn't going to think Loretta was dead 'less there was a body."

"And when Nat said it, I kinda saw that too," said Joe. "It never hit me till he said, and then I kinda saw he was right. And Loretta says what did we mean, and it just come to me, there wasn't no other female around to be a body for Loretta, so Ernie gets all the money."

"*¡Caramba!*" murmured Mendoza, awed.

"And I said that to Nat, and Loretta she started to scream and holler and I tole her shut up, but she didn't, and I just thought, if Ernie's gonna get all that money there has got to be a body in the car, so I stuck my knife in her and then she shut up—"

"I never had no such shock in my life as when you called me," said Moreno. "In the movie the guy made like an alibi, stay with people all night, and I dropped in a gamblin' joint down the pier, I ain't so much on cards but I did, and me thinkin' Loretta was up at her ma's! And then you call me, and she's dead! I called Nat soon as I got home, and he says how it happened, and I was just wild! That damn fool Joe! Well, I got to say it never crossed my mind about it not lookin' right if there wasn't no body— I kinda saw that—but he needn't have gone and killed Loretta! I was good and mad!" said Moreno.

"But there wasn't no other female around, Ernie," said Joe humbly.

"Yeah, and I been tryin' to get him come explain it ever since, him duckin' me because he knew how—I thought a hell of a lot of Loretta, she was a good woman—"

"I tole him you wouldn't like it, Ernie," said Nat. "But you know Joe, he gets an idea in his head."

"Tom," said Mendoza, "I have the feeling we've got into Looking-Glass country. You'd better go phone for a car." Without a word Landers went out to the Ferrari and called in for a squad car. This one was hard to believe, but even in the supposedly superior technological civilization of the twentieth century, the Ernies, Nats and Joes were still to be found.

They all looked surprised to be told they were under arrest. "I didn't have nothing to do with it," said Moreno, still indignant. Very likely he wouldn't know the meaning of the words, conspiracy to defraud. They were to find that there wasn't an insurance policy; he'd just signed an application. The other two were just downcast. They all climbed meekly into the black-and-white, and Mendoza and Landers followed it back to the jail to book them in. They'd apply for a warrant; this one was going to provide some amusement in the D.A.'s office tomorrow.

It provided some more at the office when they got back and told everybody else about it. "All those books," said Grace laughing, "about the shrewd master criminals—"

"You have to live with the thankless job," said Mendoza, "to realize just how stupid the little ones can be. *¡Dios, vaya historia!*"

The office never saw Piggott on Sunday until after church. As he came into the living room putting on a tie, where Prudence waited all ready, she said, "Look, Matt. There's something different about one of the tetras, that lyretail one. It's all puffed up. It looks just like that other one when— I do believe it's another female full of eggs."

"Oh, no, you don't," said Piggott. "Get me into all that again!"

"I wasn't even suggesting it, heaven forbid," said Prudence.

"Let her drop her eggs and everybody else in the tank eat them," said Piggott firmly. He ushered Prudence out the door and banged it after them.

Today, unable to go on checking on Grace's project, they were back hunting the perverts; but nobody had any deep conviction that they were going to get anywhere at that routine. Landers and Conway went back to the dairy store on Wilshire and talked to Knisely again, and the people in the stores on each side: one was a drugstore, one a newsstand, both open on Sunday. But with the normal amount of traffic passing, only the man at the newsstand had heard the shot, and thought it was a backfire; neither had seen Baby-face come out.

They went to talk to the witnesses again; sometimes after a witness had a chance to calm down, think about it, more would come out. In this case it didn't. And they both had a feeling that the sooner they dropped on this one, the better.

"He could have been hopped up, Rich," said Landers. "Going off hair-trigger like that."

"All too likely," agreed Conway.

When they got back to the office the others were taking a break, and Higgins had some snapshots to show; not the colored ones he'd taken with his Instamatic, he wouldn't get those back until Tuesday, but the black-and-white ones Steve Dwyer had shot on Friday night, and carefully developed and printed himself.

"Say, he's pretty good, isn't he?" said Grace. "They look like a pro job."

"Well, he wants to go into the lab end," said Higgins. "I think he's pretty good all right." And the rest of them had been a little amused at Higgins' humble pursuit of Dwyer's widow, but they were all thinking now that Bert would be pleased at how he was taking care of them all. And remembering that Grace had come to them as a replacement for Dwyer; Grace hadn't known Bert.

At two o'clock, with most of them just back from lunch, they had a call from Traffic. There'd been a brawl in a bar out on Third, and there seemed to be a D.O.A. Resignedly Higgins went to look at more of the stupidity. The Traffic men were holding a short skinny little man who had had a few drinks and was feeling no pain. The D.O.A. was lying quietly on the floor of the bar, and—it looked like a normally respectable place—everybody else had backed off and was watching silently. There were only a few customers, a fat bartender.

"So what happened?" asked Higgins.

"The bartender called us when they started to argue, disturb other people," said one of the uniformed men. "This one's Alfred Warner."

"He started it," said Warner. "He hadn't no call. I was just standing there at the bar, have a quiet drink or two, he come up and started laughing at my clothes, he said I looked funny. He hadn't no call. It's my own business, my clothes."

Higgins looked at the Traffic men, who were grinning. Warner, on this warm but not hot day—the heat wave had definitely departed—had chosen to don a pair of royal blue shorts, white tennis shoes, a striped canvas baseball cap and a sleeveless white T-shirt with the simple legend emblazoned on it in scarlet, back and front, KISS ME QUICK, I'M A CZECH! Almost anybody might have shared the deceased's opinion, but he needn't have said anything about it.

"I picked it up by mistake," said Warner, looking down at himself. "It's my wife's, see. The shirt, I mean. She's Czech, and her sister sent it to her—thought it was cute. I never realized I had it on till that guy come up makin' the snide remarks."

Higgins turned a laugh into a cough and said, "Did he take a poke at you, Mr. Warner?"

"Nope," said Warner. "I took a poke at him. And then he pulled a gun on me, after I kinda shoved him and knocked over his drink. He hadn't no call make snide remarks about my wife's shirt, nor he hadn't no call to pull a gun on me. But I wasn't about to get shot, I tried to grab it away from him and the bartender come and tried to get it away from both of us, and then it went off."

Higgins bent and looked at the dead man. The gun was lying on the floor beside him, an old S. and W. .45. "Well, well. Nemesis," said Higgins.

The dead man was Terry Conover, by the mug shot in circulation.

He straightened up. "You should have recognized him by the mug shot," he said to the uniformed men. "There's been an A.P.B. out on him for nearly two weeks—he got over the wall at Folsom."

"I'll be damned. We had that too— I hadn't looked at his face."

Conover had been shot in the body and shed a lot of blood. At least he'd be off their minds now. Warner would probably be charged with involuntary manslaughter and get off with a suspended sentence, but Higgins took him in now, resisting the temptation to advise him to wear his own clothes from now on. They let him make a call, and he called his wife.

Higgins was still there, getting down notes for a report, when she came. She looked upset, a little dark woman in a smart blue pantsuit, but when she saw Warner she doubled up in mirth.

"Alfred, what on earth are you d-doing in my shirt?" she demanded between whoops. "I never saw anything so ridiculous—if I could have a picture—"

"Well, you put it on top of my clean ones," said Warner.

Higgins explained matters to her, and she took it calmly. In a way, he thought, starting back to the office, it was just as well it had happened. With no death penalties getting handed out, and Conover the wild one. At least he'd be making no more trouble.

About four o'clock on Sunday afternoon, Sergeant Lake swung around from the switchboard and said, "Art! Somebody wants you or George."

Hackett shoved the right button on the phone and said, "Hackett."

"Say, Sergeant, this is Eddy Gamino."

"Oh." Hackett focused his mind back to that. Stephanie Midkiff and the damned biology textbooks. They'd expected to let that one lie until summer school opened and hopefully some more of those books came drifting in—hopefully the one in which she'd found Rex's name and phone number. "What can I do for you?"

"Vice versa," said Eddy tersely. "I'm down here at

Harry's place, and I just spotted that yellow Mustang—it's parked up the block in front of the drugstore. Oh, it's the right one, temporary license plate in the same spot and all. I just thought, if you'd like to find who owns it—"

"Thanks very much!" Hackett banged the phone down and called to Higgins. They ran, and took Higgins' Pontiac. When they got down to Seventh he went round the block to get on the right side of the street, and they saw the blinding chrome yellow car up there at the corner. But as Higgins slowed, two male figures came out of the drugstore and got into it and it took off. They passed Harry Hart's place, with Eddy standing in the doorway, and followed the Mustang.

Evidently the driver didn't notice the Pontiac. The Mustang went on up Seventh, turned on Coronado, and slid to the curb in front of a small stucco house. Higgins parked behind it, and they got out in a hurry, converged on the pair just out of the Mustang. "Is this your car?" asked Higgins, getting out the badge; but warm satisfaction spread through him as he looked at one of them. Here was Ruthie Runnells' young man too old for school, with a scrubby little dark moustache. He looked about twenty, and he was almost six feet but slender, and he had a weak girlish chin. The other one, younger, was enough like him to mark them as brothers. They were both dressed in sharp flashy sports clothes. When the younger one saw the badge he started to cry weakly.

"I knew they'd find out— I knew they'd find out—"

The older one said, "Shut up." He looked around as if for a place to run.

"Don't try it," advised Higgins.

"It was all your idea—get to know girls—I didn't want to," wept the younger one.

"So let's hear your names," said Hackett. No reply forthcoming, he went to look at the registration in the Mustang. "Rex Hubbard—that's you?"

"So what if it is?" the older one said in a thin voice.

A door slammed and a strident voice called. "What's goin' on out here? Who are those guys, Rex?" She came

246

striding at them like a man; she wasn't very tall but she had a deep-bosomed figure, grayish-white hair in an uncompromising knob on top of her head, and a harsh loud voice. She had on pants and a man's sweat shirt. "What you want with my boys?" she demanded.

Hackett showed her the badge. "A cop!" she said, taken aback. "Listen, my boys wouldn't do nothing wrong! Their dad just scalp 'em, an' so would I, they snitch anything or talk back—Jimmy, what the hell you cryin' for? I'm always tellin' you not to be such a crybaby—"

"How do you happen to be driving an expensive new car, Rex?" asked Higgins. He had been a little curious about that; this neighborhood didn't say money. The question fired the woman up again.

"What business is it of cops, we wanta give Rex a nice car? My husband, he makes good money—he's a plumber —and if he wants to—"

"Is he drunk again?" asked Rex, sounding very tired, and she turned on him.

"And so what if he is? He works hard all week, it's a dirty hard job, and if he wants get drunk on Sundays what's it to anybody? I still don't know what these cops are after— Did you get me my aspirin? Where is it? And the change from that five bucks—"

He took them both out of his pocket and handed them over.

"You're both under arrest," said Hackett, and the woman began to jabber astonishment, anger and incoherent questions. "For a start, homicide—we'll decide the degree later."

"I didn't want to do it," sobbed the younger one.

They left Mrs. Hubbard still talking into the air after them, and they wondered if maybe it was a relief to Rex and Jimmy to get away from her. They were pleased about this unexpected bonus; they'd thank Eddy better later.

Except that Rex was a little surprise, quiet and meek and gentle, it was much the sort of story they could have expected. Mendoza sat in on the questioning.

Rex was twenty, Jimmy sixteen. Jimmy went to the high

school on Ninth, and knew about that latest thing, the phone numbers in margins. They didn't get much out of him but tears and remorse. Both the boys were shy, loners, hadn't any close friends, unsure how to make any. But it had been Rex's idea to put the phone number in that book—maybe get to know some girls. It had been way last month Jimmy'd done that. And then when a girl had phoned, they didn't know exactly what to say—

They finally got Rex to open up when they took Jimmy away to wait in another interrogation room. And he didn't say much.

"I'd never—had a girl friend," he told them. "I didn't know what to say. When they met us—at that place. But that one was pretty. The other one wasn't— I don't like fat girls. I wanted the other one—kind of to myself. I made Jimmy get out—and I—just drove around—we didn't talk much—and I finally parked—just up by Echo Park. I didn't know what to say to her—so I tried to kiss her—and she started to fight me—and I guess I don't know what happened after that. Except—she was dead. I don't know."

It was an easy way to kill anybody, without meaning to. And it was a sad and stupid thing, this—the damned fool kids, one wanting adventure, one possibly queer one going out of control. It was anybody's guess what would happen to them, what the charges would be. No malice afore-thought, and Jimmy was a juvenile. But Stephanie Midkiff was just as dead.

Nothing else new, at least, came in on Sunday. Tomorrow they'd finish Grace's project, checking out those up-right male citizens living at the Hooper Avenue apartment. And so far they had all been proven shining-bright-inno-cent, and nobody felt that the list of perverts was going to give them X, so where did they go then?

They didn't know, as Higgins said afterward, that Mendoza's capricious *daemon,* for some reason, was about to take up brief residence in Hackett's subconscious mind.

* * *

When the night watch came on, they all asked Glasser about the new car. "Oh, she's a very nice little girl," said Glasser, beaming. "Very nice indeed, boys. I had her up the Malibu road forty miles, and she can skedaddle, for all she's a baby. But I'm still feeling surprised— I never won anything before in my life." He was full of statistics about the Gremlin and what a nice little girl she was. They'd given him a lime-green one with white rally stripes. "Do you know, that little thing's only two and a half inches longer than a VW, but its turning circle is three feet less, and it weighs as much as a Dodge sedan—really built, and drives like a Cadillac—" He had the advertising folder to hand around.

At ten-fifteen they discovered that the restaurant heisters had come back to their beat. The Brown Derby out on Wilshire was held up just as it was closing. They heard the same descriptions—stocking masks, big guns, two men medium-sized. They had got about four thousand bucks.

"Fast and furious you can say," said Galeano when he'd filled out a report on it.

"And this other heister—Baby-face, Tom calls him— sounds like one we'd like to get to," said Glasser. "Maybe hopped up. But not a smell of a lead on any of 'em."

"Sometimes," said Schenke, "we get lucky."

Palliser was off on Mondays. He'd picked up a copy of the *Herald* on his way home last night, and after breakfast he called three men who advertised offering to do carpentry and odd jobs. One said he had too many jobs on hand now to take on another; the second wasn't home but his wife said she'd have him call back. The third came over to look at the job. He was a lean stringy fellow in his sixties who said his name was Nethercott. He said he'd got a load of old lumber where a school had been torn down, he could put up a good stout fence for about seventy-five dollars.

Palliser closed with this offer instantly; he could always paint the fence himself if he had to. Their benefactor said, "Got all my tools in the truck, might's well start now."

"Darling," said Roberta, bouncing the baby soothingly

249

as he objected to all the hammering and sawing, "aren't you smart to have thought of the ads. Really, now it's decided, I'm dying to meet Trina."

It was, as a matter of fact, the Pallisers' real dog which triggered off the *daemon*.

On Monday, Grace, Piggott, Landers and Conway had gone ahead checking out all those men, while Hackett and Higgins had a look for the perverts on the list they hadn't found yet. The routine did break cases. By lunchtime seven more of the apartment residents had been cleared, and even Grace was feeling that this little idea wasn't about to come to anything.

They all went up to Federico's in a body, which sometimes happened. Mendoza was still talking about Moreno and his cohorts; he'd been at the jail with one of the D.A.'s deputies, getting full statements, and that really was one for the books, stupidity hardly to be believed.

The tall waiter Adam came and refilled their coffee cups, and Hackett sat back feeling slightly smug. The low-protein diet had removed five pounds so far, and his pants didn't feel so tight.

Mendoza lit a new cigarette. "Did you hear about John's dog? I'd forgotten that freeway crash last January—"

"Oh, that," said Piggott. "The dog with the funny name, yes. They're nice dogs, but I should think pretty big for the city."

"Besides, dogs will dig up things," said Grace. "Flower beds. Ginny says she'd like to get a Siamese cat. Of course, I can see anybody wanting a good watchdog these days."

"As a matter of fact," said Mendoza, "Siamese were used as—mmh—watch-cats in the palaces, and I understand they can be trained as guards. Of course, being cats, how faithful they'd be at it might depend on their current mood. I think—"

"Is that a fact?" said Grace, interested.

"Not all dogs dig up things," said Higgins, thinking of well-mannered little Brucie. "I think it depends on the breed—some do and some don't—"

Suddenly Hackett leaped up and let out a shout. "BEDS!" he yelled. They all looked at him in alarm, and Higgins half got up.

"What—"

"BEDS!" said Hackett loudly. "But where does he sleep? Two other men—and only one bedroom with twin beds—" He was convulsed by a sudden light from heaven, but only he could see it.

"Se conoce," said Mendoza, concerned, "he's drunk—what the hell are you talking about, Arturo?"

"Beds," said Hackett, breathing rapidly and still staring unseeingly at the far wall. "Only two beds—and there was a couch—I can see it plain as day—and it's got to be a daybed. *A daybed!* That opens out—"

"Art—" Higgins was worried. "Calm down and make sense. What are you talking about?"

Slowly Hackett's eyes focused; he gave a little gasp. "By God, it just hit me—out of the blue. I just *saw* it. In that apartment—up on the fifth floor—three men sharing it, and one of them works at night—and only one bedroom, so that couch in the living room must be—has got to be—a bed-davenport. And that's where—"

"¡Válgame Dios!" said Mendoza very quietly, and was on his feet like a cat.

"William Reed," said Hackett. "One of those five night workers."

"Oh, my God!" said Higgins. "You mean he put her in—" And they were all remembering that autopsy report now. Grace was on his feet too.

"Come on," said Mendoza. "We'll go look at it, Art. The rest of you'll know soon enough."

They found him there; he opened the door and let them in without protest, a dark stolid man about forty. Hackett remembered that he was a waiter somewhere. They didn't ask him any questions before they went to look at the couch in the living room. It was a bed-davenport, and Hackett found the lever and heaved it open with one yank, and of course there was nothing the naked eye could see, but the lab would find anything that was there, and there would probably be traces there.

"Was that where you put her?" asked Mendoza.

After a moment he nodded. "I been real sorry," he said simply in a soft voice. "I don't know what makes me want to do like that. I hadn't—in quite a spell. Since I come out here. But I went out—that day, 'bout noon, go down see if was any mail. She was—"

Hackett interrupted him and recited the piece about his rights; they wanted to nail this one, all legally tied up. He just waited, and nodded.

"She was in the hall, she'd just fell down and bumped her nose, it was bleedin'. She was—just awful cute," he said. "She knew me—seen me around. And I—just—had to—do that. It's like a devil inside me, I had to. And she was scared then—and I had to stop her cryin'—"

"And then you heard her mother—and the other women—calling her," said Mendoza.

A slow nod. "And then—when the policemen came—and all of you—I was scared. I see they was all looking—every place. It just come to me, I hadn't made up the bed yet, and I put her in it and folded it up, was all. And nobody looked. And I left for work same time, but then I come home, other two fellows asleep then, I just took her down there. I put her dress in a trash can up the street."

And Hackett thought back, queerly, to that bank robber who had killed Bert. They'd wanted, all the while they were hunting him, to commit mayhem on him: and then when they found him, they were just sorry for him. This was a little like that.

"I don't reckon," said Reed sadly, "they oughta let me out, when I do these things. Seems like I can't stop myself."

Mendoza called the lab; a team would come out. They took him in, and booked him. When they took his prints, they sent them to NCIC, and were shortly informed that he was William Chale, originally from Atlanta. He had a long pedigree of attempted and completed child molestation charges there before he raped a five-year-old in Pittsburgh eighteen years back; he'd got a ten-to-twenty and been out in four years. Five years later he had raped a nine-year-old in Erie, Pennsylvania, and been put in again, and was out in three years. There would be others he'd never been tagged for. He'd got off his last parole in Pennsylvania two years ago, and come out here. He said this was the first time he'd done anything here; they didn't know whether to believe that or not.

The two men who had shared the apartment with him were shaken and astonished. They were both the upright citizens, working for a big construction company. They'd met him last year, they said, at an employment agency uptown. Both of them were saving up to get married, and Reed getting a night job in that restaurant, it had seemed a pretty good arrangement. They hadn't seen much of him, but he'd always seemed like a nice, quiet guy.

"I feel, damn it," said one of them, "like I brought a rattlesnake in this place. Not knowing. That poor baby. I wouldn't know how to look Mr. and Mrs. Blaine in the face."

And Mendoza said, "I've known you to have a little hunch now and then, Art, but that was a spectacular one—¡Pues hombre!"

There weren't any leads on Baby-face, just nowhere to look. If he pulled something else, maybe they'd get a better description.

Tuesday was quiet, with only a new unidentified corpse turning up, and a suicide.

And on Tuesday night Landers took Phil O'Neill out to dinner, at The Castaway high up in the hills above Burbank, the nice place with the quiet atmosphere and the magnificent view out over the whole metropolitan area.

They were late, because when he'd started out to pick her up he'd found he had a flat tire, and feeling disinclined for the job after a shower and a clean shirt, had called the garage, which was busy. They didn't get there, to sit over preliminary drinks, until after eight-thirty.

Somehow they always had plenty to say to each other,

and he thought she looked good enough to eat, little trim Phil with her short flaxen curls and freckled upturned nose, in a plain white dress with a bright red stole. They had a leisurely dinner, and lingered over more coffee. The waitress came tactfully with the bill and said, "We close at nine-forty-five, sir."

Landers was reluctant to move. "Well, I suppose—" said Phil. "Tomorrow a weekday after all." She slid out of the booth and put the stole round her shoulders. In the lobby the manager and cashier had the register open, and a stout canvas bag was on the counter. In the middle of the week, business was evidently slow; Landers and Phil were the last to leave, and when they went out, Landers' car the only one left in the customers' lot.

They got into the Corvair; it was a nice night, the air warm with just a promise of real coolness coming later.

"It really is a lovely, lovely view," said Phil.

"It really is," said Landers, looking at her profile tenderly. A car came up the hill behind and stopped up there by the restaurant. In the parking lot, by the low parapet at the top of the hill, they sat quiet in the car admiring the view.

"Dearest darling Phil," said Landers, "I do love you such a hell of a lot. I'm not good at saying things, Phil, but please will you marry me?"

"Well—" said Phil. He could tell she was smiling. "Yes, I guess I will, Tom."

"Darling love!" said Landers, and a wild salvo of gunfire shattered the night, a bullet slammed into the side of the Corvair and confused shouts sounded from the door of the restaurant. Landers shoved Phil down on the seat and leaped out of the car, clawing for his gun. More shots, and two men came running down from the building, with a man in pursuit firing at them. One of the first two went down with a yell.

My God, those damned heisters, thought Landers, and ran, and tackled the second man with memories of high-school football, and brought him down flat.

The restaurant manager came running up, brandishing a .38 Police Positive. "It was a hold-up—they came in—

I'd heard about them, I brought my gun in just in case—"

"For God's sake," said Landers. "Of all the—"

One man had taken a bullet in the leg. The other one was just swearing.

Phil came running up excitedly. "Have you got them? Honestly, Tom! Honestly! Well, we'll never forget the night we got engaged, will we? Maybe typical, for a couple of cops!"

Landers called the night watch. They'd get some names from the heisters tomorrow; a car came up to take them in. The night watch, amused, called the boss.

Mendoza was still laughing when he came back to the living room, where Alison sat reading with Bast and Sheba in her lap. Nefertite, insulted when Mendoza put her down to answer the phone, was sitting on El Señor on the sectional washing his ears. Cedric was asleep at Alison's feet. The lamp turned her hair to burnished copper.

"Once a cop always a cop," said Mendoza.

She looked up. "¿Qué?"

He told her about Landers and Phil O'Neill, and she laughed. "And I still wonder why I'm there, at the thankless job. Watching all the stupidity and cupidity happen."

The twins, hostages to fortune, were asleep down the hall. And you couldn't help worrying, as a parent—old or young.

"Amado," said Alison, smiling, "all of you at the thankless job need reminding—always more of the good people than the other kind. Se dice—"

"It is to be hoped," said Mendoza. "And as you were about to say, mañana será otro día,—tomorrow is also a day."